The Second Generation

Studies in German History
Published in Association with the German Historical Institute, Washington, D.C.

General Editors:
Hartmut Berghoff, Director of the German Historical Institute, Washington, D.C.
Uwe Spiekermann, Deputy Director of the German Historical Institute, Washington, D.C.

Volume 1
Nature in German History
Edited by Christof Mauch

Volume 2
Coping with the Nazi Past: West German Debates on Nazism and Generational Conflict, 1955–1975
Edited by Philipp Gassert and Alan E. Steinweis

Volume 3
Adolf Cluss, Architect: From Germany to America
Edited by Alan Lessoff and Christof Mauch

Volume 4
Two Lives in Uncertain Times: Facing the Challenges of the 20th Century as Scholars and Citizens
Wilma Iggers and Georg Iggers

Volume 5
Driving Germany: The Landscape of the German Autobahn, 1930–1970
Thomas Zeller

Volume 6
The Pleasure of a Surplus Income: Part-Time Work, Gender Politics, and Social Change in West Germany, 1955–1969
Christine von Oertzen

Volume 7
Between Mass Death and Individual Loss: The Place of the Dead in Twentieth-Century Germany
Edited by Alon Confino, Paul Betts and Dirk Schumann

Volume 8
Nature of the Miracle Years: Conservation in West Germany, 1945–1975
Sandra Chaney

Volume 9
Biography between Structure and Agency: Central European Lives in International Historiography
Edited by Volker R. Berghahn and Simone Lässig

Volume 10
Political Violence in the Weimar Republic, 1918–1933: Battle for the Streets and Fears of Civil War
Dirk Schumann

Volume 11
The East German State and the Catholic Church, 1945–1989
Bernd Schaefer

Volume 12
Raising Citizens in the "Century of the Child": Child-Rearing in the United States and German Central Europe in Comparative Perspective
Edited by Dirk Schumann

Volume 13
The Plans that Failed: An Economic History of the GDR
André Steiner

Volume 14
Max Liebermann and International Modernism: An Artist's Career from Empire to Third Reich
Edited by Marion Deshmukh, Françoise Forster-Hahn and Barbara Gaehtgens

Volume 15
Germany and the Black Diaspora: Points of Contact, 1250–1914
Edited by Mischa Honeck, Martin Klimke, and Anne Kuhlmann-Smirnov

Volume 16
Crime and Criminal Justice in Modern Germany
Edited by Richard F. Wetzell

Volume 17
Encounters with Modernity: The Catholic Church in the Federal Republic, 1945-1975
Benjamin Ziemann

Volume 18
Fellow Tribesmen: The Image of Native Americans, National Identity, and Nazi Ideology in Germany
Frank Usbeck

Volume 19
The Respectable Career of Fritz K: The Making and Remaking of a Provincial Nazi Leader
Hartmut Berghoff and Cornelia Rauh
Translated by Casey Butterfield

Volume 20
The Second Generation: Émigrés from Nazi Germany as Historians
Edited by Andreas W. Daum, Hartmut Lehmann, and James J. Sheehan

THE SECOND GENERATION
Émigrés from Nazi Germany as Historians

With a Biobibliographic Guide

Edited by

Andreas W. Daum

Hartmut Lehmann

and

James J. Sheehan

First published in 2016 by

Berghahn Books

www.berghahnbooks.com

© 2016, 2018 Andreas W. Daum, Hartmut Lehmann, and James J. Sheehan
First paperback edition published in 2018

All rights reserved. Except for the quotation of short passages
for the purposes of criticism and review, no part of this book
may be reproduced in any form or by any means, electronic or
mechanical, including photocopying, recording, or any information
storage and retrieval system now known or to be invented,
without written permission of the publisher.

Library of Congress Cataloging-in-Publication Data

Names: Daum, Andreas W. | Lehmann, Hartmut, 1936- | Sheehan, James J.
Title: The second generation : Émigrés from Nazi Germany as historians / edited by Andreas W. Daum, Hartmut Lehmann, and James J. Sheehan.
Description: New York : Berghahn Books, 2016. | Series: Studies in German history ; volume 20 | Includes bibliographical references and index.
Identifiers: LCCN 2015033832| ISBN 9781782389859 (hardback : alkaline paper) | ISBN 9781782389934 (ebook)-
Subjects: LCSH: Germany—Historiography—Philosophy. | Historiography—Philosophy. | Holocaust, Jewish (1939-1945)—Historiography—Philosophy. | Historians—Biography. | Intergenerational relations. | Immigrants—Biography. | Political refugees—Biography. | German Americans—Biography. | Germans—Foreign countries—Biography. | Germany—History—1933–1945—Biography.
Classification: LCC DD86 .S53 2016 | DDC 907.2/02331—dc23
LC record available at http://lccn.loc.gov/2015033832

British Library Cataloguing in Publication Data

A catalogue record for this book is available from the British Library

ISBN 978-1-78238-985-9 (hardback)
ISBN 978-1-78920-052-2 (paperback)
ISBN 978-1-78238-993-4 (ebook)

Contents

List of Tables — ix

Preface — xi
    Hartmut Lehmann and James J. Sheehan

Introduction

Refugees from Nazi Germany as Historians:
Origins and Migrations, Interests and Identities — 1
    Andreas W. Daum

Part I. Testimonies

1. It Hardly Needs Emphasis That My Own Generation, the Second, Is Deeply Indebted to the First — 55
    Klemens von Klemperer

2. "A Wanderer between Several Worlds" — 59
    Walter Laqueur

3. External Events, Inner Drives — 72
    Peter Paret

4. Not Exile, But a New Life — 79
    Fritz Stern

5. History and Social Action beyond National and Continental Borders — 82
    Georg G. Iggers

6. Some Issues and Experiences in German-American Scholarly Relations — 97
    Gerhard L. Weinberg

7. Some Reflections on the Second Generation — 102
    Hanna Holborn Gray

8. A Life between Homelands — 114
Peter Loewenberg

9. Out of Germany — 130
Renate Bridenthal

Part II. Approaching the Second Generation

10. The Second Generation: Émigré Historians of Modern Germany in Postwar America — 143
Catherine Epstein

11. Thinking about the Second Generation Conceptually — 152
Volker R. Berghahn

Part III. Émigrés and the Writing of History

12. The Tensions of Historical *Wissenschaft*: The Émigré Historians and the Making of German Cultural History — 177
Steven E. Aschheim

13. From the Margins to the Mainstream: Refugees and the Successors on the Jewish Question, Antisemitism, and the Holocaust in German History — 197
Jeffrey Herf

14. Reluctant Return: Peter Gay and the Cosmopolitan Work of a Historian — 210
Helmut Walser Smith

15. Out of the Limelight or In: Raul Hilberg, Gerhard Weinberg, Henry Friedlander, and the Historical Study of the Holocaust — 229
Doris L. Bergen

16. Blazing New Paths in Historiography: "Refugee Effect" and American Experience in the Professional Trajectory of Gerda Lerner — 244
Marjorie Lamberti

Part IV. Comparative and Transnational Perspectives

17. German Émigré Historians in Israel — 261
Shulamit Volkov

18. German and Austrian Émigré Historians in Britain after 1933　　271
    Peter Alter

19. The Second-Generation Émigrés' Impact on German Historiography　　287
    Philipp Stelzel

20. Encounters with Émigré Historians of the First and Second Generation　　304
    Gerhard A. Ritter

21. Influences: A Personal Comment　　318
    Jürgen Kocka

Part V. Biobibliographic Guide

22. Émigrés in the Historical Disciplines: Research Perspectives　　327
    Andreas W. Daum

23. Biographies　　339
    Andreas W. Daum and Sherry L. Föhr

24. Selected Bibliography　　454

Index　　463

Tables

1. Second-Generation Émigrés as Historians in North America (107)   33

2. The Second Generation: Year of Escape/Emigration and Age at That Time   36

3. Émigré Historians of the First Generation in North America (98)   37

PREFACE

In 1973–74, Felix Gilbert invited us to spend a year at the Institute for Advanced Study in Princeton. We occupied adjoining studies where we pursued our individual projects, but there was ample time to talk during the tea break in the morning and the coffee hour in the afternoon. Felix Gilbert, the most learned of Friedrich Meinecke's many *Doktoranden,* was generous with his time. He seemed to like the idea that two young historians, who could have been his children, one from the United States and one from Germany, one from the country of his origins and one from the country to which he now belonged, began an intensive exchange of ideas and became friends.

Felix Gilbert belonged to that great generation of German historians who had completed their education in Germany and were forced into exile by the Nazis. When Hartmut Lehmann became the founding director of the German Historical Institute in Washington, DC, he chose this generation as the subject of the institute's first scholarly conference, held in December 1988. Organized with the help of James Sheehan, it had three aims: first, to explore this important chapter in the relationship between German and American history and historians; second, to celebrate the scholarly achievements of these émigré scholars; and finally, to establish an agenda for the Institute's scholarly activities for the next several years.

This conference on "German-Speaking Refugee Historians" was a moving experience. Of the émigré historians who had received their doctorate in Germany prior to 1933, several were able to attend, including Felix Gilbert. In addition, there were members of the second generation: historians who had been born in Germany, were forced into exile as children, and then studied and pursued their careers at American universities. In some cases, children of both of these cohorts were present, among them, for example, Catherine Epstein, daughter of Klaus Epstein and granddaughter of Fritz Epstein. In 1988, members of all three generations were able to meet and share their very different academic and personal experiences. Three years later, in 1991, we published the proceedings in a book titled *An Interrupted Past.*

During the German Historical Institute's first decade, the history of émigré historians remained an important topic. Catherine Epstein did research on the biographies and bibliographies of all of the members of the first generation. In

1993, she published her findings in a "Catalog of German-Speaking Refugee Historians in the United States after 1933" under the title *A Past Renewed*. Sybille Quack dealt with "Women Refugees of the Nazi Period"; her collected volume was published in 1995 under the title *Between Sorrow and Strength*. Gabrielle Simon Edgcomb, herself a member of the second generation, investigated the special destiny and academic role of "Refugee Scholars at Black Colleges," and in 1993 published her results in a book with the title *From Swastika to Jim Crow*.

We had always hoped to examine the achievements of the second generation of émigrés. But it was not until the fall of 2007 that we came back to this project, when we had a chance to meet in Berkeley. But how to go ahead? Both of us had officially retired. Fortunately, Andreas Daum, a former member of the German Historical Institute and now a professor of history at the State University of New York at Buffalo, took a strong interest in our project. As successor of Georg Iggers at Buffalo, yet another member of the second generation, he was well acquainted with the topic. Without his generous support, tactful persistence, conceptual ideas, and organizational skills, we would not have succeeded.

In May 2012, we joined with Andreas Daum to bring together members of the second generation and other historians at an international conference, which quite appropriately became part of the German Historical Institute's twenty-fifth anniversary celebrations. This is the place to express our gratitude. We thank the Academic Advisory Council of the German Historical Institute for supporting our plan, and the Institute's director, Professor Hartmut Berghoff, for offering us the Institute's premises and for taking an active part in the project's organization. Our thanks go to the Fritz Thyssen Foundation as well as the ZEIT Foundation– Ebelin and Gerd Bucerius for their generous support. We thank our colleagues from the United States, Germany, Canada, Great Britain, and Israel who provided intriguing contributions. We are especially grateful to the members of the second generation who came to Washington and shared their memories with us; these are a treasured part of this book.

In many ways, this book goes beyond its origins and now presents—recomposed and enriched by additional contributions—the first systematic exploration of the second generation from a multitude of perspectives, including substantial and new biographical research. We are grateful to Marion Berghahn for accepting this endeavor for publication. Above all, we want to use this opportunity to express our sincere thanks to Andreas Daum. His tireless efforts made the entire project and this volume possible.

Hartmut Lehmann, Kiel
James J. Sheehan, Stanford

Hartmut Lehmann taught as a professor of modern history at the University of Kiel since 1969. He was the founding Director of the German Historical

Institute in Washington, DC (1987-93) and served as director at the Max Planck Institute for History in Göttingen from 1993 to 2004. He was also a research fellow at the University of Chicago, the Institute for Advanced Study in Princeton, Princeton University, the Australian National University in Canberra, and Harvard University. Recent publications include *Die Entzauberung der Welt. Studien zu Themen von Max Weber* (2009), *Religiöse Erweckung in gottferner Zeit. Studien zur Pietismusforschung* (2010), *Luthergedächtnis 1817–2017* (2012), *Das Christentum im 20. Jahrhundert. Fragen, Probleme, Perspektiven* (^{2}2012).

James J. Sheehan is Dickason Professor in the Humanities and Professor of History Emeritus at Stanford University. He has written five books, most recently *Where Have All the Soldiers Gone? The Transformation of Modern Europe*. He edited, with Hartmut Lehmann, *An Interrupted Past: German-Speaking Refugee Historians in the United States after 1933*. He is a member of the American Academy of Arts and Sciences, the American Philosophical Society, and the Orden Pour le Mérite. In 2005 he served as president of the American Historical Association.

Introduction

REFUGEES FROM NAZI GERMANY AS HISTORIANS
Origins and Migrations, Interests and Identities

Andreas W. Daum

This book deals with the biographies, scholarly oeuvres, and intellectual interests of men and women who were both professional historians and, in a particular sense, "participants" in history.[1] They were born in the early twentieth century and grew up in Germany or the surrounding German-speaking territories usurped by the National Socialist regime before 1939. At a young age, they were forced to leave the so-called Third Reich and escaped to other countries. The families of these young refugees reacted to the discrimination and terror that the Nazis imposed on them. They were no longer wanted in Germany. With few exceptions, they were targeted as Jews. In contrast to the older, first generation of émigrés[2] who fled the Nazi dictatorship after their university training had been completed, members of the younger, or second, generation acquired their academic degrees after their emigration and in the English-speaking world. Our volume concentrates on this younger cohort, specifically those who ultimately settled, or spent the bulk of their career, in North America; we also cast a look at England and Israel.

In this second generation we encounter historians who lost their parents and family members in the Holocaust as well as scholars who escaped the Nazis via a *Kindertransport* (children's transport) abroad. We find one historian who was still a baby when his parents brought him to Shanghai, and another who parachuted as a U.S. soldier into Normandy in June 1944, seven years after his escape from Germany.[3] The second generation includes others who spent years in France, New Zealand, Bolivia, and Mexico before they found a home in America. They all demonstrated a remarkable persistence in moving on after their escape from

---

Notes from this chapter begin on page 40.

Nazi Germany. They shared some cultural capital, and there remains something distinct about them. Yet, they pursued different interests. Age, gender, family background, personal references, and the levels of support they found in the institutions of higher education all made a difference. They also negotiated their personal and professional identities in a wide variety of ways. Some, for example, quickly shed that of an émigré, while others never felt entirely assimilated in their new homeland.

This volume presents the first sustained effort to examine the second generation of refugees who became historians and to analyze their scholarly work. But it does not present one émigré narrative.[4] The various connections between personal experiences and scholarly interests resist quick generalizations. First, we provide space for nine American historians to speak for themselves; they were all born in Germany and escaped the Nazi dictatorship. The authors include Klemens von Klemperer, Walter Laqueur, Peter Paret, Fritz Stern, Georg G. Iggers, Gerhard L. Weinberg, Hanna Holborn Gray, Peter J. Loewenberg, and Renate Bridenthal. Part II offers some conceptual thoughts about this generation and the role it played in post–World War II historiography. Part III consists of case studies that deal with individual historians. The chapters in Part IV point out comparative and transnational perspectives.

Taken together, these contributions demonstrate that the historians of the younger émigré generation added important themes, experiences, and perspectives to the academic landscape that expanded after 1945. In a few cases, they played a role in the transformation of history as a discipline. For the various audiences of history in the English-speaking world, many of these scholars kept alive a critical interest in the plurality of the German and European pasts.[5] In diverse, often subtle, and mediated ways, the imprint of these pasts expressed itself in a distinct habitus, rather than in a common concentration on a few themes. Furthermore, several of these historians drew German scholars into intellectual and personal conversations that helped to open German historiography to new analytical concepts and to overcome its national orientation.

But who belonged to the second generation? Our volume offers, in Part V, for the first time a biobibliographic guide, which is based on systematic research and features 107 individuals. Chapter 22 explains the methodology used to identify them; Tables 1 and 2 at the end of this introductory essay offer a summary. This sample is much larger and far more diverse than one would assume at first glance; it includes eighty-seven male and twenty female historians. The detailed biographies in chapter 23 provide information about the origins, migrations, academic careers, international recognition, and publications of these 107 historians of the second generation, supplemented by a selected bibliography.[6]

In the following, I exploit the collected data, utilize the rich pool of autobiographical literature, as well as information obtained directly from former émigrés,[7] to present some general observations. I will trace the various origins of the young refugees and then follow their extended migrations, which in some cases led around the globe. These migrations equipped the future historians with transcultural experiences that allowed them to acquire a broad outlook on the world and make us realize the complexity of what constitutes their identity. As a result, seemingly coherent entities such as "German-American emigrants" or "German-Jewish historians" become more differentiated. We can discern more clearly elements of continuity and discontinuity that characterized these émigrés' paths to history, the diversity of their interests, and their place in the intellectual history of what Eric Hobsbawm, yet another migrant between cultures, has called the "Age of Extremes."[8]

The Second Generation

The protagonists of this book did not escape as "refugee scholars." This term has been used frequently when discussing the enforced brain drain from Nazi Germany; it encapsulates what is often called the first generation of émigrés.[9] A considerable number of works have dealt specifically with the refugee historians who escaped from the Third Reich as academically trained scholars. Hans Baron, Fritz T. Epstein, Felix Gilbert, Hajo Holborn, Ernst Kantorowicz, Hans Kohn, Paul Oskar Kristeller, Hans Rosenberg, Hans Rothfels, Selma Stern-Täubler, and Helena Wieruszowski belong to this group of ninety-eight historians (see Table 3 at the end of this essay). Studies on this older generation[10] have drawn our attention to the intellectual dynamics inherent in the process of *Wissenschaftstransfer*—that is, the transfer, exchange, and transformation of scholarly knowledge—and have suggested moving beyond older models that distinguished between losers and winners of scholarly emigration.[11] This volume focuses not on the migration of existing scholarly knowledge, but on the competencies that young refugees carried abroad.

The term "second generation" itself has also been established by previous studies.[12] We use it primarily as a heuristic category to analyze the cohort of emigrants who escaped from Nazi Germany at a young age—that is, as children, teenagers, or young adults. With few exceptions, they were born between 1918 and 1935 (see Table 1). Most of them had not even finished middle or high school when they left Germany. In our sample, the average age at the time of emigration was thirteen years and nine months (see Table 2). Speaking of a second generation, however, bears an ironic notion insofar as this term prioritizes the German perspective on those who left the Third Reich. If we concentrate on the young refugees' arrival and careers in their new countries, we see that they were often the first—that is, the first who attained a native speaker's fluency in English; the first to receive a doctorate in the English-speaking world; and the first to fight in American or British uniform against the country in which they were born (and its allies in the Pacific theater).[13] Moreover, the term "second generation" bears different meanings in other scholarly contexts. Psychologists, literary scholars, and historians apply it to describe the children of Holocaust survivors. Sociologists use the term when dealing with the children of immigrants, especially in the United States.[14]

The refugees of the second generation did not know that they would be scholars one day. While a few of them had parents who were accomplished academics, they were anything but "illustrious immigrants."[15] Their acculturation in North America, as in England and Israel, was not about adjusting an existing professional record to a new environment; it was about creating a professional future from scratch. There are individuals in this generation who rose to prominence in postwar historiography, such as Peter Gay, Gerda Lerner, or George L. Mosse—and the authors who contribute autobiographical testimonies to this volume. But there were others as well: historians who published little, were not well known outside the circle of experts, and have therefore been largely forgotten. They, too, deserve to be taken into consideration.[16]

Acknowledging this diversity means we should refrain both from construing a generation of emigrants in a biological sense and from suggesting that émigrés-turned-historians constituted a clearly identifiable group. Nor should we claim a direct causal connection between the experience of emigration and the research émigrés undertook years later. Kenneth Barkin, Catherine Epstein, Christhard Hoffmann, and James J. Sheehan have articulated similar caveats in their observations on first-generation refugee historians.[17] Epstein and Volker Berghahn confirm this caution in this volume. The emphasis on the diversity of the émigrés also separates our volume from a recent trend to design so-called generations that are defined by commonalities in life experiences and intellectual output, yet seem to derive from the common year of their birth.[18]

Numbers, Origins, Chronology

Approximately 500,000 individuals left Central Europe in the years 1933 to 1945 to escape discrimination and ultimately—as we now know—physical annihilation. Those young refugees who eventually became historians constitute numerically a tiny segment of the group of around 28,000 emigrants who were born between 1918 and 1935.[19] Only four of the second-generation refugees in our sample were born in the first decade of the twentieth century; twenty between 1910 and 1919. A total of sixty-six were born in the 1920s; seventeen in the 1930s. The oldest at the time of her emigration was Ann Frank Beck, born in 1900; she later taught history in South Dakota, Michigan, and Connecticut. The youngest is Michael A. Meyer, who was born in 1937 and became a leading scholar in the field of Jewish history.

Eighty (c. 75 percent) were born and lived in the territory of the German Reich prior to the annexation of Austria, twenty-one (c. 20 percent) in Austria, while one was born in Poland and one in Switzerland; four grew up in post–World War I Czechoslovakia.[20] This distribution corresponds roughly to that of the total number of refugees who escaped the National Socialist regime in the 1930s. It is not surprising that four major cities with strong middle-class Jewish communities feature prominently among the birthplaces in our sample: twenty-three of the young émigrés came from Berlin, sixteen from Vienna, eleven from Frankfurt/Main, and six from Breslau, today's Wrocław.

The chronology of their emigration, as well as the set of motivations that triggered it, mirror the patterns we know from the general statistics. The year 1933, when the Nazis took over in Germany, represents a first peak; twelve left Germany that year. Their parents immediately saw the consequences of the establishment of Hitler's regime. The socioeconomic situation of the families affected made a difference. Emigrating—which required not only a visa, but also the means to manage the departure logistically—was an option more available to middle-class families, especially those with connections abroad, than to others.[21] The families of George L. Mosse and Johanna Stolper belonged to this group. With disarming frankness, Mosse later described that his departure from Germany does not fit the image of an adventurous escape. Mosse grew up in the bourgeois setting of the wealthy Lachmann-Mosse family in Berlin. After he had concluded his last exam at a prestigious boarding school on Lake Constance, he took a boat to Switzerland, where he attended a boarding school for another year.[22] Stolper, the author of two stimulating books on German society in the nineteenth and twentieth centuries, is known in the profession under the name Joan Campbell. Her parents, Gustav and Toni Stolper, both originally from Vienna, had become accomplished economists and journalists in the Weimar Republic. Living in Berlin, they belonged to Weimar's liberal establishment and were close friends of the family of Theodor Heuss. The Stolpers also had ties to intellectuals abroad and were able to move to New York City in 1933.[23]

In our sample, as in the population at large, the number of emigrants remained low until the end of 1937, but it rose noticeably after the Nuremberg Laws were passed in 1935 (see Table 2).[24] The year 1938 constituted a watershed. It was epitomized by three traumatic events that accelerated the pace with which the National Socialist regime undermined the remaining legal and social status of Jews.[25] Germany's annexation of Austria on 11–12 March 1938, the so-called *Anschluss*, marked the beginning. Raul Hilberg, the analyst of the Holocaust, recalled that "giant swastika flags were draped from the upper stories of apartment houses" in Vienna the next day. His father remarked tersely: "Hitler will put us to the wall." Then, in October 1938, came the German annexation of the border region of Czechoslovakia that included a significant German-speaking population, the *Sudetenland*. This step meant a dramatic intrusion into the post–World War I order, sanctioned by the Munich Agreement of late September. For Wilma Iggers, who was born in Bohemia as the daughter of a Jewish farmer and later became a literary historian in the United States, the Munich Agreement meant "the greatest shock imaginable for my belief in the decency of the world."[26]

The attacks on Jews intensified after the pogrom of 9 November 1938, the so-called *Kristallnacht*. Werner Gundersheimer, who would serve as the director of the Folger Shakespeare Library in Washington from 1983 to 2002, was still an infant in November 1938. But through his parents' memories, he relived the terror of *Kristallnacht* for decades. His mother had already prepared the sandwiches she thought would be needed for her husband in captivity after that night. But for another nine months, the Gestapo kept Hermann Gundersheimer in custody. He was an art historian who was forced to relinquish his position as a university docent and had taken a position as curator of the Rothschild Museum of Judaica in Frankfurt/Main. The secret police wanted to exploit his knowledge of Jewish art, which had just been vandalized in the Rothschild Museum and elsewhere. The Gundersheimer family left for England in 1939 and emigrated to the United States a year later.[27]

The enforced departures of 1938 and 1939 were organized much more hastily than those in previous years. The rapidly growing external as well as psychological pressure to find a way "out of Germany," to quote Renate Bridenthal's chapter in this volume, placed an even greater burden on families with limited financial means. Roosevelt's America was the most desired destination. Many scrambled to secure an affidavit and acquire a visa to enter the United States, the country that ultimately agreed, against domestic opposition, to receive the largest contingent of refugees from the Third Reich. An estimated 130,000 came directly from Central Europe; the total number might be significantly above 200,000 if we were to count those who arrived in the United States after stays in other countries, such as England, and often with a hiatus of several years.[28]

It has been estimated that 118,000 Jews escaped from Germany in 1938 and 1939—about 42 percent of the total number of Jewish emigrants in the years 1933–45. The number of Jews living on Austrian territory shrank by about 100,000 (c. 55 percent) within twelve months after the German annexation.[29] Our sample of émigrés confirms these statistics. Twenty-three (c. 21 percent) of them left—or were deported and expelled from—the now enlarged German Reich in 1938, thirty-one (c. 29 percent) in the following year. Several escaped abroad via a *Kindertransport*. They were rescued in a series of last-minute efforts to provide a safe haven for an estimated 10,000 children who would otherwise have faced an abyss. This small group included Robert Schwarz, who taught for over three decades at Florida Atlantic University; Gerald Holton, a distinguished Harvard physicist who also immersed himself into the history of science; and George Nadel, who pursued his changing interests in Australia, the United States, and England. They were all first brought to England, while Peter Buzanski, a long-time professor of history at San Jose College in California, left Vienna for Sweden in March 1939, crammed into a railway car filled with refugee children.[30]

Diversity and the Shades of Emigration

Many of the refugees who turned into historians were part of a complex migration history, the roots of which reach back to the nineteenth century. They were not simply Germans who turned into Americans.[31] They had parents who had come to Berlin, Vienna, or other German-speaking cities from the multiethnic regions of Central and Eastern Europe, which were then part of the ethnic patchwork of the eastern parts of the German Empire and especially of the Habsburg and Russian Empires. They spoke Czech, Hungarian, or German; some, Russian or Polish; others, Yiddish or Romanian—and in many cases several of these languages.

Both Alexander Dallin, the expert on Russia at Columbia and Stanford University, and George A. Lensen, who wrote about history of Russian-East Asian relations during his tenure at Florida State University, were Berliners. And both were sons of Russian fathers, a Menshevik and a Kadet, who lived in exile from the Bolshevik Soviet Union. Raul Hilberg's father was born in what is today the western region of the Ukraine, his mother in Galicia. Theodore Hamerow, a long-time professor of history at the University of Wisconsin-Madison, was born in Warsaw. He would later entitle succinctly the last chapter of his recollections of interwar Poland "Leaving the Titanic."[32]

The refugees' diverse ethnic and socioeconomic backgrounds as well as their multifaceted cultural and linguistic heritage, in addition to their age and gender, had an impact on the timing and circumstances of their escape. For those who were old enough and willing to speak up against the National Socialists, or who directly felt the Gestapo's terror, this political experience needs to be blended into the story of emigration and escape. All these factors influenced how the refugees later remembered their early years in German-speaking Europe and whether they were willing to reconnect with the country of their birth.

A telling example is provided by Gerd Korman, who taught history in Cornell's School of Industrial and Labor Relations for decades. Korman's mother was born in today's Wuppertal, where her family—Jews from the Austro-Hungarian Empire—had immigrated in the midst of a migration of Polish workers into the industrial Ruhr valley. His father, however, had entered Weimar Germany from Polish Galicia, and counted as a Pole—and a Polish Jew. According to the German citizenship law, Gerd Korman and his immediate family were categorized as Polish citizens. In late October 1938, after the Kormans were forced to surrender their passports, making them stateless, they were ordered out of the country. They fell victim to the deportation of Poles, the so-called *Polenausweisung*, which ultimately affected about 18,000 individuals living on German territory. Korman was forced into the camp set up for Polish Jews in Zbaszyn, a Polish town close to Germany's eastern border. Under dire conditions, he began to embrace Yiddish culture and Zionist ideas. In August 1939, Korman was rescued by a

Kindertransport that brought him to England. A year later, the family reunited in New York City. Korman later felt deep ambiguities and anxieties when visiting Germany and, after decades, began to speak German again.[33]

Klemens von Klemperer and Gerda Lerner were both older and exposed to the National Socialist regime in different ways. Klemperer, the long-time professor of European history at Smith College, came from a middle-class family. At the time of the *Anschluss,* he had already graduated from a prestigious high school in Berlin, the *Französische Gymnasium,* spent two years at Oxford's Balliol College, and was enrolled at the University of Vienna. Although Klemperer realized immediately the necessity of leaving Austria, he continued to support his anti-Nazi friends. Thinking of becoming a poet, Klemperer was concerned about "losing my living tie with the German language."[34] In the fall of 1939, he packed his suitcases under the supervision of two Gestapo men and left for New York City, though with cultural baggage that was very different from Korman's. While the latter devoted much of his energies to teaching and writing about the necessity of keeping the memory of the Holocaust alive, Klemperer focused on bearing witness to those Germans who had resisted the National Socialist dictatorship; he cultivated ties to academic communities in both Germany and Austria.[35]

Gerda Lerner, born in Vienna, also arrived in New York City in 1939. She would become one of America's foremost feminist scholars and a pioneer in the field of women's history. The daughter of a Jewish pharmacist, Lerner absorbed Socialist and feminist literature as a teenager in Vienna. She engaged in political activities with her young Marxist friends. Lerner later described the German annexation of Austria as a "funeral." Desperately attempting to obtain a visa for the United States, enduring harassment by the local bureaucracy, and being held for several weeks in a Vienna prison, Lerner felt it was like "trying to fight your way out of a swamp and sinking deeper with every step."[36] Under a deportation order, she was finally able to leave Austria, exactly a month before *Kristallnacht.* In the immediate years after that experience, Lerner could no longer bear "to hear the German language without choking." Even more than six decades after her enforced departure from Vienna, Lerner was struggling to write about and emotionally confront the events of 1938. Only the resonance that her literary and scholarly works found in the German-speaking world reconciled her with her native tongue and with Austria.[37]

German-Jewish Cultures

Most of those portrayed in this volume belonged to the "Generation Exodus" as described by Walter Laqueur: the generation of young, German-speaking Jews who were old enough to witness the rise of the Nazis, but young enough to begin a new life in America, England, Palestine, and elsewhere.[38] Being Jewish had different meanings for members of this cohort. It could be a distinct religious identity or, more broadly, a set of cultural values and traditions. Jewishness could be a category imposed by the National Socialists, which might then have been strengthened by the experience of the Third Reich. For some, being Jewish was a highly mediated and partial identity, while others strongly embraced it. Can we capture, at least in nuances, what the hyphenated, seemingly familiar term "German-Jewish" signified for the refugees of the second generation?[39]

We know today that the National Socialists themselves grappled with developing a supposedly coherent racist categorization of Jews.[40] Nevertheless, from early 1933 on, being classified as Jewish was the decisive reason to be targeted by the new regime. About 90 to 95 percent of the individuals in our sample and their families fell into this category. This confirms what we know about the composition of the refugees from Central Europe at large.[41] The category of Jews included children of religiously mixed marriages and of grandparents with Christian and Jewish origins. Hans A. Schmitt, who later taught at the University of Virginia, was one of them. Until 1933 he did not care much about the fact that his mother was Jewish. Schmitt never had a bar mitzvah, and in his self-perception was "not a Jew and had no intention of becoming one." But he marched proudly in the first rank of the Jewish Boy Scouts with his "certified Nordic appearance," as he dryly put it later.[42] Others did see themselves as Jews. At least two of the émigrés in our sample had mothers who had converted from the Christian faith to Judaism before 1933.[43]

A substantial number of young refugees exemplified the cultural situation of Jews who had become part of the German *Bildungsbürgertum* whose social position largely derived from their educational achievements and economic success. These middle-class citizens embraced the value of *Bildung*, culture and education, in both their private and professional life. They often shared a sense of civic responsibilities—and pride—as German citizens. Not surprisingly, the *Bildungsbürgertum* of Jewish background displayed a high degree of assimilation. In their cultural tastes, habitus, interests, and material attributes, they had immersed themselves to a considerable extent into the dominant Protestant culture of Prussia and adjusted more generally to the surrounding Christian society and its "Germanness." Many were baptized; others reconciled respect for Christian holidays (often including a Christmas tree for their children in the living room) with their Jewish traditions.[44] Fritz Stern's childhood illustrates this sociocultural situation. He comes from a highly educated family of medical doctors and is one of several in our sample who were baptized Lutherans. Stern was named after his godfather, Fritz Haber, one of Germany's prominent scientists, who had converted from Judaism in his mid-thirties.[45]

Himself an agnostic, the Berliner Walter Simon also came from the Jewish middle class; his father was an industrialist. In the postwar era, Simon taught for twelve years as a professor at Cornell before leaving for England, where he continued to write on nineteenth-century German history. John L. Clive, too, came from the upper middle-class. The son of a Jewish lawyer, he, like Klemperer, attended the prestigious *Französische Gymnasium* in Berlin. Clive taught as professor of history at Harvard from 1965 on, while his brother Geoffrey became a professor of philosophy in the United States.[46]

The German-Jewish *bildungsbürgerlich* Eyck family in Berlin generated no fewer than three historians. Erich Eyck, a prominent lawyer and intellectual from the left spectrum of Germany's fractured liberal scene, became best known for his biographies of William Gladstone and Otto von Bismarck. He had celebrated his bar mitzvah, but rarely attended services at a synagogue. Eyck objected to the various Jewish dietary, hygienic, and Sabbath restrictions. His much younger cousin Franz Gunther Eyck emigrated first to Palestine in 1933 and then taught at various universities in the United States. Better known is Erich Eyck's son, Frank Eyck, who also focused on British and German history as a historian. Frank was allowed to join the youth wing of the *Central-Verein deutscher Staatsbürger jüdischen Glaubens*, and, after 1933, the *Kulturbund deutscher Juden*.[47] But he was exempted from learning Hebrew at school. The family had intimate Christian acquaintances who helped make them a center of sociability in Berlin's liberal circles. Among them were Elly and Theodor Heuss. Frank Eyck's "sheltered childhood ended abruptly" on 30 January 1933.[48] His father lost his position and was harassed by SA troops. Family connections allowed Frank Eyck to transition into the English school system in 1935–36.

The religious and cultural identities of the young émigrés varied considerably. They ranged from those who defined themselves as secular or agnostic, if not atheist, to Orthodox believers, from Zionists to others who described their upbringing as that of a religiously traditional but culturally assimilated family. The latter held true for Toni Oelsner, who worked with a Jewish study group at the *Freies Jüdisches Lehrhaus* (Free Jewish School) in Frankfurt/Main prior to her emigration. Lacking a doctorate, she never held a tenured position at an academic institution in the United States. Werner Angress and Werner Warmbrunn joined the Jewish youth organization *Schwarzes Fähnlein* (Little Black Flag), which initially distanced itself from Zionist groups.[49] In the post–World War II era, Angress became a professor at Berkeley and the State University of New York (SUNY) Stony Brook, while Warmbrunn taught at Pitzer College in California.

Others in our sample were drawn strongly to Judaism as a religion and equally to the political contents of Zionism. The young Georg Iggers, for example, opposed his parents' relaxed attitude toward kosher food and increasingly felt that he "was Jewish, not German." Susan Groag Bell, on the other hand, grew up with a Jewish background and bilingual in the Moravian-Silesian region of Czechoslovakia. But she was baptized, lived in a predominantly Catholic town, and celebrated the Christian holidays. Both of Bell's parents converted to Lutheranism.[50] Much later, Bell played an important role in the fields of women's and gender history in the United States.

Yet, there were also the Zionist families living in the partially German-speaking parts of Czechoslovakia: the father of Theodore K. Rabb, who taught for decades at Princeton, was a well-known Zionist intellectual and journalist.[51] While nearly all of the historians in our sample nominally retained their religious affiliation, only one, Bruno Schlesinger, converted to Christianity before emigration. This did not prevent the Gestapo from targeting him as a Jew in Vienna. Schlesinger devoted his academic life to teaching at a private Catholic college in Indiana.[52]

Still others had roots in the Orthodox and Eastern European segments of Central European Jewry. They constituted a heterogeneous group from which Western European Jews often distinguished themselves, as the historian Manfred Jonas recalled.[53] Abraham Ascher provides an intriguing example. Like Fritz Stern, Ascher grew up in Breslau, though in a very different milieu. Both his parents had moved to the city from the Polish-speaking part of Galicia. They "never regarded themselves as Germans," did not socialize with Gentiles, and raised their son as a religiously Orthodox Jew. Accordingly, the young Ascher always wore a hat. For good reasons, he concealed it on the day in March 1936 when curiosity drove him to watch Adolf Hitler speak to the local population. When he did not cheer to the *Führer*, Ascher was thrown down, yelled at ("Damn Jew"), and had to run for his life. He escaped to England in July 1939 and later had a distinguished career at Brooklyn College.

By the time Ascher arrived in England, he no longer felt particularly religious. He had discovered Marx's writings, which replaced the Old Testament for him. In the light of his personal encounters with antisemitism and the National Socialist terror, however, he was determined "to preserve the essentials of Judaism" and his attachment to Jewish culture.[54] Ismar Schorsch does not fit the type of an assimilated German Jew, either. He came from a family deeply devoted to Jewish service and learning. Schorsch fled Germany in 1938 at the age of three, after his father was released from internment in the Buchenwald concentration camp. Emil Schorsch had been ordained as a rabbi at the Breslau Jewish Theological Seminary, and Ismar Schorsch was ordained in the United States. He later became professor and chancellor of the Jewish Theological Seminary in New York and an intellectual voice of America's Conservative Judaism.[55]

In spite of the differences in their cultural and social background, all of the young refugees brought personal experiences of antisemitism to their new countries. Some encountered ardent Nazis among peers and teachers, though a surprisingly large number report a relatively protected school life and even instances of explicit solidarity with Gentiles. The gray zone in between generated its own bizarreness. For Werner Angress, this included the experience of being praised by the local teacher of *Rassenkunde* (science of race) for his Aryan head shape—"just like our Reich Propaganda Minister Dr. Goebbels."[56] Looking back at his years at Berlin's *Goethe Gymnasium*, Peter Gay pinpointed the obvious dilemma. His experiences contradicted widespread clichés; these years "attested to surviving pockets of decency in Nazi Germany, even of quiet resistance. And this further complicated our assessment of what we had to expect."[57]

Finally, there were some refugees with different cultural roots and other reasons to emigrate. Gerard Thormann, from 1959 on professor at Manhattanville College, came from a Roman Catholic, anti-Nazi family. In 1933, he followed his father, a well-known left-leaning Catholic journalist, into exile in France. Maria Schweinburg Grossmann also came from a Roman Catholic family and fled Austria after the German annexation. In the United States, she married a refugee from a Jewish family in Vienna. Maria Grossman served for years as a librarian at Harvard, while Walter Grossmann, her historian husband, became the director of the libraries of the University of Massachusetts, Boston.[58]

Neither Ursula Lamb nor Theodor von Laue were Jewish. Both came to the United States in the 1930s on temporary student visas—and they stayed, alienated by the National Socialist regime. Colleagues of Lamb, who became a distinguished historian of the Spanish Empire, report that she had already opposed the Nazis in Germany.[59] The same cannot be said of Laue. In the 1930s, he seems to have lived in a largely apolitical, private world of education, sports, and *Bildung*, protected by the well-off family around his scientist father, the Nobel Prize winner Max von Laue. Max von Laue's connection with Albert Einstein, who lived in Princeton, helped Theodor when he was admitted to Princeton University. As a historian in the postwar era, he concentrated on Russian history and became an early advocate of teaching world history.[60]

Like Laue, the Protestant Hans W. Gatzke was older than most second-generation émigrés. He does not fit into any category. Neither a descendant of an established *bildungsbürgerlich* family, nor of Jewish background, nor a left-wing opponent of National Socialism, Gatzke had belonged to the *Deutsche Freischar* in Weimar, one of the liberal branches of the German youth movement. After his return from a year at Williams College, Gatzke began to study in the Third Reich. Realizing that he did not fit into the National Socialist matrix—a realization emphasized by a Gestapo raid of his apartment—Gatzke returned to the United States for good in 1937. During his tenure at Johns Hopkins University and Yale, Gatzke gained a stellar reputation as a scholar of Germany's political history. Already in 1950, Gatzke proposed a critical analysis of imperial Germany's aims during World War I that anticipated the later writings of Fritz Fischer.[61]

Transcultural Migrations

And so they fled Germany: some officially left as emigrants with the *Reichsfluchtsteuer* (federal escape tax) paid by their parents, others were expelled, many escaped without a clear plan. All left under immense stress: deprived of their homes, robbed of all their belongings, and separated from family members whose future remained uncertain. The young refugees brought along distinct features of their socioeconomic, cultural, and political upbringing. In very different ways and mediated through their families' experiences, they brought to the English-speaking world a familiarity with diverse German-Jewish cultures—in the plural. Soon, they carried indelible memories of family members and friends murdered in the Holocaust. For many, such memories played into their motivation to study history, even when they did not deal explicitly with the Jewish genocide. For some, the memory of the past fueled their willingness to become politically engaged against new and other forms of injustice.

However, lines of continuity were broken by moments of discontinuity. Once the young refugees had left Germany, they added the experience of migration to the cultural and social capital wrapped in their mostly sparse baggage. This experience meant yet another formative period in their lives. Their migration often turned out to be much longer than expected. It generated more twists and unanticipated interruptions which offered gateways to new transcultural experiences. The enforced movement through different geographical and cultural spaces gave many refugees an understanding of themselves that was not restricted by state borders or national narratives.[62]

After his departure from Germany, it took Peter Gay more than a year and a half to arrive in the United States. He spent most of this time in Cuba. Life in Havana meant being part of both the German-Jewish refugee and the American communities while surrounded by a Spanish-speaking society. Gay used the time to improve his English and immerse himself in American popular culture. He became a fan of the New York Yankees and finally saw *Gone with the Wind*, after having read Margaret Mitchell's novel two years earlier in German. Memories of Berlin would continue to hang over him "like a sinister shadow." Still, while sitting on suitcases in Havana, it was necessary to preserve a "fixation on the future."[63]

Several of the young refugees spent considerable time in western and southern Europe before they were forced to move on again. Peter Paret spent two years in Austria, followed by two years in France, before arriving in the United States via England. Peter Amann escaped from Austria to France in 1939, a year later to Switzerland, then again to France, only to board a ship from Lisbon to New York City in 1941.[64] Mostly due to family connections, Italy provided a temporary haven for some refugees in the mid-1930s, including Robert A. Huttenback, who rose through the ranks at the California Institute of Technology, and Conrad Schirokauer, the long-time professor of Asian history at the City University of New York.[65] A large number of refugees first spent some time in the United Kingdom, primarily England, before leaving again, this time for America or Canada. Peter Alter provides a survey of those who stayed in the United Kingdom in this volume.[66]

Arrival in England, though a country familiar to some, meant entering a new "contact zone."[67] Those who had just escaped the National Socialist terror were now exposed to an asymmetrical mix of cultural influences, some friendly, others not. This mélange generated new forms of intercultural encounters, all of which took place on unfamiliar ground. There was the private English boarding school with uniform-wearing peers and a headmistress who greeted the newcomer in person, certainly a double novelty for those coming from a German *Gymnasium*. Yet other refugees perceived a "Prussian discipline" in English educational institutions. And there were the Anglican families who embraced Jewish children with their own ethical principles and religious rituals, with nonkosher food on the dinner table and the celebration of Christmas and Easter.[68]

The beginning of the war against Germany in September 1939 marked another milestone. It turned the refugees into "enemy aliens." Some soon found themselves in British internment camps, including Frank Eyck, who was held on the Isle of Man in 1940. There he was surrounded by Nazi sympathizers and victims of the Third Reich, by internees of Italian, Turkish, and Japanese descent, by rabbis, Catholic priests, and Protestant pastors. This experience made Eyck not only more sensitive to the necessity of accepting the coexistence of different cultures, but also confirmed his decision to dissociate himself politically from Germany.[69]

George L. Mosse underwent a fundamental political socialization during his six years in England. He did not experience the deprivations of an émigré's life; on the contrary, exile "energized" and "challenged" Mosse as nothing had done before. He experienced his "true political awakening" at Cambridge University and joined young socialists in the antifascist cause. Mosse's consciousness of being a German Jew, though secular in nature, became more pronounced instead of weaker—a parallel to Fritz Stern, who emigrated straight to the United States where his "sense of being a Jew became still stronger."[70]

There is substantial evidence to suggest that especially those who went to the Netherlands embraced the experience of cultural tolerance. This did not mean that they abandoned what they regarded as German traditions worthy of preservation. For no fewer than five or six individuals out of our sample, this experience was epitomized by the Eerde School, hosted in a Dutch manor not far from the German border. The result of an initiative by German and English Quakers, Eerde began its operation in April 1934. The school's primary purpose was to protect "half-Aryan" and "half-Jewish" children from discrimination by the Nazis. The predominantly German-Jewish children at Eerde received a rigorous education, oriented to the requirements of the Oxford School Certificate. They enjoyed excellent instruction in English, as well as a grounding in literature and music that firmly anchored them in European humanistic traditions. In spite of the curricular demands, girls in particular enjoyed the "feeling of freedom" at Eerde.[71] One of them was Beate Ruhm von Oppen, who would eventually come to the United States via England. She became a skillful translator of historical works, including the first volume of Konrad Adenauer's memoirs. Hans A. Schmitt, another Eerde alumnus, turned the Quaker support for refugees from Germany into the topic of a monographic study.[72]

We know about the indispensable support lent by the Quakers and Jewish aid organizations, which helped many of the individuals documented in our sample. Historians have also devoted attention to refugees' experiences in England, Palestine, and Israel: Walter Laqueur's fifteen-year passage through all three regions is instructive. In this volume, Shulamit Volkov deals with the émigrés who taught history in Israel. Yet, with the exception of the German refugee community in Shanghai, the formative experiences that some young émigrés' gained in Asia and South America have hardly been explored.[73]

Ernst Badian, Harvard's long-time professor of ancient history, escaped the Nazis to the Pacific world. In 1938, he and his parents moved to New Zealand, where he acquired his first academic degrees. Badian preserved his sympathy for New Zealand throughout his life. He maintained close ties to his alma mater and even endowed a chair in classics there. After more than two decades in England, Badian accepted a position in the United States. One can speculate whether his critical account of Alexander the Great might have been informed by his family's early encounter with Hitler's dictatorial power.[74]

Harry Benda's scholarly interests were directly connected to his experiences in the Pacific. Both of Benda's parents and most of his close relatives perished in the Holocaust. As a twenty-year-old, Benda managed to escape to Indonesia in 1939 and found employment in an import firm. In the wake of the Japanese occupation, Benda was interned in a camp together with other Jews. After his liberation, he acquired his first academic degrees in New Zealand. Benda used his first-hand knowledge of Southeast Asia to succeed in Cornell University's doctoral program in government with a thesis on Indonesian Islam under the Japanese occupation of Java. As a professor at Yale, Benda was instrumental in establishing Southeast Asian history as a major field of study in the United States and argued against the prevailing, "western" view of Asia.[75]

South America also contributed to shaping the biographies of the second-generation émigrés. Henry Blumenthal, born into a Jewish middle-class family in Mazovia, was old enough to enroll briefly at the *Hochschule für Wissenschaft des Judentums* (College for the Scholarly Study of Judaism) and at the University of Berlin, where the historian Hermann Oncken accepted him as a doctoral candidate. In 1936, he escaped to Brazil, only to encounter the wave of antisemitic measures endorsed by President Getúlio Vargas. Blumenthal was expelled to Uruguay. In 1938, he took the chance to immigrate on the Polish quota to the United States, where he discovered his interest in North American and French history.[76]

Charles W. Arnade's global itinerary first led from his hometown Görlitz to China. In Nanking, he and his father, who served in the German Military mission, witnessed the brutal Japanese invasion in 1937. Via Shanghai and Switzerland they escaped to Bolivia, where Arnade spent six years—and, in 1944, won the country's swimming championship in breaststroke. In his academic positions in Florida, Arnade promoted the teaching of the Holocaust as well as of the Spanish Empire in the Americas and, specifically, Bolivian history. Neither his memory of the Third Reich nor the itinerary of his life, which ultimately led him to Holocaust conferences and lectures around the globe, stopped at national borders.[77]

Settling in America

In 1953, the political scientist Franz L. Neumann, who belonged to the older generation of German-Jewish emigrants and, as a professor at Columbia University, advised several students of the second generation, praised the "openness of American society" when it came to integrating refugee scholars. The term reverberates in the autobiographical recollections of the younger refugees. For many, the United States presented itself as a "land of opportunity," in the words of Walter L. Arnstein, who escaped the Third Reich in 1939.[78] Arnstein excelled as a historian of Britain at the University of Illinois at Urbana-Champaign. However, once the young refugees had arrived in America and become immigrants, they noticed that there were some limits to openness—and more opportunities for some than for others. While embracing the chance to enter high school and college, they faced a plethora of new challenges, ranging from the loss of social status and distinct gender-specific obstacles to variations of antisemitism.

The overwhelming majority of immigrants in our sample, as in the refugee population at large, went through an extended period of uncertainty, during which they and their families struggled to make a living. Women in particular were forced to stay in low-paying jobs for a while. A few could make use of their family's social connections in Germany; others used the skills they had acquired during their emigration. Leonore Laan did both—and the latter even left an imprint on her historical research. After her schooling at Eerde, Laan trained as a nanny in England and then went to Italy before arriving in the United States in 1939. The émigré and theater director Max Reinhardt, acquainted with her mother, arranged part-time employment for her as a nanny in California until she could start attending the University of California at Los Angeles (UCLA). At Radcliffe College, Laan wrote a dissertation on the history of nursing legislation in the British Commonwealth.[79]

Early work experience in the United States also left its traces on the thematic interests of Herman Freudenberger, who had emigrated with an early *Kindertransport* via New York City to Chicago. As a worker in a mattress and shoe polish factory, Freudenberger experienced first hand the world of manufacturing and industrial production, which he later analyzed as an economic historian. Others faced what Gerda Lerner summed up as follows: "I had nearly gone under in the first eight months as an immigrant, unable to find work, due mostly to the fact that employers of casual labor and domestic work found me 'overqualified,' and I was too afraid of getting in trouble with the Immigration Service to seek even private assistance."[80]

The young immigrants were Germans, Austrians, or Czechs who now turned into Americans. Yet, the naturalization process could take a long time; some remained stateless for years.[81] As far as we can tell, all of them retained the capacity to read and understand German. This heritage was often encouraged, if not enforced by parents, as Hanna Holborn Gray describes it in her contribution to this volume. Thanks to their previous schooling or religious education, many could add some knowledge of Hebrew and other European languages, old and new. Particularly in some neighborhoods of New York City, where more than half of the German-Jewish refugees from the Third Reich initially settled, German could be used in everyday life well into the 1950s.[82]

Foreign language ability was another piece of cultural capital that turned out to be a plus for these immigrants on their way into academia. However, there was not only the momentum of continuity. Gerhard Weinberg recalled that he needed to refresh his German after two years of English schooling, which predated his emigration to the United States in 1940. In Albany, New York, his family spoke English so that his parents could gain a command of this language. Furthermore, a considerable number of immigrants refused to speak German at home. Emotional and political reasons played a role, but also the desire to accommodate non-German speaking partners and friends who now joined the family circle. Once reunited in New York City, the Arnstein family no longer wanted to speak German: "We were so disgusted." But this judgment did not affect their continued willingness to respect European cultures. Fritz Stern felt "no urge" either to have his children "learn the language of a country that had expelled me, a language that they were unlikely to find as easy or natural as I did." Yet he wanted his children to master French and cherished their affinity for the "Europeanness" of his parents' home.[83]

In their new professional lives, the young immigrants almost always spoke English. Ironically, this was not the case among the faculty members at the Institute for German History in Tel Aviv, whom Shulamit Volkov encountered as late as 1973.[84] English became the second-generation émigrés' primary language in America; they learned it quickly, and most spoke it without any trace of an accent. This learning process was a catalyst in their Americanization, in addition to absorbing American popular culture—practicing baseball, for example—immersing themselves in the dorm life in college, and becoming citizens of the United States.[85] In their mastery of English, the young immigrants clearly differed from the first generation of émigrés. Only a few scholars, such as Georg and Wilma Iggers, Klaus Epstein, and Felix F. Strauss, published continuously and without a translator's assistance in German.

Gender and Military Service

Gender was of paramount importance when these young people adjusted to their new environments and found a way into academia. More often for women than for men, there was continuity between their involvement in organizing the practicalities of emigration in their German homes and managing the logistics of social and economic acculturation in America.[86] They shouldered the tasks caring for siblings and children, doing errands and handling bureaucratic procedures, while contributing to the family's economic survival and supporting husbands and other male family members. This reality came at the expense of young women's chance to pursue their intellectual interests at college and delayed their earning a graduate degree.

Twenty—that is, around 19 percent—of historians in our sample are women, as opposed to only around 9 percent among the first-generation refugee historians (see Tables 1 and 3). Among these twenty female historians, five never acquired a doctorate.[87] This percentage is significantly higher than in the group of male historians. Moreover, the average age at which female historians finished their Ph.D., slightly above thirty-three, is higher than among male historians. Four female historians did not finish their doctorates until well after they turned forty: Ann Beck, Joan Campbell, Maria Grossmann, and Gerda Lerner. After completing her undergraduate and graduate training at two elite schools, Radcliffe and Oxford in England, Campbell married and soon followed her husband when his academic career took the family to New Zealand and Canada. It was only in her forties that Campbell, a devoted mother of four children, enrolled in the Ph.D. program of Queen's University, Ontario. Involuntarily, she became part of what her male colleagues in the history department condescendingly referred to as the "housewives brigade," which happened to do much of the department's teaching. With abysmal academic job prospects, she got by for several years with part-time assignments at various Canadian universities.[88]

Other women faced gender discrimination when entering university, at times reinforced by age discrimination and hostile attitudes toward what contemporaries defined as deviant sexual behavior. Renée Watkins, who was born in Berlin in 1932 and escaped Germany via the Netherlands and Portugal, was admitted to Radcliffe in the early 1950s. But she found the college's atmosphere stuffy and oppressive, which compelled her to hide her homosexuality. Still in the mid-1960s, Susan Groag Bell was turned down by the admissions committee of Stanford's graduate program in history due to her age, then thirty-nine.[89]

Military service was a distinctly gender-specific experience for a majority of men in our sample, about forty-nine out of eighty-eight.[90] Many experienced combat in the European or, as in the case of Peter Paret, in the Pacific theater of World War II. Later Paret drew on this experience in his studies of military and cultural history. He dedicated one of his seminal works, *Imagined Battles*, to the memory "of the men with whom I served, and against whom I served." Paret acknowledged explicitly how his personal experience motivated his long-standing interest in the place "war occupies in history and in the role it has played for my generation."[91]

The U.S. Army used the bilingual competence of several immigrants to deploy them for purposes of psychological warfare and to interrogate German military and Nazi Party personnel. Werner Angress, Henry Kissinger, Hans A. Schmitt, Gerard Thormann, and Guy Stern, who later became one of the foremost scholars of German literary history, all served as "Ritchie Boys." They became members of the U.S. military intelligence unit trained in Fort Ritchie, Maryland, to be deployed in Europe after the Normandy invasion. With fifteen minutes of jump training under his belt, Angress parachuted into the area behind German lines on 6 June 1944. Only a year later, when he arrived at Wöbbelin, a branch camp of the Neugamme concentration camp in Hamburg, did Angress learn about the full extent of the "Final Solution," a term—like Auschwitz—he had never before heard.[92]

Serving in the military against their homeland was for some a stepping-stone in their "Americanizing".[93] Yet, this had more complex implications. Service in intelligence units brought some together with other German Jews and opened a space to discuss responses to National Socialism. For many, military service helped to confirm the growing separation between their German past and the conscious—and desired—political separation from Germany as a state. "I could never call myself a German again," recalled Frank Eyck after the Second World War had ended.[94] He had served in the British army, as did Lewis Gann, who worked in the postwar period as an archivist in Rhodesia and a curator at the Hoover Institution in Stanford, and Guenter Lewy, who pursued his historical interests as a professor of government and political science.

The biography of Gunther E. Rothenberg exemplifies how military service for a cause outside, if not against, the country of origin became a seminal event. It meant departing from an ethnic, seemingly objective understanding of national belonging in favor of turning toward a voluntary, subjective understanding of what the commitment to a nation entailed. Rothenberg was born into an upper-middle-class family in Berlin. He left Germany in 1937 and came to the United States after years of migration via the Netherlands, Palestine, and Canada. Rothenberg served in three armies. A member of the Zionist-Socialist movement Hashomer Hatzair, Rothenberg first did a five-year stint in the British Army in the Mediterranean theater before fighting as a captain in the Haganah for an independent Jewish state in Palestine. During the early Cold War, he joined U.S. Air Force intelligence, suspicious of new fascist or other authoritarian threats. Rothenberg identified strongly as a Jew and a supporter of Israel after 1948. He followed his military experiences with a distinguished career as a military historian at the University of New Mexico.[95]

Distinctiveness and Antisemitism

Going to college turned the young American citizens into the historians we know today. They—and, again, this meant many more men than women—profited from the expansion of American higher education during and after the end of World War II. The G.I. Bill officially sanctioned the growing demand for education in 1944. This trend was fueled by high birth rates in the United States between 1946 and 1964. These political and demographic developments created a growing student population. Colleges and universities, both long-established and newly founded, expanded their programs and increased the number of faculty. The social sciences and humanities had their share in this transformation, as did new area studies and revamped foreign language programs. For some years, career prospects in one of these fields were much better than prior to World War II, even when they still influenced by gender, family circumstances, and changing economic cycles. Moreover, once the GIs had graduated in the 1950s and college and university enrollments dropped again, far fewer academic jobs were available.[96]

Did the immigrants bring to American academia a "distinctiveness advantage"[97] thanks to their European heritage? There is, at first glance, abundant evidence to support this sociological observation. They were able to infuse a distinct cultural capital into the study of history. They possessed a familiarity with European intellectual traditions, accompanied by the linguistic skills that America's liberal arts education cherished. This helps explain why immigrants such as Karl J. Weintraub, Werner Warmbrunn, Bruno Schlesinger, and John Rodes excelled as teachers in the flourishing World and Western Civilization programs. These became a key element of the general education requirements many American institutions of higher learning implemented after 1945.[98]

But the German-speaking immigrants' tangible or perceived distinctiveness must be assessed in comparison with that of others—and it was ambiguous. Since almost all of our sample were Jewish, they could face forms of antisemitism, which had its own tradition in American academia.[99] Although prejudices against Jewish students weakened from the 1940s on, many encountered the resulting impediments in one way or another, often closely coupled with their social status as refugees. It is difficult to draw general conclusions from individual recollections. Some encountered a defensive attitude, if not hostility, toward Jewish refugee students when they met a conservative professor; others, when mingling with peers; still others in the social environment of universities.

Harvard and Columbia were more open to Jewish students than other Ivy League schools, while Princeton traditionally had a very low percentage of Jewish students. The City College of New York and Brooklyn College had a predominantly Jewish student population and welcomed faculty from Jewish and German family backgrounds. Across the United States, the picture varied dramatically.[100] The newly founded Roosevelt College in Chicago, for example, welcomed Jewish and African-American students. Roosevelt College (from 1954 on called Roosevelt University) employed a considerable number of first- and second-generation émigrés from National Socialist Germany as faculty, among them the historians Helmut Hirsch, Georg Iggers, and Walter Arnstein. Rolf A. Weil, Roosevelt's long-time president, was also a Jewish refugee; he opted for economics instead of history as a senior in college. It was then evident for him that "as a Jew I would have great difficulty getting equal consideration at many institutions of higher learning." He found this situation "extremely disillusioning" in light of his previous experiences in Germany.[101]

Gerald D. Nash's experiences attest to the fact that America was not always like New York City, or Roosevelt College, for that matter. The distinguished historian of the American West was born as Gerhard Nachschön in Berlin in 1928. Nine years later he arrived via Palestine in New York City, where the family shortened its last name to Nash. Nash felt comfortable at school in Washington Heights, where many German-Jewish middle-class families settled, as well as at New York University and Columbia. Having already become acquainted with a "kaleidoscope of European emigration" in the family's second apartment in Manhattan, Nash wanted to learn more about the country and accepted a fellowship at Ohio State University in Columbus. Here he encountered a "virulent anti-Semitism" and landlords who did not rent rooms to Jewish students. Not surprisingly, Nash returned to New York City, where he wrote his master's thesis at Columbia on the Reconstruction era. Nash's early intersection with fascism surfaced much later in his critique of the New Western history and again, unexpectedly, in 1990–91, during a year as a guest professor in Göttingen. There, Nash encountered protesters rallying against the first Gulf War. Their attitude, "mass meetings," and the "shattering of glass" prompted unwelcome memories of the Nazi era.[102]

Academic Entries and Thematic Interests

As a result of the National Socialist dictatorship and World War II, American institutions of higher education realized the need to research the history of Germany, Europe, and East Asia—and to utilize the expertise of refugees. There was an urgent demand to find explanations and analytical categories that could explain the rise of the "German ideology" and the "failure of illiberalism," as Fritz Stern pointedly described the particularities of German history. There was also the desire to arrive at generalizations that would explain the character of authoritarian and totalitarian societies. Experts were needed to investigate these issues.[103]

Against this background, the immigrants from the second generation pursued careers in the historical disciplines—just as others chose neighboring fields, many of which overlapped with the interests of historians: political science, sociology, economics, art history, and psychology as well as Judaic and Jewish studies,

German studies and literature, and Romance cultures; in chapter 22 I provide examples of scholars from these areas. Out of the 100 immigrants in our sample who received a doctorate, a few, such as Benda, Hilberg, Lewy, Schlesinger, and Kissinger, did so in the fields of political science or government; they all emphasized the historical aspects of their topics. Peter Gay, strongly drawn to Franz L. Neumann, initially taught in Columbia University's government department. Most future historians began their study with a broad range of interests. Their later research foci developed over time and did not necessarily reflect their initial ideas about a possible specialization. George L. Mosse, for example, was primarily interested in European history before 1800 when he came to the United States.[104]

Only three in our sample finished their Ph.D. between 1940 and 1945: Alma Luckau Molin, who later taught at Vassar College; Herbert Moller, the demographic historian at Boston University; and Theodor von Laue. The numbers rose considerably in the following two decades. Fourteen concluded their doctoral work in the years 1946–50, thirty-three between 1951 and 1955, and thirty in the period 1956–60. Twenty received their doctorate after 1961. Columbia University tops the list of institutions that awarded doctorates to members of this group (21), nearly matched by Harvard (20, a number to which three Radcliffe dissertations could be added,) and followed, with a considerable gap, by the Universities of Chicago (8) and California, Berkeley (6). The sample includes three doctorates each from the University of Pennsylvania, the University of Wisconsin (Madison), Stanford, Yale, and Oxford (England), in addition to other institutions in the United States and three Central European universities.[105]

Many immigrants, the women among them in particular, had to live on temporary appointments for years. Others spent a considerable portion of their early careers at institutions that did not emphasize history or even the humanities. Herbert A. Strauss taught for six years at New York's Juilliard School of Music before becoming a member of the faculty at the City College of New York. Many found employment at small institutions, such as Conrad Latour at Beaver College, today's Arcadia University, and Wilhelm Reuning at Susqehanna University. Some immigrants went into fields that are important for the study of history but easily overlooked: the work of translating (Ruhm von Oppen), library service (Maria Grossmann and Agnes Peterson), bibliographical research (Eric H. Boehm), administrative work for philanthropic foundations (Gerald Freund), and research in nonacademic institutions such as the Office of the Historian at the State Department (Arthur G. Kogan). Foundations and institutions that granted aid and fellowships widely recognized the talent of many refugees and the importance of their research topics. The number of fellowships awarded to them is staggering, as documented in chapter 23; thirty (c. 28 percent) received a Guggenheim fellowship in the course of their career.

The second-generation immigrants, now American citizens, chose very different areas of specialization. Their thematic spectrum was much wider than that among the older refugees.¹⁰⁶ They came of age in an academic setting that offered them considerably more—and more varied—options. Individual preferences and the conditions at each university, where mentors needed to be found, played as much of a role in choosing research topics as did their past. Moreover, there was simply the luck of finding a supportive place to study and of entering a field in need of scholars.¹⁰⁷

Many began to research the various histories of society, politics, and culture in the German-speaking territories of Europe. A closer look, however, reveals that a relatively small number concentrated on the Third Reich and, later, the Holocaust. Gerhard Weinberg did so in his path-breaking studies on Hitler's "Second Book," National Socialist foreign policy, and the genocidal war after 1939, increasingly in global perspective. George Stein concentrated in his studies on Hitler and the *Waffen SS*. Renate Bridenthal contributed to exploring the role of gender and of biological thinking in the paths to the Third Reich and in the fabric of the National Socialist society. Several historians pointed out varieties of resistance against the National Socialist regime.¹⁰⁸

Conceptual and historical approaches to the Holocaust and genocide at large developed slowly, as Doris Bergen shows in her chapter on Henry Friedlander, Raul Hilberg, and Gerhard Weinberg, to whom we would need to add Henry Feingold, Saul Friedländer, Henry R. Huttenbach, Walter Laqueur, and the less well-known George M. Kren. Eric H. Boehm did not undertake original research in the field of Holocaust studies, but already in 1949 drew the public's attention to survivors of the Holocaust and opponents of the Third Reich. Gerd Korman also published a moving collection of testimonies by victims of the Nazis.¹⁰⁹ More often, however, the immigrants concentrated on the long and twisted roads to National Socialism. Several scholars sought its roots in a dazzling spectrum of populist and political ideologies, including Klaus Epstein, Walter Laqueur, George L. Mosse, and Fritz Stern. Others, such as Hans W. Gatzke, Manfred Jonas, and Joachim Remak, researched the diplomatic history of the decades leading to World War II.

While emotional reasons are difficult to assess, there was a fundamental methodological reason for what might seem like a reluctance to study Nazism: access to sources and their availability in print were still limited in the two immediate postwar decades. From the 1950s on, this dilemma prompted Fritz T. Epstein, the father of Klaus Epstein, as well as Raul Hilberg, Gerhard Weinberg, and others to devote their expertise to documenting important German source materials and making them accessible to future researchers. Weinberg expands on this topic in his essay in this volume.¹¹⁰ Furthermore, a considerable number of immigrants injected their familiarity with the plurality of Jewish histories in Germany and Central and Eastern Europe into historiographical works. Their studies offered analyses of a broad range of local and regional Jewish cultures and communities.¹¹¹

Equally important are studies on German antisemitism, both before and during its radicalization in the Third Reich. Herbert A. Strauss analyzed the enforced emigration of German Jews from the Third Reich. Michael A. Meyer's history of German-Jewish culture in the modern age, in addition to his more specialized studies, offered an indispensable long-term perspective. Can *German-Jewish History*, edited by Meyer with the assistance of Michael Brenner, then be seen as the sophisticated product of an "émigré synthesis," a scholarly agenda created by German-Jewish émigrés whose experience and memory was supported by the post–World War II institutional infrastructure, with the Leo Baeck Institute in New York taking the lead?[112] Perhaps such a pointed characterization suggests too easily a causal link between one specific context that helped generate such scholarship and the breadth of its contents, which derived from heterodox motives and approaches.

Although a considerable number of immigrants came to focus on modern German and Austrian history, many chose other themes. Several historians explored Eastern and specifically Russian history. In addition to Ascher, Dallin, Huttenbach, and Laue, it is important to recognize Hans Rogger, who taught at UCLA.[113] French history was researched by Peter Amann, Sabine Jessner, Ruth Kleinmann, and Dora Weiner. Robert Vogel rounds out the list of historians of Britain, which includes Arnstein, Clive, Frank Eyck, and Huttenback.

Ernst Badian, Erich S. Gruen, and Harald Reiche specialized in ancient history. Gerard Caspary, Hanns Gross, Hanna Holborn Gray, Toni Oelsner, and Reinhold Schumann all dealt with topics of medieval history.[114] We find a pronounced interest in the history of humanism, the Renaissance, and the Protestant Reformation as well. Susan Groag Bell, Maria Grossmann, Werner Gundersheimer, and Renée Watkins shared this interest, as did Gerald Strauss.[115] Gray did research in these fields while pursuing a distinguished administrative career, which culminated in the presidency of the University of Chicago. Furthermore, several historians worked in the broadly defined area of early modern history, including Hanns Gross, Walter Grossmann, and Theodore Rabb.

The remarkably diverse oeuvres of Rabb, Peter Gay, Walter Laqueur, George L. Mosse, and Peter Paret, to give only a few examples, ultimately defy any categorization along chronological, geographical, or thematic lines. Instead, all these historians pursued questions that were not prescribed by disciplinary boundaries—be they about the character of the Enlightenment, about modernity and the role of art and symbolic politics, or about the history of political ideologies.

There is one more noticeable difference, and thus another moment of discontinuity, in comparison with the first generation: the younger immigrants played a role in expanding the field of history to include geographic areas and non-European topics that had hardly been represented among the older refugee scholars. Benda, Lensen, Rabe, and Schirokauer opened new perspectives on Asian history. Arnade, Lamb, and Friedrich Katz contributed to investigating the history of the Spanish Empire and Latin American regions. Jonas, Kissinger, Nash, and Trefousse researched the history of the United States and of American foreign policy. Gay, Loewenberg, and Kren promoted the newly developing field of psychohistory, while Gerda Lerner and Renate Bridenthal explored women's history. For Lerner and Bridenthal, there was and is a pronounced link between their personal stories, the experience of National Socialism and the turn to the history of women and the traditions of feminism. Lerner was already beginning to think about issues of gender, discrimination, and otherness before her arrival in the US. This awareness, heightened by evidence of discriminatory practices in America, led her to take an active role in the feminist and civil rights movements. By contrast, Susan Groag Bell's involvement with feminist ideas came, in her words, "purely from my historical studies."[116]

The contributions to the wide field of the history of medicine and of science also deserve recognition, especially since these research areas were still relatively new in the postwar era and struggling to establish themselves.[117] Gert Brieger, for example, directed the Institute for the History of Medicine at Johns Hopkins University, where, in 1947, Ilza Veith had gained the first Ph.D. ever in the United States in the field of the history of medicine. Veith became a pioneer in exploring the history of Chinese medicine and acupuncture.[118] Ann Beck dealt with medical traditions and imperial policies in Africa, and Otto Marx instructed students in the history of medicine and psychology. Alexander Ospovat became an expert in the history of geology in the decades around 1800, while Gerald Holton added the history of science to his already distinguished portfolio as a physicist. He also contributed to making Albert Einstein's papers accessible to the public.

Intellectual Traditions

A considerable number of the émigrés-turned-historians developed an interest in the history of historiography and in the longer traditions of the discipline they made their own. Fritz Stern opened this field to readers in the 1950s with his collection of historians' texts, entitled *The Varieties of History*, one of his favorites among his many books. Others followed with monographs and anthologies.[119] Georg Iggers established himself as a leading authority in the history of historiography as a research field and collaborated increasingly with historians outside Central Europe and the United States.

Iggers's early critique of German-style historicism, both as a set of methodological assumptions and as a political ideology, remained controversial. Still, it reflected an intellectual stance that distinguished many of those who came to America at a young age from the refugee scholars of the first generation. The latter were trained by *Gelehrte* (senior scholars) in Germany who were often steeped in the traditions of historicism and German idealism. Their academic teachers conveyed to them an appreciation for writing political history in which nations and state actions, embodied by individuals, played a dominant role. Friedrich Meinecke exemplifies this cohort. While his students who escaped to the United States diversified their interests and methodological strategies, they needed to work through these traditions in order to emancipate themselves intellectually. Hans Rosenberg is particularly remarkable in breaking new ground for a broadly conceived social history.[120] The younger immigrants showed more flexibility and intellectual freedom in their engagement with the historicist heritage. For them, this heritage did not mean a commitment exemplified by their teachers, but was one among a variety of intellectual strands that deserved recognition as much as critique.

The immigrants' fresh curiosity in—and productive distance from—the traditions of the historical disciplines, which they explored and exploited rather than defended or dismissed per se, needs to be factored into our understanding of their oeuvres. This stance allowed them to position themselves largely outside what Charles S. Maier has pointedly called the "filiopietistic base lines" of attempts to write the history of historiography primarily as an organic development—that is, as a story that emphasizes precedents, and highlights what the sons and daughters have learned from their elders, and where they departed from them.[121]

I would also emphasize the moments of discontinuity that separated the second generation from previous one. Even more so than the older refugee scholars, the younger generation faced the experience of rupture and novelty. Moreover, members of the second generation were profoundly affected by the need to deal with the Holocaust, not only intellectually, but personally, as a part of their families' histories. This experience also accounts for what is implicit in the second generation's writings and seems to go without saying: that they did not—and could not—take intellectual positions marked by a *deutschnational* ideology, the apologetic belief in the righteousness of the German nation, or antisemitic leanings, which had certainly been present in German academia.[122]

It might be more remarkable that so few historians in our sample were attracted to Marxism. Certainly, some of those who promoted emancipatory ideas in the 1960s and 1970s engaged Marxism as well. But Marxist and socialist ideas seem to have had the greatest appeal for some of the older of the second-generation, largely in the early phases of their lives, and especially so when they came from urban centers such as Berlin, Breslau, and Vienna. This interest was often coupled with an enthusiasm for psychoanalysis. In his younger years, Marx and Freud appeared to the literary historian Walter H. Sokel as the two great "liberators" of the world.[123] Most of the younger immigrants, however, shared a disenchantment with socialism. They found Max Weber's writings and the post–World War II sociology more appealing than Marx and were attracted by forms of political philosophy that tackled the challenges of twentieth-century mass society and authoritarian regimes. They also acknowledged new, unorthodox forms of economic philosophy, exemplified by Albert O. Hirschman, himself an immigrant.[124]

Against this background, the story of the second-generation émigrés can hardly be framed as one in a sequence of intellectual cohorts grounded primarily in the traditions of German historiography. Certainly, some of the younger ones studied with members of the first generation. In the 1940s, Peter Paret cherished lectures by Hans Kelsen, the Austrian-born legal philosopher, and Ernst Kantorowicz, the great interpreter of the mediaeval period.[125] There is no doubt that individual historians admired the older refugee scholars, as Klemens von Klemperer and Hanna Holborn Gray, the daughter of Hajo Holborn, show in this volume. But only a few outstanding scholars of the first generation enjoyed a broad appreciation in the United States, in particular Felix Gilbert, Hajo Holborn, and Hans Rosenberg, and, in the field of research on humanism and the Renaissance, Hans Baron and Paul Otto Kristeller.[126]

Among the younger immigrants, those with a distinct *bildungsbürgerlich* background and connections were more likely than others to mingle academically and socially with émigrés of the first generation. Such connections mostly developed around individuals such as Gilbert and Hajo Holborn. Here we see social and intellectual circles that created at times a microcosmos of European (and transatlantic) intellectual life in America, especially in New York City. Furthermore, some of the second-generation historians found together to collaborate in scholarly projects, but they did so primarily because they had similar scholarly interests.[127]

Transnational Transfers and Networks

The historians of the second generation not only addressed audiences in North America, their studies reverberated into historiography in Germany; during the Cold War era, this meant primarily West Germany. While this effect cannot be explained solely by the authors' background, their capacity to communicate with colleagues across the Atlantic, along with the personal interest in reestablishing ties to Europe, contributed to the emergence of new transatlantic conversations. From the 1950s on, these took place in an ever-growing, transnational web of exchanges and transfers. This cross-border exchange was made possible by guest professorships in Germany, support from American and German foundations, such as the Ford Foundation, and the input of a new generation of transatlantic brokers.[128]

Personal encounters at a variety of research centers fueled this exchange. Particularly important were the Institute for Advanced Study in Princeton; the Center for Advanced Study in the Behavioral Sciences at Stanford, which was created in 1954; and Harvard's Center for European Studies, founded in 1969. No less important were the German Marshall Fund from 1972 on; the German Historical Institute in Washington, DC, since its inception in 1987; and the American Academy in Berlin, which opened its gates in 1994. Furthermore, the Wiener Library, located in London since 1939, and the Leo Baeck Institute, centered in London, New York City, and London, became indispensable hinges in the transatlantic research on the Holocaust and the history of European Jewry. Moreover, starting in 1958, the Conference Group for Central European History, today's Central European History Society, furthered the transnational dialogue. It originated as the American Historical Association's (AHA) Committee for the Study of War Documents, which sponsored the microfilming of the German records before their return to Germany. Finally, the German Studies Association, which emerged from the Western Association for German Studies, founded in 1976, became an engine of transatlantic exchange.[129]

American historians and German-born academics in the United States willing to reconnect with German academia increasingly utilized the expanding transatlantic topography of scholarship. They engaged scholars from the German-speaking world who departed from older traditions, as Gerhard A. Ritter and Jürgen Kocka illustrate in their essays in this volume. George L. Mosse alone advised an unmatched number of students in the United States, various European countries, and Israel, the country he felt particularly close to.[130] Prominent scholars from Germany reciprocated this interest. Karl Dietrich Bracher and Ralf Dahrendorf connected with Peter Gay and Fritz Stern already during the 1950s, while spending research time in the United States. Hans-Ulrich Wehler, the brothers Hans and Wolfgang Mommsen, Thomas Nipperdey, and, slightly later, Hartmut Lehmann and Jürgen Kocka were all intrigued by the works of American scholars, émigrés and non-émigrés alike. They conveyed this interest back to German students and colleagues.[131]

The mutual interest in exploring the cultural and political history of Germany encouraged the translation of English-language historical studies for European and, in particular, German audiences. Initiatives of farsighted editors, such as Ernst-Peter Wieckenberg at the C. H. Beck publishing house in Munich, facilitated this transfer from the 1960s on. Although many of the historians in our sample spent considerable time in Germany during their career, only one returned for good to Germany: Werner Angress, who settled in Berlin for the last two decades of his life.

However, the impact German scholars had on American historiography at large was limited. It was centered on the oeuvre of a few outstanding scholars, such as Karl Dietrich Bracher, Jürgen Habermas, and Reinhart Koselleck. The reverse effect is more noticeable.[132] Peter Gay, Georg Iggers, Gerda Lerner, Peter Loewenberg, Michael A. Meyer, George L. Mosse, Peter Paret, Fritz Stern, and Gerhard Weinberg are second-generation historians whose studies influenced students and scholars of history on an international scale and especially so in Germany. To this impressive list we need to add Arno J. Mayer and Saul Friedländer.[133] Through the critical review of German history they provided, with their commitment to the values of civil society, and fostered by their discussions with German colleagues (at times, as in the case of Fritz Stern, also with journalists and members of the political class,) they had their share in what Konrad H. Jarausch and others have called the "cultural democratization of West Germany."[134]

Identities and Habitus

Members of the second generation pursued their careers as American citizens; a few lived in Canada. Did they remain immigrants, was there something distinct about them? It might be fair to say that most of them had several identities, which could no longer be reduced to that of refugees from Germany. Each individual took his or her own path of Americanization. Many considered themselves Americans with a European or German heritage. Many embraced the transcultural experiences gained during their long journey to America. Often with divergent, if not painful, feelings, many remained emotionally and intellectually connected to their origins. Such connections were also rhetorically constructed, reminiscent of what Joan Scott has described as the "fantasy echo" that makes individuals arrange retrospectively an ever-changing identity.[135]

An in-depth probe into these complicated processes would need to employ psychological, if not psychoanalytical categories. It is not a coincidence that Peter Gay and Peter Loewenberg, both familiar with such categories, have authored particularly sensitive assessments of what the processes of acculturation meant to them. Loewenberg's essay in this volume attests to this capacity. Gay has described how he came to feeling profoundly "at home" in America, an attitude that he traces back to his youth in Berlin. Others have defined in different terms the twisted road from departure to arrival in America and their existence in this country. Theodor von Laue, for example, was an émigré, but not a refugee. He felt "uprooted from a formal German traditional culture—a positive heritage for me that was free of Nazi crudeness—and tossed into America." Laue retained the sense of remaining an "in-between person" at university. Toward the end of his life, he confessed that, in spite of having lived in the United States for over half a century, he was "not quite here yet."[136]

The students and colleagues of the historians in our sample noticed features that distinguished the latter from other academics, though perceptions varied. Some friends of Klemens von Klemperer in his hometown in Massachusetts saw him as the "prototypical American college professor who, like many others, took an occasional trip to Europe."[137] For many others, however, the scholars portrayed in this volume retained an aura, or at least a noticeable touch (and charm) of Europeanness. There remained something distinct about them. Undoubtedly, they did not have the "air of a Teutonic Herr Professor Doktor" that some of the older, first-generation refugee scholars seem to have possessed.[138] The younger ones also had an accent that marked them as people who had spent their formative years in Brooklyn or New England rather than in Berlin or Vienna.

Still, their personal and professional demeanor had facets that set them apart from their colleagues and peers. They were known to have continuous or newly assumed transatlantic connections, which led to opportunities to travel and lecture abroad. They showed a familiarity with the plurality of Jewish cultures and with themes that the German-style *humanistische Gymnasium*—in essence, a high school with a particular focus on the classics—had cultivated to a greater extent than the average American school. Gerald Holton once confessed how "unpleasant" the instruction at his *Gymnasium* had been for him—and yet how deeply it influenced him in embracing a wide variety of subjects.[139]

This sense of difference and the vestiges of otherness—that is, the former émigrés' "habitus" (Pierre Bourdieu),[140] their manners, demeanor, taste, and, more broadly, forms of social and communicative behavior—added distinctiveness to their personal and professional appearance. Many of them shared a fondness for German-style coffee and cake on weekend afternoons. Many displayed an academic vigor that their students perceived as European. They had an appreciation of high culture, encapsulated in the German term *Bildung*, and of classical music in particular. They often expressed an avid interest in cultural events on and off campus, and many displayed an impressive ability to quote from the classics and German literature. They were also interested in conveying to family members and students elements of this humanistic heritage. In front of many of his American colleagues and friends, Walter Laqueur concluded the celebration of his ninetieth birthday, arranged at Georgetown University in 2011, by reciting a long quote from Hans Sachs, taken from Richard Wagner's *Meistersinger*—in impeccable German.[141]

Yet, both the self-descriptions of former refugees and the assessments from outside defy a reduction to an "illusory sameness established by referring to a category of person . . . as if it never changed."[142] When George L. Mosse confessed in the 1990s that he would "remain an emigrant," this statement did not suggest a simple continuity between his early life in Germany and his present, quite the contrary. Mosse pointed to the many factors that shaped his life, from his early political socialization and his homosexuality to his pleasure in living and communicating in different cultures and languages, including German. All of these informed his scholarly interests and the choices he made for himself.

Not unlike Mosse's characterization of himself as an "anti-nationalist," Susan Groag Bell identified astutely the complications of demarcating identities when she explained that she felt as though she did not belong to "any nation, race, or religion." This nonbelonging was a consequence of both her multiple cultural socializations and the limits inherent in any attempt to define identities in a coherent fashion and then separate them neatly as constitutive factors of one individual's biography:

> I have lived in Czechoslovakia, in both the Sudetenland and the heartland of Czech Bohemia in Prague; I have lived in England; and I have lived in the United States. I have been, and could be, a legal citizen of any of these countries and hold passports for all of them. As a child I have also been officially affiliated with Lutheranism and Anglicanism, and my ancestors were Jews. I have thus been unusually fortunate to have had numerous possibilities to create an identity for myself and even to choose which one I would like to consider as primary. But I have also been a German among Czechs, a Continental among Britons, a European among Americans, a Protestant among Jews, and a Jew among Gentiles. So, although I have obviously taken some facets of all of them into myself, I cannot choose any one of these identities above any other, partly because they did not choose me [. . .][143]

Paths From and To History

Peter Gay once called the cohort of refugees who fled Hitler to the United States a "very heterogeneous crowd."[144] This characterization is even more appropriate when approaching the second-generation émigrés who became historians in North America. The autobiographical essays assembled in this volume reflect this diversity. They demonstrate how personal narratives and, specifically, departure from National Socialist Germany shaped both the interests that these refugees developed as students and the works they produced as scholars. But they also show that such processes varied in individual, often unpredictable ways.

Certainly, it is useful to "study the historian" before we "begin to study the facts," as Edward H. Carr recommended in a now famous remark.[145] But there is a multitude of stories to study in that regard, and we can read and construe these stories in many different ways. Sigmund Freud had it right when he wrote to Arnold Zweig that "biographical truth does not exist." His addendum ("if it did we could not use it")[146] points to the necessity of caution in defining categories to help understand particular features of an individual's life, as well as the pluralities of factors that cause an ever-changing relationship between elements of continuity and of discontinuity, in the biographies of historians as well as in their contributions to scholarship. This relationship articulates itself in the peripatetic character of the protagonists as "wanderers between several worlds," as Walter Laqueur puts it in this volume.

The young émigrés' paths to history emerged from age, gender, and talent. They were influenced by family background, socioeconomic factors, and religious and regional identities. Persistence and intellectual curiosity during the complex processes of migration, and of acculturation to new contexts, had an impact on these paths, as did the expansion of higher education in postwar America. Contingencies and luck played a role in finding a place as a historian. Even when they did not translate their personal stories into their research, the second-generation émigrés had to grapple with a past that possessed a "brooding omnipresence" (Peter Gay) and could not simply be shed.[147] This awareness encouraged several to engage in humanitarian enterprises, to support the civil rights movement from the 1950s on, as Georg Iggers did in his work with the National Association for the Advancement of Colored People (NAACP), or to endorse other civic and political causes. Fritz Stern, having experienced illiberalism first-hand in his youth and later researching it as a historian, had good reasons, as late as 1988, to mobilize the public against the danger, articulated by Ronald Reagan, of denigrating what he cherished as a core value of any democratic society: liberalism based on the value of individual freedom and the protection of minorities.[148]

Due to their emigration early in life and because of their migration through different cultural spaces and "contact zones," many of the second-generation émigrés from Germany lived "transcultural lives."[149] They developed an understanding of the histories of various continents and cultures in ways that were not defined by borders of state, ethnicity, or religion alone. Can we at all gauge their impact on the historical disciplines? We are just beginning to find answers to this question, and readers of this volume will find different ones. Steven Aschheim and Jeffrey Herf emphasize the distinctiveness of the scholarly works of émigrés who come from a German-Jewish background. Helmut Walser Smith argues that the early works of Peter Gay, especially his interpretation of the Enlightenment, derived primarily from Gay's engagement, in the 1950s, with the ideas of Franz Neumann, Ernst Cassirer, and Erwin Panofsky. Philipp Stelzel sees both similarities and differences between the critical take on German history that several émigrés articulated and that of German historians, as exemplified in the debate about a German *Sonderweg*—that is, about a peculiar path into modernity that ultimately culminated in the National Socialist regime. With a focus on Gerda Lerner's scholarly oeuvre, Marjorie Lamberti remains skeptical vis-à-vis linking the refugee experience directly with later historiographical positions.

The immediate confrontation with the National Socialist regime early in life, the ensuing emigration, and the forms of acculturation did not create unbroken lines of continuity for the second-generation émigrés. They made a difference because these men and women shared a memory of the past as well as specific forms of cultural capital, competencies, and habitus. These factors further influenced the impressively diverse themes they embraced when they became historians and transatlantic brokers. For their students and colleagues, as for us today, their stories constitute a chapter of how the study of history comes about. Yet, they also offer a panorama of the new and unexpected avenues this study—and its personal origins—opens and will continue to open, again and again.

Table 1 Second-Generation Émigrés as Historians in North America (107)

Peter H. Amann	1927 Vienna – 2012 Manchester, WI
Werner T. Angress	1920 Berlin – 2010 Berlin
John J. Appel	1921 Weimar – 1998 East Lansing, MI
Charles W. Arnade	1927 Görlitz – 2008 Leesburg, VA
Walter L. Arnstein	1930 Stuttgart
Abraham Ascher	1928 Wrocław (Breslau)
Ernst Badian	1925 Vienna – 2011 Quincy, MA
Ann F. Beck	1900 Braunschweig – 2002 Avon, CT
Susan Groag Bell	1926 Opava (Troppau) – 2015 Palo Alto, CA
Harry J. Benda	1919 Liberec (Reichenberg) – 1971 New Haven, CT
Henry Blumenthal	1911 Grudziądz (Graudenz) – 1987 New York, NY
Eric H. Boehm	1918 Hof – 2017 Santa Barbara, CA
John W. Bohnstedt	1927 Berlin – 2015 Fresno, CA
Renate Bridenthal	1935 Leipzig
Gert H. Brieger	1932 Hamburg
Peter M. Buzanski	1929 Vienna
Joan Campbell	1929 Berlin – 2013 Toronto
Gerard E. Caspary	1929 Frankfurt/M. – 2008 Berkeley, CA
John L. Clive	1924 Berlin – 1990 Cambridge, MA
Alexander Dallin	1924 Berlin – 2000 Stanford, CA
Gabrielle S. Edgcomb	1920 Berlin – 1997 Washington, DC
Klaus W. Epstein	1927 Hamburg – 1967 Bonn
Frank Eyck	1921 Berlin – 2004 Calgary
F. Gunther Eyck	1912 Magdeburg – 2009 Alexandria, VA
Henry L. Feingold	1931 Ludwigshafen
Herman Freudenberger	1922 Eberbach/Baden – 2017 Houston, TX
Gerald Freund	1930 Berlin – 1997 New York, NY
Paul G. Fried	1919 Leipzig – 2006 Holland, MI
Henry Friedlander	1930 Berlin – 2012 Bangor, ME
Lewis H. Gann	1924 Mainz – 1997 Palo Alto, CA
Hans W. Gatzke	1915 Dülken – 1987 New Haven, CT
Peter Gay	1923 Berlin – 2015 New York, NY
Hanna H. Gray	1930 Heidelberg
Hanns Gross	1928 Stockerau/Austria – 2006 Arlington Heights, IL
Maria Grossmann	1919 Vienna – 2003 Conway, MA

(*continued*)

Table 1 (*continued*)

Walter Grossmann	1918 Vienna – 1992 Conway, MA
Helmut Gruber	1928 Austria – 2014 New York, NY
Erich S. Gruen	1935 Vienna
Werner L. Gundersheimer	1937 Frankfurt/M.
Arthur G. Haas	1925 Vienna – 2016 Knoxville, TN
Theodore S. Hamerow	1920 Warsaw – 2013 in Madison, WI
Hans Heilbronner	1926 Memmingen – 2011 Durham, NH
Raul Hilberg	1926 Vienna – 2007 Williston, VT
Gerald J. Holton	1922 Berlin
Henry R. Huttenbach	1930 Worms
Robert A. Huttenback	1928 Frankfurt/M. – 2012 Camarillo, CA
Georg G. Iggers	1926 Hamburg – 2017 Williamsville, NY
Wilma A. Iggers	1921 Mirkov (Mirschikau), Bohemia
Sabine L. M. Jessner	1924 Wrocław (Breslau)
Manfred Jonas	1927 Mannheim – 2013 Schenectady, NY
Friedrich Katz	1927 Vienna – 2010 Philadelphia, PA
Henry A. Kissinger	1923 Fürth
Ruth S. Kleinmann	1929 Berlin – 1995 Brooklyn, NY
Klemens von Klemperer	1916 Berlin – 2012 Easthampton, MA
Arthur G. Kogan	1914 Vienna – 2001
Gerd Korman	1928 Elberfeld
George M. Kren	1926 Linz – 2000 Manhattan, KS
Leonore M. Laan	1919 Wrocław (Breslau) – 2016 Bethesda, MD
Ursula S. Lamb	1914 Essen – 1996 Tucson, AZ
Walter Z. Laqueur	1921 Wrocław (Breslau)
Conrad F. Latour	1923 Vienna – 1991
Theodore H. von Laue	1916 Frankfurt/M. – 2000 Worcester, MA
George A. Lensen	1923 Berlin – 1979 in Florida
Gerda Lerner	1920 Vienna – 2013 Madison, WI
Guenter Lewy	1923 Wrocław (Breslau)
Peter J. Loewenberg	1933 Hamburg
Otto M. Marx	1929 Heidelberg – 2012 Townshend, VT
Michael A. Meyer	1937 Berlin
Alma M. (Luckau) Molin	1908 Lamme – 2000 Poughkeepsie, NY
Herbert Moller	1909 Hannover – 2001 Sarasota, FL

(*continued*)

George L. Mosse	1918 Berlin – 1999 Madison, WI
George H. Nadel	1923 Vienna – 1990 Sussex
Gerald D. Nash	1928 Berlin – 2000 Albuquerque, NM
Toni F. Oelsner	1907 Frankfurt/M. – 1981 New York, NY
Alexander M. Ospovat	1923 Königsberg – 2010 Stillwater, OK
Peter Paret	1924 Berlin
Agnes F. Peterson	1923 Berlin – 2008 Los Altos, CA
Theodore K. Rabb	1937 Teplice-Šanov (Teplitz-Schönau)
Valentin H. Rabe	1930 Hannover – 2008 Geneseo, NY
Harald A. T. Reiche	1922 Germany – 1994 in Massachusetts
Joachim Remak	1920 Berlin – 2001 Santa Barbara, CA
Wilhelm Reuning	1924 Mainz – 2013 Selinsgrove, PA
John E. Rodes	1923 Frankfurt/M. – 2000 Pasadena, CA
Hans Rogger	1923 Herford – 2002 Los Angeles, CA
Gunther E. Rothenberg	1923 Berlin – 2004 Canberra, Australia
Beate Ruhm von Oppen	1918 Zurich – 2004 Annapolis, MD
Conrad Schirokauer	1929 Leipzig
Bruno Schlesinger	1911 Neunkirchen/Austria – 2010 Santa Barbara, CA
Hans A. Schmitt	1921 Frankfurt/M. – 2006 Charlottesville, VA
Ismar Schorsch	1935 Hannover
Reinhold S. A. Schumann	1919 Düsseldorf – 2010 Concord, MA
Robert Schwarz	1921 Vienna
Walter M. Simon	1922 Berlin – 1971 Ashley, UK
George H. Stein	1934 Vienna – 2007 Ithaca, NY
Fritz Stern	1926 Wrocław (Breslau) – 2016 New York, NY
Felix F. Strauss	1918 Innsbruck – 1990 New York, NY
Gerald Strauss	1922 Frankfurt/M. – 2006 Amherst, MA
Herbert A. Strauss	1918 Würzburg – 2005 New York, NY
Gerard C. Thormann	1922 Frankfurt/M. – 2011 Nyack, NY
Hans L. Trefousse	1921 Frankfurt/M. – 2010 Staten Island, NY
Ilzah F. Veith	1915 Ludwigshafen – 2013 Tiburon, CA
Robert Vogel	1929 Vienna – 1994 Montréal
Werner E. Warmbrunn	1920 Frankfurt/M. – 2009 Claremont, CA
Renée E. Watkins	1932 Berlin
Gerhard L. Weinberg	1928 Hannover
Dora B. Weiner	1924 Fürth – 2018 Santa Monica, CA
Karl J. Weintraub	1924 Darmstadt – 2004 Chicago, IL

Table 2 The Second Generation: Year of Escape/Emigration and Age at That Time

Year of Emigration	Age (at the end of year in which these individuals left the realm of National Socialist Germany)	Per Year
1929	Molin (21)	1
1930	Hamerow (10)	1
1932	Peterson (9)	1
1933	Beck (33), Campbell (4), Caspary (4), Gunther Eyck (21), Gray (3), Huttenback (15), Katz (6), Loewenberg (- 1), Mosse (25), Paret (9), Simon (11), Thormann (11)	12
1934	Boehm (16), Epstein (7), Freudenberger (12), Oppen (16), Schmitt (13)	5
1935	Frank Eyck (15), Haas (20), Jessner (11), Lamb (21), Schirokauer (6), Schorsch (3), Weintraub (11)	7
1936	Arnade (9), Blumenthal (25), Bohnstedt (9), Edgcomb (16), Huttenbach (16), Kogan (c. 22), Marx (7), Trefousse (15), Warmbrunn (16), Watkins (14)	10
1937	Angress (17), Brieger (5), Clive (13), Gatzke (22), Jonas (10), Laue (21), Nash (9), Reuning (13), Rothenberg (14), Veith (25)	10
1938	Appel (17), Badian (13), Bridenthal (3), Feingold (7), Fried (19), Gann (14), W. Grossmann (20), Holton (16), G. Iggers (12), W. Iggers (17), Kissinger (15), Klemperer (22), Korman (10), Kren (12), Laqueur (17), Lerner (18), Reiche (16), Rodes (15), Schumann (19), Stein (4), Stern (12), Weinberg (10), Weiner (14)	23
1939	Amann (12), Arnstein (9), Ascher (11), Bell (13), Benda (20), Buzanski (10), Dallin (15), Freund (9), Gay (16), Gross (11), M. Grossmann (20), Gruber (11), Gruen (4), Gundersheimer (2), Heilbronner (13), Hilberg (13), Laan (20), Latour (16), Lensen (16), Lewy (16), Moller (20), Nadel (16), Oelsner (22), Rabb (2), Remak (19), Rogger (16), Schlesinger (28), Schwarz (18), F. Strauss (21), G. Strauss (17), Vogel (10)	31
1940	Ospovat (17), Rabe (10)	2
1941	Kleinmann (12), Meyer (4)	2
1943	H. A. Strauss (25)	1
1947	Friedlander (17)	1

Table 3 Émigré Historians of the First Generation in North America (98)

Most names listed in this table are based on information provided by Epstein, *A Past Renewed* (1993). Added are ten names, set in italics, and all biographical data are updated.

Erwin H. Ackerknecht	1906 Stettin – 1988 Zurich
Paul J. Alexander	1910 Berlin – 1977 Berkeley, CA
Alexander Altmann	1906 Košice (Kaschau) – 1987 Boston, MA
Berthold Altmann	1902 Torgau/Saxony – 1977 Alexandria, VA
Alfred Apsler	1907 Vienna – 1982 Vancouver, WA
Hans Baron	1900 Breslau – 1988 Urbana, IL
Elias J. Bickerman	1897 Kishinev, Russia – 1981 Tel Aviv
Rosy R. Bodenheimer	1900 Frankfurt/M. – 2004 Baltimore, MD
Eberhard F. Bruck	1877 Breslau – 1960 Reichenau/Bodensee
Henry J. Bruehl	1879 Herford – 1946 Washington, DC
Helmut G. Callis	1906 Breslau – 1982 Salt Lake City, UT
Fritz Caspari	1914 Baden, Switzerland – 2010 London
Frederick H. Cramer	1906 Berlin – 1954 Toulouse, France
Henry G. Dittmar	1913 Cologne – 1998 Redlands, CA
Andreas Dorpalen	1911 Berlin – 1982 Columbus, OH
Ludwig Edelstein	1902 Berlin – 1965 New York, NY
Ismar Elbogen	1874 Schildberg/Posen – 1943 New York, NY
Friedrich Engel-Janosi	1893 Vienna – 1978 Vienna
Fritz T. Epstein	1898 Saargemünd, Lorraine – 1979 Lüneburg
Aron Freimann	1871 Filehne/Posen – 1948 New York, NY
Robert Friedmann	1891 Vienna – 1970 Kalamazoo, MI
Frederick Ernest Gaupp	1897 Freiburg/Breisgau – 1979 Williamson, TX
Dietrich Gerhard	1896 Berlin – 1985 Constance
Alexander Gerschenkron	1904 Odessa – 1978 Cambridge, MA
Felix Gilbert	1905 Baden-Baden – 1991 Princeton, NJ
Rudolf Glanz	1892 Vienna – 1978 Parksville, NY
Fred Hahn	1906 Stankov, Czechoslovakia – 2003 New York, NY
George W. Hallgarten	1901 Munich – 1975 Washington, DC
Fritz M. Heichelheim	1901 Gießen – 1968 Toronto
Karl F. Helleiner	1902 Wien – 1984 Toronto
Emmy Heller	1886 Frankfurt/M. – 1956 Glen Cove, NY
Frederick G. Heymann	1900 Berlin – 1983 Calgary

(*continued*)

Table 3 (*continued*)

Felix E. Hirsch	1902 Berlin – 1982 Newton, PA
Helmut Hirsch	1907 Barmen – 2009 Düsseldorf
Hajo Holborn	1902 Berlin – 1969 Bonn-Bad Godesberg
Ernest I. Jacob	1899 Göttingen – 1974 Pittsburgh, PA
Erich von Kahler	1885 Prague – 1970 Princeton, NJ
Robert A. Kann	1906 Vienna – 1981 Vienna
Ernst H. Kantorowicz	1895 Posen – 1963 Princeton, NJ
Eckart Kehr	1902 Brandenburg/Havel – 1933 Washington, DC
Guido Kisch	1889 Prague – 1985 Basel
Adolf Kober	1879 Beuthen/Upper Silesia – 1958 New York, NY
Hans Kohn	1891 Prague – 1971 Philadelphia, PA
Eric C. Kollman	1903 Vienna – 1981 Mount Vernon, IA
Paul O. Kristeller	1905 Berlin – 1999 New York, NY
Richard Krautheimer	1897 Fürth – 1994 Rome, Italy
Stephan Georg Kuttner	1907 Bonn – 1996 Berkeley, CA
Gerhart M. A. Ladner	1905 Vienna – 1993 Los Angeles, CA
Carl Landauer	1891 Munich – 1983 Oakland, CA
Richard Laqueur	1881 Strasbourg/Alsace – 1959 Hamburg
Edith Lenel	1909 Strasbourg/Alsace—1994 Langhorne, PA
Adolf F. Leschnitzer	1899 Posen – 1980 Centerport, NY
Ernst Levy	1881 Berlin – 1968 Davis, CA
Charlotte Littauer-Blaschke	1897 Leipzig – 1999 Lexington, MA
Alfred D. Low	1913 Vienna – 2003 Bellevue, WA
Christian W. Mackauer	1897 Geisenheim – 1970 Chicago, IL
Otto Maenchen-Helfen	1894 Vienna – 1969 Berkeley, CA
Golo Mann	1909 Munich – 1994 Leverkusen
Gerhard Masur	1901 Berlin – 1975 Lynchburg, VA
Franz H. Michael	1907 Freiburg/Breisgau – 1992 Monterey, CA
Carl Misch	1896 Berlin – 1965 Danville, KY
Theodor E. Mommsen	1905 Berlin – 1958 Ithaca, NY
Otto Neugebauer	1899 Innsbruck – 1990 Princeton, NJ
Fritz C. Neumann	1897 Hamburg – 1976 Libertyville, IL
Peter H. Olden	1905 Berlin – 2002 Green Valley, AZ
Henry M. Pachter	1907 Berlin – 1980 New York, NY

(*continued*)

Ernst Posner	1892 Berlin – 1980 Wiesbaden
Johannes Quasten	1900 Homberg/Niederrhein – 1987 Freiburg/Breisgau
Fritz L. Redlich	1892 Berlin – 1978 Newton, MA
Hanns Günther Reissner	1902 Berlin – 1977 Philadelphia, PA
Werner Richter	1888 Muskau/Saxony – 1969 Lugano, Switzerland
Edgar R. Rosen	1911 Berlin – 1994 Braunschweig
Arthur Rosenberg	1889 Berlin – 1943 New York, NY
Hans Rosenberg	1904 Hannover – 1988 Freiburg/Breisgau
Eugen Rosenstock-Huessy	1888 Berlin – 1973 Norwich, VT
Hans Rothfels	1891 Kassel – 1976 Tübingen
Richard G. Salomon	1884 Berlin – 1966 Mount Vernon, OH
Frederick C. Sell	1892 Bonn – 1956 in Massachusetts
Charlotte Sempell	1909 Osnabrück – 1998 Chester, CT
Erika Spivakovsky	1909 Hamburg – 1998 Westport, CT
Selma Stern-Täubler	1890 Kippenheim/Baden – 1981 Vienne, Switzerland
Raphael Straus	1887 Karlsruhe – 1947 New York, NY
Bruno Strauss	1889 Hannoversch-Münden – 1969 Shreveport, LA
Eugen Täubler	1879 Gostyn, Posen – 1953 Cincinnati, OH
H. G. Robert Ulich	*1890 – 1977 Stuttgart*
George Urdang	1882 Tilsit/East Prussia – 1960 Madison, WI
Alfred H. F. Vagts	1892 Basbeck/Hannover – 1986 Cambridge, MA
Veit Valentin	1885 Frankfurt/M. – 1947 Washington, DC
Hedwig Wachenheim	1891 Mannheim – 1969 Hannover
Luitpold Wallach	1910 Munich – 1986 Columbia, MO
Martin Weinbaum	1902 Küstrin/Brandenburg – 1990 New York, NY
Bernard Dov Weinryb	1905 Turobin, Poland – 1982 Philadelphia, PA
Helene Wieruszowski	1893 Elberfeld – 1978 Sorengo, Switzerland
Hellmut Wilhelm	1905 Qingdao, China – 1990 Seattle, WA
Mark Wischnitzer	1882 Rovno, Russia – 1955 Tel Aviv
Karl A. Wittfogel	1896 Woltersdorf – 1988 New York, NY
Hans J. Wolff	1902 Berlin – 1983 Freiburg/Breisgau
Sergius O. Yakobson	1901 Moscow – 1979 Washington, DC

Andreas W. Daum is professor of history at the State University of New York at Buffalo. His research deals with German, transatlantic, and international history, as well as the history of knowledge, from the eighteenth century to the Cold War era. His books include *Wissenschaftspopularisierung im 19. Jahrhundert* (a history of popular science in Germany; 1998, ²2002), *Kennedy in Berlin* (2003, English edition 2008), and co-edited volumes on the *Vietnam War and the World* (2003) and *Berlin – Washington, 1800-2000* (2005).

Notes

1. On the term "participants," specifically referring to emigrants from the Third Reich, see Donald Fleming and Bernard Bailyn, eds., *The Intellectual Migration: Europe and America, 1930–1960* (Cambridge, MA, 1969), 4.
   I would like to thank those colleagues and friends who have commented on earlier drafts of this essay and enriched my thinking about the topic over many years: Volker Berghahn, Georg and Wilma Iggers, Hartmut Lehmann, Peter Paret, James J. Sheehan, Fritz Stern, Gerhard Weinberg, and Sherry Föhr. I sincerely thank all the participants in the 2012 conference on which this volume is based; see Andreas W. Daum, "The Second Generation: German Émigré Historians in the Transatlantic World, 1945 to the Present," *Bulletin of the German Historical Institute* 51 (Fall 2012): 116–21. Atina Grossmann and Marion A. Kaplan kindly provided the notes of their comments presented at this conference. Special thanks go to the "participants"/historians, and in many instances their family members, who generously provided valuable feedback; they are listed in the acknowledgments to my chapter 22 in this volume. And I still appreciate it that my academic teachers Thomas Nipperdey, Gerhard A. Ritter, and Kurt Sontheimer, as well as Georg Nicolaus Knauer, shared with me stories about their experiences in America and with refugee scholars.
2. The author is aware that the terms "refugee" and "émigré" are not interchangeable and that their definition, as the semantic and political differences between them, would warrant an in-depth discussion. The overwhelming majority of this volume's dramatis personae *escaped* from Nazi Germany to avoid discrimination and ultimately annihilation—they sought refuge from terror, they were refugees, they felt as such, and they often preferred this term in self-descriptions. Only a few were not forced to escape and did not face discrimination in Germany; they were émigrés, but not refugees. For further clarification, see chapter 22 in this volume.
3. Peter Loewenberg and Werner (Tom) Angress.
4. An important starting point has been provided in *Fleeing Nazi Germany* by Allan Mitchell, who explores the (auto)biographies of Felix Gilbert, Klemens von Klemperer, Werner Angress, Peter Gay, and Fritz Stern. Recent case studies on our topic include those by Jerry Z. Muller, "American Views of German History Since 1945," in Frank Trommler and Peter Hohendahl, eds., *Whose Brain Drain? Immigrant Scholars and American Views on Germany* (Washington, DC, 2001), 14–27; Stanley G. Payne, David J. Sorkin, and John S. Tortorice, eds., *What History Tells: George L. Mosse and the Culture of Modern Europe* (Madison, WI, 2004); Steven E. Aschheim, *Beyond the Border: The German-Jewish Legacy Abroad* (Princeton, NJ, 2007); Ethan Katz, "Displaced Historians, Dialectical Histories: George L. Mosse, Peter Gay, and Germany's Multiple Paths in the Twentieth Century," *Journal of Modern Jewish Studies* 7, no. 2 (July 2008): 135–55; and Philipp Stelzel, "Rethinking Modern German History: Critical Social

History as a Transatlantic Enterprise, 1945–1989" (Ph.D. diss., University of North Carolina at Chapel Hill, 2010).
5. To vary an expression by Felix Gilbert, *A European Past: Memoirs 1905–1945* (New York, 1988).
6. Instead of citing the relevant publications of the second-generation émigrés in the endnotes to this chapter, I refer the reader to the bibliographic entries following each biography in chapter 23, as well as to the selected bibliography in chapter 24.
7. See the acknowledgments at the end of chapter 22 in this volume. For recollections of second-generation scholars from various disciplines, see Abraham J. Peck, ed., *The German-Jewish Legacy in America, 1938–1988: From Bildung to the Bill of Rights* (Detroit, 1989); Peter Suedfeld, ed., *Light from the Ashes: Social Science Careers of Young Holocaust Refugees and Survivors* (Ann Arbor, 2001); and Eileen Boris and Nupur Chaudhuri, eds., *Voices of Women Historians: The Personal, the Political, the Professional* (Bloomington, 1999). An attempt to explore historians' autobiographies in a systematic manner is offered by Jeremy D. Popkin, *History, Historians, & Autobiography* (Chicago, 2005). See also Marion A. Kaplan, "Using Memoirs to Write German-Jewish History," in Eli Lederhandler and Jack Wertheimer, eds., *Text and Context: Essays in Modern Jewish History and Historiography in Honor of Ismar Schorsch* (New York, 2005), 383–410.
8. Eric J. Hobsbawm, *Age of Extremes: The Short Twentieth Century, 1914–1991* (New York, 1994); see also Hobsbawm's autobiography, *Interesting Times: A Twentieth-Century Life* (London, 2002).
9. See Herbert A. Strauss, *Jewish Immigrants of the Nazi Period in the USA*, vol. 1 (New York, 1978), 47–63.
10. See Hartmut Lehmann and James J. Sheehan, eds., *An Interrupted Past: German Speaking Refugee Historians in the United States after 1933* (New York, 1991) and Catherine Epstein, *A Past Renewed: A Catalogue of German-Speaking Refugee Historians in the United States after 1933* (New York, 1993). A landmark in exploring the heterogeneous strands of German historiography, with due respect to émigré historians, is still Hans-Ulrich Wehler, ed., *Deutsche Historiker*, 9 vols. (Göttingen 1973–82). Specifically on émigré historians, see Georg G. Iggers, "Die deutschen Historiker in der Emigration," in Bernd Faulenbach, ed., *Geschichtswissenschaft in Deutschland. Traditionelle Positionen und gegenwärtige Aufgaben* (Munich, 1974), 97–111; Lewis A. Coser, "Hajo Holborn (1902–1969), Felix Gilbert (1905–), Hans Rosenberg (1904–), and Paul Oskar Kristeller (1905–): Refugee Historians," in *Refugee Scholars in America: Their Impact and Their Experiences* (New Haven, 1984), 278–94; Heinz Wolf, *Deutsch-jüdische Emigrationshistoriker in den U.S.A. und der Nationalsozialismus* (Bern, 1988); Volker Berghahn, "Deutschlandbilder 1945–1965. Angloamerikanische Historiker und moderne deutsche Geschichte," in Ernst Schulin, ed., *Deutsche Geschichtswissenschaft nach dem Zweiten Weltkrieg (1945–1965)* (Munich, 1989), 239–72; Peter Th. Walther, "Von Meinecke zu Beard? Die nach 1933 in die U.S.A emigrierten deutschen Neuhistoriker" (Ph.D. diss., State University of New York at Buffalo, 1989); Robert Jütte, *Die Emigration der deutschsprachigen "Wissenschaft vom Judentum." Die Auswanderung jüdischer Historiker nach Palästina 1933–1945* (Stuttgart, 1991); Wolfgang J. Mommsen, *The Return to the Western Tradition: German Historiography since 1945* (Washington, DC, 1991); Christhard Hoffmann, "The Contribution of German-Speaking Jewish Immigrants to British Historiography," in Werner Mosse, ed., *Second Chance: Two Centuries of German-Speaking Jews in the United Kingdom* (Tübingen, 1991), 153–75; Gabrielle S. Edgcomb, *From Swastika to Jim Crow: Refugee Scholars at Black Colleges* (Malabar, FL, 1993); Catherine Epstein, "Fashioning Fortuna's Whim: German-Speaking Women Emigrant Historians in the United States," in Sibylle Quack, ed., *Between Sorrow and Strength: Women Refugees of the Nazi Period* (New York, 1995), 301–23; Claus-Dieter Krohn, "Geschichtswissenschaften," in *Handbuch der deutschsprachigen Emigration 1933–1945*

(Darmstadt, 1998), 747–61; Peter Alter, ed., *Out of the Third Reich: Refugee Historians in Post-War Britain* (London, 1998); P. Th. Walther, "Die deutschen Historiker in der Emigration und ihr Einfluss in der Nachkriegszeit," in Heinz Duchhardt and Gerhard May, eds., *Geschichtswissenschaft um 1950* (Mainz, 2002), 37–47; Gabriela Ann Eakin-Thimme, *Geschichte im Exil. Deutschsprachige Historiker nach 1933* (Munich, 2005), who places emphasis on Hans Baron; Mario Kessler, ed., *Deutsche Historiker im Exil (1933–1945). Ausgewählte Studien* (Berlin, 2005); Georg G. Iggers, *Refugee Historians from Nazi Germany: Political Attitudes towards Democracy* (Washington, DC, 2006); and Axel Fair-Schulz and Mario Kessler, eds., *German Scholars in Exile* (Lanham, MA, 2011).

Some recent studies have focused on individual historians; see, for example, Marina Sassenberg, *Selma Stern (1890—1981). Das Eigene in der Geschichte. Selbstentwürfe und Geschichtsentwürfe einer Historikerin* (Tübingen, 2004); Dave Renton, *Sidney Pollard: A Life in History* (London, 2004); and Jan Eckel, *Hans Rothfels. Eine intellektuelle Biographie im 20. Jahrhundert* (Göttingen, 2005). We are still lacking a full-fledged monograph on Hans Rosenberg. On him and other students of Friedrich Meinecke who emigrated to the United States, see Gerhard A. Ritter, "Die emigrierten Meinecke-Schüler in den Vereinigten Staaten. Leben und Geschichtsschreibung im Spannungsfeld zwischen Deutschland und der neuen Heimat: Hajo Holborn, Felix Gilbert, Dietrich Gerhard, Hans Rosenberg," in *Historische Zeitschrift* 284 (2007): 59–102; and idem, *German Refugee Historians and Friedrich Meinecke: Letters and Documents, 1910–1977* (Boston, 2010).

Still foundational for any research on émigrés from the Third Reich is the *International Biographical Dictionary of Central European Émigrés 1933–1945 = Biographisches Handbuch der deutschsprachigen Emigration nach 1933*, edited by Werner Röder and Herbert A. Strauss. 3 vols. in 4 (Munich, New York, 1980–83); in the following, I use a common abbreviation (IBDCEE) for this gigantic compendium.

11. Klaus Fischer, "Vom Wissenschaftstransfer zur Kontextanalyse—oder: Wie schreibt man die Geschichte der Wissenschaftsemigration," in Rainer Erb and Michael Schmidt, eds., *Antisemitismus und jüdische Geschichte. Studien zu Ehren von Herbert A. Strauss* (Berlin, 1987), 267–93; Mitchell G. Ash and Alfons Söllner, eds., *Forced Migration and Scientific Change: Émigré German-Speaking Scientists and Scholars after 1933* (New York, 1996).

12. Horst Möller, "From Weimar to Bonn: The Arts and the Humanities in Exile and Return, 1933–1980," in IBDCEE, vol. II, part 1 (Munich, 1983), LX–LXI, LXIV; Kathleen Joy Melhuish, "The German-Jewish Emigrant and the Historian's Craft," in Konrad Kwiet, ed., *From the Emancipation to the Holocaust: Essays on Jewish Literature and History in Central Europe* (Kensington, 1987), 163; Hoffmann, "The Contribution of German-Speaking Jewish Immigrants," 154–55, 161; Alter, *Out of the Third Reich*, XIV–XVII; Krohn, "Geschichtswissenschaften," 751; Doris Ingrisch, *Der dis/kontinuierliche Status des Seins. Über vom Nationalsozialismus aus Österreich vertriebene (und verbliebene) intellektuelle Kulturen in lebensgeschichtlichen Kontexten* (Frankfurt/M., 2004), 215–28.

13. On the first-generation refugee historians and scholars who joined the American war efforts through their involvement in the Office of Strategic Service (OSS), see Barry M. Katz, "German Historians in the Office of Strategic Services," in Lehmann and Sheehan, *An Interrupted Past*, 136–39.

14. See Aaron Hass, *In the Shadow of the Holocaust: The Second Generation* (Cambridge, 1996); Alan L. Berger, *Children of Job: American Second-Generation Witnesses to the Holocaust* (New York, 1997); Alan L. Berger and Naomi Berger, eds., *Second Generation Voices: Reflections by Children of Holocaust Survivors and Perpetrators* (Syracuse, NY, 2001); and Erin McGlothlin, *Second-Generation Holocaust Literature: Legacies of Survival and Perpetration* (Rochester, NY, 2006). The term "1.5 generation," which the sociologist Rubén G. Rumbaut helped to establish, is being used today by both Holocaust and immigration researchers; see Susan Rubin

Suleiman, "The 1.5 Generation: Thinking about Child Survivors and the Holocaust," in *American Imago: Studies in Psychoanalysis and Culture* 59 (2002): 277–95.
15. Laura Fermi, *Illustrious Immigrants: The Intellectual Migration from Europe, 1930-41*, 2nd ed. (Chicago, 1971). See, in contrast, Peter Gay, *Moritz Fröhlich-Morris Gay: A German Refugee in the United States* (Washington, DC, 2nd ed., 2007).
16. See Andreas W. Daum, "Émigrés in the Historical Disciplines: Research Perspectives," i.e., chapter 22 in this volume.
17. See the extensive study by Gerhard Sonnert and Gerald Holton, *What Happened to the Children Who Fled Nazi Persecution* (New York, 2006) as well as the contributions by Sheehan, Epstein, and Barkin in Lehmann and Sheehan, *An Interrupted Past*, and Hoffmann, "The Contribution of German-Speaking Jewish Immigrants." Peter Gay casts the net more widely in his "Reflections on Hitler's Refugees in the United States: A Keynote Speech," in *Leo Baeck Institute Yearbook* 53 (2008): 117–26.
18. Those covered in our volume were born over a period of three decades. On the concept of generations see Lutz Niethammer, "Die letzte Gemeinschaft. Über die Konstruierbarkeit von Generationen und ihre Grenzen," in Bernd Weisbrod, ed., *Historische Beiträge zur Generationsforschung* (Göttingen, 2009), 13–38; A. Dirk Moses, "The Forty-Fivers: A Generation Between Fascism and Democracy," in *German Politics and Society* 17 (1999), 95–127; Barbara Stambolis, ed., *Leben mit und in der Geschichte. Deutsche Historiker Jahrgang 1943* (Essen, 2010); Thomas A. Kohut, *A German Generation: An Experiential History of the Twentieth Century* (New Haven, 2012). For the broader historiographical context, see Jürgen Reulecke, ed., *Generationalität und Lebensgeschichte im 20. Jahrhundert* (Munich, 2003); Ulrike Jureit and Michael Wildt, eds., *Generationen. Zur Relevanz eines wissenschaftlichen Grundbegriffs* (Hamburg, 2005); Volker R. Berghahn and Simone Lässig, eds., *Biography Between Structure and Agency: Central European Lives in International Historiography* (New York, 2008); and Hartmut Berghoff et al., eds., *History by Generations: Generational Dynamics in Modern History* (Göttingen, 2013).
19. Sonnert and Holton, *What Happened to the Children*, XII, 1–2.
20. Susan Groag Bell, Harry Benda, Wilma Iggers, and Theodore Rabb. Theodore Hamerow was born in Poland; Beate Ruhm von Oppen in Switzerland.
21. Wolfgang Benz, ed., *Das Exil der kleinen Leute. Alltagserfahrungen deutscher Juden in der Emigration* (Munich, 1991); Marion A. Kaplan, *Between Dignity and Despair: Jewish Life in Nazi Germany* (New York, 1998); and Doron Niederland, "Areas of Departure from Nazi Germany and the Social Structure of the Emigrants," in Mosse, *Second Chance*, 57–68.
22. Irene Runge and Uwe Stelbrink, eds., *"Ich bleibe Emigrant." Gespräche mit George L. Mosse* (Berlin, 1991), 30.
23. Author's conversation with Joan Campbell's brother, Max A. Stolper, in Alexandria, VA, 20 February 2014; letters from Dugal Campbell, Joan Campbell's husband, to the author, 26 January 2014 and 20 February 2014. See the recollections by Joan Campbell's mother, Toni Stolper, *Ein Leben in Brennpunkten unserer Zeit* (Vienna, 1960), 337–41, 473–74, as well as Joan Campbell, *The German Werkbund: The Politics of Reform in the Applied Arts* (Princeton, NJ, 1978) and *Joy in Work, German Work: The National Debate, 1800–1945* (Princeton, NJ, 1989).
24. See Herbert A. Strauss, "Jews in German History: Persecution, Emigration, Acculturation," in IBDCEE, vol. II, part 1, XV; Richard J. Evans, *The Third Reich in Power 1933–1919* (New York, 2005), 555.
25. Saul Friedländer, *Nazi Germany and the Jews*, vol. I: *The Years of Persecution, 1933–1939* (New York, 1997), 239–305; Evans, *The Third Reich in Power*, 555–610; Victor Klemperer, *I Will Bear Witness: A Diary of the Nazi Years, 1933–1941*, trans. Martin Chalmers (London, 1998), 241–63.

26. Raul Hilberg, *The Politics of Memory: The Journal of a Holocaust Historian* (Chicago, 1966), 42; Wilma and Georg Iggers, *Two Lives in Uncertain Times: Facing the Challenges of the 20th Century as Scholars and Citizens* (New York, 2006), 16.
27. Werner Gundersheimer, "Kristallnacht Revisited: A Nightmare, A Legacy," *Washington Post*, 9 November 1988, A15. I thank Werner Gundersheimer for sharing with me additional information about his family.
28. Claus-Dieter Krohn, "Vereinigte Staaten von Amerika," in *Handbuch der deutschsprachigen Emigration 1933–1945* (Darmstadt, 1998), 446.
29. Strauss, "Jews in German History," XV.
30. Letter by Peter M. Buzanski to the author, 17 March 2014; AHC Interview with Robert Schwarz, Oral History, Center for Jewish History, http://www.cjh.org/ (accessed 15 August 2015); Alexandra Ludewig, "The Last of the Kindertransports. Britain to Australia, 1940," in Andrea Hammel and Bea Lewkowicz, eds., *The Kindertransport to Britain 1938/39: New Perspectives. Yearbook of the Research Centre for German and Austrian Exile Studies* 13 (Amsterdam, 2012): 96; Ken Ingles, "From Berlin to the Bush," *The Monthly: Australian Politics, Society & Culture* (August 2010), at http://www.themonthly.com.au/monthly-essays-ken-inglis-berlin-bush—2638 (accessed 15 August 2015). On Nadel, see also Derek John Mulvaney, *Digging up a Past* (Sydney, 2011), 50–52, 60–61. For the estimated number of 10,000 rescued via a *Kindertransport* in 1938–39 see Wolfgang Benz, Claudia Curio, and Andrea Hammel, *Die Kindertransporte 1938/39. Rettung und Integration* (Frankfurt/M., 2003), 7. It is difficult to estimate the numbers precisely; see Kaplan, *Between Dignity and Despair*, 116–18.
31. See Klaus J. Bade, *Migration in European History*, trans. Allison Brown (Malden, MA, 2003); idem, ed., *Deutsche im Ausland, Fremde in Deutschland. Migration in Geschichte und Gegenwart* (Munich, 1992); Dirk Hoerder and Jörg Nadler, eds., *People in Transit: German Migrations in Comparative Perspective, 1820–1930* (New York, 1995).
32. Theodore S. Hamerow, *Remembering a Vanished World: A Jewish Childhood in Interwar Poland* (New York, 2001), 173–99. See also Hilberg, *Politics of Memory*, 22, 27; John J. Stephan, "Foreword," in George Alexander Lensen, *Balance of Intrigue: International Rivalry in Korea & Manchuria, 1884–1899* (Tallahassee, FL, 1982), IX. Karl Schlögl expands on the Russian émigrés in Berlin in his essay "Berlin: 'Stiefmutter' unter den russischen Städten," in *Der große Exodus. Die russische Emigration und ihre Zentren 1917 bis 1941* (Munich, 1994), 234–59, here p. 249 also on Dallin.
33. Gerd Korman, *Nightmare's Fairy Tale: A Young Refugee's Home Fronts 1938–1948* (Madison, WI, 2005), 12–14, 31–46. I thank Gerd Korman for providing me with additional information in late 2013 and 2014. See Sybil Milton, "The Expulsion of Polish Jews from Germany October 1938 to July 1939: A Documentation," in *Leo Baeck Institute Yearbook* 29, no. 1 (1984): 169–99, and Friedländer, *Nazi Germany and the Jews*, vol. I, 266–68.
34. Klemens von Klemperer, *Voyage Through the Twentieth Century: A Historian's Recollections and Reflections* (New York, 2009), 32. See Mitchell, *Fleeing Nazi Germany*, 15–28.
35. Klemperer, *Voyage*, 97–98; for his book publications, see chapter 23 in this volume. For Korman, see Korman, *Nightmare's Fairy Tale*, 165–67, and idem, ed., *Hunter and Hunted: Human History of the Holocaust* (New York, 1973).
36. Gerda Lerner, *Fireweed: A Political Autobiography* (Philadelphia, 2002), 83, 119.
37. "Zu der Zeit konnte ich kein Deutsch mehr hören, ohne dass mir schlecht geworden." See "Gespräch mit Gerda Lerner," *Emma* (May/June 2000), http://www.emma.de/artikel/gespraech-mit-gerda-lerner-ich-bin-ein-alien-266112 (accessed 15 August 2015); Lerner, *Fireweed*, 105.
38. Walter Laqueur, *Generation Exodus: The Fate of Young Jewish Refugees from Nazi Germany* (Hanover, NH, 2001). See Michael Brenner, "Turning Inward: Jewish Youth in Weimar Germany," in Michael Brenner and Derek J. Penslar, eds., *In Search of Jewish Community:*

Jewish Identities in Germany and Austria, 1918–1933 (Bloomington, 1998), 56–73; and, more broadly, Michael Brenner, *The Renaissance of Jewish Culture in Weimar Germany* (New Haven, 1996).

39. See Michael A. Meyer, "A Heritage Freighted across the Abyss," in Peck, *The German-Jewish Legacy*, 111–15; Marion Berghahn, *Continental Britons: German-Jewish Refugees from Nazi Germany*, rev. ed. (New York, 2007), 18–46; Shulamit Volkov, *Die Juden in Deutschland 1780–1918* (Munich, 1994); idem, "How German and How Jewish were the German Jews? Reflections on the Problem of Identity," in Lederhendler and Wertheimer, *Text and Context*, 411–31; and Michael A. Meyer, ed., with Michael Brenner, *German-Jewish History in Modern Times*, 4 vols. (New York, 1996–98).
40. Alan E. Steinweis, *Studying the Jew: Scholarly Antisemitism in Nazi Germany* (Cambridge, MA, 2006), and Thomas Pegelow, *The Language of Nazi Genocide: Linguistic Violence and the Struggle of Germans of Jewish Ancestry* (New York, 2009).
41. Strauss, "Jews in German History," XII, XV.
42. Hans A. Schmitt, *Lucky Victim: An Ordinary Life in Extraordinary Times, 1933–1946* (Baton Rouge, 1989), 28–29, 65, 66.
43. See the essay by Peter Loewenberg in this volume and Herbert Arthur Strauss, *In the Eye of the Storm: Growing up Jewish in Germany, 1918–1943. A Memoir* (New York, 1999), 7–8.
44. The literature on German-Jewish Bildungsbürger is vast; see, e.g., Elisabeth Kraus, *Die Familie Mosse. Deutsch-jüdisches Bürgertum im 19. und 20. Jahrhundert* (Munich, 1999); Simone Lässig, *Jüdische Wege ins Bürgertum. Kulturelles Kapital und sozialer Aufstieg im 19. Jahrhundert* (Göttingen, 2004); and Volkov, *Die Juden in Deutschland*.
45. Fritz Stern, *Five Germanies I Have Known* (New York, 2006), 67.
46. IBDCEE, vol. II, part 2, 1086 (for Simon), and John Leonard Clive, *Not by Fact Alone: Essays on the Writing and Reading of History* (Boston, 1991), 4–5.
47. The Central Association of German Citizens of Jewish Faith was founded in 1893 and constituted the most prominent platform for mostly middle-class Jews in Germany to articulate their civic concerns and their commitment to the German nation. The Cultural Association of German Jews was established in 1933 to channel the cultural activities of Jews.
48. Frank Eyck, *A Historian's Pilgrimage: Memoirs and Reflections*, ed. Rosemarie Eyck (Calgary, 2009), 75. Franz Gunther Eyck has couched his autobiographical recollections in the form of a literary novel in the tradition of the German-style *Bildungsroman*: see *Pantha Rei: A Century's Memoir* (Baltimore, 2010). On Erich Eyck, see Alter, *Out of the Third Reich*, XVI–XIX; Klaus Hildebrand, "Erich Eyck," in Wehler, *Deutsche Historiker*, vol. II, 98–119.
49. "Dreams of a Better Life: Interview with Toni Oelsner," *New German Critique* 20, Special Issue 2: *Germans and Jews* (Spring–Summer 1980): 31, 42–45; Werner T. Angress, *Witness to the Storm: A Jewish Journey from Nazi Berlin to the 82nd Airborne, 1920–1945* (Durham, NC, 2012), 98. On Warmbrunn, see IBDCEE, vol. II, part 2, 1209.
50. Iggers, *Two Lives in Uncertain Times*, 29; Susan Groag Bell, *Between Worlds: In Czechoslovakia, England, and America* (New York, 1991), 3–5, 11–2, 19–20. See Marsha L. Rozenblit, "Germans or German-Speaking Jews? The Case of the Jews of Moravia, 1848–1938," in Lederhendler and Wertheimer, *Text and Context*, 321–45.
51. Theodore K. Rabb, "Rabinowicz, Oskar K.," in *The Yivo Encyclopedia of Jews in Eastern Europe*, at http://www.yivoencyclopedia.org/article.aspx/Rabinowicz_Oskar_K (accessed 15 August 2015).
52. Philip Gleason, "From Vienna to South Bend: A Refugee Professor's Story," in Rick Regan, ed., *Bruno Schlesinger: A Life in Learning & Letters at Saint Mary's College, South Bend* (Raleigh, NC, 2013), 11–12.
53. Manfred Jonas, "A German-Jewish Legacy," in Peck, *The German-Jewish Legacy*, 52–53. See M. Berghahn, *Continental Britons*, 53–57.

54. Abraham Ascher, *A Community under Siege: The Jews of Breslau under Nazism* (Stanford, 2007), 4, 5, 13.
55. Michael A. Meyer, "Ismar Schorsch, The Historian: A Critical Appreciation," in Lederhendler and Wertheimer, *Text and Context*, 3–23.
56. Angress, *Witness to the Storm*, 60. See also Schmitt, *Lucky Victim*, 54–59.
57. Peter Gay, *My German Question: Growing Up in Nazi Berlin* (New Haven, 1998), 66. On this dilemma, see especially Kaplan, *Between Dignity and Despair*.
58. The papers of Gerard Thormann's father, Werner E. Thormann, are accessible at the Deutsches Exilarchiv of the German National Library in Frankfurt/Main. See also Alan Seaburg, "Maria and Walter Grossmann, Scholarly Librarians. A Biographical Bibliography," at http://www.anneminiverpress.com/content/maria-and-walter-grossmann (accessed 15 August 2015).
59. Martin Torodash, "Ursula Lamb (1914–1996)," *Hispanic American Historical Review* 77, no. 2 (May 1997): 281; Susan M. Deeds and Donna J. Guy, "Ursula Lamb (1914–1996)," *Hispanic American Historical Review* 77, no. 4 (Nov., 1997): 677.
60. Theodor von Laue's correspondence with his father clearly indicates that he had initially not planned to stay in the United States; see Jost Lemmerich, ed., *Mein lieber Sohn! Die Briefe von Max von Laue an seinen Sohn Theodor in den Vereinigten Staaten von Amerika 1937 bis 1946* (Berlin, 2011), 61, et passim. See also "Theodor H. Von Laue," [interview] in Roger Adelson, ed., *Speaking of History: Conversations with Historians* (East Lansing, 1997), 227–28.
61. Annelise Thimme and Carole Fink, "Hans W. Gatzke, Germany, and the United States," in Carole Fink, Isabel V. Hull, and MacGregor Know, eds., *German Nationalism and the European Response, 1890–1945* (Norman, 1985), 267–69. See Hans W. Gatzke, *Germany's Drive to the West: A Study of Germany's War Aims during the First World War* (Baltimore, 1950), based on Gatzke's Harvard dissertation. Gatzke's lasting influence on his students becomes evident in the acknowledgments of Isabel V. Hull, *A Scrap of Paper: Breaking and Making International Law during the Great War* (Ithaca, 2014).
62. See David A. Gerber, "Introduction," in Alan M. Kraut and David A. Gerber, eds., *Ethnic Historians and the Mainstream: Shaping the Nation's Immigration Story* (New Brunswick, 2013), 1–16.
63. Gay, *My German Question*, 154, 159.
64. See, on Paret, Andreas W. Daum, "Was Clausewitz mit Kleist und Schiller verbindet: Unmodisch und frei," *Frankfurter Allgemeine Zeitung*, no. 84, 9 April 2014, N 3, English translation in *Michigan War Studies Review*, 7 May 2014, at http://www.miwsr.com/2014-041.aspx (accessed 15 August 2015); and Joe Lunn, "Peter H. Amann (1927–2012)," *Perspectives on History: The Newsmagazine of the American Historical Association* (October 2013), 45.
65. "Robert A. Huttenback, Interviewed by Shirley K. Cohen, September 14 and November 6, 1995," Archives, California Institute of Technology, at http://oralhistories.library.caltech.edu/156/1/Huttenback_OHO.pdf (accessed 15 August 2015).
66. Alter, *Out of the Third Reich*, and Hoffmann, "The Contribution of German-Speaking Jewish Immigrants."
67. For the term "contact zone," see Mary Louise Pratt, *Imperial Eyes: Travel Writing and Transculturation*, 2nd ed. (London, 2008), 7 et passim.
68. Bell, *Between Worlds*, 80–81; Eyck, *Historian's Pilgrimage*, 112.
69. Eyck, *Historian's Pilgrimage*, 112, 145–53.
70. George L. Mosse, *Confronting History: A Memoir* (Madison, WI, 2000), 75, 79; see also page 111, and Stern, *Five Germanies*, 187.
71. Beate Ruhm von Oppen, "The Tuning Fork," *The St. John's Review* 48, no. 2 (2005): 38. See Schmitt, *Lucky Victim*, 82–126. Schmitt mentions Werner Warmbrunn as an Eerde alumnus, in addition to those whom I could identify: Klaus W. Epstein, Leonore Laan, Beate Ruhm von Oppen, Hans A. Schmitt, and Karl J. Weintraub. On the founding of Eerde and its

first principal, Katharina Petersen, see Hildegard Feidel-Mertz, ed., *Schulen im Exil. Die verdrängte Pädagogik nach 1933* (Reinbek bei Hamburg, 1983), 151–67; Peter Budde, "Katharina Petersen und die Quäkerschule in Eerde. Eine Dokumentationscollage," in Monika Lehmann und Hermann Schnorbach, eds., *Aufklärung als Lernprozeß. Festschrift für Hildebard Feidel-Mertz* (Frankfurt/M., 1992), 82–101.
72. Author's conversation with Leonore Laan, 14 June 2014, in Bethesda, MD; Hans A. Schmitt, *Quakers and Nazis: Inner Light in Outer Darkness* (Columbia, 1997).
73. Walter Laqueur, *Thursday's Child Has Far to Go: A Memoir of the Journeying Years* (New York, 1992); Jütte, *Die Emigration*; Steve Hochstadt, *Exodus to Shanghai: Stories of Escape from the Third Reich* (New York, 2012); Irene Eber, *Wartime Shanghai and the Jewish Refugees from Central Europe: Survival, Co-Existence, and Identity in a Multi-Ethnic City* (Berlin, 2012). See Claudia Curio, "'Unsichtbare' Kinder. Auswahl- und Eingliederungsstrategien der Hilfsorganizationen," in Benz, Curio and Hammel, eds., *Die Kindertransporte 1938/39*, 60–81; John Ormerod Greenwood, *Friends and Relief: A Study of Two Centuries of Quaker Activity in the Relief of Suffering Caused by War or Natural Calamity*, vol. 1 (York, 1975); and Schmitt, *Quakers and Nazis*.
74. "Ernst Badian, Professor of History Emeritus, 85," *Harvard Gazette*, 14 February 2011, at http://news.harvard.edu/gazette/story/2011/02/ernst-badian-professor-of-history-emeritus-85/ (accessed 28 August 2014).
75. George McT. Kahin, "Harry J. Benda," *Indonesia* 13 (April 1972): 211–12; Ruth T. McVey, "Harry J. Benda," *Journal of Asian Studies* 31, no. 3 (May 1972): 589–90; Robin W. Winks, "Harry J. Benda: An Appreciation," in *Continuity and Change in Southeast Asia: Collected Journal Articles by Harry J. Benda* (New Haven, 1972), VII–XII.
76. Henry Blumenthal, *Challenges along My Twentieth Century Odyssey* (New York, 1981), 13–14, 30–38; Robert M. Levine, "Brazil's Jews during the Vargas Era and After," *Luso-Brazilian Review* 5, no 1 (1968): 53–55. See Egon Schwarz, *Refuge: Chronicle of a Flight from Hitler*, trans. Philip Boehm et al. (Riverside, CA, 2002), 76–184, originally published in German.
77. My thanks go to Peter Arnade and Tim Arnade for sharing with me additional information and family documents pertaining to their father. See Donna Winchester, "Former USF Professor Charles Arnade Dies at 81," *Tampa Bay Times*, 8 September 2008, at http://www.tampabay.com/news/obituaries/former-usf-professor-charles-arnade-dies-at-81/802352 (accessed 28 August 2014). For numbers on the German-Jewish refugees who escaped to South America, see the *Holocaust Encyclopedia* at http://www.ushmm.org/wlc/en/article.php?ModuleId=10005468 (accessed 28 August 2014), and Leo Spitzer, *Hotel Bolivia: The Culture of Memory in a Refuge from Nazism* (New York, 1998).
78. Franz L. Neumann, "The Social Sciences," in Franz L. Neumann et al., *The Cultural Migration: The European Scholar in America* (Philadelphia, 1953), 18; "Walter L. Arnstein," [interview] in Adelson, *Speaking of History*, 3. I would like to thank Walter Arnstein for sharing with me recollections and materials pertaining to his career.
79. I thank Remmert, Willem, and Leonore Laan for sharing this and other information with me in June and August 2014.
80. Gerda Lerner, *Why History Matters* (New York, 1997), 38; Herman Freudenberger, "Meine Auswanderung von Eberbach in die USA als Zwölfjähriger," *Eberbacher Geschichtsblatt* 99 (April 2000): 136–41.
81. See the interview with Herbert A. Strauss, in Herbert A. Strauss, ed., *Jewish Immigrants of the Nazi Period*, vol. 5 (New York, 1986), 111–22, and Werner Bergmann and Christhardt Hoffmann, "Herbert A. Strauss—eine wissenschaftliche Biografie," *Jahrbuch für Antisemitismusforschung* 14 (2005): 17–38.
82. Jeffrey S. Gurock, *Jews in Gotham: New York Jews in a Changing City, 1920–2010* (New York, 2012), 122; Geneviève Susemihl, "... *and it became my home." Die Assimilation und Integration*

der deutsch-jüdischen Hitlerflüchtlinge in New York und Toronto (Münster, 2004), 107–12; Atina Grossmann, "Questions of Jewish Identity: A Letter from New York," in Anson Rabinbach and Jack Zipes, eds., *Germans and Jews since the Holocaust: The Changing Situation in West Germany* (New York, 1986), 174–75. On Washington Heights as a microcosm of immigrants, see Steven M. Lowenstein, *Frankfurt on the Hudson: The German-Jewish Community of Washington Heights, 1933–1983, Its Structure and Culture* (Detroit, 1989).

83. Author's conversation with Gerhard Weinberg, October 2013, and Weinberg's email to the author, 28 July 2014; Charlotte and Richard Arnstein, "'Das waren ja alles Demokraten,'" in *Emigranten in New York im Gespräch mit Ellen Küppers* (Ulm, 1995), 118; Stern, *Five Germanies*, 174.

84. See Shulamit Volkov's contribution to this volume.

85. An early attempt to assess the pace and extent of so-called Americanization is tainted by overly general (and optimistic) biases, in addition to being focused on young males, but offers some interesting materials: Maurice R. Davie, *Refugees in America: Report of the Committee for the Study of Recent Immigration from Europe* (New York, 1947), here 225.

86. Sonnert and Holton, *What Happened to the Children*, chapters 5 and 6. See the essays in Quack, *Between Sorrow and Strength*, especially the contribution by Epstein, "Fashioning Fortuna's Whim"; Kaplan, *Between Dignity and Despair*, chapter 2; and Harriet Pass Freidenreich, *Female, Jewish, and Educated: The Lives of Central European University Women* (Bloomington, 2002), 163–201.

87. Susan Groag Bell, Gabrielle S. Edgcomb, Toni Oelsner, Agnes Peterson, and Beate Ruhm von Oppen.

88. See endnote 23. The quotes by Campbell are taken from a personal memoir she wrote on the occasion of her 50th class reunion at Radcliffe in 2000. My thanks go to Campbell's husband, Dr. Dugal Campbell, for making this unpublished text—and other information—available to me, as well as to Max. A. Stolper for sharing his recollections of his sister.

89. I would like to thank Renée Watkins for her helpful communication in early 2014. See Jasmine J. Mahmoud, "A Perpetual Misfit, History Professor Embraces Homosexuality," *Harvard Crimson*, 2 June 2003, at http://www.thecrimson.com/article/2003/6/2/a-perpetual-misfit-history-professor-embraces/ (accessed 15 August 2015), and Bell, *Between Worlds*, 214.

90. It might well be possible that the actual number was higher. Examples of German-Jewish refugees fighting in the British Army during World War II are embedded in the account by Martin Sugarman, *Fighting Back: British Jewry's Military Contribution in the Second World War* (London, 2010).

91. Peter Paret, *Imagined Battles: Reflections of War in European Art* (Chapel Hill, 1997), Acknowledgments.

92. Angress, *Witness to the Storm*, 243–47, 261–62, 314; Guy Stern, "German Cultures, Jewish Ethics," in Peck, *The German-Jewish Legacy*, 28–29; Christian Bauer and Rebekka Göpfert, *Die Ritchie Boys. Deutsche Emigranten im US-Geheimdienst* (Hamburg, 2005).

93. As Henry Kissinger recalled; see Steven Karras, *The Enemy I Knew: German Jews in the Allied Military in World War II* (Minneapolis, 2009), 119.

94. Eyck, *Historian's Pilgrimage*, 298. See Deborah Dash Moore, *GI Jews: How World War II Changed a Generation* (Cambridge, MA, 2004).

95. My thanks go to Eleanor Hancock, Australian Defense Force Academy at the University of South Wales, for providing materials on Rothenberg's life and career.

96. James T. Patterson, *Grand Expectations: The United States, 1945–1974* (New York, 1996), 67–69; John S. Brubacher and Willis Rudy, *Higher Education in Transition: A History of American Colleges and Universities*, 4th ed. (New Brunswick, 1997), part IV. Christopher J. Lucas, *American Higher Education: A History* (New York, 2006), 247–51 provides figures on the growing student enrollment and the increase in the number of institutions of higher education.

97. Sonnert and Holton, *What Happened to the Children*, 144–55.
98. See Lucas, *American Higher Education*, 267–74.
99. For an overview of antisemitism in twentieth-century United States, see the essays by Marcia Graham Synnott, Harold S. Wechsler, Lewis S. Feuer, and Leonard Dinnerstein in Jeffrey S. Gurock, ed., *Anti-Semitism in America*. Part II (New York, 1998), as well as Susanne Klingenstein, *Jews in the American Academy, 1900–1940: The Dynamics of Intellectual Assimilation* (Syracuse, NY, 1998). On possible correlations between the ethnic background of immigrants and their academic careers, see Rubén Rumbaut, "Immigration Research in the United States: Social Origins and Future Orientations," *American Behavioral Scientist* 42 (1999): 1285–1301.
100. Marcia Graham Synnott, "Anti-Semitism and American Universities: Did Quotas Follow the Jews?" in Gurock, *Anti-Semitism*, 473–511.
101. Rolf A. Weil, *Through These Portals: From Immigrant to University President* (Chicago, 1991), 25, see also 20, 26, 44–46. I am grateful to Walter Arnstein for pointing out to me the importance of Roosevelt College. For Hirsch, see Epstein, *A Past Renewed*, 127–30, Helmut Hirsch, *Onkel Sams Hütte. Autobiographisches Garn eines Asylanten in den USA* (Leipzig, 1994), and Horst Schallenberger and Helmut Schrey, eds., *Im Gegenstrom. Für Helmut Hirsch zum Siebzigsten* (Wuppertal, 1977). On Columbia University in the post–world War II era, see Robert A. McCaughey, *Stand Columbia: A History of Columbia University in the City of New York, 1754–2004* (New York, 2003), 356–422, including references to the limits of opportunities and to antisemitism.
102. Gerald D. Nash, "Autobiography: Roads to the West," in Richard W. Etulain and Ferenc Morton Szasz, eds., *The American West in 2000: Essays in Honor of Gerald D. Nash* (Albuquerque, 2003), 7, 9, 15. I thank Richard W. Etulain for further information; see Richard W. Etulain, "Clio's Disciples on the Rio Grande: Western History at the University of New Mexico," *New Mexico Historical Review* 87 (Summer 2012): 277–98.
103. Fritz Stern, "German History in America, 1884–1984," *Central European History* 19 (1986), especially 153–63; Muller, "American Views of German History since 1945"; Konrad H. Jarausch, "Die Provokation des 'Anderen.' Amerikanische Perspektiven auf die deutsche Vergangenheitsbewältigung," in Arnd Bauerkämper, Martin Sabrow, and Bernd Stöver, eds., *Doppelte Zeitgeschichte. Deutsch-deutsche Beziehungen 1945–1990* (Bonn, 1998), 432–47; Catherine Epstein, "German Historians at the Back of the Pack: Hiring Patterns in Modern European History, 1945–2010," *Central European History* 46, no. 3 (2013): 599–639.
104. Mosse, *Confronting History*, 122–23.
105. Berne, Switzerland, where Herbert A. Strauss submitted his dissertation; Vienna, where Friedrich Katz received his doctorate; and Erlangen, where Paul G. Fried finished his dissertation after having served as a translator in the U.S. delegation to the post–World War II Military Tribunal in nearby Nuremberg.
106. See Catherine Epstein, "*Schicksalsgeschichte*: Refugee Historians in the United States," in Lehmann and Sheehan, *An Interrupted Past*, 116–35.
107. Strauss, *In the Eye of the Storm*, XII; [Fritz Stern], "A Conversation with Fritz Stern," *Bulletin of the German Historical Institute* 28 (Spring 2001): 44.
108. So Klaus Epstein, Theodore Hamerow, Klemens von Klemperer, Fritz Stern, and Beate Ruhm von Oppen, this last by making letters from the Moltke family accessible to audiences on both sides of the Atlantic. See Marjorie E. Lamberti, "The Search for the 'Other Germany': Refugee Historians from Nazi Germany and the Contested Historical Legacy of the Resistance to Hitler," *Central European History* 47 (2014): 402–29.
109. Eric H. Boehm, *We Survived: Fourteen Histories of the Hidden and Hunted in Nazi Germany*, rev. and updated ed. (Boulder, CO, 2003); previous editions appeared in 1949, 1966, and 1985; Korman, *Hunter and Hunted*.

110. See Astrid M. Eckert, *The Struggle for the Files: The Western Allies and the Return of German Archives after the Second World War* (New York, 2012), 343–53.
111. See the bibliographical information provided in chapter 23 on Werner Angress, Abraham Ascher, Wilma Iggers, Hans Rogger, and Henry R. Huttenbach.
112. Meyer and Brenner, *German-Jewish History*; David Sorkin, "The Émigré Synthesis: German-Jewish History in Modern Times," *Central European History* 34, no. 4 (2001): 531–59.
113. John D. Klier, "Hans Rogger: 1923–2002," *East European Jewish Affairs* 32 (2002): 149–52; Hartmut Lehmann, "Hans Rogger as a Second Generation Refugee Historian," *Jewish Social Studies* 11, no. 1 (Fall 2004): 25–31.
114. See Julie Mell, "Twentieth-Century Jewish Émigrés and Medieval European Economic History," *Religions* 3 (2012): 556–87.
115. See "Gerald Strauss: Historian," in Andrew C. Fix and Susan C. Karant-Nunn, eds., *Germania Illustrata: Essays on Early Modern Germany Presented to Gerald Strauss* (Kirksville, MO, 1992), XI–XXIII.
116. Bell, *Between Worlds*, 218. See Epstein, "Fashioning Fortuna's Whim."
117. Michael A. Dennis, "Historiography of Science: An American Perspective," in John Krige and Dominique Pestre, eds., *Science in the Twentieth Century* (Amsterdam, 1997), 1–26; *Catching Up with the Vision: Essays on the Occasion of the 75th Anniversary of the Founding of the History of Science Society* (= Supplement to *Isis* 90, 1999).
118. On Veith, whose oeuvre has hardly been recognized outside the circle of experts, see Sandra Moss, "Ilza Veith—Charter Oslerian," in *The Oslerian* 13, no. 2 (August 2012): 1–3, 10, and no. 3 (November 2012): 1–4.
119. My thanks go to Fritz Stern for sharing this and other observations with me over the years. In 2011, Stern collaborated with the German historian Jürgen Osterhammel to publish a new and expanded edition of the *Varieties of Histories*: see Fritz Stern and Jürgen Osterhammel, eds., *Moderne Historiker. Klassische Texte von Voltaire bis zur Gegenwart* (Munich, 2011). See the bibliographic information on John Clive, Peter Gay, Theodor Hamerow, Theodor von Laue, Peter Paret, Hans A. Schmitt, and Karl J. Weintraub provided in chapter 23.
120. See the studies by Gerhard A. Ritter cited in endnote 10 as well as James J. Sheehan, "Three Generations of German Gelehrtenpolitik," *Bulletin of the German Historical Institute* 39 (Fall 2006): 39–43.
121. Charles S. Maier, "Comment: Theodor Schieder," in Hartmut Lehmann and James Van Horn Melton, eds., *Paths of Continuity: Central European Historiography from the 1930s to the 1950s* (New York, 1994), 395.
122. For the discussion of antisemitism and German nationalism in the thinking of historians who were academically trained before 1945 and played a major role in German historiography after 1945, see Ingo Haar, *Historiker im Nationalsozialismus. Deutsche Geschichtswissenschaft und der 'Volkstumskampf' im Osten* (Göttingen, 2002); Nicolas Berg, *Der Holocaust und die westdeutschen Historiker. Erforschung und Erinnerung* (Göttingen, 2003); and Eckel, *Hans Rothfels*.
123. Interview with Sokel, in Beatrix Müller-Kampel, ed., *Lebenswege und Lektüren. Österreichische NS-Vertriebene in den USA und Kanada* (Tübingen, 2000), 40, see also 30–31.
124. See the references in chapter 22 and, specifically on Hirschman, Jeremy Adelman, *Worldly Philosopher: The Odyssey of Albert O. Hirschman* (Princeton, NJ, 2013).
125. See Paret's essay in this volume, and Peter Paret, "Crossing Borders," *Historically Speaking* 4, no. 2 (November 2002): 8.
126. For the second-generation's appreciation of scholars from the older émigré generation, see Leonard Krieger and Fritz Stern, eds., *The Responsibility of Power: Historical Essays in Honor of Hajo Holborn* (London, 1968), III–XIV; Klemens von Klemperer, "Hans Kohn," *Central European History* 4 (1971): 188–90; idem, "Hans Rothfels, 1891–1976," *Central European History*

6 (1976): 381–83; Peter Paret, "Felix Gilbert 1905–1991," *Journal of the History of Ideas* 52, no. 2 (1991): 341; Gerhard L. Weinberg, "Fritz T. Epstein, 1898–1979," *Central European History* 12 (1979): 399–401; Karl J. Weintraub, "Christian Wilhelm Mackauer (1897–1970)," in *A Teacher at His Best: Christian W. Mackauer* (Chicago, 1973), IV–VI. Jürgen Petersohn highlights the appreciation Baron and Kristeller enjoyed in the United States in his essay "Deutschsprachige Mediävistik in der Emigration. Wirkungen und Folgen des Aderlasses der NS-Zeit," *Historische Zeitschrift* 277 (203): 37–48.

127. See, as examples, Hans Rogger and Eugene Weber, *The European Right: A Historical Profile* (Berkeley, 1965); Stanley Chodorow, Hans W. Gatzke, and Conrad Schirokauer, *A History of the World* (San Diego, 1986); Peter Paret, ed., *Makers of Modern Strategy: From Machiavelli to the Nuclear Age* (Princeton, NJ, 1986).

128. See Volker R. Berghahn, *America and the Intellectual Cold Wars in Europe: Shepard Stone between Philanthropy, Academy, and Diplomacy* (Princeton, 2001), and Andreas W. Daum, *Kennedy in Berlin* (New York, 2008), 36–50, 156–62.

129. Andreas W. Daum, Sabine Hacke, and Bradley Prager, eds., *The GSA at Forty*. Special Issue of *German Studies Review* 39, no. 3 (2016).

130. I am grateful to John Tortorice for providing me with a long list of students who studied under George L. Mosse.

131. Andreas W. Daum, "German Historiography in Transatlantic Perspective: Interview with Hans-Ulrich Wehler," *Bulletin of the German Historical Institute* 26 (Spring 2000): 117–25; James J. Sheehan, "In Memory of Hans-Ulrich Wehler," H-German Discussion Log, H-Net, at http://h-net.msu.edu/cgi-bin/logbrowse.pl?trx=vx&list=H-German&month=1407&week=c&msg=-fO4PasPLiCt/5TDfM2l05g&user=&pw= (accessed 28 August 2014); Tim B. Müller, *Krieger und Gelehrte. Herbert Marcuse und die Denksysteme im Kalten Krieg* (Hamburg 2010); Gangolf Hübinger, "Fritz Stern zwischen Europa und Amerika. Eine Fallstudie zum Geschichts-Intellektuellen," in Peter Burschel, ed., *Intellektuelle im Exil* (Göttingen, 2011), 219–40. Nipperdey's role in the transatlantic dialogue becomes apparent in Wolfgang Hardtwig and Harm-Hinrich Brandt, eds., *Deutschlands Weg in die Moderne. Politik, Gesellschaft und Kultur im 19. Jahrhundert* (Munich, 1993). On the important role that conversations with American scholars played for German historians, see also Konrad H. Jarausch and Rüdiger Hohls, eds., *Versäumte Fragen. Deutsche Historiker im Schatten des Nationalsozialismus* (Stuttgart, 2000).

132. On the many asymmetries in the transatlantic dialogue in the field of historiography, see Muller, "American Views," and Philipp Stelzel, "Working toward a Common Goal? American Views on German Historiography and German-American Scholarly Relations during the 1960s," *Central European History* 41 (2008): 639–71.

133. See chapter 22 on Mayer and Friedländer.

134. Arnd Bauernkämper, Konrad H. Jarausch, and Marcus M. Payk, "Transatlantische Mittler und die kulturelle Demokratisierung Westdeutschlands 1945–1970," in *Demokratiewunder. Transatlantische Mittler und die kulturelle Öffnung Westdeutschlands 1945–1970* (Göttingen, 2005), 11–37. See Konrad H. Jarausch, "German Social History–American Style," *Journal of Social History* 19 (1985): 349–59, and Jarausch and Rüdiger Hohls, *Versäumte Fragen*.

135. Joan Scott, "Fantasy Echo: History and the Construction of Identity," *Critical Inquiry* 27, no. 2 (Winter 2001): 284–304.

136. Peter Gay, "At Home in America," *The American Scholar* 46, no. 1 (Winter 1977): 31–42; "Theodor H. Von Laue," [interview] in Adelson, *Speaking of History*, 227, 228, 239.

137. Mitchell, *Fleeing Nazi Germany*, 25.

138. Here in reference to the political scientist Waldemar Gurian; see Regan, *Bruno Schlesinger*, 81.

139. Gerald Holton, "Some Lessons from Living in the History of Science," *Isis*, supplement to vol. 90 (1999), S96.

140. Sonnert and Holton, *What Happened to the Children*, 144–55 et passim, have rightly emphasized the value of Bourdieu's notions of habitus and cultural capital in understanding some of the distinct features of young émigrés from Nazi Germany.
141. I thank Walter Laqueur for taking time to converse about the themes of this volume in the aftermath of this celebration.
142. Scott, "Fantasy Echo," 285.
143. Bell, *Between Worlds*, 227. See Runge and Stelbrink, *"Ich bleibe Emigrant,"* 119.
144. Gay, "Reflections," 117.
145. Edward H. Carr, *What is History? The George Macaulay Trevelyan Lectures Delivered at the University of Cambridge January–March 1961* (New York, 1961), 26, 54; Carr seems to have had only male historians in mind.
146. Sigmund Freud to Arnold Zweig, 31 May 1936, in Ernst L. Freud, ed., *The Letters of Sigmund Freud and Arnold Zweig*; trans. Elaine and William Robson-Scott (New York, 1987), 127. For the German original, see Ernst L. Freud, ed., *Sigmund Freud—Arnold Zweig. Briefwechsel* (Frankfurt/M., 1968), 137.
147. Peter Gay, "Introduction," in Karl Dietrich Bracher, *The German Dictatorship: The Origins, Structure, and Effects of National Socialism*; trans. Jean Steinberg (New York, 1970), VII.
148. Fritz Stern, "Attacks on the 'L-Word' Debase Us All," *New York Times*, 4 September 1988, E15; "A Reaffirmation of Principle," *New York Times*, 26 October 1988, A21.
149. See Dirk Hoerder, Yvonne Hébert, and Irina Schmitt, "Transculturation and the Accumulation of Social Capital: Understanding Histories and Decoding the Present of Young People," in *Negotiating Transcultural Lives: Belongings and Social Capital among Youth in Comparative Perspective* (Göttingen, 2005), 11–36, and the discussion on "Transnational Lives in the Twentieth Century," *American Historical Review* 118 (February 2013): 45–139.

Part I

TESTIMONIES

Chapter 1

IT HARDLY NEEDS EMPHASIS THAT MY OWN GENERATION, THE SECOND, IS DEEPLY INDEBTED TO THE FIRST

Klemens von Klemperer

In 1922, Friedrich Meinecke wrote in the *Historische Zeitschrift* an article on "Drei Generationen deutscher Gelehrtenpolitik."[1] An important chapter in the intriguing history of *Gelehrtenpolitik* is the part played in the historical dialogue on the American scene by the second generation of German émigré historians, the subject of this volume.

Let me comment first on the scope of the volume. It hardly needs emphasis that my own generation, the second one, is deeply indebted to the first. These seminal figures guided us in a fatherly way, helping us to make the transition from the treasury of German scholarship to the new world in which they had gained a foothold. In my case, these guides were Felix Gilbert, Hajo Holborn, and Hans Rothfels. There is, however, one important name I do miss in the listing of these mentors, namely Fritz Epstein. In the years after 1939 when I became launched at Harvard, Fritz, whose academic career was cut short in Hamburg, was a poorly paid bibliographer at Widener Library. Every so often, my friends— say Carl Schorske or Hans Gatzke—and I would get a little envelope from him filled with scraps of references, often rather esoteric ones, that were of interest to our work. Fritz was a saint among bibliographers.

Let me comment further on the process of acculturation, the process by which we young Europeans became American scholars as well. For this, too, we are indebted to an older generation of Americans. I had the fortune to be close to a formidable array of scholars—William L. Langer, my *Doktorvater*, as they say in Germany; Sidney B. Fay, who took a particular interest in my work; and Hans

---

Notes from this chapter begin on page 58.

Kohn. Both Fay and Kohn had taught many years at Smith College, where I eventually landed.

William Langer was a powerhouse, a master diplomatic historian whose seminar at Harvard came to be an institution. Unforgettable was his lecture on the first Marne Battle of September 1914. Was it "the "miracle" of the Marne" that saved the Allies? With great relish, Langer went about to debunk that myth, exposing the folly in the German conduct of the battle. After the American entry into the war, Langer became head of the Research and Analysis branch of the OSS, which combined a select group of German émigrés of both generations. Way after the war he changed course and became a pioneer in the exploration of psychohistory, demography, and the study of the impact of climate on human affairs.

The English historian Sir John Robert Seeley once said that history without political awareness is stale, but that politics without historical perspective tends to be vulgar. Hajo Holborn lived up to that balance in scholarship between historical perspective and power consciousness envisaged by Seeley. He was a humanist and man of action at the same time. He often came up to Cambridge, where he paid much attention to us neophytes. And he became a sort of mentor to my generation of émigré historians.

As for Sidney B. Fay, he was the gentlest scholar I ever knew. He went about his work quietly and did not care to assert himself. His lectures were, if anything, on the dull side. But his great work on the causes of World War I was a landmark in the history of modern diplomacy. Not surprisingly, his balanced account of the causes of World War I did not go unchallenged. It was questioned most powerfully by Fritz Fischer in what had become a *Historikerstreit* of sorts, with Fischer attacking the whole German military-industrial complex. Among his German colleagues, Fischer wrote to me, only Karl Dietrich Bracher stood by him, but the rest fell on him. He was, they maintained, not worthy to teach in a German university. Fischer had good reason to feel ostracized, much like Eckart Kehr (*Schlachtflottenbau und Parteipolitik*, 1930) in earlier days.

The younger generation of refugee scholars, notably Fritz Stern, Klaus Epstein, myself, and also Hans Gatzke, took an unambiguous stand in support of Fischer. Fischer's position, if ever there will be a last word on this most complex question of causation of World War I, certainly has become recognized as having gained legitimacy. Moreover, we have learned from the cases of Kehr and Fischer that ostracizing fellow scholars might well mean ganging up on those who today may seem troublesome, yet tomorrow might turn out to have been pioneers.

We young imports from Germany were helped in our efforts by our American contemporaries in graduate school—Carl E. Schorske, Peter Viereck, H. Stuart Hughes, and I must also add Hans W. Gatzke. Now our acculturation was completed. We lunched regularly at the *Wursthaus* in Cambridge where we consumed our bowl of beef stew for fifteen cents and, if we had enough money, fudge cake and coffee for another ten cents, arguing about historical sense and nonsense. We had a History Club where we periodically read papers to each other, sharpening our wits. After we moved from Harvard to our respective assignments, we kept in touch with one another.

To most of us youngsters, World War I was history. I, probably the eldest here, was living during just two years of it. But during the terrible decades that followed, we were not only observers, potential historians, but also actors, and in some cases victims. This brings me to another matter that lies within the scope of this discussion: my generation of German historians and the Holocaust. As I reflect on our past, I am struck by the fact that the Jewish problem hardly figured. I don't remember the Holocaust being discussed at the *Wursthaus* lunches by us graduate students, who were obviously much preoccupied with the recent events in Germany. Nor did we write History Club papers about events related to the Holocaust. I can extend this statement to include my friends in the OSS, who had the best information at their disposal. As a matter of fact, Stuart Hughes wrote in his memoir, "What amazes me is how little heed I paid to the 'Final Solution.'" In fact neither Langer nor Felix Gilbert even mentioned the Holocaust in their memoirs (1977, 1988). To be sure, we have to keep in mind here that the very term Holocaust was not commonly used in the public discourse until the 1950s.

Fundamentally, my problem has to be viewed in the context of the political climate then in the United States. During wartime there was silence, virtual silence about the Jews, even though by mid-1942 the information about the Nazi atrocities had filtered into the Western foreign offices and intelligence services (see especially Richard Breitman, *Breaking the Silence*, New York, 1986). The silence about the Jews, the "Abandonment of the Jews," as David S. Wyman called his pioneering work (Boston, 1984), was fueled by a variety of factors, partly by the apprehension even of people like Samuel I. Rosenman, special counsel of the President on Jewish matters, lest too pointed reference to the Jewish problem would fuel antisemitism. Call the immediate response, indeed nonresponse, from on high to the information on the plight of the Jews bigoted, cowardly if not scandalous. But there was also a distinctly pragmatic, indeed stringent strategic reason for withholding the information about the Holocaust: It was of paramount importance to keep secret the fact that the Allies had all their information about the Holocaust from the cipher machine Enigma. In short, the overriding objective of the American leadership was to defeat Hitler, and nothing was to divert the wartime energies from this aim.

I began with Friedrich Meinecke, and I am ending with Meinecke. After the war, he observed that he was struck by the fact that the German émigré historians were so devoid of resentment towards Germany, that in fact they were building bridges between the new Germany and America. Yes, we have done so. Might I try to comment on Meinecke's observation? Many of us served in the Armed Forces during the war. Our perspective on postwar Germany then was not confined to our being émigrés recalling the murderous regime; but we newly baked Americans had gained the benefit of recognizing across the Atlantic a Germany reborn.

Nullpunkt (Zero Hour)? I do not mean to suggest that there was any. Yehuda Elkana, the distinguished Hebrew scholar and philosopher, survivor of Auschwitz, may have been too extreme in advocating "The Need to Forget" and attacking the "morbid" cult of the Shoah. It is not morbid; it is inevitable. If I have learned something from the preparation for this contribution, it is the perception that all history after Auschwitz must directly or indirectly relate to it and that normalcy after Auschwitz is elusive. Forgetting cannot be the answer to all the horrid crimes and suffering. However, Yehuda Elkana is worth listening to when he urged politicians and teachers to side with life and dedicate themselves to the future.[2]

Klemens von Klemperer was born in Berlin in 1916 and died in 2012 in Easthampton, MA. He studied at the University of Vienna, Oxford, and Harvard University. For over three decades he taught at Smith College, where he was appointed the L. Clark Seelye Professor of History in 1979. His publications are documented in chapter 23 and include *Germany's New Conservatism, Its History and Dilemma in the Twentieth Century* (1957, ²1968), *German Resistance Against Hitler: The Search for Allies Abroad, 1938–1945* (1992), *German Incertitudes, 1914–1945* (2001), *Voyage Through the Twentieth Century: A Historian's Recollections and Reflections* (2009), and *Passion of a German Artist: Käthe Kollwitz* (2011).

Notes

1. *Historische Zeitschrift* 125 (1922): 248–83; reprinted in Friedrich Meinecke, *Werke*, vol. 9, ed. Hans Herzfeld, Walther Hofer, and Gisela Bock (Stuttgart, 1979), 476–509. Gelehrtenpolitik in Meinecke's title refers to scholars' relationship to the political realm.
2. Due to health reasons, Klemens von Klemperer was unable to revise this chapter, which has been slightly edited by Andreas W. Daum and James J. Sheehan.

Chapter 2

"A WANDERER BETWEEN SEVERAL WORLDS"

Walter Laqueur

On a rainy morning in December 1938, I presented myself at the Hebrew University on Mount Scopus, Jerusalem. I was seventeen years and six months old, I had graduated from a German humanistic gymnasium (high school) earlier that year; in the months between I had worked in a textile plant in Reichenbach, a few miles from the scene where Gerhart Hauptmann's *Die Weber* (The Weavers) takes place. I was underage according to university regulations; this I owed to Adolf Hitler, who had introduced the *Wehrpflicht* (general military service) and therefore abolished the uppermost form, the *Oberprima*. In any case, I was very lucky to be there in the first place. My parents, like most German middle-class Jews, were impoverished, and I owed the money needed for registration and two years' fees to the munificence of an uncle, who happened to be in prison at the time, having defiled the Aryan race. Being a highly decorated World War I officer, he could dispose of his money even from prison. The fact that the woman in question had wanted to blackmail him had displeased the judge, who apparently belonged to the old school.

The secretaries at the university overlooked the issue of my age (or took pity on me.) Thus I became the youngest student of this institution and shortly thereafter one of the earliest dropouts. My first choice had been medicine; there had been several physicians in my family, a few of them quite distinguished, but only two historians: one specializing in ancient Rome whom I had never met (Richard Laqueur, professor of history at the university of Giessen; he was also rector of the university for a number of years), the other had written his books in Russian and had died in the 1870s.

I was told that there were several medical research institutes at the university but no medical faculty. If I wanted to study medicine, I had to go to Beirut for

---

Notes from this chapter begin on page 70.

premedical studies (as was the custom those days) and later to Lausanne or some such place in Europe. My second choice was history, specifically Russian history. I was sent to see Professor Richard Koebner; he was the only professor of general history at the Hebrew university at the time. Koebner was born and had taught in Breslau, my home town, and, if memory serves right, he cordially received me. But his field of specialization was early medieval British history; he had written the lead essay in the Cambridge medieval history. The interview was brief. "Did you read the four volumes of Klyuchevsky, my young friend?" I answered in the affirmative, which was a slight exaggeration as I had read only the first volume. "If so, my dear Laqueur, this is all I know, I cannot teach you." I was not too dejected. It was less than a year before the outbreak of the war. One felt in one's bones that a war was coming, and it seemed pointless to start something that in all probability I would never finish, even If I had the good luck to survive the war.

This, then, was the beginning and the end of my formal education in history—no Ph.D., no M.A., not even a B.A. The next twelve years, I was a member of a kibbutz and later a journalist and political commentator. For several years I drove a tractor and a combine harvester; I also served as a mounted policeman. I dug up potatoes and picked tomatoes, irrigated an orange grove, and dealt with horses and donkeys and various animals in between. I worked for a while as a stevedore in Haifa Bay and in a brick factory that belonged to the kibbutz. I helped to build firewalls between the giant reservoirs of the oil refineries in Haifa Bay. I had to work as a second driver unloading the heavy milk can from the truck. I was not allowed to drive, not being in the possession of a driving license.

Still, I found time to read: the kibbutz had an excellent library, particularly strong in the field of modern history, especially the Weimar period, Judaica, and the history of socialism. I acquired a knowledge of Russian (and aspects of Russian life and letters), spending days and nights with natives of that country (often from Siberia.) I had a private teacher, the mother of a coworker who had been a teacher in Nikolaev—as for a time I had a broken leg and was unable to do physical labor. Living among Arabs as much as among Jews, I learned Arabic—the spoken rather than the literary language. (Unfortunately, most I have forgotten; my commitment to things Russian was much stronger than to Arabic.) As far as my further education was concerned, these were not lost years.

More important, perhaps, was the fact that they shaped my outlook and understanding in various ways. Being an autodidact, I suffered from feelings of inferiority. I knew, after all, little about the methodology of history, and my knowledge of the philosophy of history was rudimentary in those years. There were other substantial lacunae in my education—and I had read much that was unnecessary. But there was also a feeling of superiority, which I had to restrain, not always successfully. Much of the time, I lived and worked among workers and peasants, not among intellectuals. I had experienced a world that was usually a closed book to most academics. As an eighteenth-century critic once wrote, it is the main assignment of the historian to understand the actions of people who are not historians.

Living in a country where almost everyone was an immigrant, none felt like one. There was little self-consciousness and not much need to conform, no urge to change one's religion—or to hide one's past. There was no pressure, open or subtle, to change one's identity with the change of the native language (such pressure was stronger in Britain than in the United States).

To compare big things with small: there was the Edward Gibbon syndrome, the belief that being a captain of the Hampshire grenadiers had not been useless to the historian of the Roman empire. Unloading a ship in Haifa Bay and driving a tractor had broadened my horizon in a way that reading books could not have done. I had been compelled to make important decisions in contrast to those who had spent their life on university campuses and whose decision making had been confined to questions such as what universities to choose for studying and, later as a faculty member, what courses to give.

There were other influences that had an impact on my thinking predating the Palestinian-Israeli experience. My judgment had been sharpened as the result of growing up in a particularly nasty dictatorship. It was difficult for most American and British contemporaries who had grown up in calmer and more fortunate circumstances even to imagine conditions of life in a dictatorship, especially if one happened to be a victim. True, not every dictator was a Hitler, and the temptation of being excessively influenced by past disasters had to be resisted. There was the danger of usually expecting the worst, but the worst, according to an old French saying, does not always happen.

My generation had been politicized at a very early age. After I left the kibbutz as a journalist, still in my twenties, I was sent to various Middle Eastern countries. I was in Egypt when King Farouk still ruled, covered the years leading to the establishment of Israel, had witnessed a civil war, acted as war correspondent in 1948, had come to watch the leading politicians prominent in the events of those years, often from a close angle. These various experiences resulted in two books in which I tried to put the events I had witnessed into historical perspective. They were well received; they came at the right time and were among the first in the field.[1] But, in retrospect, I feel not too happy about them; some of what I then wrote I now read with embarrassment. They were amateurish, lacked distance; without strong feelings about religion and nationalism, I underrated their enduring impact in the events I had watched and which were to follow.

I mention these books because they led directly or indirectly to my entrance into academic life. I was invited to teach for a semester at the University of Chicago and for a longer period to the Russian and Middle East research centers at Harvard. We arrived in Chicago in midwinter 1956, and they gave us a big house in the very area in which only a few years earlier work on the atomic bomb had been carried out. My guide and friend at Chicago was Edward Shils, a sociologist and polymath, equally at home in German and French history as well as in philosophy. A difficult man but, as far as my wife and I and our two little children were concerned, a good Samaritan, helpful in many unfamiliar situations. Students came to see me and announced that they were not out to get credit but attended as auditors. I did not understand a word they were saying; I was bewildered—did they believe my lectures were on banking?

I was impressed by the lack of snobbery—even the young newcomer from abroad with no achievements was treated (more or less) as an equal. I remember conversations in Chicago with Leo Strauss and Hans Morgenthau. They were not historians, but both had a profound historical knowledge on which they liberally drew in their work; such knowledge was limited, as was customary in those days, to Western and Southern Europe. Conversations with Leo Strauss were not very productive; they were continued in later years when he lived in Annapolis. I wanted to benefit from the knowledge of the great political philosopher; he wanted to talk about current affairs on which he was not particularly well informed. These were the early years of the Cold War, and he believed, for instance, that there would be a convergence between the two superpowers and, as a result, an armed conflict would be prevented (I believe that Friedrich and Brzezinski's book discussing this thesis had not yet been published.)[2] Perhaps Strauss was influenced by his French-Russian émigré colleague Alexandre Kojeve's famous Hegel seminar in the 1930s. I very much doubt whether I managed to persuade him that this perspective seemed quite unlikely.

In the meantime, we had moved from Jerusalem to London. I felt I had a great deal to learn, and the British capital seemed the best place to do so. My interests had shifted from the Middle East to Russian studies. With all the importance of the Middle East then and now, the intellectual attraction of the field was not remotely as strong to me as that of Russia—not just Russian political history but more so in the cultural field. I launched a quarterly journal entitled *Survey*, mainly devoted to the Soviet era. This was an exciting period in the history of that country—the last years of Stalin, the thaw after his death, and the beginning of a new period of which no one as yet could know where it would lead.

I enjoyed these first years in London, met many intellectuals who had been known to me only through their books, and learned from them. My interests were wide; the peril of narrow specialization never existed. But there were other dangers: what did I want to be? In which field did I intend to invest my time and effort? Was it history or political science or something in between? Did I want to enter the academic world—if not, how to gain a living and bring up a family, not being a gentleman of independent means? History, after all, had been written in the twentieth century even outside the academe (in the previous century it seems to have been the rule rather than the exception.) The classic work on the history of the crusades had been written by Steven Runciman, an independent scholar; Loe de Jong, the author of the multivolume history of the Netherlands during the Second World War had been a journalist and later also an independent scholar. The same was true of Jan Romein, another important Dutch historian. But, unlike Runciman, I did not have the good fortune to receive a substantial inheritance early in life, and, unlike de Jong, I had no support from a ministry of culture. My friend George Mosse, of whom more later, did not need universities for his work, but he liked academia—not having a family of his own, it was largely a family ersatz. I need not mention Spengler, probably the most widely read historian of the century. A considerable amount of historical writing was done outside universities even in the twentieth century—for instance, Alfred Vagts on the history of militarism; and there is the danger that this aspect will be ignored in reviewing the work of émigré historians.

There was a further complication impeding my decision, since my intellectual interests tended to shift every ten or twelve years, something which was frowned upon. Serious people, it was widely believed, chose a field of work and stuck to it. But my Russian period came to a (temporary) end in the mid-sixties. It was on a family excursion in the Caucasus Mountains that I realized that time had come for a change. It had, no doubt, to do with current political developments: it was clear that in the period of stagnation under Brezhnev (*zastoi*), not much of importance was likely to change in that great country, and, if so, why not engage in some more exciting project? Such ephemeral considerations should not really influence long-term decisions of a serious scholar, but in my case they certainly did.

In the sixties and seventies, I researched modern German history, which resulted in the history of the German youth movement and the book on Weimar culture, as well as the issue of political violence (leading to a history of terrorism and guerrilla warfare), but I also pursued an interest in Jewish history, which led me to write the history of Zionism. All these books are still in print; they were historical studies but quite often, for one reason or another, attracted interest in other fields. The history of the German youth movement, for instance, has been reprinted in a series named *Classics of Sociology*. I was flattered and did not protest.[3]

Thus I continued to be a wanderer between several worlds. I very much liked history—but not all kinds of history; I had no particular interest in diplomatic history. A Russian great-granduncle of mine had written in the 1860s a history of Russian heraldry.[4] It has remained the standard work in the field and was reprinted in recent years. He even designed a coat of arms for the Russian branch of our family, which had been ennobled (landless nobility to be sure), but I have never studied his work.

I found political science fascinating but could not accept some of its basic tenets—to establish laws and communalities as often as possible; I knew from history that each situation was sui generis, that it was not really a science, and that trying to find common denominators was frequently an artificial enterprise bound to result in conclusions that were at best obvious and quite frequently mistaken. These were the years of the Cold War; emotions were running high, and personal predilections frequently got the better of common sense and objectivity.

My personal situation was further complicated by an inclination mentioned earlier on—to change my field of interest from time to time. Surely such fickleness betrayed superficiality? But I could not change my ways—I admire some historians' devoting their whole life to a specific topic and producing eventually a work or works of great profundity. But this was not my style, and I was not willing to conform. Moreover, I found academic life stifling in those years—I was interested in politics but not in university politics. Endless committee meetings put a great strain on someone who had never overcome a native inclination towards impatience. Furthermore, I suffered from both agoraphobia and claustrophobia, even if not in very severe forms. Most conferences I found a waste of time (there were as always exceptions); why listen to papers that I could read in a fraction of the time?

For these reasons (and some others), I decided not to accept occasional offers of tenured positions in England and America. I craved security (at one stage, over a few years in the 1970s I was a visiting professor simultaneously on three continents). But I wanted even more to preserve my independence despite some risks. Some accused me of ingratitude; someone without an academic background and the degrees needed should have been grateful. (The history uncle initially mentioned, the expert on Polybius and Flavius Josephus, had spent his years as an émigré washing dishes in a Chicago restaurant.) I was flattered—I felt honored—but I still preferred my freedom.

When eventually I accepted a permanent job at Brandeis University in 1968, I made it a condition that my presence would be expected only one semester per year and that this would remain the case. To my surprise, the request was accepted. If I hesitated, other reasons were also involved. I was aware of my strengths as well as my shortcomings. I was at best a mediocre lecturer (I think I was better in small seminars). Lectures were a strain; I would have been unhappy under constant pressure. For similar reasons, I never seriously considered a political or diplomatic career, which were suggested to me on a few occasions. I have been told by people in these fields that, with a little effort on my part, I could probably have gone that way. But I knew that I did not have what it takes to be a successful diplomat. And I had doubts whether I would be successful in the capacity of a full-time advisor or consultant. I had never worked in a team for any length of time, and I doubted whether I could adapt at this stage in life to such discipline, to function well in an unfamiliar framework. I preferred a life of reasonable satisfaction and do not regret the decision to have foregone greater (temporary) fame or at least the illusion of some influence and power.

And thus I preferred relative solitude, the calm life of a small backwater—or so I thought. But it did not turn out to be quite that calm either—it was the Wiener Library in London. Having written on Germany and German Jewry and with a certain background in Jewish history, I was offered in 1964 the directorship of this small institution, which I had known as a visitor well before. Some of my research on Russia and Germany and the German youth movement had been done there. The history of the Wiener Library has been written by Ben Barkow, one of my successors, and I need not go over familiar ground.[5] What I did not know at the time was that this hallowed institution was virtually bankrupt and I was expected to act above all as a fund raiser, an occupation I abhorred. Dr. Wiener, the founder, had been only partly successful in this respect—he had never managed to get the substantial support, let alone an endowment, which he should have been given by the various Jewish restitution organizations that came into being after 1945.

It was mainly the old aversion of East European Jews towards German Jews (*Kaiserjuden*, as Weizmann called them in his autobiography.) I was perhaps in a slightly stronger position—a German Jew to be sure, but my Hebrew was much better than theirs; I had even studied a bit of Yiddish in the course of my work, and in my Palestinian/Israeli years I had learned how to handle East European Jews who did not like "Jeckes."

For a little while, I was involved in a dreary struggle with some of these institutions that should have helped us but did not. This led to some mildly amusing incidents caused by the formidable Hannah Arendt. I had criticized some of her writings on the Holocaust. At the same time, she found herself under attack by the very same Jewish institutions that were my antagonists. Miss Arendt concluded that I must be their obedient servant and hatchet man. (Details about this curious incident can be found in contemporary issues of the *New York Review of Books* and in her exchange of letters with Karl Jaspers.)[6] She was adding two and two, and the result was ridiculous.

However, my heart was not in getting involved in long internecine plotting and scheming, and so I decided to try to make progress in two directions that, I thought, would benefit the Wiener Library, make it better known, and eventually secure greater support for it. The full title of the Wiener Library had always been "and Institute of Contemporary History." Why not proceed in this direction? These were the years when contemporary history was recognized as a legitimate discipline, when archives were opened and the field become of wide interest. So I decided to call a conference in London with the intention of establishing an international association of contemporary historians who wanted to further develop the field. Naively, I had forgotten to lobby for the success of my idea and get the support of leading figures. As a result, there was strong opposition headed by Alan Bullock, who suspected me of trying to dominate the new organization—a newcomer from nowhere with very little standing in the profession. How could I prove that I had no such personal ambitions? My suggestions were defeated. Eventually, such an organization came into being, but it was a halfhearted enterprise that did not last long and with which the Wiener Library had no connection.

My other initiative was more successful—the launching of the *Journal of Contemporary History*. There was at the time no journal in this field other than the German *Vierteljahrshefte für Zeitgeschichte*. It was clear to me from the beginning that I would not be able to do this singlehandedly, and the obvious coeditor of my choice was George Mosse. I had known him in London in the fifties. Our interests and our research were close at the time, and George had all the things I lacked. He was in the mainstream of historiography, he knew all the people in the field who mattered, he loved to attend conferences, he was far better known in the United States than I was, and he had many friends and no enemies. He had studied at Cambridge but was given to understand that, for people like him (whatever that meant), there was no future in British academia. Church history was his main field originally; he claimed that he could celebrate a mass. But in later years he became deeply involved in the study of Nazi Germany and fascism in general, as well as various aspects of popular culture. He was an excellent teacher, a great speaker, especially in front of large audiences. Students adored him since they felt that he was genuinely interested in their fate and was always willing to help. In Iowa, they wanted to make him sheriff without ever asking his permission, and he was almost elected. Later, there was talk about persuading him to run for a Senate seat.

It was clear that I would do most of the actual work since, in those precomputer days, the journal would be edited and produced in London. Jane Degras acted as a superb manuscript editor; she had just retired after many years in a senior position at Chatham House, the Royal Institute of International Affairs. I should have mentioned that George hailed from one of the wealthiest German Jewish families and in the years of restitution came into considerable money. But I never in my life knew a person to whom money mattered less. From time to time, my wife had to suggest tactfully that George needed a new jacket or pair of trousers. There were of course differences of opinion between us, but we never seriously quarreled.

I had persuaded George Weidenfeld in London to act as the publisher of the journal, which he did with great aplomb. No doubt this helped the circulation and the acceptance of the new journal in 1966. Almost overnight we had arrived and became known. But a price had to be paid that was high and that after several years became too heavy a burden. Weidenfeld wanted us to publish mainly special issues devoted to a central topic so that the issue could be sold as a book—in English, German, Italian, and, if I remember correctly, one or two other languages. We published such special issues on the outbreak of World War I, on generations in politics, on leftwing intellectuals in the 1920s, on fascism right and left, and other topics.[7] But after a few years, we were running out of ideas for frequent special issues; moreover, this restricted the character of the journal. It precluded the publication of articles, however interesting, that did not fit into the pattern of special issues. And so, after a while, we parted company, and Sage, a publisher of a score of respected journals, took over after a few years.

We concentrated on twentieth century Europe with an emphasis on fascism, which at that time had not yet been explored in detail. There was an emphasis on ideology and intellectual history in general. We seldom dealt with Soviet affairs and Communism since there were other publications devoted to these topics.

There were occasional contributions on social history (becoming more frequent in the course of time), again because others were focusing on these subjects.

When I look at the list of contributors to the first issues published in the 1960s, I come across the following names—chosen at random: Llewellyn Woodward, Eugen Weber, Romero Maura, Adrian Lyttelton, Pieter Geyl, Norman Stone, Norman Davies, James Joll, Herbert Luethy, Gordon Craig, Ralf Dahrendorf, Klaus Epstein, Leo Valiani, Wolfgang J. Mommsen, Arnold Toynbee, Theodor Zeldin, Anthony Burgess, C. Vann Woodward, Alain Besancon, Henri Michel, Charles Moraze, Fritz Ringer, John Roehl, William Langer, Elie Kedourie, Shlomo Avineri, Marc Ferro, William Medlicott, Alfred Sauvy, G. F. Hudson, Charles Maier, Rene Remond, J. H. Hexter, Rhodes James, and many others. We had no difficulty attracting the leading historians of the older generation (at least those we wanted), but equally the younger ones at the beginning of their career.

Scanning the tables of content of historical journals today, one will find but rarely the names of leading established historians, and the question inevitably arises: why this change? There is not one but a number of answers, and I am not at all sure that I know all of them. The 1960s were an exciting period in the historiography of contemporary Europe. Many important issues had not been tackled before, and it was also the time that a cohort of talented younger historians first appeared on the scene. Today, one is far more likely to find competent specialized articles in historical journals rather than those addressing general issues.

George remained coeditor up to his death in January 1999; I retired a decade later. Today, the journal is still going strong ("one of the outstanding learned journals in the field of history" according to the *Times Literary Supplement*), this despite the general crisis affecting periodicals in the age of the computer. It is now edited by Richard J. Evans and Stanley Payne, emeritus professor of history at the University of Wisconsin. Temporarily, a few others, such as Niall Ferguson and Arthur Marwick, acted as coeditors.

In retrospect, it has been probably one of the most lasting contributions by émigré historians; there were talented individual historians in this age cohort, and they in turn influenced a younger generation of scholars. But what we had started had a collective impact that individual scholars could not have had. The work of émigré physicists was of enormous importance developing the field and generated new impulses. There was nothing like it (nor could there be) in the field of history—with perhaps one exception, namely art history—(Nikolaus Pevsner, Ernst Gombrich, Fritz Saxl and the Warburg Institute in the UK, Erwin Panofsky and Rudolf Wittkower in the United States.) Seen in this light, the role of Eric Hobsbawm certainly had a great influence on the development of British social history, but the journal *Past and Present* would have come into existence even without him, and the same is true with regard to the Marxist school in general.

The *Journal of Contemporary History* brought prestige to the Wiener Library, which acted as its host until a few years ago, but it hardly solved its financial problems. The institution's continued existence was mainly owing to the efficiency and devotion of a few well-wishers on its board, not its director. Survival had been achieved on a modest level, but the funds for the more ambitious original plans of mine still did not exist.

Having secured the survival of the institution, I felt myself to a certain degree redundant; the librarians and the rest of the staff did not really need constant supervision and advice, which meant that I could devote more and more time to my work in the United States. I acted as head of the International Research Council of CSIS (Center for Strategic and International Studies in Washington) from the early seventies to 2001. This was combined with a university professorship at Georgetown University, where I launched what was, I believe, the first seminar on guerrilla and terrorism in an American university. Earlier on, it had apparently not been considered a legitimate subject.

Above all, it meant that I could devote more time to my own interests. Historiography had always intrigued me, and this resulted in a study of the changing interpretations of the way the Russian revolutions of 1917 had been understood and commented upon, where Pieter Geyl's work on Napoleon served as my model.[8] As the situation inside the Soviet Union became more and more volatile, the question of the rise and fall of this empire, which until recently had seemed almost invincible, intrigued me a great deal. I also studied the history of the Russian far right; the work of two other émigré historians, Hans Rogger of UCLA and Abraham Ascher of New York, were of help to me. When discussing the role of émigré historians in the United States, those who made their name in fields other than German history should not be underrated.

The two other fields of my interest were political violence (terrorism and guerrilla warfare) and the fate of the European project after World War II, with particular emphasis on the strongest European country—Germany. My books on guerrilla warfare and political terrorism were essentially historical in approach and character; in the beginning, I had believed that guerrilla warfare and terrorism were more or less two sides of the same coin. But gradually I realized that there were basic differences, and that a study of their history over the centuries was essential for an understanding of their recurrence in the last third of the twentieth century.[9]

My work on Europe, on the other hand, was essentially political science in character, albeit in a traditional way. Fashionable approaches in this field I found largely unconvincing; they did barely influence my work. Early on, I realized the weakness of the new structures that had emerged (a minority position at the time of near universal celebrations). But when the failures became obvious, I did not reach the conclusion that the European Union had been total failure. It could well be that a major crisis was needed to provide the impetus for further progress.

As old age approached, I came to think more and more about my good fortune having survived largely owing to several fortunate accidents—when most of my family and many of my friends did not. I began to work on my autobiography, covering the first thirty-five years of my life.[10] I thought that the later years had proceeded along more conventional lines and were of less interest. At the same time, I became interested in some related issues that in my opinion had not been paid sufficient attention or had been ignored altogether. This refers on one hand to the question of how the news about the Shoah had become known and how various groups of people had reacted. On the other hand, I became preoccupied with the fate of my generation—those who, like me, had the good fortune to escape death and start a new life mainly outside Europe. There had been no safety net; accident had played a major role. Often it had been a matter of being at the right place and at the right time, both as far as survival was concerned and the subsequent fate. Some had succeeded beyond their wildest dreams; in other cases, lives had been ruined as the result of being uprooted.[11]

We spent the 1990s and the years after mainly in Washington with frequent stays in Europe, and I have lived in America since. My work at CSIS brought me in touch with many academics—political scientists and economists, but also many historians. I insisted that our International Research Council should contain a fair number of historians. It also brought me in touch with leading politicians from various countries. An enumeration would be tedious; most of these meetings and conversations were fleeting and did not significantly influence my work.

I have sometimes been asked about major influences on my thinking; two names above all come to mind: George Lichtheim and Raymond Aron. The former, a leading historian of socialism, was a close friend; Raymond Aron I met only on occasion. Both influenced me with the freshness, breadth, and depth of their thinking, the clarity and elegance of their expression. George Lichtheim is not now that widely known—he spent most of his life outside the academic world; when I knew Aron first in the 1950s, he was still considered an outsider—great fame came to him only much later. The general feeling among the Paris intelligentsia still was, at the time, that it was much preferable to be wrong with Sartre than right with Aron.

What, in retrospect, do I make of my own work? Some of my books I now regret having written. They were written too close to the events I was dealing with. This was my old weakness, the impatience that made me deal with a subject too soon and also finish my work too quickly. A leading German publisher (Wolf Jobst Siedler) in a laudatio complained that the weakness of my work was that the books came often too early—if they had appeared later, their echo would have been greater (and sales more substantial). Nor did the fact that I had, on occasion, been right prematurely (from the days of the Cold War to the European crisis) add to popularity. A price had to be paid for being outside the mainstream (and not trying to join it). Since I was covering a great variety of topics in my work, I had to be prepared to face some resentment on the part of critics who did not like intrusions by outsiders in what they considered their own domain.

Reluctantly, I had to admit that critics were not always wrong and motivated by malevolence. I liked praise as much as the next person, but negative criticism, justified or not, seldom caused me sleepless nights. I knew, on the credit side, that some of my work had stood the test of time. Books of mine had been translated into many languages (twenty according to the last count, including some exotic ones such as Albanian). About half of my books were still in print many years after they had first appeared. Since the average life span of a book in our field is little more than a decade, this too has been a cause of satisfaction.

Generally speaking, the interest in history (and perhaps even more in historical biography) seems undiminished. But this is not the case with regard to history as a profession. Neither my children nor my grandchildren followed in my footsteps, and I don't think my great grandchildren will do either.

My generation suffered from a surfeit of history, and it seems in some ways natural that my life's work should have been in this field and the study of politics. Had I been born and grown up in calmer times, my interests and inclinations would probably have led me in different directions. This is probably also true for others of my generation—partly because of the politicization mentioned earlier on but also as the result of the G.I. Bill of Rights, which after 1945 enabled many to study and to opt for an academic career who in other circumstances would not have done so. But this leads us into the deep waters of the "what if," of counterfactual biography, and it may be advisable to heed the warning signs saying "Do not enter."

Walter Laqueur was founder and editor, with George Mosse, of the *Journal of Contemporary History* and founding editor of *The Washington Papers*. He was director of the Wiener Library in London from 1964 to 1993 as well as chairman of the International Research Council of the Center for Strategic and International Studies (CSIS) in Washington, DC. He taught as professor of the history of ideas at Brandeis University from 1967 to 1971, and as University Professor at Georgetown University from 1980 to 1991. His numerous book publications, documented in chapter 23, cover a wide variety of historical and political topics.

Notes

1. *Communism and Nationalism in the Middle East* (London, 1956); ed., *The Middle East in Transition: Studies in Contemporary History* (London, 1958); *The Soviet Union and the Middle East* (London, 1959).
2. Carl J. Friedrich and Zbigniew K. Brzezinski, *Totalitarian Dictatorship and Autocracy* (Cambridge, MA, 1956).

3. *Young Germany: A History of the German Youth Movement* (New York, 1962); *A History of Zionism* (New York, 1972); *Weimar: A Cultural History, 1918–1933* (London, 1974); *Guerrilla: A Historical and Critical Study* (Boston, 1976).
4. Alexander Borisovich Lakier, *Russkaya Geraldika*. First published in Saint Petersburg in 1855. Ten editions since, the most recent in Moscow, 2006.
5. Ben Barkow, *Alfred Wiener and the Making of the Holocaust Library* (London, 1997).
6. Lotte Kohler and Hans Saner, eds., *Hannah Arendt/Karl Jaspers Correspondence, 1926–1969*, translated from the German by Robert and Rita Kimber (New York, 1992).
7. Ed., with George L. Mosse, *1914: The Coming of the First World War* (New York, 1966); idem, *The Left Wing Intellectuals Between the Wars, 1919–1939* (New York, 1966); idem, *International Fascism, 1920–1945* (New York, 1966); idem, *Generations in Conflict* (London, 1970).
8. See *The Fate of the Revolution: Interpretations of Soviet History from 1917 to the Present*, rev. and updated ed. (New York, 1987); Pieter Geyl, *Napoleon: For and Against*, trans. Olive Renier (New Haven, 1949).
9. *Guerrilla: A Historical and Critical Study* (London, 1977); *The Guerrilla Reader: A Historical Anthology* (New York, 1977); *Terrorism* (Boston, 1977).
10. *Thursday's Child Has Far to Go: A Memoir of the Journeying Years* (New York, 1992).
11. With Richard Breitman, *Breaking the Silence* (New York, 1986); *Generation Exodus: The Fate of Young Jewish Refugees from Nazi Germany* (Hanover, NH, 2001).

Chapter 3

EXTERNAL EVENTS, INNER DRIVES

Peter Paret

Most members of the second generation of German émigré historians left Europe at an early age. When we are asked today to give an account of our emigration, we can either depict ourselves as inert dependents, taken by adults from one place to another, or add some words about our families and who we were as children and adolescents—even if this means doing what we were brought up not to do: talk about ourselves. On this occasion perhaps we should. As immigrants and historians-to-be, we shared in the collective act of leaving Germany for the United States as the Weimar Republic collapsed into the Third Reich, but each of us set out from particular circumstances, and each encountered the new differently. If the following remarks include too many references of a preprofessional, personal nature, I apologize. The information is offered in the hope that the details of one individual's experience add to the reality of the experience common to all. Historians, following life, link the specific with the general.

My emigration may be said to have begun with my parents' divorce in the summer of 1932, shortly after my eighth birthday. At the time, my mother, who, unlike my father, was Jewish, studied medicine at the Charité in Berlin. After the divorce, she moved with my younger sister to Vienna to continue her training, while I stayed with my father until she had settled in her new environment. I was becoming vaguely aware of the economic and political crisis invading our world. A young man my parents supported in a program to assist needy university students would occasionally visit. In the progressive school I attended, we drew crayon variations of political posters used in the two 1932 Reichstag elections; the Social Democrats' three parallel arrows were, I think, the most commonly used motif. When the class heard that a Jewish fellow student was beaten up by his parents' National-Socialist gardener, we found the news interesting

---

Notes from this chapter begin on page 78.

rather than frightening. It was not until early in January 1933 that I followed my mother and sister to Vienna. By a matter of weeks I did not experience the Third Reich directly.

In 1934, my mother married again, and she and her new husband, a psychoanalyst and educational reformer, decided to emigrate to the United States, where my stepfather had relatives and professional connections. To acquire the necessary papers took time. In Vienna, I was educated by tutors; then I attended school in France and England until, in the summer of 1937, we embarked for New York and, after a week or ten days there, continued by train to Los Angeles, and then to San Francisco. Despite much that was different and seemed strange, we took to northern California as though it was our predestined, natural environment, and my mother and stepfather soon established themselves professionally. I went to junior high school and high school in San Francisco, institutions that channeled me through adolescence; but I found the classes dull, except in the sciences, in which I struggled to keep up. The courses in history and English offered little to support my growing preoccupation with literature, art, and the past. I was reading a great deal at home, much of it over my head, but I was aware of at least some issues of structure, continuity, and character analysis, and hoped for more from school than the detached, mechanical instruction I received. The schools I attended in Europe had meshed more closely with the reality around me and how it was reflected in books. As an example of the difference in engagement, I mention the morning in my *Lycée* when our history teacher, a formidable lady, concluded a week's lectures on the French Revolution with the remark that despite its errors, the revolution would have succeeded "if only another hundred thousand men and women had been executed"—a statement that brought the past alive and linked to the present as no history teacher in Galileo High School ever could.

I graduated in 1941 and the following January entered the University of California at Berkeley. Three semesters later I was drafted, and after basic training was sent overseas, where I served in the S-2 section (combat intelligence) of an infantry battalion in New Guinea and later in the Philippines. The war was a lasting experience in my life. It Americanized me; not until then did I begin to dream in English. My section's principal duty was to conduct short- and long-range patrols and to man outposts. We were also responsible for such matters as searching Japanese corpses for the identity of their units—instead of documents, we often found minute rice-paper packages that contained fingernail clippings of the dead men's wives or parents, links to family and home a thousand miles away. Most of the men in the section were Hispanic Texans who had scored well in the Army IQ tests, but none of whom, if I remember correctly, had finished high school. They had no idea why they were in the war, and lived for the day. I, on the other hand, was both horrified and fascinated by the new world in which we found ourselves, tried as best I could to meet its challenges, and began to turn the immediate reality of combat into something intellectually and morally more acceptable by thinking about war as a general phenomenon in history. Decades later, I dedicated a book on the interpretation of war in European art to the memory of the men with whom and against whom I served in the South Pacific.[1]

I returned to the United States in February 1946, was discharged, and in the fall registered at Berkeley as a high sophomore. For the next three years I took a broad range of courses in the humanities and social sciences. Among my professors were several members of the first generation of German and Austrian émigré academics. Two, Hans Kelsen and Ernst Kantorowicz, left a lasting impression. They differed in personality and as scholars, but were alike in their power to affect both their students and their fields. Kelsen analyzed the function of law in political constitutions and international relations as though he were designing a modern traffic network through a medieval town. His positivist outlook, similar to that of the philosopher Hans Reichenbach, two of whose courses I took when I temporarily transferred to UCLA, puzzled but also intrigued many students, who, their comments indicated, tended to find the source of public morality in religion, an association that Kelsen, always expressing sympathy with the speaker, firmly rejected. In his course on medieval Sicily, Kantorowicz, whom I have never ceased to admire for his boldness as a scholar and a human being, converted facts—discovered or inferred—into insights that may at times have been more aesthetic than historical, and yet always increased our understanding of the past.

After graduating in 1949, I returned to Europe to visit my father and other relatives in Germany and Italy, who had survived the war with varying degrees of difficulty. I planned to begin graduate study in art history in England, but soon flew back to San Francisco to help my mother during my stepfather's final illness, and it was not until 1956, at the age of thirty-two, that I returned to Europe and graduate school once again. The issue of war in history continued to be in my thoughts as unfinished business, and led me away from art history. In Michael Howard, then a lecturer at King's College, London, I encountered a military historian who looked at war in a broad political and social context. The dissertation I wrote under his supervision was not about a campaign or a military commander, but on the intellectual, social, and political issues inherent in adjusting an armed force to new conditions, as illustrated by the reform of the Prussian army after the defeat of 1806. That I placed this study of modernization in the framework of German history at the beginning of the nineteenth century was probably motivated by the importance that German literature and music of the time has for me. While writing the dissertation, I retained my interest in current military topics. I became an early member of the Institute for Strategic Studies that had just been founded in London, and in its journal, *Survival,* published articles on psychological warfare and on the modern French doctrine of *guerre révolutionnaire.* Another article published the year before I received the Ph.D. did concern German history. Writing it came about by chance. I was working in the library of the Royal United Service Institution, with its exceptional holdings of eighteenth and early nineteenth-century military works, when I noticed a large, crudely bound volume used by the library attendants as a tray for their tea mugs. It turned out to be the register of a prison, established in one of the wings of the Lehrterstrasse prison in Berlin by a Gestapo *Sonderkommando* on 21 July 1944 in response to the plot of 20 July. After the surrender, the volume came to the British War Office, which eventually passed it on to the library, where it remained uncatalogued and ignored. The register contained information on the admission, transfer, release, or execution of 306 prisoners, among them Ulrich von Hassell, Albrecht Haushofer, Ewald von Kleist-Schmenzin, and several military members of the resistance, but also three Jehovah's Witnesses and a Russian POW. The information contained in the register, which I complemented with interviews of a number of former prisoners, allowed me to recreate the history of the prison, and determine the circumstances and dates of the execution of some of the inmates.[2]

My accidental discovery of this document did not divert me from what was then my main interest, the study of war as a historical force. I received my degree in 1960, and in that prosperous period of academic expansion, finding a position in the United States was not the challenge it has since become. At the Center of International Studies in Princeton I wrote on current irregular conflicts, but also a study of one of their historical precedents, the uprisings in the Vendée during the French Revolution. With a young historian of the American Revolution, John W. Shy, I collaborated on a little book on Guerrilla warfare, past and present, which to our surprise gained many readers and was assigned as a text in a number of institutions.[3] I continued to be interested in how men react under fire, their feelings about their enemies, and on a less personal level, the place of the military in society, how organized violence is shaped to support policy, the history of military theory, and its links with the society and culture of the times. The interaction of culture and war has continued to interest me. Two examples from a recent publication are the relationship of late eighteenth-century manuals and theoretical treatises on war to the *Encyclopédie,* and the impact Schiller's *History of the Thirty Years' War* had on the young Clausewitz's attempt to find or develop a methodology that allowed him to see past and present conflicts objectively, or, as he would have said, scientifically.[4] These topics may strike some as old-fashioned, but links between culture and war obviously exist, and never more so than in the ways people think about and analyze war. Such interactions deserve to be noticed. Since my dissertation, most of my studies of one or the other aspect of the history of war, including a biography of Clausewitz and subsequent essays on his work, have been written with an attention to intellectual, social, and cultural factors—not an approach of particular interest to most military historians. I chose to write about Clausewitz not because of any doctrinal value his strategic and operational teachings may or may not have today—he himself wrote not to establish and recommend a system of waging war, but to help his readers think about the subject and form their own conclusions—nor was I interested in any supposed influence of his theories on later wars. I wanted to explore how one individual, a member of the generation of German classicism, with his particular military and political experiences, analyzed a major phenomenon of the human experience and created a work that has now attracted readers for two centuries.

Despite my preoccupation with the military, eventually my old interest in art reasserted itself, and the nonmilitary sources and consequences that I encountered in writing on war turned into main subjects of some of my work. This began with an article on art politics in Wilhelmine Germany: "Art and the National Image: The Conflict over Germany's Participation in the St. Louis Exposition," which appeared in *Central European History* in 1978. Further short studies of artists and the art of that time eventually led to a monograph on the conflict over modernism in German art during the Wilhelmine era, and subsequently to two collections of essays on German modernism in the nineteenth and early twentieth century. A number of these articles, in turn, touched on developments related to the cultural concepts of National Socialism and their implementation in the Third Reich. I had long been interested in the twentieth-century German sculptor Ernst Barlach. During family visits and research trips to Germany, I explored his life and work, and, owing to the assistance of a German colleague, came across the records of the denazification trial of the National Socialist propaganda artist and functionary, Hans Schweitzer, who under the pseudonym "Mjölnir"—the battle hammer of Thor, the Norse god of thunder and war—produced posters and political cartoons from the 1920s to 1945, and on apparently personal grounds persecuted Barlach even beyond Goebbels's wishes. This resulted in a talk at the American Philosophical Society that analyzed Schweitzer's hounding of Barlach as characteristic of the mix of general ideological considerations and particular personal motives in National Socialist cultural policy.[5] The paper was an early step towards the publication, eleven years later, of a book on Barlach's life and work in the Third Reich.[6] I have continued to write about this artist, most recently a book on Barlach's drawings on the *Nibelungenlied* in collaboration with Helga Thieme of the German Ernst Barlach Foundation, the further development of an exhibition at the Princeton University Art Museum I curated in 2009.[7] Studying National Socialism almost inevitably leads one back to conflict and violence in German history from the Middle Ages to the Third Reich, a course traced by the Nibelungen myth, its conversion into powerful verse by an unknown twelfth-century poet, through German history and culture in the early modern period and the nineteenth century, to the work's degradation by twentieth-century ideologues and by Goering's use of the myth to explain and justify the German army's disaster at Stalingrad—but also to the poem's reinterpretation by great modern artists. Topics such as these narrow or even eliminate the distance between the historical study of war and of other activities by individuals or groups, whether in the area of politics, social change, or culture.

As we know, there is nothing unusual about joining different topics in historical analysis, nor is it rare for the historian to move from one area of inquiry to another. Many members of the second generation of émigré historians have done just that. And although comparing topics and bringing them together may clash with the faith in specialization and the division of knowledge, which, while necessary in research and teaching, may at times exert too great an influence on historical thought, we also know that in history disparate forces are rarely isolated, and that their coming together is revealing about each. It would be remiss of me not to add that I have greatly benefitted from this country's cultural generosity and tolerance, which—notwithstanding any compartmentalization encountered on the way—enables us to follow our interests wherever they might lead.

I fear I have written more than enough about the outside events and the inner wishes that made me into a historian. Let me conclude by returning to our focus group, the German émigré historians, and do so by recalling one of its most distinguished members, Felix Gilbert. A young historian arriving in this country in the thirties, even one who had already done significant work, could encounter considerable difficulties, and Gilbert's first years in the United States were far from easy ones. Still, he was outspoken in his gratitude for the opportunities he was offered. His person and the years he spent here vastly benefitted the study and teaching of history in the United States. In turn, he and his work gained much—a duality of giving and receiving that I suspect has characterized or at least been noticeably present in every relationship of host country and émigré historian. Gilbert's historical interests were exceptionally diverse. His early work on Johann Gustav Droysen, and his first writings on the ideas and politics of Renaissance Italy, enriched his studies of later times and other places, from the political ideas of the early American Republic to the ideology and practices of the Third Reich. His way of encountering the past, a way he inherited from his teachers and then refined, belongs to the scholarly and cultural history of the country in which he grew up and from which he fled, to survive and add to the intellectual energy of his new home. With rare specificity, his work reminds us that knowledge in one area may complement our understanding of other areas, whether linked or far apart. Interpreting the history of one time, one country, one activity, helps us see the history of other countries, other societies, related activities, more clearly. And if we look once more at the subject that partly or wholly has occupied most members of the first and second generation of German émigré historians—the history of the country from which they came—we see again that by achieving an understanding of any phase of German history, we may contribute to the recognition and understanding of its other aspects, be they sublime, ordinary and commonplace, or murderous.

Peter Paret was educated in Germany, France, Great Britain, and the United States. After serving in the U.S. Army during the Second World War and completing his Ph.D. in London, he taught at the University of California at Davis and then at Stanford University for many years. In 1986, he accepted a professorship at the Institute for Advanced Study, where he remained until becoming emeritus in 1997. His research interests range from European cultural history, art, and politics to theories of war. His publications are documented in chapter 23 and include *Clausewitz and the State* (1976, 1985, 2007), *The Berlin Secession* (1980), *Art as History* (1988), *An Artist against the Third Reich* (2003) and most recently, *Clausewitz in His Time* (2014).

Notes

1. *Imagined Battles: Reflections of War in European Art* (Chapel Hill, NC, 1997).
2. "An Aftermath of the Plot against Hitler: The Lehrterstrasse Prison in Berlin, 1944–45," *Bulletin of the Institute of Historical Research* XXXII (May 1959): 88–102.
3. *Guerrillas in the 1960s*, (Princeton Studies in World Politics No. 1, Praeger, New York, 1961, expanded ed., 1962.
4. "Aufklärung und Preussische Reform: Clausewitz' Vorlesungen über den Kleinen Krieg," in Harald Bloom, Karsten Fischer, and Marcus Llanque, eds., *Ideenpolitik. Geschichtliche Konstellationen und gegenwärtige Konflikte* (Berlin, 2011).
5. "God's Hammer," *Proceedings of the American Philosophical Society*, CXXXVI, No. 2 (June 1992).
6. *An Artist against the Third Reich: Ernst Barlach, 1933–1938* (Cambridge, 2003).
7. *Myth and Modernity: Ernst Barlach's Drawings on the Nibelungen* (New York, 2012).

Chapter 4

NOT EXILE, BUT A NEW LIFE

Fritz Stern

I am grateful to have been invited to contribute to this volume, especially as it gives me a new "identity"—a term I have always been uneasy with. I never thought of myself as an exile; an exile hopes to go back and, for all my enduring affection for and interest in Europe, I don't think I ever had the intention of returning for good. True, I had lost a *Heimat*, but that had already happened in the Third Reich. I was immensely lucky to come to a country where it seemed plausible for people to have many homes. Certainly, in the beginning of my American life was the intense anxiety about friends and relatives left in war-torn Europe, to say nothing of the intense involvement with the course of the war itself. But America became my permanent home, the more so with the birth of my children. We felt at home here, and I surmise that was true for most of my cohort. But as I have said before, Europe was enshrined in memory and heart.

My first task was to learn English. And for that enterprise I remain grateful to P.S. 152, Queens. In college and graduate school, I came to realize that my passion was in history—and I mean history in the broadest sense, undivorceable from literature. To fill one of the many gaps in my *Bildung*, I began my work in studying how major historians since Voltaire had conceived of their work. Hence, in 1956 appeared *The Varieties of History*, an early paperback that to my honest surprise caught on and has had many readers. In some ways *The Varieties* has remained my favorite book.

When I think back on those early years of graduate and postgraduate life, inevitably one of the first names that come to mind is Hajo Holborn: what erudition, what professional commitment marked him. But even more, I was deeply impressed by his integrity, his humanity, and his great kindness. He had already been a mentor to my friend Henry Roberts, Yale Ph.D., and now I could have

---

Notes from this chapter begin on page 81.

some of that experience as well. In 1950–51 I shared an office with Henry, and it was Henry who gave me the reprint Hajo had sent to him: "Der deutsche Idealismus in sozialgeschichtlicher Beleuchtung," a key text for my early work.[1] My relations with the first generation (at the time I thought of them simply as my betters) was formative and came to include more and more a friendship with Felix Gilbert, that Renaissance historian of modern Europe. Holborn and Gilbert: what unforgettable models—my debt to them is huge. I benefited also greatly from my contacts with Franz Neumann, legal advisor to the German trade unions in Weimar and political scientist at Columbia. In several ways he helped me with my dissertation. At the defense of my dissertation, Professor Lazarsfeld strongly objected to my critical remarks about the German youth movements in the 1920s. Before I had a chance to defend myself, Franz Neumann denounced these organizations much more vehemently than I had done in the text. I didn't have to change anything!

I also became something of an OSS groupie,[2] meaning that I had the good fortune to form a bond with Lenny Krieger as early as 1948, and later and at somewhat greater distance Carl Schorske, Stuart Hughes, and others. But speaking of colleagues and models—perhaps neither of the first nor second generation—I would like to mention Gordon Wright and Gordon Craig, though perhaps foremost was the continuing presence of my very close friend Richard Hofstadter, a brilliant interpreter of the American past and a great stylist and an example of what was true for all of us. His historical work reflected his involvement with the American present, a reciprocal relationship. For most of us, I suppose, the link between present and past shaped our work, even if we weren't always conscious of it. All of them were, in one way or another, my mentors after my formal and inspiriting education from Jacques Barzun and Lionel Trilling, who taught me how to write.

At the beginning of my studies, German history was an existential, urgent, and wide open field. So few books and so many quandaries! And there were splendid non-émigrés in the field: I am thinking of Alan Bullock, Gordon Craig, and my good friend James Joll. To none of these friends and colleagues would a separation between history and literature make any sense. I think via Holborn and Gilbert one had the awesome sense of somehow being partial heirs to Friedrich Meinecke, who, as Hajo told us, danced in Leopold von Ranke's house. And one more coincidence of private life and professional commitment: Germany had always to be seen in its inherent connectedness to Europe.

I must confess that, in retrospect, it all seems so natural, so harmonious, so predestined. At the time I felt appropriate uncertainty, a kind of groping towards some goal, and a good measure of pain. And one other thought: the second generation might have been old enough to learn from the masters of the first generation and young enough to assimilate the thoughts and aspirations of our American contemporaries. What good fortune!

Last point: I still feel uneasy with the identity "second generation." The great thing about life and our profession is that one goes on learning, learning from one's younger contemporaries! The best example is Jim Sheehan, from whom I have learned a great deal, as I have learned from Ralf Dahrendorf, Thomas Nipperdey, Karl Dietrich Bracher, Jürgen Kocka, Hans-Ulrich Wehler, and James Joll, and indeed from my own students! In retrospect, I feel that we European historians owe much to the first generation, but my debt to many of the younger historians in the United States and in Europe is huge. And that affords hope for the future.

Fritz Stern is University Professor emeritus and former Provost of Columbia University. He specializes in modern European history, particularly German history, Jewish` history, and historiography. His publications are documented in chapter 23 and include *The Politics of Cultural Despair* (1961), *The Varieties of History: From Voltaire to the Present* (1956), *Gold and Iron* (1977), *The Failure of Illiberalism* (1972), *Dreams and Delusions* (1987), *Einstein's German World* (1999), *Five Germanys I Have Known* (2006), and—coauthored with Elisabeth Sifton—*No Ordinary Men: Dietrich Bonhoeffer and Hans von Dohnanyi, Resisters Against Hitler in Church and State* (2013).

Notes

1. *Historische Zeitschrift* 174, 2 (1952), 359-84.
2. Office of Strategic Services.

Chapter 5

HISTORY AND SOCIAL ACTION BEYOND NATIONAL AND CONTINENTAL BORDERS

Georg G. Iggers

First a word about my identity as it influenced my formation as a historian and my social activism. I was born in December 1926 in Hamburg into a Jewish family as Georg Gerson Igersheimer; the name was changed to Iggers against my will by our sponsors when we arrived in the United States.[1] The family, both on my father's and my mother's side, had been in Germany for centuries, considered themselves religiously Jewish but were culturally fully German. I began school on 3 April 1933, two months after Hitler came to power and two days after the Nazis staged a boycott on Jewish businesses. My parents sent me not to a Jewish but to a normal German public school. I was fortunate in encountering no antisemitism in the school, which at that time was unusual. Instead, my fellow pupils, who mostly came from working class families, fully accepted me, as did the teacher, who embraced much of the ethos of the youth movement that predated the Third Reich. Our immediate neighbors, as well as the shops which we frequented, remained perfectly friendly, even after the Nazi accession to power; but, at the same time, I experienced the terrible hate propagated by the media and witnessed many stores and other facilities begin to bar Jews. Thus I could no longer go swimming or attend movies. I lived in two worlds, the world of the public school and a Jewish world. But both worlds had a lot in common. My two best friends were Christian boys from the public school.

On the other hand, I belonged to a Jewish sports club, Bar Kochba. Somewhat later, secretly and against the will of my parents, who understood themselves as *gut bürgerlich* (solidly middle-class), I joined a religious Zionist youth group with a socialist orientation. We rejected the bourgeois world of our parents and had a

---

Notes from this chapter begin on page 95.

romantic yearning for a simpler agrarian world; for me, this meant the kibbutz in Palestine. I became increasingly aware of my Jewish identity, and by October 1936 I decided that I wanted to transfer to the Jewish Talmud Torah school. The gulf between myself and my parents grew to such an extent that in December 1937 they sent me away to the Jewish orphanage and reformatory (*Erziehungsanstalt*) in Esslingen, near Stuttgart. It turned out to be a very progressive school in which I felt myself very soon more at home than with my parents; many of the children came from small towns in the surrounding area, where they were no longer permitted to attend school. In many ways, the school was also guided by the ideology of the youth movement. It followed the belief that Jews had been involved in commercial and intellectual pursuits too long, had been too urban, and now sought to prepare the children to work with their hands in an agricultural setting. I was assigned to the chicken coop. Knowing that we all would have to emigrate, the school day included intensive English and intensive modern Hebrew instruction, with the United States and Palestine in mind.

In October 1938, less than five weeks before the November pogrom, the so-called *Kristallnacht*, I emigrated with my parents and my sister to the United States. We arrived in New York almost penniless, yet with the help of the Hebrew Immigrant Aid Society relocated in Richmond, Virginia. Richmond, the former capital of the Confederacy, which fought for the preservation of slavery in the American Civil War, still maintained strict patterns of racial segregation. What I found seemed to me to resemble the discrimination I had experienced under the Nazis prior to the Holocaust. I was outspoken, and my teachers reprimanded me. When documents became available in the 1970s, I discovered to my surprise that the FBI had started a file on me in January 1941, a few weeks after my fourteenth birthday. I could not obtain the files, which, I was told, had been destroyed. Again in 1944, when I was very active in an interracial student organization in Richmond, where all schools and colleges, including the University of Richmond which I attended, were strictly segregated, the FBI again began files on me.[2]

I received my B.A. in 1944 from the University of Richmond at the age of seventeen with a major in Romance languages, but also studied German literature and philosophy. In the summer of 1944, I began my graduate studies in the German Department at the University at Chicago. My interests had shifted increasingly from the study of languages to that of literature and ideas. After receiving my M.A. in 1945, I went to New York for a year to study sociology and philosophy at the New School for Social Research and attended Paul Tillich's lectures at Union Theological Seminary. Several of my mentors, both in Chicago and at the New School, were refugee scholars. Until that point, I had had only one undergraduate course in history. When I returned to Chicago in the fall of 1946, I decided to enter the doctoral program in the interdisciplinary Committee on the History of Culture, with a concentration on Europe in the first part of the nineteenth century with fields in philosophy, literature, religion, and, for the first time, history, focusing on intellectual history. I was particularly interested in socialist movements in the first part of the nineteenth century, including the young Marx, and wrote my doctoral dissertation on the political philosophy of the Saint-Simonians; I had previously written my M.A. thesis on Heine and the Saint-Simonians. I never became a historian in the traditional sense. I rarely worked in archives but rather on published sources.

At the University of Chicago I met my future wife, Wilma. We had and have a lot in common, and although our intellectual interests have differed, mine more oriented to the history of ideas, hers to the culture of everyday life, particularly but not exclusively that of the Jews of her native Bohemia. In October 1938, she had escaped from the Nazis from the German-speaking area of Czechoslovakia to Canada. We shared our Central European background and our social and political commitments. We married in 1948. In the summer of 1950, we accepted positions at Philander Smith College, a historically black college in Little Rock, Arkansas, where I was to teach history, German, and French, and Wilma provided instruction in German and French. While white colleges and universities hired very few Jewish refugee scholars from Nazi Germany—the antisemitism current in the United States at the time undoubtedly played a role—black colleges actually hired quite a few.[3] We, of course, were the second generation, with whom this volume deals, who had their university education in the United States. Once in Little Rock, we moved into a very simple house on campus in the black community. We had no concrete plans of social action. During the first semester there, I taught a course on the world since 1918. The Korean War had begun that summer. The college library was very inadequate, but there was a very good public library that was not open to blacks. I wrote a letter to the liberal local newspaper, the *Arkansas Gazette*, asking that the public library be desegregated.[4] I did not expect a positive response, but to my surprise I was informed two weeks later by the president of the college that the public library board had decided to admit my students. As a matter of fact, they had decided to end racial bars in the library altogether, but chose not to make a public announcement. Two weeks later a small, but very impressive delegation—composed of postal employees and independent craftsmen who did not need to fear being dismissed from their jobs—from the Little Rock chapter of the NAACP came to our house. The NAACP (National Association for the Advancement of Colored People), founded in 1909, was the most important civil rights organization in the United States, committed to the abolition of all forms of legal segregation.[5] They explained to me that they badly needed someone to do research and planning and asked me whether I would be willing to become chair of the chapter's education committee. I accepted and became the first white member of the executive committee of the Little Rock branch, and Wilma and I the first white members of the organization in Arkansas; on a national level, the NAACP had always had white members. Although they were denounced by Southern racists as a movement akin in its radicalism to the Communists, in fact their aims were very moderate, to gain for American blacks the equality to which they were entitled as American citizens. They sought to achieve their goals through the courts and turned out to be very successful. It was only in the 1960s that the civil rights movement took the form of mass civil disobedience. Its main concern in Arkansas was to end legal forms of segregation, particularly in the schools. I was able to fill an important void in undertaking the research needed for the lawsuits and in organizing these suits. Without my efforts, the suit which led to the opening of the Little Rock schools, a turning point in the desegregation of school systems in the South, would not have taken place. What I did was fully accepted and supported by the local NAACP chapter. At one point, they wanted to elect me as president of the chapter, and I had to explain that this was politically impossible insofar as the Southern politicians claimed that the movement for the abolition of segregation was the work of Northern agitators who did not represent the black population. In my case, they would have claimed that I was a foreign agitator. I had to remain less visible. Instead, Daisy Bates, black, a very able and articulate person, became the spokesperson for the Arkansas chapter, and showed great courage in the face of repeated death threats. I worked very closely with her but did the actual planning.

The schools in Arkansas and in the South still operated under the "separate but equal" Plessy vs Ferguson decision of the U.S. Supreme Court in 1896, which permitted racial segregation if the facilities were equal. In fact, however, they were unequal everywhere. I set out to establish that this was so. With Wilma's assistance, I investigated several rural school districts, which led to lawsuits. But the most important school system to be studied was, of course, Little Rock. In 1952, I prepared a study of inequalities in the Little Rock high schools.[6] The inequalities were striking. Appropriations for white students were nearly double those for black students. The black high school was so badly overcrowded that students had instruction in two shifts every day. But most shocking was the difference in curriculum. Students at the main white high school were prepared for college, as well as for white-collar professions, and in addition there was a technical high school for whites; the black high school offered only the most elementary courses. My proposal was that black students would be permitted to attend courses at the white high school not offered at the black high school. The report received considerable support in liberal elements of the white community. It has sometimes been overlooked that the civil rights movement always also involved whites. It is amazing that the school board actually considered the plan seriously, but then was split three to three. It would have meant a first step to school desegregation. Although a large section of the white population of Little Rock and an even larger section in the rural areas of Eastern Arkansas were fiercely opposed to any liberalization of racial separation, many Arkansans, especially in urban

Little Rock, felt that desegregation was inevitable. They felt that Arkansas, next to Mississippi the poorest and economically least developed state in the United States, had to modernize, and modernization required an end to the existing racial pattern. This explains why the library board was ready to admit blacks and the school board was willing to talk about our proposal.

On 17 May 1954, the U.S. Supreme Court in its Brown v. Board of Education decision declared racial segregation in the schools unconstitutional, thereby repealing the Court's 1896 decision. I then arranged for a meeting with the Little Rock school board. The board declared its readiness to comply with the Supreme Court decision and presented us with its desegregation plan, which we found acceptable.[7] Two high schools were under construction. When completed in 1956, they, as well as the already existing Central High School, would be open without racial designation; the black Dunbar High School would become a desegregated junior high school. By 1960, all schools would be desegregated. But when a second decision of the Supreme Court in 1955 declared that the desegregation of the schools should proceed "with all deliberate speed," this was seen by the opponents of desegregation as a signal that they could delay the implementation of integration indefinitely resulting in growing resistance to desegregation throughout the South. The Little Rock school board caved in and announced that it would not desegregate the three high schools. We were thus reluctantly forced to file a lawsuit. I organized teams of two, who visited black families in the neighborhood of Central High School, whose children would have to make the long way past Central High to the segregated high school on the East Side, and suggested to them that their children register at Central High School. Strikingly, almost all the parents agreed; indeed, we had to advise some parents not to participate because their jobs would be in danger. We had expected twenty-eight pupils to attempt to register on the morning the semester began; instead, over eighty showed up. They were all refused registration. Thus we had no choice but to bring a lawsuit, which went up to the U.S. Supreme Court. We had problems finding a lawyer for the case because the local attorneys were afraid to handle it or were going to charge exorbitant fees. Wiley Branton, who had just graduated as the first black law student from the University of Arkansas Law School, took the case for free but needed money to file the case, money which neither we nor the local chapter had and the national office of the NAACP was not willing to let us have at this point. In order not to delay filing the suit, Wilma, in strict secrecy—because this would have been dynamite for the white segregationists—explained the case to her family in Canada, who immediately sent us the money we needed. Once the suit was filed, there was broad support from the local black community, and the national office entered the case. The NAACP won the case to a limited extent. The U.S. Supreme Court did not order the opening of Central High School as we had hoped, but the admission of nine students of color as a first step.[8] All seemed to go well.

In the meantime, we had moved to New Orleans, where we had accepted positions at Dillard University, also a black institution. We had made the move because I now taught only history, we had lighter teaching loads, and we had an arrangement with Tulane University, a research institution, by which for the first time we would teach a graduate course each semester, and where we had access to a major library and thus better conditions for our research. In the meantime, we expected desegregation of Little Rock Central High School to proceed peacefully when schools opened on 3 September 1957, the day after Labor Day. That morning, we arrived in New Orleans and were totally shocked when we learned that Arkansas governor Orval Faubus had called out the National Guard to prevent the nine pupils from entering the school, and had mobilized masses to rally against the desegregation of the school. The nine pupils were directly threatened by the mob. The moderate voices that had predominated before were now silenced. Three weeks later, after Faubus continued to disobey the Supreme Court to desist, President Eisenhower sent the airborne troops to Little Rock to enforce the Supreme Court decision.

In New Orleans, I again became chair of the education committee of the local NAACP chapter. The racial atmosphere was much more tense than it had been in Little Rock, at least before the explosion in front of Central High School. The state of Louisiana and the local authorities were all committed to massive resistance in defiance of national legislation. There were no plans for the desegregation of the schools. Buses were still segregated. The state legislature set up a commission to investigate what it defined as subversive activities. The NAACP was outlawed, although very quickly the federal courts reversed this decision. For the first and only time, we and our children were threatened physically. My main project was the desegregation of a new high school, the Benjamin Franklin School for gifted children with IQs of over 130, which was all white because the school authorities claimed that there were no black children who would qualify. I believed that the school for gifted children would be a good place to begin the desegregation of the school. With the full support of the local branch of the NAACP and the American Civil Liberties Union, which arranged for the testing, we found a fair number of students with high enough IQs to qualify; however, as expected, they were turned down. I was disappointed when in the last minute the national office of the NAACP advised against pressing the matter for the time being, a suit which I believed would have provided a good first step to desegregation. In brief, I was able to achieve much less in New Orleans than in Little Rock. I continued to work with the NAACP and am still on the board of its chapter in Buffalo, New York.

We had felt comfortable in the black community in Little Rock. We had good relations with our neighbors. All of our three children were born while we were living on the Philander Smith campus, and our children played with the children of our neighbors. One indication that we were accepted was that in 1953 I was pledged as the first white brother into a black fraternity. At the same time, we had good white friends in Little Rock—Quakers, Unitarians, Bahai, but also others. Although I fairly regularly went to Friday evening and holiday services, we had few contacts with the Jewish community. In New Orleans, we again lived on the black campus and felt fully accepted. With our links to the Tulane faculty, we were not isolated from the white community, but we had fewer friends than in Little Rock.

Although my involvement in civil rights had little to do directly with my work as a historian, I had my first excursion into historiography in the American history courses that I regularly taught at Philander Smith College and at Dillard University. I taught history not as a straight narrative, but from a problem-oriented perspective. One such problem involved the interpretation of the Reconstruction after the American Civil War, when blacks briefly played an important role in Southern politics. The students in the segregated schools had all been taught a Southern interpretation. We now read the chapter on the South Carolina legislature in James G. Randall's *Civil War and Reconstruction* (1937)[9] and in W. E. B. Du Bois's *Black Reconstruction in America* (1935).[10] Randall, not a Southerner but a Columbia University professor who regarded himself a Rankean scholar committed to a strict reliance on sources, argued that the black legislatures were total failures and ascribed this to their race; W. E. B. Du Bois, a distinguished African American historian and sociologist, showed the great contributions that the black legislatures made in the areas of social reform that survived the Reconstruction. Randall's book, notwithstanding its racist orientation, was greeted at the time as the standard work on the topic. It was clear that in both cases, ideological presuppositions played a role. This was unavoidable, although Randall, who claimed to be strictly objective, did not admit this. The question now was how to accept this and aim at as truthful a reconstruction of the past as possible.

There now followed an interlude in our lives away from the South, while we were on leave from Dillard University. From the spring of 1960 until the fall of 1962, we were in Europe, of course with the children, first in France, where with a fellowship from the Guggenheim Foundation I worked on a study of the decline of the ideas of progress, which I interrupted to work in Germany on German conceptions of history. In France, I became interested in the new historiographic directions of the journal *Annales*. I regularly attended the lectures of Fernand Braudel at the *Collège de France* and had the good fortune several times to be invited to a coffee circle afterwards, where I had an opportunity to discuss my research project with him. I became particularly interested in the political implications of historical ideas. We went to Germany with some apprehension so soon after the Holocaust, but quickly met people who had the right attitudes and with whom we felt very much at home. Germany gradually became a second home for us.

After our return to New Orleans in 1962, we became involved in the opposition to the Vietnam War, and even more after we came to Buffalo in 1965. I accepted an offer from the State University of New York at Buffalo, where for the first time I could teach in my own fields of interest—intellectual history and historiography—and work with graduate students. Wilma received a position in modern languages at Canisius College in Buffalo. We felt that the war was wrong, basically a belated colonial war of aggression. I cofounded the Buffalo Draft Counseling Center and was trained by the Central Committee on Conscientious Objectors as a draft counselor and later also as a military counselor. I counseled hundreds of war objectors in my office, at home, and in the Friends (Quakers) Meeting House and also some members of the American military in Germany. I discovered later that the FBI had taped some of my counseling sessions. Wilma was president of the Buffalo branch of the International Women's League for Peace and Freedom. She left the League after it called for a protest against Pinochet, a protest which she supported, but refused her request that they also look at violations of human rights in the Communist countries, specifically in Czechoslovakia. The League wrote her that to do so would be red baiting. Wilma's position on the Cold War was close to mine. We were critical of many aspects on both sides, probably even more of what was occurring in the countries dominated by the Soviet Union and Mao's China. But we wanted to make our contribution, however modest it was, to an understanding between the two sides.

All this had initially little to do with my work as a historian, yet increasingly it did. I wished to work with historians beyond the ideological divide. In 1966, Wilma for the first time dared to visit her native Czechoslovakia, now assured that she would be able to leave again. I already had visited her friends two years earlier and while there also met two young historians who later played a role in the Prague Spring. We applied for a transit visa through the GDR (East Germany), which was the most direct way to her part of Bohemia. To our surprise, we and the children received visas with an overnight stay in Halle. It appears that historians in Halle already knew something about me. Wilma and I were very cordially received. When I told them that I would like to meet GDR historians, they said this could be arranged and invited me to come to Halle for a week the following year. They also arranged for me to meet two Leipzig historians with whom we are still in touch, Hans Schleier and Werner Berthold. Berthold invited me to come to Leipzig the following summer and give two talks at the Karl Marx University. Several weeks later I also received an invitation to come to East Berlin. I gave the two lectures in Leipzig, stressing that the official GDR description of historians in the United States and West Germany as serving NATO was a distortion and deliberately overlooked the very critical note which historians in the United States had actually introduced in dealing with American foreign policy and with which historians such as Fritz Fischer and Hans-Ulrich Wehler in West Germany dealt with the German past. Despite the criticism of GDR positions that my lectures implied, I was regularly invited to speak in Leipzig and at the Academy of Sciences in East Berlin, occasionally also in Halle and Jena, but always in a closed circle that included distinguished historians and occasionally doctoral candidates, but no students.

At the same time, I established contact with leading historians in West Germany. When the newly founded German Studies Association in the United States began to invite scholars from West Germany, Austria, and Switzerland, I suggested that they also invite scholars from the GDR, which they did. The first scholars from the GDR, Hans Schleier and Wolfgang Küttler, arrived in 1982, and I arranged a discussion in Buffalo between them and Jörn Rüsen from West Germany. From then on, there was an annual West-East-German discussion in Buffalo, and GDR scholars began regularly attending the annual conferences of the German Studies Association. In 1983, I suggested to the Academy of Sciences of the GDR that we exchange doctoral candidates between Buffalo and the Academy, and, to my surprise, they agreed two years later. The exchange began on a small scale in 1987. In the 1970s and '80s, I also exchanged visits with Polish and Hungarian scholars. Wilma maintained contacts with Czech dissidents after the Soviet occupation of Czechoslovakia. At the International Congress of the Historical Sciences in Bucharest I, together with Charles-Olivier Carbonell from France, who had originated the idea, and Lucian Boia from Bucharest, founded the International Commission for the History of Historiography. I saw to it that both sides of the ideological divide were represented on the executive board of the commission. From the beginning, Zhang Zhilian from Beijing worked closely with us. As chair of the history department in Buffalo in the early 1980s, I was able to invite Qi Shirong from Beijing for half a year in 1982. As president of Capital Normal University, Qi later established world history as an important field of study in China. In 1984, still as a department chair, I agreed to have Gennady Dubovitsky, a young Soviet historian, come to Buffalo, where his unquestioned faith in the Soviet system was gradually replaced by an appreciation of democracy as he experienced it during his year's stay in the United States. In 1984, Qi Shirong invited Wilma and me for six weeks to his university. Since that time I have had close ties to Chinese historians, and also contacts with Taiwan and South Korea. Most recently, in March 2013, and with the same motivation to carry on critical discussions across ideological lines, I visited the history department at the University of Havana.

And now to the question of how my research and publications related to my biography. I already referred to my dissertation on the Saint Simonians. This resulted in my first book, *The Cult of Authority* (1957),[11] an analysis of the authoritarian aspects of the political philosophy of the Saint-Simonians that involved my affirmation of aspects of their socialism, but also my rejection of their advocacy of what amounted to a socialist dictatorship. What particularly interested me, however, was their conception of history that combined an idea of progress with a very pessimistic assessment of their contemporary world, involving a basic critique of Enlightenment values and of what we call civil liberties. I then agreed with Hayden White to write a small book on the idea of progress in which each of us would develop our very different positions, mine at the time basically optimistic, his much more critical. The book was never completed because we were both engaged in other projects, he in his *Metahistory: The Historical Imagination in Nineteenth-Century Europe*,[12] which soon became famous. I was able to present my own theses in an article in *The American Historical Review* in 1965, "The Idea of Progress: A Critical Reassessment."[13] From then on, my writings dealt primarily with questions of historical theory and historiography.

While working on the idea of progress, I became increasingly interested in the German historicist tradition as a form of historical optimism with strong political implications. In 1961 this motivated me to move from France to Germany and led to my *The German Conception of History: The National Tradition of Historical Thought*,[14] a critique of the German historical profession from its formation in the early nineteenth century to the 1960s. In a sense, this critique undertook for the German historical profession what Peter Novick did in *That Noble Dream*[15] for the American historical profession. Both professions viewed themselves as scholarly disciplines committed to strict objectivity. In fact, both followed ideological guidelines, in the German case propagating an aggressive authoritarian nationalism committed to the rejection of democratic institutions. I did not argue that this historiography led directly to the Nazis, but suggested that it created an atmosphere in which an academic intelligentsia and to an extent a larger public were able to reconcile themselves with broad sections of the Nazi program.

In the United States, my book was largely regarded as an academic work; in Germany it received broad attention at a time when a younger generation of historians in West Germany began to look critically at the German past.[16] The book not only examined the political ideology of the historians, but also the conception of history upon which this ideology rested. This conception, which has been identified as historism (*Historismus*),[17] prevailed from the time of Leopold von Ranke, who has been viewed as the father of the German historical profession, to Friedrich Meinecke, who, despite his own opposition to Nazism, continued to argue that German historism, with its rejection of Western democratic values, represented the highest form of historical thought and Germany's special contribution to mankind.[18] Shortly after the German edition was published, I received a letter from a German historian, who wrote that I was wrong to focus on the ideological position of the historians and not to appreciate sufficiently the solid historical work they did;[19] as I replied to him, their historical work could not be separated from their ideology. This, of course, immediately raises the question of to what extent my critique of the German national tradition had roots in my own subjective experiences, including my experiences with the Nazis. Of course, it did. But this did not necessarily invalidate it.

Although this book focused on Germany, all my further writings followed a comparative, transnational, and ultimately transcultural approach. In 1975, I published *New Directions in European Historiography*.[20] This book presented historical studies throughout Europe after 1945. Unlike other surveys of the historiography of the period, it also paid attention to Soviet-dominated Eastern Europe. It gave particular attention to new approaches to economic and social history in Poland by Witold Kula, Andrzej Wyszanski, and Jerzy Topolski, who were in their approach very close to the French *Annales* and very far from Marxist orthodoxy. I wanted to demonstrate that historical studies in the Soviet bloc could not simply be ignored, as they too often were. There were pressures for conformity, and most historians conformed, but there were also others who went in other directions. Unfortunately, I did not know yet of Aaron I. Gurevich's *Categories of Medieval Culture*,[21] which had just appeared in Moscow and which should have been included. It dealt primarily with the new school in West Germany of "Historical Social Science," which confronted what had happened in Germany in a socioeconomic context. One point of my criticism was that while the *Annales* largely ignored politics, the German school gave too little attention to the role of popular culture. That was first undertaken a decade later by the *Alltagsgeschichte* (the history of everyday life) historians. The book did surprisingly well. It was quickly translated into Italian, Danish, Greek, Korean, Japanese, and Chinese. I then rewrote it extensively for the German edition, *Vom Historismus zur Historischen Sozialwissenschaft*,[22] which gave more attention to the empirical approaches of historical social science, and, as the title suggests, to theoretical problems raised by historism and the social sciences.

Almost two decades later, I wrote an assessment of historiographical trends in the early 1990s, *Geschichtswissenschaft im 20. Jahrhundert. Ein kritischer Überblick im internationalen Zusammenhang*.[23] In a sense, the book could be regarded as an updating of *New Directions*, but it was essentially very different. While the earlier volume had focused on various forms of social science history, the historiographical situation had markedly changed with a growing postmodernist critique of the earlier social science models. I thoroughly rewrote an English version, which appeared under the title *Historiography in the Twentieth Century*.[24] As the subtitle *Scientific Objectivity and the Postmodern Challenge* suggests, this involved my critical examination of the basic objectivist assumptions of much of social science history but also of the radical denial of any form of rational inquiry. Although I agree with Hayden White, the foremost exponent of the postmodernist position, that all historical narratives have a literary character and that there are clear limits to objective historical inquiry, I have always maintained that this does not mean that history is pure literature—or, if you want, pure fiction.[25] In a sense, I continue the position that I had entertained in *The German Conception of History*, an affirmation of Enlightenment conceptions of human rights and rational inquiry. While postmodernists like Hayden White in fact affirm human rights, they deprived them of any theoretical foundation.

However, I always wanted to write a global history of historiography. I believed firmly that history needed to transcend not only national but also cultural borders. I was keenly aware of the limitations of my previous book, *Historiography in the Twentieth Century*, which had appeared in various European and East Asian languages, including Turkish and, of course, in Chinese, both in the People's Republic and Taiwan, which indicates that it was taken seriously even outside the West. It was transnational in its approach, but not transcultural, focusing on the West like most historiographical works at the time. But without the knowledge of non-European languages, I was unable to undertake such a history. In 1979, together with Harold T. Parker, I published an *International Handbook of Historical Studies*,[26] an anthology, the first work from a global perspective which included an excellent article on historiography in Sub-Saharan Africa by two leading Nigerian historians.[27] In 1984, during my first visit to China, I made the acquaintance of Qingjia Edward Wang, with whom I then conducted an extensive correspondence on questions of comparative historiography. I was very much impressed by his book *Inventing China through History* (2001),[28] which dealt with how the modernization of Chinese historical studies in the twentieth century involved the integration of Western models of historical scholarship with traditional Chinese models. Thus, when Longman asked me to write a history of modern historiography, I suggested a global approach and asked Wang to participate in the project. We convinced Supriya Mukherjee, an Indian, who had been my doctoral student, to take on the Indian part. Thus our *Global History of Modern Historiography* took shape.[29] Its basic idea, one which Wang had already pursued, was how processes of the modernization of historical studies involved the interaction of Western and indigenous ideas.

The book was guided by two theoretical presuppositions: it agreed with Dipesh Chakrabarty's thesis[30] that modernization has taken different forms in different cultural contexts, and also with his view that there are basic values with roots in the Western Enlightenment, specifically the commitment to human rights and to standards of rational inquiry.[31] Despite fundamental cultural differences, modern India cannot be conceived without these Western traditions. As I already made clear in my *Historiography in the Twentieth Century*, I disagree markedly with much of the postmodernist rejection of the Enlightenment and the totality of the Western tradition, including its radical epistemological relativism, which considers history a form of fiction. In the meantime, Wang and I completed a coedited volume on Marxist historiographies from a global perspective.[32]

A concluding observation: Wilma's and my early lives in Czechoslovakia and Germany respectively and our experiences as Jews in a very critical period contributed to the formation of our identities and to our motivation to reach across racial, political, and national borders both in our social activism and our roles as historians. But although we felt ourselves to be culturally Central European,

America, where we spent the major part of our careers, became an integral part of our lives. In the civil rights movement and later in the peace movement, we were deeply involved in American affairs. Beginning in the 1960s, we also became very much involved in Germany, during the Cold War in both parts of Germany, and we reached the decision to reclaim my German citizenship, and in Wilma's case to acquire German citizenship, without renouncing our American citizenship, wanting to be members of both societies, in Wilma's case also of her native Bohemia. For many years we had dual residences, spending approximately an equal amount of each year in Göttingen and Buffalo. We regretfully gave up our apartment in Göttingen because in our old age we want to be closer to our children and their families, but we continue to visit Göttingen frequently. I have been active in the Jewish community in Göttingen since it was revived in 1994 with the arrival of Jewish immigrants from the former Soviet Union, a liberal synagogue in which women and men are fully equal. I have established an informal cooperation between this congregation and the synagogue to which we belong in Buffalo, which has a similar liberal religious orientation. In November 2011, I accompanied our Buffalo rabbi, who had been invited to Göttingen to participate in the annual remembrance of the November pogrom of 1938, the so-called *Kristallnacht*.

Our involvements received recognition: in 2007, President Horst Köhler of Germany awarded me the *Bundesverdienstkreuz 1. Klasse* (Federal Cross of Merit 1st class), stressing my contributions to Jewish-German reconciliation, my involvement in the civil rights movement in America, and particularly my efforts to bridge the differences between the two Germanys during the division of the country. Wilma received a similar award from the Czech government for her contribution to Czech cultural history, She also became a citizen of her home town, Horšovský Týn, only the second person to receive this honor since the end of the Communist regime, recognizing her assistance to the town in restoring the memory of the Germans and Jews who once lived in the community. As a historian, I was always committed to overcoming all myths of national superiority propagated by much of professional historiography, particularly but not only in Germany, throughout the nineteenth until past the catastrophes of the twentieth century, and the accompanying notion in an age of imperialism of the inferiority of non-Western cultures. While my work always proceeded from transnational assumptions, it became truly global only with time. It is to this global perspective to which I am now firmly committed.

Georg Iggers migrated to the United States in 1938 and pursued an academic career that culminated in his current position as distinguished professor of history emeritus at the State University of New York at Buffalo. A civil rights activist, he taught at two African American colleges in Little Rock and New Orleans between 1950 and 1963. He is also the cofounder of the International Commission for the History and Theory of Historiography. His books, documented in chapter 23, include *German Conception of History* (1968, rev. ed. 1983) and *Global History of Modern Historiography* (2008).

Notes

1. On my biography, see Wilma Iggers and Georg Iggers, *Two Lives in Uncertain Times: Facing the Challenges of the 20th Century as Scholars and Citizens* (New York, 2006).
2. The FBI file was sent to me under the Freedom of Information Act: Director FBI, SAC Little Rock (100-2920), 9 June, 1953, Reports dated Richmond, VA, 1/23/41; 5/24,41;8/28/41; 9/8/41;10/2/41; New York City 11/1/41; Richmond, VA, 11/19/41, 318,44, New York City 4/10/44; Richmond, VA, 5/12/44; Norfolk, VA, 5/24/44; Richmond, VA, 0/5/44.
3. See Gabrielle Simon Edgcomb, *From Swastika to Jim Crow: Refugee Scholars at Black Colleges*, with a foreword by John Hope Franklin (Malibar, FL, 1993).
4. *Arkansas Gazette*, 23 November 1950.
5. See Manfred Berg, *The NAACP and the Struggle for Black Political Integration* (Gainesville, 2005).
6. Little Rock Council on Schools, "A Study on Equality under Segregation in the Little Rock Public School System," Little Rock, 1952. See also "The Struggle against Racial Segregation: Little Rock and New Orleans (1950–1960)," in Iggers and Iggers, *Two Lives*, ch. 4, 61–87.
7. This was the so-called Blossom Plan named after the superintendent of Little Rock schools Virgil Blossom; see Tony A. Freyer, "Politics and Law in the Little Rock Crisis, 1954–1957," *The Arkansas Historical Quarterly* 69, no. 2 (2007): 148.
8. Tony A. Freyer, *Little Rock on Trial: Cooper vs. Aaron and School Desegregation* (Lawrence, KS, 2007).
9. James G. Randall, "Reconstruction Debacle: Collapse of the Radical Regime," in *Civil War and Reconstruction* (Boston, 1937), 847–79. His assessment of the political role of blacks in the Reconstruction was summed in the two sentences: "Elections in the South became a byword and a travesty. Ignorant blacks by the thousands cast ballots without knowing even the names of the men for whom they were voting" (847).
10. W. H. B. Du Bois, "The Black Proletariat in South Carolina," in *Black Reconstruction in America: An Essay toward a History of the Part which Black Folk Played in the Attempt to Reconstruct Democracy in America (1860–1880)* (New York, 1935), 381–430. Du Bois's study, today regarded more important than that of Randall, was not even reviewed in the *American Historical Review* at the time.
11. Georg G. Iggers, *The Cult of Authority: The Political Philosophy of the Saint-Simonians, a Chapter in the Intellectual History of Totalitarianism* (The Hague, 1958)
12. Hayden V. White, *Metahistory: The Historical Imagination in Nineteenth-Century Europe* (Baltimore, 1973).
13. Georg G. Iggers, "The Idea of Progress: A Critical Reassessment," *American Historical Review* 71, no. 1 (1965–1966): 1–17.
14. Georg G. Iggers, *The German Conception of History: The National Tradition of Historical Thought from Herder to the Present* (Middletown, CT, 1968).
15. Peter Novick, *That Noble Dream: The "Objectivity Question" and the American Historical Profession* (Cambridge, MA, 1988).

16. Georg G. Iggers, *Deutsche Geschichtswissenschaft. Eine Kritik der traditionellen Geschichtsauffassung von Herder bis zur Gegenwart* (Munich, 1971; fourth revised edition, Vienna, 1997).
17. I am intentionally using the term "historism"—in German, *Historismus*—to refer to the German tradition; the commonly used term "historicism," as in Karl Popper's *The Poverty of Historicism*, has a very different meaning, involving a belief in laws of history which the German tradition, with its stress on the individual character of epochs and societies, would reject. For Popper, Marx is a historicist. Others define historicism very broadly as "the view that the nature of a thing lies in its history," as Frank Ankersmit does in *Meaning, Truth, and Reference in Historical Representation* (Ithaca, 2012), 1, who nevertheless sees Ranke as a main originator of the idea.
18. Friedrich Meinecke, *Die Entstehung des Historismus* in *Werke*, vol. 3 (Munich, 1959), 4. For the English translation, see *Historism: The Rise of a New Historical Outlook* (New York, 1972).
19. Thomas Nipperdey to Georg Iggers, 15 February 1971.
20. Georg G. Iggers, ed., *New Directions in European Historiography* (Middletown, CT, 1975).
21. Aaron I. Gurevich, *Categories of Medieval Culture* (London, 1985 [English translation of the 1972 Russian edition]).
22. (Munich, 1978).
23. (Göttingen, 1993; 4th revised edition 2007).
24. (Middletown, CT, 1997; revised edition 2005).
25. Hayden White, "The Historical Text as Literary Artifact," in *The Tropics of Discourse: Essays in Cultural Criticism* (Baltimore, 1982), 82.
26. Georg G. Iggers and Harold T. Parker, eds., *International Handbook of Historical Studies: Contemporary Theory and Research* (Westport, CT, 1979).
27. J. F. Ade Ajayi and E. J. Alagoa, "Sub-Saharan Africa," in Iggers and Parker, *International Handbook*, 403–16.
28. Q. Edward Wang, *Inventing China through History: The May Fourth Approach to Historiography* (Albany, 2001).
29. Georg G. Iggers and Q. Edward Wang, eds., *A Global History of Modern Historiography* (Harlow, UK, 2008).
30. Dipesh Chakrabarty, *Provincializing Europe: Postcolonial Thought and Historical Difference* (Princeton, NJ, 2000).
31. Chakrabarty, *Provincializing Europe*, 5.
32. Q. Edward Wang and Georg G. Iggers, eds., *Marxist Historiographies: A Global Perspective* (London, 2015).

Chapter 6

SOME ISSUES AND EXPERIENCES IN GERMAN-AMERICAN SCHOLARLY RELATIONS

Gerhard L. Weinberg

I shall use this opportunity to review three aspects of historical scholarship in the United States and Germany in which the second generation has played a significant role. If, in discussing these aspects, I concentrate on providing illustrations from personal experience, it is because, in a way, as a member of the second generation I have been very much involved in them.

First, a central issue for all who work on German history since 1871 in Germany—as in this country and every other country—is a heavy dependence on access to the sources. The decision of the four occupying powers to sign the state treaty with Austria in 1955 that ended the occupation of that country led to a critical issue when American troops left their zone. In one of the former German army barracks in the Linz area that had been utilized by the Americans and was now to be evacuated, there were some German records in the attic. These turned out to be the records of the *Pferdeeinziehungskommission*, the horse draft board, of the military district (*Wehrkreis*). When both the Austrians and German claimed the records, the judge advocate general's office in the Pentagon decided that these were American records and should be kept with the other captured German records held in Alexandria, Virginia. They were then moved and integrated with the other *Wehrkreis* records. The decision that these were legally American records had two critical implications for all the captured German records held in the former torpedo factory in Alexandria. It meant that they fell under the rules governing all United States records. Those rules included provisions for a procedure under which they could all, in stages, be returned to Germany as and when specific portions were included in "disposal schedules" submitted to a joint

---

Notes from this chapter begin on page 101.

committee of the U.S. Senate and House of Representatives and agreed to there. It was for this reason that, as a result of the still not monumentally commemorated lives of Austrian horses, when the captured German records in this country were beginning to be returned to the Federal Republic of Germany, an American Committee for the Study of War Documents was organized with the participation of such émigrés as Hans Kohn and George Hallgarten.[1] This committee, the ancestor of the Conference Group for Central European History of the American Historical Association, raised money from foundations to microfilm the records before their return to Germany to assure access to them in the future by scholars in Germany and all other countries. Most likely at the suggestion of Dr. Fritz Epstein, I was asked to organize the initiation of the microfilming of those records in 1956 under the auspices of the American Historical Association, which administered the foundation grants.

A further effect of the records having been determined to be American records, they and any microfilms of them were subject to American privacy rules. These rules were explained to me when the microfilming was about to start in the summer of 1956 and were thereupon carefully applied to the microfilms until 1995, fifty years after the end of the war. I have argued that this blanket lifting without any checking for items which might need seventy-five-year privacy protection was a mistake, but the deed has been done.

Ironically, at the time when the first large batches of records were returned to the Federal Republic, German archivists, who had not yet discovered *Datenschutz*, privacy protection, did not impose the restrictions to which the microfilms were subjected at the National Archives. The negative films from Alexandria were deposited there; then positives were made for scholars to use, and copies were for sale. Of course, as many scholars have discovered with some regret, once the issue of privacy was discovered in Germany, the *Datenschutz* rules that were enacted in the Federal Republic were especially complicated.

Of great importance for the utilization of these microfilms in all countries has been the publication by the National Archives of a series of "Guides to German Records Microfilmed at Alexandria, VA." These were distributed for free and are now available from the National Archives in electronic format. The Library of Congress, which holds the films that were made of Japanese records before their return to Japan, has yet to publish a catalog of them.

The films of the records held in Alexandria were added in the National Archives to the German Foreign Ministry microfilms that were being deposited there by the State Department from the joint British-American microfilm project at Whaddon Hall in England. When the German Auswärtiges Amt (Ministry of Foreign Affairs) decided to refuse access to its returned personnel records, treating the 1956 Transfer of Archives Agreement between the Western Powers and the Federal Republic as a "Fetzen Papier" (scrap of paper), to quote a former Reichskanzler, it was the success of the careful and enterprising scholar Hans-Jürgen

Döscher in locating relevant microfilms that changed the access situation on the German side. Since the microfilming in Whaddon Hall was selective not only between files but within files, this was and remains a critical issue for scholars who need to check the original file for individual documents related to their topic that had not been selected for filming and can be identified by not having a frame number stamped on them.

On my own first return to Germany in 1962, I noticed on the shelves of a scholar working in the Bundesarchiv, then in Koblenz, the familiar looking blue boxes of Alexandria microfilm. When I mentioned to him that the originals of those records were by then in the Militärarchiv in Freiburg, he responded that it was far easier to obtain the microfilms from Washington than the originals from Freiburg. Subsequent experience, both of other scholars and my own, has certainly shown that the Militärarchiv in Freiburg is exemplary in its provision of access and service to scholars. Surely the assurance of access and its accompanying assurance of preservation of microfilm reproductions of poor wartime paper have had a major effect on historical scholarship in Germany.

I want to suggest that in the future, this last point, the preservation issue, will be even more significant than is generally recognized now. When we began microfilming, it was originally explained to me by Albert Leisinger, the head of the Exhibits and Publications Section and thus the key figure in the National Archives. This was a major contributing factor to the decision to do almost all of the filming in Alexandria on the principle of complete rather than selective filming of individual folders, as was the general practice at Whaddon Hall. While Präsident des Bundesarchivs Dr. Wolfgang Mommsen was certain that the paper would last forever once it had been redeemed from the filthy hands of the Allies, his successor, Dr. Hans Booms, understood that, in reality, the disintegration of wartime papers has almost nothing to do with who has custody of them, and he initiated a huge program of microfilming the Reichskanzlei files. I must say that I was most pleased to learn from officials of the Innenministerium (Home Office) some years ago that, in their talks with the Russians about German records still held in the Russian Federation, they were concentrating on access to microfilm them rather than arguing about custody. The question of who eventually has the boxes with piles of dust on the bottom is surely not worth arguing over. In view of the practice of all World War II belligerents to utilize for most issues the poorest possible paper in order to save resources for more important purposes, the preservation issue is especially significant for the history of that conflict.

A second also frequently ignored broader issue is the role of the German Studies Association (GSA) in bringing together second-generation scholars with members of the GSA from Germany. In the decades that the GSA has operated, there has been a steady interaction between those American members who, like myself, came to this country as children, and the German participants. This occurs not only at the annual meetings of the GSA but also in its committees. Again, it may be helpful to cite a couple of personal experiences. When I was president of the GSA, I made sure that German members felt included by appointing the distinguished German scholar Hanna Schissler to one of the prize committees. Currently I serve as one of the members of the GSA's Archives Committee under the chairmanship of Rainer Hering of the Landesarchiv Schleswig-Holstein, who had previously served as a member of the committee when Ronald Smelser was its chairman. Other members, for example, the late long-time member and former president of the GSA Henry Friedlander, have had similar experiences. Such connections certainly have an impact on both sides of the Atlantic. Invitations in both directions often result from the development of personal ties at the GSA. It deserves to be noted in this connection that papers at the annual meeting of the GSA may be given in English or German and that the association's journal, the *German Studies Review*, accepts articles and book reviews in both languages.

The third topic that needs to be considered is that of the translation into German of scholarly works produced by those in the second-generation category. This is a topic that surely deserves some further systematic examination. Again, I cite an example from personal experience. Shortly after my general history of World War II, *A World at Arms: A Global History of World War II*, appeared in 1994, a friend in the Militärgeschichtliches Forschungsamt (Military History Research Institute), then still in Freiburg, called to tell me that the chief, General Dr. Günter Roth, had authorized a substantial sum to make possible a German translation. I cautioned him that there might in the future be some criticism in the Federal Republic because the text includes rather negative comments about the conduct of the German military in the war. He thanked me but said not to worry—"We have read the text very carefully." In 1999, Jürgen Chrobog, then the German ambassador to the United States, told me that he knew my work. He explained that this was because the German text of my book on World War II, *Eine Welt in Waffen: Die Geschichte des Zweiten Weltkriegs*, was being used by the Auswärtige Amt in the training of its recruits.

The broader subject of the influence of works, both those translated and those available only in English, that have been published in article and book form by the second generation on scholars, scholarship, and the teaching of modern German history in Germany should be the focus of further exploration. I believe that there is room here for a study that would enlighten those interested in the wider scholarly relationship of the United States and Germany in the post—World War II era. In regard to scholarship and university and school teaching, as in so many other fields, the world is indeed getting smaller. Globalization is generally discussed as an economic development. Indeed it is, but there is also an intellectual aspect that deserves the attention of those interested in the history of Germany and of German-American relations.

Gerhard L. Weinberg served in the U.S. Army from 1946 to '47, earned a history Ph.D. at the University of Chicago in 1951, worked on Columbia University's War Documentation Project, and established the program for microfilming the captured German documents. He has taught at the Universities of Chicago, Kentucky, Michigan, and North Carolina, chaired several professional organizations, and served on a number of U.S. government advisory committees. His book publications are documented in chapter 23 and include *World in the Balance: Behind the Scenes of World War II* (1981); ; *A World at Arms: A Global History of World War II* (1994, 2005); *Hitler's Foreign Policy 1933–1939: The Road to World War II* (2005, 2010), and *Visions of Victory: The Hopes of Eight World War II Leaders (2005).*

Notes

1. See the work of Astrid M. Eckert, *Kampf um die Akten. Die Westalliierten und die Rückgabe von deutschen Archiven nach dem Zweiten Weltkrieg* (Stuttgart, 2004), and several articles of this author listed in her bibliography. There is now an English language edition: *The Struggle for the Files: The Western Allies and the Return of German Archives after the Second World War* (New York, 2012).

Chapter 7

SOME REFLECTIONS ON THE SECOND GENERATION

Hanna Holborn Gray

Even at my advanced age, I am one of the younger members of the second-generation émigrés, and one of the luckiest. My family (parents, brother, and myself) arrived in New York on 28 August 1934. My father had received a faculty position at Yale; we had a definite place to go. My parents were both young at thirty-two. Among the many variables affecting the experience of emigration, the role of age must make an important difference in terms of the flexibility and adaptability people can command. I was just short of four years old. My education (if you eliminate nursery school) was entirely in the United States; my ease in learning accentless English no surprise.

But of course there are many other elements, too, that will have shaped any individual's life as a member of the second generation. Those stem from a great variety of influences: the extent to which parents embraced or resisted learning about and accepting the fundamental nature of the society and culture they had entered; the extent to which they felt or came to feel welcome or at home in their new environment; the degree of success they achieved in their professional lives; the dynamic and demands of family life in relation to the worlds of school and participation in the larger society.

In addition, émigré children responded differently and saw their heritage differently at different stages in their lives. (One should note, too, that their parents' outlook evolved over time as well. And one should observe the changes that took place in the United States; they inhabited a series of Americas.) Most adolescents, after all, tend to rebel against their parents in one way or another, and most tend to seek conformity with what they see as the characteristic ways of their peers, ways that may be inconsistent with familial attitudes and expectations. It would be astonishing if children of the second generation did not follow that pattern

---

Notes from this chapter begin on page 113.

and come to believe that they needed to reject, or were now poised to reject, older traditions and cultural values rooted in the still-European ethos of the older generation. But it would be equally astonishing if those children, as adults, did not find themselves very much affected by and very much in possession of many of the gifts bestowed by that ethos, often in quite subtle forms—and, I should add, very grateful as well to have had access to two cultures, however difficult at times the process of their integration. No matter how rebellious one might have been, the substratum of family background and its teachings remained always part of one's makeup, ready to emerge and reemerge in changing contexts. Over the years, I encountered a wide range of ideas and tastes and assumptions that had grown out of my past. I discovered, too, that assimilation to America was in no way inconsistent with retention of a European heritage and that I had learned much from the experience of my parents and their fellow émigrés.

My father, Hajo Holborn, had left his positions at the University of Berlin and the Hochschule für Politik in Berlin already in 1933 after the law of 7 April 1933 for the "restoration of the German Civil Service" that was designed to rid the service of its non-Aryan and politically unreliable members. My father clearly counted among the politically unreliable. He had published a lecture on academic freedom given in October 1932 in which he said that, should the National Socialists come to power, academic freedom would be totally lost in Germany. He was working on a history of the creation of the Weimar constitution. He had already published prolifically, and he held a chair at the Hochschule für Politik (regarded as a deeply suspect institution politically by the new regime and shortly to be taken over by the state) funded by the Carnegie Endowment for International Peace. My mother was Jewish; she came from an assimilated Lutheran family (her father a professor of medicine at Heidelberg). She held a Ph.D. in classical philology from the University of Berlin. Both parents were liberal democrats, and both saw all too clearly what the Nazi regime would mean for Germany and for their futures. My father departed for London, where he found a temporary home at the Royal Institute of International Affairs, continued his writing, and worked hard at his English while trying to see whether he might find an academic position in England. My mother went with her children to Heidelberg while waiting to see where the family might ultimately settle. London or elsewhere in England seemed a likely destination; they assumed that exile there would still keep them somehow close to home.

My father was advised that he was probably more suited to a research than to a teaching position in England. But he continued to hope for an academic career abroad and decided to go hunting in America. Stephen Duggan, then the director of the Institute for International Education and of the newly formed Emergency Committee for the Relief of Displaced Foreign Scholars told him that this was a truly foolish idea—he was too young; the Depression was displacing young faculty and making it very hard for young scholars to find any positions at all; people were resentful of foreigners taking jobs that might have been filled by these unemployed Americans. Nonetheless, my father persevered, booked passage on the R. M. S. Olympic, arrived in New York to be greeted by a youthful staff member of the Emergency Committee named Edward R. Murrow, traveled to a number of universities, and in six or seven weeks' time—it seems a kind of miracle—had the good fortune of an offer from Yale. Sad to say, given the antisemitism prevalent in the American academic world, and in the Ivy League especially, this might well not have happened had he been Jewish. And so we set down in New Haven in time for the fall semester of 1934.

In his letters to my mother from America, my father tried to reassure her that an emigration to its shores, rather than to the much more familiar England, would be excellent. The newspapers in America, he wrote, were dreadful, but the landscapes were wonderful. If he went to Yale, they could live very nicely in a house with a garden for the children to play in, far better than their living space in gray Berlin. People seemed friendly and helpful. Yale and its campus seemed most attractive, the professors welcoming. The (to me, very moving) hopefulness and determination he expressed to convince her undoubtedly convey a need for some self-persuasion as well, but the energy and optimism, the zest for a new beginning and belief that he could make it work, could teach courses in a new language in a new kind of academic setting to students with whose culture he was totally unfamiliar, tell much about why and how he made it work. The first couple of years were hard, with all the lecture preparation and the infinite other demands of establishing himself and his family securely in these new surroundings, but the many letters I have that he wrote to his sister and mother and friends abroad never convey weakening resolution. They do speak of difficulties and then, after a time, of a sense that the transition had been basically mastered. My father wrote from the outset that he found his students remarkably responsive and quite willing to put up with his English. He had immediate success in teaching both graduate and undergraduate students. He found at Yale an expanding interest, both in his department and, more generally, in European history, and found for himself a role in building on that, especially in the area of modern German history from the Reformation forward.

My parents' strong desire to adapt to their new world, to see it in a positive light but without sacrificing the values of their European culture, had a huge impact on both my brother and me. We were encouraged to learn the language quickly, to enjoy school, and to find American friends. My parents did not, as did some of their friends, confine themselves mainly to the company of other European émigrés. They adapted better than many others to the lessened social status that came with moving from the German academic system of the Herr Professor to the more democratic American one, and they very much liked the greater informality of this new world. At the same time, we continued at home to speak German, to celebrate holidays (especially Christmas) and other occasions in the

German manner, to listen to classical music, and to read German books. Twice before the war, we went to Europe, stopping in London and Paris, where we were taken (sometimes dragged) to the museums and parks, and then going on to the Engadin in Switzerland, where we stayed with our Heidelberg grandparents and were governed by my grandfather's rather severe discipline. He had very firm and precise views on how and where to hike and what to read and what to eat and when and how to speak. He assigned us reading and tested us with oral exams on books and subjects that he wanted to be sure we would learn something about. I particularly recall his insistence that we read and discuss G.E.Lessing's famous play, *Nathan der Weise*. We had to work diligently; our summer studies under his tutelage felt more demanding than those we enjoyed in our moderately progressive (and first-rate) school in New Haven.

Another strong influence came from the network of academic refugees that developed and grew in the years after our arrival. As our family had come early and had a settled home, colleagues and friends who came later often passed through our house on their way to their next stop (unfortunately often only a temporary destination). Our living room then and later became the site for many gatherings of central European academics, and my brother and I were directed to sit in the corner and listen. We were told that many of these people were absolutely remarkable and that we should always remember them. Some members of this network also taught at Yale—for example, Arnold Wolfers, Paul Hindemith, Rene Wellek, and Erich Auerbach, and, for shorter periods, Jakob Marschak and Ernst Cassirer. Hindemith invited me and my brother over to examine his collection of instruments and try some of them out. Later, I learned to drive from an instructor who seemed to have been turned permanently ashen by his terrifying (and unsuccessful) attempt to teach the Hindemiths. Mrs. Cassirer had been a seamstress, and one summer she decided that she would teach me to sew. I would go to the Cassirers' apartment where she would talk and talk while cutting out patterns. She would then finally open the door to the philosopher's study, where, looking like a movie producer's vision of a philosopher with his great mane of white hair and writing steadily in a flowing script without ever crossing out a word, Cassirer was at work. "Ernstli," his wife would say, "Himbeersaft, bitte." And he would go obediently to the kitchen, pour raspberry syrup into three glasses, add water, and join us for savoring this treat and for kindly conversation. I never did really learn to sew, however; Mrs. C., while chattering away, did all the work.

I remember most vividly among the other regular visitors Heinrich Zimmer, the Sanskrit scholar who died young, and his wife, the daughter of Hugo von Hofmannsthal; the art historians Erwin Panofsky and his wife (they were known as Pan and Pandora) and Richard Krautheimer; Paul Tillich, Hannah Arendt, Sigmund Neumann, Herbert Marcuse, Franz Neumann, Karl Löwenstein, Albert Salomon, Paul Oskar Kristeller, and Erich Franck. The historians included

Felix Gilbert, Theodor Mommsen, Dietrich Gerhard, Hans Rosenberg, Ernst Kantorowicz, and Ludwig Edelstein. But there were nonacademics as well—for example, the writer Hermann Broch.

I remember with special vividness the occasion in 1936 when Friedrich Meinecke came to the United States to receive an honorary degree at Harvard's Tercentenary. He was my father's professor and mentor (and my brother's godfather). My parents were extremely excited to have him stay with us for several days and to introduce him not only to Yale but to some of the surroundings they found so beautiful along the Connecticut shore and in the northwestern part of the state. I have photos of my father and Meinecke and his namesake standing by the Ford, recently purchased, that was my father's pride and joy, a kind of symbol for having really taken to life in America. Others of Meinecke's former students came to see him as well.

The conversations in my parents' living room covered all kinds of intellectual topics, some of which I could scarcely understand in my early years. There was of course a tremendous amount of talk devoted to the international situation, to developments in Germany and on the continent more generally, and to the New Deal. I was much encouraged, at a very early age, to learn all I could about both domestic and international politics and, when the war began, to follow its course and to become a pint-sized advocate for intervention. I believed that Franklin Delano Roosevelt was a truly great man and assumed that he was the permanent leader of the United States; I could imagine no other.

A powerful shortwave radio had been installed in my father's study by the State Department intelligence service in order that he monitor and report on German propaganda and whatever useful information he could garner from German radio. I used to listen sometimes with my father to these broadcasts and became used to hearing Hitler and Goebbels and the German news service, but also, switching the knobs, to Churchill and the BBC. We tuned out when Lord Haw-Haw addressed the world. Between the shrill voices of the leaders, German radio would play, endlessly (and ironically), the theme "Üb' immer Treu and Redlichkeit" from *The Magic Flute*.

As it happened, my grandmother had been able to come to the United States (my grandfather died in their exile in Switzerland) on one of the last ships that left Europe for New York before 7 December 1941. In consequence, we soon found that we were harboring an enemy alien, and she became subject to the regulations governing this category. The rules prohibited an enemy alien from possessing or listening to shortwave radios (spies would presumably do so to the detriment of national security). So while he listened, she would stay in her room with the door closed, my father in his study with the door also closed, in order to avoid any contamination. Enemy aliens were also not permitted to have binoculars (the dreaded spies again!), so my grandmother gave up her opera glasses to be locked away for the duration. Nor could they travel more than forty miles from their place of residence without permission from the Department of Justice, and my grandmother liked to shop at I.G. Fox in Hartford, forty-three miles from our door. She was a law-abiding woman, and I imagine her applications to travel that distance cost the DOJ a good many wasted hours.

The community of academic refugees was also a mutual help society. People tried to help one another in finding positions; my father was very active in this regard. They often raised money among themselves to enable someone to travel to a place where a position might be available. The children shared hand-me-downs. New arrivals were given support. In a letter to Friedrich Meinecke in 1935, my father wrote, "Relations among the German colleagues are . . . very pleasant; they are all quite different from one another, but all are very willing to help one another. With the rarest of exceptions, . . . the Americans are entirely approving of their growing numbers. That's very gratifying to all of us."[1]

Needless to say, things were not always rosy. Despite the united front that led to so much collaboration and mutual support, there were also internal divisions, jealousies, resentments, tensions, and conflicts over everything from politics to academic disputes to highly personal feuds. The deep sense of belonging to a group of common backgrounds and interests remained always powerful. But it was not necessarily easy for some who failed to achieve the kinds of professional careers they hoped for in the United States to watch the success of others. I think of a scholar like Hans Baron, whose deafness created an obstacle to his mastering English and whose few teaching jobs ended quickly. Although he found a secure and highly respected niche at the Newberry Library in Chicago, with plenty of time to pursue his scholarship and to publish, and although he finally did some graduate teaching at the University of Chicago and Harvard, he never felt that he had been recognized as he should have been or given the opportunities that others had enjoyed. Alfred Vagts (son-in-law to Charles Beard and essentially a private scholar) wrote about the émigré community in an unpublished memoir as follows: "In various ways, we émigré scholars remained 'Verschworene' [*sic*], sworn band helping one another as far as our reach went, telling one another of academic openings where such occurred, giving applicants a good character, keeping silence where there might be something discredible [*sic*], in American eyes, as to their past."[2] As to this last comment, one should probably note that Vagts was himself not exactly generous in his views of mankind more generally, and he offered this remark as introduction to a juicy piece of gossip he was about to recount with malicious satisfaction.

Nonetheless, that sense of a community remained, and remained strong, over the lifetimes of the first generation, and it communicated itself to at least this member of the second generation. The large personalities I observed and the debates to which I listened were a significant part of my education. In moving to Washington from 1943 to '45 to serve full-time in the OSS (Office of Strategic Services), my father joined a number of other refugees assigned to the Research and Analysis branch. In addition to encountering again such familiar people as Franz Neumann and Herbert Marcuse, I was introduced to some new faces, Otto Kirchheimer prominent among them. There were others in different sections of the OSS. Once again, in Washington, our living room was the site of many gatherings of the clan, and by then I was old enough to take it all in.

With the end of the war and the immense expansion of American higher education that followed, the situation of the refugee scholars altered markedly. They were much more in demand; a number of people who had had a terrible time finding positions now found excellent ones. For example, Felix Gilbert was appointed at Bryn Mawr College (and subsequently, of course, at the Institute for Advanced Study), Theodor Mommsen at Princeton (and later Cornell), Fritz Epstein found a home at Indiana before returning to Germany, and so on. European studies were in vogue, the expertise of European scholars sought after. At Bryn Mawr, I could study with both Felix Gilbert and Erich Franck, and I could see how the college had benefited from the presence of a number of refugee scholars. I could see also how they had in turn been affected by their integration into the American academic community.

By war's end, most refugee scholars had—to different degrees in individual cases—become Americans. When my father was asked by Meinecke in 1946 whether he would think of returning to Germany to help restore the historical profession, he responded,

> In general I would love nothing better than to help German historians to rebuild historical studies in Germany and you may call on me any time you think I could be of help. . . . However, I would not consider accepting an appointment at a German university. Our children are American children. They have spent all their formative years in this country, and if we go back to Germany they would be exiles. Knowing what that means, we certainly would not want them to go through that experience unnecessarily. Moreover, we have not become American citizens in name only. We are deeply devoted to the country of our adoption. We have been happy here after going through the first years of difficult adjustment. I have been particularly lucky in attracting a large number of unusually good students. Some of them are already teaching in various places; others, delayed by the War, will soon start their academic careers. I believe it to be my function in life to finish the task of helping to educate and train a new generation of college teachers of European history in this country and I feel that by doing this I shall contribute at least indirectly to maintaining or rebuilding German historical research.[3]

My father's postwar work as a consultant on German affairs, as a frequent visitor to Germany, as a mentor for younger historians, and as an intermediary between the United States and Germany constituted yet another phase of his career and of his bringing together the two worlds in which he was now comfortably at home. That demonstrated to me that learning to live with two cultures was an always-evolving process for the first generation as it was for the second, although the second generation came, of course, to be far more firmly rooted in the new culture as their real home. The experience of each member of course varied, and yet there was something recognizable about us, something we had in common. Among my very good friends (and fellow historians) of the second generation were John Clive, Klaus Epstein, and Jerry Caspari; we shared an identifiable history.

After arriving in New Haven, my six-year-old brother was sent to the local public school, where he picked up English by some process of osmosis. When he came home in the afternoon, he would teach me words and phrases he had learned that day. Soon he knew how to read and then how to write English, so he decided he'd better teach me all that as well. As a consequence, I was overqualified for first grade. My parents had done a very smart thing: they told us we would learn good English before they did, and we should correct their English; in turn, they would correct our German. This gave us, we felt, an important role, and it also made us proud of being bilingual so that we kept up our German. For many of the émigré children, that was the last thing they wanted, and they became American by speaking only English and losing command of German altogether. The difference between those who wanted to adapt fully to their new surroundings and those who were reluctant to do so (or whose parents were reluctant to let go) was often mirrored in the presence or absence of an accent (as witness, for example, the Kissinger brothers, one of whom sounds like a native of New York).

Our parents insisted that we read the German classics and that we speak only German on Sundays. But finally my mother heard me kicking the stairs as I came down them one Sunday, muttering loudly, "Goddamn it, another goddamned Sunday," and began to fear that she was raising a monster. By then, however, my German was firmly and permanently implanted. As time passed, we moved between the two languages, even in the same paragraph, with scarcely a thought.

We were sometimes embarrassed by our parents' accents. Now I miss them; rarely any longer does one hear them outside New York concert halls, and even there they are fewer and fewer. The German émigrés, while always hoping to improve their English, dealt with the problem by telling inside jokes. For example, one story, often repeated, that always made everyone roar with laughter was about a refugee in London who went to the grocer's and asked for "bloody oranges." "We have no oranges for juice," was the answer. Whereupon the lady turned to her companion and said "Ach, sieh mal, jetzt werden sie auch hier anti-semitisch." (Look, now they are becoming antisemitic here, too) Another story had to do with the translation from the Lutheran Bible of the passage "The spirit is willing, but the flesh is weak" as "The ghost is eager, but the meat is tender."

My parents loved much about America—its political system, its freedom, its relative informality, its diversity. But they were leery of American popular culture and anxious that we share the high European culture in which they were immersed. We did not go to movies, except for such carefully selected ones as "Fantasia," with its classical music, and (for me) "Journey for Margaret," with its wholesome attitude toward virtue's triumph over the sorrows of wartime. We were not allowed to listen to radio, except for the New York Philharmonic, the NBC Symphony, and the University of Chicago Roundtable of the Air. Fortunately, my father at some point discovered, and fell for, the Sunday evening comedians: Jack Benny, Fred Allen, Edgar Bergen (with Charlie McCarthy and Mortimer Snerd), and I was permitted to join him for these wonderful programs.

Our cuisine was German, and we were forbidden white bread (Wonder Bread was considered the epitome of barbarianism) or a number of other such unhealthy products. For a time, our clothes were German, too, quite literally. My brother suffered the humiliation of Lederhosen and I of Dirndl dresses, sent from my grandmother's seamstress in Heidelberg. The ladies of New Haven clucked over how adorable these were while we squirmed in self-conscious dismay. But after my grandparents left Germany for good in 1939, we happily began to look more like the other children at school.

At friends' houses, I luxuriated in eating sandwiches made with white bread, in having no requirement to finish what was on my plate, and in listening to afternoon radio serials like "Stella Dallas." But I did not confess these sins on returning to the more austere environment of my own home.

Despite restrictions designed to keep us from the corruptions and superficialities of popular culture, we had freedoms unknown to other children. We could read whatever we wished in the well-stocked library at home and were encouraged to keep up with the newspapers. We could roam about and visit, so long as we turned up at a stated time and did what we needed to do, and go to school on our own. School was the most important thing. Education was everything, and my parents sacrificed for the best education they could give us at the excellent private elementary school, the Foote School, in New Haven—prep school for my brother, private high school for me. It was clear to us that doing well at school mattered tremendously and that our futures, and some guarantees for those futures, were at stake. Academic and intellectual achievement was prized above all else. That was very much a common experience for the second generation.

As an adolescent, although I loved school, I determined that I would have none of this ardor for the academic. I would most certainly not become an academic myself. But once in college, I had an epiphany that shifted my aspirations to studying history. It had become clear to me that I understood and thought about the world best by trying to understand how it had come to be what it was. While as an adolescent I fretted about the limitations placed on my access to many activities that my friends took for granted, as a college student I realized how deeply my tastes for classical music and for literature and art, my internationalism, and my knowledge, incomplete as it was, of things European, defined my interests and my choices in life. I realized also that living, so to speak, between the two worlds of Europe and America, and finding myself in some ways different from my peers, growing up with a sense of difference, helped accustom me to being—and not to mind being—somewhat different, not a bad thing for a young woman with professional ambitions who was bound to encounter expectations and obstacles that could create pressure to conform to stereotype rather than to pursue one's own path.

In choosing the Renaissance as my specialization, I was entering a field that had been cultivated and given a strong impetus in the United States especially by émigré scholars, and most influentially by Felix Gilbert, Hans Baron, Paul Oskar Kristeller, and Erwin Panofsky (he was really an intellectual historian as well as a historian of art). Felix Gilbert, one of my father's oldest and closest friends since they had first met in Meinecke's seminar at Berlin, was my first professor and guide in the field. But the influence of Bryn Mawr's remarkable classics faculty was equally important in developing my mix of interests, and my Ph.D. was undertaken with Myron Gilmore at Harvard.

After graduating from college, I attended Oxford on a Fulbright scholarship and came to know something of the English academic world and its life. I met quite a few of the European scholars who had ended up in England, including such men as Ernst Gombrich and Nicolai Rubinstein and their colleagues at the Warburg Institute, and the classicist Eduard Fraenkel and his circle, which included Arnaldo Momigliano, at Oxford. Those who had gone as exiles to England rather than America seemed in some ways to have had a harder time becoming fully accepted; it was noticeable that a number of the second generation had adopted Anglicized names. There were whole colonies of refugees in London. The Warburg Institute, a wonderful place to work, often felt like one. I was at Oxford at a time marked by a considerable suspicion about, even hostility toward, Americans—the Cold War, the Korean War, the fear of the Bomb, the general opinion that Americans were uneducated and uncivilized all contributed to that—joined simultaneously to an endless fascination with America. I found that my contemporaries at Oxford often thought that I couldn't be American. I didn't quite fit their image of one, having had a good classical education and having the interests that I did in music and art and literature. So (and this was, I think, meant as politesse) it was concluded that I must be Canadian; being a citizen of the Commonwealth would explain one's being at least somewhat cultured.

For me, the experience of studying in England and of traveling on the Continent as well was both enriching and liberating. It led me to discover that I was indeed truly an American and helped round out my sense of belonging to a second generation that had retained something of the old world while becoming full citizens of the new. A trip to Germany was almost overwhelming. In Heidelberg, I met some members of the older generation, including Alfred Weber and Else Jaffe (his long-time companion and formerly his brother Max's mistress) who were entirely recognizable; I could converse with them as with my grandmother. But the next generation, that of my parents, seemed alien: their attitude toward the war and to their current situation in Germany, their lack of any sense of what the British had endured and were still suffering in austerity, their resentment of those who had left Germany in the 1930s, were simply repugnant. It was as though we shared no common vocabulary at all.

When I consider how membership in the second generation has affected my life, I see not one theme but a complex of related elements. Over the years, I have become increasingly aware of the good fortune my parents' emigration conferred on us and increasingly awed by the sense of what they accomplished in working through the complications and difficulties of their move to America.

By and large, the academic refugees embraced the American academic environment and came to prefer it to the rigid and authoritarian academic institutions they had left behind. They certainly saw the downside and the imperfections of American academia, the continuing antisemitism that tainted the system until well after the war, the potential for intrusiveness from on high, the unevenness of quality, and the excesses of campus life. They never lost their deep sense of the evil that had driven their emigration and of the evils that arise from the politicization of universities with the resulting loss of academic freedom and of the institutional autonomy on which it rests. It is no accident, I think, that in the California oath controversy of the 1950s, some of the leaders in opposition to the university's stance came from the ranks of refugee scholars at the University of California and that some of them left the university. Nor is it surprising that, with some well-known exceptions (like Herbert Marcuse who seemed to be having his second adolescence), refugee scholars tended to be among those, whatever their political persuasion, who were deeply alarmed by the rhetoric and actions of the radical left of the 1960s who wanted to transform universities into instruments of social revolution. The issue had not to do with Left or Right; it had to do with maintaining the integrity of the universities' central mission: to provide the space and the support for freedom of scholarship, thought, and learning. The refugee scholars had escaped from a society in which that independence had been crushed, to a United States in which the universities, however imperfect, held out this autonomy as a guiding principle of their existence. The émigrés were committed to the American academic ethos. They were all too well aware of its potential fragility, and they wanted to help sustain and strengthen it. The lessons they had learned and that they passed on to us cannot be learned too often.

It was in part through their example and by knowing something of the searing experience they had undergone that their goals became in substance mine as well.

Hanna Holborn Gray is a historian of Renaissance and Reformation Europe who has taught at Harvard, Yale, Northwestern, and, for over thirty years, the University of Chicago, where she also served as president from 1978 to 1993; see chapter 23. Her most recent book is *Searching for Utopia: Universities and their Histories* (2012). Born in Heidelberg, the daughter of the historian Hajo Holborn, she came to the United States with her family in 1934.

Notes

1. Gerhard A. Ritter, *German Refugee Historians and Friedrich Meinecke: Letters and Documents*, trans. Alex Skinner (Leiden, 2012), 261.
2. Alfred Vagts, Unpublished Memoir (1976?) in Hajo Holborn Papers, Box 1, Folder 5, Yale University Library.
3. Ritter, *German Refugee Historians*, 266–67.

Chapter 8

A Life Between Homelands

Peter Loewenberg

German Origins and Family

Both of my parents were born in Hamburg. Mother (1903–1972) was a public health nurse, large in heart and body, practical and efficient, a convert to Judaism from the Lutheran tradition of her north German family, idealistic, a socialist activist on the political left in a Weimar Republic increasingly threatened by a rising radical right. Father (1898–1954), the son of a distinguished German-Jewish educator, writer, and poet, was a university psychiatrist and a humanist, who wrote, among other things, on Kant, Lichtenberg, and Nietzsche. I was born in Hamburg in August 1933, seven months after Hitler's seizure of power. Although it was the first months of Nazi rule, Dad saw that it was urgent to act *now*. This prudent existential decision for early emigration, which spared me a childhood in Nazi Germany as my cousins suffered, is one of many unacknowledged debts to my parents.

I treasure the soft-covered, mottled brown notebook, which holds the record of Dad's search that 1933 Nazi spring for a place of refuge for his wife, his new baby, and himself. The depth of the Great Depression was hardly an opportune time to seek resettlement. He traveled to Great Britain, including Scotland, France, and the Netherlands in May 1933 to see what the prospects of settling were. There are melancholy lists of lands, spelled in German, organized by the prospective ease of entering medical practice—countries with "only an examination: *Albanien, Bulgarien, Ägypten, Griechenland, Haiti, Jamaica, Madras, Nicaragua, Samoa, Yukon.*" And those "without an exam: *Abessynien, Arabien, Kongo, Bengal, Bombay, Borneo, Burma, China, Zypern, Hong Kong, Irak, Madera, Marakko, Mauritius, Palästina, Panama, Persien, Salvador, Siam, Sudan, Syrien, Tanger.*" Dad's feelings of futility, despair, rejection, and desperation in seeking a refuge can only be inferred. Yet, there was courage and

---

Notes from this chapter begin on page 127.

toughness, a willingness to explore exotic *terra incognita*, strange, seemingly inhospitable, and unknown places.

My parents chose to emigrate to a distant quarter of the globe—East Asia. Their friend and colleague, Nurse Milli, came to help them pack at a time when some "friends" no longer visited Jews. Milli explains in her diary that in order to protect her position at the hospital, *Krankenanstalt Friedrichsberg*, she became a member of an SS support group. At this time, she wrote a letter to her fiancé, which as an historian I especially value because it is a contemporary account:

> Yesterday I helped Loewenbergs closing their apartment. They will be moving into a furnished room for eight days and then travel to China in the blue mist [*auf blauen Dunst*]. Fortunately there was much to do yesterday, so they weren't fully aware. Their furniture has been partly sold, another part will be auctioned. Helmut and I received two book shelves, an adjustable lamp, twelve very fine white wine glasses and many other beautiful things for our home. It is all intended as a gift, but I want to give them something for it, since otherwise I could not enjoy these things. They have been robbed of their livelihoods and their Fatherland and have only enough money to travel to China. Then comes the abyss.[1]

In October 1933, my parents emigrated from Germany to Shanghai, China, with their six-week-old infant. My childhood memories of China are smells of freshly steamed rice, the aroma of tea. I still abhor human crowding, not only in the streets, but at home—the cook, the houseboy, the chauffer, my *Amah*—servants with incomprehensible layers of authority and power to whom I could not make myself understood. When I returned for the first time to Shanghai while visiting our then twenty-two-year-old daughter who was teaching in Beijing, I saw how hard life is there, even now. There is not enough of anything, except people. I imagined how difficult life must have been for refugees eighty years ago.

Shanghai: Chinese Cosmopolitan Sanctuary, 1933–1937

Our four years in Shanghai were filled with the anxieties of emigration from Germany, the knowledge of what was happening to my parents' siblings and relatives in the "new" Germany, and adaptation to an alien non-Western culture. My daughter Anna Sophie took me and her cameraman Luke Mines to find the Astrid Apartments on 240 Route Vallon (now Fanchon Road) and visit the former Loewenberg residence, flat 20. She made a video, which is "Freud in China, Part Two" of her series "Sexy Beijing." The film records how we found the building—which I recalled from childhood as many stories high—we lived on the top floor. In fact, childhood memories of dimensions are grandiose: the building is three stories high. The shopkeepers on the street level were excited to see us and gave us gifts. They phoned upstairs and brought down the former owner, who took us to his room and talked of how he purchased the building for gold in 1949 and how it was confiscated in the Cultural Revolution. The flats are now subdivided into one-room apartments.

When the Japanese invasion began in 1937, we stood on the roof garden observing the propeller-driven Japanese planes slowly moving over the Chinese part of Shanghai and releasing their loads of bombs, the fire and plumes of smoke ascending, hearing the sirens of the fire brigades and ambulances. Chinese who fled the Japanese and could not speak the Shanghai dialect were regarded with suspicion as spies.[2] On our street corner, a Korean shop owner and his family, mistaken for Japanese, were beaten and lynched. The French arranged a truce on the Huangpu and Yangtze Rivers so they could evacuate the inhabitants of the French Concession. I recall the excitement of boarding a French gunboat with a cannon and a seaplane on deck.

San Francisco, 1937–1942

Entry to the United States was not easy in the late 1930s. Anti-refugee, nativist, antisemitic, and isolationist sentiment determined the Immigration Acts of 1921 and 1924 and colored the public attitude in the depression 1930s. The affidavits guaranteeing our support were provided by relatives in El Paso, Texas, who were the descendants of my grandfather's older siblings who came to the American West in the nineteenth century. We have a photograph of "Cowboy Carl" Loewenberg with a rifle sitting astride his horse in the Arizona Territory in 1860. They sent their daughters back to Hamburg for education in the Loewenberg *Schule*, thus maintaining regular contact with their German family. These Texans also supplied affidavits making it possible for my uncles, aunts, and cousins to enter the United States in the period 1937–1941. We enjoy attending reunions of this Southwestern/Mexican branch of the family. They have a nightly fiesta with *mariachis* and cakes spelling Löwenberg in the German manner with an *Umlaut*, which does not exist in English or Spanish.

After China, the first year of my life in San Francisco was the greatest trauma of my development as a small child. While my mother worked as a night nurse and my father was an intern living in St. Joseph's Hospital on $25 a month to get his medical license in depression America, I lived for a year with two different families of pediatricians, each of whom had two older children. My parents, being medical people, thought the care would be especially good in the households of children's doctors. For a four-year-old boy, living with families of strangers away from his parents was a major trauma of childhood separation not unlike those of urban children separated from their parents in foster homes and nurseries in Britain during World War Two described in the work of John Bowlby, Anna Freud, Dorothy Burlingham, James and Joyce Robertson, and

D. W. Winnicott.³ I am moved by Winnicott's capturing in simple everyday language the feelings of "the child who has suddenly been uprooted, seemingly turned out of his own home and dumped among strangers."⁴ Winnicott is particularly evocative of the desperate way I waited for Sunday visits from my parents when I lived in Berkeley, which seemed very far away from my parents across San Francisco Bay.

After the Japanese attack on Pearl Harbor on 7 December 1941, Americans anticipated that if the Japanese sea and air forces could reach across the Pacific to strike Hawaii, California was not safe. This presented excuses for the cruelty of children. In school, the children harassed and taunted the Japanese children, who would cry, "I am Chinese!" We practiced air raid drills in the school basement, which meant hours of waiting to be picked up by a parent. I asked Dad whether, if the Japanese invaded, we would go to the High Sierras to be Partisans like Tito. He said we would.

One morning in February 1942 on the way to school, I saw Japanese citizens with their suitcases being loaded into army trucks for internment. There was a poignant bent-over posture of older Japanese women, carrying the weight of years of toil. This was unprecedented internment of American citizens, a national disgrace for which the American government now pays compensation. My parents supported the Japanese internees by buying their bright handcrafted pins of birds. I still have a watercolor painting of the gate and purple mountain backdrop of the Manzanar Internment Camp in Owens Valley.

Rural California: High Sierras and the San Joaquin Valley, 1942–53

When the United States entered World War II, my parents were not yet citizens; therefore they were "Enemy Aliens," with their movements restricted by curfews. Due to my father's World War II service, we moved to Portola, a small railway town on the Feather River, now a national scenic byway. I recall discovering the lunch area in a grove of pine trees below the school building. It seemed so unspoiled, cool, so natural, that I could not believe my good fortune.⁵ I asked the teacher, "Is this for *us*?" In family terms, the period in the High Sierras was reunion, comfort, adventure, and security. GIs passed down letters from troop trains headed for embarkation to the war in the Pacific, asking us boys to mail them.

Bakersfield, with an economy of oil, cotton, and agriculture, was a small city of 30,000 in a plain at the southern end of the San Joaquin Valley, surrounded by mountains on three sides. The climate is scorching hot in summer, with cold, foggy winters. Many of the inhabitants were migrants from the Oklahoma Dust Bowl. Mrs. Steinbeck, the mother of John Steinbeck, author of *The Grapes of Wrath*, lived across the street.

In high school, I enjoyed debate and student government. The excitement of debate was not only the verbal combat, but the out-of-town overnight trips of the coed debate squad to tournaments. I learned something about the value of compromise as I watched our debate coach, Ed Brunson, resolve a three-way standoff of three teams after a full weekend of debate eliminations by negotiating a triple championship in which all three teams were deemed winners and we could all return home with personal medals.

The Junior Statesmen of America played at politics in the most serious sense of "play." We campaigned for civic offices and held elections. I was the city manager of Bakersfield for a day and went on the local radio to announce the new budget with no tax increase. The statewide meetings were held in the imposing California State Assembly chambers in Sacramento. We wrote and lobbied for legislation. There I met Richard Hovannisian, who would later be a colleague in the UCLA History Department. I was elected "governor" of the Central District of California.

I attended the local two-year junior college, which was in many ways an advanced high school. One of the virtues of the California educational system is vertical mobility, allowing a student to move from two-year colleges to four-year state colleges and on to the university. I was student body president of Bakersfield College, a local notable who was invited to the weekly Rotary Club lunches. I worked as a salesman in a men's store during the holiday season and as a clerk for a criminal defense lawyer. I thought I would return to Bakersfield and practice law. Our family lawyer assured me, "There is a place for you in my office, Peter."

University of California, Santa Barbara, 1953–55

Santa Barbara is a lovely California city, originally a Spanish mission, on the seaside with the mountain backdrop of the Coast Range one hundred miles north of Los Angeles. Our family regularly holidayed there to escape the Central Valley summer heat. I attended a student Visitor's Day at the University of California, Santa Barbara, went to the history department, and had a serious conversation with Wilbur Jacobs, then an assistant professor who researched colonial American history, the frontier, and Native Americans. He had personal charm, an obvious love of history, and an interest in students. On returning home, I found a friendly personal letter from him. I was hooked and enrolled at UCSB. At Will Jacobs's urging, I ran for president of the UCSB History Club, of which he was the advisor.

The momentous personal event in my college years was the sudden death of my father by stroke during a lecture at the USC department of psychiatry in 1954, at the age of 56. He had hypertension (250/150) at a time when there was no effective treatment for high blood pressure. As in all deaths, there were financial as well as emotional consequences. No more checks from home. My mother opened a nursery school in our garden. I had to work my way through college. I got a job as a short-order hamburger chef, worked as a bellhop in the Barbara Hotel, pumped gas at a Shell station, and was a clerk in a law firm. I am grateful to the people of the State of California who, to this day, continue to support a world-class university open to students of varied social classes and economic backgrounds, where students from all corners of the globe can study with distinguished scholars.

Young men who lose their fathers early often look for and find mentors who give guidance and advice, whom they admire and consider models to emulate and compete with—father substitutes. These were my professors—Wilbur Jacobs (1918–1998) in Santa Barbara, Raymond J. Sontag (1897–1972) and Carl Schorske (1915–2015) in Berkeley, and, in Los Angeles, the psychoanalyst Samuel Eisenstein (1913–1996).[6]

UC Berkeley, 1955–65

The University of California, Berkeley, was an exciting place in the late 1950s and early 60s. A student could learn more off campus than in the classroom about Marxism in all its varieties, Max Weber, psychoanalysis, anarchism, cultural relativism, the cooperative movement, racism, unions, nonviolence, environmentalism, conservation, and whatever else was in the social culture. Since Berkeley, I have been an advocate of study groups—a small group of congenial people who meet regularly to present, dialogue, contest, compare views, and dispute on given topics—which can be motivating and enlarging of one's knowledge and mental horizon.[7]

I lived in International House for two years. There I met several bright foreign students who have remained close friends, including Giorgio Freddi, a political scientist from Bologna, from whom I was stimulated to study Max Weber. Among the American students were brilliant New Yorkers who had come west. My first wife, Florence, was a gifted and sensitive poet. David Horowitz was an English grad student from a Communist home and an institutional rebel who quit the English department and wrote his own book on the existential Shakespeare. He has since become a fanatic Rightist with the same pugnacious affect that he had on the Left.[8]

When I first visited the history department at Berkeley, I saw Raymond J. Sontag sitting at a desk signing letters. He was tall, white-haired, imposing. I wondered whether I could ever study with him. I indeed studied diplomatic history with Sontag, the editor-in-chief of the *Documents on German Foreign Policy, 1918–1945*, and *Nazi-Soviet Relations, 1939–1941*. His seminar was rigorous. I was his teaching assistant for diplomatic history several semesters. I learned

German history from W. T. (Tom) Angress (1920–2010) and modern German historiography from Hans Rosenberg (1904–1988). Nicholas V. Riasanovsky (1923–2011) viewed psychoanalysis as a useful research tool for historians, so I sought him for my doctoral committee. I was attracted to China and took two of Joseph Levinson's formidable courses on Chinese intellectual history.

Carl Schorske was an empathic scholar of German Social Democracy and of the culture of early twentieth-century Vienna. He thought dialectically, was a brilliant speaker in a mellifluous baritone, filled the largest lecture halls, and was an inspiring teacher. I was his teaching assistant and shared the experience of how students adored him. Schorske was a forthright humanist who, when I once expressed doubts about the acceptability of psychodynamics in historical analysis, said to me, "Peter, never give up the fundamental principles you believe in!"

I wrote my dissertation with Schorske on Walther Rathenau (1867–1922), the German industrialist and foreign minister. I presumed it to be psychoanalytic—Rathenau's psychosocial conflicts appeared to me to invite a psychodynamic treatment. I have drawn many articles and worthwhile insights to Wilhelmine German society from that work. I was recently surprised when a documentary filmmaker interviewed me about a 1980 paper I wrote on Rathenau.[9]

I had not systematically studied psychoanalysis as a method and a professional discipline. I decided that, as soon as I could, I would seek full clinical psychoanalytic training. I felt the historical explanations were only partial; they did not go deep enough and did not explain as much as we could when we understood more about the unconscious in human motivations and behavior. The rational and the irrational are interacting and inseparable components of decision making. If psychodynamics enabled us to better comprehend personal motives, conflicts, and behaviors, why settle for rational interest explanations in history and politics?[10] I knew that I wanted psychoanalytic training.

Fulbright to the Free University Berlin

A formative event of my graduate years was an American Fulbright Fellowship to the Freie Universität Berlin in 1961–62. I had visited the Berlin enclave in 1959 and now chose FU Berlin because it was a wide-open East-West city. The university was in Dahlem in the American zone. Berlin, especially the *Mitte* (center), was still filled with war rubble. The housing shortage was severe. I was there in the days of the building of the Berlin Wall, 12 to 16 August 1961, and for the ensuing year. I will never forget the clang of tanks on paving stones, making the earth tremble, rolling up to Check Point Charlie. We expected war at any minute. My landlady was anxious about being taken care of by her butcher.

In that first year of the Wall, there was clandestine activity in smuggling Western passports to bring students over from the East. At the request of FU

Studentenpfarrer (student chaplain) Rudolf Weckerling and his wife, I hid packages of penicillin in my clothing to get them into the DDR through the American checkpoint Friedrichstrasse, I then dropped these into DDR postal boxes for sick people. I visited oppositional Evangelical youth groups. Through David Horowitz's parents I also had a connection to Adolf Deter, an old KPD (Communist Party of Germany) member of the Prussian Landtag, now head of the DDR *Ausschuss für Deutsche Einheit* (Committee for German Unity). I was in Germany in 1989 at the coming down of the Wall and the end of the DDR. In November, we traveled north on the Autobahn Bayreuth-Hof-Jena. Suddenly, as we crossed the border of the DDR with all the fortifications, check posts, and serpentines in place but abandoned, we cheered!

We took the ASTA (Allgemeiner Studentenausschuss) trains, which during the long semester break collected students from all over West Germany to travel south through the Balkans to the Mediterranean. I recall my wonder of seeing orange blossoms in Greece, evocative of Goethe, after the freezing winter in Brandenburg, where the storms seem to come out of Siberia. We enjoyed the traditional Homerian hospitality offered by Greek students.

I worked in the Central Zionist Archive, Jerusalem, and did a psychoanalytic piece on Theodor Herzl (1860–1904).[11] The director, Michael Heymann, was the best of archivists: he knew where the material was and was helpful in getting it. For several ensuing visits I taught at the Talbieh Hospital, located for the past fifty years in an old British prison on Disraeli Street. During my last visit, the Carthusian monks who owned the building repossessed it with a court order. The staff was hurt, angry, and in crisis; the repossession of the hospital was compounded by the loss of a leader and the politics of the threatened loss of the occupied Golan Heights. I did several group process sessions with them. In the Psychiatric Hospital Etanim, I interviewed several "messiahs"—a Jerusalem syndrome where tourists and visitors, or in one case an Arab taxi driver from Bethlehem, have the delusion they are the Messiah.

History at University of California, Los Angeles (UCLA)

Robert Dallek, an American historian, A. J. Slavin in Tudor history, and Isser Woloch, in French history, were close colleagues and friends and have remained so over the past half century. Two of our brightest young assistant professors in family and demographic history, Franklin Mendels (1943–1988) and Lutz Berkner (1942–2011), who were in my cohort, resigned because, as junior faculty, the department chair would not let them teach a graduate seminar.[12] From Lutz I learned the eighteenth-century origins of the Austrian "stem family," which is still the custom in my wife's Austrian farm family: the oldest son inherits the intact, unsubdivided farm on the condition of caring for his aged parents. I learned a great deal about historical demography and generational cohorts from Franklin and still mourn his premature death at only 45. One evening over a glass of wine, I asked Franklin why he had an iconic Anglo-American name. He replied, "Peter, all Jewish boys born in Paris in 1943 were named Franklin!"

My colleague in the history department, Fawn McKay Brodie (1915–1981), who taught American political biography, was an adored friend. Fawn was born into the McKay family, who are Mormon aristocracy. She wrote a nonidealizing biography of Joseph Smith, for which she suffered painful excommunication from the church and her family. Her works demonstrated how psychodynamic insight could inform and enrich biography.[13] Fawn was particularly kind to me during my marital breakup, inviting me to lunch in her and her husband's beautiful Pacific Palisades home and sharing her own story with me.

Two persons who profoundly influenced my career in history were Robert K. Webb, the editor of the *American Historical Review* (AHR), and Nancy Lane, the AHR's managing editor. Bob had a broad and tolerant view of what the premier journal of the profession should publish. He was willing to take the interdisciplinary manuscripts of an unknown young historian, send them out to historians as well as psychoanalytic professionals for evaluation, and publish two essays of this methodological maverick in the year 1971.[14] Nancy was a generous and tireless editor who devoted meticulous attention to detail and introduced photographs and illustrations with the texts in the AHR.

Psychoanalytic Training

When I applied for institute training, the incoming dean of the Southern California Psychoanalytic Institute was Samuel Eisenstein (1913–1996). He asked me to his office on a Saturday morning. We talked and went to lunch, hitting it off as though we were old friends. We became close friends. We named our first son "Samuel", and Eisenstein gave Josefine away as a bride at our wedding in 1985.

Sam Eisenstein had the idea, unprecedented in American psychoanalysis, of a research training fellowship to help young academics pay for their training in analysis. I remember the day in late 1969 when he said to me, "Peter, we should have a training fellowship for researchers." He followed through vigorously, year after year pushing the often-ambivalent membership to vote to renew the $10,000 three-year stipend so another university-based researcher could be trained in psychoanalysis. Now the New Center for Psychoanalysis is among the most successful psychoanalytic academic research training programs. Over the past forty-five years, forty-six academic researchers from UCLA, USC, Caltech, and the CSUs have completed or are currently in psychoanalytic training. When I became dean in 2001, I persuaded the board to double the stipend to $20,000, paid out over four years of training.

The birth of my first child, Samuel, in 1971 was one of the most profound experiences in my life. I felt in touch with eternity and the primordial cycle of life. Sam was born in the early hours of the morning, as so many children are. I experienced the birthing process as elemental and ineffable—we were in touch with every woman who has delivered, from the prehistoric past to our hygienic hospital present.[15] As I drove home in the gray dawn, the world seemed changed—there was a new tiny creature here whom I loved and was responsible for.

Regardless of psychoanalytical school or orientation, I believe the curative factor is the quality of the interpersonal relationship between analyst and analysand. For anyone doing analytic work, it is necessary to have a professional confidant to regularly discuss cases and consult regarding life problems and clinical countertransferences. In Joshua Hoffs I have such a trusted colleague and friend, whom I have met weekly for two-hour personal lunches for over thirty years.

Civil Rights in Mississippi: Bruin Grenada Project

In the fall of 1966, I was a new assistant professor of history at UCLA. A call came to the history department from the Reverend Martin Luther King Jr.'s Southern Christian Leadership Conference (SCLC), requesting tutors to prepare the African American children of Grenada, a city in north-central Mississippi, for school integration.[16] We put together an interracial team of ten tutors who could teach English, math, science, history, government, dance, and art. I stayed with the Allens; Willie was the principal of the segregated black elementary school.

The educational situation was worse than I anticipated. The black kids who had already been integrated were harassed so much that they often wanted to quit. They did so by failing at school or by getting into fights so they would be expelled. One boy, James Hudson, had his skull cracked. We visited him at the University of Mississippi Medical Center in Jackson. Grenada was segregated, with the center white and the periphery black. We were given young guides and cautioned on the safe ways to move around town. White locales were dangerous—not to be entered.

We taught our classes at the Holiness Baptist Church. Some of the mothers asked to join us. I taught history from a simple third-grade-level text donated by my UCLA colleague John Caughey. When I realized some of the mothers could not read, I was moved and felt these people needed to be cherished. We ate meals at the church. I noticed excitement as the folks said "chitterlings today!" It turned out these are hog intestines. They are slimy and smell strongly. I could not get them down. Mrs. Springfield took pity on me and made me fried chicken. What kept me alive was sweet potato pie, which I could get at the one black diner in town. I was called on to preach, which was accompanied by an active audience response: "That's right, Pete!" "You tell 'em!" I found that this is encouraging and becomes part of the performance.

Academic Psychoanalytic Research Training

One day I received a call from a friend on the California Psychology Licensing Board, who told me there had been a complaint filed against me for "practicing psychology without a license." Bill Winslade, who is a lawyer, an ethicist, and an analyst, went with me to visit the California Attorney General's Office. They threatened: "We will prosecute you!" So, we moved to secure a Research Psychoanalyst Law. Our legislation was sponsored by Howard Berman, the Assembly majority leader, (thereafter a congressman), who represented the district of UCLA. The most important lobby we had on our side was the University of California Student Lobby, representing the one hundred thirty thousand students of the UC system and their extended families. They argued with great understanding of the nature of academic psychoanalytic training and practice and of what was at stake for students of the university.[17]

When it came to getting our bill through the Senate and the governor's office, the adage of Tip O'Neill that "all politics is local politics" was abundantly demonstrated. Our legislation was carried in the Senate by its doyen, Senator Walter Stiern, whom I had known as my veterinarian in Bakersfield. Dr. Stiern said to me, "Write me a letter explaining what psychoanalysis is and why this is a good bill." He secured unanimous passage. After the bill's passage in the Assembly and Senate, we needed a contact who had the ear of Governor Jerry Brown. That man was Leroy Chatfield, whom I knew in Bakersfield as Brother Gilbert, the vice principal of the Roman Catholic high school, when we worked together for Cesar Chavez on the United Farm Worker's strike and grape boycott. Now, having been freed by the Vatican of his vows, he was in the governor's office as an advisor on farm labor. When I called Leroy, explained the bill, asking him for help, he said, "Peter, this sounds like a wonderful idea! I'll talk to Jerry."

On 30 September 1977, Governor Edmund G. (Jerry) Brown, Jr. (who is now again governor of America's largest state, with a population of over thirty-eight million), signed the first Research Psychoanalyst Law, which is also the first time in the history of any jurisdiction that psychoanalysis was legitimated by a state.[18] Upon the passage of the law, Anna Freud wrote, "I think this legal decision is a wonderful thing and will mark an important development in the history of psychoanalysis in America."[19] I am impressed by how, in our political system, a small group of neither rich nor influential citizens could seek and successfully obtain hearing and redress on a complex legal issue. A further historical irony is that the psychology institutes who fought us so hard are now part of the International Psychoanalytic Association and enthusiastically take advantage of the California Research Psychoanalyst Law.

I first met my current wife, Josefine, in 1979 on the telephone as the cultural secretary of the Austrian Consulate General in Los Angeles. She was arranging a luncheon date for the consul. Her voice was friendly and struck a resonance in me.

I think analytically of the significance of the mother's voice, the earliest imprint of love and tenderness. I said I would be sure to look for her at the next reception. Josefine was as good as her voice. We have been together thirty-five years, have a son, Jonathan, who studies at John Hopkins where he edits the college Literary journal *Zeitgeist*. We frequently travel, for she is now a travel agent. I like to think that I have learned from my two previous marriages and am a better partner for the experiences.

University of California Interdisciplinary Psychoanalytic Consortium

In 1991, a group of research psychoanalysts on the University of California faculty—led by Nancy Chodorow from Berkeley, Robert Nemiroff, a psychiatrist from San Diego, and myself—approached the UC statewide administration and their respective campus deans and provosts, proposing the creation of a UC Interdisciplinary Psychoanalytic Consortium (UCIPC) so we could discuss both our work as university teachers and researchers and our problems interfacing as psychoanalysts in medicine, the liberal arts, humanities, and social sciences. We gained university financial support and, for the first time, formal recognition of the role of psychoanalysis in the curriculum and research agenda of the university. Getting the first meeting off the ground would not have been possible without the competent efforts of my research assistant David Lee. The first UCIPC met at UCLA's Lake Arrowhead Conference Center in May 1993 and has convened annually since; we celebrated our twentieth anniversary in 2013. Rather than formal presentations and prepared discussions, which we know so well from our academic disciplines and guilds, the UCIPC has informal workshops focused on the various interests of the group. Today, fifty faculty and graduate students from the ten UC campuses, academics from several other schools, and interested clinicians—encompassing sixteen fields in the humanities, social, and biobehavioral sciences—participate. In thirty-one years I missed only one conference, and that was due to teaching in China.

Chair of CORST and Institute Dean

I was chair of the Committee on Research and Special Training (CORST), the gatekeeper to psychoanalytic training for academics who wish to learn analysis in institutes of the American Psychoanalytic Association (APsaA) , from 1997 to 2001. I was dean and director of education of the Southern California Psychoanalytic Institute (SCPI) and of the New Center for Psychoanalysis (NCP) from 2001 to 2006. These years accomplished the reunification and merger of a split in institutional psychoanalysis in Southern California. Sixty-four years ago, in 1950, one nascent four-year-old institute in Los Angeles split into two. Dean Mark Thompson of the Los Angeles Psychoanalytic Society and Institute and I collaborated as co-deans in the early days of the merger, convening summit meetings with committee co-chairs and one or two leaders of the still-separate groups in my study to resolve issues and iron out impasses and stalemates. We initiated the reunion by combining the two first-year classes. All officers and committee chairs were paired, being made up of one from each institute.

Today the split of 1950 has been undone, if not fully healed. The new institute lost some valuable members of the old SCPI group, but many have now rejoined the NCP, the new unified institute. We now have one president, one dean, and a single chair of each committee. We have assets of over eighteen million dollars, a state approved Ph.D., a thriving psychoanalytic psychotherapy program, and the most successful psychoanalytic research training program in the world.

My emotional/historical models of the successful functioning of creative groups are from Freud's period in the beginning of the last century, such as the early analysts around Eugen Bleuler, C. G. Jung, and Karl Abraham at the Burghölzli Hospital, Zürich.[20] The Bauhaus in Weimar and Dessau, 1919–1933, was a phenomenally creative institution in design, arts, and architecture.[21] As a personal model of conduct, I take the relationship of deep personal friendship, accompanied by fundamental theoretical disagreement, between Freud and Ludwig Binswanger (1881–1966), the founder of existential psychoanalysis (*Daseinsanalyse*). The two men met and talked often, comforted each other when Freud's son was a wounded prisoner of war and after tragic losses, such as the death of Freud's daughter and grandson and Binswanger's son in the 1920s.[22] When a leading clinician was brought to Vienna to address Freud on his eightieth birthday in 1936, it was Binswanger. His lecture was dissenting and respectful,[23] as was Freud's appreciative response.[24]

The Austromarxists Karl Renner (1870–1950) and Otto Bauer (1881–1938) offer lessons in creative adaptation.[25] They struggled with the most inflammatory issue in our world today: how may different peoples with varied cultures, languages, religions, ethnicities, live together in a polity? Their conceptual approach to a peaceful solution, which today governs the South Tyrol, was to replace the territorial primacy with a principle of personal cultural identity *Personalprinzip*, which is an internalized identity, congruent with psychoanalytic understandings of identity and self, that overlaps with others on the same territory.[26]

Psychoanalysis in China

We in the West have much to learn from China in the important realms of interpersonal relations and public tact and sensibility. The concept of *face*, wrote Lin Yutang, "abstract and intangible, it is yet the most delicate standard by which Chinese social intercourse is regulated.... it is prized above all earthly possessions."²⁷ Chinese culture has a highly developed sensibility to preserving, not humiliating, the face of others. Face may be conferred, saved, or lost. A person or group may "save" or "leave" face to another by not exposing a lapse, slip, or *faux pas*. Face may be presented as a gift.

Luo Fengli, a scholar of the methodology section of the Chinese Academy of Social Sciences, Beijing, came to study psychoanalysis and history with me in 1992–93 as a Ford Fellow.²⁸ I taught with the German psychotherapy group led by Alf Gerlach at the Shanghai Mental Health Center, with open lectures to the mental health community in Shanghai, and at the Anding Hospital in Beijing. I also taught psychoanalytic therapy for the Hospital Authority of Hong Kong in 2003, 2004, and 2005, and in major cities such as Wuhan, Kunming, and Chengdu. Chinese mental health professionals are eager to acquire the best Western talk therapies. The International Psychoanalytic Association (IPA) China Committee commenced a full curriculum of psychoanalytic training in Beijing in 2007 and in Shanghai in 2011. As part of the IPA's China program, which I chaired from 2007 to 2013, German, Norwegian, Argentine, and American analysts have taught and supervised in China since 2007. In October 2015 the Fourth Chinese Psychoanalytic Congress was held in Hefei. This is a tremendous accomplishment for an educational effort that was initiated a mere eight years ago. Carl Schorske's analogy to Matteo Ricci (1552-1610) and the Jesuits bringing to China a Western system of thought is appropriately stimulating of irony and self-reflection.²⁹

Peter Loewenberg is professor of history, emeritus, at UCLA and a former dean of the New Center for Psychoanalysis. He is the author of books (documented in chapter 23) and papers on history, psychoanalysis, and their integration, including *Decoding the Past: The Psychohistorical Approach* (1996) and *Fantasy and Reality in History* (1995). He is editor (with Nellie Thompson) of *100 Years of the IPA: The Centenary History of the International Psychoanalytical Association (1910–2010)* (2011). In 2010, he received the Nevitt Sanford Award for Professional Contributions to Political Psychology. In November 2013, he was elected an honorary member of the German Psychoanalytic Association (DPV). In 2015 he was elected an IPA Board Representative for North America.

Notes

1. Milli Wachedorf, *Mädchen, was soll aus Dir noch mal werden! Ein biographischer Versuch nach Briefen, Tagebüchern und anderen Aufzeichnungen*, ed. Helmut Wachendorf (Hamburg, 1971), 230–31.
2. Judicial and press accounts in Richard Loewenberg, "Rumors of Mass Poisoning in Times of Crisis," *Journal of Criminal Psychopathology* 1 (July 1943): 131–42.

3. Hampstead Nursery, Foster Parents Report, 1942, 1943, 1944, 1945 (4 vols.) in Anna Freud and Dorothy Burlingham, *War and Children* (1943; Westport, CT, 1973); *Infants Without Families: The Case for and Against Residential Nurseries* (New York, 1944); Margaret S. Mahler, Fred Pine, and Anni Bergman, *The Psychological Birth of the Human Infant: Symbiosis and Individuation* (New York, 1975); James Robertson and Joyce Robertson, *Separation and the Very Young* (London, 1989).
4. D. W. Winnicott, *The Child and the Outside World* (New York, 1957), 84.
5. Peter Loewenberg, "John Muir and the Erotization of Nature," *Journal of Applied Psychoanalytic Studies* 2, no. 4 (2000): 365–81.
6. Peter Loewenberg. "Emotional Problems of Graduate Education," *Journal of Higher Education* 40, no. 8 (November 1969): 610–23.
7. Hans-Georg Gadamer, *Truth and Method*, 2nd ed. (New York, 1997), 302–6.
8. David Horowitz, *Radical Son: A Journey through Our Times* (New York, 1997).
9. Peter Loewenberg, *Walter Rathenau and Henry Kissinger: The Jew as a Modern Statesman in Two Political Cultures* (New York, 1980).
10. Peter Loewenberg, "Psychohistorical Perspectives on Modern German History," *Journal of Modern History* 47, no. 2 (June 1975): 229–79.
11. Peter Loewenberg, "Theodor Herzl: Nationalism and Politics," in *Decoding the Past: The Psychohostorical Approach* (New York, 1983), 101–35.
12. Peter Loewenberg, "Love and Hate in the Academy," *The Center Magazine* V, no. 5 (September/October 1972): 4–11.
13. Fawn M. Brodie, *No Man Knows My History: The Life of the Mormon Prophet* (New York, 1945); *Thaddeus Stevens: Scourge of the South* (New York, 1959); *The Devil Drives: A Life of Sir Richard Burton* (New York, 1967); *Thomas Jefferson: An Intimate History* (New York, 1974); *Richard Nixon: The Shaping of His Character* (New York, 1981).
14. Peter Loewenberg, "The Unsuccessful Adolescence of Heinrich Himmler," *American Historical Review* 76, no. 3 (June 1971): 612–41; "The Psychohistorical Origins of the Nazi Youth Cohort," *American Historical Review* 76, no. 5 (December 1971): 1457–1502.
15. For a prehistoric birthing process alone in the present, see Marjorie Shostak, *Nisa: The Life and Words of a !Kung Woman* (New York, 1983), 209.
16. For this account I am relying on my contemporary journal notes.
17. "Students attending the University of California will benefit in the following ways: Allow these . . . professors to maintain a working knowledge of the actual practice of psychoanalysis by authorizing them to engage in psychoanalysis. (Most of these professors teach the application of psychoanalysis in the study of such academic disciplines as history, law, medicine, political science, and humanities. In the course of their teachings they also provide some instruction in the practice of psychoanalysis as it relates to the class's subject matter.) If these professors are not allowed to actually engage in the practice of psychoanalysis on a routine basis, their instruction will consist entirely of theoretical knowledge with no solid foundation in practice. If AB 246 is not enacted some 1300 students at UCLA will be deprived of a score of courses in which the application of psychoanalysis to certain academic disciplines is now taught. Similar adverse impacts will be seen at UC Berkeley and UC San Diego." Bret Hewitt, Codirector, Associated Students of the University of California Student Lobby, to Hon. Jerry Brown, Governor, 9 September 1977 (in the possession of the author).
18. Research Psychoanalysts, *California Business and Professions Code*, Division 2, Chapter 5.1, sections 2529–30.
19. Anna Freud to Peter Loewenberg, 12 October 1977 (in the possession of the author).
20. Peter Loewenberg, "The Creation of a Scientific Community: The Burghölzli, 1902–1914," in *Fantasy and Reality in History* (Oxford, 1995), 46–89.

21. Peter Loewenberg, "The Bauhaus as a Creative Play Space, Weimar, Dessau, and Berlin, 1919–1933," *Annual of Psychoanalysis* XXXIII (2005): 209–26.
22. Loewenberg, "Aggression in World War I: The Deepest Part of Sigmund Freud's Self-Analysis," in Günther Baechler and Andreas Wenger, eds., *Conflict and Cooperation: The Individual between Ideal and Reality* (Zurich, 2002), 81–92.
23. Ludwig Binswanger, "Freud's Conception of Man in the Light of Anthropology," in *Being in the World: Selected Papers*, trans. Jacob Needleman (New York, 1963), 49–181.
24. Freud to Binswanger, 8 October 1936, in Ernst Freud , ed., *Letters of Sigmund Freud* (New York, 1960), 286, 431.
25. Peter Loewenberg, "Austro-Marxism and Revolution: Otto Bauer, Freud's Dora Case, and the Crises of the First Austrian Republic," in *Decoding the Past*, 161-204.
26. Peter Loewenberg, "Karl Renner and the Politics of Accommodation: Moderation versus Revenge," in *Fantasy and Reality in History*, 119–141.
27. Lin Yutang, *My Country and My People* (New York, 1939), 200.
28. Luo Fengli, *History and Heart: Theories and Practice of Psychohistory in the West* [in Chinese] (Beijing, 1998).
29. Peter Loewenberg, "Matteo Ricci, Psychoanalysis, and *Face* in Chinese Culture and Diplomacy," *American Imago* 68, no. 4 (2012): 689–706.

Chapter 9

OUT OF GERMANY

Renate Bridenthal

A double agent, a young Czech woman, spirited me, a three-year-old, out of Leipzig and into Czechoslovakia in September 1938. When my mother put me on the train, she told me it was important not to cry, and I obeyed. My mother, father, and fourteen-year-old half-brother fled in more devious ways and sometimes over difficult terrain by foot. They picked me up again two weeks later.

My family got out of Czechoslovakia just ahead of the Nazi invasion, flying from there to France. In Paris, thousands of refugees were crowding consulates for visas to anywhere. We got them for Panama and crossed the Atlantic on the *Reina del Pacifico*, a ship filled with returning International Brigade veterans of the Spanish Civil War, with whom my brother chatted. I only remember losing my hat and the smell of oil from the engines, nothing else.

We spent nearly two years in Panama, first in Colón on the Caribbean coast, where my parents operated a *Pension* (guesthouse) for other newly arrived refugees whom my father met at the dock. They subdivided rooms into compartments, with sheets as dividers. My mother remembered cooking for as many as thirty-five people. Later, in Panama City, the capital on the Pacific coast, my father and brother, then seventeen, made a living for us by peddling cosmetics, toiletries, and perfumes door to door. At the end of his first day getting doors slammed in his face, my brother announced that "a whole world died for me today." My father slipped into depression. I turned five years old, speaking Spanish. And then the U.S. government took us so-called enemy aliens away from the militarily sensitive Canal Zone and allowed us entry to New York City in September 1940.

Soon after our arrival here, my father ended his deepening depression by committing suicide, that last adjustment he was expected to make being too much

---

Notes from this chapter begin on page 139.

for him. My brother, already a young adult, began a life of his own apart from ours, working and attending school at night, first high school and then college. My mother found work as a skilled fur finisher, the way she had made a living in Leipzig before her marriage, and I attended public elementary and high schools. From 1940 to 1951, I grew into becoming part of the "two-and-a-half generation," born Jewish in Germany with no memory of that origin, but with a historical consciousness nurtured by my mother with stories of the past.

What were the stories? Some reached back into Germany's Imperial period, when my mother remembered political arguments between her mother, a seamstress, and her stepfather, a brushmaker. Her mother supported the Kaiser; her stepfather was a Social Democrat. My mother remembered the revolution of 1918, when as a seventeen-year-old working girl in Leipzig she brought water to revolutionary students at barricades. The experience radicalized her as did the following hunger years of inflation and depression when she raised her young son alone after the end of her youthful first marriage. I first learned to see communism as an ideal for social justice and egalitarianism at her knee in later years when she was again a working woman in New York, once more raising a child alone.

The thirties, by contrast, were described to me as years of hope with my mother's second marriage to my father, whose young fur business began to thrive with the military Keynesianism of the early Nazi years. Despite increasing antisemitism, which forced my brother into a Jewish school, the family prospered and their social lives were not much narrowed by the new restrictive laws. But, of course, this couldn't last. The principal of my mother's old school, who had become a trusted friend and who recognized the looming danger for Jews, strongly advised her to get herself and her family out. My father, whose business accounts had twice been scrutinized by the Gestapo, was now also ready. Not so my Polish-born grandfather, who said, "You're all crazy. Germany is the most civilized country in the world. I'll hold the apartment for you." Still, we fled; he was deported first to Theresienstadt and later to Auschwitz, where he was murdered.

But, as for so many refugees, you could get us out of Germany, but you couldn't get Germany out of us. There it sat: the language, the culture, the memories, the homesickness. And for me who could not remember any direct experience, the history. It was why I became a German historian.

However, while I was raised speaking German at home with the prospect of eventually returning to a socialist Germany, I was growing up in America, or more specifically in a tenement in what was then a poor neighborhood on the Upper West Side of New York. The superintendents were Hungarian refugees; other tenants, some in single-room occupancies, were a diverse bunch from Puerto Rico, China, and other parts of the United States. My first preschool playmates on the street were Irish; my first close friend was a half-Philippine half-Yankee little girl. My first schoolmates at P.S. 9 in the 1940s were largely also Jewish refugees, but better off, better dressed, better housed. I felt the class difference more sharply than the ethnic one. This held true later at all-girls Julia Richman High School, where my "gang" consisted of one other Jewish girl, two Catholics, a half-Italian half-Yankee girl, a half-Jewish half-German girl, and an African-American girl. These actual relationships complemented the universalist humanism that my mother taught me. There was little religious ritual at home, mainly observance of the high holy days, although not always in synagogue, and half-guilty half-gleeful violations of Yom Kippur, when in midday we could no longer resist sausage sandwiches.

It was also America of the Cold War, of the House Un-American Activities Committee and of McCarthyism. Not a great time to be growing up socialist despite not belonging to any political party. Nevertheless, I spoke up in class. When my high school civics class trained us to read newspapers by reporting from them, I regularly brought in *The Daily Compass*, a left-leaning paper (not to be confused with the Communist Party's *Daily Worker*) that questioned official explanations about American involvement in the Korean War. So in 1951, on the eve of my graduation, a history teacher called me in to her office to show me that she had stapled shut part of my permanent record in which she had recorded my political views, lest I become "another Judith Coplon," recently tried for espionage on behalf of the Soviet Union.

It seemed the right time to leave the country. My mother, overworked and alienated here, had always planned to go "home," meaning Leipzig, which had become part of the German Democratic Republic, and I was willing too. I had shown some promise as a pianist and, encouraged by a half-hour performance on a radio youth talent show, expected to attend music school. We set sail in the summer of 1951 on the Queen Elizabeth I, where even third class was a very different experience from the *Reina del Pacifico*. My brother, whose politics were quite different and who had married and started a family, stayed here.

It was a naïve venture. It was not so easy to enter the German Democratic Republic during the Cold War. Instead, we found ourselves diverted to Frankfurt am Main, where we sublet a single room from a family. In that confined space, my mother labored at sewing linings into fur coats for many more hours than she had in unionized shops in New York, while I studied music for many more hours than I had ever done. And I met "real" Germans—other young people who had had very different childhoods from mine and a different experience of the war and who came from quite a different culture. It dawned on me that I was neither German nor American nor intensely Jewish. It didn't feel like a crisis. Rather, at seventeen, it was an awakening. But as I realized that music was not going to be my vocation, my mother finally lost her precarious mental balance and made a suicide attempt. The American consulate lent us the money for tickets "home," which was now New York.

We arrived back in Manhattan in 1953, still in a Cold War atmosphere with the executions of Ethel and Julius Rosenberg and, soon after, Senator McCarthy's Army-McCarthy hearings. I immediately found a job, established my own separate residence, and registered for the evening session at the City College of New York (CCNY). And so it remained for the next seven years while I slowly earned a B.A., majoring in European history.

At CCNY, I met my first husband, Kenneth Bridenthal, a veteran of the Abraham Lincoln Battalion of the International Brigades, which had volunteered to fight for the Spanish Republic during its civil war. Although twenty years older than I and twice divorced, he seemed the most likely intellectual and political companion available during that difficult time. He was a home-grown radical from St. Joseph, Missouri, the son of working-class parents of Welsh and German immigrant origins, and an aspiring historian. In 1959, he graduated and began to attend Columbia University. In 1960, I followed him there, the beneficiary of a Woodrow Wilson scholarship. Those were the years of post-Sputnik showers of gold on academe, the brain race with the Soviet Union that saw me through three more years of subsidized scholarship up to and including dissertation support.

My education at Columbia proceeded smoothly at first, with a focus on German intellectual history. An M.A. with Professor Rudolph Binion was followed by a Ph.D. seminar with Professor Peter Gay. But suddenly and unfortunately, life intervened into what should have been an expediently completed dissertation. In 1962, my mother was mugged in a subway station and left in a coma that took her life a month later. I fell into a depression that deepened over the next three years before being diagnosed. My dissertation stalled, my marriage dissolved, everything was put on hold. I entered psychoanalysis. My *Doktorvater* Peter Gay, himself a second-generation German Jewish historian familiar with the value of psychoanalysis, underwrote a medical leave from Columbia, which suspended the "eight years or out" rule for a Ph.D. By 1966, the clouds had lifted enough for me to find a job teaching at the Borough of Manhattan Community College and, a year later, at Brooklyn College. My professional career had begun.

It was a rousing beginning. Greeted at the campus gate by a faculty member handing out leaflets to an antiwar rally, I knew I had found my political compatriots and was soon distributing leaflets too. In the history department, by contrast, I met with a cautious, somewhat mistrustful welcome, which only deepened as time wore on. The marriage to my second husband, the department's Latin Americanist Hobart Ames Spalding, Jr., a Marxist like me and an antiwar and anti-imperialist activist despite (perhaps because of) being a scion of an old American family, intensified that mistrust in what became an ever more severely divided history department. Nevertheless, I pursued a typical professional trajectory by finishing my Ph.D. in 1970 and by starting to publish.

My first article was drawn from my master's thesis on a footnote in *The Communist Manifesto*, a reference to a little-known follower of the so-called Utopian Socialists excoriated by Karl Marx. Finding some parallels to the New Left of the 1970s, I sent "The 'Greening of Germany,' 1848: Karl Grün's 'True' Socialism" to *Science & Society*, even now the oldest Marxist journal in the world.[1] My article was not only accepted and published in 1971, but to my surprise I was invited to visit with the editorial board and, after a year's attendance and participation at biweekly meetings, the board added my name to its masthead. At a fundraising meeting of subscribers, chief editor David Goldway introduced me as a new editor especially interested in "the woman question." I responded, "We're calling it 'the man question' now. It depends on who's asking the question." Soon the journal was publishing many more articles on women than before, while I, for my part, acquired what I still consider my second graduate education there at the feet of brilliant older Marxist editors, such as John Cammett, Annette Rubinstein, and David Goldway, and my cohort of younger scholars: the economist David Laibman, now chief editor of *S&S*, and historians Gerald Markowitz and Marvin Gettleman.

Encouraged by this first success, I plumbed my dissertation on Barthold Georg Niebuhr (1776–1831), historian of ancient Rome, for another article on his theory of an oral tradition underlying Livy's histories. "Was there a Roman Homer? Niebuhr's Thesis and its Critics" was published by *History and Theory* in 1972.[2] But the dissertation had not taken me down the historiographical path I had intended, and so I abandoned it.

Meanwhile, a life-changing event was taking place: the women's movement. Enlivened by the civil rights movement, it hit society like a firestorm, academe not excepted. The Chinese Revolution's "speak bitterness" campaign for peasants to discuss their conditions inspired the consciousness-raising sessions of women, who by sharing their experiences in past and present, came to realize the limitations to which we had been held and the sexist attitudes that still prevailed. We were furious. We swung into action.

At Brooklyn College, I founded an organization of energized women who fought and won important changes on campus. We established a Women's Studies Program, a Women's Center, and a daycare center, all of which still exist. And one of us, Professor Lilia Melani, initiated the CUNY Women's Coalition, which sued the City University of New York for sex discrimination and, after a ten-year battle, won. In the history profession, I joined the Coordinating Committee of Women in the Historical Profession (CCWHP), led by Gerda Lerner, Joan Kelly, Sandi Cooper, Berenice Carroll, and other prominent women historians, fighting for stronger female representation in conferences and committees of the American Historical Association. These efforts led to the establishment of a formal Committee of Women Historians in the AHA, and lasting reforms.

A new question inspired many academic women: where were the women in their disciplines? In history, we avidly pursued new research. As a German historian, I too asked that question and, skeptical about the widely accepted "new woman" of the nineteen twenties, explored the less glamorous work world of the time, my mother's world. "Beyond Kinder, Küche, Kirche: Weimar Women at Work" was a paper I gave at the first women's history panel at the AHA, which also included Claudia Koonz and Sheila Tobias. My research revealed that in the Weimar Republic, the modern division of labor had actually caused many working women to lose ground relative to the previous paradigm. But when I sent the article to the *Journal of Social History*, it was rejected by a reader who clearly did not accept women's history as a subject (years later, he recanted). However, *Central European History* did accept it in 1973, and after that it was widely cited and reprinted.[3] The field had gained traction.

There was action on the streets, too. One day, sitting in protest on the sidewalk in front of Honeywell offices, the arms manufacturer that made cluster bombs for the Vietnam War—a particularly horrible weapon designed to maim rather than kill so that the enemy would be tied up with caretaking—I found myself next to Ruth Graham, professor of history at Queens College, who like myself was teaching women's history from the very scarce resources we had at the time. Since we weren't being arrested, we had a long time to talk, including about our new teaching focus. We agreed that we needed a textbook; spontaneously and impulsively I blurted out that I might create one. And then forgot about it. Less than a week later, she called to say she had an interested publisher: Houghton Mifflin. Alarmed by my audacity, I called Claudia Koonz to ask if she would work with me. She accepted. *Becoming Visible: Women in European History* was born in 1977. A volume of twenty articles by scholars including myself and Claudia Koonz, it was the first textbook to present women's past in Europe from antiquity to the present. Second and third revised editions appeared in 1987 and 1998.[4]

In those days, there were not many of us on the frontier. Some of us ventured onto interdisciplinary ground, and I approached family history with several articles. In "The Dialectics of Production and Reproduction in History," I applied Marxist analysis to family relationships as they changed over time, along with the ways that families made a living depending on the prevailing mode of production.[5] This took a historiographical form in "Examining Family History" and in "The Family: The View From a Room of Her Own," where I reviewed some traditional family history, summarized new feminist approaches, and noted the horizon that opened when one asked not only what do women do for family, but what does family do for women. What happens when women are no longer seen as the core of a household but as just another individual member of it?[6] These efforts culminated in my coauthoring *Household and Kin*, later republished as *Families in Flux*, in which I reviewed studies of current American family patterns.[7] I discovered that working-class families, unable to prevent intrusive investigators, were much studied and often diagnosed as pathological. Furthermore, studies faulted African-American families for being matriarchies and Hispanic families for being patriarchies, two kinds of so-called failures that supposedly explained their persistently low class ranking. Upper-class families could shield themselves from studies; information came mainly from discontented scions. Not surprisingly, middle-class families, the origin of most of the investigators, were designated the ideal model against which to measure others. Unfortunately, my own second marriage could not meet this ideal and dissolved with the pressure of two professional lives under the emotional searchlight of feminism. However, the research gave me an enlightening side visit to American culture, a small step out of Germany, to be followed later with larger ones.

Meanwhile, German women historians began to make their appearance on both sides of the Atlantic. Around 1980, Marion Kaplan, Atina Grossmann, and I formed a German Women's History Group for critical support of our own forthcoming scholarship outside of a formal academic setting. Early members included Bonnie Anderson, Jane Caplan, Amy Hackett, Deborah Hertz, Claudia Koonz, Molly Nolan, and Joan Reutershan. Over time, this group expanded with new members and has produced many well-received books.[8] Since many of us had contacts with feminist scholars in Germany, a lively interaction ensued. One early result of these communications became *When Biology Became Destiny: Women in Weimar and Nazi Germany*, edited by Marion Kaplan, Atina Grossmann, and myself, a collection of articles by American and German researchers.[9] The contributors found disturbing intimations of and precursors to fascism regarding women's issues in the democratic Weimar Republic, and we saw in these a warning against the backlash to feminism we ourselves had begun to witness in the United States in the eighties. My own contribution again questioned the novelty of the Weimar period, this time by looking at the organization of urban housewives who used feminist rhetoric when aspiring to be seen as professionals who train apprentices (actually used as servants) in what they called the craft of traditional housewifery. In an earlier article, I had published my findings about the housewives' fight against the attempts at unionization of their domestic servants.[10] A related article on the organized rural housewives appeared in another collection.[11]

But I was already beginning to move out of familiar fields into the wider world. I had begun to distance myself from my country of birth in the 1950s on my first return with my mother. In the early 1960s, research on Barthold Niebuhr took me to East Berlin, where the *Staatsbibliothek* held his papers. While the capital of the German Democratic Republic seemed culturally more like what I had envisioned an earlier Germany to be and had expected to enter when I returned in the 1950s, it remained alien to me. People resented the wall that had just gone up to divide the city, even though they valued the stability and entitlements that the socialist government offered. The West was dismissive of its Eastern sibling while itself culturally mutating in part by acquiring some American characteristics. What did being German mean? And what was still German about me? By the early 1980s, when I returned to both East and West Germany to research the urban and rural housewives' organizations, I felt even further removed. The countries kept moving on; I kept moving on.

The historical profession also moved on. The strenuous efforts of the CCWHP, which I cochaired for a year, and the official Committee on Women Historians had succeeded in not only bringing more women to panels at the annual meetings, but also into governance of the AHA. Only one woman had been president, Nellie Neilson in 1943, when nearly half a century later Natalie Davis became the second in 1987. She was followed in 1993 by Louise Tilly, in 1996 by Carolyn Walker Bynum, in 1997 by Joyce Appleby, in 2002 by Lynn Hunt, and then by five women in a row: in 2006 Linda Kerber, in 2007 Barbara Weinstein, in 2008 Gabrielle Spiegel, in 2009 Laurel Thatcher Ulrich, in 2010 Barbara Metcalf. Executive director Sandria Freitag was followed by Arnita Jones, and many of the AHA committees now included women members.

In this exciting new atmosphere, I was invited to participate in planning the program for the 1995 annual meeting. This led to my chairing the program committee for the 1996 annual meeting, which gave me the opportunity to further widen the AHA perspective beyond Europe and the United States by assembling for my committee a group of historians researching countries around the globe. The resulting conference was hailed for its many novel panels. This, in turn, led to my being appointed the official American representative to the nineteenth meeting of the International Congress of Historical Sciences in Oslo in 2000, which brought together historians from all over the world, itself a heady learning experience for me. At its business meeting there, Natalie Davis and I contributed to the pressure that ensured a woman be elected to its executive council and that panels in women's history be included in future meetings.

By now, I had become completely taken by world history—the questions it opened up and the methodological problems it presented. And so the following year, with renowned world historian Jerry Bentley, I cochaired an AHA Ford-funded group on interarea studies, which created two conferences at the Library of Congress on historical cultural contacts between different regions of the globe, both now published.[12] They fertilized my mind with two new ideas for research: one was about the place of Germans (as distinct from Germany) in world history, and the other was a hunch about the political power of crime.

One of the ways that West Germany had changed was that, since the 1960s, it had become a country of new immigrants, mostly so-called guest workers of Turkish origin who in the 1970s had brought their families. They remain the largest ethnic subgroup in united Germany. But after the fall of the Soviet Union, another set of newcomers arrived from the east, historical reminders of a much earlier emigration: the Germans from Russia. These were the descendants of farmers lured from impoverished Southwest Germany in the eighteenth century by Catherine the Great of Russia and later Tsar Alexander I to cultivate lands along the Volga River and Black Sea. They did so successfully, having been given special privileges of tax and military exemptions, self-governance, and cultural autonomy. However, they lost these when the government equalized their status to those of newly emancipated serfs and when rising nationalism in the late nineteenth century made Russo-German relations precarious. These events, soon followed by the Russian Revolutions, led a large number (one hundred twenty thousand from 1870 to 1920) to emigrate yet again, most of them this time to the United States, following the lure of public land on offer. They were a double diaspora: from Germany to Russia and from Russia to America. Those who remained in Russia suffered both the Nazi invasion and discrimination as potential traitors as well. Never fully trusted, when the Soviet Union fell they came in droves into newly united Germany. But my interest was piqued by the Russian Germans who had settled earlier in North Dakota and Nebraska, so I went there to study their archives in search of their remaining contacts with Germany. The research yielded a strong diasporic connection with political overtones through transatlantic pulpit, press, and research institutes but with a rather weaker echo among the main Americanized group. Intrigued by the diaspora question, I coedited and contributed to *The* Heimat *Abroad: The Boundaries of Germanness* with Krista O'Donnell and Nancy Reagin, who wrote about German colonists in Southwest Africa and Eastern Europe respectively. We assembled ten more contributors, who discussed German institutions and politics in Latin America and Eastern Europe as well as the legal and ideological context of diasporic nationalism.[13] With that, my intellectual emigration out of Germany was complete.

My next project came out of the hunch inspired by the two world history conferences I had cochaired with Jerry Bentley. In each, there had been a paper on piracy in early modern times, one showing how Venice and Genoa, using pirates against each other, came to claim legal sovereignty over their surrounding waters, and the other showing how Japanese territorial lords coopted local pirates into their expanded governance. Intrigued by the way these indicated a role for crime in state formation, I began to research the theme and found it to be a lively matter of debate. Thus I came to edit *The Hidden History of Crime, Corruption and States*, a collection of ten original contributions about the hugely vibrant, politically powerful underbelly of capitalism that has been active on every continent from the seventeenth century to the present.[14] My introduction reviews previous conceptualizations and asserts my own Marxist analysis of the importance of capital accumulation, even when illegal, in political history.

What is still to be done? Retiring from teaching in 2001 afforded me more time for research and some vistas remain before me. Where they will lead, I cannot say, but while I treasure the German friends with whom I am still in touch and while I remain fluent in the language, I have clearly come out of Germany.

Renate Bridenthal is emerita professor of history at Brooklyn College, The City University of New York. She has published articles and coedited volumes (documented in chapter 23) and articles on women's history, notably three editions of *Becoming Visible: Women in European History* (1977, 1987, 1998) and *When Biology Became Destiny: Women in Weimar and Nazi Germany* (1984). Most recently she has edited *The Hidden History of Crime, Corruption and States* (2013).

Notes

Previous autobiographical articles, with special emphases, have appeared in Abraham J. Peck, ed., *The German-Jewish Legacy in America, 1938–1988: From* Bildung *to the Bill of Rights* (Detroit, 1989), 179–98, and in Eileen Boris and Nupur Chaudhuri, eds., *Voices of Women Historians: The Personal, the Political, the Professional* (Bloomington, 1999), 76–84.

1. "Karl Grün's 'True' Socialism," *Science and Society* XXXV, no. 4 (Winter, 1971): 439–62.
2. "Was There a Roman Homer? Niebuhr's Thesis and its Critics," *History and Theory* XI, no. 2 (1972), 193–213.
3. "Beyond *Kinder, Küche, Kirche*: Weimar Women at Work," *Central European History* 6, no. 2 (June 1973): 148–66. Anthologized with Claudia Koonz in Berenice Carroll, ed., *Liberating Women's History: Theoretical and Critical Essays* (Urbana, 1976), 301–29, and in *When Biology Became Destiny* (see above), 153–173. Translated in James S. Amelang and Mary Nash, eds., *Historia y Género: Las Mujeres en la Europa Moderna y Contemporánea* (Valencia, 1990), 345–87.
4. Renate Bridenthal, Susan Mosher Stuard, and Merry E. Wiesner, eds., *Becoming Visible: Women in European History*, 3rd rev. ed. (Boston, 1998). Second revised edition, Bridenthal, Claudia Koonz, Stuard, eds., 1987. First edition, Bridenthal and Koonz, 1977.
5. "The Dialectics of Production and Reproduction in History," *Radical America* 10, no. 1 (March–April, 1976): 3–11, and "Notes toward a Feminist Dialectic," in Amy Swerdlow and Hanna Lessinger, eds., *Class, Race, and Sex: The Dynamics of Control* (Boston, Mass., 1981), 3–9.
6. Renate Bridenthal, Rayna Rapp, and Ellen Ross, "Examining Family History," *Feminist Studies* 5, no. 1 (Spring, 1979): 174–220; Renate Bridenthal, "The Family: The View from the Room of Her Own," in Barrie Thorne, ed., *Re-Thinking the Family: Some Feminist Questions* (Boston, 1982), 225–39.
7. Amy Swerdlow, Renate Bridenthal, Joan Kelly, and Phyllis Vine, *Families in Flux*, 2nd rev. ed. (New York, 1989). First edition, *Household and Kin*, 1981.
8. For about the last ten years, this group has also been meeting annually with an equal number of scholars from the Coalition of Women in German, for interdisciplinary perspectives on a variety of topics pertaining to German literature and history.
9. Renate Bridenthal, Atina Grossmann, and Marion Kaplan, eds., *When Biology Became Destiny: Women in Weimar and Nazi Germany* (New York, 1984).
10. "Class Struggle Around the Hearth: Women and Domestic Service in the Weimar Republic," in Michael Dobkowski and Isidor Walliman, eds., *Towards the Holocaust: The Social and Economic Collapse of the Weimar Republic* (Westport, CT, 1983), 243–64.
11. "Women and the Conservative Mobilization of the Countryside in the Weimar Republic," in James Retallack and Larry Jones, eds., *Between Reform, Reaction, and Resistance: Studies in the*

History of German Conservatism from 1789 to the Present (Providence, 1993), 375–405. Trans. as "Die Rolle der organisierten Landfrauen bei der konservativen Mobilmachung in der Weimarer Republik," *Feministische Studien* 12, no. 1 (May 1994): 110–21.
12. Jerry H. Bentley, Renate Bridenthal and Anand A. Yang, eds., *Interactions: Transregional Perspectives on World History* (Honolulu, 2005); Jerry H. Bentley, Renate Bridenthal, and Karen Wigen, eds., *Seascapes, Littoral Cultures, and Transoceanic Exchanges* (Honolulu, 2007).
13. Krista O'Donnell, Renate Bridenthal, and Nancy Reagin, eds., *The* Heimat *Abroad: The Boundaries of Germanness* (Ann Arbor, 2005).
14. Renate Bridenthal, ed., *The Hidden History of Crime, Corruption and States* (New York, 2013). Four of the essays appeared previously in the *Journal of Social History* 45, no. 3 (Spring 2012).

Part II

APPROACHING THE SECOND GENERATION

Chapter 10

THE SECOND GENERATION
Émigré Historians of Modern Germany in Postwar America

Catherine Epstein

At first glance, little unites the second generation of refugee historians in the United States. Some became historians of modern Germany, some did not. Some intensely disliked Germany, some did not. Some identified as Jews, some did not. Some were on the left, some were not. Some spent the war years in the United States, some did not. Some began their careers as historians of Germany, some did not. Some wrote directly on the Holocaust, some did not. Still, while the following focuses on historians of modern Germany (broadly conceived), these émigré scholars shared a set of experiences that shaped their historical work and their careers as professional historians.

In my definition, a second-generation refugee historian was born in Germany or what became Nazi-occupied Europe; he or she left due to Nazi persecution or opposition to the Third Reich; and he or she had his or her college and graduate education in the United States. These criteria are significant: they mean that these individuals came to the United States as children, adolescents, or young adults. Emigration and subsequent Americanization occurred at a life stage in which these individuals were striving to forge their own identities.

As a rule, these historians came to think of themselves as Americans. They were also perceived as such by their refugee parents. In correspondence, for example, my grandfather (and first-generation refugee historian) Fritz Epstein wrote my father (and second-generation émigré historian), Klaus Epstein, using phrases such as "young Americans like you."[1] Unlike their parents, the second generation experienced a profound rupture in their identities. They had been Germans, but now they were Americans. Meanwhile, many of their parents remained

---

Notes from this chapter begin on page 150.

pronounced *Bei-unskis*, those who insisted that "bei uns" (back home) everything had been better.

Many second-generation émigré historians served in the United States military, usually in Europe. Because of their native-language skills, many underwent training in intelligence operations at Camp Ritchie in Maryland. Tom Angress is featured in the documentary film *Ritchie Boys*, about German-Jewish refugees who fought the Nazis as American soldiers. Some future historians also belonged to United States occupation forces in Germany. They now occupied the very country from which they had barely escaped just a few years earlier. This, however, only underscored the sense that they were no longer Germans, but rather Americans.

All of the second-generation historians (by my criteria at least) received their Ph.D. degrees after World War II. Second-generation émigré historians studied history as it was then studied in the United States. They studied European history, not the national histories of the major European nation-states. Modern German history barely existed. Émigré graduate students did not study with historians of Germany per se—this was well-nigh impossible, given how few historians specialized in German history at the time. Still, most of those who became historians of modern Germany wrote their dissertations on German history topics. They had a burning interest to understand what happened in their native country. In the 1940s, for example, Hans Gatzke and Klemens von Klemperer wrote German history theses at Harvard under the nominal supervision of William Langer.

Most second-generation émigré historians received their graduate educations at just three institutions: Harvard, Columbia, and the University of Chicago. A few each earned their degrees at Yale, Stanford, and Berkeley. Three had a *Doktorvater* who was a first-generation refugee historian: Walter Simon and Arno Mayer both studied with Hajo Holborn at Yale, and Gerhard Weinberg studied with Hans Rothfels at Chicago. Why didn't more younger refugee historians study with their older counterparts? Besides Holborn, only Hans Rothfels, who spent a decade at Chicago between 1946 and 1956, taught in a top graduate program. Hans Rosenberg didn't get to Berkeley until 1959, when most younger refugee historians had already launched their careers.

Nonetheless, second-generation émigré historians had connections to their older counterparts. Hajo Holborn was key in this regard. While teaching at Yale, Holborn taught at least one seminar at Harvard and participated in others at Columbia. Von Klemperer recalls how Holborn was "helping us youngsters move into the profession. . . . We had to come to terms as scholars with our own experiences, and Hajo Holborn helped us in a masterful way to bring together history and political commitment."[2] Stern, too, developed a close relationship with Holborn, and eventually coedited the *Festschrift* in his honor.[3] Gatzke became Holborn's colleague at Yale in 1964.

In the 1940s, younger émigré historians came to know Fritz Epstein and Dietrich Gerhard. Fritz Epstein, then a librarian at Widener Library, was known for supplying graduate students with obscure bibliographical references. In the early 1950s, he was in charge of the War Documentation Project, the filming of captured German war documents. Gerhard Weinberg fondly recalls working under his direction.[4] Meanwhile, younger historians such as Klaus Epstein and Georg Iggers came to know Dietrich Gerhard, a first-generation refugee historian at Washington University in St. Louis. In 1960, Gerhard extended a job offer to Klaus Epstein to become an associate professor at Washington University.[5]

Yet some younger refugee historians had difficulties with older refugee historians. In his memoirs, Raul Hilberg recalled an encounter with Hans Rosenberg in an undergraduate class at Brooklyn College: "[Rosenberg] remarked, in parentheses, that Napoleonic atrocities in Spain had not been equaled since. At this point I raised my hand and asked, 'What do you call six million dead Jews?' Ah, said Rosenberg, that was an interesting problem, but one which was very complicated, and he was constrained by time and the outline of the course to forgo a discussion of my question." Hilberg was deeply agitated by Rosenberg's response—one perhaps typical of the older generation of refugee historians who didn't quite know what to make of the Holocaust. Still, Hilberg remarked, "Although I perceived in Rosenberg's remark about Napoleon a plain denial of Adolf Hitler's Germany, I used everything he taught."[6] Rosenberg may well have sparked Hilberg's interest in the bureaucratic organization of the Holocaust.

By contrast, Hilberg was scathing about Fritz Epstein. Hilberg also worked on the War Documentation Project. In his memoirs, he complained of Epstein's "limited analytical abilities," quoted a Jewish refugee coworker who hissed that Epstein "looks like a Jewish cattle dealer from Hesse," and complained that Epstein fired him because he wanted to hire "men who would be totally beholden to him."[7] I suspect that Hilberg's vituperation stemmed from his frustration that Epstein did not place the murder of Europe's Jews front and center of the War Documentation Project.

Hilberg was not the only second-generation historian to have difficult interactions with older refugee historians. At Chicago, Iggers later wrote, "I found two small seminars by Hans Rothfels very useful. . . . For the first time I was forced to study documents carefully, which I had not been required to do in my previous training. However, I had a very unpleasant exchange with him. . . . Rothfels made no secret of his rightwing and nationalistic Prusso-German views and I challenged him. . . . He called me in his office and told me, although he had given me As in both seminars, that with my views I had no understanding of history and should not pursue a doctorate."[8] Rothfels, dismayed that someone with Iggers's views might write the history of his native country in the United States, hoped to cut short his career.

Refugee historians, of course, were not the only émigré academics that the younger historians encountered. Indeed, other refugee academics had an arguably much greater influence on them. This was particularly true at Columbia, where many future historians of Germany studied with the political scientist Franz Neumann, author of *Behemoth*. Similarly, at Chicago, Iggers studied with Arnold Bergstraesser, a refugee political scientist employed in the German Department. Younger émigré historians also came into contact with Erich Auerbach, Felix Gilbert, Erwin Panofsky, and a host of other notable refugees. In their memoirs, they repeatedly praise these scholars' erudition and engagement.

Despite many connections with refugee scholars, the second generation of émigré historians had a decidedly American education. In the 1940s and 1950s, this meant that they received their graduate education in an educational environment in which the Western civilization narrative dominated. For some, Western civilization remained a lifelong passion. Karl Weintraub, for example, was a legendary lecturer in the core course on Western civilization at the University of Chicago. Students spent nights in line waiting to register for his course. Even in later decades, when "Western Civ" had become a dinosaur, Weintraub tried to save the course. He justified this with his biography. Recalling his time as a hidden child and adolescent in Nazi-occupied Holland, he quipped, "I had enough of life without civilization."[9]

As budding historians, the second generation was eager to fit into the American milieu. In keeping with prevailing trends in European history, they generally focused on intellectual history or the history of ideas. Their work solidified the *Sonderweg* paradigm—why Germany departed from the supposed norms of Western civilization. While Hajo Holborn made the most dramatic statement about the importance of the *Sonderweg* thesis in a 1952 article—"The split between Germany and the West will of necessity always be an important theme for historians"—it became something of an article of faith among younger émigré historians.[10] Fritz Stern, for example, later wrote about how this article inspired his own research.[11]

Significantly, some second-generation refugee historians did not initially focus on German history at all. George Mosse first made his reputation as a historian of early modern British constitutional history. As he later wrote of his early books, "These were certainly respectable, indeed core subjects at the time. . . . That they were also far removed from my own origins may have played an unconscious role as I tried to dive into my new Anglo-Saxon environment."[12] Mosse chose a historical field that would allow him to "fit in" to his American environment. Other budding historians may have worried that by focusing on German history, they might be accused of navel-gazing. Worse still, their refugee status, they thought, might seem to compromise their ability to write so-called objective history about their native countries. Klaus Epstein was allegedly told that as a refugee, he would never get a job if he focused on Germany history. He wrote his dissertation on modern British constitutional history. Fritz Stern wrote his Ph.D. dissertation on a German topic, but he published *The Varieties of History*—an edited volume on great historians—before *The Politics of Cultural Despair*. In his memoirs, Stern questioned the motives behind doing *The Varieties of History*: "Was I unconsciously taking a break from the Nazi past, returning to my old love of Europe itself?"[13] Perhaps Stern's decision was an unconscious attempt to first establish credentials in a field other than German history—in a field in which his motives and achievements would be less open to question.

What of their careers? Émigré historians came of age just when European history took off in the United States. Indeed, they were the first generation of American Europeanists who specialized in national subfields such as German history.[14] As Stern describes in his memoirs, when he first taught German history, there were virtually no books available. "What a remarkable opportunity for my generation!" he exclaims.[15] Émigré historians ran with the times and wrote pathbreaking books that defined the field of modern German history. In addition, they pioneered subfields of German and European history. Peter Loewenberg applied psychoanalytical methods to history. Renate Bridenthal was among the first to write women's history. Michael A. Meyer wrote landmark studies in modern German-Jewish history.

But second-generation émigré historians did not have a monopoly on German history. While they shaped the field of modern German history, they did so in conjunction with nonrefugee colleagues, such as Gordon Craig, Leonard Krieger, Otto Pflanze, and Carl Schorske. In an interview, Tom Skidmore, eventually a leading historian of Latin America, spoke of how he wrote a dissertation in German history, but jumped at the opportunity to retrain as a Latin Americanist. He felt that it would be difficult to break into the German history crowd—to an outsider, refugees dominated the German history scene.[16] But was there really a refugee historian cabal? Unlikely. True, the émigré historians had a network of sorts, but it spanned their American-born and other colleagues, too. In 1964, for example, when a group of twelve American historians wrote a letter to *Die Zeit* protesting the German Foreign Ministry's cancellation of a lecture tour by Fritz Fischer, the group included quite a mix.[17] Klaus Epstein, Hans Gatzke, Hans Kohn, Hans Rosenberg, and Fritz Stern were émigré historians. Leonard Krieger, William Langer, Otto Pflanze, Carl Schorske, and John Snell were American-born. Gordon Craig was born in Glasgow and Theodore Hamerow in Warsaw, and both came to the United States before 1933.

Still, something differentiated the émigré historians from their American-born counterparts. For one, they were tireless mediators between the German and American historical professions. In the Fischer controversy, Klaus Epstein and Fritz Stern spearheaded the American campaign on behalf of Fischer. Epstein drafted the letter to *Die Zeit*, while Stern secured funding for Fischer's subsequent lecture tour in the United States.

Second, many émigré historians became public intellectuals: they combined professional activity with civic engagement. Since political events had such a tangible impact on their early lives, many became avid followers of contemporary affairs at a very young age. Their childhood and adolescent experience of persecution in Germany also profoundly shaped their politics. Most were liberals to the core. They staunchly believed in civic engagement. Georg Iggers has suggested that his experiences in Nazi Germany inspired his work for racial equality in the United States.[18] In the 1950s, when he taught at several historically black colleges, he worked hard to end segregation in Little Rock and New Orleans. Fritz Stern has written that "at decisive moments in cold-war America, the memory of German civic passivity sliding into complicity prodded me into action."[19] In the 1960s, he was deeply involved in the antiwar movement and student protest politics at Columbia. On a more leftist note, Bridenthal has written, "The direct personal experience of flight from fascism colors all my political vision, so much so that I must factor it out sometimes. When I read that the FBI has been surveilling groups to which I give regular contributions . . . then I hear the midnight knock on the door."[20] While émigré historians were certainly not alone in their civic engagement, it seems that their early, direct experiences with persecution led many to speak out against perceived injustices.

Finally, many émigré historians felt themselves to be outsiders. They were not quite part of mainstream American life. Tom Angress titled his memoirs *Immer etwas abseits* (Always somewhat on the margins). Peter Gay famously analyzed "the outsider as insider" in his study of Weimar Culture.[21] Did a sense of "outsiderdom" shape these historians' work? In his memoirs, George Mosse repeatedly refers to the two qualities that made him an outsider: his homosexuality and his German-Jewish origins.[22] "Outsiderdom" may have influenced Mosse and other refugee historians to pursue innovative topics, new methodologies, or simply daring conclusions. Other essays in this volume speak to the enormous influence the second generation exercised on the study of modern German history in the United States and even in Germany.

But what role did émigré historians play in the now burgeoning field of Holocaust history? In the past two decades, there has been a sea change in German history. Earlier, historians of Germany were primarily preoccupied with 1933 (Hitler's rise to power), but now they are more preoccupied with 1941–42 (the Holocaust). The *Sonderweg* thesis, however, was focused on 1933—and this is where second-generation historians made their biggest contribution. Given their life histories, this should not be surprising. Most second-generation émigré historians came to the United States between 1933 and 1941. Their lives were indelibly marked by Hitler's rise to power. This was the seminal event that fundamentally changed their lives. In their later historical work, they thus wanted to know why National Socialism took root in Germany. Contrary to what other authors in this volume argue, these historians were first and foremost preoccupied with the failure of liberalism, and only secondarily (and much later in their careers) with the Holocaust. In his memoirs, for example, Mosse lists his major historical concerns. First on his list is the demise of liberalism, last is the Holocaust.[23]

Steven Aschheim and Jeffrey Herf have both argued that Stern and Mosse, along with Gay and Walter Laqueur, played a crucial role in shifting historians' attention from 1933 to 1941. Aschheim insists that their early focus on German nationalism, racism, and antisemitism, showed that, for them, "the scandal in need of accounting, was 1941–42."[24] Perhaps. But while these émigré historians' works were key for the analysis of the German cultural antecedents to the Holocaust, it is striking that none of them researched the details of the Holocaust per se. This was true even though captured German documents related to the nuts and bolts operations of the Holocaust were readily available in the National Archives. The liberal ethos for which these refugee historians are justly admired, along with their research topics, suggests that, for much of their professional lives, their primary historical concern was Germany's inability to adhere to a liberal political order.

This is not intended as an indictment, only an attempt to document historians' changing interests, in step with their times. Most second-generation refugee historians made their careers before anyone was much concerned with the Holocaust. There were, however, a few refugee historians who always had the Holocaust at the center of their professional concerns. They are just not usually mentioned in the same breath as Peter Gay, George Mosse, or Fritz Stern. Take Henry Friedlander. Unlike most refugee historians, Friedlander came to the United States only after harrowing experiences in ghettos and camps. He was always much more focused on the Holocaust than most of those historians who came to the United States in the 1930s. Henry Huttenbach, who spent the war years in England but received his higher education in the United States, was a pioneer in placing the Holocaust in the broader framework of genocide studies. Even though he wrote on the Jewish community in Worms, he is seldom grouped among historians of modern Germany. And although Raul Hilberg came to the United States in the 1930s, his preoccupation with the Holocaust made him a total outsider to the historical profession (and indeed, he was trained and taught as a political scientist).

There is no question, though, that the second-generation émigré historians trained many of the current scholars of the Holocaust. Gerhard Weinberg's list of students reads as a veritable who's who of Holocaust studies. Students of Mosse and Stern have also made extraordinary contributions to the study of the Holocaust. Many of these did their graduate work in the 1960s and 1970s, just when widespread interest in the Shoah began to percolate. Is it possible that they taught their teachers in this regard?

To conclude, second-generation émigré historians were American historians of Germany. They brought the intellectual concerns of their host country to bear on their native country's past. Their careers coincided with the extraordinary take-off and resulting specialization in European history that occurred in the quarter century following World War II. Together with American-born and other colleagues, they defined the field of German history in the postwar era. They did so, however, with a passion, commitment, insight, and understanding born of their experience of persecution in, and emigration from, Nazi Germany.

Catherine Epstein is dean of the faculty and professor of history at Amherst College. She is the author of four books on modern German history, including *Nazi Germany: Confronting the Myths* (2015); *Model Nazi: Arthur Greiser and the Nazi Occupation of Western Poland* (2010), awarded the Arthur Kronthal Prize; *The Last Revolutionaries: German Communists and their Century* (2003); and *A Past Renewed: German-Speaking Refugee Historians in the United States after 1933* (1993).

Notes

1. Fritz Epstein to Klaus Epstein, 18 October 1947, Epstein Family Papers (Private Collection), Box 5/1.
2. Klemens von Klemperer, *Voyage through the Twentieth Century: A Historian's Recollections and Reflections* (New York, 2009), 77.
3. Leonard Krieger and Fritz Stern, *The Responsibility of Power: Historical Essays in Honor of Hajo Holborn* (London, 1968).
4. Informal conversations with the author.
5. Dietrich Gerhard to Klaus Epstein, 7 November 1960, Epstein Family Papers, Box 1.
6. Raul Hilberg, *The Politics of Memory* (Chicago, 1996), 72.
7. Hilberg, *The Politics of Memory*, 81.
8. Wilma and Georg Iggers, *Two Lives in Uncertain Times: Facing the Challenges of the 20th Century as Scholars and Citizens* (New York, 2006), 57–58.
9. Andrew Patner, "Karl Joachim Weintraub: Teacher of Culture and Cultural Historian, 1924–2000," found at http://www-news.uchicago.edu/releases/04/040421.weintraub-patner.shtml (accessed 3 April 2012).
10. As quoted in Fritz Stern, "German History in America, 1884–1984," *Central European History* 19, no.2 (1986): 160.
11. Heinz Wolf, *Deutsch-jüdische Emigrationshistoriker in den USA und der Nationalsozialismus* (Bern, 1988), 81.
12. George L. Mosse, *Confronting History: A Memoir* (Madison, 2000), 142.
13. Fritz Stern, *Five Germanys I Have Known* (New York, 2006), 221.
14. For more on the development of national field specializations in the American historical profession, see Catherine Epstein, "German Historians at the Back of the Pack: Hiring Patterns in Modern European History, 1945–2010," *Central European History* 46, no. 3 (2013): 599–639.
15. Stern, *Five Germanys*, 203.
16. Interview with Thomas Skidmore, 12 January 2012.
17. "Ein Protestbrief," *Die Zeit*, no. 17 (24 April 1964).

18. David A. Gerber, "From Hamburg to Little Rock and Beyond: The Origins of Georg Iggers's Civil Rights Activism," in Konrad H. Jarausch, Jörn Rüsen, and Hans Schleier, eds., *Geschichtswissenschaft vor 2000. Perspektiven der Historiographiegeschichte, Geschichtstheorie, Sozial- und Kulturgeschichte. Festschrift für Georg G. Iggers zum 65. Geburtstag* (Hagen, 1991), 518.
19. Stern, *Five Germanys*, 198.
20. Carol Ascher, Renate Bridenthal, Marion Kaplan, and Atina Grossmann, "Fragments of a German-Jewish Heritage in Four 'Americans,'" in Abraham J. Peck, ed., *The German-Jewish Legacy in America, 1938–1988: From* Bildung *to the Bill of Rights* (Detroit, 1989), 190.
21. Werner T. Angress, *Immer etwas abseits: Jugenderinnerungen eines jüdischen Berliners 1920-1945* (Berlin, 2005); Peter Gay, *Weimar Culture: The Outsider as Insider* (New York: Harper & Row, 1968).
22. Mosse, *Confronting History*, 118.
23. Mosse, *Confronting History*, 175–85.
24. Steven E. Aschheim, *Beyond the Border: The German-Jewish Legacy Abroad* (Princeton, 2007), 49. See also Jeffrey Herf, "How the Culture Wars Matter: Liberal Historiography, German History, and the Jewish Catastrophe," in Michael Bérubé and Cary Nelson, eds., *Higher Education under Fire: Politics, Economics, and the Crisis of the Humanities* (New York, 1995), 152.

Chapter 11

THINKING ABOUT THE SECOND GENERATION CONCEPTUALLY

Volker R. Berghahn

Unlike many of the other contributions to this volume on the second generation, this chapter does not focus closely on the life and work of individual German-Jewish refugee historians. Rather, it tries to raise some broader conceptual and analytical issues about how this generation might be fruitfully examined as a cohort. It is therefore an essay in its original literal meaning and deals with tentative forays into some very difficult questions of individual biography and contingency, on the one hand, and large-scale impersonal structures and forces, on the other.[1]

There has been a truly enormous amount of writing and debate on the problem of generations in a Central European context. For a long time, and starting in the eighteenth and nineteenth centuries, German-speaking intellectuals and scholars have been discussing this notion mainly from the angle of successive young generations and their rebellions against their elders. English-speaking historians of modern Germany came along with a number of important contributions mainly after World War II. They analyzed the origins of the Wilhelmine Youth Movement, the rise of the *Wandervogel* associations of young people, the changes that they underwent during and after the Great War, and finally their relationship with National Socialism both before and after the Nazi seizure of power in 1933. The string of studies continued covering the postwar period, and most recently the youth rebellions of the late 1960s and 1970s have become a growth industry.[2]

A fairly recent examination of "Youth Revolt and Generational Formation in Germany, 1770–1968" by a group of British, American, and German historians

---

Notes from this chapter begin on page 170.

is to be found in Mark Roseman's 1995 anthology entitled *Generations in Conflict*.[3] This book continues to be a good starting point for this particular chapter, thanks both to the long and circumspect introduction by the editor and the subsequent thirteen contributions, including a number of pieces that raise not merely the older question of socioeconomic class and its relation to (male) youth rebellions, but also that of the role of young women in generational change.

In his introduction, Roseman broaches the issue of why it is that generational debates have been particularly intense in Germany. According to him, this is because "few other nations have experienced such a succession of dramatic breaks in their historical narrative."[4] By comparison, he believes that youthful rebellions in Britain have been more muted and apolitical because that country did not see as many major societal upheavals as did Germany. While this argument may still await further comparative testing with, for example, the Italian case, the Roseman volume does provide a very good survey, ranging from the generational and class conflicts in the revolutions of 1848 to the *Wandervogel* phenomenon and the *Generation of 1914* that Robert Wohl first analyzed in 1979.[5] Considerable space is then given to the myth and reality of the German "front generation" and the appearance of the New Woman after World War I, to the "Hitler Youth generation," the "generation of 1945," Helmut Schelsky's "skeptische Generation," and finally to the student and youth rebellions that set in during the late 1960s.[6]

However, the Roseman collection also had to grapple with a problem that for the past eight decades or more has preoccupied not only historians, but also social scientists: that of generations and generational change. Accordingly, most discussions of the subject tend to start with references to Karl Mannheim, who in the 1920s was among the first to try to systematize the generational phenomenon that had become so visible during the socioeconomic, political, and cultural conflicts of the Weimar Republic. For Mannheim, "youth experiencing the same concrete historical problems may be said to be part of the same actual generation which worked up the material of their common experiences in different ways" and hence "constitute separate generation units."[7] He added that "the social phenomenon of 'generations' represents nothing more than a particular kind of identity of location, embracing related 'age-groups' embedded in a historical-social process." These definitions certainly constituted a refinement of earlier arguments that had looked at generations in large blocs of sons and daughters, fathers and mothers, and grandfathers and grandmothers. These blocs were moreover assumed, for example, by the famous Dutch historian Johan Huizinga, to have existed in thirty-year time spans. Large parts of Julian Marias's book on *Generaciones y constelaciones* of 1989 and translated as *Generations* by Alabama University Press in 1970, apart from providing a survey of relevant literature, are devoted to reviving the work of Jose Ortega y Gasset with its insights, but also its pitfalls.[8] Ortega had approached the generational question "through familiar succession" and "a biological chain from father to son to grandson." Interested in a family's "rise," his work bears a resemblance with Thomas Mann's fictional treatment of several generations of a Hanseatic merchant family in *Buddenbrooks*, although Mann, reflecting the mood of cultural pessimism in Central Europe at the time, traces the decline of this family. Like Mannheim, Ortega's wrestling with the generational problem led the Spanish philosopher to view generations as "people of roughly the same age whose shared experience significantly distinguishes them from contemporaries in other age groups."[9]

It should be clear by now that social scientists' and historians' debates on the concept of generation increasingly moved away from rather crude notions of thirty-year spans and large demographic blocs toward smaller cohorts and their experiences within shorter time frames, especially if these were marked by severe crises and emergencies in which the experiences of contemporaries became compressed and intensified. This trend has been more prevalent among historians who, with the rise of sociocultural history "from the bottom up," became more interested in the fragmentation and differentiation of modern societies than in their larger structures. By contrast, social scientists, and political scientists in particular, have tended to study generations in delineated age blocs in their quest to identify, through quantitative analysis, the behavior of different larger age groups. Consequently, they have come up with some very sophisticated analyses of electoral behavior that are based on a large sample. The idea is to identify the voting record of twenty-somethings and thirty-somethings all the way up into the decennium of those over seventy.[10]

Much less interested in representative samples and rigorous quantification, sociocultural and political historians have focused increasingly on the distinctive experiences of, for example, literary cohorts and even on what Roseman has called "sub-cohorts."[11] In other words, and mindful of the need not for generalized but for differentiated research, they were prepared to cut their cloth when dealing with "age-specific behavior without asserting the identity of all these" within their cohort.[12]

Given that there has been some doubt as to whether a second generation of German-Jewish refugee historians actually existed, the above-mentioned evolution of the debate on generations and cohorts seems to offer a first justification for the writing of the essays represented in this volume. This group grew up in the 1930s as a discriminated minority among German youth that was itself by no means thoroughly Nazified and thus did not constitute a solid bloc in itself. It is a subcohort that may be profitably studied in its own right, even if the sample is small and if it will therefore be impossible to achieve something like representativeness in a strictly quantitative sense. Still, for the historian, it is already a useful clue if the group concerned spoke of itself as a generation. Their experiences were different from the first generation, who had lived, trained, and begun their careers in the Weimar Republic and who became the subject of a conference and a book more than two decades ago.[13] Although this earlier generation was examined at the time without more detailed conceptualization, Hans Jaeger's argument seems very plausible that the study of specific groups rather than larger blocs of people is most promising, in this case the group of refugee historians.[14] This is certainly the approach adopted here, and if there are various commonalities of experience, attitude, and memory, it seems legitimate to offer a number of generalizing observations.

However, before discussing the life and work of the group represented in this volume, there are two further issues to be considered. The first one has interested both historians and social scientists researching this field—that is, how far conflicts between youth and their elders are softened by intergenerational common experiences and conversations. There is a good deal of tangible evidence that, faced with Nazi discriminations, strong feelings of belonging together were created within families and also toward supportive non-Jewish friends who were opposed to the regime.

These solidarities weakened again after the escape, as the traumas suffered by the second generation as children in school and in the streets, while partially repressed in the 1930s, emerged more powerfully in the 1940s. They were stimulated by the ever more certain knowledge of Nazi crimes and the Holocaust. Here, it seems, a difference of view between parents and children became reinforced with respect to notions of the Germans and German society that will be discussed in a moment. After all, the latter received their important tertiary socialization first during the Nazi period and later in the United States, resulting in deep-seated negative feelings toward Germany after 1945 and a stronger identification with American society and its political system. They had become conscious Americans, unlike their parents, who, with their socialization into Weimar society, by and large mellowed more quickly and also had more ambivalent feelings about the United States, often reinforced by the fact that their German accent tended to give them away when they met native speakers. In this respect, it may also be significant that the members of the second generation visited West Germany, often with uneasy feelings, but they did not go back permanently, whereas some of the first generation did, either in the 1950s or later, such as Fritz Epstein and Hans Rosenberg, after their retirement from their academic positions in the United States.

With respect to the second generation, there is therefore the issue of how far their strong feelings of hatred toward Germany eroded over time after 1945. Scholars of generational research have even gone so far as to ask whether the youthful experiences of cohorts and subcohorts are really more important, as has often been assumed, than aging in later years when bitter memories begin to fade and a person may find it possible to take a less categorical and less undifferentiated view of his or her past experiences, in this case of the 1930s, perhaps also due to a growing feeling that unmitigated hatred can be self-destructive. And yet, the question remains how far feelings of suspicion ever subsided.

While the concept of generation will therefore have to be handled with care and caution in general, there is also the more specific problem of what we mean by the second generation after Alan L. Berger published a number of articles and finally a book that deployed the term in a way different from the contents of this volume and that he titled *Children of Job: American Second Generation Witnesses to the Holocaust*.[15] For him, all those who actually survived the Nazi deportations and the camps, including the extermination camps, belong to an identifiable "first generation." They comprised the children, women, and men of all ages from all over Nazi-occupied Europe who made it to the United States after 1945, where they began to raise their children. Assuming, no doubt rightly, that these actual survivors were profoundly traumatized by what they had witnessed and gone through, Berger focused his extensive research on their children. Hence his particular notion of "second generation." His approach to this generation is to study their writings (short stories, novels) and their film productions (documentaries and docudramas) in order to examine how they dealt with what they learned about the experiences of their parents.

Berger's usage of "second generation" is obviously different from that in this anthology and is therefore being mentioned here also as a way of clarifying the use of the term in this essay. After all, here the "first generation" is defined as German-Jewish refugee historians who experienced the Weimar Republic as adults and left during the 1930s in the face of increasing Nazi persecution of Germany's Jewish population. They decided sooner or later to escape and to settle, together with children born in the 1920s, in an array of foreign countries, such as Britain, the United States, Mexico, Australia, or whichever nation was prepared to accept them as refugees. If their children had experienced the Nazi dictatorship in their early schooling and in public places until their parents took them out of the country, they have been deemed a second generation different from Berger's, the more so since they have tended to define themselves as such. Applying this definition, Walter Laqueur has called these children the "generation Exodus," although his book *Generation Exodus* is more wide-ranging across the entire spectrum of German-Jewish refugees rather than just those who became academic historians.[16] In addition, some research has also been done on the third generation—that is, the children of the second generation of German-Jewish refugees and their experiences of being born and growing up in the country of their parents' refuge. This latter cohort is the one that Berger, working with a different framework, has defined as his second generation.

To be sure, he argues at one point that, in light of the larger objectives of Hitler's policies of extermination that he would have completed if he had won World War II, all European Jews are in this sense survivors. Yet, to him, this was "true only in a very broad and non-specific way."[17] Still, although he does not study refugees from Nazism but only camp survivors, his research seems to be helpful to an understanding of the second generation in the current volume. Thus, Berger found that many of the survivor parents of his second generation were either silent and remote or overprotective. They tended to move in circles in the United States that had shared their earlier experiences. For them, the ever more concrete knowledge of the realities of the Holocaust centrally shaped their Jewish identity. The Holocaust became for this second generation, just as for the parents, an "unmastered trauma" that, worse, may ultimately even have been unmasterable.[18] Looking at their trajectories after 1945, Berger quotes approvingly the title and subtitle of Albert Friedlander's book *Riders Towards the Dawn*, trajectories that led them *From Ultimate Despair to Temperate Hope*.[19] And even though these children did not experience persecution themselves, they felt compelled to transmit what they had heard to subsequent generations, even as their parents were aging and passing away. All these findings may be said to have been true also of the second generation of German-Jewish refugees who came to the United States without being survivors in Berger's sense and later became academic historians who similarly saw their writings and lectures as the means to make their often quite uninformed fellow-Americans aware of what had happened in Nazi Germany.

Berger introduced in his book two categories that may also be fruitfully employed with respect to the second generation of German-Jewish refugee historians in this volume. He sees two distinct Jewish paths: particularism and universalism. Essentially, he means by this the internal private communication within the community and family, on the one hand, and, on the other, a gradual shift over time towards a recognition of the "moral example of non-Jewish rescuers and helpers who during a time of severe testing revealed the *tikkun* of ordinary decency. Varied in their motivation, the rescuers are united in their two-fold belief that what they did was not heroic, and, given the choice between saving lives and acquiescing to death, they chose life."[20] It seems that many of the second generation discussed here experienced a similar rethinking of their earlier positions. Having raised in this way basic ethical issues relating to majority populations in Nazi-occupied Europe and their behavior towards Jewish minorities, Berger finally leads his readers to the questions that some of the refugee children in this volume would also ask themselves later on: "How would I behave" and what are the larger lessons to be learned from the Holocaust?

It is against the background of the debates about the concept of generation and of Berger's specific definition of "second generation" that we can now turn to an analysis of the tangible experiences and attitudes of German-Jewish historians. Is it possible to say anything about their lives and thoughts that goes beyond their very individual biographies and makes generalizations possible? After all, even though they were born in the 1920s and grew up in the 1930s, some of them, such as George Mosse or Peter Paret, left Germany straightaway in 1933 when their parents were either forced into exile by the authorities or decided to leave while the obstacles were not yet as huge they as they would be later. Others, such as Hans Schmitt, went to Holland in 1934, and a third group among them—Fritz Stern, Renate Bridenthal, Walter Laqueur, and Peter Gay—finally escaped with their parents in 1938. Mosse never attended an increasingly Nazified German public school. Schmitt's parents decided to send their son abroad after the racist discriminations in his school became, in their view, intolerable. A third group continued to go to public schools or were sent to purely Jewish institutions once Nazi discrimination and segregation policies began to escalate. Gerhard Weinberg, whose family hailed from Hannover and whose brother was eventually sent to a Jewish school, continued in the state system until one day in November 1938 the headmaster read out the new expulsion law, whereupon Weinberg gathered together his books and pencils and left. He recalled that the 1938 pogrom made the deepest impression on him when he read about it in the papers because of the massive physical violence that the regime unleashed on this occasion. His parents sent their three children to England at the very end of December before they followed a few weeks later. Gay's and Bridenthal's families left before the pogrom of 1938; the Sterns and many others got out thereafter, often under hair-raising circumstances.

If those refugees who later became historians actually saw themselves as a second generation, this did not mean that when it came to their social lives and perceptions of the world, they could be neatly separated from their elders. The children who stayed up to 1938 later grew up in families that tried their best to shield them from hardship. This makes it difficult to draw a clear generational line. Although they lived in different cities, they hailed from middle-class or upper-middle-class families. Bridenthal, who came from a working-class background, seems to have been an exception. The professional positions and social recognition the parents had achieved were visible evidence of their successful integration into majority society. Their families' successes, which had begun in the late nineteenth century, culminated in the Weimar Republic, when the last major obstacles that had continued to exist in Imperial Germany to their rise in the civil service, the judiciary, and the universities had finally disappeared. Most of these upwardly mobile Jews had left their lives as peddlers, small shop keepers, and cattle dealers in the provinces behind and had moved to the cities.[21] There they were able to establish close contacts not only among themselves but also with their non-Jewish socio-economic peers. In Hamburg, Berlin, and Frankfurt, these became so close that the rate of intermarriage between Jews and non-Jews was very high. Being evidently accepted by key local elites even to the point of marriage, their feelings of being part of the city—its politics, economy, and culture—were strong. This was not an illusion and probably also applied to the integration of working-class Jews into their non-Jewish neighborhoods. Some of the men had been soldiers and officers in World War I, which had merely reinforced their identification with the German nation.

But, even if their politics and their economic activities were the same as their non-Jewish peers, this did not mean that German Jews had become completely absorbed by their environment and had shed all cultural attributes of their Jewish roots. It has been one of the more serious misinterpretations of their actual status within the majority society that they had adhered to the same cultural practices as their neighbors. On the one hand, Jews all over the world adapted to the larger societal milieu to some extent, be it the larger environment of Britain, the United States, or Argentina. At the same time, Marion Berghahn and other scholars have demonstrated that the identity that refugees developed and the practices to which they adhered were not completely assimilationist.[22] They did not vanish but had hyphenated identities and constituted a new ethnicity that incorporated within itself, mostly quite comfortably and often barely consciously, the German and Jewish elements that they had inherited over time. Living these elements, German Jews simply took them as given. The cultural practices of Theodor Herzl, the father of Zionism, offer a most striking example of this hyphenated ethnicity when on one occasion he received the flabbergasted chief rabbi of Vienna in his living room in front of a Christmas tree.

Indeed, many Jewish families in Central Europe saw no tension between combining *hanukkah* with the Christmas holidays. It is therefore also no coincidence that the largest association, whose members, unlike the Zionists, were quite happily settled in Germany, called itself "Central Association of German Citizens of the Jewish Faith." Its members, insofar as they were practicing Jews, belonged to liberal or reformed synagogues. Those families or individuals who did not attend services and were more secular nevertheless tended to celebrate high holidays quietly in the family circle, just as Christian families would whose members no longer regularly went to church. The children of the latter were still baptized and later confirmed or went to communion. The small contingent of Jews in Germany and Austria-Hungary who had converted—often not out of conviction, but because they believed it would enhance their social and professional status—still found it possible to combine their Jewish and non-Jewish roots. Having referred to Susan Groag Bell, whose family converted to Protestantism in German-speaking Czechoslovakia, Bridenthal writes in her contribution about her own working-class family:[23] "There was little religious ritual at home, mainly observance of the high holy days, although not always in synagogue." Hence the "half-guilty, half-gleeful violations of Yom Kippur, when in midday we could no longer resist sausage sandwiches."

Gay's parents lived secular lives and yet they had their son circumcised, which later led the latter to wonder why.[24] From the vantage point of recent research it is much less puzzling. After all, there are many other examples showing that humans have a capacity to quite peacefully unite within themselves seemingly contradictory practices and attitudes. If the racist Nazis saw Jews as a biologically defined race, Eastern European Jews had since the late nineteenth century begun to see themselves as an ethnic group that was culturally defined. But while many of them remained isolated and ostracized in their neighborhoods, the Jews of

Central Europe, living freely in big cities, were no longer socially isolated, even if they lived in certain upscale areas, such as Harvestehude in Hamburg.

There was an important further bond that was not merely generational but intergenerational and emerged among German Jews after their flight from Nazism. It was their common front against the reproach from American Jews with an East European background that they had brought their persecution and ultimately their murder by the Nazis upon themselves because, according to their critics, they had abandoned their Jewishness. Consequently, they were said to have been blind to the deadly threat of German antisemitism. It was a criticism that could be found in the scholarly literature especially after 1945. German Jews were deemed by these studies to be responsible not only for their own tragedy, but also for the demise of Jews all over Europe once the Hitler regime and the Wehrmacht had overrun most of Europe in the early 1940s and had initiated systematic mass murder. This reproach reached a renewed pitch when Daniel Jonah Goldhagen published his bestseller entitled *Hitler's Willing Executioners* in 1995—a book that sold eighty thousand copies in the United States alone in the first four weeks.[25] Its central hypothesis was that antisemitism had traditionally been so deeply ingrained in German society that by the late nineteenth century it had become "eliminationist." This meant that the majority of Germans wanted to remove the country's small minority of half a million Jews (about one percent of the entire population) from their midst. This widespread Judeophobia, Goldhagen continued, became even more visceral after 1918. It therefore did not take the Hitler regime and its racism much to tip the eliminationist antisemitism into an exterminationist one. In short, the Holocaust was in principle on the cards in Germany since at least the late nineteenth century with the rise of eliminationism.

While the main thrust of Goldhagen's book is directed against the non-Jewish Germans who lived in this period and are hence alleged to have supported the Holocaust as perpetrators or bystanders, it also contains a criticism of Jews from Germany that is relevant to this essay. After all, if antisemitism had reached an eliminationist pitch by the late nineteenth century and the idea of extermination had already been propagated by a few radical antisemites, this was the moment for German Jews to have recognized that Germany was not the home with which they could identify and belong to. If they had analyzed their predicament more soberly, they would have known that the point of emigration was well before 1933. The outcry against this interpretation among German Jews has been intergenerational. The first generation vigorously rejected it. The second generation joined this opposition when they began to confront this criticism in their own work. By the time Goldhagen published his book in the 1990s, it was even three generations of German Jews in Europe and the United States who joined an angry chorus against his critique.

Here, as the first piece of evidence, is a longer review that Stern wrote of *Hitler's Willing Executioners* in 1996 in *Foreign Affairs*, the influential journal of the

Council for Foreign Relations.[26] In it, he charged Goldhagen with having given a distorted view of Germany's political culture and having equated Hitler with the country as a whole when Nazism in fact reflected the sentiments of "only *some* Germans"; nor did the author say more than "very little" about those who defended the Weimar Republic against Hitler. Stern reminded his readers that the regime's violence was from the start not merely directed against Jews but perhaps even more ruthlessly against the political Left. Nor, Stern added, was the road to Auschwitz "straight." German antisemitism "varied with mood and condition of German politics." Moreover, Goldhagen's focus on the members of Police Battalion 101, which was involved in atrocities in Eastern Europe, must be complemented by the findings of Christopher Browning, who based his study of *Ordinary Men* on the same court files that Goldhagen evaluated. To Stern, the book was a deliberate provocation that could shock people but could also be seen as no more than "self-promoting attacks on earlier works and professional standards."

But apart from censoring Goldhagen for riding roughshod over serious research by other scholars, American and European, or, worse, ignoring it, the author had also gotten the account of the position of Jews in German society wrong. In Stern's view, this was the "country in which Jews had made extraordinary leaps to cultural and economic prominence" an "integral element of history" that Goldhagen chose to omit from the record. The critic admits "that any hope that they [the Jews] had for complete acceptance remained unfulfilled. They knew that they were being treated as second-class citizens and that their very success heightened their vulnerability." And yet, the achievements of this minority were the "envy of Jews elsewhere."

If Stern's refutation of Goldhagen's hypotheses concerning the depth of German antisemitism and the endangered position of Germany's Jews was more indirect in his review, he was blunter in his memoirs. Ten years later, he railed at the "facile generalities, such as the 'summary judgment about German Jewry, about their putative self-surrender, their cravenness, or their opportunism.'"[27] Meanwhile, Gay in his *My German Question* spent a considerable amount of space to explaining his family's life in Berlin and why his parents waited until 1938 to leave. There was not only the high degree of integration into the social environment before 1933, but also the mixed signals that they believed the regime was sending out. Accordingly, he is really quite angry at the "critics of German-Jewish assimilation" that he "later encountered only too often in the United States."[28] He says, "For them our situation had been obvious from the start; German Jews they said (to borrow a phrase from the historian Charles Beard), without fear and research, had been culpably blind in the face of spectacular warnings and had sold out to an irresponsible fantasy known as German-Jewish symbiosis." Consequently, the "self-appointed commentators, especially in the decades after the fact, found it all too easy to reprimand German Jewry collectively: 'And you still thought, after the Nuremberg Laws and other horrors that you were Germans?'

But we were Germans; the gangsters who had taken control of the country were not Germany—we were." Referring to Gershom Scholem's reproach that German Jews had been delusionary, Gay countered that "my parents and I did not think we were living a delusion. Granted, our Germany had taken refuge in exile or was living underground at home, and resistance to Nazi oppression appeared to be impossible. But we believed that the Nazis had no right to impose their perversion of history and biology on us."

On top of these considerations came purely practical questions. After all, his father did not know any English and had no qualifications that would provide for his family in a foreign country like the United States. He was reluctant to contemplate destitution for his family. He did not know the future. Later, with more and more restrictions and chicaneries impeding emigration, where should they have gotten the required documentation for their departure and entry into another country? In the end, Gay's family found itself in Cuba and was very lucky not to be sent back. Eventually they were admitted to the United States, but had to go to Denver, Colorado. In contrast, Stern's memoirs reflect the self-confidence and pride with which his family, with its highly esteemed elders and extensive network of friends and colleagues in Breslau, were better connected than the Gays. When, after much hesitation, they finally left, they were flown out to Holland; they were able to take their furniture and other possessions with them, while many others had their property "Aryanized" and auctioned off at bargain basement prices.[29]

The most careful and extensively researched scholarly analysis of the situation of German Jews in the 1930s is by Marion Kaplan.[30] She also highlights the ambivalences, the continuing interactions with family and friends, and the constant attempts to make sense of a highly dynamic Nazi movement and its aims. Stressing that the road to Auschwitz was twisted, Kaplan concludes that "it has been common, with hindsight, to criticize German Jews for not having emigrated quickly enough, for hoping that they could remain in Germany, for loving Germany too much [and] for not seeing the writing on the wall. This is a profound and cruel distortion." Perhaps it should be noted that such conclusions do not merely contain a scholarly verdict, but also reflect a significant intergenerational consensus rather than a conflict between the young and their elders. Kaplan was born after 1945 and is thus a member of the third generation.

It looks, though, as if it was not just a question of divergent interpretations of the historical evidence, with historians of German-Jewish background arguing that, given the high degree of integration of Germany's Jews into society, economy, and culture and given also the liberal and pluralistic cultural climate of the Weimar Republic, no one could have anticipated what happened in the 1930s and 1940s. The problem of the first generation was that they just did not know a future that we have—as Berger also wrote—to live and wrestle with today. Walter Laqueur, who left the country in December 1938 for Palestine, has cast the fact that no one knew the future into a dialogue in a novel, titled *The Missing Years.* When challenged in Israel that Germany's Jews should have known, the protagonist replies angrily,[31] "No, . . . I didn't and cleverer people didn't. Every fool knows what happened yesterday, but even the greatest genius cannot tell what will occur tomorrow. Looking backwards, everything usually seems inevitable: it happened because it was bound to happen." Taking up the theme again later on in his novel of why the protagonist did not leave in 1931, the critic receives the answer "we were born there, we were part of the country, German was our language and anyway we had no other home. . . . If Hitler's plane had crashed in 1930, the Nazis might not have come to power and there would not have been a world war." This also means that the notion of industrial mass murder of millions of innocent men, women, and children was still beyond the horizon of human experience. Consequently, it was also difficult to believe the rumors of the Holocaust that by 1942 began to publicly circulate in Europe and the United States. For those of us living in the post-Holocaust period, these horrors have now become part of humankind's history, and only a few in the West deny that it actually happened.

Finally, what resurfaced in the Goldhagen debate may also have been the old tensions between the German-speaking Jews of Central Europe and the so-called *Ostjuden*, many of whom lived in orthodox communities in Poland and the Soviet Union and, insofar as they migrated to Germany after World War I, were seen, not only by the antisemites but also by many German Jews, as a group whose culture and religious practices made them unwelcome aliens. Many of them existed at the poverty line. Before 1933, these immigrants who lived in certain sections of the big cities, like the *Scheunenviertel* in Berlin, were looked down upon by many Jews who had been born in Germany. Eastern orthodox immigrants also dressed and appeared quite different from middle-class Jews in suits and ties and fashionable dresses. It was a tension that also affected relations between German-Jewish refugees and American Jews, many of whom had come to the United States from Russia to escape the pogroms of the Tsarist autocracy. These are divisions that some New Yorkers have experienced to this day. Discussing this question against the background of his experiences in Israel, Laqueur concluded that "it was mainly the old aversion of East European Jews towards German Jews (Kaiserjuden as Weizmann called them in his autobiography)."[32] But his years in Palestine and Israel taught him "how to handle East European Jews who did not like [German Jewish] 'Jeckes.'" Stern added that, while his family experienced antisemitism in the United States, "the occasional taunt made by American Jews about my having been born into a converted family hurt more."[33]

However, the stepped-up antisemitism of the Nazis had, by the mid-1930s, also become a point of tension between the first and the second generation in Germany. The former, often well-established professionally and respected in the local community, tried their best to secure the economic survival of their families, while often hoping that the regime would mitigate its persecution or be replaced by a less repressive conservative authoritarianism. Those who had served as soldiers or officers in World War I thought, erroneously as it turned out, that the protection that the regime initially afforded them would never be withdrawn. They tried to live a normal life and thus continued to pursue their earlier hobbies and foibles. This might involve watching and cheering on one's favorite German soccer team or meeting with old non-Jewish friends to play cards. The second generation was invited to join in, perhaps also to escape from the negative experiences that they had in school. But, increasingly, it was precisely the encounters with indoctrinated fellow-pupils in the schoolyard or with a few pro-Nazi teachers that generated resentment and bitterness, resulting in a reinterpretation of their identity.

Georg Iggers, who came from a *gutbürgerliche* family in Hamburg but was evidently in a rebellious mood, joined a Zionist youth group that was both religious and socialist. Although he went to a public school where his working-class classmates and teachers fully accepted him, his parents later decided to send him to a Jewish *Erziehungsanstalt*. It was only in October 1938 that he rejoined them to emigrate to Richmond, Virginia, where he experienced Southern segregation and racism. His aversion to this caused him and his wife Wilma, after receiving their doctorates at Chicago, to move to Arkansas to teach in a black college and to become politically active in the civil rights movement.[34] This trajectory may have made him an exception among his cohort. Still, overall it may be said that, unlike the first generation, the adolescents had no more than ephemeral memories and impressions of the better days under the Weimar Republic before 1933 and, in light of their experiences under Nazism, became increasingly embittered, possibly also leading to later disagreements with their parents about American politics and postwar policies toward West Germany.

The bitterness that in some cases turned into outright hatred of the Germans received a further boost once, after harboring great anxieties and experiencing often very precarious journeys, the teenagers finally reached a safe haven abroad. But even then life remained uncertain. Their fathers found it difficult to establish themselves professionally, a fate that they shared with some members of the first generation. While Hajo Holborn found an academic position at Yale soon after his arrival in the United States, Hans Rosenberg, who later taught at Berkeley, sent out some eighty applications until he was finally offered an academic job at Brooklyn College. By the early 1940s, the German-Jewish historians examined in this volume had become politically conscious young people who read American newspapers and magazines and, in a few cases, even began to write their own columns in a school or college paper. They now "Americanized" themselves.

In 1942–43, the first reports on the atrocities in Nazi-occupied Europe appeared in the American press. This news notwithstanding, at this point American public opinion was by and large not openly anti-German, but rather anti-Nazi and anti-Hitler. This changed virtually overnight when the first accounts, photos, and newsreels appeared of the liberated camps. It seems that it was also the moment when many refugees of the second generation joined the ranks of those American Jews who swore never to set foot on German soil again nor to buy German-made goods, although some continued to speak German, perhaps because their parents had difficulties in their use of the English language.[35]

This raises a related question concerning the life and thought of those wartime teenagers, who were, by the late 1940s, working hard to establish themselves professionally and to embark upon an academic career that would involve them in researching and writing about modern European and, in many cases, German history. What they began to buy into with great energy and determination was the relative openness of the American system of higher education. Highly motivated and determined to overcome the initial handicaps of their immigration, most of them shone in college before going to graduate school and obtaining their first appointment as assistant professors. It may be that their belief in the American credo that anyone can move up in society through hard work and a determination to succeed explains why structuralist interpretations of history did not appeal to most of them. Although I could not find any direct evidence that Vilfredo Pareto as a theoretician of socioeconomic change through the rise of highly intelligent and clever people from the "masses" into the ranks of the elites[36] was picked up by the second generation, we know that the work of the Italian sociologist had a very positive reception at Harvard and elsewhere.[37] His ideas certainly corresponded well with the American notion that the realization of the individual in society depends primarily on that individual's will to move up. While it must remain an open question as to whether Pareto percolated from American sociology into the self-perceptions of German-Jewish refugee historians and their attitudes toward the dynamics of American society, the general ethos of the chance to move upwards as an individual and of the relative openness of the system of higher education was something they came to appreciate and highlight later on when comparing the United States with the much more exclusive German universities and the more rigid stratification of West German society. Certainly it continued to be much more difficult to become a professor in West Germany than in the United States, and the second generation was always appreciative of this.

Such comparisons sooner or later also confronted them with the problem of whether they wanted to visit the society that had forced them into exile and return to a defeated and devastated country. Very few German-Jewish refugee historians returned permanently. Without being able to provide statistics, it seems that we can differentiate between three categories of reactions, namely (1), those who visited occupied Germany straight-away in 1946–47, in some cases with the U.S. Army, not only to revive former contacts and friendships but also to give lectures; (2), those who waited until the 1950s and even then went across the

Atlantic with ambivalent feelings; and (3), those whose reservations and, indeed, feelings of hatred remained so strong that it took until the 1960s or even longer to overcome them or at least to contemplate setting foot on German soil and accepting invitations to lecture and meet younger students, of whom it would have made no sense to ask what they had done during the war.

The reasons they decided to go back are most difficult to gauge. But this being an essay, let me try to see if certain motives and incentives can be identified within the three above-mentioned categories. George Mosse's explanation for his return to Germany as early as 1947 and again in 1950 and 1954 to give lectures is probably too simple.[38] His family, he claimed, was forced to leave in early 1933. He therefore never went to a German school and consequently had few bitter feelings toward the Germans. Perhaps we should also relate his attitudes to the academic milieu in which he began to move, first at the University of Iowa and later at Madison, Wisconsin, and to which we shall return at the very end of this chapter. This seems to be confirmed by what Theodore Hamerow, his colleague at Madison, wrote about the influence that his own "childhood stay in Germany" had on him throughout his life—"an influence whose extent and depth I cannot describe with precision, but whose existence seem to me undeniable."[39] He continued that "unlike many Jews, I have never held the Germans collectively responsible for the atrocities committed by National Socialism. Nor do I believe that they have historically been more authoritarian or more nationalistic or more anti-Semitic than most of the other people of Europe." He liked to think "that I base these views on my study of the history of Germany and on my extended visits to that country after the Second World War."

Although Francis Carsten became a historian in Britain rather than in the United States, his explanations for his very early return to postwar Germany to give lectures add another angle of vision.[40] He always saw himself as a political refugee from Nazism who had been working underground and was forced to leave in a hurry. Until then, Carsten, a member of the radical Left who had distanced himself from the Communist Party, had joined Neu Beginnen, an anti-Nazi resistance group in Berlin to which Willy Brandt also belonged for a while. As happened to many other clandestine operations that the Gestapo had begun to penetrate quickly, Carsten was tipped off in time before his arrest and could flee to France and later to Britain. If a generalization on the basis of a very small sample is permissible, this German-Jewish refuge historian, like Mosse, certainly knew of "other Germans," whom he met again after 1945 while discussing with students at West German universities both the Nazi past and the country's future. It seems that Bridenthal's leftist family also left primarily for political reasons, encouraged by friends who had no illusions about the character of the Nazi regime.[41]

The second category of second-generation refugees fled the country, often after very bad experiences in school, not for political reasons, but as Jews from middle-class backgrounds scrambling to escape Nazi racism. They had developed very strong feelings of aversion to Germany during the war that spilled over into the early postwar period. They had also tried hard to acquire a new identity and to view themselves as committed Americans, even to the extent of serving in the Armed Forces if, like Peter Paret, Hans Schmitt, or Werner Angress, they were old enough.

However, by the mid-1950s, some of them began to make the transition to a more differentiated view of what had by then become the parliamentary-democratic Federal Republic. They claimed to be supporters of the integration of Europe and to discover within themselves a growing ambivalence. True, they were Americans now, but increasingly they were also conscious of their European roots. It seems, though, that in talking about their European-American attachments, they were not merely identifying with the narratives of a transatlantic community that found itself in a confrontation with the Soviet Bloc. To be sure, they were all anti-Communist, but more of the "Cold War liberal" variety.[42] In the meantime, they had begun to study modern German history, often mentored by the first generation, who guided them, based not only on their own knowledge of the field but also on their memories of the Weimar Republic, toward a better understanding of the complexities of the country in which they, as the second generation of refugee historians, had been born.

For some, such as Stern, it was the encounter with the "Other Germany" that began to change their outlook, even if initially it was still veiled by their Europeanism.[43] As he reports in his memoirs, a crucial moment in his changing views of Germany was his visit to the site that commemorated the failed attempt to overthrow Hitler on 20 July 1944. According to his memoirs, it was at this point that he felt shame for his earlier indiscriminate hatred of the Germans. But it seems that this did not signify the end of his ambivalent feelings. After his first visit in 1950, he was invited four years later to be a guest professor at Berlin's Free University, where he arrived with "mixed emotions" after an exhilarating trip through France. He had a number of very positive meetings with Karl Dietrich Bracher and also with Ralf Dahrendorf, even if they shared his skepticism that the Germans had turned away from authoritarianism towards democracy. Indeed, when he was asked to comment on a survey that the Fulbright Commission conducted on the political views of West German students, he noted that he was rather alarmed at how uninformed and apolitical they were about the past.

There was thus a group of second-generation historians who, while not reconciling themselves immediately after 1945, slowly achieved their rapprochement with West Germany in the 1950s, while remaining vigilant, until, by the 1980s if not before, they concluded that the experiment that the United States initiated in West Germany in 1945–49 had by and large been a success. This assessment was temporarily upset during the late 1960s at the time of the student rebellion, which some of the second generation found very disturbing. Was this a younger cohort that was lapsing back into the irrationalism and violent totalitarian practices of the 1930s? Although some engaged in an energetic push-back both at their home institutions and in Europe, once they had succeeded, they returned to and in fact reinforced their defense of German society and history. Stern, for example, wrote that German history should not "forever be seen exclusively from the perspective of 1933 or 1945." To view National Socialism as the culmination of German history was not only wrong, but "would be to accept Nazism's triumphalism."[44]

The third group of refugee historians of the second generation waited even longer. Some, such as Gay, took until the 1960s, but again it was colleagues whose families had represented the "Other Germany" under Nazism that slowly swayed him in long discussions. As he wrote,[45] "It was the Brachers who supplied the much needed complications that would let me break out of my fixed pattern of response to my native land." About one occasion with them, Gay wrote, "I remember thinking—perhaps even saying—Why, you lost more members of your family to these barbarians than I did!" He goes on to clarify that he did not mean to argue that "the discovery of good Germans depended on a quantitative comparison, as though the fate of millions could be reduced to a body count," adding "I do not want to defend it. I can only say that this is how I felt. I must have been ready to listen."

This chapter has tried to conceptualize the issue of generations and its uses in this volume. It has also attempted to categorize the intellectual journeys that members of the second generation of German-Jewish refugee historians took after their escape from persecution and death. Three questions remain at the end. The first one concerns the problem of explaining how and how far they became reconciled with the history and the society that had traumatized them as children and young adults. Was it the growing wisdom of age, their scholarly immersion in the complexities of German history, the influence of the first generation and of their parents—who avoided the feelings of hatred because they had known another, pre-1933 Germany that the second generation recovered only in careful academic studies and long discussions during their visits to Germany—or the larger ideological framework in which the European-American relationship evolved, with Germany becoming more and more deeply integrated into it? To assert that it was all of the above may be the easy way out. The task of research in this field therefore is to see if these factors can be more carefully weighted.

Second, there is the point that all members of the second generation wrote their books and articles in English, even if some of them were translated into German. This may be because it was the easier language for them to handle. But there seems to have been another impetus: their decision to be American citizens and a sense of obligation to make the history of Germany in all its complexities available to an English-speaking readership as a warning against what happens if a constitution with its guarantee of civil liberties and a parliamentary-democratic order is abandoned and destroyed. They were therefore not merely always sensitive to right-wing and neo-Nazi stirrings in West Germany, but also observed American society closely for similar phenomena. The transmission of their message occurred in different academic settings. The "Mosse Milieu" at Madison was more liberal–social democratic, the intellectual climate at Columbia and Yale more liberal-conservative.[46] But all of them underwent a long-term learning process, even to the extent of admitting that at some points—for example, during the 1960s—mistakes in assessing the situation were made. As Stern put it, "In my dismay at the violent strain among West German students at that time, I may have thought too little about what provoked them: the rigidity of academic structures and the entrenched self-interest of the privileged, authoritarian professoriate."[47]

Thus, the second generation lived through traumatic experiences, and it also underwent a learning process in which their study of history played a major role. Some of them took long detours into other fields of historical writing, such as English or French early modern history. Some turned to German history right away, but more likely to periods prior to the twentieth century; others moved towards it more slowly and took detours into other regions of Europe or turned toward more general phenomena, such as nationalism or fascism. Perhaps significantly, most of them took longest to begin to work on German-Jewish history in the strict sense and to contemplate the experience of their group under National Socialism.[48] An exception, it seems, was Carsten who—as will be recalled—saw himself as a political refugee. He did not touch, as many colleagues in his generation, the history of German Jewry, but of the German working class in which he had once invested his political hopes for the future and that had moved from resistance to collaboration once the Nazi regime was firmly in the saddle.

In conclusion, I would like to come back to the first paragraph of this essay and the question of agency in a different way. As I was reading about the second generation of German-Jewish refugee historians, it was striking how strong their sense of being was—to quote the title of Hans Schmitt's book—"Lucky Victim[s]."[49] This they no doubt were in comparison to Berger's second generation, whose parents had survived the Nazi camps. But they were also fortunate to have escaped those horrors themselves when they fled from Germany in the 1930s to grow up in the United States during a period of prosperity and an opening of the system of higher education that enabled them, perhaps in Pareto fashion, to embark upon successful careers. In the process, they had been confronted with structures that profoundly limited their agency, even if they were not completely bereft of it as they tried to shape their life and their identity. These experiences, it appears, made them particularly conscious of contingency and of the small coincidences that suddenly moved their lives in new and unexpected directions. With age and looking back, they became more aware of these lucky twists and turns in their careers, and this, in turn, may also have helped them gain better understanding of the German situation under National Socialism, when many had the same experience of the unpredictability of the human condition.

Volker R. Berghahn is the Seth Low Professor of History Emeritus at Columbia University. He taught in Britain until 1988, when he moved to Brown University and ten years later to Columbia. He has written widely on modern German history and European-American relations. His *American Big Business in Britain and Germany: A Comparative History of Two "Special Relationships" in the Twentieth Century* was published in 2014. He has now begun to work on a study of influential journalists in Hamburg between 1945 and 1965.

Notes

1. See, e.g., Volker R. Berghahn and Simone Laessig, eds., *Between Structure and Agency: Central European Lives in Comparative Perspective* (New York, 2008). This being a conceptual piece, I will not be able to mention all second-generation refugee historians by name. Given my approach to a small sample, I hope that their experiences and intellectual journeys broadly fit into the frameworks developed below. I would like to thank Renate Bridenthal, Georg Iggers, Marion Kaplan, Andreas Daum, Fritz Stern, Philipp Stelzel, Mark Roseman, Gerhard Weinberg, Merel Leeman, and Marion Berghahn for their helpful comments and criticisms of this essay.
2. See, e.g., Walter Laqueur, *Young Germany: A History of the German Youth Movement* (New York, 1962); Peter Stachura, *The German Youth Movement, 1900–1945: An Interpretative and Documentary History* (London, 1981); Thomas A. Kohut, *A German Generation: An Experiential History of the Twentieth Century* (New Haven, 2012); Uta Poiger, *Jazz, Rock and Rebels: Cold War Politics and American Culture in a Divided Germany* (Berkeley, 2000); Mark Ruff, *The Wayward Flock: Catholic Youth in Postwar West Germany, 1945–1965* (Chapel Hill, 2005); Martin Klimke, *The Other Alliance: Student Protest in West Germany and the United States in the Global Sixties* (Princeton, NJ, 2010).
3. Mark Roseman, ed., *Generations in Conflict: Youth Revolt and Generation Formation in Germany, 1770–1968* (Cambridge, 1995).
4. Ibid., 1.
5. Robert Wohl, *Generation of 1914* (Cambridge, MA, 1979).
6. For the "front generation," still the best in terms of a conceptualization of the veterans associations of the Weimar Republic is Karl Rohe, *Das Reichsbanner Schwarz-Rot-Gold. Ein Beitrag zur Geschichte und Struktur der politischen Kampfverbände zur Zeit der Weimarer Republik* (Düsseldorf, 1966), and now also very good with fresh insights, Benjamin Ziemann, *Contested Memories: Republican War Veterans and Weimar Political Culture* (Cambridge, 2013). See also Hans-Peter Schwarz, *Der konservative Anarchist. Politik und Zeitkritik Ernst Jüngers* (Freiburg, 1962). On gender relations, see Renate Bridenthal et al., eds., *When Biology Became Destiny: Women in Weimar and Nazi Germany* (New York, 1984); Ute Frevert, *Women in German History* (Oxford, 1989), esp. 168–204. On the wartime and postwar generations, see Dirk Moses, *German Intellectuals and the Nazi Past* (Cambridge, 2007); and Helmut Schelsky, *Die skeptische Generation. Eine Soziologie der deutschen Jugend* (Düsseldorf 1957).

7. Karl Mannheim, "The Problem of Generations," in *Essays on the Sociology of Knowledge* (London, 1959), 276–322; quotation 304.
8. Julian Marias, *Generaciones y constellations* (Madrid, 1989). In English: *Generations: A Historical Method*, trans. Harold C. Raley (Tuscaloosa, 1970).
9. Thus Alan B. Spitzer, "The Historical Problem of Generations," *American Historical Review* 78 (1975): 1354, also for the second quotation.
10. Ibid., 1372ff.
11. Roseman, *Generations in Conflict*, 26.
12. Spitzer, "The Historical Problem of Generations," 1356.
13. See Hartmut Lehmann and James Sheehan, eds., *An Interrupted Past: German-Speaking Refugee Historians in the United States After 1933* (Cambridge, 1991). See also Heinz Wolf, *Deutsch-jüdische Emigrationshistoriker in den USA und der Nationalsozialismus* (Bern, 1988); Gerhard A. Ritter, "Meinecke's Protégés: German Émigré Historians Between Two Worlds," *Bulletin of the German Historical Institute* 39 (Fall 2006): 23–38; James J. Sheehan, "Three Generations of German Gelehrtenpolitik," *Bulletin of the German Historical Institute* 39 (Fall 2006): 39–43; Marianne Hassler and Jürgen Wertheimers, eds., *Der Exodus aus Nazideutschland* (Tübingen, 1997); Allan Mitchell, *Fleeing Nazi Germany: Five Historians Migrate to America* (Trafford, 2011), and the contributions by Catherine Epstein and Hanna Holborn Gray in this volume.
14. Hans Jaeger, "Generationen in der Geschichte," *Geschichte und Gesellschaft* 3, no. 4 (1977): 446.
15. A. L. Berger, *Children of Job: American Second-Generation Witnesses to the Holocaust* (New York, 1997). See also Helen Epstein, *Children of the Holocaust: Conversations with Sons and Daughters of Survivors* (New York, 1979).
16. Walter Laqueur, *Generation Exodus: The Fate of Young Jewish Refugees from Nazi Germany* (Hanover, NH, 2001).
17. Berger, *Children of Job*, 24.
18. See, with reference to the difficulties West Germans had with the Nazi past, Volker R. Berghahn, "The Unmastered and the Unmasterable Past," *Journal of Modern History* 63, no. 3 (1991): 546–54.
19. Albert Friedlander, *Riders Towards the Dawn: From Ultimate Despair to Temperate Hope* (London, 1993).
20. Berger, *Children of Job*, 189, also for the following.
21. Monika Richarz, ed., *Jewish Life in Germany: Memoirs from Three Centuries*, trans. Stella P. Rosenfeld and Sidney Rosenfeld (Bloomington, IN, 1991).
22. Marion Berghahn, *Continental Britons: German-Jewish Refugees from Nazi Germany* (Oxford, 1988), esp. ch. 1 and 2.
23. Renate Bridenthal in her contribution to this volume. Andreas Daum has put together a list of all German-Jewish refugee historians who came to the United States; see his biobibliographic guide at the end of this volume. This list includes a number of women whose lives and careers are also included in the broader arguments of this essay. Insofar as they hailed from Austria, such as Gerda Lerner, they pose no particular problem, for I also relied on the memoirs of Klemens von Klemperer, whose youth and later career was also rather complex. See his *Voyage through the Twentieth Century: A Historian's Recollections and Reflections* (New York, 2009). However, the question of inclusion arises in the case of historians who came, like Bell, from Czechoslovakia. Finally, mention should be made of two women who were spouses but also historians and played an important role as collaborators and critics of their husbands: Wilma Iggers, who came from Czechoslovakia, and Ruth Gay. Wilma even wrote her memoirs jointly with Georg: *Two Lives in Uncertain Times: Facing the Challenges of the 20th Century as Scholars & Citizens* (New York, 2006).
24. See Peter Gay, *My German Question: Growing Up in Nazi Berlin* (New Haven 1998), 50.

25. Daniel Goldhagen, *Hitler's Willing Executioners: Ordinary Germans and the Holocaust* (New York, 1996).
26. Fritz Stern, "The Goldhagen Controversy: One Nation, One People, One Theory?" *Foreign Affairs*, 6 (1996): 128–38, also for the following.
27. Fritz Stern, *Five Germanys I Have Known* (New York, 2006), 302.
28. Gay, *My German Question*, 111, xii, and, on the life of his family in the 1930s, passim.
29. See Frank Bajohr, "Aryanisation" in *Hamburg and Economic Exclusion of Jews and the Confiscation of Their Property in Nazi Germany* (Oxford, 2002).
30. Marion Kaplan, *Between Dignity and Despair: Jewish Life in Nazi Germany* (New York, 1998), 231. See also idem, ed., *Jewish Daily Life in Germany, 1618–1945* (New York, 2005); and Francis Nicosia and David Scrase, eds., *Jewish Life in Nazi Germany* (New York, 2010).
31. Walter Laqueur, *The Missing Years: A Novel* (Boston, 1980), 7, 98–99. See also his *Best of Times, Worst of Times: Memoirs of a Political Education* (Waltham, MA, 2009).
32. See above Walter Laqueur's contribution to this volume.
33. Stern, *Five Germanys*, 187.
34. Wilma and Georg Iggers, *Two Lives*, 29–30 and Georg's contribution to this volume.
35. Conversation with Hans Rosenberg, 13 September 1986. On American public opinion see, e.g., Thomas Reuther, *Die ambivalente Normalisierung. Deutschlanddiskurs und Deutschlandbilder in den USA, 1941–1955* (Stuttgart, 2000). Reconstructing what the second generation read as they grew up in the United States in the 1940s should be a worthwhile exercise. It seems that, apart from reading the *New York Times*, some also dipped into *The Nation* or *The New Republic*. There also seems to have been an interest in anti-German books, while Hans Schmitt, for example, tried to catch up with American novelists, such as Eugene O'Neill, Sinclair Lewis, and Tom Wolfe.
36. See Vilfredo Pareto, *The Rise and Fall of Elites* (New York, 1979).
37. My conversations with Frank Sutton, who was a graduate student at Harvard in the 1930s when Pareto's model of upward mobility and the fate of elites who did not refresh themselves with highly intelligent individuals "from below" were discussed together with Weberian ideas about the dynamics of modern industrial societies. See Volker R. Berghahn, "American Social Scientists and the European-American Dialogue on Social Rights, 1930–1979," in Alice Kessler-Harris and Maurizio Vaudagna, eds., *Democracy and Social Rights in the "Two Wests"* (Turin, 2009), 67–89, esp. 70–71. Harriet Zuckerman recalled that Robert Merton attended a Pareto seminar at Harvard and even took up Italian in order to be able to read the sociologist. Apart from a few Harvard professors and Merton, Kingsley Davis, George Homans (still an undergraduate), and Talcott Parsons (then still an instructor) were among the participants. Harriet Zuckerman to author, 30 December 2010 (Berghahn archive).
38. Merel Leeman is writing a dissertation at Amsterdam University on Gay.
39. Theodore S. Hamerow, *Remembering a Vanished World: A Jewish Childhood in Interwar Poland* (New York, 2001), 77. See also idem, "Guilt, Redemption, and the Writing of German History," *American Historical Review* 88, no. 1 (1983): 53–72.
40. See the biographical sketch in Volker R. Berghahn and Martin Kitchen, eds., *Germany in the Age of Total War* (London, 1981), 7–22.
41. See Bridenthal's contribution to this volume.
42. See Volker R. Berghahn, *America and the Intellectual Cold Wars in Europe* (Princeton, NJ, 2001), 108ff.
43. Stern, *Five Germanys*, 176, and for the description of his trip to Germany, ibid., 208ff. Walter Laqueur apparently never shared this optimistic view of the European experiment. In fact his analyses of developments have become gloomier and gloomier. See, e.g., his *The Last Days of Europe: Epitaph for an Old Continent* (New York, 2007).
44. Stern, *Five Germanys*, 271.

45. Gay, *My German Question*, 196ff.
46. See Paul Breines, "The Mosse Milieu," in Paul Buhle, ed., *History and the New Left: Madison, Wisconsin, 1950–1970* (Philadelphia, 1990), 246–51.
47. Stern, *Five Germanys*, 275–76.
48. For an analysis of these scholarly trajectories that, unlike Carsten's, culminated in books on German Jews and memoirs, see Volker R. Berghahn, "Deutschlandbilder in der amerikanischen Geschichtswissenschaft, 1945–1965," in Ernst Schulin, ed., *Deutsche Geschichtswissenschaft nach dem Zweiten Weltkrieg* (Munich, 1989), 239–72. In the British context, George Mosse's cousin Werner is a good example. He became an expert on Russian history and also wrote on great power politics in the mid-nineteenth century. It was only later that he turned to the history of German Jews and even wrote a book whose title may not have been entirely uncontroversial: Werner Mosse, *The German-Jewish Economic Elite, 1820–1935* (Oxford, 1989). However, it was perhaps also another sign of changing times that he felt free to tackle this subject. Klaus Epstein started as a historian of Britain before moving into German history, partly it seems because he was advised that there was little future in offering courses in German history. Finally, Gerda Lerner, who hailed from Austria, concentrated on American history, where she had a major influence on the creation of the Organization of American Historians and the development of gender history.
49. Hans Schmitt, *Lucky Victim: An Ordinary Life in Extraordinary Times, 1933–1946* (Baton Rouge, 1989).

Part III

ÉMIGRÉS AND THE WRITING OF HISTORY

Chapter 12

THE TENSIONS OF HISTORICAL *WISSENSCHAFT*

The Émigré Historians and the Making of German Cultural History

Steven E. Aschheim

> "Whoever deals with the past, will always have to confront himself"
> —*Reinhart Koselleck*

During the 1960s and in the decades following, the historians Peter Gay (1923–2015), Walter Laqueur (1921), George Mosse (1918–1999), and Fritz Stern (1926) virtually reinvented German cultural and intellectual history and recast our understanding of it. I want to approach this theme comparatively by contrasting their novel cultural and intellectual approach with the more or less simultaneous emergence of a new, committed "social" history developed in Germany by young German historians (exemplified by Hans-Ulrich Wehler, Jürgen Kocka, brothers Hans and Wolfgang Mommsen, Martin Broszat, Heinrich Winkler, Wolfgang Schieder, and others). This will hopefully shed light not only on the biographical influences on the production of historical knowledge but also on the ways in which different ethnonational identities, generations, and geographical locations tend to color our biases and nudge historical emphases in one direction or another. It may perhaps also shed light—rather unexpectedly—on what, somewhat clumsily, has become known as "the German-Jewish" dialogue. In its post–second World War guise, that dialogue, I suggest, becomes especially

---

Notes from this chapter begin on page 192.

interesting not when the differences are great and obvious, but when, at least on the surface, they appear to be almost nonexistent. Indeed, it becomes most intriguing when the tensions are largely unacknowledged and unspoken (perhaps even unconscious), when the discursive differences and relationships are at their most subtle. It is then that the charged moral, emotional, and intellectual stakes around the German and Jewish pasts become paradoxically most apparent.[1]

It is, of course, a truism to state that the modern German past is a particularly explosive, emotionally loaded subject, one peculiarly prone to all kinds of interested projections and transferences. Thus Peter Gay writes, "And the German historian, however bravely he attempts to see the whole picture and to see it plain . . . is bound to be emotionally involved in, and often crippled by his materials. He, more than most historians, is exposed to the risk that psychoanalysts, wary of permitting their work to be distorted by feelings of affection or aversion toward their analysands, call counter-transference. The writing of German history is laden with, mainly unexamined, counter-transferences."[2] But, at first glance, the schools under investigation here may appear as particularly inappropriate exemplifications of these tendencies. After all, all the authors I have mentioned must be considered postwar "good guys." Both groups defined themselves squarely within the liberal or Social Democratic progressive camps. Their reconfigurations of German history sought to throw off the apologetic yoke of a nationalist, politically and methodologically conservative *Zunft* (guild). The social and cultural historians alike were galvanized by the need to overcome the idealist, historicist tradition (one could, after all, hardly compose an empathic epic narrative of the Third Reich or identify with it) and to evaluate the past in essentially distanced, critical terms.[3] Above all, their commonalities sprang from, and were animated by, a single great quest: to comprehend the unprecedented rise and nature of Nazism.

To be sure, earlier on within Germany, the patricians of the *Zunft*, Friedrich Meinecke and Gerhard Ritter[4] (to name but the most prominent), and Hannah Arendt[5] from without, had also undertaken such investigations. For them, indigenous German traditions and developments played only a minor role in explaining the etiology and disposition of National Socialism; the real causes (and blame) were deflected outward onto post-1789 Europe, where the origins of a formless mass society and totalitarian democracy were to be found. To be sure, the case of Meinecke is more complex than stated here. His account did include a critique of certain aspects of the Prussian tradition and the German *Bürgertum* (middle class). Still, it rested upon the assumption of the superiority of the high humanist German cultural tradition—Nazism was a symptom of its collapse. The reconstitution of Germany rested upon renewing its Goethean cultural splendor. Nevertheless, the German catastrophe derived mainly from external sources. The victims of the catastrophe were Germans rather than those singled out by Nazism. Indeed, the Jews are here pictured as naggingly complicit in the resentment they evoked. There is no discussion of the "Final Solution" (*Endlösung*) as such.[6]

Both the social and the cultural-intellectual historians rejected these accounts as defensive and apologetic, and insisted upon intimately linking the Third Reich to immanent elements of German society itself. Both, each in their own ways, indeed formulated what became a kind of historical orthodoxy: the critical *Sonderweg* version of German history. This (by now familiar) narrative held that modern German historical and political development was fatefully peculiar, illiberal, and misshapen. It argued that an obstinately and anachronistically authoritarian society would bring forth Nazism as the extreme manifestation, the last fruits of a foiled and disfiguring modernization process. (Like all orthodoxies, this was eventually to be seriously challenged, and even revised by some of the proponents themselves—but, for present purposes, that is beside the point.)[7]

Given the rather basic commonalities between the social and the cultural historians, what is at issue? Built into all historical methods and approaches will be certain principles of selection, emphases, and omissions. They will, consciously or unconsciously, contain numerous narrative biases, interpretive strategies, and ideological preferences.[8] I would like to argue here that despite their surface similarities, the more or less simultaneous emergence in the 1960s of the increasingly influential, tone-setting school of the social history of modern Germany, and the less studied and remarked[9] émigré cultural-intellectual equivalent, represent significantly different, emotionally fraught confrontations with a traumatizing past. I will try to show here how their respective biographies, group membership, geographical location, and generational experiences played a crucial role in shaping both these historiographies, and argue that they reflect divergent experiences and interests that go far beyond mere methodological differences. The catalyst for much of the new history (of both kinds) was the Fritz Fischer affair. This was not only a battle of generations but one in which the younger critical social and cultural historians emerged and seemed to entirely agree that the German past was a deeply problematic one and that its problems and responsibilities could not be deflected outwards. Fritz Stern played a major role in this controversy. Yet, despite this apparent affinity, there was a subtle lack of reciprocity not in terms of personal relations or scholarly contact but regarding incorporation into the works themselves. What I am suggesting is that, at some—not always conscious (and almost never explicit)—level these can be also be read as interested "German" and "Jewish" counter-narratives, histories written within or beyond the geographical limits and mental boundaries of the Federal Republic, divergent readings of a contested and threatening past.[10]

Both groups focus on the same period (the Kaiserreich through the end of the Weimar Republic); both seek to grasp the historical roots of Nazism; both end up with some kind of *Sonderweg* thesis. Yet, their respective foci, the centers of attention, were strikingly different. The German social historians were overwhelmingly concerned with the conditions that resulted in the collapse of the Weimar Republic; their works analyzed in great detail the social, economic, and political structures that eventuated in the breakdown of democratic rule.[11] Their great symbolic date, the major event to be explained (and overcome), is 1933.[12] This date is also important for the cultural historians, but for them the implicit epicenter, the nodal point, the scandal in need of accounting, is 1942. Although (certainly at the beginning) they seldom directly dealt with the Holocaust per se, their emphasis on ideology, stereotypes, antisemitism, cultural breakdown, and the complex machinations of German-Jewish relations rendered that event as historically—one might say ontologically—crucial. For the social historians, if I may put it this way, the *Sonderweg* was the collapse of liberal democracy; for the cultural historians, it was antisemitism, genocide, and related Nazi atrocities. The two may have been related, but they were neither conceptually nor existentially identical.

I am aware that defining these as "German" and "Jewish"—or "home" versus "refugee"—narratives is problematic. In the first place, if anyone adopted a highly critical attitude to their own national past, it was the German social historians. That, indeed, was their defining credo. It is clear, too, that the German-Jewish distinction, apart from its potentially essentialist connotations, blurs an important datum: the cultural historians all heralded from highly acculturated, if not fully assimilated, liberal German backgrounds. Walter Laqueur's experience was typical: "My education," he writes, "was not Jewish, I did not attend a Jewish school, and most of my early friends were not Jewish either. I knew little about Judaism and was not particularly interested in the subject." Yet Laqueur adds, "It would not have occurred to me to deny that I was Jewish." Given Nazi policy, he writes, there was not so much an "identity" but rather a common bond arising from past and present persecution. Finding oneself in the same boat "was quite sufficient for me at a time when introspection had not the highest order of priority."[13] It is thus certainly not my intention to simplistically reduce the respective historiography of my subjects to their national provenance. After all, the early functional-structural study of Nazism was formulated by Ernst Frankel and Franz Neumann, and an important pioneer of German social history was Hans Rosenberg—all German-Jewish émigrés, while certain postwar German historians, such as Thomas Nipperdey and Reinhart Koselleck, demonstrated a fine sensitivity to the cultural and ideational dimensions of their history. It would thus be absurd to argue that these German social historians and the Jewish cultural historians were somehow determined—ethnically driven—to argue in the way they did. What I am suggesting, however, is that divergent experiential, situational, and identificatory factors played an important role in the genesis, nature, and emphases of their work and that any assessment of their respective achievements and biases, their historical location and legacy, will have to take these dimensions into account.

My main concern here will be the émigré historians, but, for purposes of comparison, let me briefly outline some of the history, contributions, and assumptions of the social historians. They indeed formed part of an admirable, self-conscious generation of German left-liberal public intellectuals—the names Jürgen Habermas, Günter Grass, Ralf Dahrendorf, Rainer Lepsius, and Walter Jens spring immediately to mind—a self-constituted, by now patriarchal, elite who, for over thirty years, shaped much of the intellectual, cultural, and perhaps even political tone of the Bundesrepublik.[14] It is largely they who created its intensely critical atmosphere, insisted upon a radical break from the country's questionable past, and contributed to the creation and maintenance of its constitutional, democratic norms.[15]

In retrospect, it seems clear to me that their historical emphases—on 1933, foiled and failed modernization processes, and the stubborn hold of authoritarian and conservative structures—reflected an urgent concern just as much with the contemporary and forward-looking needs of the nascent Bundesrepublik as with the past.[16] Their great concern, the imperative of the hour, was the democratic shaping of the Federal Republic. History was mobilized to learn the lessons of the failures of German democracy in the recent past. Reformist and democratic inclinations thus clearly and legitimately entered their historiographical quest. But there were also other biographical circumstances that, in some way or another, were bound to leave a more problematic imprint.

This was a generation born between 1925 and 1938. All its members were young enough to experience growing up in the Third Reich. The Second World War and ensuing total defeat occurred, for the most part, between their fifteenth and twenty-second year. They were too young to be at the front, but they were, inevitably, socialized into National Socialist institutions; some, at the end of the war, became *Flakhelfer*, even members of the Party.[17] There was, of course, nothing exceptional in all of this—this was the fate of all German citizens during this period. Like many other Germans, those who were destined to become historians also had to grapple with the fact that their parents and teachers, family and friends, were—in various ways and degrees—somehow implicated in Nazi society and policy.

What I am suggesting here is that this issue of the implicated "parents"—both literal and metaphorical[18]—has immediate relevance to the kind of social history that these historians subsequently produced. The rise of social history in the 1960s was, of course, a general phenomenon in the world of Western historiography. This undoubtedly also facilitated its prominence in Germany, but, in the light of that country's charged past, it assumed a specific coloring, one particularly suited to contemporary psychopolitical needs. For an extraordinary and uniquely German tension helped to shape a species of social history that was at once skeptical and protective. The putatively progressive, new paradigm of German social history sought somehow to negotiate and integrate this strangely conflicted situation: a highly critical, reformist impulse with an unacknowledged, perhaps unconscious, filial loyalty. Wehler has recently rendered this tension explicit: "We owe loyalty to the dead with whom we spent good years—but also in tension to another loyalty—the victims and the persecuted."[19] The structural and systemic history of the kind practiced by this generation of social historians encoded, but also contained and domesticated, this tension.[20] Retrospectively, this brand of social history can be read as a kind of (subtle and not necessarily conscious) navigation exercise: formulating a necessarily critical narrative of the past while at the same time leaving questions of personal complicity and ideological and intellectual convictions relatively untouched. A certain lip service is paid to ideational and ideological factors, but these tend to be either relegated or disappear entirely as explanatory factors of analysis. Thus intentions and convictions are effectively displaced as factors of historical action. An approach that placed transpersonal structures and processes and curiously bloodless social formations at the center and that typically gave short shrift to the role of particular events and personalities, to culture and ideology, was admirably suited to fill this mediating function.[21] As Hartmut Lehmann strikingly put it, many chose "to discuss problems of social history and structural history, as if deliberately to evade questions of moral responsibility and guilt."[22] Many of these works read like, and functioned as, "neutralized" productions.[23] The mechanics of process and the forces of structure seemed to overwhelm events and intentionality.[24] Paul Nolte has tellingly noted that the image of society created in this mold is curiously devoid of "history" and indeed becomes a kind of substitute for it.[25]

The émigré German-Jewish cultural-intellectual historians viewed matters in quite different ways. Of course, the experiential and biogenerational links to their work are both more obvious and (I would argue) less problematic than the German social historians. Of course, this does not render their personal or professional profiles less interesting or complex. Peter Gay, Walter Laqueur, George Mosse, and Fritz Stern have all by now, in one way or another, published memoir material in which the match between their forced emigration and historiography, their works and lives, is clear enough.[26] They were never, to be sure, a coherent or academically organized group (such as the Bielefeld School of German social historians). There was only one institutional link between them: Mosse and Laqueur were the founders and, for many years, the editors of the London-based *Journal of Contemporary History*. In the main, however, these historians pursued their own separate careers, and their personal relations proceeded on a spectrum ranging from close friendship to thinly veiled dislike. Nevertheless, the experiential, generational, and conceptual commonalities of their projects seems clear, and that is what I shall emphasize here (it awaits a later study to underline the individual richness, variety, obvious and important differences, and problems in their respective oeuvres). To be sure, neither their work nor their persons can or should be limited or reduced to their émigré experience. Their range makes this apparent. Of the four, Fritz Stern has remained most closely within the ambit of German cultural and political history; Mosse and Gay can rightly be considered as historians of a much wider "European" experience, while Walter Laqueur—thus far not given sufficient consideration, perhaps because of his autodidacticism and his only occasional formal attachments to university positions—has written extremely broadly on topics far removed from German and West European history. His works encompass tracts on the Soviet Union and Russian history, the Middle East, the history of Zionism, terrorism, guerilla warfare, and international relations.[27]

Whatever their differences, the commonalities are clear. Although theirs is a cohort slightly older than the social historians—they were born between 1918 and 1926—their early lives, too, were indelibly shaped by the breakdown of Weimar democracy and the advent of Nazism. But here, of course, their stories diverge, for all were (or were considered to be) Jews. All were forced to become refugees/exiles/émigrés—the choice of appellation is significant, for the reactions of these historians to this event were very different. Peter Gay and Fritz Stern regarded this experience with a sense of deep lingering resentment. In his memoir, *My German Question*, Gay speaks of it as "the story of a poisoning and how I dealt with it," and Stern states, "I was no freer than others of hatred for what Germans had done,"[28] while for Laqueur and Mosse it was, ironically, akin to liberation, an opening up to the world. "The loss of my native country at the age of seventeen," Laqueur writes, "hurt me considerably less than the loss of those I loved. Perhaps I felt, even vaguely, that the Nazis were leading the country to ruin and that the place where I was born and grown up would be lost in any case. If my country did not want me, I was reasonably sure that I could find my place elsewhere."[29] Mosse describes his last journey in Germany, as a fourteen-year-old from an exceedingly wealthy home, thusly: "Despite everything I regarded this journey not as something sad, as a blow of fate, no, I was happy to be able to see new places, ready for new adventures." Many years later he reflected that "even today I do not see this as a blow of fate, but rather as merciful providence. . . . Why such a way of thinking that goes against all clichés of Exile? Because exile tore me from wealth and left me no other choice but to make myself."[30]

However differently they may have experienced it, Nazism indelibly marked all their lives. As Gay put it, "More than a half-century after the collapse of Hitler's Thousand Year Reich, every surviving refugee remains to some extent one of his victims. In recent years, the status of victim has become widely popular, I know, exploited to elicit sympathy and sustain claims for reparation. I make no such demands. My point is a simple factual one: even the most fortunate Jew who lived under Hitler has never completely shaken off that experience."[31] Indeed, it is important to note that, like Gay, none of these historians have defined themselves as "survivors" or claimed "victim" status.

This group shared other defining characteristics. "All," as Jerry Z. Muller notes, "were all old enough to have experienced the rise and regime of Nazism but young enough to complete their studies abroad," and thus cultivated the "ability to speak and write both German and English with style and verve, a talent that is difficult to acquire for those who move into a new linguistic culture after adolescence."[32] (The first generation of émigré historians, Felix Gilbert, Hajo Holborn, Hans Rothfels, Veit Valentin, Arthur and Hans Rosenberg, and Gustav Meyer, we should note, were all trained within Germany itself.)[33]

All these historians underwent significant transformations of identifications and identities. The different nuances are interesting: Fritz Stern went on to embody a kind of critical yet sympathetic commitment to both (a reformed) Germany and the USA and the dialogue between them; Laqueur, with his Israeli, British, and American career, retains perhaps the most internationalist profile; and while Peter Gay described his integration into his new homeland as "a beneficent transformation" and demonstratively entitled one of his papers "At Home in America,"[34] a series of 1991 interviews with Mosse was published under the name *Ich Bleibe Emigrant* (I Remain an Emigrant).[35] Upon his migration to Palestine, Walter Laqueur added Ze'ev as his middle name; Gerhard became George Mosse, and, most enthusiastically, Peter Joachim Froehlich became Peter Jack Gay.[36]

"I believe," writes Walter Laqueur, "that I understood Germany better than France or Britain, even though I have spent much more time there than in Germany. This is largely a matter of instinct, of feeling in one's bones how people will react in a certain situation. But what is instinct? A little inspiration based on experience."[37] Their peculiar circumstances thus allowed these younger historians to combine tacit understanding of, and an inside feel for, German society (comprising not only high but also popular culture; as Laqueur reminds us, "Henry Kissinger or Peter Gay . . . would be able to recite fifty years later the composition of a leading German or Austrian team confronting England or Hungary or Italy"[38] with the measured distance of an external perspective. One positive legacy of exile, Mosse proclaimed, was a certain sense of overall "outsiderdom," which enabled the historian to bring to bear alternative perspectives.[39] "Perhaps," Fritz Stern reflected, "I gradually acquired something like bifocal views—others might call it impaired vision: I tend to see things German with American eyes, and things American also with German eyes."[40]

Experience encouraged a kind of insider-outsider perspective, one that crossed and, at times, transgressed physical and conceptual borders rather than being fixed within them. For instance, George Mosse's penchant for hilarity, his eye for the exotic and the outrageous, and his ongoing, always provocative critique of "normalcy" and "respectability" were clearly related to a personal awareness of a marginal Jewishness and homosexuality—but his deliberate cultivation of outsiderdom was also obviously related to a more general location beyond or between these German and American (and Israeli) borders. Mosse's drive to critique respectability—and often to do so in hilarious ways—is well known. "I like to provoke," he writes, "to break taboos, but purely theoretically . . . to get people to think—not in the practice of daily life."[41]

These, then, were the young émigrés who would go on to invent a new kind of cultural and intellectual history—unburdened by the obvious inadequacies of traditional idealist assumptions and historicist methods—able to shed novel light upon, and place into different perspective, the history of modern Germany and the shock of Nazism. To be sure, there was a period of latency. Before turning to German history (in the 1960s), most first pursued other academic interests partly out of a need to more firmly establish their new careers and identities, partly because they—like others around them—were not yet psychically and socially ready for such a confrontation. In the 1950s, as has been well documented, it was not polite to talk of such things.[42] These historians explored other fields. Fritz Stern edited a work on general trends in historiography;[43] Mosse first acquired his reputation as a leading scholar of early modern English history and the Reformation;[44] Laqueur published works on Communism and the Middle East; and Peter Gay concentrated at first on the Enlightenment and American history (it is true that he wrote his doctoral dissertation, which he later published, on Eduard Bernstein, the German Social Democratic theorist, but he did so at the time expressly because "Bernstein had been an outsider to German society both as a Jew and as a Marxist").[45]

Eventually, however, they all turned, in one way or another and in varying degrees of intensity, to the investigation of their own troubled German past. When—in their new homes—these émigrés did so, they instinctively turned to "culture" (in its broadest sense) as an explanatory key, to ideology and issues of self-definition and identity under crisis, not only because they were aware of the enormous power of these forces within National Socialism itself and because they had experienced the weight of these issues directly on their own persons, but also because, as acculturated young German Jews raised in a particular tradition of humanist *Bildung*, they shared the German-Jewish bias for "culture" in the overall human economy. In effect, here was an expression of an inherited sensibility. George Mosse's classic 1983 *German Jews beyond Judaism* is simultaneously an identification, analysis, personal credo, and critique of this mindset and disposition. Moreover, it is clear that these authors were not simply disinterested diagnosticians but were themselves exemplifications of that open cultural and experimental intellectual sprit they sought to convey.

If, across the border, these scholars were in some way the repositories and mediators of the legacy and the traditions they analyzed—presumably a source of the attractiveness these European scholars possessed for many of their American students[46]—they also engaged in criticism of this overestimation of culture. As Laqueur put it in his *Weimar Culture*, "German writers, including Thomas Mann and other leading spirits of the age, tended to attribute too much significance to *Bildung*; it dawned on them only gradually that illiterate people could be humanists and democrats by instinct whereas highly educated men could advocate cannibalistic ideologies and even become commanders of SS Einsatzgruppen."[47] This was cultural and intellectual history that operated against the idealist current, critical of various aspects of both culture and intellectuals and yet always convinced of the motivating importance of meaning-bestowing ideas and symbolism in human affairs. This became most clearly and classically apparent in Stern's *Politics of Cultural Despair* and Mosse's *Crisis of German Ideology* (both published in the early sixties). These works outline the machinations and fantasies of middle-range pamphleteers and publicists in the formulation of a (late) nineteenth-century counter-liberal *Völkisch* (ethnic) ideology and trace the multiple ways in which this semimystic, organic nationalist Weltanschauung penetrated German politics and informed various strands of its high and popular culture. [48] This also applies to Mosse and Laqueur's probings of the myopia of the youth movements and misjudgments of the educated and politically active intellectual classes, Stern's critique of the "Unpolitical German," and Peter Gay's dissection of the consequences of the "hunger for wholeness."[49]

In all this, the innovative nature of their enterprise became increasingly apparent. In their reinvention of German cultural and intellectual history, these émigrés veered away from both the historicist legacy and the rationalist "history of ideas" tradition (a fact either not registered or understood by the social historians, who, while willfully ignoring their work, continued to label and dismiss *Kulturgeschichte* (cultural history) according to its superseded conservative pedigree). Because these émigré historians had experienced Nazism and gone beyond the border, no trace of the epic, empathic, and idealist historicist narrative could be found amongst them. Rather, they radically enlarged the meaning, definition, and scope of the "cultural." No longer was the concept reserved for matters high and cultivated; rather it became broadly "anthropological." Mosse defined culture, in its Western historical context, extensively "as a state or habit of mind which is apt to become a way of life intimately linked to the challenges and dilemmas of contemporary society."[50] In this guise, cultural and intellectual history was no longer purely elite-oriented—and when it was, it was largely critical—but extended to a vast range of aspects of popular culture previously untouched: the content and diffusion of racism and stereotypes; strategies of class and religious, national, ethnic, and (later with Mosse) sexual inclusion and exclusion; antisemitism; and political myths and mass symbolism.[51]

Moreover, the work of these cultural historians betrayed few signs of a detached Lovejoyian "chain of ideas" that somehow floated above the historical process. These were always context-sensitive presentations, rooted in particular historical circumstances. For example, the emergence and percolation of *völkisch* ideology as a habit of thought, feeling, and perception was closely tied to crises of the Kaiserreich, analyzed as a response, generated by the perplexities and singularities of the German modernization experience during the latter part of the nineteenth century, and radicalized and reinforced by World War I and its traumatic aftermath. These were not presented as epiphenomena, mere reflections of class and other material interests, but active (and interactive) forces in their own right.[52]

Given the catastrophic and unprecedented nature of their subject matter, these historians—precisely because they were liberals and men of the Enlightenment—were constrained to deal with material usually quite foreign to students of the mind and, in so doing, virtually reinvented the study of German cultural and intellectual history.

For the émigrés, Nazism and genocide rendered "irrationalism"—and the history of "irrationalism"—as the basic problem and issue, as an essential, and indeed extremely appealing, driving force of mass culture and politics. They plumbed the histories of the late nineteenth and early twentieth century in search of its manifold manifestations and sought to account for their genesis and dynamics. Indeed, they became its master analysts, dissecting its various forms and trajectories. Stern's reflections on his own work applies equally to the other émigré historians discussed here: "I only wanted to emphasize that history must scientifically and rationally also research the role of the irrational, that these factors are just as real, true and objective as the interest-politics of industry or the claims of the military or the bureaucracy."[53] As opposed to the social historians, the subjects of their history were endowed with ideas, prejudices, myths, stereotypes, emotions, and, indeed, minds (even, perhaps especially, when these sometimes went astray).

We have already adverted to the fact that while the social historians in Germany more or less excluded the cultural, experiential, and phenomenological from their purview, this German-Jewish émigré group placed such issues at the center. It was, after all, at this immediate ideological and existential level that they had also personally experienced these events. Perhaps, additionally, when it came to issues related to National Socialism, German Jews, both because they were above suspicion and beyond the border, could openly address these ideological issues, the putative magnetism of right-wing radicalism and Nazi politics, in a way that would have been taboo for Germans in Germany. Concerning the content and attraction of such ideas, it was better to be mute and discrete.[54] George Mosse, on the other hand, felt free to, and often would, describe to his students the tremendous personal and group appeal of the myths of German nationalism and the pull of Nazi mass meetings. In his memoirs, he describes how his school at Salem "gave me a first taste of nationalism, which at the time I found congenial; there was a danger that it might provide the belief system that I so badly lacked. . . . When as a historian much later I wrote about German nationalism, I did have an insight into its truly seductive nature."[55] When he was about fifteen years old, he watched a Nazi demonstration in front of his home in Berlin. "The impression was so great," he later recalled, "that I ran away from home, it must have been in 1932, and went to a Hitler rally. I must admit, even today, that it was an experience. I was swept away. First there were the masses of people; that was very captivating to be in the middle of it all. But it was also Hitler."[56] Fritz Stern has claimed that as a "victim," he is able to say what few German historians could allow themselves to say. In his lecture on "National Socialism as Temptation," he was able to cheerfully acknowledge that he was saved from that temptation by dint of not being a full-blooded Aryan.[57]

Clearly then, this reconfiguration of modern German cultural and intellectual history reflected, to some degree, the personal memories and trajectory of its creators. "I vividly remember the speeches," Laqueur has written, "the demonstrations, the torchlight parades that hailed the dawn of the new era. The teachers told us, with varying degrees of conviction, what bliss it was to be alive in that dawn." "Gibbon," he commented later, "once said that his service as captain of the Hampshire grenadiers had not been useless to the historian of the Roman Empire; attending school from 1933 to 1938 was of use to the future student of the Third Reich and totalitarianism."[58]

The émigré scholars were of course particularly sensitive to the changing forms and functions of antisemitism. This, they insisted, was in various ways and degrees tied into numerous and basic strands of German self-definition. Mosse later extended this historical net to an analysis of the pernicious dynamics of what he termed "bourgeois respectability" and the infiltration of middle-class morality into national self-definition, with its exclusionary constructions of insiders and outsiders, its dichotomies of normalcy and abnormality, health and disease, beauty and ugliness. Startlingly, he proclaimed that "the new man of national socialism was the ideal bourgeois."[59] In his *Nationalism and Sexuality* (1985), the victimization of the Jew remains both central and most extreme but is comprehensible as part of a continuum and dynamic affecting the stereotypical bourgeois creation of other outsiders.[60]

It is clear that the narrative biases of these historians, their emphases on "culture," exclusion, and the ideological dimension, sprang, at least in part, from their liberal Jewish backgrounds and émigré experience. Yet they were careful not to allow dislocating personal experience to warp their viewpoint. They remained acutely aware of the dangers of teleology, and warned against linear history: Auschwitz was not a necessary inscription of an incurably infected past, not inherent in Germany's cultural and political fabric.[61] Peter Gay put it thusly: "To say that the Third Reich was grounded in the German past is true enough; to say that it was the inescapable result of that past, the only fruit that the German tree would grow is false."[62] Rather, with differing emphases, they sought to identity potentialities, the multiple forces and building-blocks that moved the society in the direction it did without ever reducing it to it. Contingency, too, played a role. Thus George Mosse never tired of asserting that if, at the beginning of the twentieth century, one were to predict which Central or West European country would perpetrate a Holocaust against the Jews, the answer, in all likelihood, would have been France!⁶³ It was absolutely crucial to trace the steps that led to Auschwitz—while always remembering that the road there was never simply straight, but twisted and quite unpredictable.

Not surprisingly, these émigrés, more than any other group of scholars, did not limit themselves to the study of antisemitism but sought to grasp the wider history of German-Jewish relations as such, consistently and insistently bringing to light their complex and subtle nature, stressing always the coimplicated nature of the nexus, its ironies, limitations, and problems, but also its achievements, possibilities, and richness. These writings, let me suggest, represent in part a commemorative project written after the catastrophe and in every way from beyond the border. Employing the tools of their historical profession and without indulging in apologetic or so-called contribution history, these emigrants nevertheless sought to restore to German Jewry something of the dignity of their history. This applies not only to their various forays into pre-1933 Germany. Walter Laqueur has become the biographer—in *Generation Exodus: The Fate of Young Jews From Nazi Germany*— of his own generation's collective displacement and relocation, the role of luck in its members survival and their (not always) successful, highly diverse adaptation throughout the world (ranging from stories such as that of Henry Kissinger to a German-Jewish "Benedictine Abbot, Hindu guru, and West African chieftain").⁶⁴

Yet the commemorative seldom lost sight of the critical perspective. Mosse's ironic piece on Jewish internalizations of the *völkisch* idea, Stern's depiction of the intricate and loaded modes of Jewish entry into the higher realms of German economic, political, and scientific life, Gay's ruminations on the complex relations between German Jews and modernism, and Walter Laqueur's biting assessment of the insensitivity and irresponsibility of Jewish radicals such as Kurt Tucholsky represent only a few examples of this kind of work.⁶⁵

None of the émigrés claimed to be internal Jewish historians; they could hardly be said to be familiar with, or particularly interested in, traditional Jewish texts (although Walter Laqueur has not dwelled upon the tradition, he may be a partial exception here. By virtue of his early emigration to Palestine, he is the only one of these historians with a thorough knowledge of Hebrew). In many ways, their liberal, acculturated backgrounds are reflected in their historiographical emphases and accounts. They all exemplify what Dan Diner has called the individualist, emancipated Western European Jewish narrative as against the collective, pre-emancipationist East European Jewish conceptual framework.⁶⁶ For all sought, as it were, to deghettoize Jewish existence while at the same time making European history sensitive to that Jewish presence. As Peter Gay put it, "Jews lived in a world larger than themselves, and just as it is impossible to understand that larger world without its Jews, it is impossible to understand its Jews without that larger world."⁶⁷

Their perspectives were always based upon the same—albeit self-critical—liberal and acculturated *Bildung* assumptions with which they were raised. Perhaps because of this, in differing degrees of intensity they confronted, rejected or, at the very least, modified and refined, or sought to find some saving grace in, the uncompromisingly Zionist terms of Gershom Scholem's tone-setting and highly controversial thesis—that the German-Jewish project, the putative "dialogue" and "symbiosis," had been doomed from the outset and was a purely one-sided delusion.[68] Thus Fritz Stern could comment "that though the 'German-Jewish partnership or collaboration' may have been an illusion, it was an enticing illusion, an illusion productive of greatness."[69] For Mosse, the dialogue (with its ideals of self-cultivation and liberal outlook on society and politics, and based upon the need to transcend the gulf between the history of the Jews and the German tradition) "became an integral part of the European intellectual tradition . . . [and] served to produce a unique heritage for the Jews themselves and for intellectuals all over Europe, but also became a part of the German Jewish identity, infiltrating . . . most aspects of Jewish life in Germany."[70] Similarly, Walter Laqueur has declared that "[w]ithout the Jews there would have been no 'Weimar culture.'"[71]

Peter Gay, of course, has been the most vehement opponent of the Scholem thesis. In his view, Jewish integration was at the very least a partial reality; the rise of Nazism was not inevitable, nor was the Holocaust predictable. Accusing German-Jews of self-delusion, he argues, is really "an attack, an accusation. . . . What Hitler did to the Jews so goes the reproach—they deserved."[72] In this debate, it is difficult to separate historical analysis from personal experience. Thus, Scholem, caustically dismissing his father's belief in the purported symbiosis, reports that he had no real non-Jewish friends nor had any non-Jews ever entered their house. As if in direct riposte, Gay declared that his "father found his closest friends in business and sports, and his professional associates and the soccer players and sprinters he knew and liked were nearly all gentiles. And without the help of some of them, we would probably have ended up in the gas chambers."[73]

It is worth noting parenthetically, however, that whatever their views on Scholem's thesis, their particular refugee and generational experience inclined them toward a certain sympathy for (a liberally conceived) Zionism and the State of Israel. Clearly, the degree and intensity of such a commitment differs considerably amongst them. It is well known that Laqueur and Mosse, though critical of certain aspects of Zionist history and Israeli attitudes, have been actively identified with its political and intellectual life. Laqueur was the only member of this cohort, during the years of Nazism, to emigrate to Palestine, where (before moving on to London and Washington, DC) he spent many years and became a well-known journalist and, later, also taught at Tel Aviv University. He has written extensively on the Middle-East, the Arab-Israel conflict, *A History of Zionism* (1972), and, most recently, a highly informed combination of memoir, history, and contemporary analysis entitled *Jerusalem Beyond Zionism*.[74] With Mosse this commitment is rendered even more powerful by the tensions between his intellectual predispositions and his biographically laden emotional attachment ("a sense of belonging, close even to love," as he put it). Mosse, amongst other things, wrote incisively about and identified with the humanism of the Zionist binationalists. Mosse, to be sure, always questioned conventional conceptual borders, yet his emigrant history rendered palpable the need for secure physical ones. "There was always a certain pull toward realism," he recalled in his memoirs, "to the feeling that if one did not belong to a strong nation one could slide back into the statelessness I had experienced. Thus, an emotional engagement always threatened that liberalism to which I remained faithful." Mosse, moreover, later became one of the great analysts and critics of the discourse and functions of the ideology of masculinity. Yet, confronted in Israel with what he half-mockingly referred to as "Muskeljuden"(Max Nordau's term), the muscular "new Jew," he confessed that this "represented a normalization, an assimilation to general middle-class ideals and stereotypes which otherwise I professed to dislike. But I could not help myself; faced with this Zionist ideal my reason and historical knowledge were overcome."[75]

Stern and Gay too, perhaps more ambivalently and surprisingly, have also revealed their intellectual and emotional investment. Of his 1942 meeting with the Zionist leader and first president of the State of Israel, Chaim Weizmann, Stern wrote, "I have never forgotten that moment. I felt that I was in the presence of a great man with a great, transcending cause." And Gay, perhaps the most assimilationist of these émigré historians, has written—in response to Ernst Nolte—that the latter "has no grasp of the essentially defensive drive for Palestine; no sense that Zionism is an ideal born amidst pogroms and amidst persecutions in which Nolte's countrymen particularly distinguished themselves. . . . Zionism or not, securing the survival of Israel is a moral obligation on the Western world since that world, after all, made that refuge, quite literally, a matter of life and death."[76]

I hope to have shown how and why these émigré scholars turned to certain methodologies and foci of attention in their quest to understand the nature and traumas of modern German and German-Jewish history. Just like their German social historian counterparts, their biographies, personal backgrounds, and experiences nudged them in particular directions, biased them towards certain questions and interpretations, rendered the cultural and ideational dimensions so centrally relevant and significant and made them an absolutely integral part of the ways in which we come to grips with many of the most crucial issues that characterized the German—indeed European—twentieth century.[77]

Steven E. Aschheim is emeritus professor of history at the Hebrew University, Jerusalem, where he held the Vigevani Chair of European Studies. He also served as director of the Franz Rosenzweig Research Center for German Literature and Cultural History. His book publications include *Brothers and Strangers: The East European Jew in German and German-Jewish Consciousness, 1800–1923* (1982), *The*

Nietzsche Legacy in Germany, 1890–1990 (1992), *Culture and Catastrophe: German and Jewish Confrontations with National Socialism and Other Crises* (1996), *In Times of Crisis: Essays on European Culture, Germans and Jews* (2001), *Beyond the Border: The German-Jewish Legacy Abroad* (2007), and *At the Edges of Liberalism: Junctions of European, German and Jewish History* (2012).

Notes

1. This essay is based upon, and a radically shortened version of, chapter 2 of my *Beyond the Border: The German-Jewish Legacy Abroad* (Princeton, NJ, 2007). The epigraph is from Reinhart Koselleck, "Wozu noch Historie? Vortrag auf dem deutschen Historikertag in Köln am 4 April 1970," in Wolfgang Hardtwig, ed., *Über das Studium der Geschichte* (Munich, 1990), 361.
2. See his preface to *Freud, Jews and Other Germans: Masters and Victims in Modernist Culture* (New York, 1978), ix. See also Saul Friedlander, "Trauma and Transference," in *Memory, History, and the Extermination of the Jews of Europe* (Bloomington, 1993), 117–37. Dominick LaCapra has analyzed many of these issues in *Representing the Holocaust: History, Theory, Trauma* (Ithaca, 1994). Of course, with regard to the German-Jewish cultural historians, acknowledged emotional engagement will differ in intensity—compare Peter Gay's highly charged attitude with that of Walter Laqueur as presented in his memoir: "My attitude to Germany has remained markedly unemotional; I have been interested in German affairs since the war, but much of the time I've been even more interested in other countries and cultures." See his *Thursday's Child Has Far to Go: A Memoir of the Journeying Years* (New York, 1992), 105.
3. Sebastian Conrad characterizes historicism thusly: (1) a belief in the "objectivity" of the study of the past that is, however, facilitated by the historian's present standpoint; (2) an idealist conception of history in which ideas are seen as the carrier of historical events; (3) a method in which past events are seen as part of a hidden continuity; (4) an epic form of narrative; (5) whose goal is the construction of a national identity. See his *Auf der Suche nach der verlorenen Nation. Geschichtsschreibung im Westdeutschland und Japan 1945–1960* (Göttingen, 1999), 38.
4. See *The German Problem* (Columbus, 1965). See also the massive study by Christoph Cornelissen, *Gerhard Ritter. Geschichtswissenschaft und Politik im 20 Jahrhundert* (Dusseldorf, 2001).
5. *The Origins of Totalitarianism* (New York, 1951).
6. Friedrich Meinecke, *The German Catastrophe* (Boston, 1950).
7. Since the pioneering work by David Blackbourn and Geoff Eley, *The Peculiarities of German History: Bourgeois Society and Politics in Nineteenth-Century Germany* (Oxford, 1984), it has become necessary to argue and substantiate such a *Sonderweg* rather than simply asserting it.
8. These issues are well explored in Conrad, *Auf der Suche nach der verlorenen Nation*.
9. There is one such (insufficiently known) study by Heinz Wolf, *Deutsch-jüdische Emigrationshistoriker in den USA und der Nationalsozialismus* (Bern, 1988). See also David Sorkin, "'Historian of Fate': Fritz Stern on the History of German Jewry. An Appreciation," in Marion F. Deshmukh and Jerry Z. Muller, eds., *Fritz Stern at 70* (Washington, DC, 1997); and Stanley G. Payne, David J. Sorkin, and John S. Tortorice, eds., *What History Tells: George L. Mosse and the Culture of Modern Europe* (Madison, WI, 2004).
10. I should note here that my approach differs slightly from that of Hartmut Lehmann—one of the few German observers who, it must be said, is perceptively sensitive to the issue at hand. He argues that it was only with the generation under examination that German and

émigré historians became serious dialogical partners. I would claim that while personal and professional contacts were, indeed, created, this was not reflected particularly in the works themselves. See Hartmut Lehmann, "Kooperation und Distanz: Beobachtungen zu den Beziehungen zwischen der deutschen under der amerikanischen Geschichtwissenschaft im 19. und 20. Jahrhundert," in *Alte und Neue Welt in wechselseitiger Sicht. Studien zu den transatlantischen Beziehungen im 19. und 20. Jahrhundert* (Göttingen, 1995), 150–65, especially 153. It should also be apparent here that my concern differs—and, in part, dissents—from Theodor Hamerow's rather naive assessment of social history. His identification of the phase of a highly critical "social history" as that of a reflection of German "guilt" does not get to the interesting ambiguities and defensive postures that have revealed themselves over the last few years and that are also explored here. See his otherwise perceptive review essay, "Guilt, Redemption, and Writing German History," *American Historical Review* 88 (1983): 53–72.
11. Perhaps the most representative of these is Hans-Ulrich Wehler's *Das Deutsche Kaiserreich* (1973); see *The German Empire 1871–1918*, trans. Kim Traynor (Leamington Spa, 1985).
12. Jürgen Kocka has correctly argued that the *Sonderweg* approach is helpful in explaining why there were so few barriers to fascism in Germany but less so when accounting for Nazism's unique radical impulse. He does not, however, inquire as to why this should be so. See his "German History before Hitler: The Debate about the German Sonderweg," *Journal of Contemporary History* 23 (1988): 3–16.
13. See Laqueur, *Thursday's Child*, 100–6.
14. See Dirk Moses, "The Forty-Fivers: A Generation between Fascism and Democracy," *German Politics and Society* 17 (1999), 94–126. See also Ulrich Herbert, "Liberalisierung als Lernprozesse. Die Bundesrepublik in der deutschen Geschichte—eine Skizze," in *Wandlungsprozesse in Westdeutschland. Belastung, Integration, Liberalisierung 1945–1980* (Göttingen, 2002).
15. See the fascinating piece by Michael Jeismann, "Im Schatten alter Männer Blüte. Über die Nicht Vererbare Vernunft der Vater," *Kursbuch* 135 (March 1999): 172–80, especially 172–73. I thank Till van Rahden for this reference.
16. See Herbert, *Wandlungsprozesse*, 47, for a slightly different but related point. See also Gerhard A. Ritter: "We intensively and consciously engaged the question of what led to a totalitarian State and a dictatorship and the presupposition and conditions necessary for the functioning of a democracy," in *Versäumte Fragen*, 137.
17. Apart from the aforementioned piece by Jeismann, see Paul Nolte, "Die Historiker der Bundesrepublik. Rückblick auf eine 'lange Generation,'" *Merkur* 53 (May 1999): 413–32. Jürgen Kocka was born in 1941, later than the rest of this group. He must nevertheless be considered a member less by dint of birth and circumstance than choice and sensibility.
18. This is graphically illustrated in the superb volume of interviews, *Versäumte Fragen*.
19. See his "Nationalsozialismus und Historiker" essay in *Umbruch und Kontinuität. Essays zu 20. Jahrhundert* (Munich, 2000), 41.
20. Long before these revelations about the "parents" became known, Heinz Wolf, in *Deutschjüdische Emigrantenhistoriker*, 420, perceptively noted that this kind of history writing was perfect for avoiding "a genuine confrontation with National Socialism." It constituted, he wrote, a kind of "refuge" historiography.
21. Winkler, in *Versäumte Fragen*, 381, writes that Hermann Lübbe's 1983 "communicative silence [*beschweigen*]" also demonstrated that one could have a scientific and public political confrontation with National Socialism that went together with a silent acceptance of individual burdens. In the same volume, Kocka, 393, correctly points out that there is a difference between examining the paradigms and methods of a school and investigating their political enterprises and biographical guilt. This is certainly so but does not exempt us from nevertheless tracing the extrascholarly, generational connections and inquiring as to how these impinge upon scholarly concerns.

22. See his piece in Hartmut Lehmann, ed., *Felix Gilbert as Scholar and Teacher* (Washington, DC, 1992), 6.
23. The term is Dan Diner's. See the symposium between German and Israeli historians, "The End of Social History," in the Hebrew journal *Historia* (2004): 93–112, but see especially 101–4.
24. Indeed, as Wolf argues, the very evasion of intentionality derives from a strategic, defensive intention of the historian. See his *Deutsch-jüdische Emigrantenhistoriker*, 421.
25. Nolte, "Die Historiker der Bundesrepublik," 426.
26. I have already mentioned Laqueuer's *Thursday's Child*. See also idem, *Jerusalem Beyond Zionism: Recollections and Reflections, 1938–2003* (New York, 2004), and idem, *Best of Times, Worst of Times: Memoirs of a Political Education* (Hanover and London, 2009). For the rest of the group, see Peter Gay, *My German Question: Growing Up in Nazi Berlin* (New Haven, 1998); George L. Mosse, *Confronting History: A Memoir* (Madison, 2000), and Fritz Stern, *Five Germanys I have known* (New York, 2006), and *Reden über das eigene Land* (Munich, 1997). I thank Jerry Muller for providing me with these latter references.
27. See the entry on Laqueur in Andreas Daum's "Biobibliographic Guide" at the end of this volume.
28. Gay, *My German Question*, ix; Stern, *Five Germanies*, 11.
29. Laqueur, *Thursday's Child*, 105.
30. See Mosse's "Politisches Erwachen. Berlin, das Exil und dis antifaschistiche Bewegung," in Wolfgang Benz and Marion Neiss, eds., *Die Erfahrung des Exils. Exemplarische Reflexionen* (Berlin, 1997), 67–80, see especially 72. See also his chapter on "Experiencing Exile," in *Confronting History*, 71–93, especially 75, where Mosse states that "exile energized me and challenged me as nothing had ever challenged me before."
31. *My German Question*, 21.
32. See Jerry Z. Muller, "American Views of German History since 1945," in Frank Trommler and Peter Hohendahl, eds., *Whose Brain Drain? Immigrant Scholars and American Views on Germany* (Washington, DC, 2001), 14–27.
33. Again, see Andreas W. Daum's "Biobibliographic Guide," in this volume. The complicated story of Hans Rothfels has lately become the object of much controversy in Germany. Most of this is in German. For a convenient, extremely critical, English-language treatment, see Nicolas Berg, "Hidden Memory and Unspoken History: Hans Rothfels and the Postwar Restoration of Contemporary German History," *Leo Baeck Institute Yearbook* 49 (2004): 195–220.
34. *My German Question*, 4–5; "At Home in America," *The American Scholar* 46, no. 1 (Winter 1976–77): 31–42.
35. Irene Runge and Uwe Stelbrink, eds., *"Ich Bleibe Emigrant": Gespräche mit George L. Mosse* (Berlin, 1991).
36. Gay, *My German Question*, 4–5.
37. Laqueur, *Thursday's Child*, 367.
38. The presence of sports in their recollections is striking, see Laqueur, *Generation Exodus: The Fate of Young Jews from Nazi Germany* (Hanover, 2001), 8.
39. Mosse, "Politisches Erwachen," 80.
40. Stern, *Five Germanies*, 14.
41. See Mosse, *Confronting History*, 180–81.
42. For a graphic account of this resistance, see Raul Hilberg, *The Politics of Memory: The Journey of a Holocaust Historian* (Chicago, 1996).
43. *The Varieties of History: From Voltaire to the Present* (New York, 1956).
44. See *The Struggle for Sovereignty in England from the Reign of Queen Elizabeth to the Petition of Right* (Oxford, 1950); *The Reformation* (New York, 1953); *The Holy Pretense: A Study in Christianity and Reason of State from William Perkins to John Winthrop* (Oxford, 1957).

45. Peter Gay, *Voltaire's Politics: The Poet as Realist* (Princeton, 1959); *The Party of Humanity: Essays in the French Enlightenment* (New York, 1964); *A Loss of Mastery: Puritan Historians in Colonial America* (Berkeley, 1966). See also Gay, *My German Question*, 191. His dissertation, completed in 1951, was published as *The Dilemma of Democratic Socialism: Eduard Bernstein's Challenge to Marx* (New York, 1952).
46. This theme is pursued in the insightful article by Paul Breines, "Germans, Journals and Jews/Madison, Men, Marxism and Mosse: A Tale of Jewish-Leftist Identity Confusion in America," *New German Critique*, no. 20 (Spring–Summer 1980): 81–103.
47. Laqueur, Weimar Culture, 30–31.
48. See Fritz Stern, *The Politics of Cultural Despair: A Study in the Rise of Germanic Ideology* (Berkeley, 1961), and George L. Mosse, *The Crisis of German Ideology: Intellectual Origins of the Third Reich* (New York, 1964). These two works are usually, and correctly, grouped together. Yet their differences may be as significant as their similarities. Stern examines in detail three *völkisch* intellectuals (Paul de Lagarde, Julius Langbehn, and Moeller van den Bruck), while Mosse's canvas is much wider, taking in a panoply of political, educational, cultural, and recreational institutions and organizations and examining the diffusion and variations of this ideology therein.
49. See Laqueur, *Young Germany*; Gay, *Weimar Culture*; and Stern, "The Political Consequences of the Unpolitical German," in *The Failure of Illiberalism: Essays on the Political Culture of Modern Germany* (Chicago, 1975; originally published in 1971).
50. See his *The Culture of Western Europe: The Nineteenth and Twentieth Centuries* (Boulder, 1988), 2. The work was originally published in 1961.
51. It seems clear that in all this, Mosse was really the pioneer, forging paths of research that were later followed by other scholars. See Aschheim, "George Mosse at 80"; Payne, Sorkin, and Tortorice, *What History Tells*.
52. In this earlier period, the cultural historians, too, viewed matters in this *Sonderweg* light. The analyses of the social historians would have received confirmation and been deepened by referring to this dimension. They were reluctant to do so for reasons elucidated in this chapter and relegated such matters basically to epiphenomena. For a critique of this reductive social-historical view in terms of its understanding of antisemitism, see Till van Rahden, "Words and Actions: Rethinking the Social History of German Antisemitism, Breslau, 1870–1914," *German History* 18, no. 4 (2000): 413–18.
53. See Stern's *Um eine deutsche Vergangenheit*, Konstanzer Universitätsreden 57 (Konstanz, 1972), 181. Stern also wrote, in his *Politics of Cultural Despair*, x, "Specific studies . . . have shown that cultural, spiritual and psychic factors must be taken into account if we are to understand the triumphs of irrationality that marked fascism." See Aschheim, "George Mosse at 80."
54. I owe this suggestion, which places a slightly different, more benign light upon the motivations of the social historians, to Anson Rabinbach.
55. Mosse, *Confronting History*, 70.
56. George L. Mosse, *"Ich bleibe Emigrant."* Quoted in Emilio Gentile, "A Provisional Dwelling: The Origin and Development of the Concept of Fascism in Mosse's Historiography," in Payne, Sorkin, and Tortorice, *What History Tells*, 44.
57. See Stern, *Five Germanies*, 9.
58. See *Thursday's Child*, 91.
59. See the book-length interview with Michael A. Ledeen, *Nazism: A Historical and Comparative Analysis of National Socialism* (New Brunswick, 1978), 43.
60. George L. Mosse, *Nationalism and Sexuality: Respectability and Abnormal Sexuality in Modern Europe* (New York, 1985).
61. This is, quite clearly, a crucial distinguishing mark between these historians and Daniel Jonah Goldhagen. See Fritz Stern's critique, "The Past Distorted: The Goldhagen Controversy," in

Einstein's German World (Princeton, 1999), 272–88. My own assessment can be found in chapters 9, 12, and 13 of *In Times of Crisis: Essays on European Culture, Germans and Jews* (Madison, WI, 2000). I should add here that while—like many others historians—I dismiss Goldhagen's highly one-dimensional account of modern German history and culture as monolithically antisemitic, his critique of "structural" and "functional-systemic" accounts of the Holocaust as lacking "agency" and "willing executioners" is a necessary and salutary corrective.

62. See Gay, *Freud, Jews*, 9.
63. See my "George Mosse at 80."
64. See *Generation Exodus*.
65. See, respectively, George L. Mosse, "The Influence of the Volkish Idea on German Jewry," in *Germans and Jews: The Right, the Left and the Search for a 'Third Force' in Pre-Nazi Germany* (London, 1971), 77–115; Fritz Stern, *Dreams and Delusions: The Drama of German History* (New York, 1987), especially section I; Peter Gay, *Freud, Jews and other Germans: Masters and Victims in Modernist Culture* (New York, 1978).
66. See Dan Diner, "Hannah Arendt Reconsidered: On the Banal and the Evil in Her Holocaust Narrative," *New German Critique* 71 (Spring–Summer 1997): 177–90.
67. Gay, *Freud, Jews and other Germans*, ix.
68. See Gershom Scholem, "Jews and Germans," reproduced in Gershom Scholem and Werner J. Dannhauser, eds., *On Jews and Judaism in Crisis: Selected Essays* (New York, 1976). I have examined these views in greater detail in my *Scholem, Arendt, Klemperer: Intimate Chronicles in Turbulent Times* (Bloomington, 2001) and "The Metaphysical Psychologist: On the Life and Letters of Gershom Scholem," *Journal of Modern History* 76, no. 4 (December 2004): 900–33.
69. Stern, *Dreams and Delusions*, 114.
70. Mosse, *German Jews Beyond Judaism*, 1–2.
71. Laqueur, *Weimar: A Cultural History*, 73.
72. See Gay, "In Deutschland zu Hause," in Arnold Paucker, ed., *Die Juden im nationalsozialistischen Deutschland/The Jews in Nazi Germany, 1933–1943* (Tübingen, 1986), 33.
73. Gay, *My Jewish Question*, 49. I have discussed this debate in greater detail in my *Scholem, Arendt, Klemperer*, 37–40.
74. Amongst others see, most relevantly, Walter Laqueur, *A History of Zionism* (London, 1972), and *Jerusalem Beyond Zionism: Recollections and Reflections, 1938–2003* (New York, 2004).
75. The respective quotes appear in Mosse, *Confronting History*, 190–91. I have also analyzed in greater depth and detail Mosse's relationship to Zionism and the State of Israel in "George Mosse at 80."
76. See Stern's "Chaim Weizmann and Liberal Nationalism," in *Einstein's German World*, 223. For the Peter Gay quote, see his preface to *Freud, Jews*, xiii–xiv.
77. It is worth remarking that the positions adopted by these cultural historians are remarkably similar to the émigré literary *Germanisten*, as Mark Anderson has characterized them: all shared "the commitment to Germany's Enlightenment tradition; the interest in modernist, exile and Jewish culture; a political and historical consciousness that resists purely formalist readings; an insistence on differentiating positive and negative forces in German culture; and an aversion to generalizations about 'the Germans.'" See his "The Silent Generation? Jewish Refugee Students, Germanistik, and Columbia University," *The Germanic Review* 78, no. 1 (Winter 2003): 20–38, quote on 32.

Chapter 13

FROM THE MARGINS TO THE MAINSTREAM
Refugees and the Successors on the Jewish Question, Antisemitism, and the Holocaust in German History

Jeffrey Herf

In the United States in the past thirty years, the issues of the Holocaust and the history of antisemitism in German history have moved from the periphery to the center of the historical discipline. German-Jewish refugee historians and Jewish scholars, some refugees from other European countries and others born in this country, as well as succeeding generations, played a key role in bringing this shift about. The leading figures of the German refugee generation in this effort were Walter Laqueur, George Mosse, Raul Hilberg, and, in a less direct manner, Fritz Stern and Peter Gay.[1] Lucy Dawidowicz and Saul Friedlander, two other historians of the generation that survived the Holocaust, also played a major role in this shift.[2] Raul Hilberg, author of *The Destruction of the European Jews,* was a political scientist at the University of Vermont. Dawidowicz worked at the American Jewish Committee and taught Jewish, not German, history at Yeshiva University in New York. Hannah Arendt's *Origins of Totalitarianism* drew attention to the ideological dimensions of the Nazi regime, yet the cumulative impact of her work on research on the Holocaust was more ambiguous.[3] That said, in the four decades following World War II and the Holocaust, the beginnings of historical writing on the Holocaust were due to the efforts of relative outsiders.

In the United States, the shift took place for the following reasons. First, to use Walter Laqueur's apt phrase, the members of "generation exodus" had the good fortune to find refuge from Nazi persecution here. Second, they felt an acute sense of responsibility to see that the truth about what had happened in Germany and Europe enter historical scholarship and that historians attempt to explain

---

Notes from this chapter begin on page 207.

how and why these events took place. In so doing, they inspired the succeeding generations. Third, they began their careers in the 1950s and 1960s, when American antisemitism was declining following the revelations of the Holocaust, and when American university faculties were expanding. The conjuncture of the two developments made it possible for some of the Jewish refugee scholars to get positions at major research universities. There they had time to do their research and were able to train a succession of doctoral students who built on and developed further research, teaching, and writing about these issues. In these postwar decades, Jews in the profession went from being outsiders to becoming part of its establishment.

However, the works that most directly concerned the Holocaust in the refugee generation came from relative outsiders to the American historical profession. Hilberg was a political scientist. Dawidowicz was a historian of the Jews who worked at the American Jewish Committee from 1948 to 1960 and then became a professor at Yeshiva University in New York. Walter Laqueur, a historian whose broad interests included important work on the Holocaust, had visiting professorships at major universities, but in the postwar decades, his primary base of employment and research was the Wiener Library in London and, thereafter, the Center for Strategic and International Studies in Washington, DC. Of the German-Jewish refugees in the discipline of history who achieved great national and international prominence and were not specialists in modern Jewish history, Mosse was the only one who wrote extensively and continuously about the history of antisemitism, Nazism, and the ideological origins of the Holocaust. In that sense, he was the key path breaker within the broader discipline.

One direct consequence of the Holocaust was that if "the Jewish question" and the history of antisemitism and the Holocaust were going to emerge among historians after 1945, it was not going to happen in Germany. As Nicholas Berg's study of the response of non-Jewish German historians in West Germany revealed, the resistance in the West German discipline to paying attention to Jewish scholars such as Joseph Wulf was considerable.[4] In East Germany, in the course of the "anti-cosmopolitan purges" of the early 1950s, the specificity of the murder of Europe's Jews was marginalized in the public rhetoric and scholarship, and the Communist regime began to pursue a longstanding policy of intense antagonism to Israel.[5] It was the exceptional German historian—Karl Dietrich Bracher or Eberhard Jaeckel in West Germany and Helmut Eschwege in East Germany—who decided to devote time to the anti-Jewish policies of the Nazi regime or to the history of antisemitism in German history.[6] The absence of Jews in West Germany made this all the more unusual. As Peter Novick explained well in his study of the issue of objectivity in the American historical profession, until the 1950s, research on the history of racism and slavery was conducted primarily by African-American historians, such as W. E. B. Du Bois and John Hope Franklin, working mostly in historically black colleges and universities.⁷ It took almost a century after the Civil War for the issues to move into the center of the American profession. Similarly, the emergence of "the Jewish question" in the history of the Nazi regime was primarily due to efforts of Jewish historians in Israel, France, England, and the United States and, as Laura Jockusch has recently pointed out, by Jewish researchers and historians who survived the Holocaust and established the first research centers devoted to work on the subject. The emergence of these issues among American historians of modern German history was primarily due to the German-Jewish refugee scholars and other Jewish historians of that generation who decided to work on it and who had gained a foothold within the profession.

The key texts that stand at the beginning of the shift from periphery to center were Stern's 1961 study, *The Politics of Cultural Despair,* and Mosse's 1964 work, *The Crisis of German Ideology.* While Stern's focus was on German illiberalism, of which antisemitism was one aspect, and Mosse concentrated on what he called "the anti-Jewish revolution" at the heart of *Völkisch* and Nazi ideology, both of these two canonical works illustrate the points I made above. Both raised the issue of the revolt against liberal modernity in Nazism's ideological origins and thus also of the subsequently controversial view of the cultural and intellectual special path—the *Sonderweg*—on which significant portions of Germany's political and intellectual elites combined nationalism with opposition to political liberalism and Enlightenment values. These two excellent works came from professors at major institutions, Columbia and Wisconsin. Stern and Mosse went in rather different directions thereafter, directions which are prefigured in their early works. Stern, as is evident in his 1987 essay on "National Socialism as Temptation," focused on multiple reasons why the German elites were tempted by National Socialism, followed Hitler, leapt "from despair to utopia," and sought "the clarity of authority" and unity as opposed to liberalism's supposed fragmentation.⁸ It was liberalism and the illiberal revolt against it that remained at the center of his concerns. Mosse, in his multiple works on fascism, racism, and antisemitism, was more preoccupied with the specifics of the Jewish question, of antisemitism, and of the origins of the Holocaust. One of Mosse's central arguments in these works concerned the centrality of Jewish questions to the broader intellectual and cultural history of not only Germany in the twentieth century but Western and European history over a period of many centuries.⁹

In addition to these canonical works, the *Journal of Contemporary History* (*JCH*), founded and edited for four decades by Mosse and Laqueur, was crucial in fostering the shift to the center. While the *Leo Baeck Institute Yearbook* published a great deal on antisemitism and the Holocaust, it was the *JCH* that, more than any other mainstream journal of the historical profession, brought these issues to the attention of an international, especially European and American, network of scholars working on the history of Nazism, fascism, and totalitarianism, such as Karl Dietrich Bracher, Eberhard Jaeckel, and Emilio Gentile, who had positions at prominent universities in the United States, Britain, Italy, Israel, and West Germany. Bracher was another example of the outsider—again a political scientist preoccupied with the theory of totalitarianism as well as with the impact of ideas and ideologies on political history.

Yet, despite their differences of nuance and focus, Mosse, Stern, and Laqueur had a number of important shared conceptual approaches that contributed to the shift from periphery to center. They all argued that ideas, which they examined in the German elites and which Mosse examined in popular mentalities as well, had played a role in the susceptibility of the German establishment and public to Hitler and Nazism. Laqueur, was an early and prominent example of an intellectual in Washington preoccupied with the impact of ideas on government policies and decision making. All three criticized economic reductionism. All wrote intellectual history with an eye towards its political significance. They agreed that ideas had played a major causal role in Nazism's rise to power, the consolidation of the dictatorship, and, of course, in the Holocaust itself. They were, more or less implicitly, all Weberians in insisting that a causal explanation must also be "adequate at the level of meaning."[10] Their focus on the political import of ideological fanaticism put them at odds with three different orientations in the historical profession: traditional political historians who viewed ideologies as clever tools used in a Machiavellian, cynical fashion by political leaders and which thus ought not to be taken seriously as causal factors; varying strands of Marxism, which viewed ideas as tools used to advance class interests; and the emerging wave of social historians who shared such skepticism as well as a disinterest in research on intellectual and political elites. Yet for Mosse, Stern, and Laqueur, to dismiss the role of ideology left the historian without an adequate causal explanation of why and how these major political events took place. In their common view, the tools of intellectual history and the determination to take ideas seriously were necessary for historical interpretations of the origins and implementation of the Holocaust.

The German scholar who understood this point best did not teach in a department of history. Rather, it was the historically oriented political scientist Karl Bracher who, in what became a classic essay in a volume edited by Laqueur, famously wrote that the history of National Socialism was the history of its underestimation. That is, both Hitler's contemporaries and too many subsequent scholars failed to take his ideas seriously as the basis for his actions and decisions. For the Jewish question and the history of the Holocaust to move from periphery to center, as Bracher began to do in his 1969 work, *Die Deutsche Diktatur*, Hitler's ideological obsessions about the Jews had to assume center stage. In retrospect, the famous juxtaposition of "intentionalists and functionalists" was a euphemism for a deeper and more important debate, namely whether or not historians were going to look closely at the causal significance of antisemitism in the history of Nazism.[11] It was a willingness to do so, more than a methodological debate about intentions and functions, that marked the importance of Eberhard Jäckel's 1969 work, *Hitler's Weltanschauung*, one in which Jaeckel succinctly yet powerfully made the case that Hitler's ideas, however repulsive, comprised a coherent and, most importantly, causally important factor in the history of the Nazi regime.[12]

Raul Hilberg, in his classic work, *The Destruction of European Jewry*, inaugurated another scholarly tradition—that is, the immersion in the facts of official decision making and the machinery mass murder based on the massive documentary record left behind by the Nazi regime, a tradition continued in the next generation by Christopher Browning and Richard Breitman, among others.[13]

The Jewish refugees from Germany were historiographical liberals in two senses of that term. First, Stern and Mosse, and Peter Gay even more so, wrote about the liberalism and the Enlightenment, which fascism and Nazism had attacked. Second, there was a conservative element to their liberalism, namely a concern, articulated in Freud's later writings about the fragility of civilization, as well as in Mosse and Stern's work on the intellectual and cultural aspects of Nazism, about the importance of nonrational and irrational factors in life and politics. They shared a skepticism about mass movements. While they were supportive of the civil rights movement in the United States, their skepticism about social movements and popular mentalities put them a bit at odds with an enthusiasm for revolts from below that emerged among American historians who came of age in the 1960s and since. While they stood in the traditions of European antifascism, their publications focused primarily on those intellectual and cultural figures who supported fascism and Nazism. Indeed, one of the key themes of many articles in *The Journal of Contemporary History* was that fascism and Nazism in fact were part of Europe's intellectual and cultural history. The German-Jewish refugees were critics of the counter-enlightenment in Europe and were not tempted by the revival of the counter-enlightenment traditions offered by the postmodernists in the United States. They remembered the attacks on the Enlightenment and norms of objectivity from Joseph Goebbels, Martin Heidegger, Carl Schmitt, and other German intellectuals who found reason superficial compared with emotion, who thought truth claims could not be separated from the identity of the speaker or writer, and who wanted to place the university in the service of political goals.[14] In *Nazi Germany and the Jews*, Saul Friedlander stressed that understanding the role of multiple perspectives in historical explanation did not mean agreement with relativism and loss of a historian's ability to establish the factual reality of past events. Within the American historical profession, few issues did more to bring the postmodernist fad to an end than did the specter of Holocaust denial that would logically follow if historians agreed that various interpretations of the past were simply narratives that reflected power but had no basis in facts that could be established with certainty.

The German-Jewish refugees have been criticized for writing teleological history. To be sure, Mosse and Stern believed that there were ideological origins to the Holocaust that needed to be examined, though their work eschewed a deterministic view that the die was cast long before the crises of the last years of Weimar. They sought to strike a balance, captured in Thomas Nipperdey's important phrase "multiple continuities," in German and European history.[15] In so doing, they reminded American students that not all of European or German history was the prehistory of Nazism. They also examined European and German traditions that would have led in other directions but which were defeated and derailed. In American universities today, that balance needs to be restored so that our students again have knowledge of multiple continuities. Gay's volumes on the Enlightenment, Stern's collection of classic and modern works of historiography, and Mosse's work on the culture of Western Europe were efforts to do so. An important task for historians now and in years to come is to think about how we can best strike a balance—that is, how to offer an unflinching gaze at the history of Nazism and the Holocaust while also writing and teaching about the cultural and political traditions of Europe that contributed to the theory and practice of freedom and human rights.

The work of Walter Laqueur points to another aspect of the Jewish question, namely that of persecution of the Jews in the Soviet Union and in Eastern Europe and the antagonism to Israel by the entire Soviet bloc during the Cold War. The German-Jewish refugees were understandably preoccupied with Nazism and the Holocaust. Many were uncomfortable with unambiguous anti-Communism. Yet the history of antisemitism did not end with the defeat of Nazi Germany. Laqueur's work on Soviet policy in the Middle East stood at the beginning of what has become a large scholarly literature on Communism and the Jewish question.[16]

We, the successors of what this volume is tentatively calling "the second generation," built on the foundation established by the refugees. Not everyone in the succeeding generation who made significant contributions to the history of the Jewish question, antisemitism, and the Holocaust studied or knew Laqueur, Mosse, and Stern, but many did. Those who studied with Mosse included Stephen Aschheim, who produced a continuing stream of work on the intersection of German and Jewish history and on Jewish intellectuals in German intellectual life;[17] Christopher Browning, whose "modified functionalism" shed new light on the decisions that launched the final solution (Browning's enormously influential work also builds on the project that Hilberg began, yet it also displays a welcome effort to integrate ideological factors in what he called a "modified functionalism"); Anson Rabinbach, who played an important role both in his many essays on intellectual life before, during, and after the Nazi era as well as in his work as an editor of *New German Critique*.[18] I studied with Mosse as an undergraduate and examined how antisemitism moved from an ideology of persecution to one of extermination. Robert Wistrich, at the time of his death in 2015 was the preeminent historian of antisemitism. He worked with Laqueur at the Wiener

Library and on *The Journal of Contemporary History* in London.[19] My own work on Nazism is another example of an impetus that came from the margins of the discipline. My book *Reactionary Modernism* was a doctoral dissertation in interpretive sociology at Brandeis University advised by two Jewish refugees, Kurt Wolff from Germany and Egon Bittner from Czechoslovakia. I must also mention Hans Gerth, a non-Jewish German refugee, who introduced students at the University of Wisconsin to the Weberian tradition of comparative and interpretive sociology. *Reactionary Modernism* emerged from the ferment in social theory in the 1970s on both sides of the Atlantic and a set of puzzles posed but left unresolved by Stern and Mosse's canonical works on cultural despair and *völkisch* ideology.[20] My study *The Jewish Enemy: Nazi Propaganda during World War II and the Holocaust* also built on the work of the refugees yet asked why antisemitism had become an ideology justifying mass murder and not "merely" persecution.[21]

Stern's students have made important contributions to the shift. One thinks of Marian Kaplan's study of women and family life under the Nazis in the 1930s, Jerry Muller's work on intellectual life in the Nazi era and on the views of Jews in European writings about capitalism,[22] and the work of Helmut Walser Smith, who studied with Peter Gay and Henry A. Turner and examined the place of antisemitism in his study of the continuities of German history.[23] Richard Breitman is that rare Harvard Ph.D. who made significant contributions to the history of the Holocaust. He did so first in *The Architect of Genocide*, his important study of Himmler and Holocaust decision making; in *The Terrible* Secret, his collaboration with Walter Laqueur on efforts to reveal the secrets of the Holocaust and Allied responses and lack thereof to them; as editor of the journal *Holocaust and Genocide Studies*; and in the past decade as a leader of the team that has declassified millions of U.S. government documents dealing with the Nazi and Japanese Imperial regimes.[24] Peter Hayes, Atina Grossman, Marion Kaplan, and Omer Bartov were a step or two removed from the direct influences of these refugee historians but not from their focus on the role of antisemitism in Nazi policy, evident in Hayes work on I. G. Farben during the Holocaust,[25] Grossman's work on Jewish survivors in the displaced person's camps,[26] Kaplan's study of the Jews and in particular Jewish families in 1930s Germany,[27] and Bartov's examination of the diffusion of Nazi ideology from the Nazi leadership to the German General staff down to millions of soldiers on the Eastern Front in World War II.[28] Hans Rosenberg was one of the refugee historians known for his work on the social structure of the Kaiserreich, yet his student, the Israeli historian Shulamit Volkov, produced important work on the cultural codes of antisemitism and played a significant role in the shift from periphery to center in the United States and in West, and then unified, Germany.[29]

Gerhard Weinberg's work on the diplomacy and international history of the Nazi regime took Hitler's ideology seriously as a causal factor to an extent that was then not so common among the very practically minded scholars of diplomatic and military history. His work was integrative in several dimensions. First, he took Hitler's ideology seriously in writing the history of the diplomacy of Nazi Germany. As a result he integrated the history of the conventional diplomatic and military history of World War II with the history of the Holocaust. Just as the traditions emerging from Hilberg, Stern, and Mosse formed the beginnings of bridge between the history of the Holocaust and the main currents of intellectual history, Weinberg's work bridged the history of the Holocaust and the role of antisemitism to the main currents of diplomatic history.[30] His students who have continued that labor of integration include Norman Goda and Doris Bergen.[31]

No discussion of the intellectual effects of the second generation would be complete without mention of Daniel Goldhagen's *Hitler's Willing Executioners*.[32] The refugee scholar who most influenced this work was his father, Erich Goldhagen, who survived the ghetto in Czernowitz and taught a course on the Holocaust for many years at Harvard. Historians had written more about the relationship between antisemitism and the Holocaust than he suggested, and his generalizations from his study of Police Battalion 101 to German society and history went beyond his evidence. Yet despite its methodological problems, no book of the past several decades has done more to bring the issue of antisemitism to the center of public debate. This impulse also came from political science. The impact of his book was perhaps even greater in West Germany than here, for there it was a major challenge to West German historians of Nazism who were reluctant to give due weight to antisemitic ideology and who recoiled from an idea that was more firmly embedded in the work of American historians of Germany, namely that Nazi ideology had struck various chords in significant parts of German society, not only in German elites.

All of the refugee historians were interested in, and some wrote about, American-German relations or the Atlantic Alliance, yet Laqueur was the only one who focused his scholarship on the Middle East and who made scholarly contributions to the history of the Arab-Israel conflict.[33] In his 2006 work *The Changing Face of Anti-Semitism*, he examined the shift in geography and cultural coordinates of antisemitism from Europe to Islamists in the Middle East, Iran, and Europe, and to parts of the secular left as well.[34] Weinberg had also played a pioneering role in drawing attention to Nazi Germany's failed efforts to extend the Holocaust to the Middle East. In the succeeding generation, Wistrich has examined what he called "the shift of gravity" from antisemitism's historic home in Christian Europe to Iran and the Arab Middle East. In *Nazi Propaganda for the Arab World*, I built on important work by German historians Martin Cuppers, Klaus Gensicke, and Klaus Mallmann, as well as on the work of Israeli historians Zvi Elpeleg, Meir Litvak and Ester Webman and on the files of the American, German, and British foreign ministries and intelligence agencies, in order to document and interpret the collaboration between Arab nationalists and Islamists with the Nazi regime.[35] Richard Breitman and Norman Goda, as part of the important work with declassified

OSS (Office of Strategic Services) and CIA files related to Nazi war crimes, have offered further evidence regarding Haj Amin el-Husseini's collaboration with the Nazi regime as well as of the role played by ex-Nazi officials in the propaganda ministries of Arab governments in the post-Holocaust decades.[36] Paul Berman in this country and Mathias Küntzel and Bassam Tibi in Germany have written important works that connect the Jew-hatred of Germany and Europe's past to contemporary, Islamist antisemitism and totalitarian politics.[37]

It remains to be seen whether the shift from periphery to center will remain an enduring component of the study of modern German history or if it was the temporary result of the efforts of the refugee and successor generations. One indication that fosters its continued centrality in the discipline is the presence in Germany of historians such as Martin Cuppers, Norbert Frei, Ulrich Herbert, and Michael Wildt, whose focus is on the Nazi era as well as the Holocaust.[38] The existence of centers for research on Jewish history in Leipzig, Potsdam, and Heidelberg also creates a larger critical mass of scholars interested in these issues. Though the impulse to address Jewish questions in German history now no longer comes only from scholars outside Germany, the one-sided irritation with Israel that has become fashionable among many European and American intellectuals may eventually push Jewish questions back to the periphery of the discipline or perhaps the preoccupation with dead Jews will fit quite well into a mood of hostility to live Israelis. Time will tell. In this country, in view of the presence of the U.S. Holocaust Memorial Museum and the increased interest in work on the Holocaust on both sides of the Atlantic, the question of whether these issues will remain central to the discipline seems odd. Yet there is reason to wonder whether the integration of the history of antisemitism and the Holocaust will remain in the main narrative of German and European history. Whether it will stay there and whether antisemitism when expressed by the far left and by Islamists will receive the attention it deserves remain open questions. Will the hostility to Israel that is now an enduring feature of left-wing and much liberal sentiment in the universities on both sides of the Atlantic erode an interest in scholarship on these matters? As history departments in this country turn more resources to the study of Asia, Africa, Latin America, and the Middle East, the focus on Europe as a whole becomes relatively less central to the historical profession. We want to avoid the emergence of a double standard, one which combines sharp criticism of antisemitism in the European and German past with excuses and apologia when it emerges from non-European sources, from the Soviet bloc, and from the Communist dictatorship in East Germany,[39] or from the West German radical left of the 1960s and 1970s. The enlightenment principles which the refugee generation defended in various ways call for a uniform standard regarding this stubborn and persistent hatred, namely that of critique and rejection regardless of its origins. Of central importance in this regard, are Wolfgang Kraushaar's series of impressive and important works on anti-Zionism and antisemitism in the ideology and practice of the West German radical left, especially in the years of terrorism in the 1970s. Kraushaar, a scholar at the independent Hamburg Institute for Social Research, displays, as do many of the refugees and successors, the pattern of the outsider as insider who works to push these issues from the periphery to the center of the historical profession.[40]

We also face a problem of cultural discontinuity. Very few American universities still require undergraduates to take a sequence of courses in Western political and intellectual history. Far too few of our students, including students studying history, are learning about the cultural and intellectual traditions that we assume belong to the definition of an educated person, and thus too few can understand the place of Jewish questions in the longer history of Europe and Germany. Before the shift of the Jewish question from periphery to center, many American undergraduates learned very little, if anything, about the history of antisemitism and the Holocaust. After the shift, they are learning too little about the multiple continuities of European and German history. A determination to keep both dimensions in mind, that of the better and the worse Germany and Europe, was one of the defining features of the German-Jewish refugee historians. Striking that balance while sustaining the shift from periphery to center of the last half century will be a continuing challenge for current and future generations of historians.

Finally, it is important to note that the historians who, in my view, did most to push the issues of antisemitism and the Holocaust from the periphery to the center of the historical profession were either intellectual historians or were historians of politics who paid close attention to the causal impact of ideas and ideologies. While social historians have contributed greatly to understanding the impact of Nazi policies and the diffusion of Nazi ideology into German and European society, the specificity of the mass murder of the Jews remains incomprehensible if one ignores or dismisses the causal impact of Hitler's world view. Cultural and intellectual historians in the second decade of the twenty-first century have incorporated the insights of their colleagues working in social, economic, and certainly political and international history. The continued centrality of Jewish questions in German history rests on the continuation of labors of integration and synthesis in which, however, the Nazis' core ideological motivations retain the causal centrality they possess in the scholarship of the refugees and their successors.

Jeffrey Herf is Distinguished University Professor in the department of history at the University of Maryland, College Park. His research and teaching focus on the intersection of ideas and politics in modern European and German history. His books include *Reactionary Modernism* (1984), *War by Other Means* (1991), *Divided Memory* (1997), *The Jewish Enemy* (2006), and *Nazi Propaganda for the Arab World* (2009). His book *Undeclared Wars with Israel: East Germany and the West German Radical Left, 1967–1989* is forthcoming with Cambridge University Press in spring 2016.

Notes

1. Important works include Walter Laqueur, ed., *The Holocaust Encyclopedia* (New Haven, 2001); George L. Mosse, *The Crisis of German Ideology* (New York, 1964); Raul Hilberg, *The Destruction of the European Jews* (London, 1961); Fritz Stern, *The Politics of Cultural Despair* (Berkeley, 1961); Peter Gay, *Weimar Culture: The Outsider as Insider* (New York, 1968). The bibliographical listing of important works by the refugee historians and the successor generations could expand well beyond what I am presenting in the notes in this essay. See also the "Biobibliographic Guide" by Andreas W. Daum at the end of this volume.
2. See Lucy Dawidowicz, *The War Against the Jews, 1933–1945* (New York, 1975); Saul Friedlander, *Nazi Germany and the Jews*. Vol. 1, *The Years of Persecution, 1933–1939* (New York, 1997); Vol. 2, *The Years of Extermination, 1939–1945* (New York, 2007).
3. Hannah Arendt, *The Origins of Totalitarianism* (London, 1951).
4. Nicolas Berg, *Der Holocaust und die westdeutschen Historiker. Erforschung und Erinnerung* (Göttingen, 2003).
5. On Jewish questions in East German history see Jeffrey Herf, *Divided Memory: The Nazi Past in the Two Germanys* (Cambridge, MA, 1997); and Sigrid Meuschel, *Legitimation und Parteiherrschaft. Zum Paradox von Stabilität und Revolution in der DDR 1945–1989* (Frankfurt/M., 1992).
6. Karl Dietrich Bracher, *Die Deutsche Diktatur. Enstehung, Struktur, Folgen des Nationalsozialismus* (Cologne, 1970, [7]1993); Eberhard Jäckel, *Hitlers Weltanschauung. Entwurf einer Herrschaft* (Tübingen, 1969).
7. Peter Novick, *That Noble Dream: The 'Objectivity Question' and the American Historical Profession* (New York, 1988).
8. Fritz Stern, "National Socialism as Temptation," in *Dreams and Delusions: The Drama of German History* (New York, 1987), 147–92.
9. Of particular importance are George L. Mosse, *Toward the Final Solution: A History of European Racism* (New York, 1978); idem, *The Fascist Revolution* (New York, 1999); and on the place of Jewish questions in European cultural history, see his *The Culture of Western Europe: The Nineteenth and Twentieth Centuries* (New York., 1961). Also see Jeffrey Herf, "The Historian as Provocateur: George Mosse's Accomplishment and Legacy," *Yad Vashem Studies* XXIX (2001): 7–26. Jewish questions are not only questions in German history. They are issues in the history of the West. David Nirenberg has made a significant contribution to the history of Jewish questions in the cultural and intellectual history of the West in his *Anti-Judaism: The Western Tradition* (New York, 2013).
10. Max Weber, *The Theory of Social and Economic Organization* (New York, 1964), 98-99; and *Gesammelte Aufsätze zur Wissenschaftslehre* (Tübingen, 1988), 550-52.
11. Karl Dietrich Bracher, "The Role of Hitler: Perspectives of Interpretation," in Walter Laqueur, ed., *Fascism, A Reader's Guide: Analyses, Interpretations, Bibliography* (Berkeley, 1976), 211–25; idem, *Die deutsche Diktatur* (1970, [7]1993). See also idem, *The Age of Ideologies: A History of Political Thought in the Twentieth Century*, trans. Ewald Osers (London, 1982).
12. Jäckel, *Hitlers Weltanschauung*.
13. Among their numerous works see Christopher Browning, *The Origins of the Final Solution: The Evolution of Nazi Jewish Policy, September 1939–March 1942* (Lincoln, 2004); Richard Breitman, *The Architect of Genocide: Himmler and the Final Solution* (New York, 1991).
14. On intellectuals, the counter-enlightenment, and Nazism, see Richard Wolin, *The Seduction of Unreason: The Intellectual Romance with Fascism from Nietzsche to Postmodernism* (Princeton, NJ, 2004).
15. Thomas Nipperdey, "1933 und die Kontinuität der deutschen Geschichte," in *Nachdenken über die deutsche Geschichte* (Munich, 1986), 186–205.

16. See for example, Walter Laqueur, *Communism and Nationalism in the Middle East* (New York, 1956); and idem, *The Struggle for the Middle East: The Soviet Union and the Middle East, 1958–1970* (Harmondsworth, 1972).
17. Stephen E. Aschheim, *Culture and Catastrophe: German and Jewish Confrontations with National Socialism and Other Crises* (New York, 1996).
18. Anson Rabinbach, *In the Shadow of Catastrophe: German Intellectuals between Apocalypse and Enlightenment* (Berkeley, 1997).
19. Robert S. Wistrich, *A Lethal Obsession: Anti-Semitism from Antiquity to the Global Jihad* (New York, 2010).
20. Jeffrey Herf, *Reactionary Modernism: Technology, Culture and Politics in Weimar and the Third Reich* (New York, 1984).
21. Jeffrey Herf, *The Jewish Enemy: Nazi Propaganda during World War II and the Holocaust* (Cambridge, MA, 2006).
22. Jerry Muller, *The Other God that Failed: Hans Freyer and the Deradicalization of German Conservatism* (Princeton: Princeton University Press, 1987).
23. Helmut Walser Smith, *The Continuities of German History: Nation, Religion, and Race across the Long Nineteenth Century* (New York, 2008).
24. Richard Breitman et al., *US Intelligence and the Nazis* (New York, 2005); and idem, *Official Secrets: What the Nazis Planned, What the British and Americans Knew* (New York, 1999).
25. Peter Hayes, *Industry and Ideology: IG Farben in the Nazi Era* (New York, 1987); also Peter Hayes and John K. Roth, eds., *The Oxford Handbook of Holocaust Studies* (New York, 2010).
26. Atina Grossmann, *Jews, Germans and Allies: Close Encounters in Occupied Germany* (Princeton, 2009).
27. Marion A. Kaplan, *Between Dignity and Despair: Jewish Life in Nazi Germany* (New York, 1998).
28. Omer Bartov, *The Eastern Front, 1941–1945: German Soldiers and the Barbarization of Warfare* (New York, 1986).
29. Shulamit Volkov, *Antisemitismus als kultureller Kode: Zehn Essays* (Munich, 2000).
30. Gerhard L. Weinberg, *Germany, Hitler, and World War II: Essays in Modern German and World History* (New York, 1995); and idem, *A World at Arms: A Global History of World War II* (New York, 1994).
31. Norman J. W. Goda, *The Holocaust: Europe, the World and the Jews, 1918–1945* (Boston, 2012); Doris Bergen, *Twisted Cross: The German Christian Movement in the Third Reich* (Chapel Hill, 1996).
32. Daniel Jonah Goldhagen, *Hitler's Willing Executioners: Ordinary Germans and the Final Solution* (New York, 1997).
33. Walter Laqueur and Barry Rubin, eds., *The Israel-Arab Reader: A Documentary History of the Middle East Conflict* (New York, 1976), and subsequent editions.
34. Walter Laqueur, *The Changing Face of Anti-Semitism from Ancient Times to the Present Day* (New York, 2008).
35. Jeffrey Herf, *Nazi Propaganda for the Arab World* (New Haven, 2009). Also see Klaus Michael-Mallman and Martin Cuppers, *Halbmond und Hakenkreuz. Das Dritte Reich, die Araber und Palästina* (Darmstadt, 2006); Klaus Gensicke, *Der Mufti von Jerusalem und die Nationalsozialisten* (Darmstadt, 2007); Meir Litvak and Esther Webman, *From Empathy to Denial: Arab Responses to the Holocaust* (London, 2009); Zvi Elpeleg, *The Gran Mufti: Haj Anim al-Hussaimi and the Palestinian National Movement* (London, 1993), and *Through the Eyes of the Mufti: The Essays of Haj Anim* (London, 2009).
36. Richard Breitman and Norman J. W. Goda, *In Hitler's Shadow: Nazi War Criminals, U.S. Intelligence and the Cold War* (Washington, DC, 2010), and online: United States National Archives at www.archives.gov/iwg/reports/hitlers-shadow.pdf.

37. Paul Berman, *Terror and Liberalism* (New York, 2003); Matthias Küntzel, *Jihad and Jew-Hatred: Nazism, Islamism and the Roots of 9/11,* trans. Colin Meade (New York, 2007).
38. See, for example, Cuppers, *Halbmond und Hakenkreuz*; Norbert Frei, *Adenauer's Germany and the Nazi Past*, trans. Joel Golb (New York, 2002); Ulrich Herbert, ed., *National Socialist Extermination Policies: Contemporary German Perspectives and Controversies* (New York, 2000); and Michael Wildt, *An Uncompromising Generation: The Nazi Leadership of the Reich Security Main Office*, trans. Tom Lampert (Madison, 2009).
39. On the anti-Israeli policies of the East German regime, see Jeffrey Herf, *Divided Memory*; and idem, "At War with Israel: East Germany's Enthusiastic Participation in the Soviet Policy in the Middle East," *Journal of Cold War Studies* 16, No. 3 (2014): 129–163.
40. Wolfgang Kraushaar, *Wann Endlich beginnt bei Euch der Kampf gegen die Heilige Kuh Israel? München 1970. Über die antisemitischen Wuzeln des deutschen Terrorismus* (Hamburg, 2013); idem, *Die Bombe im Jüdischen Gemeindehaus* (Hamburg, 2005); and idem, ed., *Die RAF und der linke Terrorismus* (Hamburg, 2006).

Chapter 14

Reluctant Return
Peter Gay and the Cosmopolitan Work of a Historian

Helmut Walser Smith

Peter Gay, who passed away on May 12, 2015, was one of the most distinguished historians of Europe of the postwar era. His historical writings include a dissertation and first book on the political theories of the reform socialist Eduard Bernstein; a monograph on the politics of Voltaire; a two-volume general interpretation of the Enlightenment; a biography of Sigmund Freud; a five-volume psychoanalytically informed cultural history of the bourgeoisie in the nineteenth century; short books on Wilhelmine and Weimar culture, on modernism, on art history, and on music (a biography of Mozart); three books on historiography and method; a fictional dialogue between Lucian, Erasmus, and Voltaire; an extended autobiographical essay; a magisterial work on modernism, and, shortly before his death, a small book on Romanticism. Consistently original, varied, learned, and beautifully crafted, his books have both fared well with general readers and have influenced the thinking of his professional peers. That influence is especially noticeable in discrete fields—in the history of the Enlightenment, in psychoanalytically informed history, in modern German history, in the cultural history of the nineteenth century, and in the history of modernism. In these subjects, there is hardly a historian who has not grappled with Gay's writings.

The result has not always been unqualified assent. Although Gay's work has received its share of accolades and Gay has enjoyed a prominent position within the academy—first as a professor at Columbia, then at Yale—it cannot be said that his work always strolled in the gardens of academic consensus. It is easily forgotten what a departure his arguments about the Enlightenment represented, how daring the shift to psychoanalysis was, and how writing elite cultural history

---

Notes from this chapter begin on page 225.

when most other historians were computing serial data or excavating the forgotten symbols and rituals of popular culture had the effect of making the insider into an outsider of sorts.

In many ways, Gay's work less shadowed the turns of the American historical profession than offered a looking glass onto other ways of doing things. His work on the Enlightenment was a case in point. Revisionist in its day, holding the field for a short period, indeed becoming the definitive interpretation, it harvested ever more criticism for its seemingly forced insistence on the unity and coherence of the Enlightenment; for its loftiness, emphasizing major figures over minor; for emphasizing the radicalism of the Enlightenment while stopping short before the blood and muck of revolution; for its scant attention to institutions and to outsider groups and to how ideas are spread; for its focus on France and England to the exclusion of the European and colonial periphery; and for its all too evident assertion of the close ties between Enlightenment and postwar liberalism, a tie that led one recent historian to call the work "a liberal justification for America in the Cold War."[1]

Some of the criticisms may seem accurate enough. But such labels as "liberal justification" also have the effect of shellacking a genuinely complex interpretation with coats of undifferentiated analysis, with a monochrome sense of context, and with little feel for how the life experience of the émigrés, first and second generation, created intellectual investments and generated genuinely rich interpretations of the past. Against interpretations that plot history writing as little more than past politics, I want to argue that the early Peter Gay, whose work was centered on the Enlightenment, found his coordinates in the intellectual and political maelstrom of the 1950s, in a context at once American and émigré European. I also want to suggest that the major contentions of the early work have little to do, as has been argued, with the Cold War, or the liberal ascendancy of the 1960s, or, as has also been argued, with a German-Jewish cultural history counter-narrative to a social history-centered *Vergangenheitsbewältigung* in the Federal Republic, or with modernization theory, or with identity politics of any kind.[2] Rather, the early work was shaped by such figures as, in order of importance, Ernst Cassirer, Richard Hofstadter, Franz Neumann, Aby Warburg, Erich Auerbach, and, as a foil, Carl Becker; further, that McCarthyism, as much as National Socialism, backlit Gay's thinking about the Enlightenment; and, further still, that it was not the American sixties but the changed Federal Republic, prior to 1968, that allowed Gay to begin to look back, not as a victim but as an actor (to slightly alter his words) and to write a searing essay on Weimar Culture. That essay placed Germany, if only for a moment of "precarious glory," into a narrative of enlightened modernity.[3]

When in April 1939 Peter Fröhlich fled Berlin with his family, he vowed not to even read any more German.[4] He never kept that vow, and Peter Gay's first book, *The Dilemma of Democratic Socialism: Eduard Bernstein's Challenge to Marx*, was squarely in the field of German thought. But in this intellectual biography, Gay never missed a chance to underscore the importance of the exile experience to the explanation of Bernstein's revisionism. Gay emphasized the proximity of Bernstein's revisionism to Fabianism, noted how crucial the London years of Bernstein's exile were to the development of his central ideas, and underscored how England's less harsh state and police apparatus allowed Bernstein to glimpse that gradual change was possible. Conversely, Gay pointed out the inhospitable environment into which Bernstein returned to Germany in 1901. Many, including Rosa Luxemburg and Karl Kautsky, wanted Bernstein kicked out of the party; and not a few, including Bebel, denounced revisionism as too English. Without overstepping what the sources allow, Gay largely drained Bernstein of his grounding in a German tradition, taking under scalpel Bernstein's famous turn to Kant and revealing it to be based on a faulty understanding.[5] What Bernstein did possess, in Gay's view, was a fine historical sense, analytical and empirical honesty, and an enlightened "critical spirit."[6]

The Bernstein book first appeared in 1952, and it garnered Gay the first of his many academic awards. At Columbia, he had had been teaching since 1947 in the department of public law and government, and researched and wrote the dissertation and book while teaching. The book did not win him promotion. There was, at that time, no precisely calibrated tenure track but instead a coterie of older men deciding the fate of a cadre of younger men. The department, as Gay later wrote, "chose to promote only one of us, and I was not their choice."[7] But Gay's friends in the department of history, particularly Richard Hofstadter and the Russian historian Henry Roberts, invited him to join them as a modern Europeanist, and the rest of Gay's scholarly life was spent in history.

In 1952 and 1953, Gay still thought and wrote as a young scholar of political theory and remained indebted to Franz Neumann's seminar and his many suggestions. It was in this time of transition that, upon Neumann's urging, Gay read Ernst Cassirer, whose work enjoyed an explosion of English-speaking interest. Exiled first in England, then in Sweden, and then in the United States, Cassirer had been a visiting professor at Yale before receiving a permanent position at Columbia in the year before his death in April 1945. His last book, *The Myth of the State*, was written in English in 1944 and published posthumously in 1946. A number of his other works, including *The Problem of Knowledge*, *Language and Myth*, *The Philosophy of the Enlightenment*, and the first volume of the *Philosophy of Symbolic Forms* were translated at this time and eagerly discussed.[8] Drawing on the empathetic hermeneutics of Dilthey, Cassirer's method required that the researcher search for a dynamic center of a thinker's thought, typically in a seeming contradiction, and that he comprehend ostensibly diverse expressions as various manifestations of a person's conceptual world. The key was finding the central contradiction, which opened the door not to the content but to the dynamics of a person's ideas.[9] This involved a more patterned sense of chronological context than Arthur O. Lovejoy's string of ideas and a fuller reading of a person's major and minor publications and correspondences than was ordinarily the case with practitioners of the sociology of ideas. Especially suited for the study of the thinking of individuals, Cassirer's approach could also be extended to intellectual movements. Especially against the thin and arid landscape of intellectual history as then practiced in the United States, it was impossible not to be impressed with the depth of Cassirer's erudition and the quality of his insights. And it is not too much to say that Cassirer, second only to Freud, shaped Gay's approach to the past—then, and subsequently.

In the early 1950s, Gay also contributed to the explosion of interest in Cassirer, translating Cassirer's epoch making essay of 1932, "The Question of Jean Jacques Rousseau."[10] Wrought in 1953, the translation appeared in the following year and exemplified Cassirer's method of relating diverse strands and drawing them into a contained dynamic relationship, a whole. In Cassirer's essay, central antinomies in the interpretation of the works of Rousseau, such as the irreducible uniqueness of the individual versus the necessity of life in the community, are brilliantly resolved and shown by dint of perceptive differentiation to interlock. "The bond connecting man with the community is 'natural,' but it belongs to his rational, not his physical nature," Cassirer, in Gay's translation, informs his readers.[11] Precisely Cassirer's higher differentiation leading to resolution inspired Gay. In the introduction to Cassirer's essay, Gay's first published work on the Enlightenment, the barely thirty-year-old scholar introduced a distinction "between Rousseau's political theory as a critical instrument and as a constructive device."[12] The differentiation allowed Gay, following a suggestion of Neumann, to see Rousseau's ideas as inspiration for democratic movements but not as a blueprint for democratic states. Moreover, it allowed for the claim that the "critical instrument" was not merely one facet of Rousseau, but the dynamic center of Rousseau's oeuvre. Indebted to Cassirer, likely discussed in seminar with Neumann, the differentiation also opened an insight—which Gay directed against the conservative detractors of Rousseau and of the Enlightenment generally—that the fundamental contribution of enlightened thinking inhered in the critical oppositional spirit and that its value was in providing weapons for a democratic armory. The contribution was not—and against recent interpretations of Gay's work this point must unfortunately be stressed—in pointing the way toward or showing what liberal democracy should look like.[13]

Sometime in late 1953, Gay outlined, if *ex negativo*, major arguments he would make over the next fifteen years. In "The Enlightenment in the History of Political Theory," an essay he would later marvel at for its brashness and wince at for the thinness of its source base, and included nowhere in his published volumes, Gay argued that contemporary scholarship rested on four mistaken assumptions: that the philosophes had a naïve faith in reason; that they believed in the inevitability of progress; that they lacked historical sensibility; and that they eagerly embraced enlightened despotism. The young Gay did not mince words. "A crowd of critics, of compilers, of commentators, darkened the face of learning," he wrote, quoting Gibbons against fellow historians' interpretations of Locke and Rousseau.[14]

To Gay, the platitude that the philosophes possessed a naïve belief in reason proved particularly pernicious. A wide array of contrary evidence ranged against it. There was Hume's skeptical epistemology, Diderot's interest in the passions, and Kant's concern to limit reason's domain. Nor could reason be thought of as system and opposed to empiricism. "*La Raison*," Gay approvingly quotes Voltaire as writing in his *Philosophical Dictionary*, "*consiste à voir toujours les choses comme elles sont.*"[15] Enlighteners likewise did not possess a naïve belief in progress—a view that could only be held if one foregrounded Turgot and Condorcet against the skepticism of Voltaire and Gibbon and neglected the lack of attention paid to the concept of progress in the works of Locke, Montesquieu, Hume, and Diderot. The myth, as Gay called it, confused the distinction between belief that progress is possible with the superstition that it is inevitable. Following Cassirer, Gay also maintained that major philosophes possessed a sense of causation and change in the past and that their appreciation of the pastness of the past was not as anemic as the Romantics, and their twentieth-century followers, contended. Finally, on the question of governmental form, Gay likewise argued that the palette of enlightened positions was richer than often supposed, and that even Voltaire, of whom Gay conceded a certain "Voltaire Problem" and the necessity of further research, "transcended" the doctrine of enlightened despotism.[16]

Crucial—at this stage, likely in late 1953—was not only the critical volleys against the ramparts of an undifferentiated historiography, but also the first formulation of an overall positive conception of the philosophes. Gay's words deserve full citation: "They championed free inquiry, they upheld the right to free thought and expression, they believed in diversity, they were secular, they despised superstition and fanaticism, they believed in the possibilities of reform, and they were passionately humane. Indeed, if Enlightenment thinkers can be summed up in one phrase, I would call them the 'the party of humanity.'"[17]

In view of current interpretations, it helps to note what is, and is not, contained in this brief, emphatic summary: positive is the struggle of freedom and liberty, however defined; negative is the foil of superstition and fanaticism, here as mainly embodied in religion; absent is as yet an assertion of the place of the enlightenment in a narrative of history that concludes with liberal democracy; and completely absent is a "modernization" thesis about the inevitability of enlightenment.

In 1953, serious intellectuals in the United States turned to two texts when trying to make sense of thinkers between Locke and Condorcet: one by Cassirer, the other by Carl Becker, and they were both published thirty years earlier, in 1932. Despite chronological coincidence, they could not have differed more in style, emphasis, and context. One was a serious, tightly argued plea for the continuing relevance of the Enlightenment as mythic ideologies seemed to be overtaking one polity after the next in Europe; the other an erudite *jeu d'esprit* that ranged widely but reflected an American mood of impatient despair.

In *The Philosophy of the Enlightenment*, Cassirer argued that the Enlightenment was not one of many but in fact the decisive step to the modern world, and crucial to this step was the activity of criticism. "The form and manner of intellectual activity itself," Cassirer argued, is what made the Enlightenment worthy of defense, indeed indispensable to modern man.[18] Cassirer traced the emergence of this activity through Leibniz and Baumgarten to Kant, and Gay would later complain that in Cassirer's work the Enlightenment became a "procession of thinkers who all somehow prefigured Kant."[19] Nevertheless, Cassirer advanced three essential, durable arguments: that the Enlightenment's historical sense was more profound than typically assumed, that it represented the beginning of modern thinking, and that the activity, not the product, of independent thought mattered. Cassirer's synthesis also rendered the Enlightenment dynamic and forward-oriented; it placed it in our world, not in a past already past.

In the past: that is where Enlightenment had been placed by Carl Becker—in his day, along with Charles Beard, among the most influential historians in the United States. A brilliant stylist with a gift for using ordinary words and simple sentences to punctuate balloons of academic pretension, Becker became famous (or infamous) for his "relativist" critiques of objectivity. Directed against epistemological simpletons who thought facts speak for themselves, Becker countered that the fact is in the historian's mind or it is nowhere, and that far from the historian sticking to the facts, the facts stick to him.[20] The assault culminated in what remains the most famous presidential speech to the American Historical Association, Becker's "Everyman His own Historian," delivered in 1931. Becker argued that "there is no fact until someone asserts it," that history has always been a "convenient blend of truth and fancy," and that as historians claim the validity of now this fact, now another, they are closer to the bards and storytellers of old than they dare admit.[21] But by 1931, this relativist attack was already an old saw. What irked contemporaries was Becker's pragmatism. Just as Mr. Everyman knows things in order to make his way in the world, historians use, and ought to use, history in order to help understand and shape the present. Claims to just tell the truth about the past scented of false innocence.

Becker's most influential work was a short book that brought together a series of lectures delivered at Yale Law School in 1931 and published as *The Heavenly City of the Eighteenth-Century Philosophers* in the following year by Yale University Press.[22] By the mid-fifties, the book was in its tenth printing, its reception enthusiastic.[23] In *The Heavenly City*, Becker argued that to enter the Enlightenment meant to step into a climate of opinion different from that of Becker's present; and that to understand it historically entailed "showing that it was related to something that came before and to something else that came after."[24]

"Substituting humanity, perfectibility, and faith in reason for God, church, and atonement," the Enlightenment was, according to Becker, "nearer the Middle Ages, less emancipated from the preconceptions of medieval Christian thought than they [the philosophers] quite realized."[25] Put epigrammatically, as Becker liked to do, the thirteenth century was "an age of reason as well as of faith," the eighteenth century an age of "faith as well as of reason."[26] Closer to the very distant past, the Enlightenment was also further away from the present. In the course of the nineteenth century, faith in reason, and the view of the world as a well-functioning machine, was replaced by belief in struggle, by metaphors of dynamics, by Marx and Darwin, and by magnetic fields and relativity. As this occurred, an epistemological gap opened. Then came the challenge of the Russian Revolution, the collapse of the international order, the experience of economic decline, and the advent of new key words such as planning and organization. Taken together, they widened the breach and made the Enlightenment into a past already past. [27]

In 1953, Gay had already written of this "perverse little book" that it prevented serious thinking about the Enlightenment.[28] Then, in 1956, at a conference at Colgate University devoted to the twenty-fifth anniversary of Becker's thesis, Gay mounted his criticism in greater detail. Becker, Gay argued, had failed to understand the vast difference between reason as understood in the thirteenth and the eighteenth centuries. To the medieval scholastics, reason meant deduction; to the eighteenth century *philosophes*, no more than confidence in the potential of rational inquiry to advance knowledge and improve society. Becker's supposedly brilliant thesis depended on clever, ahistorical word play, Gay told an unreceptive audience. But when brushed at with ordinary philology and a historian's insistence on the epoch-specific meaning of concepts, its dazzle quickly dulled.

Recriminations came hard and fast, and Gay later wrote "the frequency, vehemence, and unanimity of the comments to which I was exposed gave me confidence," and a sense that "I had been right all along."[29] Yet Gay's refutation was hardly airtight. If Becker made the philosophes into unwitting ersatz Christians, Gay made them into confident pagans and deists—a characterization that covered some, but not others, and tended to give the whole Enlightenment a greater irreligious cast than it actually had.[30] Although no one argued the point at the time, it is now widely considered that when taken as a European phenomenon, and major and minor figures are included, the Enlightenment was mainly populated by Christian Enlighteners still struggling within the tradition to reform it. Hume, d'Alembert, and Voltaire were brilliant secular exceptions, whom a later, more worldly age canonized as standing *pars pro toto* for the whole epoch. Becker was moreover not entirely wrong to see in the tradition of natural law something grounded in Christian ethics—even if of a kind that tried to navigate through a world decimated by religious warfare.

But to referee a past debate with what may be the differently flawed understanding of the present is to miss the large issue. What separated Gay from Becker was not a dispute about detail, though Gay's interpretation would eventually come with deeper understanding, a much richer source base, and more serious attention to the social and cultural world in which a wide range of philosophes thought and wrote. Rather, the difference was one of what Max Black called "root metaphor": the underlying worldview structuring the image of Enlightenment.[31] For Becker, the progressive historian facing the coming challenges of his era and not yet having a sense how serious they were, enlightened faith seemed misplaced, wanting in realism, a futile argument against the future. It was not so much dangerous as beside the point. It also evidenced an immature attitude toward truth—the noble but mistaken dream of objectivity that Charles Beard would, following Becker, skewer in another famous relativist address to the American Historical Association in 1935.[32] For Gay, steeped in Cassirer, and having a Jewish émigré's sense for just how high the stakes were, the enlightened commitment to reason, which was not naïve but critical and open to the range of human passions, was the *sine qua non* of modern life in the face of the Nazi dictatorship. The National Socialists had for a time pushed the Enlightenment, and the values of tolerance and criticism it stood for, into an unilluminated corner. But for Gay, the Enlightenment belonged nowhere if not at the very center of modern history. Getting it right was as crucial as relativism was irresponsible.[33]

There was, as well, an American context. As certainly as the early thirties had for Becker cast doubt on the utility of a naïve belief in reason, the early fifties demanded for Gay its forceful reaffirmation. The issue was McCarthyism, a serious intellectual and political threat in Gay's newly adopted country. While careful not to echo overblown cries of a pervasive witch-hunt, Gay recognized its corrosive effect on intellectuals inside and outside the university: now this person, now that, often in America's smaller colleges, being fired, denied tenure, shunned. It is nowadays easy to imagine that all academics opposed McCarthyism. But the issues were at the time subtler. In one of his few printed public stands of the 1950s, Gay criticized David Riesman's denigration of liberal intellectuals for whom anti-McCarthyism and cries of persecution were becoming a road to in-group cohesion. However insightful Riesman's analysis, Gay retorted in the pages of *The American Scholar*, it was cowardly to allow real persecutions to pass uncommented upon. What was necessary was to leaven space for a critical, realistic public sphere in which it was possible to be, for example, both anti-Franco and anti-Stalin, and at the same time to question the constitutionality of the Smith Act, which established criminal penalties for advocating the overthrow of the U.S. government.[34]

Finally, recalling McCarthyism suggests what the context of Gay's centering of Enlightenment was not. It was not, as has been argued, a counter-narrative to postwar liberal thinking in Germany centered on explaining 1933. As Gay formulated his central ideas on the Enlightenment, he was not yet reading new German work (save perhaps for the reflections of the aged Meinecke) on the import of the eighteenth-century Enlightenment for understanding the twentieth-century misdirection of Germany. He had also not read Horkheimer and Adorno's *Dialectic of Enlightenment*—it is nowhere cited in Gay's prodigious bibliographical commentaries of the fifties or the sixties.[35] Nor was the Holocaust, as such, the dark other to which the Enlightenment was held up as a beacon. While the Holocaust no doubt shaped a great deal of thinking at the time, Gay more immediately experienced the first years of National Socialist rule and the McCarthyism of the 1950s. Yet Gay never thought of McCarthyism as an American version of Nazism. Rather, he believed that McCarthyism demonstrated that societies must wage constant battles against obscurantism, deceit, and cowardice, and that it exposed the fragility of political freedom, especially troubling since it occurred in the United States.[36]

The general atmosphere of McCarthyism, which poisoned public discussions and rendered universities rife with denunciation and fear, also imparted urgency to Gay's strident formulations about religion. There were, of course, background factors to these formulations: Gay came from Berlin, one of the most secular cities in the world, and grew up in a family that self-identified not as Jewish but as *konfessionslos* (nondenominational); and Gay's father was, in Gay's words, a principled, aggressive, atheist.[37] Nowhere does Gay indicate unease with the ordinary anticlericalism typical of this environment. Yet during the 1950s, that general anticlerical sentiment assumed a more important, even causal, function in Gay's historical understanding. One place to see this is in his essay "The Party of Humanity," published in 1959, an expanded, significantly reworked version of his "The Enlightenment in the History of Political Theory" of 1954. Substantially added was the claim of the contemporary relevance of Enlightenment as an antidote to "an age of timid return to dependence on the supernatural, to tradition and authority."[38] Partly, Gay echoed Cassirer's distinction between the mythic and the critical. Partly, Gay aimed at conservative and neoliberal detractors of Enlightenment, such as Russell Kirk, who read the Enlightenment through Edmund Burke, and Jacob Talmon, who traced totalitarianism to the *volonté general* of Jean Jacques Rousseau.[39] Mostly, however, Gay imagined the excesses of organized religion as the true precursor to the persecutions of the present. Against Talmon's genealogy of modern totalitarianism, Gay asked, rhetorically, "Which was more totalitarian, the institutions that burned dissenters, or the movements that tried to save them?"[40]

Soon after Gay had finished his first programmatic article, he began to sketch out the wider interpretation. At first, he thought of writing a three-volume work on Enlighteners of second rank, men such as Lessing and Holbach, Gibbons and Lichtenberg, and Helvetius.[41] In this project one can perhaps discern the intellectual pull of his close friend and mentor, Richard Hofstadter, who in American history wrote brilliantly about characteristic middlebrow thinkers. Perhaps fate, perhaps coincidence, but precisely then the first volumes of Theodore Besterman's critical editions of Voltaire's letters appeared. Reading them, Gay later recalled, proved a revelation. They disclosed a Voltaire deeply involved in politics, in mortal fear of the authorities, and a dissident deliberately disguising the subversive messages in his poems, letters, and plays.

When Gay arrived in Princeton as a fellow in fall 1954, "the larger project was in shambles," and he instead focused on Voltaire alone.[42] Scouring Princeton's Firestone Library, he discovered in little-known pamphlets telling evidence of how the philosophe had veiled his political convictions. The finds were invigorating, and Gay began to immerse himself in Voltaire's world. One set of influences and two publications from that time further sharpened his thinking. The influence was the Warburg school, personified at the Advanced Institute at Princeton by Erwin Panofsky, about whom Gay wrote in almost reverent tones. The authors of the Warburg school sharpened Gay's insights about the transmission of the classical heritage through the Middle Ages and into the Renaissance—a set of concerns that played a minor role in Gay's Voltaire book but emerged centrally in the first volume of his wider interpretation of the Enlightenment; indeed, the careful calibration of the relationship of the Enlightenment to the classical contributed to the power and sweep of that interpretation. There was, as well, an article by Hajo Holborn, an émigré historian at Yale who had been widely considered one of the most brilliant of the Meinecke students, but who is now better known for his three-volume *History of Modern Germany*, a sprawling, uneven work. In the *Historische Zeitschrift* in 1952, Holborn had published a seminal article entitled "German Idealism in Light of Social History."[43] The baleful tradition of the unpolitical German had already begun in the eighteenth century and had hardened by 1840, Holborn contended, and the failed intellectual engagement with society and politics marked a fateful divergence between German and western European traditions of thought. Decisive to Gay was the argument, still more the method: it brought intellectual history away from wandering among the peaks, as Meinecke practiced it, and into closer contact with society. It is from reading this essay that Gay derived his concept of the "social history of ideas," an unfortunate misnomer (more felicitous would have been the cultural history of ideas) since as yet emerging concepts of social history, whether inspired by the *Annales* School, E. P. Thompson, or the new American social history, used different kinds of documents and possessed a very different understanding of the social. Finally, Gay had in the summer of 1954 read with great "excitement" Erich Auerbach's *Mimesis: The Representation of Reality in Western Literature*.[44] As a consequence of the separation of literary styles, high and low, Western literature, Auerbach showed, resisted with few and incomplete exceptions the convergence of tragic seriousness with everyday life, and instead cultivated a literature exclusively concerned with the affairs of one class, the nobility. The full emancipation from this doctrine only occurred in the nineteenth century, according to Auerbach: in France, with the great realist tradition of Stendahl, Balzac, and Zola, and then in prose, not verse. It did not occur in Germany, where historicism, while theoretically capable of bridging the gap, resisted the details of the everyday. Precisely the convergence of literature and life, poetry and politics, style and representation was then at the center of Gay's thinking, and Voltaire's letters. When Gay later subtitled his study "The Poet as Realist," he announced Voltaire's circumspect but pragmatic and engaged involvement in politics. But the reverberation of Auerbach was also audible. The hidden criticism of Auerbach's thesis was of the German intellectual tradition for its failures in the face of real world challenges. Is it too much to suggest that the hidden criticism likewise echoed in Gay's subtitle?

Voltaire's Politics appeared in 1959 and represented an unflinchingly positive revision of Voltaire's place in the Enlightenment. Against Voltaire's detractors based on the philosophe's supposedly doctrinaire penchant for enlightened despotism, Gay argued that Voltaire in his *Lettres Anglaise* provided the "first radical critique of the old regime," and his involvement with monarchs such as Frederick of Prussia and Catherine of Russia was pragmatic and realist.[45] The rule of law and free expression constituted Voltaire's "most strongly held political convictions," and lent his politics, in Gay's reading, "close affinities to the liberal and democratic traditions."[46] The same held for Voltaire's histories—often criticized for an anemic sense of the pastness of the past and for glorifying an absolutist present. Gay showed the subtle criticism that inhered in these histories and that revealed Voltaire as hardly an "indiscriminate royalist" and more than willing to criticize the kings of France, especially when they brushed law and common humanity aside. Finally, Gay showed a secular Voltaire who believed the organized church to be the fount of intolerance, repression, and a brake on human improvement. The attack was less theological than political. Holborn had discerned the origins of the nonpolitical German; in Voltaire, Gay showed the opposite—a poet realist who believed in reasoned reform and was open to democratic possibilities.

In *The Enlightenment: An Interpretation*, which appeared in two volumes, *The Rise of Modern Paganism* in 1966 and *The Science of Freedom* in 1969, Gay broadened his analysis.[47] Following the method expounded by Cassirer, Gay discerned the dialectical center holding together the Enlightenment in an admixture of "classicism, impiety, and science," which bound an otherwise "wholly unorganized coalition of cultural critics, religious skeptics, and political reformers."[48] Not merely a convenient frame, the argument for unity was central to Gay's Cassirer-inspired method. The philosophes, Gay argued, were revolutionaries, but respectable ones. They were at home in urban Europe, especially in England, Holland, France, and America. They were hardworking. They were cosmopolitan. They practiced serious criticism. And they were modern. By modern, Gay meant not medieval and not religious. The modernity of the Enlightenment derived from its indebtedness to the classical, whether Stoic or Epicurean; from its carrying to a close the break of the Renaissance; and from its connection to the liberal temperament of the present. There was nothing preordained about the trajectory of this narrative. The Enlighteners, according to Gay, possessed a dualistic historical vision. They saw the past as alternating between periods of faith and periods of criticism, and they never assumed criticism would win over faith; instead, they actively fought for that victory. The resonance of Cassirer, particularly his analysis of the struggle between the "mythic" and the "critical," informs Gay's larger argument and tells why the assertion of Enlightenment remained crucial to modernity.

But Gay's contribution fundamentally differed from Cassirer's. If Cassirer's celebrated work on the Enlightenment centered on German *Aufklärer* (Enlighteners), Gay's synthesis stopped for only the briefest sojourn in Germany. "The German *Aufklärer* were isolated, impotent, and almost wholly unpolitical," Gay argued, and endorsed Georg Christoph Lichtenberg's famous notebook entry that a "heavy tax, at least in Germany, rests on the windows of the Enlightenment."[49] And if Cassirer ended with Kant as his hero-skeptic, Gay settled on Hume, who, unlike Kant, was a "complete modern pagan" asserting "that God is silent" and "man is his own master."[50] In Gay's view, the leaders of the German Enlightenment, unlike the French philosophes, still sought what Aby Warburg had called a "compromise formula," the characteristic attempt of sixteenth-century humanists to mediate between a classical and a religious view of the world.[51] The drift of history was elsewhere, Gay contended, and drew the boundaries between the secular and religious spheres with a sharper stylus. Gay also delved deeper into what he called the social context of ideas but is more recognizable as the cultural underpinnings of thought. Finally, Gay's mental map of the Enlightenment possessed an unmistakable western orientation, with centers in Paris, London, Edinburgh, and Geneva. Telling, Gay concludes the second volume with America, "the hope of civilized men everywhere in the eighteenth century," with a meditation on the Federalist Papers, and with the philosophe's declaration—based on the American, not the French, Revolution—that the "Enlightenment had been a success."[52]

Gay's work on the Enlightenment was a product of nearly two decades of reading, writing, and reflection, even if its outlines and coordinates were squarely set in the 1950s. The same may be said of his interest in Freud, even if this was less apparent from the published work. Gay first began to think about Freud as a young man in Denver, and deepened his thinking about him in Franz Neumann's seminar at Columbia in 1950. In his article on the political theory of the Enlightenment, published in 1954, Gay had already referred to Freud as "the greatest child of the Enlightenment which our century has known"; in the same year he had translated Neumann's "Anxiety and Politics," a lecture given upon conferral of an honorary doctorate at the Free University that appropriated psychoanalytic insights to analyze modern alienation.⁵³ Gay also conceived of a study, never carried out, on "Love, Work, and Politics," and in his many intense conversations with Richard Hofstadter, whom Gay once described as "drenched in Freud," the use of psychoanalysis to understand the irrational in politics was a central topic.⁵⁴ Yet Freud was largely absent from Gay's study of Voltaire, and reappeared in the two-volume synthesis only as a light interpretive thread, mainly in volume 2, and mainly with respect to individual thinkers and to the loose, general post-Christian identity crisis of the family of philosophes. One can make too much of these references, as Robert Darnton perhaps does in his important criticism of Gay's two volumes.⁵⁵ The interpretive architecture of Gay's Enlightenment stands without them. Moreover, what shot out to later historians was quite ordinary in its time. Freud, now outside the mainstream of historical interpretation, then commanded significant attention. Combining Marx and Freud was at the center of pleas for the next agenda of cultural and intellectual history; one can see it, for example, in a 1954 grant application of a young scholar at Harvard, Carl Schorske, hoping to receive funding for a project aiming to understand "the uniquely anti-humanistic movements of our time," and it emerged in the interpretive floorplan of the first work Gay wrote since his dissertation that focused on Germany: the short book on Weimar Culture.⁵⁶

The book owes its existence to Bernard Bailyn and Donald Fleming's request that Gay write a background essay for an edited collection entitled "The Intellectual Migration." The commission to write about very recent history—Weimar then was as far back as the 1970s is now—likely resulted from Gay's general reputation as a historian and his evident interest in the intellectual world of the émigrés.⁵⁷ But his acceptance signaled the beginning of a distance from Gay as the "*dixhuitiemiste* with his heart in Paris," as one student put it, to the historian of Europe that included, more insistently than before, Gay as "*ein Berliner.*"⁵⁸ The book was, after all, part eulogy and part summons of a Germany, centered in Berlin, that Gay, following Karl Mannheim, compared to the Athens of Pericles. In the 1960s, Gay's attitude towards Germany, as he recounts in *My German Question*, shifted, slowly but certainly. He had returned to Berlin for the first time in 1961—but only for four nightmare-filled days. Much that had occurred in the Federal Republic was not reassuring. Nazi professors were still, or again, in their positions. Herbert Karajan, who joined the Nazi Party not once but twice, conducted the Berlin Philharmonic Orchestra. And Hans Globke, coauthor of the official commentary on the Nuremberg Laws, was director of the Federal Chancellery and as such one of Adenauer's closest aids. But there were indicators of change, too. When in 1963–64 Gay was a fellow at the Advanced Institute in the Behavioral Sciences at Stanford, he became close friends with the Brachers—Karl Dietrich, whose books on the dissolution of Weimar and on the Nazi seizure of power constituted the first serious, sober, scholarly assessments of Nazism from the pen of a historian from the Federal Republic, and his wife

Dorothee—whose mother, Ursula, was Dietrich Bonhoeffer's sister and whose father, Rüdiger Schleicher, was killed after the plot to assassinate Hitler failed. It was on the urgings of the Brachers that Peter Gay and his wife Ruth returned to Germany in 1967, and thereafter regularly.[59] It is also in this period that Gay, whose work had been ignored in the Federal Republic, began to make connections with German scholars.

Gay first employed the term "cosmopolitan work" in *A Loss of Mastery: Puritan Historians in Colonial America*, one of Gay's least well-known books and especially interesting for its spatial, temporal context.[60] It is the only book Gay ever wrote explicitly about American history. It comes as he was beginning to rethink the place of Germany. And it contains a remarkable page-filling dedicatory sentence that begins "to the many thousands of pilgrims, Jewish and not Jewish, German and Austrian and Polish, whom Hitler compelled to discover America."[61] Focusing on the historical writing of three famous Puritans—William Bradford, Cotton Mather, and Jonathan Edwards—Gay argues that they clung to mythic preoccupations when critical history offered alternative models. It is a story of provincialism overpowering cosmopolitanism, of ideology getting in the way of honesty, and of the lure of myth overwhelming the call of criticism. It is a story of loss, its title at once a psychoanalytic turn of phrase and a reminder of what is forfeited when societies set realistic introspection aside. And it is an indictment of historians who saw themselves as "victims, not as actors."[62] It is, I think—though no documentary evidence supports my contention, and therefore it remains nothing more than a speculative private insight—also a book about postwar Germany. The Puritans succumbed to myth. It could have been otherwise. For the Germans it might still be otherwise.

Gay wrote *Weimar Culture* in a blaze, both the eighty-page torso for Bailyn and Fleming, and the book, about twice as long.[63] The difference between the two contributions is one of emphasis. For the book publication, Gay added material on Stefan George and his circle, a treatment of Rilke's poetry, a description of the renaissance of critical interest in Hölderlin, Kleist, and Büchner, an excursion on the unpolitical German, and more extended reflections on Thomas Mann, a section on Heidegger, and a unit on expressionist theatre and art. The shorter version emphasizes the contributions of Jews somewhat more—though Gay never thought of Weimar culture as an "inner-Jewish dialogue to which few gentiles listened," as George Mosse, echoing George Lichtheim, once put it.[64] In both versions, there is preciously little on the specifically Jewish dimension of Weimar: nothing on Rosenzweig or Scholem, nothing on Leo Baeck or Joseph Roth, a mere mention of Walter Benjamin, and Martin Buber only insofar as he commented on Stefan George. Moreover, the shorter essay contained a great deal that could never be misunderstood as "inner-Jewish": there are extended treatments of Meinecke, Hintze, and Kehr; of Marc, Klee, and Grosz; of Mann, Brecht, and Harry Graf Kessler. And there are critical addendums to the Jewish dimensions of Weimar, such as the Frankfurt School, to which Gay affixed in the book a question mark not in the essay: "but was it a group of powerful intellectuals?"[65]

When the chapter, and book, appeared in 1968, they resonated not for their coverage of Jewish or non-Jewish Weimar, but for their telling of the promise and peril of generational revolt. Gay did not purposely chart the contemporary parallel—and in fact in a *New York Times* letter he chided one reviewer, Nathan Glazer, the former husband of Peter Gay's wife Ruth, for making the parallel explicit. "America is not Weimar," Gay retorted, and American students of the left in the 1960s were not German students of the right in the 1920s and '30s.[66] Superficial similarities of rhetoric and method aside, they shared neither social aspirations nor political programs, and the issues were different. Yet the deeper pull of psychoanalytic categories, especially pertaining to generational conflict, was more central to the analysis of Weimar than it had been to any of Gay's previous works. This was even more fleshed out in the book than in the chapter. The chapter for Bailyn and Flemming is divided into recognizably psychoanalytic, in fact oedipal, categories: the trauma of birth, the roles (later "community") of reason, the hunger for wholeness, and the revenge of the father. The organization of the book heightens the oedipal drama further still: Gay inserted a chapter on "The Secret Germany: Poetry as Power" and interleaved "Revolt of the Son: The Expressionist Years" between the "The Hunger for Wholeness" and "The Revenge of the Father." As he had not done before, Gay laced *Weimar Culture* with psychoanalytic insight. There was the severity of the trauma of birth, and the November Revolution as a revolt against paternal authority. There was the hunger for wholeness—"a great regression born of a great fear: the fear of modernity"—and that hunger fed by any number of smaller regressions.[67] And there was the wish for death—as the fascination with Kleist evidenced. There was, as well, the positive side: plotting the politics of socialists and republicans as the son's bid for rational freedom against irrational authority, seeing the expressionist as the son's revolt against the father; and everywhere emphasizing the struggle, the necessity, for mastery, and insisting on the Enlightenment's great lesson: "that the cure for the ills of modernity is more, and the right kind of modernity."[68]

Still now, it is difficult not to be impressed by the virtuosity of Gay's *Weimar Culture*. Yet it also seems, at least to me, to be a partisan book—its judgments rest too secure, and the language of psychoanalysis shored up, rather than unsettled, what Gay already knew and felt. Perhaps this is a danger of contemporary history more generally. Perhaps it jeopardizes psychoanalytically informed history. The book, in any case, was to be a start. In its introductory pages, he had already announced a "more complete history of the Weimar Renaissance."[69] He also, at this time, considered going back into German history to write a cultural history of the Imperial period, without which the renaissance of Weimar could not be understood.[70] That project, too, was never carried out. Yet it shows what might have been Gay's scholarly trajectory, and it suggests that at least part of the "cosmopolitan work" he was engaged in at the end of his Columbia years was the attempt to write Germany back into a history of modernity centered on the Enlightenment. If a road not taken, it remains a road to consider—powerful for its essentially comic mode asserted against tragic experience. Like the *philosophes*, the young Gay was a wry-smiled optimist—in a way that we, who have perhaps endured less, are not.

Helmut Walser Smith is the Martha Rivers Ingram Professor of History at Vanderbilt University and the author of *German Nationalism and Religious Conflict: Culture, Ideology, Politics, 1870–1914* (1995), *The Butcher's Tale: Murder and Anti-Semitism in a German Town* (2002), *The Continuities of German History: Nation, Religion and Race across the Long Nineteenth Century* (2008), and, as editor, *The Oxford Handbook of Modern German History* (2011). He is currently working on a study of German conceptions of the nation before, during, and after the era of nationalism.

Notes

This essay was written before Peter Gay's death. He read an earlier version and offered his appreciation and criticism, for which I am grateful.

1. Quote from Harold Mah, *Enlightenment Phantasies: Cultural Identity in France and Germany* (Ithaca, 2003), 182, n. 5, see also his critique on 3–6; further, Dorinda Outram, *The Enlightenment* (Cambridge, 1995), 4–6; Robert Darnton, "In Search of Enlightenment: Recent Attempts to Create a Social History of Ideas," *The Journal of Modern History* 43 (March, 1971): 113–32.
2. On the importance of the 1950s as an intellectual context, see Merel Leeman, "Discovering a Lost Intellectuals' Project: George Mosse and Peter Gay on Myth and Mind in History," in Carolina Rodriguez-Lopez and Jose M. Feraldo, eds., *Reconsidering a Lost Intellectuals' Project: Exiles' Reflections on Cultural Differences* (Cambridge, 2012), 13–36. On the counter-narrative, Steven E. Aschheim, *Beyond the Border: The German-Jewish Legacy Abroad* (Princeton, 2007), 45–80; on the Enlightenment as modernization, Annelien de Dijn, "The Politics of Enlightenment: From Peter Gay to Jonathan Israel," *The Historical Journal* 55 (2012): 785–805, where it is also emphasized that "the cold war context is crucial to understanding Gay's work" (789). The best analysis of Gay's career is Robert L. Dietle and Mark S. Micale, "Peter Gay: A Life in History," in *Enlightenment, Passion, Modernity: Historical Essays in European Thought and Culture* (Palo Alto, CA, 2000), 1–23. My analysis differs mainly in its focus on the intellectual context of the 1950s.
3. Victors and actors in Peter Gay, *A Loss of Mastery: Puritan Historians in Colonial America* (New York, 1966), 25; Volcano in Peter Gay, *Weimar Culture: The Outsider as Insider* (New York, 1968), xiv.
4. Peter Gay, *My German Question: Growing Up in Nazi Berlin* (New Haven, 1998), 191.
5. Peter Gay, *The Dilemma of Democratic Socialism: Eduard Bernstein's Challenge to Marx*, reprint (New York, 1962), 159.
6. Ibid., 155.

7. Peter Gay, "A Life of Learning," Charles Homer Haskings Lecture. ACLS Occasional Paper no. 58 (New York, 2004), 2.
8. Peter Gay, "Introduction," in Ernst Cassirer, *The Question of Jean Jacques Rousseau*, ed. and trans. with an introduction by Peter Gay (New Haven, 1954), 21. On Cassirer's early reception in the United States, see Thomas Meyer, *Ernst Cassirer* (Hamburg, 2006), 233–44.
9. See Peter Gay, "The Social History of Ideas: Ernst Cassirer and After," in Kurt H. Wolff and Barrington Moore, Jr., eds., *The Critical Spirit: Essays in Honor of Herbert Marcuse* (Boston, 1967), 111. On Cassirer's philosophical assumptions and his commitment to Enlightenment, see especially Peter E. Gordon, *Continental Divide: Heidegger, Cassirer, Davos* (Cambridge, 2010), 291–322.
10. Ernst Cassirer, *The Question of Jean Jacques Rousseau*.
11. Ibid., 126.
12. Ibid., 27.
13. The connection drawn too closely in Annelien de Dijn, "The Politics of Enlightenment: From Peter Gay to Jonathan Israel," 785–805.
14. Peter Gay, "The Enlightenment in the History of Political Theory," *Political Science Quarterly* 69 (1954): 374.
15. Peter Gay, *Voltaire's Politics: The Poet as Realist*, 2nd ed. (New Haven, 1988), 377. "Reason consists of always seeing things as they are."
16. Gay, "The Enlightenment in the History of Political Theory," 386.
17. Ibid., 389.
18. Cassirer cited in Gordon, *Continental Divide*, 293.
19. Peter Gay, "The Unity of the French Enlightenment," in *The Party of Humanity: Essays in the French Enlightenment*, reprint (New York, 1971), 114.
20. Carl L. Becker, "Detachment and the Writing of History," in *Detachment and the Writing of History: Essays and Letters of Carl L. Becker*, ed. Phil L. Snyder (Ithaca, 1958), 24.
21. Carl L. Becker, "Everyman his own Historian," in *Everyman His Own Historian: Essays on History and Politics*, reprint (Chicago, 1966), 251, 248.
22. Carl L. Becker, *The Heavenly City of the Eighteenth-Century Philosophers* (New Haven, 1932).
23. Peter Gay, "Carl Becker's Heavenly City," in Raymond O. Rockwood, ed., *Carl Becker's Heavenly City Revisited* (Ithaca, 1958), 29.
24. Becker, *The Heavenly City*, 29.
25. Ibid., 25.
26. Ibid., 8.
27. Ibid., 165–67.
28. Gay, "The Enlightenment in the History of Political Theory," 376.
29. Gay, "A Life of Learning," 5.
30. See especially David Sorkin, *The Religious Enlightenment: Protestants, Jews, and Catholics from London to Vienna* (Princeton, NJ, 2008); Jonathan Sheehan, *The Enlightenment Bible: Translation, Scholarship, Culture* (Princeton, NJ, 2007); and Michael Printy, *Enlightenment and the Creation of German Catholicism* (New York, 2009), though these works more advocate the integration of the religious back into our understanding of the Enlightenment than offer integrating syntheses.
31. Max Black, *Models and Metaphors: Studies in Language and Philosophy* (Ithaca, 1962), 239–41, drawing on Stephen C. Pepper.
32. Charles A. Beard, "That Noble Dream," *American Historical Review* 41, no. 1 (Oct. 1935): 74–87.
33. Of his two-volume *The Enlightenment: An Interpretation*, Gay would later write "I suppose '*The Interpretation*' would have sounded immodest; but it would have been what I meant." Peter Gay, *Style in History* (New Haven, 1974), 211, n. 26.

34. Peter Gay, letter to the editor, in "More about Freedom and Loyalty," *The American Scholar* 23 (Summer, 1954): 376–78. See also Peter Gay, "Home in America," *American Scholar* 46 (1977): 31–42, esp. 39–40.
35. Max Horkheimer and Theodor Adorno, *Dialektik der Aufklärung. Philosophische Fragmente* (Amsterdam, 1947). As far as I can make out, Reinhart Koselleck's *Kritik und Krise* (Freiburg, 1959) is the first scholarly work on the Enlightenment to cite Horkheimer and Adorno's *Dialektik der Aufklärung*. It was first published in mimeograph form as "Philosophical Fragments" in New York in 1944, then as a book in Amsterdam in 1947.
36. Gay, *The Party of Humanity*, 187. The context also tells us that Gay's understanding of Enlightenment had nothing to do with early versions of modernization theory. In this period, Gay nowhere cited progenitors such as Talcott Parsons or Seymour Martin Lipset, and underscored not the inevitably but the fragility of Enlightenment.
37. Peter Gay, "The German-Jewish Legacy—and I," in Abraham J. Peck, ed., *The German-Jewish Legacy in America, 1938–1988* (Detroit, 1989), 17.
38. Gay, *The Party of Humanity*, 137.
39. See, for example, Russell Kirk, *The Conservative Mind: From Burke to Santayana* (Washington, DC, 1953); Jacob L. Talmon, *The Origins of Totalitarian Democracy* (Boston, 1952).
40. Gay, *The Party of Humanity*, 282.
41. Gay, *Voltaire's Politics*, xi.
42. Ibid., xii.
43. Hajo Holborn, "Der deutsche Idealismus in sozialgeschichtlicher Beleuchtung," *Historische Zeitschrift* 174 (1952): 359–84.
44. On reading Erich Auerbach, *Mimesis: Representations of Reality in Western Literature*, trans. William Trask (Princeton, NJ, 1953), see Gay, "The German-Jewish Legacy—and I," 22.
45. Gay, *Voltaire's Politics*, 48, 180.
46. Ibid., 14.
47. Peter Gay, *The Enlightenment: An Interpretation*, 2 vols. (New York, 1966, 1969).
48. Peter Gay, *The Enlightenment: An Interpretation*, vol. 1, *The Rise of Modern Paganism*, (New York, 1966), 8, 3.
49. Ibid., 4.
50. Ibid., 401, 419. On this aspect of Gay's interpretation, see Martin Jay, "Modern and Postmodern Paganism: Peter Gay and Jean-François Lyotard," in Dietle and Micale, *Enlightenment, Passion, Modernity*, 256.
51. Gay, *The Enlightenment: An Interpretation*, vol. 1, *The Rise of Modern Paganism*, 270. Warburg's term was *Ausgleichsformel*.
52. Peter Gay, *The Enlightenment: An Interpretation*, vol. 2, *The Science of Freedom* (New York, 1969), 567–68.
53. On Freud as the greatest child of the Enlightenment, Gay, "The Enlightenment in the History of Political Theory," 379; the translation of Neumann in Friedrich Neumann, "Anxiety and Politics," in *The Democratic and the Authoritarian State: Essays in Political and Legal Theory* (Glencoe, IL, 1979), 270–300.
54. Peter Gay, "History, Biography, Psychoanalysis," in Elizabeth Fox Keller, Peter Gay, and E. H. Gombrich, eds., *Three Cultures: Fifteen Lectures on the Confrontation of Academic Cultures* (Rotterdam, 1989), 94.
55. Robert Darnton, "In Search of Enlightenment: Recent Attempts to Create a Social History of Ideas," *The Journal of Modern History* 43 (March 1971): 120.
56. Carl Schorske, "Proposed Plan for Study," Jan. 1954, Folder S, Box 13, William Langer Papers, Harvard University Library.
57. Gay, "A Life of Learning," 12; Email communication from Bernard Bailyn, 15 February 2014.

58. D*ixhuitiemiste* (specialist in the eighteenth century) in Dora B. Weiner, "A Provincial Doctor Faces the Paris Establishment," in Dietle and Micale, *Enlightenment, Passion, Modernity*, 66.
59. Gay, *My German Question*, 196–98.
60. Gay, *A Loss of Mastery*, 6.
61. Ibid., v.
62. Ibid., 25.
63. Peter Gay, "Weimar Culture: The Outsider as Insider," in Donald Fleming and Bernard Bailyn, eds., *The Intellectual Migration: Europe and America, 1930–1960* (Cambridge, 1969), 11–93. This publication contains a 1968 copyright as *Perspectives in American History*, volume 2, publications of the Charles Warren Center, Harvard University.
64. George Mosse, "The End Is Not Yet: A Personal Memoir of the German-Jewish Legacy in America," in Peck, *The German-Jewish Legacy*, 14.
65. Gay, *Weimar Culture*, 43. On Marcuse, Gay, "The German-Jewish Legacy—and I," 22–23.
66. Peter Gay, "America and Weimar," *New York Times*, 12 October 1969. Gay worked out the limits of the analogy in a short essay entitled "The Weimar Resemblance," *Horizon* 12, no. 1 (1970): 4–14.
67. Peter Gay, *Weimar Culture*, 96.
68. Ibid., 101
69. Ibid., xiv.
70. Dietle and Micale, "Peter Gay: A Life in History," 7. Gay mentions this project in the introduction to Peter Gay, *Freud, Jews, and other Germans: Masters and Victims in Modernist Culture* (Oxford, 1978), 6.

Chapter 15

OUT OF THE LIMELIGHT OR IN
Raul Hilberg, Gerhard Weinberg, Henry Friedlander,
and the Historical Study of the Holocaust

Doris L. Bergen

The phrase "second generation" has a particular meaning in Holocaust studies circles, where it refers to the children of Holocaust survivors.¹ In this sense, the three scholars who are the subject of this chapter are not of the second generation: they are the first. Raul Hilberg's immediate family fled Vienna in 1939, chased out of their home at gunpoint. They managed to get to Cuba and then in 1940 to the United States.² Gerhard Weinberg was ten years old when he saw his family's synagogue in Hanover destroyed in the *Kristallnacht* pogrom. He, his brother, and their parents escaped to England and subsequently to the United States.³ Almost all members of both Hilberg's and Weinberg's extended families were murdered in the Shoah. Henry Friedlander, born in 1930 in Berlin, was transported with his parents in 1941 to the Łódź ghetto. The Friedländers, as they were then called, managed to stay alive for almost three years only to be sent to Auschwitz-Birkenau in 1944, where Henry's mother and sister were killed upon arrival. He and his father were shuffled through a series of other camps and subcamps—Neuengamme, Ravensbrück—and eventually liberated. He came to Canada on his own as a teenager and from there moved on to the United States.⁴

Neither Hilberg, Weinberg, nor Friedlander focus on these personal experiences in their scholarship—indeed, they rarely if ever mention such things at all. But I raise them here because they are central to the main point of this essay. It is a simple one: these three scholars—second-generation German/Austrian Jewish exiles, in the vocabulary of this volume—shaped the historical study of the Holocaust in North America and beyond. They were not alone, of course: others made

---

Notes from this chapter begin on page 239.

key contributions, notably the survivor scholars Saul Friedländer, born in Prague in 1932,[5] although his most influential work came after theirs;[6] and Nechama Tec, born in Lublin, writing in English but, atypically for the field, as a sociologist.[7] Hilberg, Weinberg, and Henry Friedlander established central questions, identified key sources and made them accessible to others. And they opened the field in crucial ways that transcended issues of identity. From their base in the United States and through their publications in English, they made study of the Holocaust an international project, linked to scholars and institutions in Israel, Germany, and elsewhere in Europe but not dependent on them. Their combination of absolute scholarly rigor and personal engagement created a field of unusual strength and dynamism.

Questions and Sources

Raul Hilberg, Gerhard Weinberg, and Henry Friedlander all engage the big question: how did the Holocaust happen? But they do so in very different ways and with very different results. For Hilberg, the social scientist, trained at Columbia and influenced by Franz Neumann, the author of *Behemoth: The Structure and Practice of National Socialism*,[8] the key sources were the records of the German bureaucracy—and the answer to "how" was that bureaucracy itself. Systems, mechanisms, dynamics—these are the phenomena that caught Hilberg's attention. How did it happen? Hilberg famously responded, "step by step." Familiarity ("ordinariness"), chronology, division of labor, competing authorities (polycracy), "working toward the Führer," modernity, banality, center and periphery—all of these concepts, celebrated later as innovations in the field, appear in Hilberg's 1961 work, *The Destruction of the European Jews*, which might be called the greatest book about the Holocaust that is the least read.[9] Much of what scholars in the field claim as original he thought of already and addressed somewhere in those multiple editions of the three volumes.[10] A truly foundational work, *The Destruction of the European Jews* established lines of inquiry and identified the sources to go with them.

For Hilberg, evidence was everywhere, and for that reason, he found relevant material in both likely and unlikely places. In his words, as a researcher of the Holocaust, "you cannot skip anything: you cannot omit any place or organization."[11] He was adept at noticing and highlighting details that could illuminate the whole. For instance, to illustrate how petty measures isolated Jews, Hilberg observed that as of September 1941, in the German client state of Slovakia, even letters mailed by Jews were to be marked with a Star of David, so that they could be opened by police and destroyed.[12] Hilberg pioneered the field as eclectic; there is no knowing where a resourceful researcher might find insight. At the same time he recognized that incompleteness was, as he put it, "inherent in the sources." In his dramatic formulation, "Empirical history is by definition salvage. It cannot be more."[13]

It is often said that Hilberg opposed using Jewish sources, but this is not the case. His last book, on sources of the Holocaust, included extensive discussion of Jewish materials,[14] and he also included contemporaneous Jewish records in the reader he edited.[15] The most compelling evidence is the masterful edition of the diary of Adam Czerniaków that Hilberg coedited and then presented to a mass audience in Claude Lanzmann's award-winning film *Shoah*.[16] Czerniaków, head of the Jewish Council in the Warsaw Ghetto, committed suicide in July 1942, tormented by his inability to save the orphans, the weakest members of his community, from murder. According to Hilberg, before his suicide, Czerniaków wrote a note in which he said of the German request that he organize removal of the orphans from the Warsaw ghetto to be sent to Treblinka: "They want me to kill the children with my own hands."[17] In an extensive conversation with Lanzmann, Hilberg not only reported on Czerniaków's words but in an uncanny way became Czerniaków. Speaking for Czerniaków and as him, Hilberg embodied the Jewish leader's anguish at his inability to save the orphans, and indeed anyone, in the Warsaw ghetto.

Hilberg's answer to the question of how the Holocaust happened neither ignored nor blamed Jewish victims. With his emphasis on bureaucratic structures, however, he demonstrated that every organization and institution, including the Jewish councils, was swept along by the massive momentum of destruction. In this regard his work anticipated the sociologist Zygmunt Bauman's celebrated analysis of modernity and the Holocaust.[18] Published decades later, Bauman's book did not spark controversy for its depiction of the Jewish Councils.

Gerhard Weinberg comes at the question of "how" from a very different angle. Weinberg's interest is in the context of the Holocaust—that is, for him, how it happened is inextricably linked to the war of which it was a part and to its global setting. In Weinberg's analysis, the Holocaust was not the destruction of European Jews, as in the title of Hilberg's book, but an attack on all Jews everywhere as part of the Nazi German drive to remake the world. Indeed Weinberg, whose acquaintance with Hilberg goes back to the early 1950s, has criticized precisely the limitations of Hilberg's scope.[19]

Key to Weinberg's interpretation is Hitler's role as leader and Hitler's worldview, ideology, and vision of the future—his plans for the world after the war.[20] Hitler's words, Weinberg demonstrates, were plans for action, and they must be taken seriously and examined in that light, as Weinberg models with Hitler's "second book," which he discovered, annotated, translated, and published.[21] If Hilberg brought to study of the Holocaust a keen awareness of bureaucratic processes and dynamic structures, then Weinberg brought an insistence on ideology, leadership, and direction from the centers of power. The two approaches are, or at least can be, complementary. Consider the image of the train, so central to

Lanzmann's *Shoah* and also to Hilberg's oeuvre;[22] Weinberg shifts our attention to the individuals who designed and built that train, laid the tracks, started the engine, and drove it on its path of annihilation.

The war that Hitler unleashed had a purpose, Weinberg emphasizes with a pithy claim: "Hitler did not conquer France so he could visit the Eiffel Tower." If you think about this framing of the Holocaust, it, too, opens up literally a world of possibilities, questions, and sources. As Weinberg masterfully shows, the two theatres of the war were linked; [23] military developments in North Africa had direct repercussions for the situation of Jews in Palestine; the Battle of Stalingrad had deadly implications for the Jews of Byelorussia and Poland.[24] This approach points to the importance of intentions but also draws our attention to the force of contingency and unforeseen consequences.

In a short and uncharacteristically personal passage in an essay in the volume edited by David Bankier and Dan Michman, Weinberg attributes his insistence on studying the Holocaust and the war together to his childhood experience. As a child in a boarding school in England, he saw bombs falling and heard and read of battles raging, all the while knowing his relatives were trapped in Germany, and later learning that they had been murdered. How could he not see that the war and the destruction of Jews were connected, he asks?[25]

For Weinberg, sources are crucial, and without access to sources, no meaningful study of the Holocaust is possible. He played a key role in the National Archives project to microfilm captured German records in Alexandria, Virginia, and the elegant and sensible organization of that collection owes much to his signature combination of erudition and common sense.[26] As director of the microfilming project, he worked with, in fact supervised, Raul Hilberg, Henry Friedlander, and many other scholars, and it was in that capacity that he found Hitler's second book. Meanwhile, for many scholars of the period, those records on microfilm were the foundation of their studies. They can be viewed anywhere there are microfilm readers and interlibrary loan services.

Gerhard Weinberg has devoted enormous energy over decades to determined efforts to declassify records of all the countries involved in the war—and that means practically everyone. For him too, sources are everywhere. His extensive and creative research, coupled with his eye for telling details, give his work a vivid human face. For instance, to illustrate his observation that Pope Pius XII indeed did speak out on matters he deemed essential, Weinberg used correspondence from after June 1944, in which Pius urged the Allies not to use black troops in the occupation of Rome.[27] The crucial letter was found, not in the papal archives in Rome, which are closed for that period, but in the files of the recipient, in London. Weinberg's commitment to the accessibility of sources has contributed powerfully to the democratization of the field, to its internationalization, and to critical analysis, which is only possible if scholars can see for themselves where others got their information.

Henry Friedlander tackles the question of "how" from yet another angle. How did killing start and who carried it out? His signal contribution is his pathbreaking study of the so-called Euthanasia Program, *The Origins of Nazi Genocide*, published in 1995.[28] In that book and a series of articles and conference presentations that preceded it, Friedlander demonstrated the many ways the first program of mass killing, the murder of disabled people inside Germany, was connected to the subsequent annihilation of Jews, the so-called Final Solution. His concept and approach were revolutionary and have still not fully been incorporated into the mainstream of Holocaust studies. Central to Friedlander's response to the question how did it happen was the role of professionals and professions: physicians, scientists, nurses, social workers, lawyers, and judges. In his analysis, bureaucracy and ideology receded in importance, though they remained factors, and he added emphasis on careerism, competition, and institutions.[29]

Sources are also important to Friedlander. His work is notable for its use of postwar trials of all kinds, and in particular utilization of the records of investigations and prosecutions.[30] In his publications and presentations, Friedlander drew attention to the availability of such materials and their richness.[31] A vivid illustration is the address he gave as president of the German Studies Association, based on investigations into crimes committed during the *Kristallnacht* pogrom.[32] Of course, locating and obtaining access to records of this kind requires patience, determination, and relationships of trust that can take years to build. These qualities formed part of Friedlander's historical methodology. Also with his late wife, the historian Sybil Milton, he coedited a multivolume set of documents of the Holocaust, now available in many libraries, bringing sources from archives in Germany and elsewhere to college students and interested lay readers around the world.[33]

Setting a Tone

How does one write about the Holocaust—the brutality, violence, shock, suffering, betrayal, devastation, solidarity, shame, death, and isolation—in a scholarly way? Since Thucydides struggled to find the words to describe the misery of war and plague,[34] historians have faced the challenge of analyzing agony and evil. When Hilberg, Weinberg, and Friedlander embarked on their early work, there were precious few models and only a handful of studies specifically on the Holocaust in English or German. Their publications—and, at least as much, their many presentations—set a tone that has endured in much (though not all) of the now voluminous scholarship in the field.

The remarkable prose style of all three scholars merits attention. None was writing in his first language, the language of his childhood, or even the language of his sources. Yet all write in a style that is clear, precise, authoritative, even scientific. In this regard, Hilberg, Weinberg, and Friedlander were products of the social science training of mid-twentieth-century America, with its privileging of objectivity and balance. Yet their writing is neither detached nor cold, and it consciously avoids reproducing the perpetrators' gaze, although all three scholars used perpetrator sources.

In Hilberg's work, passion, outrage, and anger are contained yet conveyed by the rigor of his analysis. But at times they burst through to the surface. An outspoken atheist, Hilberg chose to dedicate the German edition of his book *Perpetrators, Bystanders, Victims* to Fr. Bernhard Lichtenberg, a Roman Catholic priest who died in 1943 on a transport to Dachau, after a parishioner denounced him for praying publicly for Jews sent from Germany to the east to be killed.[35] In the third edition of *Destruction of the European Jews*, Hilberg indicated that the Holocaust had lost its singularity. With the 1994 genocide of the Tutsi in Rwanda, he concluded, "history has repeated itself."[36] These and other passages have led the philosopher John Roth to characterize Hilberg's approach as fundamentally ethical.[37]

Hilberg took a lot of criticism, much of it in tandem with Hannah Arendt, for his description of the Jewish leadership and its failures, and for his disinterest in resistance[38] (and not just Jewish resistance: regarding 20 July 1944, he famously commented, "It was irrelevant"). Yet there is a kind of strange dignity in his refusal to permit the excuse of victimization; in his moral world, all human beings are actors, all are responsible. Put differently, there is an existential commitment beneath Hilberg's structuralist approach, and the machinery of destruction he depicts, though relentless, is not inevitable.[39]

Weinberg's writing and, even more, his oral presentations rely on irony and often a quirky humor. This trait serves as a distancing technique, yet it also draws attention to contradictions, myths, and the shared humanity of people on all sides of the perpetrator, victim, witness, collaborator, rescuer divide. Regarding the Soviet winter Weinberg has frequently observed, "It only snowed on the Germans."[40] In a discussion of how Germans became mass killers, he concludes, "If all of this does not sound very nice it is because these were not very nice people."[41] Weinberg's commitment is to understanding the human costs of history; he refuses to reduce war to a game of chess or to depict killers as aliens. His characteristic understatement serves to detract attention from himself and the brilliance of his insights and instead to let his readers and listeners feel they are the clever ones who have figured something out. All of his work reflects an extraordinary ability to see the obvious that everyone else overlooks and then show its implications. A prime example is his insight that the death marches in the last phase of the war were motivated by the vested interests of perpetrators eager to get away from the front.[42]

Henry Friedlander's writing has more the tone of a reporter: rational, richly informed, yet cautious about drawing conclusions. He provides complex information but pulls back from making big claims about it. In this regard, he is the inverse of Hilberg, who told Lanzmann on film, "In all my work I have never begun by asking the big questions because I was always afraid I would come up with small answers."[43] In contrast, Friedlander asks all manner of big questions but does not claim to provide big answers and often seems reluctant to risk overstating his case or to tell his readers what to think. In a presentation at the inaugural conference of the Center for Advanced Holocaust Studies in Washington, DC, Friedlander made a striking admission of the limits he perceived to his comprehension of Nazi killers:

> When all is said and done, I am still unable to fathom why seemingly normal men and women were able to commit such extraordinary crimes. Neither ideology nor self-interest is a satisfactory explanation for such behavior. Attempts to replicate their actions in the laboratory must fail, even if experiments seem to show, as did the one by Stanley Milgram, that ordinary men anywhere can commit such crimes. But there is a fundamental difference between the antiseptic experimental setting and the grisly reality of the killing centers, The T-4 killers confronted real human beings as victims and saw their agony, the blood and gore of the killing process. In Milgram's social science experiment, the subjects might lack the imagination to understand the pain that they could inflict, but the Nazi killers, even if they lacked all imagination, could not avoid knowing what they were doing. They understood the consequences of their deeds.[44]

Humility is not what scholars tend to project or reward, and Friedlander's attitude offers a stark contrast to the certainty of Daniel Goldhagen or Timothy Snyder, bestselling authors on the Holocaust.[45] But such reticence is profoundly important in the field: Elie Wiesel speaks of silence and unknowability; Saul Friedländer, Lawrence Langer, and Dominick LaCapra discuss something different but related: the need to resist closure.[46] Michael Rothberg offers "multidirectional memory."[47] Henry Friedlander would scoff at all those terms and resist Wiesel's mystification and the theoretical vocabulary of LaCapra et al. No doubt he would prefer to call what he does something else: common sense, not overreaching his evidence, and avoiding the brutal thoughtlessness of Nazi language, which he analyzed in an essay in 1980.[48] But by whatever name, stylistic humility is an essential quality to the openness of the field of Holocaust studies and to ongoing inquiry.

An Open Field

Study of the Holocaust is an enormously active area of historical inquiry, and seventy years after the war ended, people all over the world are engaged in work of the highest quality.[49] Much of that dynamism is thanks to the openness of the field, and Raul Hilberg, Gerhard Weinberg, and Henry Friedlander have each in significant ways contributed to that open quality.

To some readers, this claim may seem misplaced or even a flight of hagiographic fantasy. On the surface at least, Hilberg hardly looks like a paragon of scholarly openness, with his undisguised animosity toward Hannah Arendt and Lucy Dawidowicz and his disdain for what he deemed "soft" approaches. "The study of the Holocaust is not for philosophers," he asserted in an interview shortly before his death.[50] Nor does Weinberg automatically fit an image of genial openness, with his seeming old-fashioned focus on military, diplomatic, and political matters and his biting criticisms of certain scholars. His book reviews are legendary for their dismissal of work he deemed lacking as "silly" or "nonsense," and assertions such as, "those who stand on their heads see things upside down." Likewise, Henry Friedlander was known to be contemptuous of the many people he deemed to "know nothing," including some of his own colleagues. But I stick to my claim, even if it may appear paradoxical or idiosyncratic.

Consider where and how these scholars spent their careers. Hilberg was told by his advisor at Columbia, Franz Neumann, when he insisted on writing a dissertation on the Holocaust (without even the name to give the topic credibility), "It's your funeral." He struggled to find a publisher and a job and then spent the rest of his career at the University of Vermont, where he supervised no doctoral students because there was not a Ph.D. program in political science (his department) or in history. "We have studied the Holocaust when it was out of the limelight," he said at the United States Holocaust Memorial Museum in 1994, "and we have studied the Holocaust when it was in the limelight." His preference, Hilberg reported, was the former.

Gerhard Weinberg completed his Ph.D. at the University of Chicago when he was still in his early twenties. He too was supervised by an émigré scholar, Hans Rothfels, although it appears Rothfels was fairly hands-off. Weinberg then spent eight years in temporary positions, some of them only one semester long, before getting his first tenure-track job at the University of Kentucky, followed by positions at the Universities of Michigan and North Carolina, Chapel Hill. These were not comfortable, well-funded Ivy League schools but big public institutions where his teaching and administrative duties were heavy.

Henry Friedlander received his Ph.D. from the University of Pennsylvania in 1968 with a dissertation on the German revolution of 1918.[51] He acquired that degree during and after a series of short-term appointments—at McMaster University in Hamilton, Canada; at Louisiana State in New Orleans; then for the rest of his career at Brooklyn College, where he was based in Judaic Studies. In short, these were no pampered academics. They taught all kinds of students and held them to their own high standards. Hilberg, Weinberg, and Friedlander in different ways helped make the teaching of the Holocaust not a luxury but a staple. It is no coincidence that the first course on the Holocaust in the United States was taught at Brooklyn College (though it was taught by Yaffa Eliach, not Henry Friedlander); that Vermont became a major center for Holocaust research;

and that the University of North Carolina in Chapel Hill, under Weinberg and his successor Christopher Browning, produced a significant number of the professors teaching courses on the Holocaust in North America.

What can look like closed-mindedness—and must have felt to those on the receiving end like mean-spiritedness—in a backhanded way reflects a commitment to opening the field. Hilberg reserved some of his most public criticism for Lucy Dawidowicz, author of *The War against the Jews, 1933-1945*.[52] Her claim that love of the Jewish people was necessary for writing Jewish history, and by extension the history of the Holocaust, was anathema to him. Not because (as some people have charged), he was a self-hating Jew, but because to him this claim sounded the death knell for a field of inquiry he and others had worked so hard to make academically respectable. If one had to be Jewish to study the Holocaust, or if the Holocaust was confined to a chapter of Jewish history, it was not a real field of scholarship; it was not *wissenschaftlich* (scientific or scholarly); it was about commemoration, memory, and piety, a kind of private club where people made up versions of the past they found comforting.

Hilberg insisted on something different: on a field open to anyone with the persistence, training, rigor, and the stomach to do the work. Germans, Poles, Russians, Chinese—all were welcome, and indeed essential because of the languages required to access the relevant documents. According to Hilberg, there were at least twenty languages of the Holocaust, and he specifically mentioned Chinese as among them. Shortly before his death, when asked where the most significant scholarship on the Holocaust was being done, he said in Germany and Austria.

To Hilberg, the field also had to be open in the sense of no taboos. There was to be no lionizing of every act as resistance, no special pleading for members of Jewish councils, no covering up, no sentimentalizing or profiting from the suffering of others. He hated the whole wave of restitution cases and massive claims in the 1990s and said so openly, and he detested instrumentalization of the Holocaust to whatever end. He also had no problem with swimming against the tide. When the controversial scholar Norman Finkelstein was denied tenure at DePaul University in Chicago, Hilberg emerged as his most outspoken supporter.[53]

Gerhard Weinberg has fought for different kinds of openness, in addition to advocating access to sources. He has spoken at every kind of school, college, community club, synagogue, church, and university imaginable. He has briefed heads of state on World War II and lectured to Roman Catholic priests on Pius XII. He is a model of the public engagement many people have come to expect from scholars of the Holocaust. It has something to do with Weinberg that the U.S. Air Force and Naval Academies and West Point have a tradition of involving faculty and cadets in a study of World War II that pays attention to the Holocaust. A familiar presence on the History Channel, he popularizes the Holocaust without condescending to his readers and audiences. Yet, as with

Hilberg, there is a hard edge to Weinberg's openness. His role in the David Abraham affair in the 1980s made him enemies.[54] If you cannot trust the footnotes, Weinberg told his graduate students, you have nothing—no possibility of engaging a historian in debate.

Weinberg has been instrumental in connecting North America with Europe, especially Germany, to try to keep scholars in the same conversation. By training young scholars from Germany, being a visiting professor there, and maintaining professional and personal relationships with German academics, his generosity and loyalty have opened doors in both directions.[55] To Weinberg, seeing what Nazi Germans did in the past does not dictate attitudes toward Germany or Germans in the present. Citing the story of Jonah and the fish, read on Yom Kippur, he points out the lesson: if people repent and show they are trying to do better, we need to respect that.

Henry Friedlander's definition of the Holocaust—including persecution and killing of disabled people and Sinti and Roma as well as Jews—has opened the field in other ways, although in this regard not many scholars have followed. Still, together with Sybil Milton,[56] he had a significant impact on the United States Holocaust Memorial Museum, where the permanent exhibit since it was opened has been viewed by so many millions of people that one cannot keep track. And his work also influenced scholars on both sides of the Atlantic to investigate the treatment and killing of disabled people and the roles of professionals.[57] Not everyone has always been enthusiastic: Friedlander tells about presenting his work on T-4 and being accosted by an angry audience member who shouted, "Are you saying Jews are just like crazy people?"

Hilberg, Weinberg, and Friedlander brought immense integrity to study of the Holocaust, exacting standards that had to live up to skeptics, critics, and non-Jews suspicious of what some perceived as special pleading. In that climate, there was little room and no reward for revealing the vulnerable self. Nevertheless, part of the greatness of their scholarship is a product of the combination of insights from personal experience, knowledge embodied in their own families and their own bodies, and the immense discipline required to contain and channel that insight. They lived the reality and embodied the ideal described by Saul Friedländer, who has remarked that every scholar has a subject position but must be able to muster the self-discipline to see beyond it.[58]

Of the three men discussed here, only one was able to contribute to this volume: Gerhard Weinberg. Raul Hilberg died in 2007. Henry Friedlander suffered a series of strokes and spent the last years of his life in nursing homes, unable to speak. He died in 2012. Some of his last speaking appearances are relevant to this discussion. In 2008, at a conference at the German Historical Institute in Washington, DC, he presented to Gerhard Weinberg a copy of a guidebook they had worked on together for the Captured German Records microfilm collection. That same year in Evanston, at the Lessons and Legacies

Conference on the Holocaust, he arrived disoriented, with no luggage, but determined to speak in public about his time in Auschwitz. "I'm ready," he said to one of the organizers.

What Friedlander told was the following: in the fall of 1944, with the help of a kapo from Wedding, the Berlin district where the Friedlanders had also lived, he managed to escape from a selection that targeted teenaged boys for the gas chambers. Friedlander recounted how he had approached the kapo in the death barracks and said to him, in the Berlin dialect they shared, the first words that came into his head: "I don't belong here." The man ordered him to go to his barracks and not make a sound. There the fourteen-year-old Henry lay on the bare cement, afraid even to breathe. He could hear the screams and cries of the boys being loaded onto trucks to be taken to the gas. "Sometimes I still hear them," he told his listeners. "I am a historian," he continued. "I know how to write about the Holocaust. But how do I write about that?"[59]

Whether we call it "first" or "second," the generation of Raul Hilberg, Gerhard Weinberg, and Henry Friedlander produced remarkable scholars: erudite across an enormous range, brilliantly eloquent in more than one language, fiercely committed to independent thought. By refusing to focus on themselves and instead sublimating their personal memories and private grief from the Holocaust to the cause of scholarship as they understood it, they opened the way for study of the Holocaust to be part of academic history.

Doris L. Bergen is the Chancellor Rose and Ray Wolfe Professor of Holocaust Studies at the University of Toronto. Her research focuses on issues of religion, gender, and ethnicity in the Holocaust and World War II. Her books include *Twisted Cross: The German Christian Movement in the Third Reich* (1996); *War and Genocide: A Concise History of the Holocaust* (2003, 2009, 2016); *The Sword of the Lord: Military Chaplains from the First to the Twenty-First Centuries* (edited, 2004); *Lessons and Legacies*, vol. VIII, *From Generation to Generation* (edited, 2008); and *Alltag im Holocaust. Jüdisches Leben im Großdeutschen Reich 1941-1945* (co-edited with Andrea Löw and Anna Hájková, 2013).

Notes

1. The classic study is Helen Epstein, *Children of the Holocaust: Conversations with Sons and Daughters of Survivors* (New York, 1979); see also Aaron Hass, *In the Shadow of the Holocaust: The Second Generation* (Ithaca, NY, 1990); Dan Bar-On, *Fear and Hope: Three Generations of the Holocaust* (Cambridge, MA, 1995); and Alan L. Berger and Naomi Berger, eds., *Second Generation Voices: Reflections by Children of Holocaust Survivors and Perpetrators* (Syracuse, NY, 2001).
2. Biographical information in Raul Hilberg, *The Politics of Memory: The Journey of a Holocaust Historian* (Chicago, 1996).

3. See Gerhard L. Weinberg, "Kristallnacht 1938: As Experienced Then and Understood Now," Monna and Otto Weinmann Annual Lecture, 13 May 2009, U.S. Holocaust Memorial Museum Center for Advanced Holocaust Studies Occasional Paper (Washington, DC, 2009).
4. See Nathan Stoltzfus and Doris L. Bergen, "In Memoriam: Henry (Heinz Egon) Friedlander, 1930-2012," *German Studies Association Newsletter* 37, no. 2 (Winter 2012-13): 61-79. I am deeply indebted to Nathan Stoltzfus for information and insights about Henry Friedlander.
5. See Saul Friedländer, *When Memory Comes*, trans. from French by Helen R. Lane (New York, 1979).
6. Saul Friedländer, *Nazi Germany and the Jews*, 2 vols., *The Years of Persecution, 1933-1939* (New York: HarperCollins, 1997) and *The Years of Extermination: Nazi Germany and the Jews, 1939-1945* (New York, 2007).
7. Tec is also atypical in that she began her work on the Holocaust with a memoir, then moved to academic projects. Most of her contemporaries moved in the opposite direction. See Nechama Tec, *Dry Tears: The Story of a Lost Childhood* (New York, 1982); followed by, most importantly, *When Light Pierced the Darkness: Christian Rescue of Jews in Nazi-Occupied Poland* (New York, 1986); *Defiance: The Bielski Partisans* (New York, 1993); and *Resilience and Courage: Women, Men, and the Holocaust* (New Haven, CT: Yale University Press, 2003).
8. Franz Neumann, *Behemoth: The Structure and Practice of National Socialism, 1933-1944*, with a new introduction by Peter Hayes (Chicago, 2009; originally published 1942).
9. Raul Hilberg, *The Destruction of the European Jews*, 3rd ed. (New Haven, CT, 2003; originally published 1961).
10. For an analysis of the different editions, see Christopher R. Browning, "Spanning a Career: Three Editions of Raul Hilberg's *Destruction of the European Jews*," in Doris L. Bergen, ed., *Lessons and Legacies*, vol. VIII, *From Generation to Generation* (Evanston, IL, 2008), 191-202.
11. Hilberg, "The Development of Holocaust Research—A Personal Overview," in David Bankier and Dan Michman, eds., *Holocaust Historiography in Context: Emergence, Challenges, Polemics, and Achievements* (Jerusalem, 2008), 25-36, quotation on 29.
12. See Raul Hilberg, *Die Vernichtung der europäischen Juden*, vol. 2, trans. Christian Seeger et al. (Frankfurt/M., 1982), 774-75.
13. Raul Hilberg, "Incompleteness in Holocaust Historiography," in Jonathan Petropoulos and John K. Roth, eds., *Gray Zones: Ambiguity and Compromise in the Holocaust and Its Aftermath* (New York, 2005), 81-92.
14. Raul Hilberg, *Sources of Holocaust Research: An Analysis* (Chicago, 2001).
15. Raul Hilberg, ed., *Documents of Destruction: Germany and Jewry, 1933-1945* (Chicago, 1971).
16. Raul Hilberg, Stanislaw Staron, and Josef Kermisz, eds., *The Warsaw Diary of Adam Czerniakow*, trans. Stanislaw Staron and the Staff of Yad Vashem (Chicago, 1999; originally New York, 1979).
17. On 22 July 1942, Czerniaków wrote, "The most tragic dilemma is the problem of children in orphanages, etc. I raised this issue—perhaps something can be done." Hilberg et al, eds., *Diary of Czerniakow*, 385; also see remarks by Raul Hilberg in *Shoah*, dir. Claude Lanzmann, Les Films Aleph (1985); transcript in Lanzmann, *Shoah: An Oral History of the Holocaust* (New York, 1985): 188-90. For discussion of this scene from *Shoah* and Hilberg's identification with Czerniaków, see Marianne Hirsch and Leo Spitzer, "Gendered Translations: Claude Lanzmann's *Shoah*," in Stuart Liebman, ed., *Claude Lanzmann's Shoah: Key Essays* (New York, 2007), 183-4.
18. Zygmunt Bauman, *Modernity and the Holocaust* (Ithaca, NY, 1989).
19. Gerhard L. Weinberg, "A Commentary on Gray Zones in Raul Hilberg's Work," in Petropoulos and Roth, *Gray Zones*, 71-80, esp. 72-74.
20. Gerhard L. Weinberg, "The World Through Hitler's Eyes," in *Germany, Hitler and World War II* (Cambridge, 1995), 30-53; idem, *Visions of Victory: The Hopes of Eight World War II Leaders*

(New York, 2005); also idem, "Hitler's Role in the Holocaust Reassessed," in Sara R. Horowitz, ed., *Lessons and Legacies*, vol. X, *Back to the Sources* (Evanston, IL, 2012), 3-12.
21. Gerhard L. Weinberg, ed., *Hitler's Second Book: The Unpublished Sequel to Mein Kampf* (New York, 2003).
22. Raul Hilberg, "German Railroads/Jewish Souls," *Society* 314, no. 1 (November–December 1976), 60-74; see also idem, *Sonderzüge nach Auschwitz*, trans. from English by Gisela Schleicher (Mainz, 1981).
23. Gerhard L. Weinberg, *A World at Arms: A Global History of World War II* (New York, 1994 and 2005).
24. Gerhard L. Weinberg, "The 'Final Solution' and the War in 1943," in *Germany, Hitler*, 217-44; idem, "Germany's War for World Conquest and the Extermination of Jews," Meyerhoff Lecture Series (Washington, DC, 1995); idem, "The Holocaust and World War II: A Dilemma in Teaching," in Donald G. Schilling, ed., *Lessons and Legacies*, vol. II, *Teaching the Holocaust in a Changing World* (Evanston, IL, 1998), 26-40.
25. Gerhard L. Weinberg, "Two Separate Issues? Historiography of World War II and the Holocaust," in Bankier and Michman, eds., *Holocaust Historiography*, 379-401.
26. Astrid M. Eckert, *The Struggle for the Files: The Western Allies and the Return of German Archives after the Second World War* (New York, 2012).
27. Gerhard L. Weinberg, "Pope Pius XII in World War II," unpublished paper, 13-14.
28. Henry Friedlander, *The Origins of Nazi Genocide: From Euthanasia to the Final Solution* (Chapel Hill, NC, 1995).
29. Henry Friedlander, "The Exclusion and Murder of the Disabled," in Robert Gellately and Nathan Stoltzfus, eds., *Social Outsiders in Nazi Germany* (Princeton, NJ, 2001), 145-64; idem, "Physicians as Killers in Nazi Germany: Hadamar, Treblinka, and Auschwitz," in Francis R. Nicosia and Jonathan Huener, eds., *Medicine and Medical Ethics in Nazi Germany: Origins, Practices, Legacies* (New York, 2002), 59–76; and idem, "The Administrators in the Concentration Camps," in Ronald M. Smelser, ed., *Lessons and Legacies*, vol. V, *The Holocaust and Justice* (Evanston, IL, 2002), 88-99.
30. See Nathan Stoltzfus and Henry Friedlander, eds., *Nazi Crimes and the Law* (New York, 2008).
31. Henry Friedlander, "The Judiciary and Nazi Crimes in Postwar Germany," *Simon Wiesenthal Center Annual* 1 (1984): 27-44.
32. Henry Friedlander, "'Eine Berliner Pflanze': An Unusual Kristallnacht Story," *German Studies Review* 26, no. 1 (Feb. 2003): 1-14.
33. Henry Friedlander and Sybil Milton, eds., *Archives of the Holocaust: An International Collection of Selected Documents*, 22 vols. in 26 (New York, 1990-1995). Friedlander and Milton also coedited several volumes of the Simon Wiesenthal Center Annual (1984-1990).
34. Thucydides, *History of the Peloponnesian War*, trans. David Grene (Chicago, 1989), 117.
35. Hilberg, *Perpetrators, Victims, Bystanders: The Jewish Catastrophe, 1933-1945* (New York, 1992). On Lichtenberg, see Kevin P. Spicer, "The Unique Path of Bernhard Lichtenberg," ch. 7 in *Resisting the Third Reich: The Catholic Church in Hitler's Germany* (DeKalb, 2004).
36. Raul Hilberg, *Destruction of the European Jews*, 3rd ed., quoted in Doris L. Bergen, "Introduction," in *Lessons and Legacies*, vol. VIII, xxiii.
37. John K. Roth, "Raul Hilberg's Ethics," in *Ethics During and After the Holocaust: In the Shadow of Birkenau* (Houndmills, Basingstoke, 2005), 54-74.
38. See Nathaniel Popper, "A Conscious Pariah," *The Nation* (19 April 2010).
39. Instructive here is the chapter on "The Jewish Leaders" in Raul Hilberg, *Perpetrators, Victims, Bystanders: The Jewish Catastrophe, 1933–1945* (New York, 1992), 105–17.
40. Also, "the weather was identical on both sides of the Eastern Front." Gerhard L. Weinberg, "Some Myths of World War II," The 2011 George C. Marshall Lecture in Military History, *The Journal of Military History* 75 (July 2011): 701-718; quotation from 704.

41. Gerhard L. Weinberg, "Crossing the Line in Nazi Genocide: On Becoming and Being a Professional Killer," Occasional Paper, Center for Holocaust Studies, University of Vermont, Burlington (1997): 9-10.
42. Gerhard L. Weinberg, "Ignored and Misunderstood Aspects of the Holocaust," paper presented at the annual meeting of the German Studies Association, 2010.
43. Raul Hilberg in *Shoah* (1985), disc 2.
44. Henry Friedlander, "The T4 Killers: Berlin, Lublin, San Sabba," in Michael Berenbaum and Abraham J. Peck, eds., *The Holocaust and History: The Known, the Unknown, the Disputed, and the Re-Examined* (Bloomington, 1998), 249. "T4" was the code name for the Nazi German program of killing disabled people, also known euphemistically as the "Euthanasia" program.
45. Daniel Jonah Goldhagen, *Hitler's Willing Executioners: Ordinary Germans and the Holocaust* (New York, 1996); Timothy Snyder, *Bloodlands: Europe Between Hitler and Stalin* (New York, 2010).
46. On the subject of closure, see Saul Friedländer, "Trauma, transference and 'working through,'" *History and Memory* 4 (1992): 39-55; Lawrence L. Langer, *Holocaust Testimonies: The Ruins of Memory* (New Haven, CT, 1991); Dominick LaCapra, *Representing the Holocaust: History, Theory, Trauma* (Ithaca, 1994), esp. 205-223; and idem, *History and Memory after Auschwitz* (Ithaca, 1998), 42. For discussion of Wiesel and silence, see Naomi Seidman, *Faithful Renderings: Jewish-Christian Difference and the Politics of Translation* (Chicago, 2006), esp. 216-31.
47. Michael Rothberg, *Multidirectional Memory: Remembering the Holocaust in the Age of Decolonization* (Stanford, 2009).
48. Henry Friedlander, "The Manipulation of Language," in Friedlander and Sybil Milton, eds., *The Holocaust: Ideology, Bureaucracy, and Genocide* (Millwood, NY, 1980), 103-13.
49. Michael Marrus deserves my gratitude for many stimulating conversations on this point.
50. "Is There a New Anti-Semitism? A Conversation with Raul Hilberg," *Logos* (Winter–Spring 2007), at http://www.logosjournal.com/issue_6.1-2/hilberg.htm. See also Popper, "Conscious Pariah," and of course Hilberg, *Politics of Memory*.
51. Henry Friedlander, *The German Revolution of 1918* (New York, 1992).
52. Lucy S. Dawidowicz, *The War Against the Jews, 1933-1945* (New York, 1975); also her memoir, *From That Time and Place: A Memoir, 1938-1947* (New York, 1989).
53. Norman Finkelstein, "There Went a Man: Remembering Raul Hilberg," *Counterpunch* (22 August 2007).
54. See the back-and-forth between Gerald Feldman and David Abraham in *Central European History* 17 (1984): 159-290.
55. See, for instance, Gerhard L. Weinberg, "Forum: Gerhard L. Weinberg: Nicolas Berg, Der Holocaust und die westdeutschen Historiker. Comments," in *H-Soz-Kult*, 25 February 2004, http://hsozkult.geschichte.hu-berlin.de/forum/id=417&type=diskussionen.
56. See Sybil H. Milton, "'Gypsies as Social Outsiders in Nazi Germany," in Robert Gellately and Nathan Stoltzfus, eds, *Social Outsiders in Nazi Germany* (Princeton, 2001), 212-32.
57. Among others, Patricia Heberer, "'Exitus heute in Hadamar': The Hadamar Facility and 'Euthanasia' in Nazi Germany" (Ph.D. dissertation, University of Maryland, 2001); Dieter Kuntz and Susan Bachrach, eds., *Deadly Medicine: Creating the Master Race* (Chapel Hill, 2006); Sheila Faith Weiss, *The Nazi Symbiosis: Human Genetics and Politics in the Third Reich* (Chicago, 2010); and Winfried Süß, *Der "Volkskörper" im Krieg. Gesundheitspolitik, medizinische Versorgung und Krankenmord im nationalsozialistischen Deutschland 1939-1945* (Munich, 2003).
58. Saul Friedländer, "Prologue," in Jonathan Petropoulos, Lynn Rapaport, and John K. Roth, eds., *Lessons and Legacies*, vol. IX, *Memory, History, and Responsibility* (Evanston, IL, 2010), 3. He wrote, "My own work, begun in 1990, was meant to show that no distinction was warranted among historians of various backgrounds in their professional approach to the Third Reich,

that *all* historians dealing with this theme had to be aware of their unavoidably subjective approach, and that all could muster enough self-critical insight to restrain this subjectivity."

59. Henry Friedlander's remarks in Evanston, IL, November 2008, reproduced from notes taken while he spoke. He subsequently spoke in Germany about his experiences in Auschwitz; see "Zur Wiederherstellung des Rechts. Ausstellungsbericht," an account of the opening of an exhibition about the Auschwitz Trial and the Bergen-Belsen Trial in the Niedersächsischen Landtag, Hannover, in January 2009, in *Nachrichten und Berichte. Information und Kommunikation*, Fritz Bauer Institute.

Chapter 16

BLAZING NEW PATHS IN HISTORIOGRAPHY
"Refugee Effect" and American Experience in
the Professional Trajectory of Gerda Lerner

Marjorie Lamberti

"My craft and my profession are inseparable from the road I have come and the life I have led."

"I am an outsider as a woman, a Jew, an immigrant and a radical. I have also been a successful insider, an institution-builder and a respected member of my profession."

—*Gerda Lerner*

Gerda Lerner, a self-described "outsider" as a women and Jewish refugee from Austria, became a trailblazer in American historiography and academia in the years after her emigration to the United States.[1] Lerner's critique of the sexist bias and deficiencies of traditional history and her writings on historical methodology and conceptualization for the study of women's history contributed significantly to the development of women's history as an academic discipline. After she joined the faculty at Sarah Lawrence College in 1968, she launched, with a grant from the Rockefeller Foundation and the school's own resources, a program in women's history in 1972, which served as a model for the teaching of women's studies in other institutions of higher education across the country.[2] Her pioneering scholarship and institution-building talent led the University of

---

Notes from this chapter begin on page 254.

Wisconsin in Madison to hire her in 1980 to establish a doctoral program in women's history. Possessed of an inner urgency and a passionate ambition, Lerner withstood fearlessly the ridicule with which some members of the historical profession responded at first to her views on the patriarchal values that shaped the writing of traditional history and on the empty spaces and distortion within it.[3] A pragmatic "mover and shaker," Lerner worked tirelessly to change the "undemocratic structures and practices" of the historical profession's associations from within. In 1969, she led the vanguard who organized the Coordinating Committee on Women in the Historical Profession, a pressure group that lobbied to make the hiring process for academic employment open and nondiscriminatory and to increase representation for women on organizational committees and the editorial boards of history journals.[4] In her own lifetime, she won the recognition of her profession and was elected president of the Organization of American Historians in 1981.

Gerda Lerner (1920–2013) grew up in an upper middle-class home of assimilated Jews in Vienna and received a classical education at a *Gymnasium* (high school) there. In her adolescent years, she showed a lively curiosity to know "other worlds out there" and developed a political consciousness. Unafraid of making choices, she became involved in a Marxist underground movement after the civil war in February 1934, when fascists and conservatives in Austria assaulted the strongholds of Social Democracy in the cities and replaced the parliamentary democracy of the postwar republic with an authoritarian corporatist government. After Nazi Germany's annexation of Austria in 1938, she witnessed the eruption of violent antisemitism in Vienna and was imprisoned for six weeks as a hostage, until her father, who had fled to Liechtenstein, signed away his property and business. At the age of nineteen, she emigrated alone and arrived in the United States in the spring of 1939.[5] What effect did her background as a refugee from National Socialism have on her highly successful and pathbreaking professional career? To what extent did her Central European cultural heritage affect her writing of women's history? How conscious was she of a connection between her professional work and a "refugee effect" derived from the experience of persecution, forced migration, loss of homeland, and economic insecurity?[6]

Collective biographies of the second generation in the Central European emigration justly highlight the success and extraordinary accomplishments of many men and women in this group, four of whom won a Nobel Prize in science. To account for their stellar achievements, Gerhard Sonnert and Gerald Holton, a sociologist of science and a historian of science, respectively, in the physics laboratory at Harvard, formulate a theoretical explanation based on the concepts of "cultural capital" and "partial assimilation." As they contend, the young refugees arrived in America with, and retained as immigrants and naturalized citizens, "the cultural baggage" that they had received in Central European schools and from their parents. Adult refugees transmitted to them a strong work ethic, a high appreciation of the value of education, and a deep commitment to "an intellectual homeland defined by the landmarks of German *Kultur*" in literature, music, philosophy, and science. The transmission of the cultural values of "German *Kultur* without Germany" prevented refugees of the second generation from becoming totally Americanized in their basic outlook. The great socioeconomic success of this group "occurred because of that incomplete assimilation," Sonnert and Holton contend.[7]

In this essay, I intend to problematize the question of "refugee effect" through an analysis of the extent to which Lerner experienced and remembered the influence of her Central European heritage and her background as a refugee.[8] Lerner's biography suggests a more complex weave of connections between the lives and the professional writings and achievements of second-generation refugees than the explanation offered by Sonnert and Holton.[9] What did she emphasize and omit in the narratives of her career? How can one explain the silences? Lerner came to an expanded consciousness of the impact of her refugee experience on her work in women's history later in her life. What were the circumstances of her awakening to this connection? Finally, what insights does this case study offer for writing the history of the second generation in the Central European emigration?

Throughout her professional life, Lerner wrote autobiographical essays to illuminate the connection between her life and her scholarship in women's history.[10] She began to examine this linkage long before the age when former refugees, in their seventies and eighties, generally felt the urge to remember and write memoirs.[11] In her later years, she connected "[her] own life experience as a Jewish refugee with [her] work as a scholar concerned with race, class and gender."[12] The impact of her Jewish refugee background on her practice of the historian's craft is not clearly drawn in her writings from the 1960s up to the 1980s. It is an emphasis in her self-representation and narrative that emerges sharply only in the 1990s.[13]

Gerda Lerner reinvigorated the study of women's history through her incisive comments on the inadequacies and limited usefulness of older conceptual models, which focused on women as an oppressed group, the political battle in America leading up to the right to vote in 1920, or the contributions of notable women. She wanted to expand the agenda in women's history beyond the campaign for women's suffrage. She thought that this movement, dependent on educated, middle-class women, placed so much emphasis on the ballot to the neglect of other reforms. It grew in isolation from the most downtrodden groups of women and did not speak for mill workers and black women.[14] In studying women at any time in history, it was important to consider their family and economic circumstances and the factors of class and race as well as their political-legal status.

Lerner acknowledged that "women often participated in their own subordination by internalizing the ideology and values that oppressed them." But she also contended that the question of oppression should never be regarded as the central aspect of women's history, and she rejected the perception of women as a powerless minority, passive or reacting to the restraints of patriarchal society. She called for a new conceptual framework for studying women in history, which would elicit the story of "their ongoing functioning in that male-defined world *on their own terms*."[15] New kinds of questions have to be framed, and hitherto underappreciated and unexploited sources have to be used, to bring to light the various ways in which women have been active agents in history and wielded power. A new periodization should be devised that would be more appropriate to the experience of women than is the periodization in political and military history. Lerner's conceptualization of women's history, in effect, pointed to a paradigm shift and a reevaluation of the assumptions and methodology of traditional history.[16]

Nowhere was Lerner more innovative and daring than in her pathbreaking writings, from the late 1960s and early 1970s, on the history of black women and the relations between black and white women in America. When Lerner acquired her doctoral degree in 1966 at the age of forty-six and set her research priorities, she decided that the absence of African American women from the historiography of the United States should be corrected. Raising the visibility of African American women in history was a compelling research agenda for Lerner, whose support for the civil rights movement dated back to the 1950s.[17] Writing to Walter Fisher, an African American historian, in 1968, she expressed her desire to attend the annual meeting of the Association for the Study of Negro Life and History the following year and proposed a panel on the history of black women in America.[18] She knew that there were questions in women's history that could only be addressed by comparing the experiences of white and black women. Is the oppression of women universal and does it go across class and race lines? Do women of different racial groups have the same history or is there a difference? From her research, she learned that white and black women experience their historical subordination differently and that generalizations about the oppression of women have to be qualified by the factors of race and class. For black women, "race oppression has been experienced as the primary burden."[19]

At the annual meetings of the American Historical Association and the Organization of American Historians in 1972 and 1973 respectively, Lerner urged the profession to make the history of black women an integral part of all American history. She discussed the race oppression of black women and deplored the denial of their history. Whenever they appeared in history textbooks, it was "merely as victims, as helpless sufferers of conditions imposed upon them by others," she stated.[20] In the early 1970s, she proved that African American women have a rich and accessible history by publishing an anthology of historical sources, "almost wholly unexplored and widely scattered" in archives and manuscript collections.[21] From her excavating research she learned that black women were far from being merely passive victims of oppression.

"They were active participants in the social struggles of their day, provided leadership, and, more importantly, helped build and maintain welfare and educational institutions in their communities," she declared.[22] She called attention to the historical significance of the local and regional black women's clubs and said, "Contrary to widely held racist myths, black communities have a continuous record of self-help, institutional building, and strong organizations to which black women have made continuous contributions."[23]

Lerner addressed painful historical questions that few white scholars in the United States would have tackled at that time. She examined the sexual exploitation of black women by white men of the planter class in the time of slavery and in the period after Emancipation, and the way in which this abuse affected the relations of black and white women on the plantations in the Old South and the psyche of black men, who were humiliated and prevented from defending their wives, mothers, or sisters.[24] Could white historians truly understand the African American past? In the midst of the civil rights movement, African Americans wanted to define themselves autonomously and to interpret their own history. Lerner agreed that "black people and white people in America represent two separate cultures . . . and oftentimes diametrically opposed past experiences." Historians who are members of the culture about which they write bring a special quality to their research. This fact, she wrote, did not mean that the interpretation of the history of African Americans can or should only be made by someone of that race. Scholars from outside a culture frequently have "a more challenging vision than those closely involved in and bound by their own culture." A fuller and more solidly based history would emerge from the juxtaposition of different interpretations and the debates about them.[25]

In these years, Lerner received little or no encouragement from the gatekeepers of the historical profession's premier journals, whose editorial boards seemed unprepared to accept scholarship on the history of black women in nineteenth-century America as substantive and objective. The editors who rejected Lerner's manuscripts claimed that her work was marred by "presentism" and "politicized rhetoric."[26] One referee for the *Journal of American History* stated in 1970 that the "ideological and historical perimeters [of Lerner's essay] need to be separated" in order to keep it "from becoming a track [sic] for the time or merely a collection of ideological pronouncementos [sic]." Another referee for the same journal—reviewing another manuscript that she had submitted in 1972—declared, "The opening and closing assertions about black self-help *could* be criticized as no less 'racist' than the myths against which the article is directed. . . . If published as it is, [the article] would be likely to cast discredit on the women or the blacks, or both, that it seeks to praise."[27]

Contrary to these dismissive reactions, Lerner brought to the study of women's history intellectual rigor and sophistication. She showed no hesitation in chiding feminists who claimed the universality and priority of sexual oppression as an experience common to all women. She argued, "However useful that concept may be as an agitational tool, it does not work as a tool for historical analysis. The study of black women in American history illustrates that generalizations about sex oppression as *universal* are invalid. The nature of sex oppression differs for women of the dominant and oppressed races. It also differs for women of different classes. Working-class women of all races have always expressed their oppression in class terms rather than in sex terms and have organized around their work; but black working-class women experienced their oppression as *black* workers much more seriously than as women workers."[28] Lerner was unimpressed by the Marxist approach of some women's history workshop groups in Europe when she attended the fifth international conference of women historians in Vienna in 1984.[29] Noting the limitations of the Marxist model, she stated, "In the case of women, just as in the case of racial castes, ideology and prescription internalized by both women and men seem to be as much a causative factor as are material changes in production relations. . . . Unless such changes are accompanied by changes in consciousness, which in turn result in institutional changes, they do not favorably affect the lives of women."[30]

Lerner communicated her views in so distinctly an American "voice" that many of her colleagues gave little or no thought to her Austrian origins. After her marriage to an American in the early 1940s, she had assimilated into American culture and gave up reading German literature and hardly ever spoke German.[31] Recalling her decision to become an American writer at that time, she wrote, "I embraced America with gratitude and fascination, as I embraced its primary language. If that meant suppressing and denying some of my European habits in thought and attitude, so be it. I was young enough to start anew."[32] After she entered the academic profession, she referred to her life as a refugee without making any connection to her development as a historian. Instead, she noted the bias and provincialism of her European education. The history and culture of the United States were barely acknowledged and were "marginal to the ethnocentric definition of humanist knowledge of pre–World War II Austria." In her youth, it was possible to be a well-educated European intellectual and "yet to be ignorant of the history and culture of several continents."[33]

Lerner attributed her historical approach to the influence of an American woman historian. Mary Beard collaborated with her husband, Charles Beard, in widening the frame of historical analysis and in integrating women in their narratives of American civilization.[34] When Lerner read Mary Beard's *Women as Force in History*, she was "struck, as by a sudden illumination, by the simplicity and truth of [Beard's] insight" that women have always been active and at the center of history and that their contribution to human culture cannot be found by seeing them only as victims of oppression.[35] In Beard's account of women in history, Lerner recognized a world that she knew from working with women in grassroots community-building and political activism. While Lerner placed considerable emphasis on the impact of this activity on her conceptualization of women's history, she remained silent on precisely what she had done.[36]

It was not until the publication of her autobiography in 2002 that Lerner filled this empty space in her narrative. She began to work in the peace movement as a result of the atomic bombing of Hiroshima and Nagasaki in August 1945 and joined the Communist Party USA in 1946 and remained a member until 1958. Her husband, Carl, a film editor in Hollywood, had joined the party before she met him in New York City. She made this decision not out of any particular love for the Soviet Union but owing to the fact that the American Communists whom she knew personally were stronger fighters for the issues that were important to her—resistance to nuclear weapons and war, the fight against racism, the struggles of California's trade unions, and the need for low-cost childcare and decent housing.[37] She served as an officer of the Los Angeles chapter of the Congress of American Women, a popular front organization that was dedicated to the causes of peace, social reform, race justice, and women's rights. The national and local leadership levels at the founding of the Congress of American Women in 1946 represented a coalition of New Deal liberals, Communists, and activists from the African American community and trade unions. The organization had a deep awareness of class and race issues and identified itself with the history of women's struggles for equality and justice.[38] In her autobiography Lerner confessed, "Looking back on it now, it seems that my interest in the history of American women and my future career as a historian date from this period and the ways in which the Congress of American Women consistently incorporated women's history in its work."[39]

In the 1990s Lerner began to describe more distinctly the effect of her refugee background on her work in women's history. In a lecture entitled "A Personal Journey: Jewish Otherness and Women's History," which she gave at Brandeis University in 1993, she discussed the antisemitic definition of the Jews as "the Other, the outsider, the deviant." Recalling her experience of persecution and expulsion from her native land under Nazi rule, she confessed that being a stateless and destitute Jewish refugee had firmly fixed her outsider status in her consciousness.[40] She said, "It is this understanding of 'Otherness' and of the denial of self-definition which led me to the study of the history of women. For women have, for longer than any other human group, been defined by others and have been defined as 'the Other.' . . . I have, for the past 35 years, tried to comprehend analytically what I experienced and learned as a prototypical outsider—a woman, a Jew, an exile."[41]

What accounts for the expansion of Lerner's consciousness of this strand in the weave of connections at this time? The recovery of her mastery of the German language—her mother tongue—enabled her to retrieve buried, distressing memories. Her visits to Austria and Germany prompted reflection on the effects of exile and refugee status on her work. Undergoing years of psychoanalysis reawakened her consciousness of traumatic experiences, as her comments on "forgotten trauma" and the healing methods of psychotherapy suggest.[42] Speaking in Vienna in 1992, she lamented the loss of her native language and with it the culture of her homeland and "the knowledge of the unconscious, which speaks only in the mother tongue."[43]

Two years after her arrival in the United States, Lerner gave up speaking and reading German. As she explained in a lecture in Salzburg in 1995, "I no longer wanted to speak German; I was repelled by the sound of it; it was now the language of the enemy and could no longer be distinguished from that which was done in its name."[44] For nearly fifty years, she did not read any German books or newspapers. When Austrian women historians invited her to participate in an international conference in Vienna in 1984, she agreed to offer two papers with considerable anxiety and uncertainty about her competence in conversational and academic German. She eventually hired a student in the German department at the University of Wisconsin to translate the lectures that she read from the podium there.[45] She had to learn her native language all over again when she edited the translation of her book, *The Creation of Patriarchy*, which a German publishing house issued in 1991.[46]

The process of recovering her fluency in German made Lerner realize what she had lost when she gave up her mother tongue—deep memories, the communications of the unconscious, and the sounds of childhood affective experiences—and what she had suppressed: the trauma of her arrest by the Nazis in 1938, her expulsion from her homeland, and her emotionally complicated relationship with her mother, who died in Liechtenstein in 1943.[47] Lerner came to America alone with the help of a boyfriend's family. While her father, Robert Kronstein, found refuge in Liechtenstein after the Nazis seized power in Austria, her mother, Ilona, unhappily married, settled in southern France and pursued her aspiration to be an artist. Especially stressful for Gerda were the letters from her mother, who was reluctant to join her husband and wanted to keep her options open in 1939–40. When Ilona decided to emigrate to America in 1941, she sought her daughter's help in finding a sponsor who could provide an affidavit, and assumed that Gerda could persuade officials in Washington to grant her a preferential visa. The tone of Ilona's correspondence became reproachful, as she increasingly expressed despair and complained that Gerda was not answering her letters.[48]

Married to Carl Lerner and beginning a new life in California in 1942, Lerner ceased to dwell on the emotional entanglement with her mother and her feeling of guilt over her inability to help her parents. Describing her state of mind at that time during the Second World War, she wrote in her autobiography, "In actuality we lived in a black pit of false facts and forced forgetting, which gradually became a sort of cocoon. What one does not know does not hurt. So goes a charitable explanation. I think otherwise. What one does not know hurts all the more—it becomes a slow, seeping poison, which tinges every happy moment with guilt and casts a fog over joy and hope."[49] The return to her mother tongue opened the door to memories. As she wrote in 1997, "It was through language that I was able to begin the process of healing from the hidden cost of my life as a refugee."[50]

Lerner's visits to Austria and Germany enlivened her consciousness of the effects of her refugee experience. In 1992, the *Literaturhaus* in Vienna mounted an exhibition on Austrian writers who were forced into exile under National Socialism, and invited Lerner to give a public talk related to her experience.[51] Thus, in May of that year, Lerner returned to her native land with mixed feelings and spoke about her life as a refugee, a subject that she had not discussed in her earlier presentations at the 1984 conference in Vienna. She spent six weeks in Germany in the fall of 1993, when the *Campus Verlag*, her German publisher, arranged a book tour that brought her to Bonn, Bremen, Dortmund, Frankfurt am Main, and other cities there.[52] This trip was her first visit to Germany in more than fifty years; over the decades, she had drawn the line on going there. As she noted afterwards, "So it was actually through my books that I began the process of return." The University of Bielefeld invited her to become a visiting professor for a semester. On an impulse, she agreed instead to give an intensive seminar for two weeks during this tour. The earnest response of the students, born after the Third Reich and yet wrestling with the burden of their country's history, to her lectures on sexism, racism, and antisemitism had a "healing" effect on her.[53]

From the mid-1990s on, Lerner returned to Austria with greater frequency and was honored there as a pioneering scholar in women's history. On these occasions, she impressed upon her audience the connection between her experience as a Jewish refugee from Hitlerism and her work in women's history. She declared in Vienna in 1995, "Experiencing antisemitism and fascism led me to Women's History, for I learned firsthand what it means to be defined as 'the Other,' the deviant."[54] Lerner made this connection again when she accepted the prestigious Bruno Kreisky Prize in 2007, and proceeded to add that those who experienced racial hatred and persecution bear an obligation to remember as a heavy burden throughout their lives. She indicated how she understood this obligation as a historian when she recalled her own experiences and offered reflections in a universalist scope on the issue of selective remembering, invisibility, and forgetting in the writing of history. She observed that women were "not the only group who had been 'forgotten' in history." The marginalization of slaves, peasants, workers, and colonized peoples in the construction of historical narratives in the past had been accompanied by forceful domination and oppression. It was out of this system that gender discrimination, disdain for the lower classes, racism, and antisemitism drew their "poisonous nourishment." She associated the new women's history with the striving for a holistic view of the historical past.[55]

The connection between Lerner's Jewishness and work in women's history is more complicated than some of her statements suggest. By her own admission, she had an ambivalent definition of her Jewishness. She considered herself a Jew belonging to the Jewish community, but did not see that common fate tied to religion. As a youth in Vienna, she questioned the exclusionary practices related to women in synagogue services and was critical of the distinction between wealthy and poor Jews in the seating and the calling to read the Torah. She was unwilling to accept the role that traditional Judaism assigned to women, and had been an agnostic since that time.[56] Coming out of her Central European experience, her conviction that political ethnonationalism led to conflict and war "made [her] unable for a long time to accept the ideological premise of Zionism." She "wanted to get away from nationalistic allegiances [and] transcend differences of race, ethnicity, religion, and nationalism."[57] She did not make ethnicity the focus of her historical scholarship. She employed the concept of "Otherness" to discuss the problems that arise from stigmatizing any human group as a deviant outgroup.

In addition to her identity as a Jewish refugee, Lerner also experienced "Otherness" as a "political person" who stood against injustice and Cold War beliefs.[58] In the postwar era of McCarthyism, American citizens suspected of Communist leanings were subjected to charges of conspiracy and government investigations. Lerner, now a mother of two children, lived under a hovering anxiety of "witch-hunting," denunciation, and blacklisting. The Un-American Activities Committee of the United States House of Representatives cited the Congress of American Women as a subversive, pro-Communist "front organization." Many decades later, Lerner wrote, "I can write long essays about the social construction of deviant outgroups, about the social use of stereotypes to maintain the maldistribution of resources. But in my bones there is this knowledge of what it is like when what you are is taken from you and distorted and denied, held up for shame, ridicule and contempt."[59]

What insights does this analysis of the professional trajectory of Gerda Lerner offer for the history of the second generation in the Central European emigration? When women and men in that group spoke or wrote about the formative influences in their lives in relation to their professions and achievements, they were constructing narratives that sometimes changed over time. They emphasized what made sense in their current interpretation of their lives and omitted what at that time seemed less relevant or what they had thrust down the hole of oblivion. Lerner came to a consciousness of the connection between her experiences as a Jew and an exile and her work as a historian late in her life. Historians need to be alert to the silent, empty spaces in these narratives and to consider the omissions and the possible reasons for the silence. The effect of the second generation's refugee background on their professional work forms just one of the strands in a complex weave of multiple connections. It would be a mistake to reduce their experiences in the United States to "the opportunity structure"[60] and to underestimate the significance of their education in American schools and their assimilation into American society and culture. The claim that émigré intellectuals in the second generation carried the normative and conceptual baggage of the German humanist idea of *Bildung* should not ignore the possibility that they responded to new circumstances and influences in their new locations.[61] Indeed, some second-generation refugees have reacted with skepticism to the speculation about the transplantation of such a German-Jewish legacy in exile.[62] The search for a common denominator to explain the stellar accomplishments of the second generation is a tempting endeavor for sociologists and historians. Lerner's life and career and the memoirs of other refugees in this cohort who became successful academics remind us that this group was not homogeneous.[63]

The survival skills that Lerner applied effectively in Austria under Nazi rule and in emigration gave her courage, psychological stamina, and self-assurance. The experience of violent antisemitism made her morally alert to the evil consequences of designating the difference of an ethnic or religious minority as deviance and inferiority. These personal qualities grew stronger in America through her political activities outside the "Cold War consensus," her earnest concern about issues of race prejudice and injustice, and her identity with the history of women's struggles for equality and self-definition. In her experiences in Central Europe as well as in America are to be found the formative influences for her bold reconceptualization of history and for her dual commitment to correcting selective memory on the part of historians and "seeking a holistic worldview in which differences among people are recognized and respected and which records the commonality of human striving in all its variety and complexity."[64]

Marjorie Lamberti is the emerita Charles A. Dana Professor of History at Middlebury College. She is the author of *Jewish Activism in Imperial Germany: The Struggle for Civil Equality* (1978); *State, Society, and the Elementary School in Imperial Germany* (1989); and *The Politics of Education: Teachers and School Reform in Weimar Germany* (2002). Articles based on her research on academic and political refugees from Nazi Germany have been published in *Jewish Social Studies* in 2006, *Central European History* in 2007 and 2014, and *German Studies Review* in 2008.

Notes

1. The first epigraph is from Lerner's presidential address to the Organization of American Historians, April 1982, in Gerda Lerner, *Why History Matters: Life and Thought* (New York, 1997), 115. The second is from Lerner's Charles Homer Haskins lecture in 2005 in idem, *A Life of Learning*, American Council of Learned Societies Occasional Paper no. 60, 1.
2. "A Graduate Program Sets Out to Find History's Women," *New York Times*, 20 March 1973.

3. Gerda Lerner, "The Challenge of Women's History," in *The Majority Finds Its Past: Placing Women in History* (New York, 1979), 169–74.
4. Gerda Lerner, "Women Among the Professors of History: The Story of a Process of Transformation," in Eileen Boris and Nupur Chaudhuri, eds., *Voices of Women Historians: The Personal, the Political, the Professional* (Bloomington, 1999), 1–10; Catherine Clinton, "Gerda Lerner," in Robert Rutland, ed., *Clio's Favorites: Leading Historians of the United States, 1945–2000* (Columbia, MO, 2000), 98–110.
5. On her life in Austria, see Gerda Lerner, *Fireweed: A Political Autobiography* (Philadelphia, 2002).
6. Gerhard Sonnert and Gerald Holton, *What Happened to the Children Who Fled Nazi Persecution* (New York, 2006), 9, note the distinction between an immigrant effect and a refugee effect.
7. Sonnert and Holton, *What Happened to the Children*, 20–21, 93, 130–31. Some of the statistical data that Sonnert and Holton gathered in a survey of more than two thousand former refugees do not actually provide evidence to substantiate this theory. In comparison, Walter Laqueur refrains from formulating an overarching theory to account for the high achievers in the second generation. Walter Laqueur, *Generation Exodus: The Fate of Young Jewish Refugees from Nazi Germany* (Hanover, 2001), xiii, 141, 296.
8. Catherine Epstein identifies sixteen women historians of the two refugee generations and notes how emigration influenced their work in "Fashioning Fortuna's Whim: German-Speaking Women Emigrant Historians in the United States," in Sibylle Quack, ed., *Between Sorrow and Strength: Women Refugees of the Nazi Period* (Cambridge, 1995), 301–23.
9. This point is also borne out in the recollections of academic researchers in the social and behavioral sciences in Peter Suedfeld, ed., *Light from the Ashes: Social Science Careers of Young Holocaust Refugees and Survivors* (Ann Arbor, 2001).
10. Gerda Lerner, "Autobiographical Notes," in *The Majority Finds Its Past*, xiii–xxxii; see also idem, *Why History Matters*, ch. 1–4.
11. Laqueur, *Generation Exodus*, 270.
12. Lerner, "A Weave of Connections," in *Why History Matters*, 15.
13. "A Personal Journey: Jewish Otherness and Women's History," MC 498, box 13, folder 6, Gerda Lerner Papers, Schlesinger Library, Radcliffe Institute, Harvard University. In this lecture delivered at Brandeis University on 15 March 1993, Lerner admitted that until very recently she had "never given a moment's thought" to the question of how her life and identity as a Jewish refugee had influenced her work in women's history. See also Joyce Antler, *The Journey Home: Jewish Women and the American Century* (New York, 1997), 287.
14. Lerner, "The Feminist: A Second Look," in *The Majority Finds Its Past*, 33–34.
15. Lerner, "Placing Women in History: Definitions and Challenges," in *The Majority Finds Its Past*, 145–48; idem, "The Majority Finds Its Past," 164–66. One of the themes in Lerner's *The Creation of Feminist Consciousness: From the Middle Ages to Eighteen-seventy* (Cambridge, 1993) was the "survival knowledge [and] skills" that women, like other subordinate groups, developed to "maneuver in a world in which they are excluded from structured power" (12).
16. Lerner, "The Challenge of Women's History," 172–75.
17. Lerner, *Fireweed*, 352–62. Lerner assisted her husband in the making of a film documentary on the "Prayer Pilgrimage for Freedom" to Washington, DC, in the spring of 1957, which was organized by Martin Luther King, Jr., and other civil rights leaders.
18. Lerner to Professor Walter Fisher at Morgan State College in Baltimore, 9 September 1968, box 8, folder 6, Gerda Lerner Papers.
19. Lerner, "Women's Rights and American Feminism," in *The Majority Finds Its Past*, 56–58. This essay was first published in *The American Scholar* in the spring 1971.
20. Lerner's papers "Community Work of Black Club Women" and "Black Women in the United States: A Problem in Historiography and Interpretation" were published as essays in chapters 5 and 6 in *The Majority Finds Its Past*.

21. Gerda Lerner, "Notes on Sources," in *Black Women in White America: A Documentary History* (New York, 1972), xxix.
22. Lerner, "Black Women in the United States," 67.
23. Lerner, "The Community Work of Black Club Women," 84. Lerner opened up new directions in the study of African American history in her essay on black women's clubs, which was first published in *The Journal of Negro History*. Lerner's influence is clearly evident in Darlene Clark Hine, "Lifting the Veil, Shattering the Silence: Black Women's History in Slavery and Freedom," in *The State of Afro-American History: Past, Present, and Future* (Baton Rouge, 1986), 236–38.
24. Lerner, "Black Women in the United States," 69–72. The scholarship of some American historians in the 1960s minimized the suffering that the sexual aggression of white plantation masters caused black women and men in the antebellum South. See this contention in Susan Tracy, *In the Master's Eye: Representations of Women, Blacks, and Poor Whites in Antebellum Southern Literature* (Amherst, 1995), 244. On the historiography of that era, see Jay Saunders Redding, "The Negro in American History: As Scholar, as Subject," in Michael Kammen, ed., *The Past Before Us: Contemporary Historical Writing in the United States* (Ithaca, 1980), 292–307.
25. Lerner, "Preface," in *Black Women in White America*, xviii–xix.
26. Peter Stearns, editor of the *Journal of Social History*, to Lerner, 2 March 1974, box 15, folder 17, Gerda Lerner Papers.
27. Martin Ridge to Lerner, 16 March 1970, box 15, folder 15, Gerda Lerner Papers; Martin Ridge to Lerner, 29 January 1973, box 15, folder 20, Gerda Lerner Papers.
28. Lerner, "Black Women in the United States," 81.
29. Gerda Lerner, "International Report: the 5th Annual Meeting of Women Historians," *Women's Studies Quarterly* 12, no. 3 (1984), 23.
30. Lerner, "Placing Women in History," 156. Lerner became a "post-Marxist" when she began her work in women's history. See her criticism of Marxist theory in respect to questions of gender, race, and ethnicity in Lerner, *Fireweed*, 370–71.
31. On her "Americanization," see Lerner, *Fireweed*, 189–90, 214, 222–24.
32. Lerner, "Living in Translation," in *Why History Matters*, 38.
33. Lerner, "Autobiographical Notes," xvii.
34. Margaret Smith Crocco, "Forceful Yet Forgotten: Mary Ritter Beard and the Writing of History," *The History Teacher* 31, no. 1 (1997): 15–16.
35. Lerner, "Autobiographical Notes," xx–xxiii; idem, "New Approaches to the Study of Women in American History," in *The Majority Finds Its Past*, 5; idem, "Placing Women in History," 147–48. Mary Beard's *Women as Force in History: A Study in Traditions and Realities* was published in 1946. When Lerner was invited to give the Charles Homer Haskins Lecture for 2005, she called Beard her principal mentor as a historian and credited Beard for raising her feminist consciousness. Lerner, *A Life of Learning*, 12.
36. Lerner, "Autobiographical Notes," xvi.
37. Lerner, *Fireweed*, 243–64.
38. Lerner, *Fireweed*, 244–45, 256. See also Amy Swerdlow, "The Congress of American Women: Left-Feminist Peace Politics in the Cold War," in Linda K. Kerber, Alice Kessler-Harris, and Kathryn Kish Sklar, eds., *U.S. History As Women's History* (Chapel Hill, 1995), 296–312. The Congress of American Women's dissenting views on America's Cold War foreign policy made it a target of the House of Representatives Un-American Activities Committee. The organization disbanded in 1950, when the United States Justice Department ordered it to register as an enemy agent.
39. Lerner, *Fireweed*, 257.
40. Lerner, "A Weave of Connections," 11.
41. Ibid., 15.

42. Lerner, *Why History Matters*, 200. Lerner referred to her years in psychoanalysis in *Fireweed*, 292.
43. "Ein Besuch in die alte Heimat," lecture at the *Literaturhaus*, 21 May 1992, box 13, folder 2, Gerda Lerner Papers.
44. "Leben in Übersetzung: Über den Sprach- und Identitätsverlust durch den Wechsel in einen anderen Kulturkreis," box 14, folder 27, Gerda Lerner Papers.
45. Lerner to Igrun Bohle in Vienna, 23 March 1984, box 10, folder 17, Gerda Lerner Papers; Lerner, "Living in Translation," 47.
46. The German translations of Lerner's *The Creation of Patriarchy* (New York, 1986) and *The Creation of Feminist Consciousness* (New York, 1993) were published in Frankfurt am Main in 1991 and 1993 respectively.
47. Lerner, "Living in Translation," 38–40, 47–48; Gerda Lerner, "Autobiography, Biography, Memory, and the Truth," in *Living with History/Making Social Change* (Chapel Hill, 2009), 149. On Lerner's feeling of guilt over having misunderstood her mother, see *Fireweed*, 205–7.
48. Robert Kronstein to Gerda, 15 October 1939, AR 25149, box 1, folder 6, Gerda Lerner Family Papers (GLFP), Leo Baeck Institute, New York City; Ilona Kronstein to Gerda, 1 October 1939, box 1, folder 7, GLFP; Ilona Kronstein's letters to Gerda in 1940, box 1, folder 8, GLFP; Ilona Kronstein to Gerda, 10 January 1941, 30 January 1941, 17 May 1941, and 24 June 1941, box 1, folder 8, GLFP. Lerner described the tensions in her correspondence with her parents in *Fireweed*, 160–61, 178–79, 193.
49. Lerner, *Fireweed*, 236.
50. Lerner, "Introduction," in *Why History Matters*, xiii.
51. Material related to the exhibition and program at the *Literaturhaus* and the text of her lecture, box 13, folder 2, Gerda Lerner Papers.
52. Correspondence related to the arrangements for her lectures during her tour in Germany in 1993, box 13, folders 8 and 9, Gerda Lerner Papers.
53. Lerner, "In the Footsteps of the Cathars," in *Why History Matters*, 18–20, 31.
54. See the text of her address in 1995 when she received the Käthe Leichter Prize in Vienna, in Lerner, *Why History Matters*, 154.
55. *Preisrede von Gerda Lerner anlässlich der Verleihung des Bruno-Kreisky-Preises für das politische Buch 2006* (Vienna, 2007), 4–6.
56. Lerner, "A Weave of Connections," 7–8; idem, *Fireweed*, 35–36, 40–42.
57. Lerner, "A Weave of Connections," 16. She concluded, "But now, what must survive is no longer the small group, the kin, the *shtetl*, the *Landsmannshaft*, even the nation. All of us must survive in a world in which difference is the norm and no longer serves as an excuse for dominance or we will not survive at all. And in order to survive in this interconnected global village we must learn and learn very quickly to respect others who are different from us and, ultimately, to grant to others the autonomy we demand for ourselves" (17).
58. This aspect of her identity, emphasized so strongly in her autobiography, is missed when *Fireweed* is analyzed in the context of "the broader literature of Jewish or Holocaust memory" or interpreted under the theme of "recalling home," a metaphor for the recovery of Jewish ethnic identity. See, for example, Jeremy Popkin, "Holocaust Memories. Historians' Memoirs: First-Person Narrative and the Memory of the Holocaust," *History and Memory* 15, no. 1 (2003): 49–84; Janet Handler Burstein, "Recalling Home: American Jewish Women Writers of the New Wave," *Contemporary Literature* 42, no. 4 (2001): 800–24.
59. Lerner, *Fireweed*, 300, and for her recollections of McCarthyism and the "witch-hunting" against Communists, 277–300, 326–38. On the "human wreckage" of the anticommunist crusade, see Ellen Schrecker, *Many Are The Crimes: McCarthyism in America* (Boston, 1998), 359–73.
60. Sonnert and Holton, *What Happened to the Children*, 9, 174.

61. See, for example, Steven Aschheim, *Beyond the Border: The German-Jewish Legacy Abroad* (Princeton, 2007), 76–77, also 63, 65, 72, in which the values and biases of "German humanist, Enlightenment, and Bildung culture" play a key role in his interpretation of the upbringing and self-identification of four émigré historians of the second generation and their writing of German history.
62. Several contributors to Abraham Peck, ed., *The German-Jewish Legacy in America, 1938–1988: From Bildung to the Bill of Rights* (Detroit, 1989) responded skeptically to this claim. See the critical comments of the former refugees, Henry Feingold (57–61), Manfred Jonas (51, 56), Tom Freudenheim (148), and Theodore Wiener (153, 155). Feingold, a scholar in the field of American Jewish history, states, "Some go as far as attributing the postwar American explosion in technology and culture to the intellectual capital carried in the baggage of the refugee scientists, scholars, and sundry cultural agents. . . . There may be some measure of truth in such self-aggrandizing assessments, but I suspect that the contribution was made after the German-Jewish spirit was altered so that it could work in America. It is only in that sense that we can think of it as still being alive in America. I find discomfort in speaking of the 'German-Jewish spirit in exile.' It gives that spirit an autonomy and particularity it did not possess in reality" (59).
63. Werner Angress, *Immer etwas abseits. Jugenderinnerungen eines jüdischen Berliners 1920–1945* (Berlin, 2005); Peter Gay, *My German Question* (New Haven, 1998); Georg and Wilma Iggers, *Two Lives in Uncertain Times: Facing the Challenges of the 20th Century as Scholars and Citizens* (New York, 2006); George L. Mosse, *Confronting History: A Memoir* (Madison, 2000); Fritz Stern, *Five Germanys I Have Known* (New York, 2006); Klemens von Klemperer, *Voyage through the Twentieth Century: A Historian's Recollections and Reflections* (New York, 2009).
64. Lerner, *Why History Matters*, 211.

Part IV
COMPARATIVE AND TRANSNATIONAL PERSPECTIVES

Chapter 17

German Émigré Historians in Israel

Shulamit Volkov

Historians normally deal with people they know only through their written remains. The life stories and the achievements of the men and a few women we wish to reconstruct in this book are all too often known to us personally. They are part of our life. In a small country such as Israel, this is perhaps particularly so. Let me therefore begin with a personal reminiscence.

I completed my Ph.D. at Berkeley in the fall of 1972 and in March of the following year I was back in Israel, planning to take on my new position as a lecturer (parallel to an American assistant professor) in the history department of Tel Aviv University. When I first arrived on campus, I was told that on that very day and exactly at that very hour, members of the newly founded Institute for German History were having a meeting at the Institute's modest quarters on the first floor of the humanities building. Why not go over and participate, the departmental head suggested to me in a friendly tone. Not knowing my way around, it took some time before I found myself knocking and then bravely walking into this meeting. Outside the door, I could hear some of the loud conversation that was going on inside, not surprisingly for that time—all male voices, but quite surprising at that time and place—all in German. Embarrassed silence fell as I walked in. This is a faculty meeting, someone tried to explain. Would I be kind enough to wait outside?

Eventually I was admitted, not yet thirty and with a stylish miniskirt. Four men participated in the meeting, chaired, rather informally, by the founder and first head of the institute, Professor Dr. Walter Grab. Grab was born in Vienna in 1919 and was by then fifty-three years old. Almost ten years older, sixty-two at the time, was his colleague Shlomo Na'aman—born in Cologne in 1912, and the two other men present—relatively younger, both born in 1921—were Charles

---

Notes from this chapter begin on page 269.

Bloch, a native of Berlin, and Jehuda Wallach, ex–army colonel, originally from a small town, south Germany. Missing on this occasion were the two Rumanian-born members of the institute, not exactly German émigrés but clearly of the central European *Kulturraum*: Michel Harsegor, born 1924, and Shimon Shamir, born 1929. I was born in Tel Aviv at the end of 1942. The only one I knew from among those present was Na'aman, who had interviewed me—very thoroughly, I should add—when I had offered my services, so to speak, a few months earlier. He then took care of my appointment through those rather unclear channels that had been applied at the time, and was now friendly and encouraging. Needless to say, I felt completely out of place, but in the end I am not really sure who felt more ill at ease that day: I, a complete novice, young, and a woman to boot, or the four gentlemen into whose comfortable milieu I had suddenly intruded.

In any case, the men in that room that day well represent the second-generation émigré historians in Israel, teaching and conducting research in the field of German history. If I were then to step across the lawn and move from the department of history to the department of Jewish history, which in fact I did only—and with much hesitation—a number of years later, I would have encountered at least two additional members of the group: Jacob Toury, once Franz Königsberger, born in 1915 in Beuten, Upper Silesia, and the younger Uriel Tal, born in 1926 in Vienna—both teaching German Jewish history, while also well versed in German history, of course, and roughly belonging to the same generation. I will use them here as part of my sample, encompassing almost the entire relevant group.

It must be made clear at the outset: until members of my generation began to fill in academic positions at the two existing Israeli universities at that time, namely during the early 1970s, every faculty member in Israel was an émigré. The Hebrew University in Jerusalem was established in the mid-1920s.[1] By then, fewer than one hundred fifty thousand Jews lived under the rule of the British mandate in Palestine, and when it was decided that the institution on Mount Scopus would also accept students, beyond its dedication to research, their number—in all three existing faculties—was 141. When the State of Israel was established, some twenty years later in 1948, one could count only a little more than a thousand students, and despite a very fast rate of growth in the following years, by the time Tel Aviv University was established in the mid-1950s, there were fewer than ten thousand students in the entire country, including the by then well-established technical university in Haifa, the Technion.

The discipline of history, in any event, was definitely not considered a top priority at this stage. The Center for Jewish Studies at the Hebrew University, trying to combine scholarship with ideology, was initially dedicated to the study of Jewish religion and law, Hebrew language and literature, philosophy, and "the Land of Israel," *Eretz-Ysrael*, in any event not to history. Nevertheless, by the early

1930s, Avigdor Cherikover, born in St. Petersburg and educated first in Moscow and then in Berlin, was teaching ancient Jewish history with emphasis on the time of the Second Temple there; Yzchak Beer—a native of Halberstadt, later a student and then a teacher at the *Hochschule für die Wissenschaft des Judentums* (School of Jewish Studies) in Berlin, taught the medieval period, and a couple of years later, Ben-Zion Dinburg (later Dinur), born in the Ukraine and likewise educated in Berlin, joined the staff, appointed to teach modern Jewish history. Finally, it was in 1935 that Richard Koebner, an established scholar who had been dismissed by the Nazis from his position at the University of Breslau, was appointed professor of modern history and the official head of the department of general history, as distinct from Jewish history, in Jerusalem.[2] For some time this department included only him, while Beer and Cherikover were teaching in it as part-time collaborators. Luckily, Koebner was an extremely creative, knowledgeable, and prolific historian.[3] While still in Germany, he had written extensive monographs on a number of city communities in medieval times and on various aspects of the German colonization of the East. He published numerous essays in the field of *Begriffsgeschichte* (the history of concepts) and later on wrote on the economic sides of imperialism as well as on a variety of theoretical and methodological issues.[4] Moreover, he was by nature hardworking and utterly dedicated. Coming to Palestine in his fifties, Koebner managed to make a complete break with his past and, although teaching in Hebrew remained a problem for him for a long time, took on an enormous load, covering every conceivable topic from the Reformation to the First World War, including matters of economic, social, diplomatic, cultural, and colonial history. He gave lecture courses, seminars, and what were then called pro-seminars—on campus as well as at his private home, where, with the permission of his students, he often taught in German. In fact, if one did not count those teaching Jewish history, the first generation of German émigré historians in Palestine consisted of one man: Richard Koebner. All those who later joined the faculty as so-called general historians, coming either from Eastern or from Central Europe, were—at least initially—his students: Joshua Prawer, Jakob Talmon, Joshua Arieli, and many more.

The men who founded the university at Tel Aviv studied with him, too. First and foremost among them was Zvi Yaavetz, the founding father of the history department. Having arrived from Chernovich, just managing to escape the Nazis in his teens, Yaavetz began studying at the Hebrew University, and soon found himself an assistant to Koebner, helping him prepare the manuscript for his future book on imperialism. He was asked to write a piece on the changing meaning of "imperium" in ancient Rome and on the ways it was being applied in modern historiography, and ended up a historian of ancient Rome.[5] The men in that ground-floor room of the Institute for German History whom I already mentioned all studied with Koebner, and they seemed never to have forgotten their debt to him.

Fate would have it that Shlomo Na'aman, the oldest member of this group, born in 1912, began his academic education in Jerusalem in 1954, only a year before Koebner's early retirement. He just managed to meet him there. Son of a German-Jewish mother and a Galician father, Na'aman grew up in a Zionist family with clear socialist leanings and matriculated from a special *Realgymnasium* that put a particular stress on the humanities—a so called *Reformgymnasium*, in Essen.[6] Na'aman immigrated to Palestine as early as June 1932 and studied at the Teachers' Seminary in Jerusalem before becoming a teacher of some fame himself, working in a number of kibbutzim in the northern part of the country and finally settling down as member of Kibbutz Kineret, on the shores of the Sea of Galilee. Some twenty-two years passed between his arrival in Palestine and the beginning of his academic studies, over thirty years between this date and the launching of his professional career at Tel Aviv University. Untypically, he taught both medieval history and modern history there, eventually focusing ever more clearly on his research themes dealing with the history of the German liberal and social-democratic movements. Leaving the kibbutz empty-handed, Na'aman first moved with his family (his wife, two daughters, and a son) to the mixed Arab-Jewish town of Lod, not far from Tel Aviv, and later on, when his economic situation somewhat improved, to Ramat Aviv, near the new campus of Tel Aviv University. He published a fine biography of Lassalle, a book on the German *Nationalverein*, and during the last years of his life, while he was already seriously ill, a book on what had truly preoccupied him throughout his life: the link between Marxism and Zionism. In a number of interesting and original essays, he investigated Marx's and then the Marxist movement's changing attitude and relationships to Jews, Judaism, and Zionism.[7]

But what seems at first glance outstanding in Na'aman's life story, namely the long break between his immigration to Palestine and the beginning of his academic career, was in fact typical of the whole group. From among them, we have details and relatively full information only about Walter Grab's life. His autobiography, *Meine vier Leben*, was published in 1999, just over a year before his death in December 2000.[8] Grab was born in Vienna, son of a father from Bohemia and a mother from Galicia. His family tree succinctly characterizes the difference between these two backgrounds: the father was called Emil and his brothers were Rudolf, Alois, Arthur, and Ernst; the father's sister was named Bertha. His mother, on the other hand, was called Zippora, and her brothers, David, Israel, Ruben, and Nathan. In the end, however, the entire Grab family had given up all contacts with Judaism, though—as was so often the case—socialized almost exclusively within the similarly assimilated Viennese Jewish milieu. Walter attended a humanistic gymnasium and excelled in history and in German literature, both forever the loves of his life. Following the Anschluss in March 1938, having experienced a series of humiliations at the hands of local Nazis, he managed to leave for Palestine, arriving there in June of that same year.

Grab never tired of stressing that his emigration to Palestine was nothing other than a flight for his life. He had not been, and never became, a Zionist. He remained entirely loyal to his German roots, to his cultural background, and to his radical left-wing leanings, acquired in his youth on the streets of "Red Vienna." And in the twenty years following his arrival in Tel Aviv, he in fact lived within two rather isolated social milieus: the one consisting of old and new friends, sometimes relatives too, who all remained attached to their German past as much as he did, and the other, the small radical political left in Palestine, organized in the local Communist Party. The first circle was typified by the monthly meetings of the *Kreis für fortschrittliche Kultur*, meeting regularly in Tel Aviv to listen to lectures on such topics as "Hamlet and the 20. Jahrhundert," "From Rembrandt to Picasso," or "Stefan Zweig's Human Tragedy as a Reflection of a fighting Humanism."[9] In contrast, the Communists, strongly supervised and directed from Moscow, were thinly spread in the country and, wherever they were, busily debating among themselves the various political options at the time, or rather what they considered the available options, and undergoing repeated inner splits.[10] The subgroup to which Grab and his wife eventually belonged preferred the establishment of a binational Arab-Jewish state, led, naturally, by the left and under the auspices of the Russian Soviet regime. In any event, these two milieus, only rarely interacting, were islands within the Jewish mainstream at the time. Belonging to either of them, and certainly belonging to both, unavoidably made one feel an outsider. And this must have made life in the new country strenuous, sometimes even depressing.

Still, in the end, what really made life difficult for Grab was the need to make ends meet. Immediately upon arriving in Palestine, he did manage to study one year at the university in Jerusalem, with Cherikover, Beer, and Koebner, of course. But later, following the November Pogrom of 1938, some relatives arranged for the necessary papers for his parents, who landed in Palestine in March 1939, and Walter was forced to interrupt his studies and move from Jerusalem to Tel Aviv in order to help them settle down in the new, and for them very unwelcoming, country. They had left everything behind. Now the father, a leather goods producer in Vienna, attempted to establish a new business in Tel Aviv and in their small apartment, the Grabs were producing leather handbags of all kinds, trying to sell them to the various shop owners up and down the country. Business, however, was very slow, profits were meager, and, above all, none of it all fit the son's hopes and aspirations. He was miserable. Even later on, when the little workshop began to prosper and better income doubtlessly proved comforting, none of it seemed sufficient. It was 1958 and, as in Na'aman's case, twenty years after emigration that Grab began to study history at the newly founded, and at first barely existing, university of Tel Aviv. Having impressed his teachers with a phenomenal memory and unexpected wealth of knowledge, he later managed to get some minimal stipend and left for Germany to work on his doctoral dissertation.

Grab chose Hamburg, where he studied under the supervision of Fritz Fischer and soon managed to establish himself as a central figure among historians of the French Revolution in Germany. He became a world expert on the so-called German Jacobins and then traveled widely and lectured in both West and East Germany, where he was welcomed as a comrade-in-arms whose work was not only up to standards but also fitting the party line.[11]

The pattern of his career was thus established: Grab began teaching in Tel Aviv in 1965, but his academic milieu was in Germany. In 1971, with the establishment of the Institute of German History at Tel Aviv University, he was made head of the institute. Still, his lecture trips in the German-speaking lands of Central Europe, the German colleagues that he managed to invite to the institute, the conferences he organized, and his enormous correspondence with German colleagues—these constituted the real focus of his life. Although his Hebrew was good and he was an active teacher and an authoritative institute head, although he had many friends in Israel—especially but by no means only among German-speaking colleagues—although he was by then an old-time Israeli, Grab no doubt remained an outsider in many ways. Preparing for this lecture, I looked for his autobiography in the university library. It was not there. No one ordered it for the general collection, and Grab himself apparently never saw fit to give it as a present, not even to the small library in his own institution on that ground floor of the humanities building on the Tel Aviv campus.

Likewise an outsider by choice, though different from Grab in every other way, was his one-time university teacher Charles Bloch.[12] Bloch was born in Berlin in 1921 to a family of Social-Democratic activists. His uncle Joseph, for many years the editor of the *Sozialistische Monatsschriften,* had apparently greatly influenced him in early years. The family managed to immigrate to Palestine in 1934, following a stay of one year in Paris, and it was this year that made the thirteen-year-old Charles a Francophile for life. Upon arrival in Palestine and after finishing high school, he studied at the Hebrew University on Mount Scopus with the usual cadre, of course, but then left for France to work there as a newspaper correspondent, returning to Tel Aviv in 1955 with a Ph.D. from the Sorbonne, just in time to become the first lecturer in modern European history at the new history department there. Bloch, who was also fluent in Arabic and had worked to promote the study of Islam and the Arab world at the new university, taught courses on various topics in European history, with emphasis on foreign policy and international relations, stressing the period between the wars and the years of the Weimar Republic—the two topics that stood at the center of his research as well. For the whole period between 1955 and his death in 1987, Bloch commuted between Tel Aviv and Paris, teaching political science at Nanterre and history at Tel Aviv, staying ever longer periods away from Israel. Why? It is not entirely clear. Unlike Grab, Bloch was devoted to the Jewish state and felt a part of its mainstream Social-Democratic milieu in those days. Perhaps his family obligations and surely his attraction to France played some role in this, as probably did the strong academic roots he had struck there and his growing sense of alienation in view of Israel's changing political atmosphere and character. This alienation surely intensified after the Six Days War in 1967 and especially after the Labor Party's loss at the elections of 1977.

Our next protagonist provides yet another fascinating personal story.[13] The fifteen-year-old Yehuda Wallach, born near Mannheim, left Germany in 1936 and immigrated with his parents to Palestine. Having absorbed a Zionist atmosphere at home, he then fulfilled all the expected roles placed upon a young pioneer in the new country. He was among the founding members of Kibbutz Ein Dor, not far from mount Tabor, between Nazareth and the southern tip of lake Kineret, and having joined the Haganah, the Jewish military force during the British mandate, he fought in 1948 at the head of one of the brigades on the southern front and went on to become a professional soldier, commander of the Israeli army's first armored division. Wallach participated in the war of 1956, and, like most of the men in our sample, began his academic studies only in his forties. It was during the late 1960s that he began studying history and sociology at the Hebrew University and then took his Ph.D. at Oxford, focusing on military theories during the nineteenth and twentieth centuries. In 1970, almost fifty years old, he became a professor of history at Tel Aviv University, dividing his time between his research on various aspects of military theory and on the various Israeli wars, publishing many books and articles—in German, English, and Hebrew, the latter usually printed by the Israeli Army's official publishing house.

If we take yet another example, we shall be able to observe again strict similarities and important differences. In 1935, Yaakov Toury came to Palestine as a twenty-year-old Zionist youth from Silesia.[14] He then immediately picked up his interrupted studies and enrolled as a student at the Hebrew University, graduating in 1940 and then working for almost twenty years as a *Gymnasiallehrer*, teaching a variety of humanistic subjects at an elite high school in Haifa, while writing and publishing some of the best-known and much-used history textbooks for that school level. Only in his forties did he finally go back to complete his academic training in Jerusalem, receiving his Ph.D. in 1958 under the supervision of Jacob Katz, some ten years his elder, who had himself by then just managed—also after some fifteen years as a school teacher—to get a position at the Hebrew University.[15] Toury's dissertation on the political orientation of German Jewry enabled him in turn to join the small cadre of historians at the budding Tel Aviv University, where he taught German-Jewish history with other scholars born in Germany, mostly younger men, such as Shlomo Simonson, born in Breslau and by then an expert on Italian Jewry in the Middle Ages, and Uriel Tal, born in Vienna and just then moving from Jerusalem to Tel Aviv as tenured tracks in the older university seemed blocked for the time being.

The pattern seems clear. Members of the second-generation émigré historians in Palestine, men who were too young to have had a career in the academy before their enforced exit from Germany, did not experience a smooth transition. Like those coming from England or the United States, they moved from a country with a flourishing university system to another, that in fact had none. During the 1930s, as they were coming over one by one, there was only one small university in Jewish Palestine, and that university was at the time rather uninterested in taking up students in general, and students in the field of what was then called "general history" in particular. It was a poor country, torn by ethnic strife, ruled from and by Britain rather unwillingly and often capriciously, soon conceived as a burden in view of the mighty war that went on at the time on so many fronts. Most of these immigrants had to learn a language that was foreign to them and difficult, and to make a living in an economy permanently in crisis. Some joined the kibbutz movement, such as Shlomo Na'aman, Yehuda Wallach, and, somewhat later, Michel Harsegor, one of the two Romania-born historians at the Institute for German History. Others stayed in one of the country's urban centers, preferably as teachers, but sometimes, as in the case of Grab, as traders and artisans. Yet another group first joined the kibbutz movement and then served in the armed forces—not only Yehuda Wallach, but also for instance Jeshoshua Arieli, later of the Hebrew University.[16] Following his immigration, Arieli was first a member of the Haganah and then joined the Jewish Brigade that operated under British command in the battlefields of Europe. He was captured in Greece and spent some four years as a prisoner of war in various camps in Germany and Austria. Coming back after the war, he was enlisted again for a variety of military tasks and only later studied at the university, got his Ph.D. from Harvard, and finally taught in Jerusalem both American and European history, though rarely specifically German history. These men became historians after years of involvement in the life of the country. They often had very pronounced political views and an unusually rich, often unconventional life experience.

When I started to study history at the Hebrew University in the fall of 1962, none of the first-generation scholars was there, but by then the system seemed to be operating on an entirely different basis. The university now had a large faculty of history teachers covering all periods and most, if not all, aspects of the discipline. The second generation was then in full bloom, providing a diverse and comprehensive curriculum. Not all of the teachers, to be sure, were German émigrés, though all came from abroad, all were surely émigrés: Yaakov Talmon was born in Poland, Arieli in Carlsbad—by then on the northwestern border of the new Czechoslovakia—and Michael Confino in Bulgaria. They all taught modern history with great flourish and impressive scholarship. Shmuel Ettinger, born in St. Petersburg, taught Jewish history and the history of antisemitism, and Yehoshua Bar-Hillel, yet another Viennese native, first a kibbutz member and then a soldier both of the Jewish Brigade and during the war of 1948—taught me philosophy, logic above all. There was nothing logical in the career of these men. Their life was an adventure—often including painful stretches, sometimes exhilarating, never what we, of the third generation, would ever consider normal or even possible.

Shulamit Volkov is professor of modern European history emerita at Tel Aviv University (TAU) and member of the Israel Academy of Science and the Humanities. She was head of the Institute for German History at TAU and for a number of years edited its *Jahrbuch*. She wrote on aspects of German social history, German Jewish history, antisemitism, and various historiographical issues. Her *Walther Rathenau: Weimar's Fallen Statesman* was published in 2012.

Notes

1. For details on the establishment of the Hebrew University in Jerusalem and its early years, see especially the collection of essays in Shaul Katz and Michael Heyd, eds., *History of the Hebrew University in Jerusalem: Roots and Beginnings* [in Hebrew] (Jerusalem, 1997). See also Michael Heyd, "The Early History of the Hebrew University: Between National and Universal Orientation, between Research and Teaching," in Rivka Feldhai and Immanuel Etkes, eds., *Education and History: Cultural and Political Contexts* [in Hebrew] (Jerusalem, 1999), 355–76.
2. For a critical and controversial view of this group's scholarly project, see David Myers, *Re-inventing the Jewish Past: Jewish Intellectuals and the Zionist Return to History* (New York, 1995).
3. See the two introductory essays: Helmut D. Schmidt, "Richard Koebner (1885–1958): Von Breslau nach Jerusalem," and Jehoshua Arieli, "Richard Koebner—Zeitwende und Geschichtbewußtsein," in Richard Koebner, *Geschichte, Geschichtsbewußtsein und Zeitwende. Vorträge und Schriften aus dem Nachlaß* (Gerlingen, 1990), 11–21, 22–48.
4. A list of his publications can be found in the volume of his collected essays: Koebner, *Geschichte*, 295–99.
5. Yaavetz describes his time with Koebner succinctly in his preface to Koebner, *Geschichte*, 7–9.
6. See the introduction to Hans-Peter Harstick, Arno Herzig, and Hans Pelger, eds., *Arbeiterbewegung und Geschichte. Festschrift für Shlomo Na'aman* (Trier, 1983).
7. Shlomo Na'aman, *Marxismus und Zionismus* (Gerlingen, 1997).
8. Walter Grab, *Meine Vier Leben. Gedächtniskünstler, Emigrant, Jakobinerforscher, Demokrat* (Cologne, 1999).
9. See ibid., 90–98.
10. Ibid., 78–90. For the Palestinian Communist Party at that time, see Shmuel Dotan, *Reds: The Communist Party in Eretz Ysrael* [in Hebrew] (Kfar-Saba, 1991); and a recent reprint of Musa Budeiri, *Palestine's Left before Israel 1919–1948: Arab and Jew in the Struggle for Internationalism* (Chicago, 2010).
11. On this and other aspects of Grab's career, see Iris Nachum, "Es muss nicht immer Wiedergutmachung sein—Walter Grab und das Minerva Institut für deutsche Geschichte an der Universität Tel Aviv," in José Brunner and Iris Nachum, eds., *"Die Deutschen" als die Anderen. Deutschland in der Imagination seiner Nachbarn*, Tel Aviver Jahrbuch für deutsche Geschichte, vol. 40 (Göttingen, 2012), 237–76.

12. It was indeed Walter Grab who wrote on Bloch's life and intellectual development in a volume published in his memory. See Walter Grab, "The Roots of Charles Bloch's Political Conceptions: Recollections of my Friend and Teacher," in Haim Shamir, ed., *France and Germany in an Age of Crisis, 1900–1960* (Leiden, 1990), 8–15.
13. The following information was collected from obituaries in the Israeli press following Wallach's death on 10 August 2008. See also, "Zum sechzigsten Geburtstag von Jehuda Wallach," in *Jahrbuch des Instituts für Deutsche Geschichte* X (1981): 15–16. For biographical details I have also used here, as in some other cases, a few *Wikipedia* articles, when proven reliable. .
14. I have myself written on Toury's life. See Shulamit Volkov, "Jacob Toury—zum 75. Geburtstag," in *Tel Aviver Jahrbuch für Deutsche Geschichte* XX (1991): 13–21.
15. Katz was born in Hungary in 1904 and completed his academic studies at the University of Frankfurt am Main in 1934. He can therefore be best seen as a member of the first generation, though he began teaching at the sociology department of the Hebrew University only in 1950, eventually becoming the most influential historian of German Jewry in Israel. On his life and work, see Jay M. Harris, ed., *The Pride of Jacob: Essays on Jacob Katz and His Work* (Cambridge, MA, 2002), and Israel Bartal and Shmuel Feiner, eds., *Historiography Reappraised: New Views on Jacob Katz's Oeuvre* [in Hebrew] (Jerusalem, 2008).
16. On Arieli, see Michael Heyd, "Yehoshua Arieli as a Teacher and Scholar," in Hedva Ben Israel et al., eds., *Religion, Ideology, and Nationalism in Europe and America: Essays Presented in Honor of Yehoshua Arieli* (Jerusalem, 1986), 9–11, and various publications in Hebrew, including interviews, short biographies, and after his death on 8 August, 2002, a number of obituaries.

Chapter 18

GERMAN AND AUSTRIAN ÉMIGRÉ HISTORIANS IN BRITAIN AFTER 1933

Peter Alter

On their arrival in Britain in the dramatic years after 1933, most immigrants from Central Europe were bewildered, disoriented, even traumatized—an experience shared by men and women, adults and children. Physically threatened and deprived of fundamental rights as citizens, they had left Germany and, a few years later, Austria in a hurry. In most cases, they were practically penniless, deeply shaken by the disturbing revelation that a seemingly stable world could tumble and fall to pieces within a couple of weeks or months, if not days.

For example, immediately after the infamous pogrom of "Crystal Night" in November 1938, the Feuchtwanger family of Munich decided to send their fifteen-year-old son Edgar to the safety of England. In February 1939 he was hastily put on a train to the Hook of Holland and there boarded a boat across the North Sea to Harwich. Edgar Feuchtwanger recalled his departure: "My father accompanied me as far as the Dutch frontier, and I remember him being admonished by an *SS* border guard, who examined his passport, that he also should get the hell out of it as soon as possible. My parents in fact did so two-and-a-half months later, in early May 1939. In the meantime, arrangements had been made, through refugee organizations, for me to live with a doctor's family in Cornwall. I was conveyed across London from Liverpool Street Station to Paddington by family friends in a taxi, slightly startled to find it driving on the wrong side of the road, put on the Cornish Riviera Express to Truro and thus started a completely new phase in my life."[1]

In almost identical terms, the Germanist and historian Charlotte Jolles, interviewed more than sixty years after her emigration, described her sudden arrival in

---

Notes from this chapter begin on page 284.

Britain on a visitor's permit at practically the same time as Edgar Feuchtwanger: "In January 1939 I reached England with little luggage and ten *Reichsmark* in my pocket. . . . This was the first flight of my life. . . . Little luggage, yes—however, I had brought with me my typewriter. . . . Hardly favourable circumstances for a new start in a foreign country!"[2]

Jolles was then twenty-nine years old. The academic career in Berlin that she had envisaged, based on her pioneering study on *Fontane und die Politik*,[3] had come to an abrupt, though not entirely unexpected, end. As a so-called "non-Aryan Christian," she did not escape the racial policy that the new men in power in Germany had inaugurated since the promulgation of the notorious Nuremberg Laws in 1935. Ignoring the fact that her command of English was still very poor, Charlotte Jolles found work as a secretary and assistant to the female director of a home for orphaned children from Central Europe in the small town of Watford in Hertfordshire. While she was working at this charitable foundation, supported by Dr. George Bell, the Bishop of Chichester, she benefited from the chance to prepare for a career in teaching after the war. She soon began teaching German part-time at Watford Grammar School for Girls, and this had, according to her reminiscences, the potential to be turned into a full-time position shortly after the termination of war in Europe.

At the same time, Charlotte Jolles continued to attend evening classes at London's Birkbeck College, where she had enrolled as a student shortly after arriving in Britain. This laid the foundations for a master's degree, which she obtained there in 1947, and for a career as a lecturer and then professor of German studies at the same institution from 1955 until 1976. What had been denied to her in Berlin in the late 1930s thus materialized in London in the 1950s and 1960s: she became "one of the most erudite, humane and beguilingly charming representatives of German studies in the UK."[4] She helped to strengthen an academic discipline that has often been described as "relatively weak and neglected in Britain."[5]

From Trickle to Flood

Hardly any enforced migration of people from one country to another has been so well documented and so unanimously celebrated as a success story as the emigration from German-speaking Central Europe to Britain between the Nazi seizure of power in January 1933 and the outbreak of the European war in September 1939. Without neglecting the psychological problems and human tragedies behind each individual case, practically all studies on the exodus of thousands of men, women, and children from Germany, Austria, and the Sudeten areas of Czechoslovakia praise the extraordinary achievements of these refugees. They point to their substantial contributions to the cultural life and economic prosperity of their land of settlement as well as to the remarkable speed with which they assimilated after they set foot on British soil.[6]

Simultaneously, many historians stress the more-than-generous welcome given these refugees from Nazism in Britain and emphasize the hospitality and tolerance of British society in the difficult times of the 1930s, in the aftermath of the Great Depression and under the threatening omens of rising fascism and a new military conflict in Europe. In retrospect, the refugees from Central Europe are referred to as "Hitler's loss" and "Hitler's gift to Britain," as "illustrious immigrants," as "Europe's cultural exiles," or simply as "continental Britons," the latter term hinting at the refugees' obvious role as bridge-builders between different cultures and mentalities.[7]

However, terms like "Hitler's loss" or "Hitler's gift" imply more substance than simply building bridges between two countries, two societies, and two cultures. The overwhelmingly-middle-class[8] refugees from Nazism who permanently settled in Britain represented, perhaps more so than earlier waves of immigrants into Britain, the influx of an elite. Their impact on their new country seems to have been without parallel in modern history. In fact, their exodus from Central Europe had put an end to decades of German-Jewish acculturation on the one hand and signified, on the other, the beginning of a remarkable new symbiosis in Britain. Again in retrospect, one is not so sure whether the British public fully realized what was going on in their relationship with the continent of Europe in the 1930s. The English, pronounced the writer Stephen Spender, had shut their eyes to current events in Europe. Instead, they were "preoccupied during the inter-war years with Empire exhibitions, royal occasions and sport, preferring to regard what happened on the Continent as 'none of their business.'"[9] Spender's scathing observation certainly did not mirror the whole truth and was definitely over the top.

The sheer number of those who came to Britain within just six years after 1933 was, by all accounts, extraordinary. Although the figures of the available statistics differ, it is safe to say that there were about seventy-four thousand refugees from Central Europe in Britain at the beginning of the war, among them an estimated twenty-one hundred academics. A year later, fifty-five thousand were given official refugee status by the authorities. About ninety percent of the refugees were Jews, at least according to the Nazi definition.

Nevertheless, until Hitler's annexation of Austria in March 1938, the Munich Agreement and the pogrom of "Crystal Night" in November of the same year, the number of refugees from Central Europe was just a trickle. They began to arrive in Britain soon after Hitler took office as Reich chancellor. At that early stage, labor permits were given only for specific jobs. Immigration officers were under instruction to prevent anyone from entering the country who might become a public liability. British policy vis-à-vis the mounting refugee problem boiled down to the simple rule that those who were prepared to work in domestic service or were craftsmen had a better chance of being admitted into Britain than those who belonged to the professional classes.

By the end of 1937, the number of refugees from Nazi-dominated Central Europe was estimated by the Home Office in London to be around fifty-five hundred people. The persecution of democratic politicians in Germany, the book-burning, the boycott of Jewish businesses, and the legislation relating to Jews in the German civil service, law, medical practice, and education had begun as early as April 1933. Approximately 90 percent of the emigrants up to September 1939 thus entered Britain after the shocking events of 1938, an *annus horribilis* in European history of the twentieth century.

Until the momentous watershed of 1938, the decision to emigrate, the timing, and the choice of destination were, to a large extent, still left up to the individual. The assumed chances of professional and economic absorption in the receiving country were, of course, paramount in the deliberations of potential emigrants. Furthermore, the aim of the British government—to attract "desirable, industrious, intelligent and acceptable persons"[10] and to harvest the "capital in the form of skill, knowledge and foreign technical processes"[11]—proved comparatively easy for some refugees to meet. Famous scientists, eminent intellectuals, architects, musicians, dentists, and entrepreneurs with money and expertise were clearly more welcome than others. Prospective immigrants who were small shopkeepers, minor musicians, or rank and file lawyers—people without means or with less useful skills—were consigned to the back of the queue.

British immigration policy obviously followed a rather selfish line. As early as April 1933, the British Cabinet had accepted the policy that it was in the public interest to try to secure "for this country prominent Jews who were being expelled from Germany and who had achieved distinction whether in pure science, applied science, such as medicine or technical industry, music or art. This would not only obtain for this country the advantage of their knowledge and experience, but would also create a favourable impression in the world, particularly if our hospitality were offered with some warmth."[12] With hindsight, this much-quoted statement sounded almost cynical. In any case, the British policy of a "half-open door" was maintained until 1938.[13]

In early 1938, when the "push" factors gradually overcame the natural tendency of individuals to avoid the hardships of emigration, Britain introduced even more detailed restrictions. Beginning in May 1938, the new visa requirements for all German and Austrian nationals stipulated, in more general terms, that immigration officials determine "whether or not an applicant is likely to be an asset to the U.K."[14] Henceforth only a very few occupational groups who had financial guarantees or some financial backing from organizations or individuals resident in Britain could obtain visas easily. To repeat what has been said earlier: until the autumn of 1938, Britain upheld an immigration policy that was based first and foremost on its own economic and political interests. Nonetheless, after

Munich and the "Crystal Night" pogrom the number of immigrants into Britain increased dramatically as Whitehall's immigration policy relaxed in response to recent developments in Central Europe and the new visa requirements were no longer strictly adhered to.[15]

Uprooted: The Refugee Historians

What happened to those academics among the immigrants who, at first glance, did not represent "an asset to the U.K."? No contemporary could succumb to the illusion that university teachers in the humanities, solicitors, and those like them would be welcome or have an easy start in their host country. This was true all over the world, and Britain was no exception. The exemplary group of immigrants on whom this chapter will focus, namely the historians and historians-to-be, were, of course, a tiny minority among the refugees from German-speaking Central Europe. Their adaptation to the host society, either slow and painful or sometimes quick and smooth, is an instructive illustration of the process of assimilation into a culture, more or less unfamiliar, that every refugee has to undergo in order to survive, often in a very literal sense.

The select group of refugees who came to Britain and were able to continue or to start an academic career as professional historians during or after the war can roughly be divided into two categories. There were those—the first generation of émigré historians, as we may call them—who had completed their university studies in Germany or Austria and had, in almost all cases, begun working in an academic environment. Those who came to Britain as children or adolescents and turned into historians in later life will be defined as the second generation of émigré historians.

We know from autobiographical and biographical evidence that the uprooted historians who were stranded in Britain faced profound difficulties in their efforts to resume their interrupted academic career. What else could they aim for due to the simple fact that, in general, they had no skills other than teaching, writing, and researching? For a number of reasons, universities in prewar Britain had only very limited opportunities to appoint immigrants to appropriate positions, especially as their linguistic skills were often not good enough for lecturing to English-speaking students. Until the Second World War, French was the first modern language taught in German grammar schools, with English a possible second.

Moreover, the great majority of the émigré historians considered their stay in Britain as an interlude. Mentally, they felt like "transit migrants" who were waiting for an American visa to enter the United States as soon as possible. Only when they possessed one did they have a chance to obtain a job offer from an American university—and this is what they really wanted. From their perspective, the United Kingdom, that strange land of which they knew so little, was a sort of *"Durchgangsland,"* a country of transit.[16] The British government could not agree more: for Whitehall Britain was definitely not a "country of settlement" for immigrants from Central Europe.

For example, one first-generation émigré historian, Hans Baron, whose works on the Italian Renaissance had won him much acclaim in Germany and abroad, stayed in Britain for almost three years from December 1935. He was supposed to be made "fit for America"; in other words, he should prepare, with some outside help, for a professional life in Anglo-American academia. Apparently, Baron had reached that coveted status in May 1938 when his sponsor, the English Society for the Protection of Science and Learning (known initially as the Academic Assistance Council, set up by William Beveridge in May 1933), observed that Baron had made "excellent progress with his publications, with improving his English and in establishing contacts with American scholars."[17] Some weeks before he left for America in late 1938, Baron summed up his early experiences of exile in Britain by writing to the Renaissance historian Paul Oskar Kristeller, who had emigrated to Italy: "Even if the difficulties are quite great, for those who came here in person ultimately something happened, at least so far. Furthermore, for people like us the easiest road to America goes through London."[18]

The available figures outline the story. Half of the first-generation historians who found refuge in the United Kingdom after 1933 went on to the United States, among them Ernst Kantorowicz and Hajo Holborn in 1934, Hans Rosenberg in 1935, Felix Gilbert in 1936, Fritz Epstein in 1937, Arthur Rosenberg and George L. Mosse in 1939, and Veit Valentin and Hans Rothfels in 1940. Two of the first-generation historians left Britain after the war: Fritz Moritz Heichelheim, who had worked as a lecturer at the University of Nottingham after 1942, left for Canada in 1951, and Ernest Kohn-Bramstedt left for Australia in 1952. After retirement, Kohn-Bramstedt returned to England (1969).

The very few who stayed behind in Britain found it extremely hard to obtain permanent jobs in or outside academia—as teachers or temporary guest lecturers, with the BBC or the Political Intelligence Division of the Foreign Office. This was no surprise. Only some of them were lucky and could rely on private means or the help of relatives and friends. In order to illustrate the situation in the 1930s, here are two examples. Erich Eyck, born in Berlin in 1878 and a lawyer by training, arrived in Britain in 1937. The distinguished author of works on Bismarck, Gladstone, the Pitts and the Foxes, and the short-lived Weimar Republic would occasionally lecture in Oxford and London, thanks to the help of British colleagues whom he had contacted. Financially, his teaching and writing were not enough to live on. However, Eyck could enjoy a comparatively comfortable life as a scholar because his wife ran a flourishing boarding house in London.

The second example: Eva G. Reichmann, who was born in Upper Silesia in 1897, reached Britain just before the outbreak of war. She had the good fortune to become director of research at the Wiener Library, transferred from Amsterdam to London in 1939, and was actually one of the few women who were able to continue their professional career after emigration, albeit in an institution run by immigrants. The library provided the environment in which she could write her great study *Hostages of Civilisation: The Social Sources of National Socialist Anti-Semitism* (1950). Eva Reichmann died in 1998 at the age of 101.[19]

Quite a number of émigré historians, however, were dependent on financial support from newly founded philanthropic organizations. A statement that Esther Simpson, then the secretary of the Society for the Protection of Science and Learning, made in April 1939 has often been quoted. "Next to law," she wrote, "history is the most difficult of all categories to place and we have not succeeded in finding a permanent position here for a single historian. We gave one of our research fellowships to one of the most eminent of the displaced German historians as we were confident that if any historian could find a permanent berth he would; now after about five years in this country he is almost exactly where he was at the beginning."[20]

Esther Simpson was referring to Veit Valentin, who, in 1930–31, had published a major study on the German revolution of 1848–49. With his outspoken political views and involvement in pacifist organizations, Valentin was clearly *persona non grata* with the Nazi regime and therefore had come to Britain as early as the summer of 1933, shortly after his dismissal as archivist at the *Reichsarchiv* in Potsdam, where he had been working since 1920. During all his years in Britain, Valentin's position remained highly precarious. He did some lecturing at London University and received grants from the Society for the Protection of Science and Learning. Valentin finally crossed the Atlantic in search of an academic job in 1940. But again all his efforts in this respect in his second country of exile came to nothing. He died in Washington, DC, in early 1947, age sixty-two, embittered and demoralized.

The story of the first generation of émigré historians in the United Kingdom is a rather mixed one, at times even depressing. Success stories are not easy to find. For the historians, deeply rooted in the German academic tradition, the professional job market in Britain was restricted. Only a few succeeded in continuing a career in their chosen field of learning after arrival in Britain. According to Christhard Hoffmann's assessment, it seemed "that it was easier to gain admission to the more internationalized areas of historical research, like classical studies, ancient and oriental or even medieval history than to modern history, where national styles and differences played a greater role."[21]

The majority of the historians who settled in Britain, permanently or temporarily, were hardly able to support themselves and their families. The generosity of London-based relief organizations such as the Society for the Protection of Science and Learning, the German Jewish Aid Committee, or the Jewish Professional Committee proved to be extremely helpful. In many cases, they provided the essential means for surviving and assisted when the immigrants were facing all the hurdles and problems of assimilation and adaptation.[22] Nonetheless, eminent scholars such as Gustav Mayer, historian of the German labor movement, and the medievalist Wilhelm Levison led troubled lives in their host country. Both died, disappointed and lonely, shortly after the war, Mayer in London in 1948 and Levison in Durham in 1947.[23]

There was one thing that practically all emigrants of the older generation had in common: the never-ending feeling of an impaired identity, intertwined by that of having successfully overcome some of the limitations of traditional national stereotypes. After more than two decades of settling in Britain, Eva G. Reichmann summed up this peculiar mixture of emotions. "I am no longer a German," she said about her identity in a speech given in Germany in 1960, "and I will never be an Englishwoman, for all that England gave me the right to live when my native land denied it me."[24] She defined herself as a Jew, of formerly German and now of British nationality. The three layers of identity kept struggling to resolve themselves into a new personality. The economic historian Sidney Pollard expressed the same widespread sentiment in one simple sentence: "Though fully at home in Britain, I never lost the feeling that I was not quite like those born here."[25]

The Younger Émigré Historians in Postwar Britain

In comparison with the first generation of émigré historians and their difficult lives in enforced exile, the so-called second generation faced a somewhat easier task in the pursuit of their expectations and ambitions and their integration into the host society. They came to Britain at a young age and hardly shared the feeling of having been forcibly uprooted that overshadowed the lives of so many in the first generation. Most of them received their schooling and university education in their host country or, if they already had acquired a German or Austrian degree, attended a British university at least temporarily. Among this younger generation of émigré historians who started their academic career after the war were Geoffrey Elton, Edgar Feuchtwanger, John Grenville, E. P. Hennock, Helmut Koenigsberger, Karl Leyser, Werner E. Mosse (a distant cousin of George L. Mosse), Sidney Pollard, Peter Pulzer, and Nicolai Rubinstein.

The sixteen scholars who could be identified as belonging to the second generation of émigré historians in Britain had four things in common. First, they were all born in German-speaking Central Europe and had witnessed the consolidation of the Nazi regime after Hitler had come to power. Second, they all had escaped from Germany and Austria, mostly under dramatic and tragic circumstances, often unaccompanied by their parents on one of the *Kindertransporte* (children's transports) shortly before the outbreak of war. Third, the fact that they went to school and/or university in the United Kingdom gave them an advantage that had been denied to the older generation of refugee historians: the strong feeling that Britain was their homeland and a command of English that they had acquired quickly.

When the then twenty-eight-year-old legal historian and medievalist Walter Ullmann, for instance, met a colleague in Cambridge for the first time, he is said to have tried to converse in Latin because he had no English.[26] This may be anecdotal. But it is certain that Geoffrey Elton, at that time still Gottfried Ehrenberg, arrived in Britain at the age of seventeen knowing hardly a word of English. Nevertheless, after four years he had obtained an external B.A., awarded with first class honors, from the University of London. Werner E. Mosse and Helmut Koenigsberger received their respective B.A. degrees six years after arriving in Britain. Only in a few cases did the tinge of an accent continue to hint at a very distant past.[27]

Finally, most émigré historians of the younger generation, just like those of the older generation, were either interned for some time early in the war (mostly on the Isle of Man) or served in the British Army, Royal Navy, or Royal Air Force. A few of them, such as Helmut Koenigsberger, Karl Leyser, and Werner E. Mosse, had both experiences.

Geoffrey Elton and Sidney Pollard changed their names when they joined the army on the advice of their superiors. Their German names would have put them in great danger if they fell in the hands of the enemy. John Grenville was too young to enlist. He changed his name for other reasons. "With my German name [Hans Gubrauer]," he later recalled, "I could find no employment in 1945."[28] Like Grenville and Peter Pulzer, some historians-to-be escaped internment and military service. They were simply too young at the time. In 1944, Grenville, then age sixteen-and-a-half, worked as a gardener at Peterhouse, Cambridge. He applied and was granted permission to use the college library on condition, as he remembered, "that I would not attempt to enter Cambridge University as a student."[29] Rather puzzled by this reaction, Grenville instead entered London's Birkbeck College in 1947, where Eric Hobsbawm was one of his history lecturers. Later, he went on to the London School of Economics, where he earned his Ph.D. supervised by the famous professor of international relations, Sir Charles Webster.

Sometimes it is difficult to draw a clear line between the older and the younger generation of émigré historians. A good example is Francis L. Carsten, born in Berlin in 1911. He received his legal training in Berlin, Geneva, and Heidelberg. Only as an emigrant did he become a historian when, after 1935, during an extended stay in Amsterdam at the International Institute of Social History and under the influence of Norbert Elias, he turned his attention to the history of early modern Prussia. In April 1939, he sailed to Britain. By October 1940, he had gained a research scholarship to Wadham College, Oxford, with the help of influential friends in academia and politics. Interrupted by a short internment as a "friendly enemy alien" in 1940, he completed his Ph.D. thesis in 1942. Carsten spent the rest of the war with the Political Warfare Executive, a secret government department with its headquarters at Woburn Abbey. In 1947, he won a lectureship at Westfield College, London. Thus was launched a distinguished academic career that ultimately, in 1961, took him to the Masaryk Chair of Central European History at the School of Slavonic and East European Studies in the University of London. He held this position until his retirement in 1978.

At Westfield College, one of Carsten's colleagues was Nicolai Rubinstein, who was born in the same year as Carsten and had been with him at the same grammar school in Berlin. Later they were close neighbors in Hampstead. Like Francis Carsten, Rubinstein may be considered a link between the older and younger generation of émigré historians in postwar Britain. After taking his doctorate at the University of Florence in 1935, Rubinstein soon became one of the world's leading scholars on Renaissance Italy. He was able to support himself after his arrival in Britain in 1939 by teaching at Oxford and Southampton University College before he got his tenured position in London. Rubinstein himself once hinted at the fact that some discreet help from English friends had put his career in Britain on the right track. He declined, however, to disclose their names.[30]

Influence and Impact

This leads to the question of what impact émigré historians of the first and second generation had on British and, in no way less importantly, on postwar German and Austrian historiography.[31] Unfortunately, the answer must remain rather vague and inconclusive. After all, there is no reliable yardstick for assessing the significance and impact of a historian or group of historians on colleagues working in the same field of study. Nevertheless, when one is asked what success and influence the émigré historians in their entirety had in Britain, the answer must be that in many cases both academic success and influence on students and young colleagues seem to have been striking.

Given the difficult circumstances of the times, this general statement must perhaps be qualified to some extent when one scrutinizes the first generation of émigré historians. They either could not work as university teachers at all or, at most, could work only for a short period of time. Therefore, the greatest impact the first generation in Britain had was probably through their scholarly publications. However, even on this level their influence was often limited. The work of Veit Valentin and Gustav Mayer does not appear to have left a lasting impression in Britain. Erich Eyck, on the other hand, with his numerous publications on German and British history, seems to have fared somewhat better. His liberal historiography, modeled on the British Whig tradition, found an audience in his host country. Later on, particularly in the 1950s and 1960s, his books on Gladstone, Bismarck, the Emperor William II, and the Weimar Republic were widely read and discussed in postwar Germany.

Naturally, the academic climate in Britain had changed after the war. As scholars and university teachers, the second generation of émigré historians in Britain had therefore something of a head start. This observation raises the intriguing question of what actually distinguishes them, if at all, from British-born historians of the same age group. Did their origin, by then already rather distant and perhaps no longer fully conscious, have any significance for them personally and their academic work?

The question can probably be answered with a "yes" and this for one simple reason. With one or two notable exceptions, all the historians of the second generation in Britain have displayed a strong and enduring interest in the history of Central Europe. This assessment applies to Francis Carsten, Arnold Paucker, and Peter Pulzer, as well as to Edgar Feuchtwanger, Karl Leyser, Helmut Koenigsberger, and Werner E. Mosse. A number of them have worked on British as well as German history. Examples are Edgar Feuchtwanger, Hellmut Pappe, and Peter Pulzer, but also Francis Carsten and E. P. Hennock. Many saw themselves explicitly as mediators between two cultures and bridge-builders. "In my writings on German history," Edgar Feuchtwanger, the nephew of the writer Lion Feuchtwanger, once observed, "I have seen myself more as an interpreter and transmitter for an English-speaking readership, rather than as an innovative researcher.... It seemed to be a bonus to have access to two cultures."[32]

With some émigré historians of the second generation in the United Kingdom, an interest in German history or at least in writing comparative history seems to have developed at a later stage of their academic careers. Examples are Sidney Pollard and John Grenville. Maybe Christhard Hoffmann is right when, in summing up, he writes, "The younger generation of refugee historians helped to raise the subject of European history in England to a very respectable level."[33]

The same scholar assesses Francis Carsten's importance as a historian in the following words: "With his contributions, Professor Carsten has set new standards in research on German history in Great Britain. Through his long teaching experience, especially the training of graduate students, Carsten has had considerable influence upon the study of Central European history in Great Britain."[34] There is also a lot of truth in what John Grenville, in a reflective mood, once remarked about himself (and probably having in mind many of his fellow émigré historians): "A non-British background made me look at national history from the point of view of an insider as well as from that of an outsider with an acute sense that the individuality of any country is only revealed by comparison. The enforced ability to be bi-lingual, and learning other languages, pointed me towards the study of foreign policy and international history."[35] However, in the last years of his life Grenville wrote a moving history of the Jews in Hamburg over the previous one hundred fifty years. This masterly book is the closest study by any of the second-generation historians in Britain on the subject of the Holocaust.[36]

Within this context, one may therefore raise again the question that has already been referred to: has the second generation of émigré historians in the United Kingdom helped to overcome what Edward Carr in 1961 denounced rather pointedly as "the parochialism of English history"?[37] More than half a century after Carr's verdict on English history-writing in his time, one hesitates to go so far. Perhaps Daniel Snowman's judgement is fairer. In his excellent book on the *Hitler Émigrés*, he writes, "The presence of the Central Europeans brought a range of vital new perspectives to British historiography and contributed to a resurgence of interest in the subject."[38] How ambiguous, and ultimately, how impressionistic, such judgements necessarily are becomes clear when Christhard Hoffmann concludes, "In comparison with other disciplines, such as psychoanalysis and art history, the impact [refugee] historians had on British academic life was less spectacular and rather heterogeneous."[39]

The most notable exception to these sweeping generalizations about the teaching, scholarly work, and influence of second-generation émigré historians in Britain was, of course, Geoffrey Elton, son of the classical scholar Victor Ehrenberg. His writing focused exclusively on Britain. Elton became the authority on early modern English history in postwar Britain. It has been said that his studies revolutionized the traditional view of the Tudor era. No one who reads Elton's books and articles would ever trace his approach, his arguments, or his conclusions back to the author's distant roots in Central Europe. However, this statement may be somewhat superficial, even misleading. Reflecting on his work, one might go so far as to argue that Elton's concentration on government and the state actually puts him into the main tradition of German history writing. One may speculate that this application of the putative "German" approach to early modern English history would thus be an essential ingredient of his undeniable originality as a British historian.

Geoffrey Elton, who mastered the English language (and English manners) so brilliantly, achieved everything that is attainable in British academic life. By the end of his remarkable career, he had been knighted (in 1986) and elected to be Regius Professor of Modern History at the University of Cambridge. Some even considered him to be one of "the two greatest historians of the post-war era."[40] What Elton failed to achieve, however, was to stimulate and influence the postwar historiography of German-speaking Central Europe. Other second-generation émigré historians, such as Francis Carsten, Helmut Koenigsberger, Peter Pulzer, Sidney Pollard, Arnold Paucker, and Werner E. Mosse, provided this sort of stimulus from which modern German and Austrian historians have greatly benefited.

There can hardly be any doubt that the second generation of émigré historians represents a recognizable group among historians in postwar Britain. This brief discussion suggests that they had a noticeable impact on researching, teaching, and writing history in Britain and beyond in the second half of the twentieth century. They had and have, of course, very diverse interests and highly individual approaches to their fields of scholarship. However, they never aspired to form a closely-knit network based on their shared heritage, albeit the Leo Baeck Institute in London, founded in 1955, served as a kind of focus for research and social meetings for many of them. They also never showed an ambition to establish a school of like-minded scholars. Perhaps Francis Carsten alone had an interest in gathering around him a number of students working on German history. Nicolai Rubinstein and Walter Ullmann succeeded in promoting some of their students to academic positions in Britain and North America.

In general, the achievements of the émigré historians of the second generation in Britain were solidly founded on outstanding individual work, academic professionalism, and a natural ability to look—free from prejudice and with exemplary empathy—beyond the shores of the British Isles. In that respect, they offered and still offer a memorable inspiration to colleagues and students.

Second-Generation Émigré Historians in the United Kingdom

Julius Carlebach, b. 1922 in Hamburg; arr. in UK 1939; d. 2001 in Brighton
Francis L. Carsten, b. 1911 in Berlin; arr. in UK 1939; d. 1998 in London
Sir Geoffrey Elton (Gottfried Ehrenberg), b. 1921 in Tübingen; arr. in UK 1939; d. 1994 in Cambridge
Edgar J. Feuchtwanger, b. 1924 in Munich; arr. in UK 1939
John A. S. Grenville (Hans Gubrauer), b. 1928 in Berlin; arr. in UK 1939; d. 2011 in Birmingham
E. P. Hennock (Ernst Peter Henoch), b. 1926 in Berlin; arr. in UK 1939; d. 2012 in Horsham, Sussex
Helmut G. Koenigsberger, b. 1918 in Berlin; arr. in UK 1934; d. 2014 in London
Karl J. Leyser, b. 1920 in Düsseldorf; arr. in UK 1937; d. 1992 in Oxford
Wolf Mendl, b. 1927 in Berlin; arr. in UK 1936; d. 1999 in Watford
Werner E. Mosse, b. 1918 in Berlin; arr. in UK 1933; d. 2001 in Gloucester
Hellmut Pappe, b. 1907 in Liegnitz; arr. in UK 1962; d. 1999 in Brighton
Arnold Paucker, b. 1921 in Berlin; arr. in UK 1950
Sidney Pollard (Siegfried Pollak), b. 1925 in Vienna; arr. in UK 1938; d. 1998 in Sheffield
Peter G. J. Pulzer, b. 1929 in Vienna; arr. in UK 1939
Nicolai Rubinstein, b. 1911 in Berlin; arr. in UK 1939; d. 2002 in London
Walter Ullmann, b. 1910 in Pulkau, Lower Austria; arr. in UK 1938; d. 1983 in Cambridge

Peter Alter is emeritus professor of modern European and contemporary history at the University of Duisburg-Essen, Germany. He has taught at universities in

Germany (Cologne, Freiburg) and Britain (Sussex, Cambridge). From 1976 to 1994 he was research fellow and deputy director of the German Historical Institute in London. Among his many publications on nationalism and Irish, British, and German history are *The German Question and Europe: A History* (2000), and *Winston Churchill. Leben und Überleben* (2006).

Notes

1. Edgar J. Feuchtwanger, "Recovering from Culture Shock," in Peter Alter, ed., *Out of the Third Reich: Refugee Historians in Post-War Britain* (London, 1998), 46. See also idem, *Hitler, mon voisin* (Neuilly-sur-Seine, 2013).
2. Peter Alter, "Über Abschied und Neubeginn. Ein Gespräch mit Charlotte Jolles," *Fontane Blätter* 74 (2002): 136.
3. Charlotte Jolles, *Fontane und die Politik. Ein Beitrag zur Wesensbestimmung Theodor Fontanes* (reissued Berlin, 1983).
4. Obituary of Charlotte Jolles, who died on 31 December 2003, *The Times*, 23 January 2004, 34.
5. Rodney Livingstone, "The Contribution of German-speaking Jewish Refugees to German Studies in Britain," in Werner E. Mosse et al., eds., *Second Chance: Two Centuries of German-speaking Jews in the United Kingdom* (Tübingen, 1991), 137.
6. See, for example, the contributions in Mosse, *Second Chance*.
7. Tom Ambrose, *Hitler's Loss: What Britain and America Gained from Europe's Cultural Exiles* (London, 2001); Paul Johnson, "Hitler's Gift to Britain," *The Sunday Telegraph*, 29 January 1995; Laura Fermi, *Illustrious Immigrants: The Intellectual Migration from Europe, 1930–1941* (Chicago, 1968); Jarrell C. Jackman and Carla M. Borden, eds., *The Muses Flee Hitler: Cultural Transfer and Adaptation, 1930–1945* (Washington, DC, 1983); Marion Berghahn, *Continental Britons: German-Jewish Refugees from Nazi Germany*, 3rd ed. (Oxford, 1988); John Medawar and David Pyke, *Hitler's Gift: Scientists Who Fled Nazi Germany* (London, 2001).
8. See Anthony Grenville, *Jewish Refugees from Germany and Austria in Britain, 1933–1970: Their Image in AJR Information* (London, 2010).
9. Quoted in Daniel Snowman, *The Hitler Émigrés: The Cultural Impact on Britain of Refugees from Nazism* (London, 2002), 48.
10. Quoted in Ari J. Sherman, *Island Refuge: Britain and Refugees from the Third Reich, 1933–1939* (London, 1973), 260; and Bob Moore, "Areas of Reception in the United Kingdom: 1933–1945," in Mosse, *Second Chance*, 71.
11. Home Secretary Sir Samuel Hoare in 1936, quoted in Mitchell G. Ash, "Central European Émigré Psychologists and Psychoanalysts in the United Kingdom," in Mosse, *Second Chance*, 104.
12. Quoted in Charmian Brinson, "Science in Exile: Imperial College and the Refugees from Nazism. A Case Study," *Leo Baeck Institute Yearbook* 43 (1998): 135, and Livingstone, "Contribution," 138.
13. Michael Marrus, *The Unwanted: European Refugees in the Twentieth Century* (Oxford, 1985), 87. Bernard Wasserstein, "The British Government and the German Immigration 1933–1945," in Gerhard Hirschfeld, ed., *Exile in Great Britain: Refugees From Hitler's Germany* (Leamington Spa, 1984), 63–81.

14. Sherman, *Island Refuge,* 90–91.
15. Louise London, *Whitehall and the Jews, 1933–1948: British Immigration Policy, Jewish Refugees and the Holocaust* (Cambridge, 2000); idem, "British Immigration Control Procedures and Jewish Refugees 1933–1939," in Mosse, *Second Chance,* 485–517.
16. Gerhard Hirschfeld, "Durchgangsland Großbritannien? Die britische 'Academic Community' und die wissenschaftliche Emigration aus Deutschland," in Charmian Brinson et al., eds., *"England, aber wo liegt es?" Deutsche und österreichische Emigranten in Großbritannien 1933–1945* (Munich, 1996), 59–70.
17. Quoted in Kay Schiller, "Made 'fit for America': The Renaissance Historian Hans Baron in London Exile 1936–1938," in Stefan Berger et al., eds., *Historikerdialoge. Geschichte, Mythos und Gedächtnis im deutsch-britischen kulturellen Austausch 1750–2000* (Göttingen, 2003), 358.
18. Quoted in ibid., 348.
19. Arnold Paucker, "History in Exile: Writing the Story of German Jewry," in Siglinde Bolbecher et al., eds., *Zwischenwelt 4: Literatur und Kultur des Exils in Großbritannien* (Vienna, 1995), 241–66; Kirsten Heinsohn, "Erfahrung und Zeitdeutung. Biographie und Werk der Soziologin Eva G. Reichmann," in Henning Albrecht et al., eds., *Politische Gesellschaftsgeschichte im 19. und 20 Jahrhundert. Eine Festgabe für Barbara Vogel* (Hamburg, 2006), 205–308. See also Ben Barkow, *Alfred Wiener and the Making of the Holocaust Library* (London, 1997).
20. Quoted in Alter, *Out of the Third Reich,* xvi.
21. Christhard Hoffmann, "The Contribution of German-Speaking Jewish Immigrants to British Historiography," in Mosse, *Second Chance,* 163.
22. Gerhard Hirschfeld, "'The Defense of Learning and Science': Der Academic Assistance Council in Großbritannien und die wissenschaftliche Emigration aus Nazi-Deutschland," *Exilforschung. Ein internationales Jahrbuch* 6 (1988): 28–43. Shula Marks et al., eds., *In Defense of Learning: The Plight, Persecution, and Placement of Academic Refugees, 1933–1980* (Oxford, 2011).
23. Gottfried Niedhardt, "Gustav Mayers englische Jahre: Zum Exil eines deutschen Juden und Historikers," *Exilforschung. Ein internationales Jahrbuch* 6 (1988): 98–107; Hans-Ulrich Wehler, "Gustav Mayer," in *Deutsche Historiker* (Göttingen, 1973), vol. 2, 120–32; Theodor Schieffer and Horst Fuhrmann, eds., *In Memoriam Wilhelm Levison (1876–1947). Reden und Grußbotschaften bei der Gedenkfeier der Universität [Bonn] zum 100. Geburtstag am 31. Mai 1976* (Cologne, 1977).
24. Grenville, *Jewish Refugees,* 188.
25. Sidney Pollard, "In Search of a Social Purpose," in Alter, *Out of the Third Reich,* 215. Also David Renton, *Sidney Pollard: A Life in History* (London and New York, 2004).
26. Walter Ullmann, "A Tale of Two Cultures," in Alter, *Out of the Third Reich,* 247–60; Elizabeth Ullmann, *Walter Ullmann: A Tale of Two Cultures* (Cambridge, 1990); Horst Fuhrmann, "Walter Ullmann," in *Biographische Begegnungen* (Munich, 1996), 143–47.
27. See, for example, the amusing and sharp observations by Arnold Paucker, "Speaking English with an Accent," in Brinson, *"England, aber wo liegt es?"* 21–31.
28. Letter to the author, 24 April 1995.
29. J. A. S. Grenville, "From Gardener to Professor," in Alter, *Out of the Third Reich,* 64.
30. See Nicolai Rubinstein, "Germany, Italy, and England," in Alter, *Out of the Third Reich,* 237–45.
31. The important volume *Second Chance: Two Centuries of German-Speaking Jews in the United Kingdom* aims, according to Peter Pulzer, one of the editors, at giving "the story of the impact German-speaking Jews made on British life and of the impact British life made on them" (9).
32. Feuchtwanger, "Recovering," 53 and 51.
33. Hoffmann, "The Contribution," 164.
34. Ibid.

35. Grenville, "Gardener," 69.
36. J. A. S. Grenville, *The Jews and Germans of Hamburg: The Destruction of a Civilization 1790–1945* (London, 2012).
37. Edward H. Carr, *What is History? The George Macaulay Trevelyan Lectures Delivered in the University of Cambridge January–March 1961* (London, 1961), 145.
38. Snowman, *Hitler Émigrés*, 327.
39. Hoffmann, "The Contribution," 172.
40. John Kenyon, *The History Men: The Historical Profession in England since the Renaissance* (London, 1983), 273.

Chapter 19

THE SECOND-GENERATION ÉMIGRÉS' IMPACT ON GERMAN HISTORIOGRAPHY

Philipp Stelzel

When Hans-Ulrich Wehler received the American Historical Association's Honorary Foreign Membership in 2000, he emphasized the influence of American historians on their German colleagues during the previous half century: "The transatlantic dialogue between American and German historians since the late 1940s is based on the fundamental experiences of the political generations that lived through the Nazi dictatorship, World War II, the postwar years, and the founding of the Federal Republic. These common experiences led to close contacts; I am someone who has profited immensely from them. The generations of Carl Schorske, Leonard Krieger, Hajo Holborn, Arno Mayer, Jim Sheehan, Henry Turner, Gerald Feldman, Charles Maier, and others, have influenced in a lasting way the political generation in Germany to which I belong."[1]

Other observers, such as Ernst Schulin or Wolfgang J. Mommsen, have echoed Wehler's assessment of the significance of American impulses for West German historiography.[2] First- as well as second-generation émigré historians were an integral part of this transatlantic scholarly community.[3] Twenty-five years ago, the volume *An Interrupted Past* detailed the manifold impact that émigrés of the first generation exerted on younger historians on both sides of the Atlantic. This chapter analyzes the various roles that the second-generation émigré historians came to assume for their German colleagues—those of Wehler's age group as well as of others—between the 1950s and 1980s. "German" during that period meant West German, as closer contacts between American and East German historians hardly existed until the late 1970s and early 1980s, when Georg Iggers initiated the first exchanges with colleagues such as Fritz Klein.[4]

Notes from this chapter begin on page 299.

It is difficult to provide generalizations about the second-generation émigrés, as they constituted a group of scholars who differed in their research interests as well as in their methodological and political orientations. Nevertheless, I argue that second-generation émigré historians supported the interpretive and methodological diversification of the German historical profession, the former most notably during the *Fischer-Kontroverse* (Fischer controversy). Perhaps as a result of their immersion in American academia, they did not tend toward the German *Schulenbildung* (the habit of forming distinct schools). While these émigrés contributed and supported critical perspectives on the recent German past, they never became partisans of any of the West German historiographical camps that faced each other with considerable hostility, especially during the 1970s and 1980s. Ultimately, therefore, the second-generation émigrés helped shape a nuanced interpretation of modern German history.

The first part of this chapter analyzes the various roles second-generation émigré historians came to assume vis-à-vis the German historical profession. Since the early 1950s, when they began their careers, these historians observed German developments and communicated them to an American audience. In addition, they served as intermediaries between the two sides of the Atlantic and they intervened in scholarly debates taking place in Germany or within the transatlantic scholarly community. Needless to say, significant overlaps between these categories existed, and many of the émigrés rightly belong in more than one.

Shifting the perspective, the second part of the analysis focuses on how West German historians received and responded to the émigrés' writings. Up until the mid-1960s, Germans occasionally criticized some of the émigrés' interpretations of modern German history for a supposed lack of empathy (*Einfühlungsvermögen*) while praising others for displaying such empathy. By the late 1960s, however, most historians began to regard such criticism as inappropriate.

Related to the question of German responses to American interpretations, the third and final part of the chapter focuses on the intellectual history contributions to the *Sonderweg* debate. Here we will encounter examples of—an arguably surprising—German nonreception of American studies on German history. Yet as representatives of the historical profession in the United States and as proponents of critical views on German history, the émigrés were also invoked by some of their German colleagues, in particular during some heated controversies within West German academia. Unlike the protagonists of the 1970s *Kritische Geschichtswissenschaft* in West Germany, none of the émigrés used the term "critical" as a self-designation. The label nevertheless seems appropriate because, since the early 1950s, second-generation émigrés—whether as diplomatic, social, cultural, or intellectual historians—provided new answers to the big question haunting historians at the time: how the rise of National Socialism had been possible.[5] Apart from the understandable eagerness of the émigrés to analyze and reinterpret the course of German history, particularly in the nineteenth and early twentieth centuries, there was also an increased American demand for such studies. Yet at the time, during the early 1950s, very few historical works on German history existed in English—"a remarkable opportunity for my generation," as Fritz Stern observed.[6]

This chapter cannot offer a comprehensive treatment of the personalities and oeuvres of a group of exceptionally accomplished scholars. The analysis therefore focuses on those émigrés who were most engaged in the transatlantic scholarly community and will only touch upon some of the others who did not display that involvement. Occasionally, my arguments will pertain to the entire American community of historians of Germany, as the Germans usually viewed the émigrés as part of that community. Nevertheless, as we will see, in some instances the émigré status of these scholars acquired significance for their West German colleagues.

Émigrés' Roles

Some second-generation émigré historians regularly observed German developments and communicated them to an American audience by reviewing in leading American journals many key works written by their German colleagues. One of them was Theodore Hamerow, who familiarized an American readership with the works of scholars such as Günther Franz, Hans-Joachim Schoeps (himself an émigré), Karl-Georg Faber, and Hans-Ulrich Wehler. Soon after the end of World War II, Hamerow first came into contact with the German historical profession. Having received his Ph.D. under Hajo Holborn's supervision at Yale in 1951, he spent a year—through the University of Maryland's overseas program—in Germany, where he heard Franz Schnabel lecture at the University of Munich.[7] In the 1960s, Hamerow also assumed a leading role within the Conference Group of Central European History and was instrumental in the establishment of its journal, *Central European History*, which soon offered space to younger German historians, such as Hans-Ulrich Wehler and Wolfgang J. Mommsen, to publish their research in English.[8] Later in his career, Hamerow became increasingly skeptical of what he perceived as excessive moralizing in historical writing, a position triggered by his experiences with the New Left in Madison, but which he also expressed explicitly with regard to historiography on modern Germany.[9]

Another important observer of West German historiography was Klaus Epstein. Not all émigré historians of the second generation maintained or established working relationships with colleagues in West Germany early in their careers; in *My German Question*, Peter Gay discusses his strong reservations about visiting West Germany at all.[10] Yet Klaus Epstein immediately immersed himself in the transatlantic intellectual community.[11] Already in 1955–56, only two years after he had received his Ph.D. at Harvard, Epstein spent a year at the University of Hamburg on a Fulbright lectureship. Throughout his career, Epstein authored not only regular reviews of studies published by German historians, but also a number of influential review essays, which almost became his trademark. A collection of these essays on studies of the German Empire, the Weimar Republic, and Nazi Germany was issued posthumously in German—an unusual publication and testament to Epstein's status in the eyes of German historians at the time of his tragic death.[12]

Klaus Epstein's emotional connection to Germany was closer than that of many of his fellow émigrés, and this became apparent in his essay on William Shirer's simplistic yet immensely successful *The Rise and Fall of the Third Reich*.[13] Epstein's comprehensive assessment in *The Review of Politics* was at least as negative as Martin Broszat's in *Historische Zeitschrift*, and its tone was even more blunt. Epstein argued that Shirer's "one-sided misjudgments on Germany's political history appear[ed] relatively insignificant when compared with his systematic prejudice when dealing with Germany's cultural heritage," and accused Shirer of "rewarming of the wartime tale that German history is a one-way road leading from Luther to Hitler."[14]

Another influential observer was Georg G. Iggers, who in 1968 articulated a comprehensive critique of the "German conception of history" during the nineteenth and early-twentieth centuries. With this seminal study Iggers also helped legitimize an alternative conception, ultimately manifesting itself in the "Kritische Geschichtswissenschaft" à la Bielefeld.[15] Shortly before the publication of this *magnum opus*, Iggers had already declared the "decline of the classical national tradition in German historiography" in the wake of the *Fischer-Kontroverse*.[16] Throughout the 1970s and 1980s, Iggers remained a decidedly sympathetic observer of the West German social historians, and since he was the leading American authority on German historiography, his views contributed significantly to the American perception of the social historians, and in particular the "Bielefeld School," as the vanguards of progressivism.[17]

During the post-World War II decades, German historians also recognized that a favorable reception by American colleagues could be advantageous if one held views at odds with the majority of German historians. In March 1966, Fritz Fischer wrote a letter to several American colleagues including Fritz Stern, Hans Gatzke, and Klaus Epstein. Fischer announced that he would soon send them a copy of his assistant Helmut Böhme's dissertation, *Deutschlands Weg zur Großmacht*, and asked whether they would be willing to review it in one of the leading American journals.[18] Böhme's study on socioeconomic aspects of the German unification contained a strong ideological and methodological critique of the extant German historiography on the German Empire, which he—and Fischer—saw as dominated by old-fashioned diplomatic historians who revered the Iron Chancellor. Fischer apparently anticipated a negative reaction from the West German historical profession and attempted to rally American support.[19]

Klaus Epstein replied that he expected "to be able to place a review in either the *Journal of Modern History* or the *Review of Politics*." He added that he thought it to be "of the greatest importance that the unmasking of the unsalutary features of German history—which is the cherished specialty of the Fritz Fischer school—[was] extended into the Bismarckian period."[20] Hans W. Gatzke responded to Fischer that he had been "following [his] good fight with great interest and sympathy from afar."[21] In a comprehensive review essay, Epstein called Böhme's study "a pioneering achievement in the too-long-neglected field of German social history."[22] This positive reception, as well as the author's close association with Fritz Fischer, seemed to have paid off: two years later, Böhme, at the age of only thirty-two, was considered for an appointment as a full professor at State University of New York (SUNY) at Buffalo.[23]

In addition to their role as observers of the German *Zunft* (guild), second-generation émigrés at times played an important role as interventionists in German academic debates. Gerhard Weinberg, for example, participated in the scholarly dialogue through frequent publications in German journals, often battling apologetic historical interpretations widely popular in West Germany. In the 1950s, he strongly opposed German historians who claimed that *Operation Barbarossa*, Nazi Germany's invasion of the Soviet Union, had been a "preventive war." Ten years later, Weinberg was similarly outspoken in his condemnation of David L. Hoggan's attempt to portray the outbreak of World War II as a result of the supposedly conspiratorial diplomacy of Great Britain and Poland.[24]

The best example of an American and second-generation émigré intervention, however, was the *Fischer-Kontroverse* about the origins and the course of World War I, with Klaus Epstein and Fritz Stern leading the American opposition to the German censorship of Fischer's views. Without a doubt, this controversy marked the most striking example of a transatlantic fight for a historiographical cause.[25] Early in 1964, Fritz Fischer's lecture tour to the United States, funded by the *Goethe Institut*, was cancelled due to the intervention of Fischer's German opponents. They convinced the German Foreign Office that is was not in the Federal Republic's interest to let Fischer advance in the United States his critical reinterpretation of the German Empire's role in the outbreak of World War I. Only the organizational efforts of several American historians (among them Klaus Epstein and Fritz Stern) enabled Fischer eventually to realize the tour. Later in the same year, Fritz Stern appeared at the convention of the German Historical Association and backed Fischer's position at a panel discussion on World War I that attracted fifteen hundred listeners. In his magnum opus on the German Empire's war aims during World War I, *Griff nach der Weltmacht*, Fischer had challenged the notion of the Third Reich as a *Betriebsunfall* (accident) in German history, an interpretation many German historians still adhered to.[26] Commenting on this issue at the *Historikertag* (the German Historical Association's convention), Fritz Stern famously remarked, "Is it in fact possible to have a series of accidents without coming to the surmise that there may be something wrong with the whole enterprise?"[27]

American support for Fischer's lecture tour and Stern's widely publicized speech at the *Historikertag* were crucial for Fischer, who initially had been isolated within Germany. Yet one also has to mention that many of the Americans who intervened in this debate were not uncritical supporters of Fischer's views. Rather, as they made clear in their letters to German diplomats in the United States, their intervention was motivated primarily by concerns about academic freedom in the Federal Republic.[28] American responses to Fischer's talks given during his tour were also more mixed than the public intervention on his behalf might have suggested. Writing to Hans Herzfeld several weeks after Fischer's United States lecture tour, Hans Rosenberg provided a candid—and devastating—assessment: "Fischer's appearance here [at Berkeley], as I indicated already, turned out to be a great intellectual and scholarly disappointment [*eine große geistig-wissenschaftliche Enttäuschung*]. Had the German Foreign Office not tried to silence him, he would have encountered strong criticism over here. But given the political background we all turned a blind eye on his assumptions and at times sloppy methods, even though we by no means endorse them."[29] And Klaus Epstein, in a generally favorable, comprehensive review essay of *Griff nach der Weltmacht*, also worried that "some of his readers will pounce upon his material to corroborate an *a priori* prejudice against the 'eternally wicked German.'"[30]

Fifteen years after the controversy, Theodore Hamerow provided an apt summary of what had been at stake back then, when he labeled it the "declaration of independence" for younger German historians.[31] He was certainly correct: to follow Hamerow's analogy, by the late 1960s, younger German historians had declared their independence from their conservative predecessors, but the revolutionary wars were just about to begin. By contrast, American historians regarded the controversy as a sign that West German historians had finally achieved the long overdue pluralization of their profession. Many Americans no longer saw the front lines as running between apologetic reactionaries on the one side and revisionist progressives on the other. For the Americans, by the late 1960s the revolution was already nearing its conclusion, and thus in their view there was little need for the acrimonious debates between German historians throughout the 1970s and 1980s.

German Perceptions of the Émigré Historians

The Fischer-Kontroverse is an appropriate event to shift the focus and ask how German historians during the post–World War II decades perceived and responded to the émigré historians and their writings. In many ways, they viewed these émigrés as part of the American scholarly community, yet at times the émigré background came to assume a more important role for the West Germans' colleagues.

For the period between the end of World War II and the mid-1960s, it is safe to say that the more conservative an émigré was, the more attractive he was for the postwar West German historical profession. This was simply a reflection of the political leanings of the overwhelming majority of German historians. By the early 1950s, the conservative Hans Rothfels fit into the field much better than the liberal Hans Rosenberg ever could. These German preferences became apparent among both the first and the second generation of émigrés. It was significant, therefore, that Theodor Schieder, who due to his towering significance within the West German historical profession certainly had greater influence on job distributions than any of his colleagues, suggested Klaus Epstein (who was, of course, not a conservative like Rothfels) when asked for the names of promising younger scholars who could occupy a German *Lehrstuhl*. Commenting on possible candidates for a chair at the University of Bonn, Schieder recommended Epstein, who had not only an "extraordinarily sharp mind," but also, and more importantly, an "impressive ability to empathize with the German conditions, from which he had been removed through his course of life."[32] By hiring Epstein, the German historical profession would have been able to signal its openness toward foreign perspectives without running the risk of pushing revisionism too far. Schieder's remark also suggests that not all émigré historians could be trusted to express the same empathy and understanding. After all, throughout the first two postwar decades, German conservatives often accused scholars who advanced disagreeable views of harboring "*emigrantisches Ressentiment*" (émigré resentment).[33]

To Schieder's credit, he did point out that an Epstein appointment would constitute "eine wichtige Bereicherung für die deutsche Geschichtswissenschaft" ("a significant addition to the German historical profession")—his position vis-à-vis Epstein was in line with his relative openness toward different methodologies and interpretations. Yet the exact nature of his assessment of Epstein also points to the limits of what kind of émigré historian was acceptable for a moderate conservative like Schieder.

By contrast, it is difficult to imagine Fritz Stern or George Mosse being considered for an appointment at a German history department in the early 1960s. Their interpretations of modern German history, particularly ideological currents in late nineteenth- and early twentieth-century Germany, their outspoken liberal political positions, and—at least in Stern's case—their participation in German debates were not acceptable for most of their influential German colleagues during that decade. What West Germany's leading historians thought about Stern became apparent during the *Fischer-Kontroverse*. In October 1964, the publisher of the journal *Geschichte in Wissenschaft und Unterricht* (GWU) suggested including Stern's *Historikertag* contribution, which had strongly supported Fritz Fischer's position, in a forthcoming issue. GWU's editor, Karl Dietrich Erdmann, responded that Stern's paper was merely emotional in nature and contained not a single argument about the issue at hand ("Appell an Emotionen, kein einziges Argument zur Sache"). Eventually, GWU decided not to print Stern's paper.[34] Gerhard Ritter voiced a similar sentiment, complaining to Erdmann about "Mr. Stern's babble" ("das Geschwätz von Herrn Stern") at the *Historikertag*, which had deeply annoyed him.[35]

The perceived ability to empathize with the peculiarities of German history, which apparently distinguished Klaus Epstein from others, was an appealing quality to be found in an American scholar. It was also a yardstick that some German historians used until the early 1960s to assess their foreign colleagues, and the second-generation German émigrés were not an exception.

Even German-born-and-trained historians teaching overseas were suspected of having lost their *Einfühlungsvermögen* (empathy with Germany and German history), as Gerhard Ritter found it necessary to tell Yale historian Hajo Holborn when the first volume of Holborn's "German History" was published in 1960: "Ihnen ... muss man nachrühmen, dass Sie trotz Ihres Amerikanismus und trotz der großen Distanz, in die Sie seit den dreißiger Jahren Deutschland gegenüber geraten sind, sich ein echtes und warmes Verständnis für die Geschichte Ihres deutschen Vaterlandes bewahrt haben, soviel ich sehe."[36]

These "compliments," which were paid to a number of historians based in the United States throughout the first two postwar decades, reveal a persistent belief among German scholars that the different personal backgrounds and experiences of both American-born and émigré historians might pose some obstacles to an appropriate *Einfühlen* into the conditions of German history. In his review of Koppel Pinson's survey *Modern Germany*, Hans Herzfeld acknowledged that Pinson had provided "one of the most serious foreign attempts to grapple with the difficult problems of nineteenth and twentieth century German history," but he "inevitably"—as Herzfeld put it—fell short in some respects as well.[37]

Even some émigré historians, such as Klaus Epstein himself, would not shy away from such a claim. In a review essay on three American studies of German socialism in the early twentieth century, Epstein argued that American scholars sympathizing with the left wing of the SPD (Sozialdemokratische Partei Deutschlands) had, because of their nationality, difficulties understanding the no-win situation in which the moderate Social Democrats had found themselves. In Epstein's words, "American historians are handicapped when dealing with German developments by the deep-rooted American faith that all problems can be solved by intelligence and good will. . . . American historians have underestimated the impersonal forces and conditions which have made German socialists act the way they did, and they have engaged in the futile search for villains."[38] Ironically, one of the historians charged with having such a handicap was Epstein's fellow émigré Peter Gay, who, in contrast to his critic (who had left Germany at the age of eight), had spent most of his teenage years in Germany.

By the late 1960s, however, most historians of Epstein's age cohort, and certainly the overwhelming majority of scholars of the succeeding generations, deemed such an argument to be inappropriate; at least, it began to disappear from book reviews. This may have been a result of increasing German familiarity with first-rate scholarship on German history produced in the United States, or of—to follow Georg Iggers—"the decline of the classical national tradition" of German historiography.[39]

The *Sonderweg* Debates

Needless to say, the second-generation émigrés also influenced their German colleagues through their work, as they produced a large number of important monographs. In this context, it is worth looking at the émigrés' contribution to the intellectual and cultural history of modern Germany. They deserve special attention not only as scholarly achievements per se, but also as examples of a genre that was underrepresented among West German historians during the same period. By contrast, Fritz Stern's *Politics of Cultural Despair* and George Mosse's *Crisis of German Ideology* became required reading for many American graduate students of German (and arguably European) history in the 1960s and 1970s.[40]

Stern's study focused on three representatives of late nineteenth- and early twentieth-century cultural criticism, Paul de Lagarde, Julius Langbehn, and Arthur Moeller van den Bruck.[41] Stern argued that while historians in their search for the causes of National Socialism had thus far examined everything "from the dangers of Article 48 of the Weimar constitution to the role of Big Business," they had not "sufficiently reckoned with the politically exploitable discontent which for so long has been embedded in German culture."[42] Lagarde, Langbehn, and Moeller van den Bruck were, according to Stern, uprooted intellectuals who felt alienated from the progress of modernity, rationalism, and science, and who hated, above all, liberalism. They wanted to overcome these evils of modernity by a "conservative revolution," and their ideas taken together constituted what Stern termed the "Germanic ideology."[43] What proved fatal for the course of German history was that the National Socialists appropriated some elements of this ideology. Furthermore, the ideology also affected the "educated, civilized classes," who were thus likely to be attracted by at least some elements of National Socialism.[44] Finally, while Stern conceded that "the conservative revolution was a European phenomenon," he emphasized that "only in Germany did it become a decisive intellectual and political force."[45]

In contrast to Stern, George Mosse focused not only on intellectuals (or, as Stern had dubbed Lagarde, Langbehn, and Moeller van den Bruck, "'anti-intellectual' intellectuals") but on figures of high and popular culture alike.[46] Mosse explicitly rejected Gerhard Ritter's attempted Europeanization of National Socialist ideology and stated that "rather than to explain away this fact [that the *völkisch* movement had 'deeply penetrated into the national fabric'], it would seem more profitable to ask how this could have been accomplished."[47] Like Stern, Mosse emphasized that historians thus far had not taken National Socialist ideology seriously enough, either because they had regarded it as mere propaganda, or because they had "found these ideas so nebulous and incomprehensible that they have dismissed them as unimportant."[48] The essential element in the "völkisch" ideology for Mosse was "the linking of the human soul with its natural surroundings, with the 'essence' of nature."[49] Mosse also devoted considerable attention to the dissemination of these ideas, for "education preeminently institutionalized the ideology. Before 1918, no political organization or group of like-minded people was as important as educators in anchoring the Germanic faith within the German nation."[50] And since "völkisch" ideas in the 1920s permeated not only the National Socialists but the entire German Right, the Nazi seizure of power in 1933 was anything but an accident for Mosse, even though he made it clear that it was not inevitable, either.[51]

Incidentally, two other second-generation émigrés reviewed Stern's and Mosse's studies in the leading American journals, and their reviews illustrated the diversity of opinions among them. Klaus Epstein characterized Stern's *The Politics of Cultural Despair* as an "important contribution to the understanding of the roots of National Socialism" which at the same time paid attention to cultural pessimists outside of Germany.[52] However, Klemens von Klemperer, who praised Stern's study as "superb cultural history" which placed "the politics of cultural despair within the context of broader European developments,"[53] criticized Mosse sharply for the latter's "vastly exaggerated" conclusions, especially regarding Wilhelmian Germany that had been forced by Mosse "into a Volkish strait jacket."[54] Klemperer added, "Just because it is understandable and indeed inevitable that in these days German history should be written with the catastrophe in mind, it is up to the historian to exercise the necessary restraint."[55] But Klemperer's criticism should not detract from the fact that Mosse's book was extremely influential. As Saul Friedländer has indicated, "For those of us who, in the mid-1960s, started teaching modern history, particularly the history of Nazism, Nazi anti-Semitism, and the origins of the Final Solution, *The Crisis [of German Ideology]* opened new vistas."[56]

In contrast to the United States, the reception of Stern's and Mosse's studies in Germany was by and large a non-reception. *Historische Zeitschrift* reviewed neither of the two, and even though *The Politics of Cultural Despair* was published in German in 1963, it does not seem to have stimulated further research among German historians.[57] Several factors might account for this fact. First, historians of Gerhard Ritter's generation, whose influence was waning anyway during the 1960s, were likely to ignore studies that all too critically examined the ideological orientations of the German *Bildungsbürgertum*. Second, if German historians in the 1960s examined the roots of National Socialism, they generally focused on the Weimar Republic, debating, for example, whether the Social Democrats in the 1918 revolution had failed to push through more democratic reforms, which might have decisively weakened anti-democratic forces in Germany instead of making the Nazi rise to power possible in 1933.[58] Alternatively, they argued about missed opportunities and misguided policies at the end of the Weimar Republic.[59] And third, historians of National Socialism were caught up in the fascism/totalitarianism debate, and both concepts did not pay much attention to ideology in a long-term perspective. Similarly, most of the younger German historians such as Martin Broszat and Hans Mommsen focused on the structure of the National Socialist regime rather than its ideological roots.[60]

And yet the non-reception of the American studies in intellectual and cultural history by the German contemporaries remains puzzling for another reason. After all, Stern and Mosse (like Hans Kohn and Leonard Krieger) outlined a German *Sonderweg*, and even though theirs was ideological, one might have expected the German historians who in the 1970s developed a social and political *Sonderweg* thesis to pay more attention to it. This lack of reception is even more surprising when one considers that these German scholars were generally very aware of American literature on German history because of their contacts with American historians.

In the debates about the "brown roots" of German social history, some German observers have explained the social historians' focus on structures and processes instead of agency and ideology by their allegiance to their teachers, above all Werner Conze and Theodor Schieder. Conze and Schieder had compromised themselves during the Nazi years and thus were not very interested in questions of agency and individual responsibility.[61] By resorting to structural and process-oriented approaches, their students avoided these tricky issues—and remained in their advisers' good graces. While these views on social history have been developed within the German context as an exercise in "intellectual parricide,"[62] as Charles Maier has termed it, Steven Aschheim has provided a less polemical yet similar explanation. In his comparison of German-Jewish intellectual and cultural historians and German (non-Jewish) social historians, Aschheim has labeled Wehler's and others' brand of social history as being "at once *skeptical* and *protective*" and "a navigation exercise: formulating a necessarily critical narrative of the past while at the same time leaving questions of personal complicity and ideological and intellectual convictions relatively untouched."[63]

The interpretation advanced in this chapter differs from these critics: younger German social historians tended to view intellectual history as an inappropriate approach for less opportunistic or even implicitly apologetic reasons. German historians of Wehler's generation associated intellectual history—or rather *Geistesgeschichte* and *Ideengeschichte*—with an older German historiographical tradition, namely Friedrich Meinecke's, which they considered either potentially apologetic or simply not very fruitful heuristically.[64] Within the German historiographical context of the 1950s and early 1960s, this assessment was certainly not entirely unfounded.

One also has to note the age difference of ten to twenty years between intellectual and cultural historians (born in the late 1910s to mid-1920s) and social historians (born between c. 1930 and 1940). As students, the latter encountered historical professions that had begun to pay more attention to the social sciences. These observations are neither a verdict in favor of social history nor one against intellectual and cultural history. Yet they offer an explanation that does not suspect the German social historians of Hans-Ulrich Wehler's generation a priori of ulterior motives. More generally, to label certain methodologies per se "apologetic" seems only possible through a very selective reception of historiographical developments of recent decades.

Yet despite the divergence of the socio-political and the intellectual-cultural *Sonderweg* paradigms, there was a strong sense among young German historians in the late 1960s and 1970s, especially social historians in one way or another associated with a *kritische Geschichtswissenschaft*, that American historians of modern Germany, including the émigrés, were in interpretive agreement with them.[65]

This then leads us to an argument about the post–World War II German-American community of historians more generally: the postwar decades witnessed the establishment and consolidation of a large and diverse German-American scholarly community. The creation of a continuous transatlantic conversation, significantly shaped by second-generation émigrés as intermediaries, in which the national background of the participants became less and less important, unquestionably constitutes an impressive achievement. To dismiss American historians as lacking the proper understanding of the peculiarities of German history today would be perceived as unacceptable.

As German historians realized that intellectual isolation and the dismissal of American—and other foreign—perspectives on German history was no longer a viable option, they increasingly co-opted American colleagues who happened to share their views. These remarks are not meant to reduce international scholarly cooperation to its function within academic politics. German historians reached out to their colleagues on the other side of the Atlantic because of shared interests and approaches as well. But American colleagues often became supposedly impartial scholarly arbiters, whose opinion conveniently served to bolster the respective German position—of conservatives or of progressives.[66]

Of course, this is a broader argument—about the role of American historians of modern Germany in general, not only about the second-generation émigrés. These émigrés as a group, despite—or perhaps rather because of—their methodological, interpretive, and political diversity, supported the pluralization of the German historical profession (most notably during the Fischer-Kontroverse).

They contributed and reinforced critical perspectives on the recent German past, even though they were not necessarily the perspectives of the Bielefelder Schule and other self-declared progressive Germans of the next generation. Thus the second-generation émigrés contributed significantly to what amounts today to a critical yet nuanced interpretation of modern German history.

Philipp Stelzel is Assistant Professor of History at Duquesne University. He previously taught at Boston College and Duke University. His research focuses on post-1945 German and German-American intellectual and political history, historiography, and transnational history. His publications include articles in *Central European History* and *Storia della Storiografia*. Currently, he is completing a book project on the intellectual exchange between German and American historians from the end of World War II to the late 1980s.

Notes

1. I would like to thank Andreas Daum, Stephen Milder, and James J. Sheehan for their comments on an earlier version of this chapter. Andreas W. Daum, "German Historiography in Transatlantic perspective: Interview with Hans-Ulrich Wehler," *Bulletin of the German Historical Institute* 26 (2001): 121.
2. Ernst Schulin, "German and American Historiography in the Nineteenth and Twentieth Centuries," in Hartmut Lehmann and James J. Sheehan, eds., *An Interrupted Past: German-Speaking Refugee Historians in the United States after 1933* (New York, 1991), 8-31; Wolfgang J. Mommsen, *The Return to the Western Tradition: German Historiography since 1945* (Washington, DC, 1991).
3. First-generation émigrés are those who had received their academic training prior to their forced emigration from Germany. This group includes, among others, Hajo Holborn, Felix Gilbert, Hans Rosenberg, and Hans Rothfels. Second-generation émigrés left Germany as children and teenagers and were trained in the United States (or England and the United States, as was the case for George Mosse); see the biobibliographical guide by Andreas W. Daum in this volume.
4. See Georg Iggers, *Two Lives in Uncertain Times: Facing the Challenges of the 20th Century as Scholars and Citizens* (New York, 2006), 143-68; Fritz Klein, *Drinnen und Draußen. Ein Historiker in der DDR* (Frankfurt/M., 2000), 274-90.
5. See Kenneth Barkin's article "German Émigré Historians in America: The Fifties, Sixties, and Seventies," in Lehmann and Sheehan, *An Interrupted Past*, 149-69, in which he observed that for this generation of historians, this "big question" was inescapable (158).
6. Fritz Stern, *Five Germanys I Have Known* (New York, 2006), 203.
7. Theodore S. Hamerow, note to the author, 1 December 2006.
8. Douglas Unfug, the journal's first editor (1968-1991), recalled submitting a proposal for editorship to Hamerow. Douglas A. Unfug, note to the author, 29 August 2009.
9. Theodore Hamerow, "Guilt, Redemption, and the Writing of German History," *American Historical Review* 88 (1983): 53-72; Hamerow, note to the author, 1 December 2006. See also his *Reflections on History and Historians* (Madison, WI, 1987).

10. Peter Gay, *My German Question: Growing Up in Nazi Berlin, 1933-1939* (New Haven, CT, 1998), 1-20.
11. See Kenneth L. Barkin, "Klaus Epstein's Contribution to German History Forty Years Later: An Assessment," paper delivered at the Annual German Studies Association Conference, San Diego, 7 October 2007.
12. This is also emphasized by his obituary: see Klaus Schwabe, "Klaus W. Epstein," *Historische Zeitschrift* 206 (1968): 262-64. The collection of his review essays appeared as *Geschichte und Geschichtswissenschaft im 20. Jahrhundert. Ein Leitfaden* (Berlin, 1972).
13. For the reception by the nonprofessional audience, see Gavriel Rosenfeld, "The Reception of Williams Shirer's *The Rise and Fall of the Third Reich* in the United States and West Germany, 1960-62," *Journal of Contemporary History* 29 (1994): 95-128.
14. Klaus Epstein, "Shirer's History of Nazi Germany," *The Review of Politics* 23 (1961): 230–45, quotes on 232 and 245; Cf. Martin Broszat, "William Shirer und die Geschichte des Dritten Reiches," *Historische Zeitschrift* 196 (1963): 112-23.
15. Georg G. Iggers, *The German Conception of History: The National Tradition of Historical Thought from Herder to the Present* (Middletown, CT, 1968).
16. Georg G. Iggers, "The Decline of the Classical National Tradition of German Historiography," *History and Theory* 6 (1967): 382-412.
17. These texts include Georg G. Iggers, *New Directions in European Historiography* (Middletown, CT, 1975); idem, "Introduction," in *The Social History of Politics: Critical Perspectives in West German Historical Writing Since 1945* (Middletown, CT, 1984), 1-45, as well as numerous book reviews.
18. On 14 March 1966, Fischer wrote letters to Klaus Epstein, Hans Gatzke, Otto Pflanze, and Fritz Stern; NL Fischer, Box 9, Bundesarchiv Koblenz (hereafter BAK).
19. Helmut Böhme, *Deutschlands Weg zur Grossmacht. Studien zum Verhältnis von Wirtschaft und Staat während der Reichsgründungszeit 1848-1881* (Cologne, 1966).
20. Klaus Epstein to Fritz Fischer, 17 March 1966, NL Fischer, Box 9, BAK. Epstein's review appeared as "The Socioeconomic History of the German Empire," *The Review of Politics* 29 (1967): 100-12.
21. Hans W. Gatzke to Fritz Fischer, 18 March 1966, NL Fischer, Box 9, BAK. Gatzke added, "As a matter of fact, I am giving a talk on German historiography after both world wars to a group of historians in the South, and the 'Fischer case' will be an important part of it."
22. Klaus Epstein, "The Socioeconomic History of the German Empire," *Review of Politics* 29 (1967): 100-12, quote on 112.
23. See the letter by Robert A. Lively, the chair of the history department at SUNY Buffalo, to Fritz Fischer, 4 November 1968, NL Fischer, Box 11, BAK, in which Lively asks for an evaluation of Böhme. Böhme remained in Germany, where he became a professor at the University of Darmstadt in 1969 and its president in 1971.
24. Weinberg published his critique of the so-called "Präventivkriegsthese," whose proponents claimed that the Soviet Union was on the verge of attacking Nazi Germany when Hitler decided early in 1941 to preventively invade the Soviet Union as "Der deutsche Entschluss zum Angriff auf die Sowjetunion," *Vierteljahrshefte für Zeitgeschichte* 1 (1953): 303-18. For the controversy surrounding Hoggan, see the review by Gerhard Weinberg and the subsequent exchange between Weinberg, Hoggan, and Hoggan's defender, Harry Elmer Barnes, in *American Historical Review* 68 (1962): 104-5 and 914-18.
25. Klaus Große Kracht, *Die zankende Zunft. Historische Kontroversen in Deutschland nach 1945* (Göttingen, 2005), 47-68, provides the most recent survey of the *Fischer-Kontroverse's* German dimension; for the American dimension, see Philipp Stelzel, "Fritz Fischer and the American Historical Profession: Tracing the Transatlantic Dimension of the Fischer-Kontroverse," *Storia della Storiografia* 44 (2003): 67-84.

26. Fischer, *Griff nach der Weltmacht. Die Kriegszielpolitik des kaiserlichen Deutschland 1914/18* (Dusseldorf, 1961), 93.
27. Fritz Stern, "German Historians and the War: Fischer and His Critics," in *The Failure of Illiberalism: Essays on the Political Culture of Modern Germany* (London, 1972), 156.
28. The predominant American attitude was expressed by John Snell (Tulane University), who wrote to Hans Marmann, German Consul General in New Orleans, "If, now, the trip cannot be arranged, many historians in the United States, I among them, will conclude that Professor Fischer is being kept in Germany because of his 'nonconformist' ideas. . . . Let me add that I do not endorse all of Professor Fischer's book. He is basically right, but I suspect that he is somewhat extreme in his tendency to find consistent imperialist policies in Bethman [sic] Hollweg and some other important Germans of 1914–1918. Several other American historians share my qualifying attitude toward the Fischer thesis." John L. Snell to Hans Marmann on 18 February 1964, Nachlass Fritz Fischer, N 1422, Vol. 92, Bundesarchiv Koblenz. See the correspondence quoted in Philipp Stelzel, "Fritz Fischer and the American Historical Profession."
29. Hans Rosenberg to Hans Herzfeld, 24 May 1964, NL Herzfeld, Box 12, BAK.
30. Klaus Epstein, "German War Aims in the First World War," *World Politics* 15 (1962): 163-85, quote on 184.
31. Theodore Hamerow, "Guilt, Redemption, and Writing German History," *American Historical Review* 88 (1983): 53-72, quote on 66.
32. Theodor Schieder to Dekan H. Moser, 5 February 1964, NL Schieder, Box 115, BAK. As early as 1963, Schieder had recommended Epstein for a position at the University of Frankfurt. See the letter from Theodor Schieder to Dietrich Geyer (History Department, University of Frankfurt), 30 January 1963, NL Schieder, Box 115, BAK.
33. For example, Gerhard Ritter rejected Helmuth Plessner's *Verspätete Nation*, considering it "not real history, but the product of an émigré's imagination" (nicht echte Historie sondern Konstruktion aus Emigrantenfantasie). Gerhard Ritter to Theodor Schieder, [undated, c. 1961], NL Schieder, Box 506, BAK. Helmuth Plessner (1892-1985), was a sociologist whose study *Verspätete Nation* (Belated Nation) analyzed what Plessner considered the belated and defective form of modernization of German economy and society (in particular of the *Bürgertum*). See Carola Dietze's biography *Nachgeholtes Leben. Helmuth Plessner, 1892-1985* (Göttingen, 2006).
34. See the letters from Friedrich Dieckmann to Karl Dietrich Erdmann, 21 October 1964, and from Karl Dietrich Erdmann to Friedrich Dieckmann, 1 November 1964, NL Erdmann, Box 21, BAK.
35. Gerhard Ritter to Karl Dietrich Erdmann, 14 October 1964, NL Ritter, Box 270, BAK.
36. "One has to praise you for having preserved true sympathy and understanding for the history of your German fatherland, as far as I can see, despite your Americanism and the great distance, in which you have been put since the 1930s. Gerhard Ritter to Hajo Holborn, 13 October 1960, NL Ritter, Box 350, BAK.
37. Hans Herzfeld, Review of Koppel Pinson, *Modern Germany*, *Historische Zeitschrift* 182 (1956): 402-05, quotes on 402.
38. Klaus Epstein, "Three Studies of German Socialism," *World Politics* 11 (1959): 650-651. The studies under review were Peter Gay, *The Dilemma of Democratic Socialism: Eduard Bernstein's Challenge to Marx* (New York, 1952); Carl Schorske, *German Social Democracy, 1905-1917: The Development of the Great Schism* (Cambridge, MA, 1955); and Joseph Berlau, *German Social Democracy, 1914-1924* (New York, 1949).
39. Iggers, "The Decline of the Classical National Tradition," n. 16.
40. The significance of Mosse's *Crisis* emphasizes Saul Friedländer, "Mosse's Influence on the Historiography of the Holocaust," in Stanley G. Payne et al., eds., *What History Tells: George L. Mosse and the Culture of Modern Europe* (Madison, WI, 2003), 135. See also Steven Aschheim,

"The Tensions of Historical Wissenschaft: The Émigré Historians and the Making of German Cultural History," in *Beyond the Border: The German-Jewish Legacy Abroad* (Princeton, NJ, 2007), 45-80; interview with Jeffrey Herf, 12 September 2006.
41. Fritz Stern, *The Politics of Cultural Despair: A Study in the Rise of the Germanic Ideology* (Berkeley, 1961).
42. Stern, *The Politics of Cultural Despair*, xv. Article 48 of the Weimar constitution granted the *Reichspräsident* far-reaching political power. Some historians argued that this constitutional element had weakened the Weimar Republic from the outset.
43. Stern, *The Politics of Cultural Despair*, 267.
44. Ibid., 292-94.
45. Ibid., xxiii.
46. Ibid., 276; George L. Mosse, *The Crisis of German Ideology: Intellectual Origins of the Third Reich* (New York, 1964).
47. Mosse, *The Crisis of German Ideology*, 8.
48. Ibid., 1.
49. Ibid., 4.
50. Ibid., 152.
51. See ibid., 8.
52. Klaus Epstein, "Review of Fritz Stern, *The Politics of Cultural Despair: A Study in the Rise of the Germanic Ideology*," *American Historical Review* 67 (1962), 713.
53. Klemens von Klemperer, "Review of *The Politics of Cultural Despair: A Study in the Rise of the Germanic Ideology*," *Journal of Modern History* 34 (1962): 350.
54. Klemens von Klemperer, "Review of George Mosse, *The Crisis of German Ideology: Intellectual Origins of the Third Reich*," *American Historical Review* 71 (1966): 609.
55. Klemperer, "Review of George Mosse, *The Crisis of German Ideology*," 609.
56. Saul Friedländer, "Mosse's Influence on the Historiography of the Holocaust," 135.
57. Fritz Stern, *Kulturpessimismus als politische Gefahr. Eine Analyse nationaler Ideologie in Deutschland* (Bern, 1963).
58. See the studies on the German Soviets (1918–19) that were published at the same time: Eberhard Kolb, *Die Arbeiterräte in der deutschen Innenpolitik, 1918-1919* (Dusseldorf, 1962); and Peter von Oertzen, *Betriebsräte in der Novemberrevolution. Eine politikwissenschaftliche Untersuchung über Ideengehalt und Struktur betrieblicher und wirtschaftlicher Arbeiterräte in der deutschen Revolution 1918/19* (Dusseldorf, 1963).
59. In the 1950s and early 1960s, Karl Dietrich Bracher and Werner Conze clashed about the role of Chancellor Heinrich Brüning. Compare Bracher's seminal *Die Auflösung der Weimarer Republik. Eine Studie zum Problem des Machtverfalls in der Demokratie* (Villingen, 1955) and Conze's articles "Die Krise des Parteienstaates in Deutschland 1929/30," *Historische Zeitschrift* 178 (1954): 47-83, and "Brünings Politik unter dem Druck der großen Krise," *Historische Zeitschrift* 199 (1964): 529-50.
60. See Martin Broszat, *Der Staat Hitlers. Grundlegung und Entwicklung seiner inneren Verfassung* (Munich, 1969); and Hans Mommsen, *Beamtentum im Dritten Reich* (Stuttgart, 1966). Eberhard Jäckel's studies *Hitlers Weltanschauung* (Tübingen, 1969) and *Hitlers Herrschaft* (Stuttgart, 1986) do not engage Mosse's and Stern's studies, as they focus on the dictator rather than the broader Nazi or *völkisch* milieu.
61. See Peter Schöttler, "Von der rheinischen Landesgeschichte zur nazistischen Volksgeschichte oder die 'unhörbare Stimme des Blutes,'" in Winfried Schulze and Otto G. Oexle, eds., *Deutsche Historiker im Nationalsozialismus* (Frankfurt/M., 1999), 89-113; Götz Aly, "Theodor Schieder, Werner Conze oder die Vorstufen der physischen Vernichtung," in Schulze and Oexle, *Deutsche Historiker*, 163-82; Berg, *Der Holocaust und die westdeutschen Historiker*, 563ff.

62. Charles S. Maier, "Comment," in Hartmut Lehmann and James van Horn Melton, eds., *Paths of Continuity: Central European Historiography from the 1930s to the 1950s* (New York, 1994), 395.
63. Aschheim, "The Tensions of Historical Wissenschaft," 52.
64. See Paul Nolte, "Die Historiker der Bundesrepublik. Rückblick auf eine 'lange Generation,'" *Merkur* 53 (1999): 413-432; for Wehler's statements on intellectual history, see his "Geschichtswissenschaft heute," first in Jürgen Habermas, *Stichworte zur geistigen Situation der Zeit* (Frankfurt/M., 1979), and later in Hans-Ulrich Wehler, *Historische Sozialwissenschaft und Geschichtsschreibung. Studien zu Aufgaben und Traditionen deutscher Geschichtswissenschaft* (Göttingen, 1980), 13-41. For the debate about "structure" vs. "agency"/"intention" in a different context, see also Norbert Frei, ed., *Martin Broszat, der "Staat Hitlers" und die Historisierung des Nationalsozialismus* (Göttingen, 2007).
65. See, for example, the statement by Hans-Ulrich Wehler quoted at the beginning of this article. See also Ernst Schulin's assertion that "Anglo-American critical interest in German history influenced and assisted in the modernization of West German historical writing." Schulin, "German and American Historiography," 8-31; quote on 31.
66. Other foreign historians could serve in the same role. This constitutes one of two main reasons why Geoff Eley's, David Blackbourn's, and Richard J. Evans's critiques of the *Sonderweg* paradigm warmed the hearts of German conservatives. British historians could hardly be accused of an apologetic stance toward Imperial Germany. The critics' neo-Marxist orientation provided even more reason for satisfaction, since the Bielefelder were attacked by fellow progressives.

Chapter 20

Encounters with Émigré Historians of the First and Second Generation

Gerhard A. Ritter

Before I turn to my relationship with the second generation of émigré historians, let me say a few words about the first generation, which had a much larger impact on my life and work. Next to my doctoral advisor Hans Herzfeld, who as a so-called "quarter Jew" had been marginalized under the National Socialist dictatorship, my most important academic teachers were Hans Rosenberg and Ernst Fraenkel.

I got to know Rosenberg as a guest professor at Berlin's Free University in 1949. A "half Jew" in the view of the Nazis and a committed left-leaning democrat, he had emigrated to Great Britain in 1933. He put a critical approach to German history at the center of his teaching. Rosenberg focused on illuminating the social and economic reasons for the structural weaknesses of democracy in Germany and thus the National Socialists' seizure of power in 1933. This provided me with a new perspective on German history and its international context. I assume that many of my fellow students felt the same. Among these were Gilbert Ziebura, Gerhard Schulz, Wolfgang Sauer, Otto Büsch, Friedrich Zunkel, and Helga Grebing. All of them eventually became professors of history or political science.

It was particularly important that Rosenberg emphasized the value of engaging the social sciences, especially those generated abroad. But he also emphasized the research done by Otto Hintze, whom he saw as the foremost German historian of the first half of the twentieth century, ahead even of Friedrich Meinecke. Rosenberg thus helped us to move beyond the German historical profession's deep provincialism. Moreover, it was a special treat when Rosenberg invited us,

---

Notes from this chapter begin on page 316.

his seminar participants, to the restaurant of the Maison de France in Berlin, which, at that time, Germans could only enter in the company of Allied hosts. In later years, Rosenberg often returned to Berlin, even without any teaching obligations. He continued to engage his former students in long, individual conversations and provided stimulating and at times very pointed scholarly advice.

Rosenberg's critical comments on my doctoral thesis, which dealt with the labor movement in the Wilhelmine Empire,[1] were important to me as well. His overall response was positive. Rosenberg appreciated that my work put this movement into the larger context of German history and tried to explain Social Democracy's ultimate integration into German social and political life. However, his comments also demonstrated to me that I had not sufficiently connected the political history of the workers' associations to the social history of workers at large and the impact of economic transformations on German trade unions. From then on, I sent all my scholarly work to Rosenberg and always waited eagerly for his judgment. Rosenberg's emphasis on long perspectives, on placing any specific topic in the larger political, economic, and societal context of its time, and on international comparisons has guided me in my own research. This was clearly the case when I wrote my book about the emergence and transformation of the modern welfare state.[2] Rosenberg was in the audience when I first presented the thoughts for this book in 1985 at the opening of the International Congress of the Historical Sciences in Stuttgart.

What had been initially a relationship between an academic teacher and his student eventually developed into a close, personal friendship. In the fall of 1971, I substituted for Rosenberg during his sabbatical at the University of California at Berkeley. Since his American students addressed him as "Hans," Rosenberg thought it was awkward if we were to continue addressing each other as "Herr Rosenberg" and "Herr Ritter." In later years, we repeatedly spent our vacations together in the Black Forest. We exchanged many letters and began talking on the phone on a weekly basis.

Since the mid-1960s, Hans Rosenberg sent me his books and essays as well, and he asked me to comment on them. I recall a long letter in which I criticized his book *Große Depression und Bismarckzeit* (1967). This opus had enormous heuristic importance for the entire discipline of history and a profound impact on those advocating a new—and critical—social history. I pointed out that, in fact, the 1880s had not been a time of economic depression, in spite of smaller economic downturns. In a letter of 21 March 1970, Rosenberg acknowledged that he should have used the more precise, less misleading term "Great Deflation." I convinced my doctoral student Jürgen Kocka to stay away from Rosenberg's original term "Great Depression" when Kocka wrote his brilliant dissertation, published in 1969 as *Unternehmensverwaltung und Angestelltenschaft am Beispiel Siemens. 1847–1914*. Kocka had initially planned to use Rosenberg's category as the underlying structural concept. Yet, the 1880s were a boom period for Germany's electrical industry at large and certainly for Siemens, which then expanded into an enterprise on the European and ultimately world market.

I have always been particularly fascinated by Rosenberg's relationship with Friedrich Meinecke, his academic teacher. Initially, Meinecke seems to have been a kind of ersatz for Rosenberg's coolly distant father, who had died early. In a series of case studies that he undertook from 1927 to 1929, Rosenberg critically engaged Meinecke's *Geistesgeschichte*, his mentor's brand of the history of ideas; these essays were compiled much later in a volume entitled *Politische Denkströmungen im deutschen Vormärz* (1972). Meinecke provided a history of ideas that was based on a fine-grained analysis of the thoughts of leading individuals of the time. Rosenberg, in contrast, focused on thinkers from lower and middle classes and aimed at replacing Meinecke's approach with a collective history of ideas. More than any of Meinecke's other students, Rosenberg departed from the concept of a history of ideas and turned toward social history. This development found expression in Rosenberg's pioneering work *Die Weltwirtschaftskrisis von 1857–1859* (1934)[3] and his massive study on the Prussian *Junker* from the middle ages to 1945, almost finished in 1947,[4] though only the middle part was published in a heavily edited form as *Bureaucracy, Aristocracy and Autocracy: The Prussian Experience 1660–1815* (1958). The *Great Depression*, too, was far apart from Meinecke's work in terms of method and contents. Rosenberg's personal relationship with Meinecke remained very close, as documented in the correspondence between the two[5] as well as Meinecke's attempt to bring Rosenberg to the Free University in Berlin as his successor. I recall that Rosenberg, during his first postwar visits to Berlin, rented a room near Meinecke's apartment, just on the opposite side of the street. Rosenberg regularly met Meinecke for breakfast. A photograph of a bust of Meinecke always remained the only picture on Rosenberg's desk. Today, it hangs in my office under images of Jacob Burckhardt and Hans Rosenberg.

Hans Rosenberg became the nestor of the *Gesellschaftsgeschichte*, the critical history of society that has been enshrined in the history of German historiography, in Germany as well as abroad, as the Bielefeld School. But we should not overlook the earlier roots of social history in the works of political economists around the turn of the century as well as the fact that important foundations for the new social history were laid at the Free University in Berlin. Here—nearly ten years before the establishment of the Bielefeld School—the approach of critical social history was practiced in the dissertations, undertaken under my supervision, by Jürgen Kocka, Hans-Jürgen Puhle, Hartmut Kaelble, and Karin Hausen. There, they had close professional relationships with the economic historian Wolfram Fischer and the Swiss historian Rudolf Braun, who researched the processes of protoindustrialization and its social consequences.

The lawyer and political scientist Ernst Fraenkel was the second émigré of the first generation who decisively influenced my academic development. Fraenkel had immigrated to the United States in 1938. Since his training in German law was now useless, he studied law in America as well. Fraenkel's study *The Dual State*, published in 1941, was one of the first and most astute analyses of the National Socialist political system.[6] Fraenkel's interpretation was heavily influenced by his experiences as a lawyer for Jewish victims in the 1930s.[7] From the end of 1945 to 1950, Fraenkel worked in Korea as an advisor in the field of constitutional law for the United States and later for the Korean national assembly, thus contributing to the formation of the new state of South Korea, from which he was evacuated after the outbreak of the Korean War. Otto Suhr, later ruling mayor of Berlin, was instrumental in extending to Fraenkel an offer to teach at the *Deutsche Hochschule für Politik* in Berlin and, then from 1953 on, at the Free University with a full professorship for "politics as a science." Fraenkel became one of the founding fathers of political science in Germany, a discipline that was newly formed after World War II. Frankel was a splendid academic teacher. He presented a positive image of the United States in his lectures—as well as his now classic book—on *Das amerikanische Regierungssystem* (1960). Many of his profound essays contributed to anchoring liberal, democratic values and institutions in the new Federal Republic of Germany.[8] He emphasized the idea of political pluralism as an essential element of a viable democracy and highlighted that this pluralism relied on the conflict between, yet ultimate balances of, different interests and ideas. Fraenkel developed this idea as a counter model to totalitarian and authoritarian societies. It influenced the self-understanding of the Federal Republic and was ultimately seen as a foundational principle of the Basic Law.

My close relation with Fraenkel began when he invited me, before I had finished the *Habilitation*, to offer jointly—and in English—a seminar on the "Federalist Papers," that is, the series of articles that Alexander Hamilton, James Madison, and John Jay published in 1787–88 to make a case for the recently drafted American constitution. I realized that Fraenkel's engagement with this body of texts, a classic in the history of political theory, had decisively influenced his concept of pluralism. Fraenkel thus helped me intensify my interests in law—especially constitutional law, and later labor and employment law—as well as in political science. This growing interest contributed to the fact that the Free University accepted my *Habilitation* in two fields, modern history and political science. Not coincidentally, I received my first full professorship, at the age of thirty-two, at the Otto Suhr Institute of the Free University, the successor of the *Deutsche Hochschule für Politik*; it was nominally devoted to the historical foundations of politics. In 1968, Fraenkel tried to convince me to become his successor as both a professor of "theory and comparative history of political systems" and as a professor of American politics at the John F. Kennedy Institute at the Free University, which he had helped to constitute. Both positions came with a large support staff. In his attempt to draw me to Berlin, Frankel even came personally to Münster, where I was now teaching modern German history. In anticipation of this visit, my wife had sworn him to secrecy; she did not want our sons to hear anything about returning to Berlin, which might have impeded their willingness to adapt to the new surroundings in Münster. In spite of my deep admiration for Fraenkel, I did not accept the Berlin offer since I felt that I was more a historian than a political scientist. Moreover, I had just begun to offer lectures about the history of the United States, but had not published anything about the subject. Finally, I felt that I could not live up to what Fraenkel expected from me, which was to contain almost singlehandedly the student rebellion that in the meantime had engulfed the Free University.

The student rebellion, which had emerged at the Otto Suhr Institute in the mid-1960s and assumed a particularly radical character there, hit Fraenkel deeply. He thought this movement was doctrinaire and antidemocratic. Students storming lectures and seminars reminded him of SA troops who had once roamed the streets and broke up lectures of Jewish professors at universities even before 1933. During a six-hour walk in a park in Berlin Dahlem, Fraenkel explained his deep concerns to me. He indicated that he and his wife were seriously considering an emigration back to the United States. This did not happen, but Fraenkel retreated from the Free University and died detached from public life on 28 March 1977.

There were other émigré scholars of the first generation with whom I had close contact. Dietrich Gerhard was one of them. In early 1965, he invited me to substitute for him as a professor at Washington University in St. Louis and, as it turned out, left us not only his house, but also his collie. Gerhard introduced me to the international research on early modern estates (*Stände*) and also to Helmut Koenigsberger, yet another émigré scholar who had gone to England. Furthermore, Richard Löwenthal, the writer and expert on Eastern European and Soviet politics, became a close colleague and friend at the Otto Suhr Institute. I also established a personal relationship with Adolf Leschnitzer, who founded a program for German-Jewish history at the Free University.

I had fewer encounters with émigré historians of the second generation. The younger ones, roughly my age, were colleagues but dealt with topics different from mine. In the center of my research stood the question of why democracy in Germany had been so weak, especially seen in the light of the collapse of the Weimar Republic, which Karl Dietrich Bracher had analyzed so convincingly in his seminal book of 1955.[9] I also wanted to explore how we could identify political traditions, institutions, and ideas that could be used to create a viable democracy in the Federal Republic. I therefore concentrated my attention on the history of the German labor movement, parliamentarism, and the development of political parties. I later expanded my interests to include the emergence of the concept and practices of *Sozialstaat* and federalism in Germany. My focus was on the history of Imperial Germany, the revolution of 1918–19, and the Weimar Republic, but also on British history, which offered an example of successfully expanding parliamentary and democratic practices. Later, my interests included the history of the Federal Republic and the German unification of 1989–90. Rosenberg and Fraenkel had certainly encouraged my interest in the social, economic, and political reasons for the specific development of state and society in Germany. I never did serious research on the ideological origins of radical nationalism, Fascism and National Socialism, the National Socialist dictatorship, and the terrible consequences of the National Socialist rule in Europe. All these were topics central to the work of most emigrant historians in the second generation, understandably so given that they, as children and teenagers, had experienced the National Socialist dictatorship first hand.

I also developed close relations to American historians of Germany; among these were Gordon A. Craig, Otto Pflanze, James J. Sheehan, Margaret L. Anderson, Roger Chickering, and especially Gerald D. Feldman. For many years I collaborated with Feldman, as well as with Carl-Ludwig Holtferich and Peter-Christian Witt, in directing an international research project, initiated by Feldman, that dealt with "Inflation and Reconstruction in Germany and Europe." In contrast, my connections to those American historians who belong to the second generation of émigrés were rather sporadic.

Like many contributors to this volume, I deeply appreciated the work done by Klaus Epstein. With his seminal books on Matthias Erzberger, the leading politician of the Center Party (1959), and on *The Genesis of German Conservatism* (1966), Epstein contributed in important ways to understanding the history of political thinking and political parties in Germany. Even more influential were Epstein's substantial review essays. They contributed to publicizing in the English-speaking world the work done by the younger generation of German historians and thus helped to overcome the isolation of the historical discipline in Germany. Around 1960, Epstein and his wife visited me in Berlin during one of their many stays in Germany. I was deeply impressed by him and hoped to be able to collaborate with him in the future. I was shocked when he died in a car accident. This incident motivated me to have seat belts installed in my car long before this became a requirement by law.

I became acquainted with George L. Mosse in the late 1950s when we met by chance on a plane from Berlin to Cologne and started a conversation. I told him what I knew from my wife about the palace-like building, with a large, adjacent park, that his grandfather Rudolf Mosse had founded as an educational institution for about one hundred orphans in the Berlin neighborhood of Wilmersdorf in the 1890s. In later years, it was transformed into a home for young apprentices and, temporarily, a hospital. During the Nazi period, the building was renamed *Knesebeck Children's Hospital*. George Mosse was delighted to hear that even during that time people in Berlin continued to speak of the "Mosse Stift" (Mosse Foundation). In 1958, the city of West Berlin renamed the surrounding square "Rudolf Mosse Platz" and the adjacent street "Rudolf Mosse Street," and added a plaque commemorating Emilie and Rudolf Mosse.

Guided by my own research on the history of political ideas in sixteenth- and seventeenth-century England, I had learned a lot from Mosse's early scholarly works, alas often forgotten today, on *The Struggle for Sovereignty in England* (1950) and *The Holy Pretence* (1957), which dealt with the intellectual world of the Puritans. Of course, I also knew Mosse's more recent path-breaking studies on the *Crisis of German Ideology* (1964), the völkisch origins of National Socialism, and the *Nationalization of the Masses* (1975). I was impressed by Mosse's identification of the ideological and cultural origins of Fascism, especially of National Socialism, and his skillful use of the popular literature of the time as a source. I also appreciated his investigations into the importance of political symbols, myths, and political language. Yet, these works differed from my approach, which put more emphasis on economic and social factors, and on deficiencies of institutional effectiveness and political integration.

From the 1970s on, Mosse visited Munich regularly and did research in the Bavaria State Library. In spite of the damages caused by bombing during the Second World War, it offered Mosse the most comprehensive collection of nineteenth- and twentieth-century German publications. In 1983, I was delighted to support the initiative of Thomas Nipperdey, my colleague in Munich, to offer Mosse the first guest professorship for Jewish history at the university of Munich. Mosse succeeded as a splendid academic teacher and found a great deal of resonance among students. Much later, after Nipperdey's death, we were able to transform this guest position into a permanent, full professorship for Jewish history and culture that is held by yet another German-born, highly qualified scholar, Michael Brenner, who had made his early career in the United States.

George L. Mosse always reflected on his role as an outsider, both as a Jew and as a homosexual. After his emigration, he oscillated between his identity as an American citizen of the Midwest and a perennial emigrant.[10] For me, Mosse was primarily a fascinating conversationalist and a representative of one of the great Jewish families in pre-Nazi Germany. Still, I was aware of the profound impact he had on our profession—and of the success he enjoyed in his various capacities: as the author of many seminal books on topics already mentioned above; as the decade-long coeditor of the *Journal of Contemporary History*; and as a historian whose works reached broader audiences in the United States, but also in other countries such as Great Britain, France, Italy, Germany, and Israel.

My closest contact with émigré scholars of the second generation in the United States was not a historian but a Germanist: Egon Schwarz, whom I got to know during my time as guest professor at Washington University in St. Louis and with whom I remained in close contact ever since. Under adventurous circumstances Schwarz had escaped from Vienna in 1938. He made his way through Prague and Paris to South America, where he survived as a migrant worker for about ten years in Bolivia, Chile, and Ecuador.[11] Schwarz did not arrive in the United States until years after the end of the Second World War. In 1964, he edited, together with Matthias Wegner, the first large collection of notes by literary writers who had to emigrate from Nazi Germany and ultimately became one of the most important American interpreters of nineteenth- and early twentieth-century German and Austrian literature.[12] Like many other emigrants, Schwarz got involved in the American civil rights movement. Together with his wife, Dorle, and his three children, who were about the same ages as our sons, he made it possible for us to become quickly accustomed to life in St. Louis and to feel very much at home there. Egon Schwarz is a brilliant conversationalist and superb writer who always illuminates the historical context of those literary authors whose works he analyzes; I am indebted to him for a deeper understanding especially of Austrian literature of the Fin-de-Siècle.[13]

It was only after my retirement in 1994 that, thanks to Jürgen Kocka, I made the acquaintance of Georg Iggers, who had distinguished himself as a historian of German historiography, and finally of Fritz Stern, although I had read the works of both earlier. My reading of Stern's fascinating autobiography, *Fünf Deutschland und ein Leben* (2007), motivated me to write him a long letter. Stern, who is only three years older than I am, has had much greater impact on the general public. I provided him with some reflections on the significant differences, but also parallels in our careers. We have stayed in touch since then. Fritz Stern and I share the belief that history is always open-ended, an assumption proven by the unexpected case of German unification in 1990, and that coincidences play a role in history as well. Stern's famous dictum about Germany receiving a "second chance" after unification has deeply moved me as an expression of reconciliation, but also as a reminder of the obligation not to squander this chance.

My encounters with émigré historians of the second generation in Great Britain were mediated through academic institutions. I do not recall that I was in contact with British historians who had been born in Germany and fled the National Socialist regime when I spent two years at St. Antony's College in Oxford in 1952–54. I need to say this because this stay established a lifelong relationship with many British historians. When I organized a student excursion to Britain at the end of the 1950s, a trip nominally led by Hans Herzfeld, we visited the Wiener Library in London and I got to know Alfred Wiener and Eva Reichmann. Both left a deep impression on me, no less than on our students. I later met many émigré historians of the second generation in England[14] when I served as one of the cofounders of the German Historical Institute in London and as the deputy chairman of the institute's academic advisory board. As a member of the German board (*Kuratorium*) of the Leo Baeck Institute, I have also had for some decades a close connection with this institute's London branch.

With Francis Carstens, whom I first visited on the recommendation of Richard Löwenthal and who was almost two decades older, I shared interests in the early history of parliamentarism, specifically that of corporate estates (*Stände*) from the fifteenth to the eighteenth centuries, as well as in the history of the revolution of

1918–19 and of the German labor movement. Peter Pulzer attracted my attention through his studies about *The Rise of Political Anti-Semitism in Germany and Austria* (1964) in the period between 1867 and 1914. In later years, I was increasingly impressed by his books on the political system in Britain and especially by his analyses of politics in the Federal Republic, which he presented to the British public with great competence. For me, Pulzer exemplified the identity of an emigrant who was fully integrated in his new country, yet never dismissed his origins in the German and Austrian *Bildungsbürgertum*. When I visited him at All Souls College in Oxford, I noticed that he had pinned on the wall of his office two huge, crossed oars, an award for his particular success as a member of his college's rowing team during his study at Cambridge University.

I also developed close personal connections with Helmut Koenigsberger, who later presided over the International Commission for the History of Representative and Parliamentary Institutions. At that time, this commission was one of the very few bridges between east and west in the field of historical research. I had been interested in Koenigsberger's work since I had taught in Berlin, together with Gerhard Oesterreich, a seminar that dealt with the great Anglican theologian and political thinker Richard Hooker (c. 1554–1600.) I also met Geoffrey Elton at an international historians' congress. Together with his father, the famous historian of the ancient world, Victor Ehrenberg, Elton emigrated in 1939 to England. His superiors in the British army recommended changing his name so as to protect him in case he were to became a prisoner of war. After the war, Elton became the foremost authority in the field of British history during the Tudor era. His very positive take on an article of mine about the "Divine-Right und Prärogative der englischen Könige (1603–1640)"[15] made me proud, especially since Elton had a very critical mind. Ultimately, my research on British history, which I had initially pursued parallel to that in German history, shifted to the margins of my work. A main reason was that, in Britain, interest in publications written in German was lacking, a phenomenon grounded in a broader deficit in the command of foreign languages.

Via the German Historical Institute in London and the London branch of the Leo Baeck Institute, I also got to know Edgar J. Feuchtwanger, whose biographies of Disraeli and Gladstone I cherished; Werner E. Mosse, an exquisite scholar of Russian as well as German-Jewish history; and finally Arnold Paucker. Paucker had left Berlin in 1936. He immigrated to Palestine and arrived in England in early 1950 only after an extended stint in the British army, having served from 1941 to 1946 in the Middle East and India. In 1959, Pauker was appointed director of the London Leo Baeck Institute and, in 1970, editor of the Institute's *Yearbook*, which was instrumental in professionalizing research in the field of the history of the German Jewry. He himself focused on the history of Jewish resistance during the time of the Third Reich, a topic that had been much neglected before.

My closest professional relationship was with E. P. Hennock. He had arrived in England in early 1939 with one of the famous children's transports brokered by the Evangelical Church. An English family received him affectionately like their own son, and within a very short period of time he became completely Anglicized. Initially, his interests were geared toward urban history in England and the social meaning of religion, as well as the origins of the welfare state in Great Britain. In his research, he then repeatedly came across parallel developments in Prussia and the German empire. This led Hennock to explore more systematically the much-debated question of how much Lloyd George borrowed from the German model when he introduced welfare reforms and the concept of collective social insurance in Britain before the First World War. In his book on *British Social Reform and German Precedents: The Case of Social Insurance, 1880–1914* (1987), Hennock demonstrated that British social reforms had critically engaged with German models, yet exemplified a distinctly British strand based on liberal traditions.

Obviously, there was initially a certain scholarly rivalry between the two of us since I had also once undertaken a comparison between German and English social reforms in my book about *Sozialversicherung in Deutschland und England* (1983).[16] I emphasized commonalities and mutual influences between these two countries, next to the obvious differences. Still, the fact that our interests overlapped ultimately led to a close exchange of ideas and publications. I ultimately used a review essay to recommended Hennock's magnum opus *The Origins of the Welfare State in England and Germany, 1850–1918* (2007) to German readers.[17] We became friends, and Hennock even sent me the draft of the first chapter of his autobiography, which dealt with his childhood in Berlin. Alas, a severe sickness and his death have left these memoirs unfinished.

With regard to historians of the second generation who emigrated to Israel, my first contacts emerged from my time as the first guest professor in the spring of 1973 at the newly founded Institute for German History at Tel Aviv University, initiated by the ancient historian Zvi Yavetz. Based on this experience, I can only confirm what Shulamit Volkov writes in this volume about the German orientation of her older colleagues. After we had concluded the first session of my seminar about the "German Revolution of 1918–19," a delegation of participants approached me and requested that all succeeding sessions be held in German instead of English. Obviously, this suggestion was not triggered by any limits on my part in the command of the English language. I vividly remember this particular seminar for another reason. One of the students, a former chief medical doctor at a hospital, opened the discussion with the words, "When I compare my experience of the Russian Revolution in St. Petrograd with my witnessing the Revolution in Berlin 1918/1919, I come to the following observations." Teaching students who, with the exception of one, were all older than I was and had already had diverse professional careers under their belt was certainly a new experience for me.

That held true as well for my colleagues at the university's Institute for German History. Walter Grab is a good example. After he had to interrupt his university training in Vienna in 1938 to emigrate to Palestine, Grab worked for many years as a businessman before he resumed his academic studies at the age of forty-three; he soon became a lecturer and then a professor. He made his scholarly reputation particularly in the Federal Republic of Germany and the German Democratic Republic as a specialist on German Jacobines and early democratic movements in Germany. Grab was not a Zionist. He never fully embraced his exile in Israel after the enforced expulsion from Austria. He was brilliant in telling jokes; on those rare occasions his excellent memory failed, he used to pull out a book in which he had noted some keywords. Grab invited us to the wedding of his talented, attractive daughter; it was celebrated with about three hundred guests—a small circle as Grab emphasized. Together with her husband, a car mechanic, Grab's daughter later emigrated to Berlin.

In terms of professional interests, I worked most closely with Shlomo Na'aman. As a convinced Zionist and member of a Zionist youth organization, he had emigrated to Palestine in 1932, before the National Socialist seizure of power in Germany. Born as Hans Salomon Goldreich, he assumed in Palestine the maiden name of his mother: Treu—in Hebrew, Na'aman. In Palestine, later Israel, he was an elementary and high school teacher in kibbutzim before he began his university training at the age of forty-one. Na'aman studied geography and history, including Jewish history, at Hebrew University in Jerusalem. Following a one-year research stay at the International Institute of Social History in Amsterdam, a turning point in his life, Na'aman received his doctorate in Jerusalem in 1962 with a dissertation about Ferdinand Lassalle. At the age of fifty, he started his academic teaching at Tel Aviv University, initially as a lecturer, later as a full professor. Na'aman's work focused on the early history of the German workers movement and culminated in his profound biographies of Lassalle and Moses Hess, a study about political associations in the early Socialist movement, and the German *Nationalverein*. Though my own work concentrated on later periods, we had many interesting conversations about the continuities, rightly emphasized by him, between the labor movement in the revolution of 1848–49 and the dual founding of Socialist parties in Germany: Lassalle's *Allgemeiner Deutscher Arbeiterverein,* constituted in 1863, and the Social Democratic Workers Party of 1869, largely at the initiative of August Bebel and Wilhelm Liebknecht. I contributed a short biographical essay about Na'aman's life and oeuvre for the Festschrift that honored him on the occasion of his seventieth birthday.[18] In 1997, four years after Na'aman's death, his impressive work on *Marxism und Zionism* was published posthumously; it offered a summa of his life's work.

Shulamit Volkov, not Grab, Na'aman, or Bloch, is the Israeli scholar with whom I have maintained the closest personal and professional relationship. Herself a student of Hans Rosenberg, she belongs to the third generation of emigrants, already born in the country to which her parents emigrated but influenced in her choice of topic and her educational background by her German Jewish heritage.

Finally, I would like to comment on some differences I have noticed between the second generation of émigré historians in Great Britain and in Israel. Those in Israel often began their university studies and arrived in academia only in their midlife, often over the age of forty. In contrast, and with few exceptions, those who emigrated to England were able to begin their training and academic teaching without much delay. They were expected to adapt to the long tradition of the historical sciences in England and often began their career with studies in British history, whereas immigrants in Israel needed to establish, first and foremost, the historical discipline at their respective university, and they concentrated in their research on German history. Furthermore, émigré historians of the second generation in England could rely on the London Leo Baeck Institute as an institutional center when working on German-Jewish history. It seems that the second generation of émigré historians in Israel largely ignored the Leo Baeck Institute in Jerusalem, founded by immigrants of the first generation. Their relationship with their new home was tense at times, as in the case of Grab or—in a different way—Bloch. In contrast, identifying with the country that had received them after their immigration came rather easily to those who lived in England; they, too, did not shy away from establishing contacts with German historians early on in their careers.

For me personally, as probably for many historians in the Federal Republic who began studying at a university after the end of the Second World War, it was important to be able to meet historians who had had to leave Germany due to persecution by the National Socialist regime. In my case, these were mostly scholars from the first, rather than the second generation. It was through these emigrants that we could regain the contact with the western intellectual world and find a way into the international community of scholars.

Translated from German by Andreas W. Daum

Gerhard A. Ritter (1929-2015) was professor emeritus at the Ludwig Maximilians University in Munich and held honorary doctorates from the University of Bielefeld and the Humboldt University in Berlin. His most recent books include *Social Welfare in Germany and Britain* (1986), *Der Sozialstaat* (^{3}2010), *German Refugee Historians and Friedrich Meinecke* (2010), *The Price of German Unity: Reunification and the Crisis of the Welfare State* (2011), and *Hans-Dietrich*

Genscher, das Auswärtige Amt und die deutsche Vereinigung (2013). In 2007 he received the *Deutscher Historikerpreis*.

Notes

1. Gerhard A. Ritter, *Die Arbeiterbewegung im Wilhelminischen Reich. Die Sozialdemokratische Partei und die Freien Gewerkschaften 1890–1900*. 2nd ed. (Berlin, 1963).
2. Gerhard A. Ritter, *Der Sozialstaat. Entstehung und Entwicklung im internationalen Vergleich* (Munich, 1989); a third edition was published in 2010.
3. The second edition included a *new preface* and was published under the title *Die Weltwirtschaftskrise 1857–1859* (Göttingen, 1974).
4. On 5 January 1947, Rosenberg had sent Meinecke a detailed table of contents and mentioned that he was working on the thirteenth of ultimately fifteen chapters in the hope of finishing the manuscript during the summer of 1947. The manuscript is to be found in the Rosenberg Papers at the Bundesarchiv (Federal Archives) in Koblenz. See Gerhard A. Ritter, ed., *German Refugee Historians and Friedrich Meinecke: Letters and Documents, 1910–1977* (Leiden, 2010), 380–82; and idem, "Hans Rosenberg," *Geschichte und Gesellschaft* 15 (1989): 292–93.
5. Ritter, *German Refugee Historians*, 330–447; also see Gerhard A. Ritter, ed., *Entstehung und Wandel der modernen Gesellschaft. Festschrift für Hans Rosenberg* (Berlin, 1970), v–x.
6. Ernst Fraenkel, *The Dual State: A Contribution to the Theory of Dictatorship* (New York, 1941); the book was published in German under the title *Der Doppelstaat. Recht und Justiz im "Dritten Reich"* (Frankfurt/M., 1974).
7. See Douglas G. Morris, "The Dual State Reframed: Ernst Fraenkel's Political Clients and His Theory of the Nazi Legal System," *Leo Baeck Institute Yearbook* 58 (2013): 1–17. This essay is a partial publication of a much longer study on Fraenkel and his close contacts with the early resistance against National Socialism during the years 1933 to 1938. I thank Douglas Morris for granting me access to his profound study.
8. A collection of these essays was published under the title *Deutschland und die westlichen Demokratien* (Stuttgart, 1964).
9. Karl Dietrich Bracher, *Die Auflösung der Weimarer Republik. Eine Studie zum Problem des Machtverfalls in der Demokratie* (Villingen, 1955); a sixth edition was published as a paperback in 1978.
10. George L. Mosse, *Confronting History: A Memoir* (Madison, WI, 2000), 6.
11. For these early years, see Egon Schwarz, *Keine Zeit für Eichendorff. Chronik unfreiwilliger Wanderjahre* (Königstein i. Ts., 1979). The Büchergilde Gutenberg published a new edition in 1992 with a postscript and an essay by Hans-Albert Walter. There is now another new edition, with a postscript by Uwe Timm, published as *Unfreiwillige Wanderjahre. Auf der Flucht vor Hitler durch drei Kontinente* (Munich, 2005).
12. Egon Schwarz and Matthias Wegner, eds., *Verbannung. Aufzeichnungen deutscher Schriftsteller im Exil* (Hamburg 1964).
13. Egon Schwarz, *Wien und die Juden. Essays zum Fin de Siècle* (Munich, 2014).
14. See Peter Alter, ed., *Out of the Third Reich: Refugee Historians in Post-War Britain* (London, 1998).
15. Published in *Historische Zeitschrift* 196 (1963): 584–625; reprinted with slight changes in Gerhard A. Ritter, *Parlament und Demokratie in Großbritannien. Studien zur Entwicklung und Struktur des politischen Systems* (Göttingen, 1972), 11–58.

16. Published in an expanded English translation as *Social Welfare in Germany and Britain: Origins and Development* (Leamington Spa, UK, 1986).
17. Gerhard A. Ritter, "Die Ursprünge des Sozialstaats in Deutschland und England vor dem Ersten Weltkrieg," *Geschichte und Gesellschaft* 34 (2008): 292–300.
18. Gerhard A. Ritter, "Shlomo Na'aman als Historiker der deutschen Arbeiterbewegung," in Hans-Peter Harstick, Arno Herzig, and Hans Pelger, eds., *Arbeiterbewegung und Geschichte. Festschrift für Shlomo Na'aman zum 70. Geburtstag* (Trier, 1983), 9–19.

Chapter 21

INFLUENCES
A Personal Comment

Jürgen Kocka

By persecuting, expelling, and murdering Jewish scholars and intellectuals in the 1930s and 1940s, Germany inflicted not only unprecedented suffering upon millions of human beings but also did immeasurable damage to its own social and cultural life. It was a profound intellectual and moral self-mutilation with detrimental consequences lasting to this day. Conversely, many of the victims of this persecution who survived the Nazi dictatorship, the Holocaust, and the World War in the United States, Britain, and other host countries have greatly contributed to the reconstruction of Germany after 1945. This is certainly true of many historians among the refugee scholars of the first and second generations[1] in the United States who had fled Nazi Germany as adults or as children, but maintained or rebuilt relations with their country of origin. They contributed to the development of the historical profession not only in the United States, but also in Germany—for example, by influencing younger German historians whose views and convictions were shaped in the decades after 1945. I want to illustrate this by referring to my personal experiences as a student in the 1960s and a teacher in the 1970s.

After studying political science at the University of North Carolina at Chapel Hill during the academic year of 1964–65,[2] I traveled across the country and used a short stay on the West Coast to visit Hans Rosenberg. I had heard about him and his work from Gerhard A. Ritter, with whom I had been studying at the Free University in Berlin from 1962. Gerhard A. Ritter had belonged to a group of students (among them Otto Büsch, Gerhard Schulz, and Gilbert Ziebura) whom Rosenberg had deeply influenced when he was a visiting professor in

---

Notes from this chapter begin on page 323.

West Berlin in 1949–50. In the following decades Ritter became a central figure in the development of social history in the Federal Republic by working on the history of the German labor movement and training more social historians of the next generation than anyone else. He greatly appreciated Rosenberg's outstanding work and the innovative impulses and transmitted this appreciation to his students, including me. Now, in 1965, traveling to California, I had the privilege of meeting Hans Rosenberg at Berkeley and was invited to his house in El Cerrito. I met him often in the following years when his influence in West Germany had become enormous, particularly after his *Grosse Depression und Bismarckzeit* appeared in 1967. I remember how the galley proofs of this seminal book circulated among us graduate students in Berlin. It deeply influenced my dissertation on the history of white-collar workers and management of the Siemens Company (1969), just as it influenced scholars such as Hans-Ulrich Wehler, Hans-Jürgen Puhle, and others. It was the type of social history which found its home at the University of Bielefeld in the early 1970s. Clearly, Hans Rosenberg's approach to social history (in a very broad sense of the word), his ability to integrate theories offered by the systematic social sciences, his critical view of the history of German elites in comparative perspective, and his scholarship in general shaped my understanding of historical studies as well as that of many others of the so-called "Bielefeld School" during the 1970s and 1980s. He is rightly seen as one of the founding fathers of West German social history.[3]

That same year (1965), I met Ernst Borinski at Tougaloo College, located in the northern outskirts of Jackson, Mississippi. Born into a Jewish family in Kattowitz in 1901, he had studied and practiced law in the Weimar Republic. He had also developed close contacts with German Social Democrats and became active in adult education programs—for example, by teaching Labor Law to workers of the Zeiss firm in Jena. He got out of Germany in 1938, reached the United States after a long waiting period in Havana, served in the American army, and then received an M.A. in sociology and education from the University of Chicago in 1946 and later a Ph.D. in sociology from the University of Pittsburgh. The American Missionary Association helped him to get a job at Tougaloo College, a historically black private college founded in 1869, where he taught sociology (as well as German and Russian) between 1947 and 1983. He became not only a major figure in providing higher education and professional training to a large number of African-Americans, but also a strong supporter of civil rights and desegregation. By 1964–65, Tougaloo had become a center of the civil rights movement in the South. On an excursion from Chapel Hill through the South, I happened to meet Ernst Borinski, who invited me to teach a German language course to Tougaloo students in the summer of 1965. These months were a formative period for me: I learned a great deal about the United States, about the problems and the strengths of this country, and I became an admirer of Ernst Borinski. He used his position of "multiple marginality"—this is how he described his status as a white person in a predominantly black community, as a Jew among Christians, and as someone from abroad with a heavy German accent—for doing immensely beneficial educational work which emerged from his legendary "social science laboratory" in the basement of an old wooden building on campus. Ernst Borinski brought the academic world to this then still relatively isolated place. He served not only as an influential supporter of the civil rights movement, but also as a bridge builder between the African-American and the (slowly changing) white communities. He compared his situation as a Jew in Germany with the racial constellation in the American South. To some extent, his educational and political work at Tougaloo seemed to be inspired by his experience as a Social Democratic activist in adult education at Erfurt and Jena in the 1920s and early 1930s. Ernst Borinski, with whom I stayed in close contact, deeply influenced my views of the United States, including my appreciation of the remarkable capability of this country to make use of the talents and the energy of refugee scholars during a deep domestic crisis and its gradual resolution.[4]

I met Georg and Wilma Iggers, an academic couple who had also taught in the South, in the early 1970s, when I was still a *Wissenschaftlicher Assistent* (research assistant) at the University of Münster. Georg Iggers's *The German Conception of History: The National Tradition of Historical Thought from Herder to the Present*, published in 1967, had offered a sharp criticism of "Historismus," that is, of the historiographical paradigm from which the strand of social history with which I identified also tried to distance itself programmatically and practically. I have learned a lot from Georg Iggers's work about the methodology and the history of historical studies. Since the 1970s, he keenly observed and critically commented upon the developments and fresh departures in the study and the writing of history, first on a European and Western, then finally on a global, scale. He had great sympathy for the social history we tried to develop, especially in Berlin and Bielefeld.[5] In the 1980s, we cooperated on joint projects, such as the history and culture of the nineteenth-century European bourgeoisie. Georg Iggers has done more than anyone else to make new developments in German historiography—in both West and East—internationally known. He strongly influenced the way in which German social history, especially its Berlin-Bielefeld variety, was perceived in other parts of the world, especially in the United States. By presenting our case to international audiences, he continuously helped to shape it.[6]

It was at the World Congress of Historians in San Francisco in 1975 that I met Fritz Stern for the first time. We tried to get a document accepted by the Congress in favor of more freedom of research and expression for historians in Eastern Europe. Major works by Fritz Stern in that period—*The Politics of Cultural Despair* (1963), *The Failure of Illiberalism* (1973), *Gold and Iron* (1977)—have substantially contributed to a critical and balanced interpretation of German history before Hitler. I had read his texts as attempting to develop, in the field of intellectual and cultural history, a view that some of us in Germany tried to practice in social history. I have used Fritz Stern's collection *The Varieties of History* throughout my professional life, from its first edition in 1956 to the most recent revised and enlarged German edition that he published together with Jürgen Osterhammel in 2011. Over the years and decades, I have had the privilege of close contact and numerous conversations with Fritz Stern. I have learned a lot from him. He has succeeded, more than most others, in combining his professional work as a historian with the role of an intellectual who regularly intervenes in public debates on political, historical, and moral issues. He practices a specific form of *histoire engagée* which, in other ways, was also practiced by some German historians who were sympathetic to critical social history.[7]

Georg Iggers and Fritz Stern were born in Hamburg and Breslau respectively in the same year (1926) and had to leave Germany as young boys. They clearly belong to the second generation of refugee scholars from Germany. Though very different in many ways, their publications and interventions have focused on German culture and politics, past and present, in broader contexts and viewed from a liberal point of view. Their work as scholars of history and their lives as citizens have been intertwined, and both of them have pondered this interconnection intensively. In the 1960s, 1970s, and 1980s, they significantly contributed to the emergence of a critical interpretation of modern German history in which the Nazi period loomed large as a fundamental problem and as a structuring point of reference, but did not dominate their analysis as a whole. Comparisons with the U.S.A. and other Western countries, implicitly or explicitly, helped to structure their views, but they were far from glorifying the United States or the West as an impeccable model beyond criticism. Both of them combine historical reconstruction with an evaluation of present-day developments. Their comments—at once critical and encouraging—have received much attention and great respect in the historical profession and beyond.

I could comment on other refugee scholars who have influenced me in that period: Ernst Fraenkel, whose writings and lectures in the early 1960s did much to shape my views of a German *Sonderweg* in the sense of a "German divergence from the West"; Fritz Redlich, the non-Jewish and relatively conservative economic historian (an émigré, not a refugee scholar) from whom I learned much in the field of entrepreneurial history during my stay at Harvard in 1969–71; Felix Gilbert, who invited me to the Princeton Institute of Advanced Study in the mid-1970s and who was one of the very few persons I know who found the architecture of Bielefeld University beautiful when he saw it for the first time; Albert Hirschman, who discussed with me the relationship between capitalism and fascism; George Mosse, Peter Gay, and, later, Egon Schwarz and others.

Certainly, these were and are very different individuals, representing different opinions, methods, and messages. But all these scholars resembled one another in their ability to connect—though again in very different forms and amalgamations—European, especially German, traditions and an interest in Europe, especially in Germany, on the one hand, with formative experiences in the United States, in American universities, and in education, as well as with American ways of life, on the other. To visitors like me, they appeared to be Europeans and Americans at the same time. When they wrote and spoke about German history, they did so from a position in which familiarity and distance balanced each other: it was a combination that is favorable for historical understanding and analysis.

The comparative perspective was built into their biographies: the difference between Germany and their host country had literally saved their lives. Being deeply shaped by their experience of the Nazi period in a repressive and damaging—or at least deeply challenging—way, they brought specific wisdom, knowledge, and legitimacy to an intensifying transatlantic discourse among historians in which the Nazi period with its dictatorship, war, and genocide was increasingly recognized not only as a catastrophic "Zivilisationsbruch" (rupture of civilization) but also as a decisive period of reference which could structure major narratives of German, Jewish, European, and even world history.

While German at least by origin, these historians stood for a scholarly culture that was not yet well established in Germany in the third quarter of the twentieth century: a relatively cosmopolitan, open, liberal, and democratic, modern culture of scholarship, which was not the rule in German institutions of the time and which fascinated not only me but also many other scholars in the Federal Republic. It was my experience that refugee scholars were likely to support those of us who were engaged in developing certain critical approaches to modern German history and in practicing new departures and attempts at modernizing historical studies. They offered support on the basis of their research and writing, and—perhaps even more importantly—by using their status in the international academic community to give recognition and encouragement. In contrast to the period after World War I, the German historical profession (in the Federal Republic) has opened itself up to the West after World War II. Refugee scholars have substantially contributed to this and to the emerging connections. There is much reason to be grateful.

Jürgen Kocka taught modern history, especially German social and comparative history since the eighteenth century, in Bielefeld (1973–1988) and at the Free University of Berlin (1988–2009). He is a permanent fellow of the International Research Center "Work and Lifecycle in Global Historical Perspective" at the Humboldt University Berlin. His publications include *Facing Total War: German Society 1914–1918* (1984), *Industrial Culture and Bourgeois Society: Business, Labor, and Bureaucracy in Modern Germany* (1999), *Civil Society and Dictatorship in Modern German History* (2010), and *Capitalism: A Short History* (English edition 2016).

Notes

1. For this distinction, see Andreas Daum's introduction to this volume.
2. I had successfully applied for the position of a graduate assistant advertised at the Berlin Otto-Suhr-Institut by the political scientist Charles B. Robson of the University of North Carolina, Chapel Hill. Robson had come to Berlin with the American army in 1945, where he served as a reeducation officer. Afterwards, he kept in touch with German developments and helped to bring German students to his university.
3. See Gerhard A. Ritter, "Hans Rosenberg 1904–1988," *Geschichte und Gesellschaft* 15 (1989): 282–302; Philipp Stelzel, "Rethinking Modern German History: Critical Social History as a Transatlantic Enterprise, 1945–1989." Ph.D. diss., University of North Carolina, Chapel Hill, 2010, ch. 4.
4. See Maria Lowe, "An Unseen Hand: The Role of Sociology Professor Ernst Borinski in Mississippi's Struggle for Racial Integration in the 1950s and 1960s," *Leadership* 4 (2008): 27–47, http://lea.sagepub.com/content/4/1/27, accessed at SUNY Buffalo 18 February 2013; Donald Cunnigen, "The Legacy of Ernst Borinski: Production of an African-American Sociological Tradition," *Teaching Sociology* 31 (October 2003): 397–411. Borinski was not the only refugee scholar landing in a southern black college. See Gabrielle S. Edgcomb, *From Swastika to Jim Crow: Refugee Scholars at Black Colleges* (Malabar, FL, 1993).
5. On the notion of a Berlin-Bielefeld school of social history, see Jürgen Kocka, "Wandlungen der Sozial- und Gesellschaftsgeschichte am Beispiel Berlins 1949 bis 2005," in Jürgen Osterhammel et al., eds., *Wege der Gesellschaftsgeschichte*, special issue, *Geschichte und Gesellschaft* 22 (Göttingen, 2006), 11–31.
6. E.g., Georg G. Iggers, *New Directions in European Historiography* (Middletown, CT, 1975). See Georg and Wilma Iggers, *Two Lives in Uncertain Times: Facing the Challenges of the 20th Century as Scholars and Citizens* (New York, 2006).
7. Fritz Stern, *Five Germanies I Have Known* (New York, 2006); Fritz Stern and Jürgen Osterhammel, eds., *Moderne Historiker. Klassische Texte von Voltaire bis zur Gegenwart,* rev. and enlarged ed. (Munich, 2011); Gangolf Hübinger, "Fritz Stern zwischen Europa und Amerika. Eine Fallstudie zum Geschichts-Intellektuellen," in Peter Bursche et al., eds., *Intellektuelle im Exil* (Göttingen, 2011), 219–40.

Part V

BIOBIBLIOGRAPHIC GUIDE

Chapter 22

ÉMIGRÉS IN THE HISTORICAL DISCIPLINES
Research Perspectives

Andreas W. Daum

The biobibliographic guide that concludes this volume also marks a beginning. For the first time, it provides a substantial database of those historians in North America who were born in German-speaking Europe and escaped, in their early years, the Third Reich. The 107 biographies compiled in chapter 23 feature each individual in detail. They document the émigrés' origins, migration, university education, professional career, scholarly oeuvre, and public appreciation.

Goals

While this guide cannot be comprehensive, it does enable us to move beyond the scattered references to second-generation émigrés currently available in the secondary literature.[1] The biographies include prominent historians as well as others who are less well known. It puts into context scholars whose writings became important reference points for historians in the transatlantic world, and it helps to rediscover dramatis personae and works we have forgotten. The collected data therefore both serve as a companion to this volume and create a platform for future research.

Specifically, the information provided aims at gaining a more nuanced understanding of the enforced brain drain from Nazi Germany and, in particular, of the youngest cohort of refugees with their often extended, transnational migrations—a historical subject we are only beginning to explore. This guide also connects the intellectual history of historiography with the sociological profile of

---

Notes from this chapter begin on page 336.

those who undertook historical research; as such, it wants to contribute to a social history of historiography. The biographical data might help us in understanding better the development of the historical disciplines in the post–World War II era as well as the extent to which academic institutions in the United States and Canada were receptive to refugees from Nazi Europe, who in the overwhelming majority were of Jewish background.

Furthermore, detailed biographical information contributes to charting the transnational landscape of scholarship in the decades following the Second World War. Information about fellowships, the translations of English-language publications, guest lectures, book prizes, visiting professorships in other countries, etc., all add to our understanding of how historians have acted in multiple public spheres since the mid-twentieth century. By establishing links and networks among academic institutions and scholars worldwide, they have fueled the transnational traffic of ideas across state and cultural borders, especially between North America, England, Central Europe, and Israel.

Finally, this guide situates the life stories of historians in the history of the twentieth and early twenty-first centuries at large. It provides a starting point to investigate how the personal experiences, cross-border migrations, and intellectual journeys of professional observers of history intersected with the history of the "Dark Continent" (Mark Mazower's term for twentieth-century Europe) as much as with that of the United States and of the transatlantic world. Specifically, we can use this information to research further the impact that the Cold War era—which included pressure for political conformity no less than a new social dynamic alongside the rise of feminism and other social movements—and the ensuing decades had on the writing of history. The collected data also attest to the extent to which our post–World War II and post–Cold War societies have acknowledged traditions of emigration and how these relate to the political climate of the time.

Selection Criteria

This guide neither creates an ideal type, in Max Weber's definition, nor an essentialist definition of the "émigré" as a historical persona or a "generation" as a biological category.[2] Instead, it uses eight criteria to define a heterogeneous sample of individuals who, in the overwhelming majority of cases,

- were German-speaking, even if not exclusively, and lived in the realm of the National Socialist regime prior to the outbreak of the Second World War
- escaped—and were forced to leave—the Nazi-dominated territories of Central Europe because of this regime's increasing terror and practices of exclusion
- primarily faced racial discrimination targeting them as Jews

- left at a young age—that is, as children, teenagers, and young adults, born mostly between 1918 and 1935
- departed in the years 1933 to 1941
- gained their first academic degree as well as a Ph.D. in history, or a closely related field, only after their emigration
- contributed to the study of history, at least for some time during their professional life, through academic research and teaching, university service, library and archival work, publications, or other activities
- worked as historians in the United States and Canada, or spent at least a substantial portion of their careers in North America.

However, some flexibility in applying these criteria is needed to capture the dynamics of individual life and the historical complexity of emigration, expulsion, and ensuing acculturation in a new environment. In cases of doubt, we have opted to be as inclusive as possible. This seemed particularly appropriate in dealing with individuals who became victims of a racial thinking that put antisemitism at center stage, yet was often terminologically imprecise and arbitrary. Furthermore, we have come across a very small number of émigrés to whom most of the criteria mentioned above apply, but who were either not prompted to leave Germany because they faced (racial) discrimination, or could emigrate without the pressure of immediate terror and theoretically with the option of returning without risking their life.[3] It is important to note the distinction between refugees and, in a strict sense, nonrefugees. But even then we cannot always easily draw the dividing line. How to categorize a student who entered the United States to study at an American university, but remained in the country because he or she was appalled by the occurrences in Germany? Again, we opted to include such cases.

With these criteria in mind, we arrived at a sample of 107 individuals; Tables 1 and 2 in my introductory chapter in this volume provide an overview. Twenty (c. 19 percent) are female, as opposed to nine out of ninety-eight (c. 9 percent) in the sample of the older, first-generation émigré historians that Catherine Epstein put together two decades ago and that we have supplemented by adding ten names; see Table 3, also in the introductory chapter. Apart from Alma M. Luckau Molin, who came to the United States with a student visa in the late Weimar years, Theodore Hamerow, who joined his parents in New York City in 1930, and Agnes F. Peterson, who went to Switzerland in 1932, all but two of the individuals featured in chapter 23 left Germany between January 1933 and 1941: Herbert A. Strauss studied at the *Hochschule für die Wissenschaft des Judentums* (College for the Scholarly Study of Judaism) in Berlin until the Nazis shut it down in 1942. He then went underground together with Lotte Schloss, his soon-to-be wife. In 1943, Strauss managed to escape to Switzerland, where he received his doctorate in 1946. In the same year, he immigrated to the United States. Henry Friedlander was deported from Berlin to the Łódź ghetto in 1941.

After three years, he was sent to Auschwitz-Birkenau and subsequently to other camps and subcamps; he came to the United States in 1947.

With these two notable exceptions, this guide does not include individuals who left German-speaking Europe for North America after the end of World War II. Uta-Renate Blumenthal, Jurgen Herbst, Konrad H. Jarausch, Arno W. F. Kolz, Karl Wilhelm Luckert, Ernest A. Menze, Johanna Menzel Meskill, Dietrich Orlow, Diethelm Prowe, Fritz K. Ringer, and Gerald Stourzh belong to this cohort, as do Peter Hoffmann, Michael H. Kater, and Annelise Thimme, who settled in postwar Canada. Nor have we included persons whose date of emigration we could not verify or for whom we could only find little relevant information.[4]

The biographies document individuals who left the realm of National Socialist rule as defined geographically by the borders of the German Reich prior to the German invasion of Poland on 1 September 1939. This definition includes Austria, which became a part of the German Reich after the so-called *Anschluss*—that is, the annexation—of the Austrian territories in March 1938.[5] Included, too, are those territories that the National Socialist regime appropriated by annexing parts of Czechoslovakia following the Munich Agreements of September 1938, specifically its border regions with a significant number of German speakers (*Sudetenland*), and by annexing the Memel Territories in March 1939. The guide also includes individuals from the so-called Reich Protectorate of Bohemia and Moravia, which the Nazis also created in March 1939 by destroying what the Munich Agreements had left of Czechoslovakia. Yet, the complicated ethnic mix and the no-less-complicated history of family connections and cross-border migrations across Central Europe made clear-cut distinctions at times impossible.

Chapter 23 does not feature individuals who were born, or spent most of their youth, in Italy and the countries that the German military invaded after 1939. Poland, where the historian Richard Pipes was born, Luxembourg, the home state of Arno J. Mayer, and the Netherlands belong to this group of countries. So does France, where Saul Friedländer, born in Prague, survived the German occupation and where the political scientist Stanley Hoffmann, who was born in Vienna, grew up. We refrain, too, from documenting individuals born in Denmark, Norway, Greece, and Yugoslavia, from where Ivo John Lederer, born in Zagreb, escaped as a boy. German-speaking emigrants from Hungary were not included either. Last, but not least, this guide applies a broad definition of North America and includes individuals who emigrated to or settled for good in Canada later in life.

History and Other Disciplines

Whom does this data collection regard as a historian? It concentrates on those men and women who sought to acquire a doctorate in the historical studies, with various regional foci. We include those few who had enrolled at a German or Austrian university prior to their emigration. As demonstrated in my introductory, the second-generation émigrés immersed themselves into a broad range of fields and themes. Our documentation includes some doctoral students who nominally graduated in neighboring disciplines (political science, government) as long as their topics were clearly historical.

Casting the net widely means acknowledging in particular the increasingly close relationship between post–world War II historiography and the social sciences. This interaction characterized important branches of postwar political science and political philosophy. A number of first-generation German émigrés, especially Hannah Arendt, Ernst Fraenkel, Carl J. Friedrich, and Franz L. Neumann, exemplified this intellectual dynamic. Across the disciplines, these scholars profoundly influenced contemporaries in their analysis of the National Socialist regime. Leo Strauss may have had an even broader, though more diffuse, intellectual impact on the postwar generation. Karl W. Deutsch is often regarded as belonging to the first generation of émigrés, though he left Czechoslovakia for the United States in 1938 after the completion of his doctorate in Prague. Like Eric Voegelin and Hans Morgenthau, he had a lasting impact on many historians and political scientists. Harry H. Eckstein, Guenter Lewy, and Curt F. Beck, the son of Ann Frank Beck who is featured in our biographies, belong to the second generation of émigrés who taught political science.[6]

It would be easy to expand the list of the scholars with an émigré background by looking at other academic fields. There were those émigrés of the first generation who adopted varied Marxist intellectual positions and are often grouped together under the label "Frankfurt School": Herbert Marcuse, Leo Löwenthal, and Theodor Adorno.[7] The economist-philosopher Albert O. Hirschman, who was born in Berlin and received his doctorate in Europe, stands between the generations as much as between the disciplines. Among those who immigrated to the United States prior to completing a doctorate we find Reinhard Bendix, Lewis A. Coser, Herbert J. Gans, and Manfred Wolfson in the field of sociology, as well as Herbert C. Kelman, an exponent of social psychology. This cohort includes the archaeologist Karl W. Butzer, the feminist economist Marianne A. Ferber, the legal scholar Gerald Gunther, and Leon A. Feldman, who concentrated on the study of Hebraic culture. W. Michael Blumenthal fled Germany in 1939 and spent the war years in China. He studied economics, had an illustrious career in both the private and the public sectors, including a stint as the United States secretary of the treasury from 1977 to 1979, and served as the director of the Jewish Museum in Berlin from 1997 to 2014.[8]

Refugee scholars of the first generation contributed in significant ways to the discipline of art history in the United States, with Erwin Panofsky as the most prominent figure. Several of the second generation of émigrés entered this field as well, or became museum curators, including Colin T. Eisler, Lorenz Eitner,

Philipp Fehl, Tom L. Freudenheim, Joseph Gutman, Howard Saalmann, and Peter Selz. The study of Romance cultures occupied émigrés of the second generation as well, including Claude K. Abraham, Max Bach, Arthur Bieler, Gerda R. Blumenthal, Edward Glaser, Wolfgang W. Holdheim, John W. Kronick, Paul A. Mankin, Karl-Ludwig Selig, and Albert Sonnenfeld.[9]

Not surprisingly, in the broad area of German studies we encounter many scholars who fled the Third Reich early in their lives, including Dorrit Cohn, Peter Heller, Wilma A. Iggers, Herbert Lederer, Michael Metzger, Henry H. H. Remak, Peter Salm, Egon Schwarz, Walter H. Sokel, Guy Stern, and Harry Zohn. Among the literary historians, too, there are émigrés who held an academic position in more than one country, such as Hans Eichner, who went from England to Canada in 1950; Erich Heller, who taught first in England, then in the United States; and Hans S. Reiss, who taught in Ireland, Canada, and England. Peter Demetz, born in Prague in 1922, one of America's most prominent scholars of German literature, came to the United States in 1952.[10]

Unless otherwise noted, most of the 107 scholars listed in the ensuing biographies taught in departments of history. Yet, confining our picture to these, and to university faculty alone, would underestimate the field's heterodoxy as well as the diversity of the career paths chosen by young émigrés after the completion of a Ph.D. We therefore intentionally include historians with a modest publication record or no book publications at all, as well as seven individuals who never acquired a doctorate[11] and others who worked primarily as academic librarians, bibliographers, or translators, in the private sector, or in state service. Here we depart from the more restricted criteria Catherine Epstein applied in her compilation of first-generation émigrés.[12] Moreover, both a sole focus on history departments and the exclusion of less-published historians would have disproportionately bypassed women.

Research Traditions and New Perspectives

Our collection of biographies is indebted to two standard works in the field which are very different in scope and based on dramatically different resources. A generation ago, in 1983, the last of the three-volume *International Biographical Dictionary of Central European Émigrés 1933–1945* (hereafter IBDCEE) was published.[13] The IBDCEE emerged from a decade-long collaborative project that involved institutions and scholars on both sides of the Atlantic. It relied on the resources of the Research Foundation for Jewish Immigration in New York and of the Institute of Contemporary History in Munich, then under the leadership of Martin Broszat. After Willy Brandt's election as chancellor in 1969, the planners of the IBDCEE capitalized on a political climate in the Federal Republic of Germany that had become receptive to the idea of researching the life of emigrants from Nazi Germany.[14]

The IBDCEE remains unsurpassed in its depth, precision, and the sheer volume of information it provides. It covers the entire range of academic and artistic disciplines as well as a long list of political refugees and other emigrants, totaling approximately eighty-seven hundred biographies. Historians form only a small segment of the IBDCEE, and they are not singled out as such. Yet, the IBDCEE offers a starting point for scholars interested not only in the history of emigration from the Third Reich, but also in the transnational traffic of people and knowledge in the twentieth century. Herbert A. Strauss, the driving force behind the IBDCEE, himself belonged to the cohort of émigrés documented in our volume.

Ten years after the IBDCEE became available in its entirety, Catherine Epstein concluded her ground-breaking *Catalogue of German-Speaking Refugee Historians in the United States after 1933*. Her work was supported by the German Historical Institute (GHI) in Washington, DC. It must be read in conjunction with a volume on refugee historians, entitled *An Interrupted Past*, that Hartmut Lehmann and James J. Sheehan had published a couple of years earlier.[15] Both publications placed the history of émigré historians into the center of a critical review of the historiography of Germany. In the meantime, new reference works and biographic guides, in addition to a growing number of specialized monographs and collected volumes, have given us a better understanding of emigrants from other professions.[16]

Our volume's contribution to this discussion has its origins in the conference on second-generation émigrés that took place in May 2012 and coincided with the twenty-fifth anniversary of the GHI in Washington, DC.[17] In its aftermath, my main objective was to expand the initial, small set of biographies to create a broad and reliable database. Lacking institutional support, its results are necessarily more focused than its two predecessors, the IBDCEE and Epstein's *Catalogue*, and it does not replicate any of the entries in Epstein's catalogue.[18] Soon it became clear that we needed to move from documenting those whom we recalled to finding those whom our memory had bypassed and who are only sparsely documented. This led to a systematic search during which we drew on a plethora of sources and verified all relevant information through various forms of cross-checking. Some biographical dictionaries and electronic databases allowed us to identify the birth place and year of individuals born in Europe who later became historians.[19] We consulted autobiographical testimonies, original dissertation manuscripts, obituaries, entries in departmental and alumni newsletters, prefaces and acknowledgments in book publications, college catalogues, archival materials, published U.S. census records, and other sources. Personal inquiries to members of the second generation, their family members and colleagues—and the impressive generosity in sharing information on the part of all of them—greatly helped in this process. Many of these inquiries led to extensive correspondences, in several cases also to personal conversations. Ultimately, around seventy individuals could be added in the second phase of research.

The biographies are presented in a template designed expressly for this volume. The first line displays the full name, including middle name and additional first names. The first paragraph tells the reader when and where the person was born and whether he or she has passed away. It mentions whether the person's birth name was different, wherever we could verify this information, and provides the names of the parents (including the maiden name of the mother, where available) as well as the main stops in the often extended migration to America. The second paragraph features the major steps in the individual's education (undergraduate and graduate degrees, doctorate) and professional career—that is, the positions held at various institutions, supplemented by the years of military service where applicable. The third paragraph, entitled "Ad Personam," highlights major awards, fellowships, visiting professorships, guest lectures, book prizes, and professional activities, all in chronological order. This paragraph ends with a note, where applicable, on relevant archival holdings, *Festschriften*, and autobiographical texts other than those published as a book.

The final paragraph lists in chronological order selected English- and German-language publications by title and publication year, and it includes information about other foreign-language editions. The confines of space made it necessary to focus on books, monographs and edited volumes (plus, in some cases, issues of scholarly journals edited by the author) with more than fifty pages. This limitation cannot do justice to the fact that the historians documented here published essays, articles, book chapters, and book reviews. Future researchers may easily expand the publication list with the help of modern catalogues. The selected bibliography in chapter 24 documents relevant reference works, source materials, autobiographical texts, and secondary literature.

Acknowledgments

My warm thanks go to a number of individuals who have supported this research project from its inception on: James J. Sheehan and Hartmut Lehmann, who offered thoughtful comments; Volker Berghahn, who provided substantial advice and encouragement; Catherine Epstein and Gerhard L. Weinberg, who kindly shared their expertise with me; and, last but not least, Georg Iggers, my predecessor at the State University of New York, and Wilma Iggers, both sources that never run dry of information about the history of European culture. Sincere thanks, too, are due to all authors of this volume who gave additional feedback, as well as to Uta-Renate Blumenthal, Arno W. F. Kolz, Eduard A. Menze, Johanna Meskill, and the late Diethelm Prowe for providing information about their immigration to the United States after World War II. I would like to extend my thanks to Perry E. Beardsley, April Kiser, Axel Steensen, and Friederike Steensen for their assistance at the beginning of this project. Sherry L. Föhr deserves special thanks for her willingness to engage fully with it from the second phase on; our endeavor greatly benefited from her broad expertise as a bicultural historian.

In preparing our collection of data, Sherry Föhr and I contacted all individuals who could still be reached and asked them to review our drafts. We owe sincere thanks for generously sharing information to Walter L. Arnstein, Abraham Ascher, Susan G. Bell, Eric Boehm, Renate Bridenthal, Gert H. Brieger, Peter M. Buzanski, Henry Feingold, Erich Gruen, Werner Gundersheimer, Gerald J. Holston, Henry Huttenbach, Georg and Wilma Iggers, Gerd Korman, Walter Laqueur, Guenter Lewy, Peter Loewenberg, Michael A. Meyer, Peter Paret, Theodore Rabb, Conrad Schirokauer, Ismar Schorsch, Fritz Stern, Renée Watkins, Gerhard Weinberg, and Dora B. Weiner.

We would like to thank sincerely the numerous family members, former colleagues, and acquaintances of the second-generation émigrés, as well as colleagues, librarians, and archivists who provided important information necessary to amend the biographical entries, especially Cheryl Adams, Peter Arnade, Tim Arnade, Curt F. Beck, Ron Boehm, Barbara Bono, James J. Bono, James Brophy, Suzanne Brown-Fleming, John C. Burnham, Dugal Campbell, Susan Carr, Tom Cheetham, Charles d'Aniello, Peter Dennis, Paul Elovitz, William Epstein, Richard W. Etulain, Brian Fay, Marc Föcking, Roger des Forges, Amy Garrett, David A. Gerber, Carol Gould, Atina Grossmann, Roswitha Haas, Eleanor Hancock, Dorothy O. Helly, Johannes Helmrath, Thomas Hertfelder, Margaret Hughes, Polina E. Ilieva, Andrew Johnston, Marion A. Kaplan, Peter J. Katzenstein, Andreas Killen, Elizabeth von Klemperer, James von Klemperer, Georg Nicolaus Knauer, Sally G. Kohlstedt, Arno R. Kolz, John Kovach, Margo Kren, Remmert Laan, Willem Laan, Merel Leeman, Marjorie Lightman, Rani Marx, Tanja Michalsky, David B. Morris, David Myers, Jennifer Nadel, Lynn Nyhart, Nele Pollatschek, Sarah Roberts, Margaret W. Rossiter, Stephanie Schütze, Thomas A. Schwartz, Peter Sehlinger, Carole Shaffer-Koros, Tracy Snow, Abby Stambach, Joachim Stieber, Nathan Stolzfus, Max A. Stolper, Jacques Szaluta, John Tortorice, Liz Townsend, Rob Utzschneider, Mark Walker, Judith Walkowitz, Allen Ward, Richard Weiner, Katy O'Brian Weintraub, Meike G. Werner, Fordyce Williams, Nanci Young, and Ute Zimmermann.

We are indebted to all the libraries and archives that provided valuable support along the way: the Library of Congress, Lauinger Library of Georgetown University, the library of the United States Holocaust Memorial Museum, and the library of the German Historical Institute, all in Washington, DC; the Leo Baeck Institute Library and Archives in New York City; Lockwood Memorial Library at the State University of New York at Buffalo; the library of the University of Heidelberg; and the Bibliothek Albert Einstein of the Hochschule für Jüdische Studien, Heidelberg.

Finally, some caveats need to be mentioned. We cannot make any claim to comprehensiveness. Also, the more data we have collected, the more likely it is that mistakes have crept in—in addition to the fact that personal recollections, as well as the curricula vitae provided by the individuals concerned, differed at times from information given in other sources. Ultimately, the responsibility for selecting and drafting the biographies—and thus for all remaining omissions and errors—remains ours, and we would welcome corrections and addenda.

Andreas W. Daum is professor of history at the State University of New York at Buffalo. His research deals with German, transatlantic, and international history, as well as the history of knowledge, from the eighteenth century to the Cold War era. His books include *Wissenschaftspopularisierung im 19. Jahrhundert* (a history of popular science in Germany; 1998, ²2002), *Kennedy in Berlin* (2003, English edition 2008), and co-edited volumes on the *Vietnam War and the World* (2003) and *Berlin – Washington, 1800-2000* (2005).

Sherry L. Föhr runs the Writing Resources Center at the University of Heidelberg, Germany. She completed her Ph.D. in history at Georgetown University in 1999. After a stint as Assistant Dean at the Edmund A. Walsh School of Foreign Service, she began teaching history for the European Division of the University of Maryland University College. In 2009, she joined the English Studies department of the University of Heidelberg, where she has taught writing courses and done editorial work on publications in fields ranging from disability studies to linguistics.

Notes

1. See my introduction to this volume and the selected bibliography, i.e., chapter 24, at the end of this volume.
2. See this volume's introduction and the chapter by Volker R. Berghahn.
3. Hans Gatzke, Arthur Haas, Ursula Lamb, Theodore von Laue, and Reinhold Schumann might belong to this second group; in the case of Ilza Veith, the relevant information could not be obtained.
4. This group includes, for example, Sylvia Strauss, born in 1931 in Berlin and academically trained at CUNY, Columbia University, and Rutgers University. Strauss later taught at Keane College (University) where she coordinated the women's studies program.
5. The growing secondary literature on emigrants from Austria who turned into scholars can be easily captured through the recent works by Beatrix Müller-Kampel, ed., *Lebenswege und Lektüren. Österreichische NS-Vertriebene in den USA und Kanada* (Tübingen, 2000); Johannes Feichtinger, *Wissenschaft zwischen den Kulturen. Österreichische Hochschullehrer in der Emigration 1933–1945* (Frankfurt/M., 2001); and Doris Ingrisch, *Der dis/kontinuierliche Status des Seins. Über vom Nationalsozialismus aus Österreich vertriebene (und verbliebene) intellektuelle Kulturen in lebensgeschichtlichen Kontexten* (Frankfurt/M., 2004), 215–28.
6. In addition to Alfons Söllner, *Deutsche Politikwissenschaftler in der Emigration. Studien zu ihrer Akkulturation und Wirkungsgeschichte* (Opladen, 1996), see Peter Graf Kielmansegg, ed.,

Hannah Arendt and Leo Strauss: German Émigrés and American Political Thought after World War II (New York, 1995); Wilhelm Bleek, Geschichte der Politikwissenschaft in Deutschland (Munich, 2001), 246–307; and Arnd Bauerkämper, "Americanisation as Globalisation: Remigrés to West Germany after 1945 and Conceptions of Democracy. The Cases of Hans Rothfels, Ernst Fraenkel and Hans Rosenberg," Leo Baeck Institute Yearbook 49 (2004): 153–70. The discussion of Leo Strauss's works and legacy has intensified in recent years—see only the massive compendium by John A. Murley, ed., Leo Strauss and His Legacy: A Bibliography (Lanham, MD, 2005).

7. See Mary King and Lisa Saunders, "An Interview with Marianne Ferber: Founding Feminist Economist," Review of Political Economy 11 (1999): 83–98; Jeremy Adelman, Worldly Philosopher: The Odyssey of Albert O. Hirschman (Princeton, NJ, 2013); Rolf Wiggershaus, Die Frankfurter Schule. Geschichte. Theoretische Entwicklung. Politische Bedeutung (1st ed. 1986; Munich, 2008); Eva-Maria Ziege, Antisemitismus und Gesellschaftstheorie. Die Frankfurter Schule im amerikanischen Exil (Frankfurt/M., 2009); Thomas Wheatland, The Frankfurt School in Exile (Minneapolis, 2009); Tim B. Müller, Krieger und Gelehrte. Herbert Marcuse und die Denksysteme im Kalten Krieg (Hamburg, 2010); and John Abromeit, Max Horkheimer and the Foundations of the Frankfurt School (Cambridge, 2011).

8. W. Michael Blumenthal, From Exile to Washington: A Memoir of Leadership in the Twentieth Century (New York, 2013). Some of the scholars mentioned provide intriguing autobiographical reflections in Peter Suedfeld, ed., Light from the Ashes: Social Science Careers of Young Holocaust Refugees and Survivors (Ann Arbor, 2001).

9. I thank Marc Föcking, University of Hamburg, for his valuable comments on this particular group of scholars.

10. See Walter Schmitz, ed., Modernisierung oder Überfremdung? Zur Wirkung deutscher Exilanten in der Germanistik der Aufnahmländer (Stuttgart, 1994); Jost Hermand, "Germanistik," in Claus-Dieter Krohn, ed. Handbuch der deutschsprachigen Emigration 1933–1945 (Darmstadt, 1998), 736–46; Stephen D. Dowden and Meike G. Werner, eds., German Literature, Jewish Critics. The Brandeis Symposium (Rochester, NY, 2002); Ingrisch, Der dis/kontinuierliche Status des Seins, 215–28. From the group of scholars of German literary history we include in this guide only Wilma Iggers. She collaborated throughout her life closely with her historian husband, Georg Iggers.

11. Susan Groag Bell, Gabrielle S. Edgcomb, Frank Eyck, Walter Laqueur, Toni Oelsner, Agnes Peterson, and Beate Ruhm von Oppen.

12. Catherine Epstein, A Past Renewed: A Catalogue of German-Speaking Refugee Historians in the United States after 1933 (New York, 1993), 14.

13. International Biographical Dictionary of Central European Émigrés 1933–1945 = Biographisches Handbuch der deutschsprachigen Emigration nach 1933, edited by Werner Röder and Herbert A. Strauss. 3 vols. in 4 (Munich, New York, 1980–83), abbreviated as IBDCEE.

14. According to Herbert A. Strauss, ed. Jewish Immigrants of the Nazi Period in the USA, vol. 5 (New York, 1986), 117.

15. Epstein, A Past Renewed; Hartmut Lehmann and James J. Sheehan, eds., An Interrupted Past: German Speaking Refugee Historians in the United States after 1933 (New York, 1991).

16. Apart from those newer works listed in my introductory chapter, see for the academic disciplines mentioned Ilja Srubar, ed., Exil, Wissenschaft, Identität. Die Emigration deutscher Sozialwissenschaftler 1933–1945 (Frankfurt/M., 1988); Söllner, Deutsche Politikwissenschaftler; Harald Hagemann and Claus-Dieter Krohn, eds., Biographisches Handbuch der deutschsprachigen wirtschaftswissenschaftlichen Emigration nach 1933. 2 vols. (Munich, 1999); Karen Michels, Transplantierte Kunstwissenschaft. Deutschsprachige Kunstgeschichte im amerikanischen Exil (Berlin, 1999); Ulrike Wendland, Biographisches Handbuch deutschsprachiger Kunsthistoriker im Exil. Leben und Werk der unter dem Nationalsozialismus verfolgten und vertriebenen Wissenschaftler,

2 vols. (Munich, 1999); Hans Helmut Christmann and Frank-Rutger Hausmann, *Deutsche und österreichische Romanisten als Verfolgte des Nationalsozialismus* (Tübingen, 1989); Mitchell G. Ash and Alfons Söllner, *Forced Migration and Scientific Change: Émigré German-Speaking Scientists and Scholars after 1933* (New York, 1996). On publishers and booksellers, see Ernst Fischer, *Verleger, Buchhändler & Antiquare aus Deutschland und Österreich in der Emigration nach 1933. Ein biographisches Handbuch* (Elbingen, 2011).

17. Andreas W. Daum, "The Second Generation: German Émigré Historians in the Transatlantic World, 1945 to the Present," *Bulletin of the German Historical Institute* 51 (Fall 2012): 116-21.
18. Approximately one third of the 107 biographies we present are not included in the IBDCEE.
19. The various editions of the *Dictionary of American Scholars* and the obituaries published in the *Perspectives*, the newsletter of the American Historical Association, are important sources in this regard.

Chapter 23

BIOGRAPHIES

Andreas W. Daum and Sherry L. Föhr

*With the Assistance of Perry E. Beardsley, April Kiser,
Axel Steensen, and Friederike Steensen*

Readers will find the following abbreviations in the biographical entries:

AAAS	American Academy of Arts and Sciences
ACLS	American Council of Learned Societies
AHA	American Historical Association
CUNY	City University of New York
DAAD	Deutscher Akademischer Austauschdienst
HUC-JIR	Hebrew Union College-Jewish Institute of Religion
JTS	Jewish Theological Seminar
NAACP	National Association for the Advancement of Colored People
NEH	National Endowment for the Humanities
OAH	Organization of American Historians
OSS	Office of Strategic Services
SSRC	Social Science Research Council
SUNY	State University of New York
UCLA	University of California, Los Angeles

Peter Heinrich Amann

Born 31 May 1927 in Vienna; died 14 June 2012 in Manchester, MI
Parents: Paul Amann and Dora Iranyi
1939 to France; 1940 to Switzerland, again to France; 1941 to the U.S.

1947	A.B. Oberlin College
1953	M.A. University of Chicago
1956–59	Instructor, Bowdoin College

1958	Ph.D. University of Chicago, "A French Revolutionary Club in 1848: The Société Démocratique Centrale"
1959–65	Assistant to associate professor, Oakland University, MI
1965–68	Professor, SUNY Binghamton
1968–92	Professor, University of Michigan-Dearborn
1979–84	William E. Stirton Professor, University of Michigan-Dearborn

Ad Personam

1963	Fulbright fellowship
1963	Guggenheim fellowship
1975	Distinguished Teaching Award, University of Michigan-Dearborn
1982	NEH fellowship

Peter H. Amann Collection, 1929–80, Archives of Labor and Urban Affairs, Walter P. Reuther Library, Wayne State University

Peter H. Amann Collection, 1909–2009, Leo Baeck Institute Archives, New York

Selected Publications

The Eighteenth Century Revolution: French or Western? (1963)
The Modern World: 1650–1850 (1967)
Revolution and Mass Democracy: The Paris Club Movement in 1848 (1975)
The Corncribs of Buzet: Modernizing Agriculture in the French Southwest (1990)
The French Revolution at the Grassroots: A Critical Bibliography of Recent Works on Village, Small Towns, and Small Rural Regions during the Revolutionary Period (2006)

Werner Thomas Angress

Born Werner Karl Angreß, 27 June 1920 in Berlin; died 5 July 2010 in Berlin
Parents: Ernst Hermann Angreß and Henny Kiefer
1937 to the Netherlands, 1939 to the U.S.

1939–41	worked on cooperative farm, Virginia
1941–45	served in U.S. Army
1949	B.A. Wesleyan University
1950	M.A. University of California, Berkeley
1954	Ph.D. University of California, Berkeley, "The German Government and the Communist Uprisings, 1921–1923"
1954–57	Lecturer, Wesleyan University and University of California, Berkeley
1957–69	Assistant to associate professor, University of California, Berkeley
1969–88	Professor, SUNY Stony Brook

Ad personam

1944	Bronze Star and Purple Heart
1969–70	Travel grant, American Philosophical Society
1972–74	Member, editorial board, *Central European History*
1975	SUNY Chancellor's Award for Excellence in Teaching
1976	Member, board of directors, Leo Baeck Institute
1994	Honorary member, Förderverein der Mahn- und Gedenkstätten Wöbbelin

Werner Tom Angress Collection, Leo Baeck Institute, New York
A Celebration of Life: Professor Dr. Werner Tom Angress 27. Juni 1920 – 5. Juli 2010. Mit einem Verzeichnis seiner Veröffentlichungen (2011)

Selected Publications

Stillborn Revolution: The Communist Bid for Power in Germany, 1921–1923 (1963, ²1972). German edition: *Die Kampfzeit der KPD. 1921–1923* (1973)
Generation zwischen Furcht und Hoffnung. Jüdische Jugend im Dritten Reich (1985). English edition: *Between Fear and Hope: Jewish Youth in the Third Reich* (1988)
. . . immer etwas abseits. Jugenderinnerungen eines jüdischen Berliners 1920–1945 (2005). English edition: *Witness to the Storm: A Jewish Journey from Nazi Berlin to the 82nd Airborne, 1920–1945* (2005)

John J. Appel

Born Joachim Appel, 11 August 1921 in Weimar; died 6 April 1998 in East Lansing, MI
Parents: Jakob Appel and Susanna Ortweiler
1938 to the U.S.

	served in U.S. Army
1949	B.A. University of Miami
1951	M.A. University of Miami
1960	Ph.D. in American civilization, University of Pennsylvania, "Immigrant Historical Societies in the United States, 1880–1950"
1951–52	and 1954–56: Instructor, University of Miami
1952–54	Teacher, Dade County Schools
1959–60	Director of Adult Education, Baltimore Jewish Community Center
1960–62	Instructor, Essex County Community College
1962–67	Assistant professor of American Thought and Language, Michigan State University
1967–70	Associate professor, James Madison University
1970–87	Professor, Michigan State University, University College

Ad Personam

	Dissertation grant, Conference on Jewish Material Claims against Germany Harrison Fellowship in American Civilization
1969–70	Visiting Scholar, Smithsonian Institution
1972–73	Ford Foundation grant
1973–74	Visiting Professor, Graduate Program, Cooperstown, NY

John J. Appel Papers, 1931–1968, Library of Congress
John and Selma Appel Collection of Ethnic American Caricatures, Michigan State University Museum

Selected Publications

Immigrant Historical Societies in the United States, 1880–1950 (1960, 1980)
The New Immigration (1971)
Ed., with Alfred de Grazia and R. Eric Weise, *Old Government, New People: Readings for the New Politics* (1971)

Charles Wolfgang Arnade

Born Karl-Wolfgang Julius Kurt Arnade, 11 May 1927 in Görlitz; died 7 September 2008 in Leesburg, VA
Parents: Kurt Conrad Arnade and Johanna Giersch
1936 to China; 1939 to Switzerland, then Bolivia; 1946 via Chile to the U.S.

1936–37	in Nanjing (German School), then Shanghai
1938	left China via Hong Kong, returned to Europe (Italy)
1939	to Switzerland, then departure for Bolivia
1945	graduated from Colegio La Salle, Cochabamba, Bolivia
1946–50	studied at University of Texas and University of Michigan
1950	B.A. in political science, University of Michigan
1952	M.A. in history, University of Michigan
1953–55	Adjunct instructor, University of Florida, Gainesville
1955	Ph.D. University of Florida, "The Creation of the Republic of Bolivia"
1955–56	Assistant professor, University of Tampa
1956–58	Assistant professor, Florida State University
1961–94	Associate to full professor, University of South Florida, Tampa
1994–2003	Distinguished Professor of International Studies, University of South Florida

Ad Personam

1952	Research year in Bolivia
1959–62	Associate editor, *Florida History Quarterly*
1959–60	Visiting associate professor, University of Florida

1960	Visiting professor, University of Iowa
1961–62	SSRC grant
1962–	provided training for Latin American Peace Corps
1965–66	Senior Fulbright Scholar, University of Madrid
1966–68	President, American Association of University Professors, University of South Florida
1968	Founding member, Pasco County NAACP chapter
1968	Travels and lecture tours in Asia, Americas, Caribbean, Europe (including both German states) and Africa
1968–69	Visiting professor, University Ife, Nigeria
1972	Visiting professor, Tribhuvan University, Nepal
1987	Teacher of the Year Award, University of South Florida
2003	Lifetime Award, Florida Historical Society

Charles W. Arnade Collection of Boliviana, University of South Florida

Selected Publications

The Emergence of the Republic of Bolivia (1957, 1970)
Florida on Trial, 1593–1601 (1959)
The Siege of St. Augustine in 1702 (1959)
with Josef Kühnel, *El problema del humanista Tadeo Haenke: Nuevas perspectivas en la investigación haenkeana* (1960)
La historia de Bolivia y la de los Estados Unidos de América: Una comparación (1962)
La dramática insurgencia de Bolivia (1964, 1972)
Bolivian History (1984)
Escenas y episodios de la historia: Estudios bolivianos, 1953–1999 (2004)
Historiografía colonial y moderna de Bolivia, ed. Laura Escobari (2008)

Walter Leonard Arnstein

Born 14 May 1930 in Stuttgart
Parents: Richard Arnstein and Charlotte Heyman
1939 to the U.S.

1951	B.A. City College of New York
1951–53	served in U.S. Army
1954	M.A. Columbia University
1961	Ph.D. Northwestern University, "The Bradlaugh Case: A Study in Late Victorian Opinion and Politics"
1957–66	Assistant to associate professor, Roosevelt University, Chicago
1966–68	Professor, Roosevelt University, Chicago
1968	Professor, University of Illinois at Urbana-Champaign
1989–98	Jubilee Professor of the Liberal Arts & Sciences, University of Illinois at Urbana-Champaign

Ad Personam

1956–57	Fulbright Scholar, University of London
1963–64	and 1966: Visiting professor, Northwestern University
1967–68	ACLS fellowship
1973–	Fellow, Royal Historical Society
1976–2000	Member, editorial board, *The Historian*
1977–80	President, Midwest Victorian Studies Association
1980–82	President, Midwest Conference on British Studies
1982	John Gilmary Shea Prize, American Catholic Historical Association
1989	Honorary fellow, Institute for Advanced Studies in the Humanities, University of Edinburgh
1995–97	President, North American Conference of British Studies
1992–	Walter L. Arnstein Prize for Ph.D. students in Victorian Studies, Midwest Victorian Studies Association
2006–	Walter L. Arnstein Graduate Essay Award, Midwest Conference on British Studies, Member, editorial board, *Albion*

Splendidly Victorian: Essays in Nineteenth- and Twentieth-Century British History in Honour of Walter L. Arnstein, ed. Michael H. Shirley and Todd E. A. Larson (2001)

Selected Publications

The Bradlaugh Case: A Study in Late Victorian Opinion and Politics (1965, repr. 1983)
Britain Yesterday and Today: 1830 to the Present (1966, ⁸2001)
with William Bradford Willcox, *The Age of Aristocracy, 1688 to 1830* (³1976, ⁸2001)
Ed., *The Past Speaks: Sources and Problems in British History*. Vol. II, *Since 1688* (1981, ²1993)
Protestant Versus Catholic in Mid-Victorian England: Mr. Newdegate and the Nuns (1982)
Ed., *Recent Historians of Great Britain: Essays on the Post-1945 Generation* (1990)
Queen Victoria (2003)
Ed., *Lives of Victorian Political Figures*. Vol. III, *Queen Victoria* (2008)

Abraham Ascher

Born 26 August 1928 in Wrocław (Breslau)
Parents: Jakob Ascher and Feiga Storch
1939 to the U.K., 1943 to the U.S.

1950	B.S.S. City College of New York
1951	M.A. Columbia University
1953–57	Instructor, Brooklyn College and Rutgers University
1957	Ph.D. Columbia University, "National Solidarity and Imperial Power: The Sources and Early Development of Social Imperialist Thought in Germany, 1871–1914"
1957–58	Research analyst, U.S. Department of State
1958–60	Assistant professor, SUNY Stony Brook

1960–70	Assistant to associate professor, Brooklyn College
1970–2003	Professor and Distinguished Professor, Brooklyn College

Ad Personam

1963–64	Rockefeller Foundation fellowship
1966	Friedrich-Ebert-Stiftung fellowship
1968–69	ACLS grant and resident fellowship, Russian Center, Harvard University
1974–75	NEH senior fellowship
1984	ACLS grant-in-aid
1987	ACLS grant-in-aid
1997	Regional director, Andrew W. Mellon Fellowship in Humanistic Studies

Selected Publications

Pavel Axelrod and the Development of Menshevism (1972)
The Kremlin (1972). German edition: *Der Kreml* (1975)
with Tibor Halasi-Kun and Béla K Király, *The Mutual Effects of the Islamic and Judeo-Christian Worlds: The East European Pattern* (1979)
Studying Russian and Soviet History (1987)
The Revolution of 1905: Russia in Disarray (1988)
The Revolution of 1905: Authority Restored (1992)
P. A. Stolypin: The Search for Stability in Late Imperial Russia (2000)
Russia: A Short History (2002, ²2009). German edition: *Geschichte Russlands* (2005)
The Revolution of 1905: A Short History (2004)
A Community under Siege: The Jews of Breslau under Nazism (2007). Polish edition 2009
Was Hitler a Riddle? Western Democracies and National Socialism (2012)

Ernst Badian

Born 8 August 1925 in Vienna; died 1 February 2011 in Quincy, MA
Parents: Joseph and Salka Badian
1939 to New Zealand, c. 1946 to the U.K., 1968 to the U.S.

1945	B.A. Canterbury University College, Christchurch, New Zealand
1946	M.A. Canterbury University College
1947–48	Junior lecturer in Classics, Victoria University of Wellington, New Zealand
1950	B.A. University College, Oxford
1950–52	Rome Scholar in Classics, British School at Rome
1954	M.A. University College, Oxford
1954–64	Lecturer, University of Durham
1956	D.Phil. University College, Oxford, "Foreign clientelae in Roman foreign policy and internal politics (264–70 B.C.)"
1962	Litt.D., Victoria University of Wellington, New Zealand
1965–69	Professor, University of Leeds

1969–71	Professor of history and classics, SUNY Buffalo
1971–98	Professor of history, Harvard University
1973–98	also professor, Department of Classics, Harvard
1982–98	John Moors Cabot Professor of History, Harvard

Ad Personam

1958	Conington Prize, Oxford University, for *Foreign clientelae (264–70 B.C.)*
1961	Visiting professor, University of Oregon
1972–73	and 1992–93: ACLS fellowship
1973	Leverhulme Fellow, British Academy
1974–	Fellow, AAAS
1974	Cofounder, Association of Ancient Historians
1975–76	Sather Professor of Classics, University of California, Berkeley
1976–2001	Cofounder and editor, *American Journal of Ancient History*
1978	Cofounder, New England Ancient History Colloquium
1991	endowed the L. G. Pocock Prize in Classics, Canterbury University College, Christchurch, New Zealand
1999	Cross of Honor for Science and Art, Austria
1999	Honorary Litt.D., Canterbury University College, Christchurch, New Zealand

Fellow of the American Numismatic Society, corresponding member of the Austrian Academy of Sciences, honorary fellow of University College Oxford, honorary member of the Society for Roman Studies, corresponding member of the German Archeological Society, foreign member of the Finnish Academy of Sciences

Ernst Badian Collection of Roman Republican Coins, Special Collections and University Archives, Rutgers University Libraries
Transitions to Empire: Essays in Greco-Roman History, 360–146 B.C. in Honor of E. Badian, ed. Robert W. Wallace and Edward M. Harris (1996)
The Legacy of Ernst Badian, ed. Carol G. Thomas (2013)

Selected Publications

Foreign clientelae (264–70 B.C.) (1958, various later editions)
Ed., *Studies in Greek and Roman History* (1964, 1968)
Ed.: Polybius, *The Histories* (1966)
Ed., *Ancient Society and Institutions: Studies Presented to Victor Ehrenberg on His 75th Birthday* (1966)
Roman Imperialism in the Late Republic (1968, ²1971). German edition: *Römischer Imperialismus in der späten Republik* (1980)
Titus Quinctius Flamininus: Philhellenism and Realpolitik (1970)
Publicans and Sinners: Private Enterprise in the Service of the Roman Republic (1972, 1983), German edition: *Zöllner und Sünder. Unternehmer im Dienst der römischen Republik* (1997)

Ed., with Albert B. Bosworth, *Alexandre le Grand: Image et réalité* (1976)
et al., *Gibbon et Rome aÌ la lumieÌre de l'historiographie moderne: 10 exposeìs suivis de discussions* (1977)
Ed., with Robert K. Sherk, *Translated Documents of Greek and Rome*, vols. 1–3 (1977)
Ed.: Ronald Syme, *Roman Papers*, vols. 1–7 (1979–91)
From Plataea to Potidaea: Studies in the History and Historiography of the Pentecontaetia (1993)
Ed., *Collected Papers on Alexander the Great* (2012)

Ann Frank Beck

Born 5 August 1900 in Braunschweig; died 10 August 2002 in Avon, CT
Parents: Willy Frank and Claire Hirsch
1933 to Czechoslovakia, 1938 to the U.S.

1946	M.A. University of Illinois
1948	Ph.D. University of Illinois, "The Beginning of Public Health Control in England, 1870–1890: A Study of the Extension of the Functions of Government in the Later Nineteenth Century"
1948–50	Historian, Centenary College, Arkansas
1950–52	and 1953–54: Instructor, University of Connecticut
1952–53	Research associate, Columbia University
1954–57	Associate professor, Detroit Institute of Technology
1957–60	Associate professor, Dakota State College
1960–73	Associate to full professor, University of Hartford, CT

Ad Personam

1960	1962 and 1968: Research grant, American Philosophical Society
1964–68	Travel grants, National Institute of Health
1971–74	Fellow, National Library of Medicine
1976–78	Research grant, U.S. Department of Health, Education and Welfare

Selected Publications

A History of the British Medical Administration of East Africa: 1900–1950 (1970)
Medicine and Society in Tanganyika, 1890–1930: A Historical Inquiry (1977)
Medicine, Tradition, and Development in Kenya and Tanzania: 1920–1970 (1981)

Susan Groag Bell

Born Susanne E. Groag, 25 January 1926 in Opava (Troppau); died 24 June 2015 in Palo Alto, CA
Parents: Friedrich and Edith Luise Groag
1939 to the U.K., 1957 to the U.S.

1964   A.B. Stanford University
1970   M.A. University of Santa Clara
1971–81   Adjunct lecturer, University of Santa Clara
1982–   Lecturer, Stanford University
1978–   Senior Scholar, Michelle R. Clayman Institute for Gender Research, Stanford University Senior Scholar, Stanford Institute for Research on Women and Gender

Ad Personam

1978   NEH grant for analysis of British Women's Autobiographies
1983   NEH grant (with Karen Offen) to direct 1984 NEH Summer Seminar for College Teachers at Stanford

Susan Groag Bell Correspondence 1946–1996, Hoover Institution Archives and Stanford University Archives

Selected Publications

Women from the Greeks to the French Revolution (1972, ²1983)
with Karen Offen, *Women, the Family and Freedom: The Debate in Documents 1750–1950* (1983)
Ed., with Marilyn Yalom, *Revealing Lives: Autobiography, Biography, and Gender* (1990)
Between Worlds: In Czechoslovakia, England, and America (1991)
"An Annotated Bibliography of British Women's Autobiographies 1790–1950: Research and Reference Materials 1986–1998," Stanford University Libraries, Department of Special Collections and University Archives (1998)
The Lost Tapestries of "The City of Ladies": Christine de Pizan's Renaissance Legacy (2004)

Harry Jindrich Benda

Born 28 October 1919 in Liberec (Reichenberg); died 26 October 1971 in New Haven, CT
Parents: Robert Benda and Elisabeth Frank
1939 to Indonesia, 1949 sent to New Zealand, 1952 to the U.S.

–1939   attended Gymnasium in Liberec and Prague
1939–43   worked in Indonesia for Dutch trading firm
1943–45   interned by Japanese military
1949   B.A. Victoria University, Wellington, New Zealand
1952   M.A. University of New Zealand
            Junior lecturer, Victoria University, New Zealand
1953–54   Instructor, Government Department, Cornell University
1955   Ph.D. in government, Cornell University, "The Crescent and the Rising Sun: Indonesian Islam under the Japanese Occupation of Java, 1942–1945"
1955–59   Assistant professor of history and coordinator, nonwestern civilizations program, University of Rochester

| 1959–66 | Associate professor, Yale University |
| 1966–71 | Professor, Yale University |

Ad Personam

1952–55	Southeast Asia fellow, Cornell University
1961–62	Guggenheim fellowship
1963–66	Assistant editor, *Journal of Asian Studies*
1963–	Visiting lecturer, Foreign Service Institute, Washington, DC
1968–69	First director, Institute of South East Asian Studies, Singapore
1977–	Harry J. Benda Prize in Southeast Asian Studies, Association for Asian Studies

Selected Publications

The Crescent and the Rising Sun: Indonesian Islam under the Japanese Occupation, 1942–1945 (1958, 1983)

Ed., with Ruth T. McVey, *The Communist Uprisings of 1926–1927 in Indonesia: Key Documents* (1960, new ed. 2009)

Ed., with James K. Irikura and Kōichi Kishi, *Japanese Military Administration in Indonesia: Selected Documents* (1965)

Ed., with John A. Larkin, *The World of Southeast Asia: Selected Historical Readings* (1967)

et al., *Islam di Indonesia: Sepintas lalu tentang beberapa segi* (1974)

with John Bastin, *A History of Modern Southeast Asia: Colonialism, Nationalism, and Decolonization* (1968, ²1977)

Continuity and Change in Southeast Asia: Collected Journal Articles of Harry J. Benda (1972)

Henry Blumenthal

Born Heinz Blumenthal, 21 October 1911 in Grudziądz (Graudenz); died February 1987 in New York, NY
Parents: Edwin Blumenthal and Regina Cronheim
1936 to Brazil, 1937 to Uruguay, 1938 to the U.S.

–1933	studied with Hermann Oncken at the University of Berlin
1943	M.A. University of California, Berkeley
1943–46	served in U.S. Army
1949	Ph.D. University of California, Berkeley, "Diplomatic Relations between the United States and France, 1836–1861"
1949–	Instructor, Rutgers University
1953–59	Assistant to associate professor, Rutgers University
1962–65	Director, division of social sciences, Rutgers University
1963	Professor, Rutgers University
1969–71	Dean at Rutgers-Newark

Ad Personam

Selman A. Waksman fellowship to study archival materials in France
1960 First recipient of the Rutgers University's "Outstanding Teacher of the Year" award
1979 First recipient of Rutgers University Award

Selected Publications

A Reappraisal of Franco-American Relations, 1830–1871 (1959, 1980)
France and the United States: Their Diplomatic Relations, 1789–1914 (1970)
American and French Culture, 1800–1900: Interchanges in Art, Science, Literature, and Society (1975)
Challenges along my Twentieth Century Odyssey (1981)
Illusion and Reality in Franco-American Diplomacy, 1914–1945 (1986)

Eric Hartzell Boehm

Born with last name Böhm, 15 July 1918 in Hof; died 11 September 2017 in Santa Barbara, CA
Parents: Karl Boehm and Bertha Oppenheimer
1934 to the U.S.

1940	B.A. Wooster College
1942	M.A. Fletcher School of Law and Diplomacy
1942–46	served in U.S. Army
1946–47	Member, Presidential Scrutiny Board, U.S. Military Headquarters, Berlin
1950–51	Instructor, Yale University
1952	Ph.D. Yale University, "Policy-Making of the Nazi Government: A Study in the Determination of Decisions of State"
1951–55	Analyst for U.S. government, Vienna, Austria
1955–58	with U.S. government in Munich
1955–	Founder, then editor, *Historical Abstracts*
1960–	Founder, then president and chairman of the board, American Bibliographic Center – Clio Press (ABC–Clio)
1961–2003	Founder, then chairman of the board, International Academy, Santa Barbara
1964–	Editor, *America: History and Life*
1970	President and chairman of the board, European Bibliographical Center
1987–94	Founder, then president, International School of Information Management (ISM)
2006–	Chairman, Boehm Biography Group

Ad Personam

1973 Honorary D.Litt., Wooster College
1986–87 Vice president, then president, Association for the Bibliography of History

1990   Distinguished Alumnus Award, Wooster College

Selected Publications

We Survived: Fourteen Histories of the Hidden and Hunted in Nazi Germany (1949, 1966, 1985, rev. ed. 2003)
Ed., *Bibliographies on International Relations and World Affairs: An Annotated Directory* (1965)
Ed., *Blueprint for Bibliography: A System for Social Sciences and Humanities* (1965)
Ed., *Historical Abstracts* (1955–83)
Ed., *America: History and Life* (1964–83)
Ed., *Twentieth Century Abstracts* (1971–)
Ed., *Art Bibliography: Current Titles and Modern* (1972–)
Ed., with Lalit Adolphus, *Historical Periodicals: An Annotated World List of Historical and Related Serial Publications* (1961)

John Wolfgang Bohnstedt

Born Wolfgang Hans Bohnstedt, 22 February 1927 in Berlin; died 25 February 2015 in Fresno, CA
Parents: Werner A. Bohnstedt and Bertha Norden
1936 to Panama via Belgium; 1940 to the U.S.

1945–47	served in U.S. Army, Panama Canal Department
1950	B.A. Michigan State University
1952	M.A. University of Minnesota, "Peaceful Relations between Muslims and Latin Christians in Syria, 1101–1154"
1955–56	Instructor to assistant professor, University of South Dakota
1956–97	Instructor to professor, Fresno State College, CA
1959	Ph.D. University of Minnesota, "The Turkish Menace in German Public Opinion, 1522–1542"
2002	Professor emeritus, Fresno State College

Ad Personam

1953–54	Fulbright scholar, Austria
1965	Grant, American Philosophical Society
1965–67	California State Research Grant
1966	Distinguished Teaching Award, Fresno State College

Selected Publication

The Infidel Scourge of God: The Turkish Menace as Seen by German Pamphleteers of the Reformation Era (1968)

Renate Bridenthal

Born Renate Rubin, 13 June 1935 in Leipzig
Parents: Elchunon Rubin and Irene Quittner Rubin
1938 to Czechoslovakia; 1939 to France, then Panama; 1940 to the U.S.

1960	B.A. City College of New York
1961	M.A. Columbia University
1970	Ph.D. Columbia University, "Barthold Georg Niebuhr, Historian of Rome: A Study in Methodology"
1966–67	Lecturer, Borough of Manhattan Community College
1967–74	Lecturer, Brooklyn College, CUNY
1974–86	Assistant to associate professor, Brooklyn College, CUNY
1986–2001	Professor, Brooklyn College, CUNY

Ad Personam

1973–	Member, editorial board, *Science and Society*
1974	Cofounder, CUNY Women's Coalition
1974–75	National cochairwoman of the Conference Group on Women's History
1974–79	Cofounder and coordinator, Brooklyn College Women's Studies program
1980	PSC-BHE research award, CUNY
1983	International Research and Exchanges Board (IREX) award
1983–84	NEH fellowship
1983–84	Fulbright fellowship (declined)
1999–2000	PSC-BHE research award, CUNY

"Fragments of a German-Jewish Heritage in Four 'Americans,'" in *The German-Jewish Legacy in America, 1938–1988: From Bildung to the Bill of Rights*, ed. Abraham J. Peck (1989), 179–98.

"Making and Writing History Together," in *Voices of Women Historians: The Personal, the Political, the Professional*, ed. Eileen Boris and Nupur Chaudhuri (1999), 76–84.

"Out of Germany," in *The Second Generation: Émigrés from Nazi Germany as Historians*, ed. Andreas W. Daum, Hartmut Lehmann, and James J. Sheehan (2016), 130–140.

Selected Publications

Ed., with Claudia Koonz, *Becoming Visible: Women in European History* (1977). 2nd rev. ed. with Claudia Koonz and Susan Stuard (1987). 3rd rev. ed. with Susan Mosher Stuard and Merry E. Wiesner (1998)

with Amy Swerdlow, Joan Kelly, and Phyllis Vine, *Household and Kin* (1981; 2nd rev. ed.: *Families in Flux*, 1989)

Ed., with Atina Grossmann and Marion Kaplan, *When Biology Became Destiny: Women in Weimar and Nazi Germany* (1984)

Ed., with Krista O'Donnell and Nancy Ruth Reagin, *The Heimat Abroad: The Boundaries of Germanness* (2005)

Ed., with Jerry H. Bentley and Anand A. Yang, *Interactions: Transregional Perspectives on World History* (2005)

Ed., with Jerry H. Bentley and Karen Wigen, *Seascapes, Littoral Cultures, and Transoceanic Exchanges* (2007)
Ed., *The Hidden History of Crime, Corruption and States* (2013)

Gert Henry Brieger

Born Gert Heinrich Brieger, 5 January 1932 in Hamburg
Parents: Carl H. Brieger and Ylse Fuchs
1937 to the U.S.

1953	A.B. University of California, Berkeley
1957	M.D. UCLA
1962	M.Ph. (master in public health) Harvard University
1966–67	Assistant professor, Johns Hopkins University
1968	Ph.D. Johns Hopkins University "Stephen Smith, Surgeon and Reformer"
1970–75	Associate professor, Duke University
1975–84	Professor and director, Department of the History of Health Sciences, University of California, San Francisco
1984–2002	William H. Welch Professor of the History of Medicine; director, Institute of the History of Medicine; and chair, Department of the History of Science, Medicine, and Technology, Johns Hopkins University

Ad Personam

1982–84	President, American Association of the History of Medicine
1994–2004	Editor, *Bulletin of the History of Medicine*
1985	Elected member, Institute of Medicine
1993	Nicholas E. Davies Memorial Scholar Award, American College of Physicians
2000	John P. McGovern Award, American Osler Society

Selected Publications

Ed., *Medical America in the Nineteenth Century: Readings from the Literature* (1972, pbk. 2009)
Ed., *Theory and Practice in American Medicine: Historical Studies from the Journal of the History of Medicine & Allied Sciences* (1976)
et al., *A Model of Its Kind*. Vol. I, *A Centennial History of Medicine at Johns Hopkins*. Vol. II, *A Pictorial History of Medicine at Johns Hopkins* (1989)

Peter Michael Buzanski

Born Peter Buzanski, 29 May 1929 in Vienna
Parents: Isaias Buzanski and Susanne Ehrenberg
1938–39 several attempts to escape via France, Switzerland, and Belgium; 1939 to Sweden; 1940 to the U.S.

1950	B.A. University of California, Berkeley
1952	M.A. University of California, Berkeley, "American Magazine Opinion toward the Third Reich, 1933–1939"
1960	Ph.D. University of California, Berkeley, "Admiral Marl L. Bristol and Turkish-American Relations, 1919–1922"
1956–59	Instructor, American River Junior College, Sacramento, CA
1960–92	Instructor to full professor, San José State College (later: University)

Ad Personam

1971–72	American Council of Education, Fellow in Academic Administration
1965	Visiting professor, summer session, University of Colorado
1965–62	Member, Academic Council, San José State College (University)
c. 1965–75	Evening instructor, San José Junior College
1971	Visiting professor, summer quarter, California State University, Hayward
1998	Member, Executive Board, State University-Emeritus and Retired Faculty Association

Joan Campbell

Born Johanna Maria Stolper, 22 June 1929 in Berlin; died 3 March 2013 in Toronto, Ontario
Parents: Gustav Stolper and Antonie (Toni) Kassowitz
1933 to the U.S., 1950 to the U.K., 1957 to New Zealand, 1960 to Canada

1950	A.B. Radcliffe College
1952	M.A. Oxford University, U.K.
1975	Ph.D. Queen's University, Ontario, "The German Werkbund: The Politics of Cultural Reform in the Applied Arts, 1907–1934"
1975–c. 90	taught, without a tenured position, at the University of Toronto, University of Western Ontario, and Ryerson University

Ad Personam

Grants from the Social Science and Humanities Research Council of Canada, the Historische Kommission Berlin, and Wilfried Laurier University

See the account by Joan Campbell's mother, Toni Stolper, *Ein Leben in Brennpunkten unserer Zeit. Wien, Berlin, New York, Gustav Stolper, 1888–1947* (1960)

Selected Publications

The German Werkbund: The Politics of Reform in the Applied Arts (1978). German edition: *Der Deutsche Werkbund. 1907–1934* (1981, pbk. 1989)
Joy in Work, German Work: The National Debate, 1800–1945 (1989)

Gerard Ernest Caspary

Born 10 January 1929 in Frankfurt/M.; died 6 April 2008 in Berkeley, CA
Parents: Ernst Caspary and Sophie Krautheimer
1933 to France, 1946 to the U.S.

1950	B.A. Swarthmore College
1952	M.A. Harvard University
1957–62	Instructor, Smith College
1962	Ph.D. Harvard University, "The King and the Two Laws: A Study of the Influence of Roman and Canon Law on the Development of Ideas on Kingship in Fourteenth Century England"
1962–70	Assistant to associate professor, Smith College
1970–77	Associate professor, University of California, Berkeley
1978–2004	Professor, University of California, Berkeley

Ad Personam

1962	Guggenheim fellowship

Gerard E. Caspary Papers, 1983–2003, University of California, Berkeley, Bancroft Library

Selected Publication

Politics and Exegesis: Origen and the Two Swords of Luke (1979)

John Leonard Clive

Born Hans Leo Kleyff, 25 September 1924 in Berlin; died 7 January 1990 in Cambridge, MA
Parents: Bruno Kleyff and Rose Rosenfeld
1937 to the U.K., 1940 to the U.S.

1937–40	Buxton College, Derbyshire
1943	A.B. University of North Carolina
1943–46	served in U.S. Army, OSS Junior Member
1947	M.A. Harvard University
1952	Ph.D. Harvard University, "The Edinburgh Review (1802–1815) and its Background"
1952–60	Instructor to associate professor, Harvard University
1960–65	Assistant to associate professor, University of Chicago
1965–75	Professor of history and of history and literature, Harvard University
1978–89	William R. Kenan Jr. Professor of History and Literature, Harvard University

Ad Personam

1957–58	Guggenheim fellowship
1962–63	ACLS grant
1964–65	Fellow, Center for Advanced Study in the Behavioral Sciences, Stanford
1974	National Book Award for *Thomas Babington Macaulay*
1976	Robert Livingston Schuyler Prize, AHA, for *Thomas Babington Macaulay*
1975–82	Senior fellow, Harvard Society of Fellows
1974–	AAAS fellow

After the Victorians: Private Conscience and Public Duty in Modern Britain. Essays in Memory of John Clive, ed. Susan Pedersen et al. (1994)

Selected Publications

Scotch Reviewers: The Edinburgh Review, 1802–1815 (1957)
Ed. and trans., with Oscar Handlin: Gottlieb Mittelberger, *Journey to Pennsylvania* (1960)
Ed.: Thomas Carlyle, *History of Friedrich II of Prussia Called Frederick the Great* (1969)
Thomas Babington Macaulay: The Shaping of the Historian (1973)
Not by Fact Alone: Essays on the Writing and Reading of History (1989)

Alexander Dallin

Born Alexander Dalin, 21 May 1924 in Berlin; died 22 July 2000 in Stanford, CA
Parents: David J. Dallin and Eugenia Bein
1939 to France, 1940 via Portugal to the U.S.

1943–46	served in U.S. Army
1947	B.A. City College of New York
1948	M.A. Columbia University
1949	Russian Area Studies Certificate, Russian Institute, Columbia University
1950–51	Research associate, Russian Research Center, Harvard University
1951–53	Harvard Émigré Interview Project, Harvard University
1951–54	Associate director, New York Research Program on the U.S.S.R
1953	Ph.D. Columbia University, "German Policy and the Occupation of the Soviet Union, 1941–1944"
1954–56	Senior analyst, 1955 director of research, War Documentation Project, Alexandria, VA
1956–58	Visiting assistant professor of political science, Columbia University
1958–61	Associate professor, Columbia University
1961–65	Professor and (1962–67) director, Russian Institute, Columbia University
1965–71	Adlai Stevenson Professor of International Relations, Columbia University
1971–94	Professor of history and political science, Stanford University
1971–85	Senior research fellow, Hoover Institution, Stanford
1985–89	and 1992–1994: Director of Center for Russian and East European Studies, Stanford University

1994–96   Raymond A. Spruance Professor of International Relations, Stanford University

Ad Personam

1950–52   SSRC fellowship
1957   George Lewis Beer Prize, AHA, for *German Rule in Russia*
1961–62   Guggenheim fellowship
1965–66   Fulbright fellowship
1970–71   Fellow, Center for Advanced Study in the Behavioral Sciences, Stanford University
1978–79   Kennan Institute fellowship, Woodrow Wilson International Center for Scholars
1978–80   President, Western Slavic Association
1984–85   President, American Association for the Advancement of Slavic Studies
1985–90   Chairman, National Council for Soviet and East European Research
1985–90   President, International Council for Soviet and East European Studies
1994   Cofounder, European University, St. Petersburg, Russia

Alexander Dallin Papers, 1933–1972. Hoover Institute Archives, Stanford University
Alexander Dallin Papers, 1934–1935. Butler Library, Columbia University
Reexamining the Soviet Experience: Essays in Honor of Alexander Dallin, ed. David Holloway and Norman Naimark (1996)

Selected Publications

with the assistance of Conrad F. Latour, *The German Occupation of the USSR in World War II: A Bibliography* (1955)
German Rule in Russia, 1941–1945: A Study of Occupation Policies (1957, ²1981)
Soviet Conduct in World Affairs: A Selection of Readings (1960)
The Soviet Union at the United Nations: An Inquiry into Soviet Motives and Objectives (1962)
Russian Diplomacy in Eastern Europe, 1914–1917 (1963)
Ed., with Jonathan Harris and Grey Hodnett, *Diversity in International Communism: A Documentary Record, 1961–1963* (1963)
Ed., with Alan F. Westin, *Politics in the Soviet Union: 7 Cases* (1966)
Ed., with Thomas B. Larson, *Soviet Politics since Khrushchev* (1968)
with George W. Breslauer, *Political Terror in Communist Systems* (1970)
Ed., with Dorothy Atkinson and Gail Warshofsky Lapidus, *Women in Russia* (1977)
Ed., *The Twenty-Fifth Congress of the CPSU: Assessment and Context* (1977)
Black Box: KAL 007 and the Superpowers (1985)
Ed., *The Gorbachev Era* (1986)
Ed., with Bertrand Patenaude, *Soviet Scholarship under Gorbachev* (1988)
Ed., with Philip J. Farley, *U.S.-Soviet Security Cooperation: Achievements, Failures, Lessons* (1988)
Ed., with Gail Warshofsky Lapidus, *The Soviet System in Crisis: A Reader of Western and Soviet Views* (1991)
Ed., *The Khrushchev and Brezhnev Years* (1992)
Ed., *The Nature of the Soviet System* (1992)

Ed., *Soviet Foreign Policy, 1917–1990* (1992)
Ed., with Bertrand Patenaude, *Stalin and Stalinism* (1992)
Ed., *Political Parties in Russia* (1993)
Odessa, 1941–1944: A Case Study of Soviet Territory under Foreign Rule (1998)
Ed., *Dimitrov and Stalin, 1934–1943: Letters from the Soviet Archives* (2000)

Gabrielle Simon Edgcomb

Born 23 June 1920 in Berlin; died 22 May 1997 in Washington, DC
1936 to the U.S.

	B.A. University of Chicago
1951	M.A. University of Chicago
	Research specialist and bibliographer, AAAS
1984–	Research consultant, Smithsonian Institution, Washington, DC
	Resident scholar, Anson Phelps Stokes Institute
1988–	Research associate, German Historical Institute, Washington, DC

Ad Personam

1960s   to 1980s in Washington, DC: executive director, Committee for a Sane Nuclear Policy; high school teacher; public relations officer, National Welfare Rights Organization; member DC Civilian Complaint Review Board of the DC Police

Gabrielle Simon Edgcomb Collection, United States Holocaust Memorial Museum

Selected Publications

Comp., *Man-made Lakes: A Selected Guide to the Literature. An Aid to Planning Multi-Disciplinary Research on New African Reservoirs* (1965)
with Mayra Lourdes Buvinic and Cheri Storton Adams, *Women in Development: Preliminary Annotated Bibliography* (1975)
with Mayra Buvinic, Cheri S. Adams, and Maritta Koch-Weser, *Women and World Development: An Annotated Bibliography* (1976)
Working Cultures (1984)
From Swastika to Jim Crow: Refugee Scholars at Black Colleges (1993)
Trans., with Eric A. Plaut and Kevin Anderson: Eric A. Plaut and Kevin Anderson, eds., *Marx on Suicide* (1999)

Klaus Werner Epstein

Born 6 April 1927 in Hamburg; died 26 June 1967 in Bonn

Parents: Fritz Theodor Epstein and Herta Bertelsmann
1934 to the Netherlands, 1937 to the U.S.

1934–37	attended boarding school, Eerde, Netherlands
1945	served in U.S. Navy
1948	B.A. Harvard University
1950	Teaching fellow, Harvard University
1953	Ph.D. Harvard University, "The British Constitutional Crisis: 1909–1911"
1953–57	Instructor Harvard University
1957–60	Assistant professor, Harvard University
1960–63	Associate professor, Brown University
1963–67	Professor, Department of History, Brown University

Ad Personam

1953	Jay Prize, Harvard University
1955–56	Fulbright lecturer, University of Hamburg
1959	SSRC fellowship, University of Cologne
1962–63	Visiting professor, University of Bonn
1966–67	Guggenheim fellowship

Selected Publications

Matthias Erzberger and the Dilemma of German Democracy (1959). German edition: *Matthias Erzberger und das Dilemma der deutschen Demokratie* (1962)
Germany after Adenauer (1964)
The Genesis of German Conservatism (1966). German edition: *Die Ursprünge des Konservativismus in Deutschland. Der Ausgangspunkt: Die Herausforderung durch die Französische Revolution 1770–1806* (1973)
Vom Kaiserreich zum Dritten Reich. Geschichte und Geschichtswissenschaft im 20 Jahrhundert. Ein Leitfaden (1972)
The British Constitutional Crisis: 1909–1911 (1987)

Frank Eyck

Born Ulrich Franz Joseph Eyck, 13 July 1921 in Berlin; died 28 December 2004 in Calgary, Alberta
Parents: Erich Eyck and Hedwig Kosterlitz
1936 to the U.K., 1968 to Canada

1936–40	St. Paul's School, London
1940–46	served in British Army
1949	B.A. Worcester College, Oxford
1949–56	Journalist with BBC, London
1954	M.A. Worcester College, Oxford

1956–58	Research fellow, St. Antony's College, Oxford
1958	B.Litt. Oxford
1958–59	Assistant lecturer, University of Liverpool
1959–68	Lecturer in modern European history, Exeter University
1968–87	Professor of history, University of Calgary, Alberta

Ad Personam

1962	Research grant, DAAD
1965	Grant, British Academy
1974–79	Vice-Chairman, Council of the Inter-University Center of Postgraduate Studies in Dubrovnik, Yugoslavia
1982	Visiting professor, University of Würzburg
2013–	Annual Frank Eyck Memorial Lecture, University of Calgary

Selected Publications

The Prince Consort: A Political Biography (1959). German edition: *Prinzgemahl Albert von England. Eine politische Biographie* (1961)
The Frankfurt Parliament 1848–1849 (1968). German edition: *Deutschlands große Hoffnung. Die Frankfurter Nationalversammlung 1848–1849* (1973)
Religion and Politics in German History: From the Beginnings to the French Revolution (1998)
The Revolutions of 1848–49 (1972)
Ed.: Frederick Hertz, *The German Public Mind in the Nineteenth Century: A Social History of German Political Sentiments, Aspirations, and Ideas* (1975)
G. P. Gooch: A Study in History and Politics (1982)
A Historian's Pilgrimage: Memoirs and Reflections, ed. Rosemarie Eyck (2009)
A New Look at History: A Collection of Essays, ed. and trans. Rosemarie Eyck (2011)

Franz Gunther Eyck

Born 10 July 1912 in Magdeburg; died 18 October 2009 in Alexandria, VA
Parents: Hans Eyck and Erna Kallmann
1933 to Palestine, 1947 to the U.S.

1932–33	attended Berlin University
1941–46	served in the British Army, Royal Corps of Signals
1946	Instructor, British Council
1948	B.A. Alma College, Michigan
1950	M.A. New York University
1952	Ph.D. New York University, "The Political Theories and Activities of the German Academic Youth between 1815 and 1819"
1955	M.Sc. in library science, Columbia University
1956–60	Central Intelligence Agency, Area and Language School
1959–2006	Lecturer to distinguished adjunct professor at American University, departments of history and political science and the School of International Service

1960–82	United States Information Agency
	Lecturer, New York University, Rutgers University, University of Texas, U.S. Navy War College and George Washington University
1969–70	Henry L. Stimson Chair of Political Science, U.S. Army War College

Ad Personam

1950	Penfield Scholarship
1976	Distinguished Service Award, American University
1997	American University Faculty Award for Outstanding Teaching
2010–	F. Gunther Eyck Award, American University

Selected Publications

The Voice of Nations: European National Anthems and Their Authors (1995)
Loyal Rebels: Andreas Hofer and the Tyrolean Uprising of 1809 (1986)
The Benelux Countries: An Historical Survey (1959)
External Information and Cultural Relations Programs [of the] Federal Republic of Germany (1973)
Pantha Rei: A Century's Memoir (2010)

Henry Leo Feingold

Born Heinrich Leo Feingold, 6 February 1931 in Ludwigshafen
Parents: Marcus Feingold and Frieda Singer
1938 to Belgium, 1939 to the U.S.

1953	B.A. Brooklyn College
1953–65	Teacher of history in secondary school system, New York
1954	M.A. Brooklyn College
1954–57	and 1966: served in U.S. Army
1955–56	Lecturer, University of Maryland, extension program in Germany
1966	Ph.D. New York University, "The Politics of Rescue: A Study of American Diplomacy and Politics Related to the Rescue of Refugees, 1938–1944"
1967–68	Lecturer, CUNY
1968–76	Lecturer and assistant to associate professor, Baruch College
1976–98	Professor, Baruch College
1998–	Director, Jewish Resource Center at Baruch College

Ad Personam

1966	Founders' Day Award, New York University
1971–73	Adjunct professor, Yeshiva University
1972	Leon Jolson Award, Jewish Book Council, for *The Politics of Rescue*

1973–76	Adjunct lecturer, Institute for Advanced Studies in the Humanities, Jewish Theological Institute of America
1983–88	Chairman, Academic Council of the American Jewish Historical Society
1986	Presidential Award for Excellence in Scholarship, Baruch College
1989–92	President, Labor Zionist Alliance
1994	Lee Friedman Award in American Jewish History
1995	Morim Award, Jewish Teachers Association

Selected Publications

The Politics of Rescue: The Roosevelt Administration and the Holocaust, 1938–1945 (1970, ²1980)
Zion in America: The Jewish Experience from Colonial Times to the Present (1974)
A Midrash on the History of American Jewry (1982)
Did American Jewry Do Enough during the Holocaust? (1985)
A Time for Searching: Entering the Mainstream, 1920–1945 (1992)
Ed., *The Jewish People in America*, 5 vols. (1992)
Lest Memory Cease: Finding Meaning in the American Jewish Past (1996)
Silent No More: Saving the Jews of Russia: The American Jewish Effort, 1967–1989 (2006)
Jewish Power in America: Myth and Reality (2011)

Herman Freudenberger

Born Hermann Freudenberger, 14 April 1922 in Eberbach, Baden; died 10 February 1917 in Houston, TX
Parents: Alfred Freudenberger and Frieda Grünebaum
1934 to the U.S.

–1934	attended secondary school in Eberbach
1939–42	worked as clerk and in mattress factory, Chicago
1942–46	served in U.S. Army
1946–49	worked in shoe polish factory
1950	B.S. Columbia University
1951	M.A. Columbia University, "The Patent of Toleration (1782) and Its Background"
1955–56	Lecturer, School of Insurance, New York
1956–60	Instructor in history, Brooklyn College
1957	Ph.D. Columbia University, "A Case Study of the Government's Role in Economic Development in the Eighteenth Century: The Brno Fine-Cloth Factory"
1960–62	Assistant professor, Montana State University, Missoula
1962–	Associate to full professor, Department of Economics, Tulane University

Ad Personam

1953–55	Fulbright scholar, Vienna

1959	Fellowship, American Philosophical Society, Prague and Vienna
1968	ACLS-SSRC fellowship
1974–75	Visiting lecturer, Vienna

Selected Publications

The Waldstein Woolen Mill: Noble Entrepreneurship in Eighteenth-Century Bohemia (1963)
with Gerhard Mensch, *Von der Provinzstadt zur Industrieregion (Brünn-Studie). Ein Beitrag zur Politökonomie der Sozialinnovation, dargestellt am Innovationsschub der industriellen Revolution im Raume Brünn* (1975)
The Industrialization of a Central European City: Brno and the Fine Woollen Industry in the 18th Century (1977)
Ed. and trans., with Emmet Larkin, *A Redemptorist Missionary in Ireland, 1851–1854: Memoirs by Joseph Prost* (1998)
Lost Momentum: Austrian Economic Development 1750s–1830s (2003)

Gerald Freund

Born Gerhard Freund, 14 October 1930 in Berlin; died 4 May 1997 in New York, NY
Parents: Kurt Freund and Annelise Josephthal
1939 to the U.K., 1940 to the U.S.

1952	B.A. Haverford College
1955	D.Phil. Oxford University, "Germany's Political and Military Relations with Soviet Russia, 1918–1926: From Brest-Litovsk to the Treaty of Berlin"
1955–56	Research fellow, St. Anthony's College, Oxford
1958–60	Assistant professor, Haverford College
1960–69	Administrator with Rockefeller Foundation, New York
1969–70	Assistant to Kingman Brewster Jr., president of Yale University
1970–71	Executive vice president, Film Society of Lincoln Center, NY
1971–80	Dean of the humanities and arts, Hunter College
1980–83	Vice president, John D. and Catherine T. MacArthur Foundation, first director of the MacArthur Foundation's Prize Fellows Program
1985–97	Director, Whiting Writers' Awards, Mrs. Giles Whiting Foundation
1989–96	Executive director to senior consultant, Harlem Educational Activities Fund
1996	President, Private Funding Associates

Ad Personam

1952–54	Fulbright fellowship
1956–57	and 1959–60: Rockefeller Foundation fellowship
1956–57	Research associate, Institute for Advanced Study, Princeton
1957–58	Research fellow, Council on Foreign Relations, New York
1957–59	Carnegie Endowment fellow
1996–	Gerald Freund Fellowship of the MacDowell Colony

Selected Publications

Unholy Alliance: Russian-German Relations from the Treaty of Brest-Litovsk to the Treaty of Berlin (1957)
Germany between Two Worlds (1961)
Narcissism & Philanthropy: Ideas and Talent Denied (1966)

Paul Georg Fried

Born 4 April 1919 in Leipzig; died 24 July 2006 in Holland, MI
Parents: Paul Markus Fried and Emilie Grünhaut
1938 deported to Czechoslovakia, 1939 to England, 1940 to the U.S.

1940–42	and 1945–46 studied at Hope College, Michigan
1942–45	served in U.S. Army
1947	M.A. Harvard
1947–49	Chief translator, Foreign Office section, Nuremberg Military Tribunal
1949	Dr. phil. University of Erlangen, "Die tschechische Frage in den Akten des Auswärtigen Amtes"
1951–52	Lecturer, University of Maryland, extension program in Germany
1951–53	Civilian consultant, United States Air Force Historical Research Division in Germany
1953–84	Instructor to professor, Hope College
1956–69	and 1971–73, Director, Vienna Summer School, Hope College
1964–81	Director of international education, Hope College

Ad Personam

	Member, Michigan Academy of Science, Arts and Letters
	Chairman, International Education Committee, Great Lakes Colleges Association
1968	Gold Medal of Merit for outstanding accomplishments for the Republic of Austria
1981	Paul G. Fried Fund to promote international programs at Hope College
1984	Distinguished Alumni Award, Hope College

Paul G. Fried Collection, De Pree Art Center, Hope College
Into All the World: Hope College and International Affairs. Essays in Honor of Paul G. Fried, ed. Robert J. Donia and John M. Mulder (1985)

Selected Publication

Ed., *Die Welt des Rolf Italiaander* (1973)

Henry Friedlander

Born Heinz Egon Friedländer, 24 September 1930 in Berlin; died 17 October 2012 in Bangor, ME
Parents: Bernhard Fritz Friedländer and Ruth Löwenthal
1947 to the U.S.

1953	B.A. Temple University
1954	M.A. University of Pennsylvania
1957–58	worked for the AHA's War Documentation Project, Alexandria, VA
1958–64	Instructor, Louisiana State University
1964–67	Assistant professor, McMaster University
1967–70	Assistant professor, University of Missouri, St. Louis
1968	Ph.D. University of Pennsylvania, "The German Revolution 1918–1919"
1970–72	Faculty, CUNY
1975–2001	Professor, Judaic Studies, Brooklyn College
1997–2009	Faculty, The National Judicial College

Ad Personam

1955–56	Harrison fellow
1956–57	SSRC fellow
1971–72	Fellow, Research Foundation for Jewish Immigration
1996–97	Ruth Meltzer Senior fellow, U.S. Holocaust Memorial Museum
1996	Bruno Brand Tolerance Book Award, Simon Wiesenthal Center, for *The Origins of the Nazi Genocide*
1997	DAAD Book Prize, German Studies Association, for *The Origins of the Nazi Genocide*
2000	Henry Frank Guggenheim Foundation Research Grant
2001–07	Director, International Commission of Experts on the Reconstruction of the Documentation Center at the Bergen-Belsen Concentration Camp
2009	Niedersächsischer Verdienstorden

Selected Publications

Détente in Historical Perspective: The First CUNY Conference on History and Politics (1975)
Ed., with Sybil Milton, *The Holocaust: Ideology, Bureaucracy, and Genocide. The San Jose Papers* (1980)
Classified and Annotated Bibliography of Books and Articles on the Immigration and Acculturation of Jews from Central Europe to the U.S.A since 1933 (1981)
Ed., with Sybil Milton, *Archives of the Holocaust: An International Collection of Selected Documents* (1989)
The German Revolution of 1918 (1992)
The Origins of Nazi Genocide: From Euthanasia to the Final Solution (1995). German edition: *Der Weg zum NS-Genozid. Von der Euthanasie zur Endlösung* (1997)

Ed., with Nathan Stoltzfus, *Nazi Crimes and the Law* (2008)

Lewis Henry Gann

Born Ludwig Hermann Ganz, 28 January 1924 in Mainz; died 17 January 1997 in Palo Alto, CA
Parents: Hermann Ganz and Charlotte Fromberg
1938 to England, 1954 to Zimbabwe (then Rhodesia), 1964 to the U.S.

1943	and 1947–50, Domus scholar, Balliol College, Oxford
1944–47	served in British Army
1950	B.A. Balliol College, Oxford
1950–52	Researcher in North Rhodesia with Rhodes-Livingstone Institute
1952–54	Assistant lecturer, University of Manchester
1954–63	Archivist and editor, National Archives of Rhodesia and Nyasaland
1954	M.A. Oxford
1955	M.Litt. Oxford
1964	D.Phil. Oxford, "The Growth of a Plural Society: Social, Economic and Political Aspects of Northern Rhodesian Development 1890–1953, with Special Reference to the Problem of Racial Relations"
1964–66	Research associate, Hoover Institution, Stanford
1966–93	Deputy curator, African Collection, Hoover Institution
1993–95	Curator, West European Collection, Hoover Institution

Ad Personam

1963–66	Grant, Relm Foundation
1968	Member, editorial board, *International Journal of African Historical Studies*
1973	Grant, Earhart Foundation
1973–75	NEH grant
1974–75	Stipendary consultant, Historische Kommission, Berlin
1995	Officers' Cross of the Order of Merit, Federal Republic of Germany
	Fellow, Royal Historical Society, London

Selected Publications

The Birth of a Plural Society: The Development of Northern Rhodesia under the British South Africa Company, 1894–1914 (1958, 1981)
with Peter Duignan, *White Settlers in Tropical Africa* (1962)
A History of Northern Rhodesia: Early Days to 1953 (1963, 1969)
with M. Gefand, *Huggins of Rhodesia: The Man and His Country* (1964)
with Peter Duignan, *Burden of Empire: An Appraisal of Western Colonialism in Africa South of the Sahara* (1967)
Ed., with Peter Duignan, *Colonialism in Africa, 1870–1960*, 5 vols. (1969–1975)
Central Africa: The Former British States (1971)

Guerrillas in History (1971)
with Peter Duignan, *Africa: The Land & The People* (1972)
with Peter Duignan, *Africa and the World: An Introduction to the History of Sub-Saharan Africa from Antiquity to 1840* (1972)
with Peter Duignan, *The Rulers of German Africa, 1884–1914* (1977)
with Peter Duignan, *The Rulers of British Africa, 1870–1914* (1978)
with Peter Duignan, *South Africa: War, Revolution, or Peace?* (1978)
with Peter Duignan, *The Rulers of Belgian Africa, 1884–1914* (1979)
with Peter Duignan, *African Proconsuls: European Governors in Africa* (1978)
with Peter Duignan, *Africa South of the Sahara: The Challenge to Western Security* (1981)
with Thomas H. Henriksen, *The Struggle for Zimbabwe: Battle in the Bush* (1981)
with Peter Duignan, *The Middle East and North Africa: The Challenge to Western Security* (1981)
with Peter Duignan, *Why South Africa Will Survive: A Historical Analysis* (1981)
with Peter Duignan, *Africa between East and West* (1983)
with Peter Duignan, *The United States and Africa: A History* (1984)
with Peter Duignan, *The Hispanics in the United States: A History* (1986)
Ed., with Arthur J. Knoll, *Germans in the Tropics: Essays in German Colonial History* (1987)
Ed., *The Defense of Western Europe* (1987)
with Peter Duignan, *Hope for South Africa?* (1991)
with Peter Duignan, *The Rebirth of the West: The Americanization of the Democratic World, 1945–1958* (1992)
with Peter Duignan, *Eastern Europe: The Great Transformation, 1985–1991* (1992)
with Peter Duignan, *The United States and the New Europe, 1985–1992* (1992)
with Peter Duignan, *The USA and the New Europe, 1945–1993* (1994)
with Peter Duignan, *Contemporary Europe and the Atlantic Alliance: A Political History* (1998)
with Peter Duignan, *The Spanish Speakers in the United States: A History* (1998)
Ed., with Peter Duignan, *The Debate in the United States over Immigration* (1998)
with Peter Duignan, *Africa and the World: An Introduction to the History of Sub-Saharan Africa from Antiquity to 1840* (2000)

Hans Wilhelm Gatzke

Born 10 December 1915 in Dülken; died 11 October 1987 in New Haven, CT
Parents: Wilhelm Gatzke and Else Schwab
1937 to the U.S.

1934–35	Exchange student, Williams College, MA
1935–37	studied at Universities of Munich and Bonn
1938	B.A. Williams College
1939	M.A. Harvard University
1939–43	Teaching fellow and tutor, Harvard University
1944–46	served in U.S. Army
1947	Ph.D. Harvard University, "Drang nach Westen: A Study of Germany's Western War Aims during the First World War"
1947–56	Assistant to associate professor, Johns Hopkins University

1956–64   Professor, Johns Hopkins University
1964–86   Professor, Yale University

Ad Personam

1941–42   Sheldon Traveling fellowship
1950   Herbert Baxter Adams Prize, AHA, for *Germany's Drive to the West*
1951–52   Member, Institute for Advanced Study, Princeton
1954–57   Member, editorial board, *Journal of Modern History* and *Current History*
1956–57   Guggenheim fellowship
1962–63   ACLS and Rockefeller Foundation grant
1969–76   American Committee on the History of the Second World War
1969   Editorial board, *Documents on German Foreign Policy, 1918–1945*

German Nationalism and the European Response, 1890–1945, ed. Carole Fink, Isabel Hull, and MacGregor Knox (1985)

Selected Publications

Ed. and trans.: Carl von Clausewitz, *Principles of War* (1942, 2003)
Germany's Drive to the West: A Study of Germany's War Aims during the First World War (1950, repr. 1967 and 1978)
Stresemann and the Rearmament of Germany (1954)
with William L. Langer, *An Encyclopedia of World History, Ancient, Medieval and Modern, Chronologically Arranged.* (1952, 3rd ed. 1956, rev. ed. 1963)
The Present in Perspective (1957, ²1961, ³1965, ⁴1968)
with Joseph Strayer and Elmore Harris Harbison, *The Mainstream of Civilization* (1969, ²1974, ³1979, ⁴1984)
Ed., *European Diplomacy between Two Wars, 1919–1939* (1972)
Germany and the United States: A "Special Relationship?" (1980)
with Stanley Chodorow and Conrad Schirokauer, *A History of the World* (1986)

Peter Gay

Born Peter Joachim Fröhlich, 20 June 1923 in Berlin; died 12 May 2015 in New York, NY
Parents: Moritz Peter Fröhlich and Helga Kohnke
1939 to Cuba, 1941 to the U.S.

1946   B.A. University of Denver
1947   M.A. Columbia University, Instructor, Columbia University
1951   Ph.D. Columbia University, "The Dilemma of Democratic Socialism: Eduard Bernstein's Challenge to Marx"
1953–62   Assistant to associate professor, Columbia University
1962–69   Professor, Columbia University
1967–69   William R. Shepard Chair, Columbia University

1969–84   Durfee Professor of History, Yale University
1984–93   Sterling Professor of History, Yale University
1997–2003   Director, New York Public Library's Center for Scholars and Writers

Ad Personam

1950–51   SSRC fellowship
1955–56   Alfred Hodder Jr. fellowship, Princeton University
1959–60   ACLS fellowship
1963–64   Member, Center for Advanced Study in the Behavioral Sciences, Stanford
1966   National Book Award for *The Rise of Modern Paganism*
1967   Melcher Book Award for *The Rise of Modern Paganism*
1967–68   Guggenheim fellowship
1969   Ralph Waldo Emerson Award of Phi Beta Kappa for *Weimar Culture*
1970–71   Overseas fellow, Churchill College, Cambridge
1978   Rockefeller Foundation fellowship
1978   Fellow, Institute for Advanced Study, Berlin
1990   Dr. A. H. Heineken Prize for History
1996   Gold Medal, American Academy of Arts and Letters
1999   Geschwister-Scholl-Preis, Munich
2004   Award for Scholarly Distinction, AHA

Peter Gay Papers, [c. 1954]–1969. Butler Library, Columbia University
Enlightenment, Passion, Modernity: Historical Essays in European Thought and Culture, ed. Mark S. Micale and Robert L. Dietle (2000)

Selected Publications

The Dilemma of Democratic Socialism: Eduard Bernstein's Challenge to Marx (1952, repr. 1962). German edition: *Das Dilemma des demokratischen Sozialismus. Eduard Bernsteins Auseinandersetzung mit Marx* (1954)
Voltaire's Politics: The Poet as Realist (1959, ²1988). Italian edition 1991
The Party of Humanity: Essays in the French Enlightenment (1964)
Ed., with Shepard B. Clough and Charles K. Warner, *The European Past*. 2 vols. (1964)
Age of Enlightenment (1966). German editions: *Zeitalter der Aufklärung* (1967) and *Dichter, Denker, Jakobiner. Aufklärung und Revolution* (1973). French edition 1974
The Enlightenment: An Interpretation. Vol. 1, *The Rise of Modern Paganism* (1966, 1995)
A Loss of Mastery: Puritan Historians in Colonial America (1966)
Weimar Culture: The Outsider as Insider (1968). German edition: *Die Republik der Außenseiter. Geist und Kultur in der Weimarer Zeit. 1918–1933* (1970, 2004). Japanese edition 1970. Portuguese edition 1978. Spanish edition 1984
Ed., *Deism: An Anthology* (1968)
The Enlightenment: An Interpretation. Vol. 2, *The Science of Freedom* (1969, 1996)
The Bridge of Criticism: Dialogues among Lucian, Erasmus, and Voltaire on the Enlightenment—On History and Hope, Imagination and Reason, Constraint and Freedom—and on Its Meaning for Our Time (1970)
Ed., *Eighteenth-Century Studies Presented to Arthur M. Wilson* (1972)

Ed., with John A. Garraty, *The Columbia History of the World* (1972). Spanish edition 1981
Ed., with Gerald J. Cavanaugh (vols. 2 and 3 with Victor G. Wexler), *Historians at Work* (1972–75)
with R. K. Webb, *Modern Europe* (1973)
Ed., *The Enlightenment: A Comprehensive Anthology* (1973)
Style in History (1974, 1988)
Art and Act: On Causes in History—Manet, Gropius, Mondrian (1976)
Freud, Jews, and Other Germans: Masters and Victims in Modernist Culture (1978). German edition: *Freud, Juden und andere Deutsche. Herren und Opfer in der modernen Kultur* (1986). Japanese edition 1987. Italian edition 1990
The Bourgeois Experience: Victoria to Freud. Vol. 1, *Education of the Senses* (1984). German edition: *Erziehung der Sinne. Sexualität im bürgerlichen Zeitalter* (1986)
Freud for Historians (1985). German edition: *Freud für Historiker* (1994). Dutch edition 1987. Portuguese edition 1989. Japanese edition 1995
The Bourgeois Experience: Victoria to Freud. Vol. 2, *The Tender Passion* (1986). German edition: *Die zarte Leidenschaft. Liebe im bürgerlichen Zeitalter* (1987)
A Godless Jew: Freud, Atheism, and the Making of Psychoanalysis (1987). German edition: *"Ein gottloser Jude." Sigmund Freuds Atheismus und die Entwicklung der Psychoanalyse* (1988). French and Italian editions 1989. Portuguese and Japanese editions 1992. Spanish edition 1993
Freud: A Life for Our Time (1988). German edition: *Freud. Eine Biographie für unsere Zeit* (1989, [4]2001, new ed. 2006). Italian edition 1988. Dutch edition 1989. Spanish edition 1989, [2]1990. Finnish edition 1990. French and Danish editions 1991. Hebrew edition 1993. Portuguese edition 1995
Ed., *The Freud Reader* (1989)
Reading Freud: Explorations & Entertainments (1990). German edition: *Freud entziffern* (1992)
Sigmund Freud and Art: His Personal Collection of Antiquities (1993)
The Bourgeois Experience: Victoria to Freud. Vol. 3, *The Cultivation of Hatred* (1993). German edition: *Kult der Gewalt. Aggression im bürgerlichen Zeitalter* (1996)
The Bourgeois Experience: Victoria to Freud. Vol. 4, *The Naked Heart* (1995). German edition: *Die Macht des Herzens. Das 19. Jahrhundert und die Erforschung des Ich* (1997)
The Bourgeois Experience: Victoria to Freud. Vol. 5, *Pleasure Wars* (1998). German edition: *Bürger und Boheme. Kunstkriege des 19. Jahrhunderts* (1999)
My German Question: Growing Up in Nazi Berlin (1998). German edition: *Meine deutsche Frage. Jugend in Berlin, 1933–1939* (1999)
Mozart (1999). German edition: *Mozart* (2001)
Schnitzler's Century (2002). German edition: *Das Zeitalter des Doktor Arthur Schnitzler. Innenansichten des 19. Jahrhunderts* (2002)
Modernism: The Lure of Heresy (2007). German edition: *Die Moderne. Eine Geschichte des Aufbruchs* (2008)
Why the Romantics Matter (2015)

Hanna Holborn Gray

Born 25 October 1930 in Heidelberg
Parents: Hajo Holborn and Annemarie Bettmann
1933 to the U.K., 1934 to the U.S.

1950	B.A. Bryn Mawr College
1950–51	Fulbright Scholar, Oxford University
1953–54	Instructor, Bryn Mawr College
1955–57	Teaching fellow, Harvard University
1957	Ph.D. Harvard University, "History and Rhetoric in Quattrocento Humanism"
1957–59	Instructor, Harvard University
1959–60	Assistant professor, Harvard University
1961–72	Assistant to associate professor, University of Chicago
1972–74	Dean, college of arts and sciences and professor of history, Northwestern University
1974–78	Provost and professor of history, Yale University
1977–78	Interim president, Yale University
1978–93	President and professor of history, University of Chicago
1993–2000	Harry Pratt Judson Distinguished Service Professor, University of Chicago

Ad Personam

1960–61	Fellow, Newberry Library
1963–64	Visiting lecturer, Harvard University
1965–66	Visiting lecturer, Northwestern University
1965–70	Coeditor, *Journal of Modern History*
1966–67	Fellow, Center for Behavioral Studies, Stanford
1970–71	Visiting associate professor, University of California, Berkeley
1970–71	Visiting scholar, Center for Behavioral Studies, Stanford
1971–76	Chair, board of directors, ACLS
1972–78	Trustee, Institute for Advanced Study, Princeton
1973–	Fellow, AAAS
1976	Radcliffe Graduate Medal
1978	Yale Medal
1978	Honorary fellow, St. Anne's College, Oxford
1981–	Fellow, American Philosophical Society
1986	Medal of Liberty
1990	Great Cross of Merit, Federal Republic of Germany
1991	Presidential Medal of Freedom
1991	Sara Lee Frontrunner Award
1993	Jefferson Medal, American Philosophical Society
1993	Charles Frankel Prize, NEH
1994	Centennial Medal, Harvard Graduate School of Arts and Sciences
1994	Distinguished Service Award, International Institute of Education
1996	Quantrell Award for Excellence in Undergraduate Teaching, University of Chicago
1997	M. Carey Thomas Award, Bryn Mawr College
2000	Medal of Distinction, Barnard College
2004	Fritz Redlich Distinguished Alumni Award
2006	Gold Medal, National Institute of Social Sciences
2006	Newberry Library Award

2008   Chicago History Maker Award, Chicago History Museum

Over 60 honorary degrees, including honorary doctorates from Dartmouth College and Yale University 1978; Brown University and Oxford University 1979; University of Notre Dame and University of Southern California 1980; University of Michigan 1981; Duke University and Princeton University 1982; Brandeis University and Georgetown University 1983; Washington University 1985; Columbia University 1987; New York University 1988; University of Toronto 1991; McGill University 1993; Indiana University 1994; Harvard University and CUNY 1995; University of Chicago 1996; Pontifical Institute of Mediaeval Studies 2005; Rockefeller University 2010

Board member (selected) of Yale Corporation (1971–74), Harvard Corporation (1996–2005), Howard Hughes Medical Institute (chair, 1984–2012), Bryn Mawr (chair, 1978–96), Smithsonian Institution Board of Regents, Andrew W. Mellon Foundation (chair, 1982–2002), Marlboro School of Music (1990–), Council on Foreign Relations, Newberry Library (2007–)

"Some Reflections on the Second Generation," in *The Second Generation: Émigrés from Nazi Germany as Historians*, ed. Andreas W. Daum, Hartmut Lehmann, and James J. Sheehan (2016), 102–113.

Selected Publications

History and Rhetoric in Quattrocento Humanism (1956, ²1980)
Three Essays (1978)
The Liberal Arts Revisited (1981)
The Higher Learning and the New Consumerism (1983)
Educational Diversity and the Unity of Learning (1990)
with Robert E. Streeter, *One in Spirit: A Retrospective View of the University of Chicago on the Occasion of Its Centennial* (1991)
Searching for Utopia: Universities and Their Histories (2012)

Hanns Gross

Born 20 June 1928 Stockerau, Austria; died 12 July 2006 in Arlington Heights, IL
Father: Arthur Gross
1939 to the U.K., 1961 to the U.S.

1950	B.A. University of London
1963	M.A. University of Chicago
1966	Ph.D. University of Chicago, "The Debate About a German Public Law 1600–1676: An Examination of the Declining Influence of Roman Law Principles and Roman Imperial Traditions in the Constitutional and Political Thought of Lutheran Germany"
1966–67	Assistant professor, Southern Illinois University, Carbondale
1967–78	Assistant and associate professor Loyola University, Chicago

1978–99   Professor of history, Loyola University, Chicago

Selected Publications

Empire and Sovereignty: A History of the Public Law Literature in the Holy Roman Empire, 1599–1804 (1973, repr. 1975)
Rome in the Age of Enlightenment: The Post-Tridentine Syndrome and the Ançien Regime (1990)

Maria Grossmann

Born Maria Gertrude Schweinburg, 12 June 1919 in Vienna; died 31 March 2003 in Conway, MA
Parents: Fritz B. Schweinburg and Adele Geringer
1939 to the U.K., 1940 to the U.S.

1938	attended law classes at University of Vienna
1942	B.A. Smith College
1943	M.A. Radcliffe College
1947	Founder, with Walter Grossmann, Erga Foreign Books, Cambridge, MA
1956	M.S. in library science, Simmons College
1956–60	Acquisitions librarian, Andover-Harvard Theological Library
1960	Ph.D. Radcliffe College, "Humanism at Wittenberg, 1486–1517"
1960–65	Assistant librarian and head of technical services, Harvard Divinity School
1965–73	Librarian, Andover-Harvard Theological Library; member of faculty, Harvard Divinity School
1973–79	Librarian, Collection Development, Harvard University
1979–86	Librarian of the Andover-Harvard Theological Library

Ad Personam

c. 1964–65	Fellowships by the ACLS, American Philosophical Society and Deutsche Forschungsgemeinschaft; research stay in Germany
1968–69	President, American Theological Library Association
1973–79	Representative of Harvard University in Research Libraries Group

Selected Publications

Wittenberger Drucke. 1502–1517. Ein bibliographischer Beitrag zur Geschichte des Humanismus in Deutschland (1971)
Humanism in Wittenberg, 1485–1517 (1975)

Walter Grossmann

Born 5 June 1918 in Vienna; died 29 May 1992 in Conway, MA

Parents: Otto and Valerie Grossmann
1938 to Czechoslovakia, 1939 to the U.S.

1936	Matura (high school diploma) in Vienna
1941	B.A. Yankton College, South Dakota
1943	M.A. Harvard College
1947–51	Associate professor of history, Simmons College
1947–51	Founder, with Maria Grossmann, Erga Foreign Books, Cambridge, MA
1951	Ph.D. Harvard University, "Schiller's Idea of History"
1952–64	Specialist in book selection, Harvard College Library
1961	M.S. in library science, Simmons College
1961–64	Lecturer on history and literature, Harvard University
1964–66	Archibald C. Coolidge Bibliographer, Harvard University
1966–84	Professor of history, University of Massachusetts, Boston
1969–84	Director of libraries, University of Massachusetts, Boston

Ad Personam

1963	Guggenheim fellowship; 1964–65 research stay in Germany
1966–78	Visiting lecturer, School of Library Science, McGill University, Montreal
1970	Fellow, Humboldt Gesellschaft, Germany

Selected Publications

Ed.: Johann Christian Edelmann, *Sämtliche Schriften in Einzelausgaben*, 12 vols. (1969–87)
Abschied von Österreich. Ein Bericht (1975)
Johann Christian Edelmann: From Orthodoxy to Enlightenment (1976)

Helmut Gruber

Born 20 July 1928 in Judenburg, Austria; died 15 March 2014 in New York, NY
Parents: Henrich and Marie Gruber
1939 to the U.S.

1950	B.S.S. City College of New York
1951	M.A. Columbia University, "The Annexation of Austria: A Study of Its Antecedents and Results"
1956–59	Instructor, Department of History, Polytechnic Institute of Brooklyn
1959–65	Assistant to associate professor, Polytechnic Institute of Brooklyn
1962	Ph.D. in history, Columbia University, "The Politics of German Literature 1914 to 1933: A Study of the Expressionist and Objectivist Movements"
1962–	Professor and (1962–72) head, Department of Social Sciences, Polytechnic Institute of Brooklyn (since 1973: Polytechnic Institute of New York; since 1985: Polytechnic University, New York)

Ad Personam

1964	Cofounder, Socialist Scholars Conference, New York
1974–75	Visiting professor, New York University
1980	Visiting professor, Maison des sciences de l'homme, Paris
1984–99	Coeditor, *International Labor and Working-Class History*
1991–92	Center for Austrian Studies Book Prize for *Red Vienna*
1994	Visiting fellow, Institute for Human Sciences, Vienna

Selected Publications

International Communism in the Era of Lenin: A Documentary History (1967–72)
Ed., *Soviet Russia Masters the Comintern: International Communism in the Era of Stalin's Ascendancy* (1974)
Léon Blum, French Socialism and the Popular Front: A Case of Internal Contradictions (1986)
Ed., with Wolfgang Maderthaner, *Chance und Illusion. Studien zur Krise der westeuropäischen Gesellschaft in den dreissiger Jahren = Labor in Retreat: Studies on the Social Crisis in Interwar Western Europe* (1988)
Red Vienna: Experiment in Working Class Culture, 1919–1934 (1991)
Ed., with Pamela Graves, *Women and Socialism, Socialism and Women: Europe between the Two World Wars* (1998)

Erich Stephen Gruen

Born Erich Grünberger, 7 May 1935 in Vienna
Parents: Siegfried and Irma Grünberger
1939 to the U.S.

1957	B.A. Columbia University
1960	M.A. Oxford University
1964	Ph.D. Harvard University, "Criminal Trials and Roman Politics, 149–78 BC"
1964–66	Instructor, Harvard University
1966–72	Assistant to associate professor, University of California, Berkeley
1972	Professor, University of California, Berkeley
1986–	Gladys Rehard Wood Professor of History and Classics, Berkeley

Ad Personam

1957	Rhodes Scholarship
1965–72	Consultant, Education Development Corporation
1968–70	1984 and 1996: NEH fellowship
1969–70	and 1989–90: Guggenheim fellowship
1973–74	Member, Institute for Advanced Study, Princeton
1974	1978 and 2009: Visiting fellow, Merton College, Oxford
1986–	AAAS fellow

1987	Distinguished Teaching Award University of California, Berkeley
1992	President, American Philological Association
1996	Winston Fellow, Institute for Advanced Studies, Hebrew University of Jerusalem
1999	Austrian Cross of Honor for Arts and Letters
2000–	Member, American Philosophical Society
2006	Honorary member, Roman Society of London
2007–08	Villa Professor, Getty Villa
2009	Corresponding Member, German Archaeological Institute
2010	Sackler Visiting Scholar, Tel Aviv University
	Visiting professor at University of Colorado, Boulder (1981), Princeton University (1987–88), Cornell University (1991), University of Minnesota (1994), Stanford University (2006)

Selected Publications

Roman Politics and the Criminal Courts, 149–78 BC (1968)
The Last Generation of the Roman Republic (1974, 1995)
The Hellenistic World and the Coming of Rome, 2 vols. (1984, 1986)
Studies in Greek Culture and Roman Policy (1990, 1996)
Culture and National Identity in Republican Rome (1992, 1994)
Ed., with Anthony W. Bulloch, A. A. Long, and Andrew Stewart, *Images and Ideologies: Self-Definition in the Hellenistic World* (1993)
Ed., with Paul Cartledge and Peter Garsney, *Hellenistic Constructs: Essays in Culture, History, and Historiography* (1997)
Heritage and Hellenism: The Reinvention of Jewish Tradition (1998)
Diaspora: Jews amidst Greeks and Romans (2002). Hebrew edition 2004
Ed., *Cultural Borrowings and Ethnic Appropriations in Antiquity* (2005)
Rethinking the Other in Antiquity (2011)
Ed., *Cultural Identity in the Ancient Mediterranean* (2011)

Werner Leonard Gundersheimer

Born 7 April 1937 in Frankfurt/M.
Parents: Hermann S. Gundersheimer and Frieda Siegel
1939 to the U.K., 1940 to the U.S.

1959	B.A. Amherst College
1960	M.A. Harvard University
1963	Ph.D. Harvard University, "Vicissitude and Variety: The Life and Works of Louis Leroy"
1963–64	Visiting assistant professor of history, University of Wisconsin, Madison
1964–66	Junior fellow, Society of Fellows, Harvard University
1966–72	Assistant to associate professor, University of Pennsylvania
1972–	Professor, University of Pennsylvania
1983–2002	Director, Folger Shakespeare Library, Washington, DC

Ad Personam

1959–60	Woodrow Wilson scholar
1961–62	Rotary Foundation fellowship
1967–68	Visiting associate professor, Johns Hopkins University
1968	Grant, American Philosophical Society
1970–71	Member, Institute of Advanced Study, Princeton
1971–73	Visiting professor, Swarthmore College
1974	Cavaliere della Stella Solidarieta Italiana, Italy
1974–75	Guggenheim fellowship
1974–75	I Tatti fellow, Harvard Center for Renaissance Study
1976–77	Member, Carter Mondale Task Force on Humanities
1982	Visiting professor, Tel Aviv University
1986–2002	Adjunct professor of history, Amherst College
1994–97	President, Independent Research Libraries Association (IRLA)
1996–2000	President, National Humanities Alliance
1998–	Member, American Philosophical Society
2003	Visiting professor of history, Williams College
2004	Visiting professor, George Washington University
2004–	Member, AAAS

Honorary doctorates from Amherst College (1984), Williams College (1989), Muhlenberg College (1991), Davidson College (1998), Washington College (2003).

Member, board of trustees, British Institute of America and the Medici Foundation; board member, Rosenbach Museum and Library; member, Council of the Renaissance Society of America; member, Executive Council, American Jewish Historical Society

Selected Publications

Ed., *The Italian Renaissance* (1965)
The Life and Works of Louis Le Roy (1966)
Ed., *French Humanism, 1470–1600* (1969)
Ed., *Art and Life at the Court of Ercole I d'Este: The De triumphis religionis of Giovanni Sabadino degli Arienti* (1972)
Ferrara: The Style of a Renaissance Despotism (1973)

Arthur Gustav Haas

Born 21 July 1925 in Vienna; died 23 February 2016 in Knoxville, TN
Parents: Arthur Erich Haas and Emma Beatrice Huber
1935 to the U.S.

1944–46	attended U.S. Navy Japanese/Oriental Language School, University of Colorado, Boulder

1945	Bachelor of Navy Science, University of Notre Dame
1945–47	served in U.S. Army
1949	A.M. University of Notre Dame
1950–51	Lecturer in European history, Loyola University, IL
1953–54	Lecturer, Indiana University
1961	Ph.D. University of Chicago, "Metternich: Reorganization and Nationality, 1813–1818"
1963–69	Assistant to associate professor, University of Tennessee, Knoxville
1969–99	Professor, University of Tennessee, Knoxville

Ad Personam

1961–62	Research fellow, Institute of European History, Mainz

Book Publication

Metternich, Reorganization and Nationality, 1813–1818: A Story of Foresight and Frustration in the Rebuilding of the Austrian Empire (1963)

Theodore Stephen Hamerow

Born 24 August 1920 in Warsaw; died 16 February 2013 in Madison, WI
Parents: Chaim Shneyer Hamerow and Bella Rubinlicht
1930 to the U.S. via France

1938	Townsend Harris High School, New York, NY
1942	B.A. City College of New York
1943–46	served in U.S. Army in Europe
1947	M.A. Columbia University
1952	Ph.D. Yale University, "Social Conflict and Adjustment in the German Revolution of 1848–49"
1950–51	Instructor, Wellesley College
1951–52	Lecturer, University of Maryland University College – Europe
1952–58	Instructor and assistant to associate professor, University of Illinois
1958–91	Professor, University of Wisconsin, later G. P. Gooch Professor of History

Ad Personam

	Founding president, Wisconsin Association of Scholars
1962–63	Fulbright scholarship and SSRC fellowship
1978	Chair, Modern European History Section, AHA
1998	Cofounder, The Historical Society
1992–2000	Member, NEH Council
2002–	Theodore S. Hamerow Best Dissertation in European History Prize, Historical Society

In Search of a Liberal Germany: Studies in the History of German Liberalism from 1789 to the Present, ed. Konrad H. Jarausch (1990)

Selected Publications

Restoration, Revolution, Reaction: Economics and Politics in Germany, 1815–1871 (1958)
Otto von Bismarck: A Historical Assessment (1962, ²1972)
Social Foundations of German Unification, 1858–1871, 2 vols. (1969, 1972)
Ed., *The Age of Bismarck: Documents and Interpretations* (1973)
Reflections on History and Historians (1987)
From the Finland Station: The Graying of Revolution in the Twentieth Century (1990)
Ed., with David Wetzel, *International Politics and German History: The Past Informs the Present* (1997)
On the Road to the Wolf's Lair: German Resistance to Hitler (1997). German edition: *Die Attentäter. Der 20. Juli – von der Kollaboration zum Widerstand* (1999, pbk. 2004)
Remembering a Vanished World: A Jewish Childhood in Interwar Poland (2001)
Why We Watched: Europe, America, and the Holocaust (2008)

Hans Heilbronner

Born 31 January 1926 in Memmingen; died 8 June 2011 in Durham, NH
Parents: Alfred Heilbronner and Helen Liebschuetz
1939 via Switzerland to the U.K., 1940 to the U.S.

1944–46	served in U.S. Army
1949	B.A. University of Michigan
1950	M.A. University of Michigan
1954	Ph.D. University of Michigan, "The Administrations of Loris-Meilkov and Ignatiev, 1880–1882"
1954–64	Lecturer to assistant and associate professor, University of New Hampshire
1964–91	Professor, University of New Hampshire

Ad Personam

1953–54	Fulbright award, University of Paris
1961–62	SSRC grant
1968–69	Fulbright-Hays award, Athens, Greece

Raul Hilberg

Born 2 June 1926 in Vienna; died 4 August 2007 in Williston, VT
Parents: Michael Hilberg and Gisela Schachter
1939 via Cuba to the U.S.

1944 served in U.S. Army
1948 B.A. Brooklyn College
1950 M.A. Columbia University
1955 Ph.D. Columbia University in political science, "Prologue to Annihilation: A Study of the Identification, Impoverishment, and Isolation of the Jewish Victims of Nazi Policy"
1954 Instructor, Hunter College
1954–55 Instructor, University of Puerto Rico in Mayaguez
1955–56 Researcher, War Documentation Project, Alexandria, VA
1956–91 Professor, Department of Political Science, University of Vermont in Burlington

Ad Personam

1955 Clark F. Ansley Award for Dissertation
1968 Anisfield-Wolf Award, for *The Destruction of the European Jews*
1978–79 President's Commission on the Holocaust
1980–88 Member, United States Holocaust Memorial Council
1986 Leon Jolson Award for *The Destruction of the European Jews* (revised and definitive edition)
1994 Bernard Heller Prize, Hebrew Union College
1999 First recipient of Marion-Samuel-Preis, Stiftung Erinnerung Lindau
2002 Geschwister-Scholl-Preis, Munich
2002 Great Cross of Merit, Federal Republic of Germany
2005– Fellow, AAAS
2006 Raul Hilberg Distinguished Professorship of Holocaust Studies established at the University of Vermont
2007– Raul Hilberg fellowship, United States Holocaust Memorial Museum

Raul Hilberg Papers, University of Vermont Archives
Perspectives on the Holocaust: Essays in Honor of Raul Hilberg, ed. James S. Pacy (1995)
Auf den Trümmern der Geschichte. Gespräche mit Raul Hilberg, Hans Mommsen, Zygmunt Baumann, ed. Harald Welzer (1999)
Reflections on the Holocaust: Festschrift for Raul Hilberg on His Seventy-Fifth Birthday, ed. Wolfgang Mieder (2001)

Selected Publications

The Destruction of the European Jews (1961, ^{2}1985, ^{3}2003). German edition: *Die Vernichtung der europäischen Juden* (1982, ^{10}2007). French edition (1985, ^{2}2006). Italian edition 1999
Documents of Destruction: Germany and Jewry, 1933–1945 (1971)
with Stanislaw Staron and Joseph Kermish, *The Warsaw Diary of Adam Czerniakow* (1979)
Sonderzüge nach Auschwitz (1981, ^{2}1987)
Perpetrators, Victims, Bystanders: The Jewish Catastrophe, 1933–1945 (1992). German edition: *Täter, Opfer, Zuschauer. Die Vernichtung der Juden 1933–1945* (1992, ^{5}2011)
The Politics of Memory: Journey of a Holocaust Historian (1996). German edition: *Unerbetene Erinnerung. Der Weg eines Holocaust-Forschers* (1994, pbk. 2008)

Sources of Holocaust Research: An Analysis (2001). German edition: *Die Quellen des Holocaust. Entschlüsseln und interpretieren* (2009).

Gerald James Holton

Born 23 May 1922 in Berlin
Parents: Emanuel Holton and Regina Rossmann
1938 with a *Kindertransport* to the U.K., 1940 to the U.S.

–1938	attended Humanistische Gymnasium in Vienna
1940	National certificate in electrical engineering, School of Technology, Oxford
1941	B.A. Wesleyan University
1942	M.A. Wesleyan University
1942–43	Instructor, Brown University
1943–46	Office of Scientific Research and Development, Harvard University
1946	M.A. Harvard University
1947–49	Instructor, Harvard
1948	Ph.D. Harvard, "Ultrasonic Propagation in Liquids at High Pressures"
1949–59	Assistant to associate professor, Harvard
1959–75	Professor of physics, Harvard
1970–	also faculty, Department of the History of Science
1975–92	Mallinckrodt professor of physics and professor of history of science, Harvard

Ad Personam

1956–	Member, AAAS
1958–61	Founding editor, *Daedalus*
1960–61	National Science Foundation faculty fellow, Paris
1962	Exchange professor, Leningrad University and consultant UNESCO
1964	and 1967: Member, Institute for Advanced Study, Princeton
1967	R. A. Millikan Medal, American Association of Physics Teachers
1967–71	Member, board of directors, AAAS
1975–80	Member, U.S. National Commission for UNESCO
1975–76	Fellow, Center for Advanced Study in the Behavioral Sciences, Stanford
1976–94	Visiting professor, MIT, and founding member of the MIT Science, Technology, and Society Program
1979–95	Member, Council of Scholars, Library of Congress
1980	Oersted Medal
1980–81	Guggenheim fellowship
1980–95	Member, editorial committee, *The Collected Papers of Albert Einstein*
1981	Jefferson Lecture, NEH
1981–88	Vice president, Académie Internationale d'Histoire des Sciences
1983	Member, National Commission on Excellence in Education, coauthor of *A Nation at Risk*
1983–84	President, History of Science Society
1987–	Member, Leopoldina, Halle

1989	J. D. Bernal Prize, Society for Social Studies of Science
1989	George Sarton Medal, History of Science Society
1989	Andrew Gemant Award, American Institute of Physics
1994	Joseph Priestley Award, Dickinson College
1996	Member, American Philosophical Society
1998	Joseph H. Hazen Prize, History of Science Society
2008	Abraham Pais Prize, American Physical Society
2008	Republic of Austria's Ehrenkreuz
	Editor, *Science, Society and Human Values*
	Life Honorary fellow, New York Academy of Sciences

Eight honorary degrees, including from Grinnell College (1967), Kenyon College (1976), Bates College (1979), Wesleyan University (1981), Duke University (1981)

Gerald Holton Papers, Harvard University Archives
"Some Lessons from Living in the History of Science," *Isis* 90 (1999): 95–116.

Selected Publications

Introduction to Concepts and Theories in Physical Science (1952; 2nd ed. rev., and with new material by Stephen G. Brush 1973)
with Duane H. D. Roller, *Foundations of Modern Physical Science* (1958, ³1965). Spanish edition 1963
Ed., *Science and the Modern Mind: A Symposium* (1958, 1971)
Ed., *Science and Culture: A Study of Cohesive and Disjunctive Forces* (1965)
et al., *The Project Physics Course* (1970–2000)
Ed., *The Twentieth-Century Sciences: Studies in the Biography of Ideas* (1972)
Thematic Origins of Scientific Thought: From Kepler to Einstein (1973, rev. ed. 1988)
Ed., with William A. Blanpied, *Science and Its Public: The Changing Relationship* (1976)
The Scientific Imagination: Case Studies (1978, new ed. 1998)
Ed., with Robert S. Morison, *Limits of Scientific Inquiry* (1979)
Thematische Analyse der Wissenschaft. Die Physik Einsteins und seiner Zeit (1981)
Ed., with Yehuda Elkana, *Albert Einstein, Historical and Cultural Perspectives: The Centennial Symposium in Jerusalem* (1982, 1997)
Themata. Zur Ideengeschichte der Physik (1984)
The Advancement of Science and Its Burdens: The Jefferson Lecture and Other Essays (1986, new ed. 1998)
Science and Anti-Science (1993). German edition: *Wissenschaft und Anti-Wissenschaft* (2000)
Einstein, History, and Other Passions (1995, 2000). German edition: *Einstein, die Geschichte und andere Leidenschaften. Der Kampf gegen die Wissenschaft am Ende des 20. Jahrhunderts* (1998). Spanish edition 1998
with Gerhard Sonnert, *Gender Differences in Science Careers: The Project Access Study* (1995)
with Gerhard Sonnert, *Who Succeeds in Science? The Gender Dimension* (1995)
with Stephen G. Brush, *Physics, the Human Adventure: From Copernicus to Einstein and Beyond* (2001)
with David Cassidy and James Rutherford, *Understanding Physics* (2001)
with Gerhard Sonnert, *Ivory Bridges: Connecting Science and Society* (2002)

Victory and Vexation in Science: Einstein, Bohr, Heisenberg, and Others (2005)
with Gerhard Sonnert, *What Happened to the Children Who Fled Nazi Persecution* (2006).
    German edition: *Was geschah mit den Kindern? Erfolg und Trauma junger Flüchtlinge, die von den Nationalsozialisten vertrieben wurden* (2008)
Ed., with Peter L. Galison and and Silvan S. Schweber, *Einstein for the 21st Century: His Legacy in Science, Art, and Modern Culture* (2008)
with Gerhard Sonnert, *Helping Young Refugees and Immigrants Succeed: Public Policy, Aid, and Education* (2010)

Henry Rudolf Huttenbach

Born Heinrich Rudolf Hüttenbach, 15 October 1930 in Worms
Parents: Otto Hüttenbach and Gertrud Moldenhauer
1936 to Italy, 1939 to the U.K., 1947 to the U.S.

1947–51	B.A. Gonzaga University
1951–53	studied at Fordham University
1953–55	served in U.S. Army as musician and assistant conductor in 7th Army Corps, Stuttgart
1956–59	Instructor, University of Washington, Seattle
1961	Ph.D. University of Washington, Seattle, "The Zemsky Sobor in Ivan IV's Reign"
1959–60	Assistant professor, Gonzaga University
1960–61	Assistant professor, East Texas State University
1961–66	Assistant professor, Louisiana State University
1966–78	Assisstant to associate professor, CUNY
1978–	Professor, CUNY
	Director of the Center for the Study of Ethnopolitics and Ethnonationalism

Ad Personam

1955–56	Fulbright fellow, University of Heidelberg, Germany
1958–59	Rockefeller Foundation Grant
1960–73	Visiting professorships at University of Nebraska, University of Washington, New School for Social Research, Hebrew University, Rutgers University, Brooklyn College
1964–65	and 1975: U.S. State Department cultural exchange scholar, Moscow State University
1972–73	Fellow, Memorial Foundation for Jewish Culture
1975	and 1977: ACLS travel grants
1999–	Founder, editor, *Journal of Genocide Research*
2006–	Cofounder and chairman, International Academy for Genocide Prevention, NY

"Vita Felix, Via Dolorosa: An Academic Journey towards Genocide," in *Pioneers of Genocide Studies*, ed. Samuel Totten and Steven Leonard Jacobs (New Brunswick, 2002), 47–58.

Selected Publications

World Communism in Review (1960)
The Emigration Book of Worms: The Character and Dimension of the Jewish Exodus from a Small German Jewish Community, 1933–1941 (1974)
The Destruction of the Jewish Community of Worms, 1933–1945: A Study of the Holocaust in Germany (1980)
The Life of Herta Mansbacher: A Portrait of a Jewish Teacher, Heroine, and Martyr (1980). German edition: *Herta Mansbacher. Porträt einer Jüdischen Lehrerin, Heldin und Märtyrerin, 1885–1942* (1981)
Introduction and Guide to the Riga Ghetto Archive Catalogue (1984)
Ed., *Soviet Nationality Policies: Ruling Ethnic Groups in the USSR* (1990)
Ed., *A Symposium of Social Movements in the USSR* (1990)
Ed., *The Gypsies in Eastern Europe* (1991)
Ed., with Alexander J. Motyl, *The Soviet Nationalities despite Gorbachev: Proceedings of a Conference Sponsored by the Program on Nationality and Siberian Studies* (1991)
Ed., with Erika Dailey, *Religious Consciousness in the Glasnost Era* (1992)
Ed., with Charles F. Furtado, *The Ex-Soviet Nationalities without Gorbachev* (1993)
Ed., with Peter Vodopivec, *Voices from the Slovene Nation, 1990–1992* (1993)
Ed., with Gabriele Simoncini, *Ethnopolitics in Poland* (1994)
The Caucasus: A Region in Crisis (1996)
Ed., with Francesco Privitera, *Self-Determination from Versailles to Dayton: Its Historical Legacy* (1999)
Ed., with Marcia Esparza and Daniel Feierstein, *State Violence and Genocide in Latin America: The Cold War Years* (2010)

Robert Arthur Huttenback

Born Robert Huttenback, 8 March 1928 in Frankfurt/M.; died 10 June 2012 in Camarillo, CA
Parents: Otto Huttenbach and Dorothy Marcuse
1933 to Italy, 1934 to the U.K., 1939 to the U.S.

1951	B.A. University of California, Los Angeles
1951–53	served in U.S. Army
1954–56	Teaching fellow, University of California, Los Angeles
1958–60	Lecturer, California Institute of Technology, Pasadena
1959	Ph.D. University of California, Los Angeles, "British Relations with Sind, 1799–1843: A Case Study in the Dynamics of Imperialism"
1960–66	Assistant to associate professor of history, California Institute of Technology, Pasadena
1966–77	Professor, California Institute of Technology, Pasadena
1969–72	Dean of students, California Institute of Technology
1972–77	Chairman, division of humanities and social sciences, California Institute of Technology

1977–86   Professor of history and chancellor, University of California, Santa Barbara

Ad Personam

1956–57   Fulbright grant, School of Oriental and African Studies, University of London
1957–58   Ford Foundation grant to India and Pakistan
1962–63   Carnegie Endowment grant
1965   American Institute of Indian Studies grant, India
1966   ACLS-SSRC grant

Oral History Interview, 14 September and 6 November 1995, Archives California Institute of Technology

Selected Publications

British Relations with Sind, 1799–1843: An Anatomy of Imperialism (1962, new ed. 2007)
with Margaret W. Fisher and Leo E. Rose, *Himalayan Battleground: Sino-Indian Rivalry in Ladakh* (1963)
The British Imperial Experience (1966, 1975)
Gandhi in South Africa: British Imperialism and the Indian Question, 1860–1914 (1971)
Racism and Empire: White Settlers and Colored Immigrants in the British Self-Governing Colonies, 1830–1910 (1976)
with Lance E. Davis, *Mammon and the Pursuit of Empire: The Political Economy of British Imperialism, 1860–1912* (1986, abbr. ed. 1988)
Kashmir and the British Raj 1847–1947 (2004)

Georg Gerson Iggers

Born Georg Gerson Igersheimer, 7 December 1926 in Hamburg; died 26 November 2017 in Williamsville, NY
Parents: Alfred Igersheimer and Lizzie Minden
1938 to the U.S.

1944   B.A. University of Richmond
1945   A.M. University of Chicago
1945–46   studied at New School for Social Research, New York
1951   Ph.D. University of Chicago, "The Social Philosophy of the Saint-Simonians (1824–1832)"
1948–50   Instructor, University of Akron
1950–57   Associate professor, Philander Smith College
1957–63   Associate to full professor, Dillard University
1960–65   Visiting associate professor, Tulane University
1963–65   Associate professor, Roosevelt University, Chicago
1965–78   Professor, SUNY Buffalo

1978–97 Distinguished Professor, SUNY Buffalo

Ad Personam

1951–56 Chair, Education Committee, NAACP, Little Rock, AR
1953–56 Chair, Executive Committee, NAACP, Little Rock
1956–2002 Visiting appointments and professorships at University of Arkansas, Tulane University, University of Rochester, Beijing Teachers' College, Historische Kommission zu Berlin, Technische Hochschule Darmstadt, Universität Leipzig, Moscow State University, Aarhus University, Zentrum für Zeithistorische Forschung/Potsdam, University of New England at Armidale/Australia, University of Vienna
1957–60 and 1962–63: Chair, Education Committee, NAACP, New Orleans
1960 Grant, American Philosophical Society
1960–61 Guggenheim fellowship, Paris
1961–62 Rockefeller fellowship, Göttingen
1961–2008 Visiting scholar, Max Planck Institute for History, Göttingen
1962–63 Cochair, Council for Peaceful Alternatives, New Orleans
1964 Newberry Library fellowship
1965–75 Chairman, Education Committee NAACP, Buffalo, NY
1971–72 1978–79 and 1985–86: NEH fellowship
1978–79 and 1985–86: Honorary Fulbright fellowship
1986–87 Fellow, Zentrum für interdisziplinäre Forschung, University of Bielefeld
1987 Fulbright fellowship
1988 Erasmus Kittler Award, Technische Hochschule, Darmstadt
1990 Foreign member, *Akademie der Wissenschaften der DDR*
1993–94 Fellow, Woodrow Wilson Center
1995–96 Alexander von Humboldt Foundation Research Prize
1995–2000 President, Commission for the History of Historiography of the CISH (Comité international des sciences historiques)
2000 Fellow, Internationales Forschungsinstitut Kulturwissenschaften, Wien
2001 Doctor of Letters, University of Richmond
2002 Doctor of Humane Letters, Philander Smith College
2006 Honorary Doctorate, Technische Universität Darmstadt
2007 Cross of Merit First Class, Federal Republic of Germany

Geschichtswissenschaft vor 2000. Perspektiven der Historiographiegeschichte, Geschichtstheorie, Sozial- und Kulturgeschichte. Festschrift für Georg G. Iggers zum 65. Geburtstag, ed. Konrad H. Jarausch, Jörn Rüsen, and Hans Schleier (1991)
Historiographischer Rückblick. Georg Iggers zum 70. Geburtstag, ed. Gerald Diesener (1997)
Crossing Boundaries: The Inclusion and Exclusion of Minorities in Germany and America, ed. Larry E. Jones (2001)
The Many Faces of Clio: Cross-Cultural Approaches to Historiography. Essays in Honor of Georg G. Iggers, ed. Q. Edward Wang and Franz L. Fillafer (2007)
"History and Social Action Beyond National and Continental Borders," in *The Second Generation: Émigrés from Nazi Germany as Historians*, ed. Andreas W. Daum, Hartmut Lehmann, and James J. Sheehan (2016), 82–96.

Selected Publications

The Cult of Authority: The Political Philosophy of the Saint-Simonians (1958, ²1970)
The German Conception of History: The National Tradition of Historical Thought from Herder to the Present (1968, rev. ed. 1983). German edition: *Neue Geschichtswissenschaft. Deutsche Geschichtswissenschaft. Eine Kritik der traditionellen Geschichtsauffassung von Herder bis zur Gegenwart* (1971, ²1972, ³1976, exp. ed. 1997). Hungarian edition 1988. Korean edition 1992. Chinese and Japanese editions
Ed., with Konrad von Moltke, *Leopold von Ranke: The Theory and Practice of History* (1973; rev. & updated version 2011 with new translations by Wilma A. Iggers)
New Directions in European Historiography (1975, rev. ed. 1984). German edition: *Vom Historismus zur historischen Sozialwissenschaft. Ein internationaler Vergleich* (1978). Also translations into Danish, Italian, Korean, Japanese, Chinese, and Greek
Ed., with Harold T. Parker, *International Handbook of Historical Studies* (1979)
Ed., *The Social History of Politics: Critical Perspectives in West German Historical Writing since 1945* (1985)
Ed., with James M. Powell, *Leopold von Ranke and the Shaping of the Historical Discipline* (1990)
Ed., *Ein anderer historischer Blick. Beispiele ostdeutscher Sozialgeschichte* (1991)
Geschichtswissenschaft im 20. Jahrhundert. Ein kritischer Überblick im internationalen Zusammenhang (1993, ²1996, new ed. 2007). Spanish and Chinese editions 1995. Japanese edition 1996. For the expanded English version see below: *Historiography in the Twentieth Century*
Ed., with Wolfgang Bialas, *Intellektuelle in der Weimarer Republik* (1996, ²1997)
Historiography in the Twentieth Century: From Scientific Objectivity to the Postmodern Challenge (1997, 2005 with a new epilogue). Greek and Turkish editions 2000. Czech edition 2002. Icelandic edition 2004. Chinese edition 2005. New revised Spanish edition 2012
with Wilma A. Iggers, *Zwei Seiten der Geschichte. Lebensbericht aus unruhigen Zeiten* (2002); English edition: *Two Lives in Uncertain Times: Facing the Challenges of the Twentieth Century as Scholars and Citizens* (2006). Also translated into Czech and Spanish. Chinese edition 2014
with Qingia Edward Wang, *A Global History of Modern Historiography* (2008, ²2017). German edition: *Geschichtskulturen. Weltgeschichte der Historiografie von 1750 bis heute* (2013). Chinese edition 2011. Russian edition 2012. German edition 2013

Wilma Abeles Iggers

Born Wilhelmina Abeles, 23 March 1921 in Mirkov (Mirischkau), Bohemia
Parents: Karl Abeles and Elsa Ornstein
1938 to Canada, 1942 to the U.S.

1942	B.A. MacMaster University, Hamilton, ON
1943	M.A. University of Chicago
1946	Instructor, University of New Brunswick, Fredericton
1947–48	Instructor, Gary College and Navy Pier College
1949	Lecturer, John Carrol University, Cleveland
1952	Ph.D. University of Chicago, "Karl Kraus: A Viennese Critic of the Twentieth Century"

1950–56   taught at Philander Smith College
1956–57   Visiting professor, University of Arkansas
1957–63   Associate professor, Dillard University and taught at Tulane University
1963–65   Associate professor, Loyola University Chicago
1965–91   Assistant to full professor, Canisius College, Buffalo, NY

Ad Personam

1968–69   President, Women's International League for Peace and Freedom, Buffalo
1978   DAAD fellowship
1979   Grant, American Philosophical Society
1985   International Research and Exchanges Board (IREX) grant, Leipzig
2002   Honorary Citizen of hometown Horšovský Týn
2004   *Gracias agit* prize from Czech government

Selected Publications

Karl Kraus: A Twentieth Century Viennese Cultural Critic (1967)
Die Juden in Böhmen und Mähren. Ein historisches Lesebuch (1986). English edition: *The Jews of Bohemia and Moravia: A Historical Reader* (1992)
Ed.: Joseph Seligmann Kohn, *Der jüdische Gil Blas* (1993)
Women of Prague: Ethnic Diversity and Social Change from the Eighteenth Century to the Present (1995). German edition: *Frauenleben in Prag. Ethnische Vielfalt und kultureller Wandel seit dem 18. Jahrhundert* (2000)
with Georg G. Iggers, *Zwei Seiten der Geschichte. Lebensbericht aus unruhigen Zeiten* (2002). English edition: *Two Lives in Uncertain Times: Facing the Challenges of the Twentieth Century as Scholars and Citizens* (2006). Also translated into Czech and Spanish. Chinese edition 2014

Sabine Luise Marianne Jessner

Born 27 July 1924 in Wrocław (Breslau)
Parents: Max Jessner and Marianne Herzog
1935 to Switzerland, 1941 to the U.S.

1945   B.A. Wellesley College
1946   M.A. Columbia University
1947–48   Secretarial work and substitute teaching, City College of New York
1948–53   Instructor, Smith College and Mount Holyoke College
1958–67   taught at Brooklyn College
1963   Ph.D. in French history, Columbia University, "Edouard Herriot: Patriarch of the Republic"
1967–68   Visiting professor, Kent State University
1968–89   Assistant and associate professor, Department of History, Indiana University-Purdue University, Indianapolis (IUPUI)

Ad Personam

1986–89	President, Swiss-American Historical Society
1988–89	President, Indiana Academy of the Social Sciences

Selected Publications

Edouard Herriot: Patriarch of the Republic (1974)

Ed., with Giles Reid Hoyt and Claudia Grossmann, *Minutes of the Freethinker Society of Indianapolis – Das Protokollbuch des Freidenker Vereins von Indianapolis, Indiana, 1870–1890* (1988)

Manfred Jonas

Born 9 April 1927 in Mannheim; died 25 August 2013 in Schenectady, NY
Parents: Walter Jonas and Antonie Dannheisser
1937 to the U.S.

1945–46	served in U.S. Navy
1949	B.S. City College of New York
1951	A.M. Harvard University
1951–54	Intelligence analyst, Department of Air Force, Salzburg, Austria
1954	Lecturer, University of Maryland European Division
1959	Ph.D. Harvard University, "The Isolationist Viewpoint 1935–1941: An Analysis"
1959–62	Visiting professor, Amerika Institut, Free University Berlin
1962–63	Associate professor, Pennsylvania Military College Chester
1963–67	Assistant to associate professor, Union College
1967–81	Professor, Union College
1981–86	Washington Irving Professor in Modern Literature and Historical Studies, Union College
1986–96	John Bigelow Professor of History, Union College

Ad Personam

1950	Visiting lecturer, City College of New York
1958	Visiting lecturer, Northeastern University
1965	Grant, American Philosophical Society
1965–76	Member, board of directors, Freedom Forum Inc.
1969	and 1981: Ford Foundation faculty development grant
1973	Fellow, Fulbright-Hays Program, University of the Saarland
1977–78	Fellow, Charles Warren Center, Harvard University
1983–84	Dr. Otto Salgo Visiting Professor of American Studies, University of Budapest

Selected Publications

Isolationism in America, 1935–1971 (1966, repr. 1972)
Ed., *American Foreign Relations in the Twentieth Century: Documents* (1967, repr. 1969)
Ed., with Francis L. Loewenheim and Harold D. Langley, *Roosevelt and Churchill: Their Secret Wartime Correspondence* (1975)
Ed., with Robert V. Wells, *New Opportunities in a New Nation: The Development of New York After the Revolution* (1982)
The United States and Germany: A Diplomatic History (1984)

Friedrich Katz

Born 13 June 1927 in Vienna; died 16 October 2010 in Philadelphia
Parents: Leo Katz and Bronislawa Rein
1933 to France; 1938 to the U.S.; 1940 to Mexico; to the U.S. in 1945; back to Mexico in 1948; 1949 to Austria; 1956 to the German Democratic Republic; 1970 to the U.S.

1945	graduated from Liceo Franco-Mexicano
1948	B.A. Wagner College, Staten Island
1948–49	postgraduate studies at Instituto Nacional de Antropología e Historia, Mexico
1954	Dr. phil. University of Vienna, Austria
1956–66	Instructor, Institut für allgemeine Geschichte, Humboldt University, Berlin
1962	*Habilitation*, Humboldt University
1966–70	Professor, Humboldt University
1970	resigned position at Humboldt University
1971–83	Professor, University of Chicago
1983–2004	Morton D. Hull Distinguished Service Professor, University of Chicago
1992–2004	Chair, Center for Mexican Studies, University of Chicago
2004–	Morton D. Hull Distinguished Service Professor Emeritus, University of Chicago

Ad Personam

1968–69	Visiting professor of history, Facultad de Filosofía e Letras, Universidad Nacional Autónoma de México
1970–71	Visiting professor, University of Texas
1980	and 1988: Visiting Professor, El Colegio de México
1985	Visiting Professor, University of Vienna, Austria
1988	Orden de Aguila Azteca (Order of the Aztec Eagle), Republic of Mexico
1999	Albert J. Beveridge Award, AHA, and Bolton Prize, Conference on Latin American History, for *The Life and Times of Pancho Villa*
2000	Bryce Wood Book Award, Latin American Studies Association, for *The Life and Times of Pancho Villa*
2002	Honorary doctorate, Freie Universität Berlin
2004–	Katz Center for Mexican Studies at the University of Chicago
2004	Goldenes Doktordiplom, University of Vienna

2004	Medalla Isidro Fabela, Faculty of Law, Universidad Nacional Autónoma de México
2010	Distinguished Service Award, Conference on Latin American History
2010	Cátedra Cultural México-Katz (Katz Program on Mexican Culture), Mexican National Council for Culture and the Arts (CONACULTA) and the University of Chicago
2012–	Friedrich Katz Dissertation Prize, Institute for Latin American Studies, Free University Berlin
2013–	Friedrich Katz Prize in Latin American and Caribbean History, AHA

Revolución y exilio en la historia de México: Del amor de un historiador a su patria adoptive. Homenaje a Friedrich Katz, ed. Javier Garciadiego and Emilio Kourí (2010)

Selected Publications

Die sozialökonomischen Verhältnisse bei den Azteken im 15. und 16. Jahrhundert (1956)
Deutschland, Diaz und die mexikanische Revolution. Die deutsche Politik in Mexiko 1870–1920 (1964)
Situación social y económica de los aztecas durante los siglos xv y xvi (1966)
Ed., *Der deutsche Faschismus in Lateinamerika. 1933–1943* (1966)
Las relaciones socio-económicas de los Aztecas en los siglos XV y XVI (1967)
Vorkolumbische Kulturen. Die grossen Reiche des alten Amerika (1969). English edition: *The Ancient American Civilizations* (1972)
Pre-Columbian Cultures (1969)
La Servidumbre agraria en México en la época porfiriana (1976)
The Secret War in Mexico: Europe, the United States, and the Mexican Revolution (1981)
Ed., *Porfirio Díaz frente al descontento popular regional, 1891–1893: Antología documental* (1986)
Ed., *Riot, Rebellion, and Revolution: Rural Social Conflict in Mexico* (1988)
The Life and Times of Pancho Villa (1998)
Imágenes de Pancho Villa (1999). English edition: *The Face of Pancho Villa: A History in Photographs and Words* (2007)
et al., *Pancho Villa, la revolución y la ciudad de Chihuahua* (2000)
Madero y los Estados Unidos: El gobierno de los Estados Unidos y el derrocamiento del Presidente Francisco I. Madero (2003)
De Díaz a Madero (2004)
Nuevos ensayos mexicanos (2006)
with Claudio Lomnitz, *El Porfiriato y la Revolución en la historia de México: Una conversación* (2011)

Henry Alfred Kissinger

Born Heinz Alfred Kissinger, 27 May 1923 in Fürth
Parents: Louis Kissinger and Paula Stern
1938 via England to the U.S.

1943–46	served in U.S. Army
1946–47	Lecturer in German history, European Command Intelligence School, Oberammergau
1950	B.A. Department of Government, Harvard University
1950–54	Teaching fellow, Harvard University
1951–69	Director, Foreign Studies Project, Harvard (later: Harvard International Seminar)
1952	M.A. Department of Government, Harvard
1954	Ph.D. Department of Government, Harvard, "Peace, Legitimacy, and the Equilibrium: A Study of the Statesmanship of Castlereagh and Metternich"
1954–55	Lecturer, Department of Government, Harvard
1955–56	Director, Study Project "Nuclear Weapons and Foreign Policy," Council on Foreign Relations, New York
1956–58	Director, Special Studies Project, Rockefeller Brothers Fund, New York
1957–60	Associate director, Center for International Affairs, Harvard
1957–62	Lecturer to associate professor, Department of Government, Harvard
1958–71	Director, Harvard Defense Studies Program
1961–62	Advisor, National Scurity Council
1962–71	Professor, Harvard (1969–71 on leave)
1969–75	U.S. National Security Advisor to President Richard Nixon
1973–77	U.S. Secretary of State
1982–	Founder and chairman, Kissinger Associates, New York

Ad Personam

1947–54	Fellowships from Harvard University and Rockefeller Foundation
1950–	involved as consultant, advisor and in other capacities in various governmental projects and activities on the federal level and in the State of New York
1952–69	Editor, *Confluence: An International Forum*
1954	Charles Sumner Prize for dissertation, Harvard
1958	Woodrow Wilson Prize, Overseas Press Club, for *Nuclear Weapons and Foreign Policy*
1961–68	Consultant, Rand Corporation
1965–66	Guggenheim fellowship
1969	Honorary doctorate, Brown University
1973	Nobel Peace Prize, together with Lê Đức Thọ
1973	American Institute for Public Service Award
1973	International Platform Association Theodore Roosevelt Award
1973	Dwight D. Eisenhower Distinguished Service Medal, Veterans of Foreign Wars
1973	Hope Award for International Understanding
1973	Golden Medal of Honor, City of Fürth
1977	Presidential Medal of Freedom
1977	Great Cross of the Order of Merit, Federal Republic of Germany
1977	Lecturer, Institute for Strategic and International Studies, Georgetown University
1977–81	Director, Council on Foreign Relations

1977–   Member of board of directors of various nongovernmental institutes and centers, especially in the field of foreign policy
1980   National Book Award for *The White House Years*
1986   Medal of Liberty
1987   Karlspreis, Aachen
1988   Honorary doctorate, Universität of Erlangen-Nürnberg
1996   Franz-Josef-Strauss Preis
1998   Honorary citizenship, city of Fürth, and honorary member, Spielvereinigung Greuther Fürth
2000   Sylvanus Thayer Award
2000–06   Chairman, board of trustees, Eisenhower Fellowships
2005   Bayerischer Verdienstorden
2006   Woodrow Wilson Award for Public Service
2007   Verdienstmedaille des Landes Baden-Württemberg
2007–   Henry A. Kissinger Prize, American Academy Berlin
2009   Ewald von Leist Award, Munich Security Conference
2011   McCloy Lifetime Achievement Award
2012   Israel President's Medal
2013   Henry A. Grunwald Award for Public Service, Lighthouse International

Henry A. Kissinger Papers, Yale University
Henry A. Kissinger Papers, Library of Congress

Selected Publications

Nuclear Weapons and Foreign Policy (1957). German edition: *Kernwaffen und auswärtige Politik* (1959, ²1974)

A World Restored: Metternich, Castlereagh and the Problems of Peace, 1812–22 (1957, 1973). German editions: *Großmachtdiplomatie. Von der Staatskunst Castlereaghs und Metternichs* (1962); *Das Gleichgewicht der Grossmächte. Metternich, Castlereagh u.d. Neuordnung Europas 1812–1822* (1986)

The Necessity for Choice: Prospects of American Foreign Policy (1961). German edition: *Die Entscheidung drängt. Grundfragen westlicher Außenpolitik* (1961)

The Troubled Partnership: A Re-Appraisal of the Atlantic Alliance (1965). German edition: *Was wird aus der westlichen Allianz?* (1965)

American Foreign Policy: Three Essays (1969). German edition: *Amerikanische Außenpolitik* (1969). French edition 1970

The White House Years (1979). German edition: *Memoiren 1968–1973* (1979)

For the Record: Selected Statements, 1977–1980 (1981). Expanded German edition: *Die weltpolitische Lage. Reden und Aufsätze* (1983)

Years of Upheaval (1982). German edition: *Memoiren*. Vol. 2, *1973–1974* (1982)

Observations: Selected Speeches and Essays, 1982–1984 (1985). German edition: *Weltpolitik für morgen. Reden und Aufsätze 1982–1985* (1986)

Die sechs Säulen der Weltordnung (1992)

Diplomacy (1994). German edition: *Die Vernunft der Nationen. Über das Wesen der Aussenpolitik* (1994)

Years of Renewal (1999). German edition: *Jahre der Erneuerung. Erinnerungen* (1999)

Does America Need a Foreign Policy? Toward a Diplomacy for the 21st Century (2002). German edition: *Die Herausforderung Amerikas. Weltpolitik im 21. Jahrhundert* (2002, ²2003). Russian edition 2002
Crisis: The Anatomy of Two Major Foreign Policy Crises (2003)
Ending the Vietnam War: A History of America's Involvement in and Extrication from the Vietnam War (2003)
On China (2011). German edition: *China. Zwischen Tradition und Herausforderung* (⁴2011)

Ruth Sara Kleinman

Born (last name Kleinmann) 23 July 1929 in Berlin; died 7 November 1995 in Brooklyn, NY
Parents: Abraham Isaak Kleinmann and Frieda Maria Anna Schmidt
1941 via Portugal to the U.S.

1951	A.B. Barnard College
1952	M.A. Columbia University
1957–58	Instructor, Bucknell University
1958–59	Instructor, Brooklyn College
1959	Ph.D. Columbia University, "Saint François de Sales and the Protestants"
1959–62	Instructor, Connecticut College
1962–65	Instructor, Brooklyn College
1965–75	Assistant to associate professor, Brooklyn College
1975–	Professor of history, Brooklyn College

Ad Personam

1955–56	Fulbright Grant, University of Grenoble
1979–80	NEH fellowship

Kleinman Family Papers, Archives and Special Collections, Brooklyn College Library

Books Publications

Saint François de Sales and the Protestants (1962)
Anne of Austria: Queen of France (1985). French edition 1993

Klemens Wilhelm von Klemperer

Born 2 November 1916 in Berlin; died 23 December 2012 in Easthampton, MA
Parents: Herbert Otto von Klemperer and Frieda Kuffner
1938 to the U.S.

1934	Abitur, Französisches Gymnasium, Berlin

1935–37	Balliol College, Oxford
1937–38	studied at the University of Vienna
1940–43	and 1946–49: student and teaching fellow, Harvard University
1940	M.A. Harvard University
1943–46	served in U.S. Army
1949	Ph.D. Harvard University, "The Conservative Revolution in Germany, 1913 through the Early Years of the Republic; the History of an Idea"
1949	Instructor, Smith College
1950–61	Assistant to associate professor, Smith College
1961–79	Professor, Smith College
1979–87	L. Clark Seelye Professor of History, Smith College

Ad Personam

	Refugee Scholarship, Harvard University
1957–58	Guggenheim and Fulbright fellowship, Austria
1960	Visiting professor, Stanford University
1963–64	Visiting professor, University of Bonn
1973–74	Overseas fellow, Churchill College, Cambridge University
1980	Visiting fellow, Trinity College, Oxford University
1987	Fellow, Wissenschaftskolleg Berlin
1990	Five College Professor
1997	Austrian Cross of Honour for Science and Art First Class
1998	Queen's Lecture at Westminster Abbey
2000–05	Member, board, Volkswagen Stiftung
2000–12	Member, advisory board, Forschungsgemeinschaft 20. Juli 1944
2010	Dorothee Fliess Prize for Resistance Research

Klemens von Klemperer Papers, c. 1950–[ongoing], Smith College, Northhampton, MA
"It Hardly Needs Emphasis That My Own Generation, the Second, is Deeply Indebted to the First," in *The Second Generation: Émigrés from Nazi Germany as Historians*, ed. Andreas W. Daum, Hartmut Lehmann, and James J. Sheehan (2016), 55–58.

Selected Publications

Germany's New Conservatism, Its History and Dilemma in the Twentieth Century (1957, ²1968). German edition: *Konservative Bewegungen. Zwischen Kaiserreich und Nationalsozialismus* (1957, 1962)
Ignaz Seipel: Christian Statesman in a Time of Crisis (1972). German edition: *Ignaz Seipel. Staatsmann einer Krisenzeit* (1976)
Ed., *Demokratisierung und Verfassung in den Ländern 1918–1920* (1983)
Ed., *A Noble Combat: The Letters of Shiela Grant Duff and Adam von Trott zu Solz, 1932–1939* (1988)
German Resistance Against Hitler: The Search for Allies Abroad, 1938–1945 (1992). German edition: *Die verlassenen Verschwörer. Der deutsche Widerstand auf der Suche nach Verbündeten, 1938–1945* (1994)

Ed., with Enrico Syring and Rainer Zitelmann, *Für Deutschland. Die Männer des 20. Juli* (1993)
German Incertitudes, 1914–1945: The Stones and the Cathedral (2001)
Voyage through the Twentieth Century: A Historian's Recollections and Reflections (2009)
Passion of a German Artist: Käthe Kollwitz (2011)

Arthur Gustav Kogan

Born 2 May 1914 in Vienna; died 8 July 2001
1940 via France to the U.S.

1933–37	attended University of Vienna
1942	A.M. Harvard University
1942–46	graduate and research assistant, Harvard University
1946	Ph.D. Harvard, "Socialism in the Multinational State"
1946–49	taught at Reed College, Portland, OR
1948–49	Assistant professor, University of Oregon, Eugene
1949–65	Historian for the U.S. Department of State; member, board of editors, *Documents on German Foreign Policy 1918–1945*
1966–71	Chief, Record Guidance-Review Division, U.S. Department of State
1971–80	Special Assistant to the Director of the Historical Office U.S. State Department

Gerd Korman

Born Adolf Gerd Korman, 24 July 1928 in Elberfeld
Parents: Max Osias Korman and Rosa Laufer
1938 forced to leave Germany for Poland, 1939 with a *Kindertransport* to England, 1940 to the U.S.

1951	B.A. Brooklyn College
1953	M.A. University of Wisconsin, Madison
1956–62	Assistant professor of history, Elmira College
1959	Ph.D. University of Wisconsin, Madison, "A Social History of Industrial Growth and Immigrants: A Study with Particular Reference to Milwaukee, 1880–1920"
1962–	Professor of American history, Cornell University, School of Industrial and Labor Relations

Ad personam

1955–56	and 1958–59: SSRC fellowship
1961	David Clark Everest Prize in Wisconsin Economic History for dissertation
1968–69	and 1970–71: Guest professor, University of Tel Aviv

1980   Fellow in Holocaust Studies, Oxford Centre for Hebrew and Jewish Studies

Selected Publications

Industrialization, Immigrants, and Americanizers: The View from Milwaukee, 1866–1921 (1967)
Ed., *Hunter and Hunted: Human History of the Holocaust* (1973)
Comp., *Labor History Documents*, 3 vols. (1974–75)
Nightmare's Fairy Tale: A Young Refugee's Home Fronts, 1938–1948 (2005)

George Michael Kren

Born 3 June 1926 Linz; died 24 July 2000 Manhattan, KS
Parents: Frank (Franz) Kren and Gertrud(e) Bloch
1938 to England, 1940 to the U.S.

1944–46	served in U.S. Army in Europe
1948	B.A. Colby College
1949	M.A. University of Wisconsin, Madison
1954–56	Research editor, *American Peoples Encyclopedia*
1956	Research editor, Bertelsmann Verlag
1958–59	Instructor, Oberlin College
1959–60	Assistant professor, Elmira College
1960	Ph.D. University of Wisconsin, Madison, "The Image of the Middle Class in the German Novel, 1774–1865"
1960–65	Assistant professor, Lake Forest College
1964–65	Lecturer, Roosevelt College, Chicago
1965–76	Associate professor, Kansas State University
1976–2000	Professor, Kansas State University

Ad personam

1961	Visiting professor, University of New Mexico
1970	Visiting professor, SUNY Buffalo

Kren Collection of photographs, Marianna Kistler Beach Museum, Kansas State University

Selected Publications

Ed., with Leon H. Rappoport, *Varieties of Psychohistory* (1976)
with Leon H. Rappoport, *The Holocaust and the Crisis of Human Behavior* (1980, rev. ed. 1994)
with George Christakes, *Scholars and Personal Computers: Microcomputing in the Humanities and Social Sciences* (1988)

Leonore Maria (Roon) Laan

Born Leonore Maria Hamburger, 28 January 1919 in Wrocław (Breslau)
Parents: Max Hamburger and Katharina Rosenstock alias Karin Roon
1939 to the U.S.

	attended Quaker School, Eerde, Netherlands
1944	B.A. University of California, Los Angeles
1945	M.A. University of California, Los Angeles
1945–47	Researcher, International Council of Nurses, New York
1948–49	Instructor, Smith College
1949–52	Instructor, Russell Sage College, Troy, NY
1952	Ph.D. Radcliffe College, "The History of Nursing Legislation in the British Commonwealth 1891–1939"
1952–61	African intelligence research specialist, U.S. State Department
1961–c. 66	African research specialist, U.S. Department of Health

Selected Publication

Comp. [under last name Roon], *Nursing Legislation of the World (Collection of Laws and Basic Regulations Concerning Registration of Nurses and their Training in all Countries of the World)*, ed. Vladimir Gsovski (1947)

Ursula Schäfer Lamb

Born 15 January 1914 in Essen; died 8 August 1996 in Tucson, AZ
Parents: Waldemar Joachim Schäfer and Maria Katharina Hoffmann von Fallersleben
1935 to the U.S.

1933–35	studied history of art in Berlin
1935–36	Exchange student, Smith College
1937	M.A. University of California, Berkeley
1949	Ph.D. Berkeley, "Nicolas Colas de Ovando, Comendador Mayor of Alcantara and Governor of the Indies"
1944–51	Lecturer in history, Barnard College
1958–61	Lecturer and tutor, Brasenose College, Oxford University
1961–74	Lecturer and research associate, Yale University
1974–84	Professor, University of Arizona, Tuscon

Ad Personam

1943	SSRC grant
1947	ACLS travel grant
1968–69	Guggenheim fellowship
1972–73	NEH senior fellow

1975	Travel grant, American Philosophical Society
1975–77	President, Society for the History of Discoveries
1976–80	Associate editor, *Hispanic American Historical Review*
1978–79	Grant, National Science Foundation
1981	Eva G. R. Taylor lecturer, Royal Institute of Navigation
1984	Honorary member, Mortar Board
1985	Jeannette Black Fellow, John Carter Brown Library
1990	Distinguished Service Award of the Conference on Latin American History

Selected Publications

Frey Nicolás de Ovando, Gobernador de las Indias: 1501–1509 (1956)
Trans.: Pedro de Medina, *A Navigator's Universe: The Libro de Cosmographía of 1538* (1972)
Cosmographers and Pilots of the Spanish Maritime Empire (1995)
Ed., *The Globe Encircled and the World Revealed* (1995)

Walter Ze'ev Laqueur

Born 26 May 1921 in Wrocław (Breslau)
Parents: Fritz Laqueur and Else Berliner
1938 to Palestine, 1955 to England, 1967 to the U.S.

1930–38	attended Gymnasium (high school) in Wrocław (Breslau)
1938–39	studied at Hebrew University, Jerusalem
1939–44	Agricultural worker on Kibbuz
1944–53	Political journalist with newspapers in Palestine, then Israel
1957	Visiting professor, Johns Hopkins University, and research fellow, Harvard University
1958	Visiting professor, University of Chicago
1958–59	Fellow, Harvard Russian Research Center and Middle East Research Center
1964–93	Director, Institute of Contemporary History and Wiener Library, London
1967–71	Professor, Brandeis University
1970–82	Professor, University of Tel Aviv
1973–2001	Director, International Research Council, Center for Strategic and International Studies, Washington, DC
1976–77	Visiting professor, Harvard University
1980–91	University professor, Georgetown University

Ad Personam

1955–65	Founding editor, *Survey*
1957	and 1962: Rockefeller Foundation fellowship
1965–2005	Founder and editor, *Journal of Contemporary History*
1970	Guggenheim fellowship
1973–2001	Editor, *Washington Papers*

1978–2001   Editor, *Washington Quarterly*
1984   Inter Nationes Prize
2001   Association of American Publishers, Professional/Scholarly Publishing Division Award for *The Holocaust Encyclopedia*
2005–   Walter Laqueur Prize of the *Journal of Contemporary History*

Amos Jordan, *Walter Laqueur: A Bibliography of His Work* (1986)
The Impact of Western Nationalisms: Essays Dedicated to Walter Z. Laqueur on the Occasion of His 70th Birthday (1992)
"A Wanderer Between Several Worlds," in *The Second Generation: Émigrés from Nazi Germany as Historians*, ed. Andreas W. Daum, Hartmut Lehmann, and James J. Sheehan (2015), 59–71.

Selected Publications

Ha-Nefṭ veha-Mizraḥ ha-Tikhon (1950)
Communism and Nationalism in the Middle East (1956, ²1957)
The Middle East in Transition: Studies in Contemporary History (1958, ²1971)
The Soviet Union and the Middle East (1959)
Young Germany: A History of the German Youth Movement (1962, new ed. 1984). German edition: *Die deutsche Jugendbewegung. Eine historische Studie* (1962, ²1983)
Ed., with Leopold Labedz, *The Future of Communist Society* (1962)
Ed., with Leopold Labedz, *Polycentrism: The New Factor in International Communism* (1962)
Heimkehr. Reisen in die Vergangenheit (1964)
Ed., *Neue Welle in der Sowjetunion. Beharrung und Fortschritt in Literatur und Kunst* (1964)
Russia and Germany: A Century of Conflict (1965, new ed. 1990). German edition: *Deutschland und Russland* (1965)
Ed., with Leopold Labedz, *The State of Soviet Studies* (1965)
Ed., with George L. Mosse, *The Left Wing Intellectuals between the Wars, 1919–1939* (1966). German edition: *Linksintellektuelle zwischen den beiden Weltkriegen* (1969)
Ed., with George L. Mosse, *International Fascism, 1920–1945* (1966). German edition: *Internationaler Faschismus* (1966)
Ed., with George L. Mosse, *Socialism and War: The Dismissal of Jellicoe. Munich: The Czech Dilemma. Russians in Germany, 1900–1914* (1966)
Ed., with George L. Mosse, *1914: The Coming of the First World War* (1966). German edition: *Kriegsausbruch 1914* (1970)
The Fate of the Revolution: Interpretations of Soviet History (1967, rev. ed. 1987). German edition: *Mythos der Revolution. Deutungen und Fehldeutungen der Sowjetgeschichte* (1967)
Ed., with George L. Mosse, *Education and Social Structure* (1967)
Ed., with George L. Mosse, *The New History: Trends in Historical Research and Writing since World War II* (1967)
Ed., with George L. Mosse, *Literature and Politics in the Twentieth Century* (1967)
Ed., with George L. Mosse, *History Today in USA, Britain, France, Italy, Germany, Poland, India, Czechoslovakia, Spain, Holland, Sweden* (1967)
The Road to War 1967: The Origin and Aftermath of the Arab-Israel Conflict (1968, published in the U.S. as *The Road to Jerusalem*). German edition: *Nahost – vor dem Sturm. Die Vorgeschichte des Sechstage-Krieges im Juni 1967* (1968)

Ed., with George L. Mosse, *The Middle East* (1968)
Ed., with George L. Mosse, *Reappraisals: A New Look at History. The Social Sciences and History* (1968)
The Struggle for the Middle East: The Soviet Union in the Mediterranean, 1958–1968 (1969)
Ed., (later editions with Barry Rubin), *The Israel-Arab Reader: A Documentary History of the Middle East Conflict* (1969, ^{7}2008)
Ed., with George L. Mosse, *The Great Depression* (1969)
Ed., with George L. Mosse, *Urbanism: The City in History* (1969)
Europe since Hitler (1970, ^{2}1982). German edition: *Europa aus der Asche. Geschichte seit 1945* (1970)
Ed., with George L. Mosse, *Generations in Conflict* (1970)
Out of the Ruins of Europe (1971)
Ed., *A Dictionary of Politics* (1971, rev. ed. 1973)
A History of Zionism (1972, ^{2}1989, ^{3}2003). German edition: *Der Weg zum Staat Israel. Geschichte des Zionismus* (1975, ^{2}1981). French edition 1994
Ed., with Bernard Krikler, *A Reader's Guide to Contemporary History* (1972)
Weimar: A Cultural History (1974, ^{2}2012). German edition: *Weimar. Die Kultur der Republik* (1976). French edition 1978
Confrontation: The Middle East and World Politics (1974)
Ed., with George L. Mosse, *Historians in Politics* (1974)
Ed., *Fascism: A Reader's Guide. Analyses, Interpretations, Bibliography* (1976)
Guerilla: A Historical and Critical Study (1976, ^{4}1997)
Ed., with Barry M. Rubin, *The Human Rights Reader* (1977, ^{2}1990)
Terrorism (1977). German edition: *Terrorismus* (1982). French edition 1979
Ed., *The Guerilla Reader: A Historical Anthology* (1978)
Zeugnisse politischer Gewalt. Dokumente zur Geschichte des Terrorismus (1978). English edition: *The Terrorism Reader: A Historical Anthology* (1979)
A Continent Astray: Europe 1970–1978 (1979). German edition: *Europa vor der Entscheidung* (1978). Italian edition 1979
The Political Psychology of Appeasement: Finlandization and Other Unpopular Essays (1980)
The Missing Years: A Novel (1980). German edition: *Jahre auf Abruf* (1982)
Farewell to Europe: A Novel (1981)
The Terrible Secret (1980, ^{2}1988, ^{3}2012). German edition: *Was niemand wissen wollte. Die Unterdrückung der Nachrichten über Hitlers "Endlösung"* (1981). Italian editions 1983 and 2011. French edition 2010
Ed., *The Second World War: Essays in Military and Political History* (1982)
America, Europe, and the Soviet Union: Selected Essays (1983)
Ed., *Looking Forward, Looking Back: A Decade of World Politics* (1983)
Ed., *The Pattern of Soviet Conduct in the Third World* (1983)
Germany Today: A Personal Report (1985). German edition: *Was ist los mit den Deutschen?* (1988)
A World of Secrets: The Uses and Limits of Intelligence (1985). Italian edition 1986
Ed., with Robert Hunter, *European Peace Movements and the Future of the Western Alliance* (1985)
with Richard Breitman, *Breaking the Silence: The Secret Mission of Eduard Schulte, Who Brought the World News of the Final Solution* (1986, new ed. 1994). German edition: *Der Mann, der das Schweigen brach. Wie die Welt vom Holocaust erfuhr* (1986)
The Age of Terrorism (1987). German edition: *Terrorismus. Die globale Herausforderung* (1987). Italian edition 1987

Ed., with Brad Roberts, *America in the World, 1962–1987: A Strategic and Political Reader* (1987)
The Long Road to Freedom: Russia and Glasnost (1989). German edition: *Der lange Weg zur Freiheit. Russland unter Gorbatschow* (1989)
Stalin: The Glasnost Revelations (1990). German edition: *Stalin. Abrechnung im Zeichen von Glasnost* (1990)
Soviet Realities: Culture and Politics from Stalin to Gorbachev (1990)
Ed., with John Erickson, *Soviet Union 2000: Reform or Revolution?* (1990)
Europe in Our Time (1992). German edition: *Europa auf dem Weg zur Weltmacht* (1992)
Black Hundred: The Rise of the Extreme Right in Russia (1993). German edition: *Der Schoß ist fruchtbar noch. Der militante Nationalismus der russischen Rechten* (1995). French edition 1996
The Dream that Failed: Reflections on the Soviet Union (1994)
Thursday's Child Has Far To Go: A Memoir of the Journeying Years (1992). German edition: *Wanderer wider Willen. Erinnerungen 1921–1951* (1995)
Fascism: Past, Present and Future (1996). German edition: *Faschismus. Gestern, Heute, Morgen* (1997, ²2000)
Fin De Siècle and Other Essays on America & Europe (1997)
Dawn of Armageddon (1998). German edition: *Die globale Bedrohung. Neue Gefahren des Terrorismus* (1998, ²2001)
The New Terrorism: Fanaticism and the Arms of Mass Destruction (1999, ³2002)
Geboren in Deutschland. Der Exodus der jüdischen Jugend nach 1933 (2000). English edition: *Generation Exodus: The Fate of Young Jewish Refugees from Nazi Germany* (2001). Hebrew edition 2007
Ed., *The Holocaust Encyclopedia* (2001). Italian edition 2007
No End to War: Terrorism in the Twenty-First Century (2003, ²2004). German edition: *Krieg dem Westen. Terrorismus im 21. Jahrhundert* (2003)
Jerusalem beyond Zionism (2004). German edition: *Jerusalem. Jüdischer Traum und israelische Wirklichkeit* (2004)
Ed., *Voices of Terror: Manifestos, Writings, and Manuals of Al Qaeda, Hamas, and Other Terrorists from Around the World and Throughout the Ages* (2004)
Die letzten Tage von Europa. Ein Kontinent verändert sein Gesicht (2006, ²2010). English edition: *The Last Days of Europe: Epitaph for an Old Continent* (2007). Italian edition 2008
Dying for Jerusalem: The Past, Present and Future of the Holiest City (2006)
The Changing Face of Anti-Semitism: From Ancient Times to the Present Day (2006). German edition: *Gesichter des Antisemitismus. Von den Anfängen bis heute* (2008)
Best of Times, Worst of Times: Memoirs of a Political Education (2009). German edition: *Mein 20. Jahrhundert. Stationen eines politischen Lebens* (2009, ²2011)
Harvest of a Decade: Disraelia and Other Essays (2012)
After the Fall: The End of the European Dream and the Decline of a Continent (2012). German edition: *Europa nach dem Fall* (2012)
Optimism in Politics: Reflections on Contemporary History (2014)
Putinism: Russia and its Future with the West (2015)

Conrad Franchot Latour

Born 17 November 1923 in Vienna; died 18 April 1991
1939 to U.S.

1943	B.A. Hobart College
1943	served in U.S. Army
1951	M.A. Stanford University
1951–54	Staff member, Operations Research Office, Johns Hopkins University
1953–55	Instructor, American University
1954–55	Researcher, War Documents Project, Alexandria, VA
1955	Ph.D. American University, "Germany, Italy and the South Tyrol, 1938–1945"
	Area representative, Division of Exile Relations, Free Europe Committee, France
1960–67	Lecturer, University of Maryland, European Division
1967–76	Professor of History, Beaver College, PA (since 2000: Arcadia University)
1976–88	Resident Director, Beaver College Program in Vienna

Ad Personam

1951	Consultant, Department of Intelligence Research, U.S. State Department
1955–56	Consultant, Rand Corporation
1956–	Consulting Editor, *Historical Abstracts*
1965–67	Consultant, Volkswagen Foundation of Germany

Selected Publications

The German Occupation of the USSR in World War II: A Bibliography. Comp. by Alexander Dallin with the assistance of Conrad F. Latour (1955)

Südtirol und die Achse Berlin-Rom, 1938–1945 (1962)

with Thilo Vogelsang, *Okkupation und Wiederaufbau. Die Tätigkeit der Militärregierung in der amerikanischen Besatzungszone Deutschlands, 1944–1947* (1973)

Theodor Hermann von Laue

Born 22 June 1916 in Frankfurt/M.; died 22 January 2000 in Worcester, MA
Parents: Max von Laue and Magdalene von Milkau
1937 to the U.S.

1936–37	studied history at University of Freiburg
1937–44	studied at Princeton University
1939	B.A. Princeton University
1944	Ph.D. Princeton University, "The Beginning of Social Insurance in Imperial Germany: A Study of Social Adjustment in the Dynastic State"
1943–45	and 1947: Instructor, Princeton University
1945–46	served in U.S. Army
1948–49	Assistant professor, University of Pennsylvania
1949–51	Assistant professor, Swarthmore College
1952–54	Assistant professor, Bryn Mawr College

1954–64   Assistant to full professor, University of California, Riverside
1964–70   Professor, Washington University, St. Louis
1970–82   Frances and Jacob Hiatt Professor of European History, Clark University, Worcester

Ad Personam

1951–52   Fellow, Russian Institute, Columbia University
1953   Lecturer, Free University, Berlin
1954–55   Fulbright scholar, Finland
1962–63   and 1974–75: Guggenheim fellowship
1967–68   Ford Foundation visiting professor, M.I.T.
           Founding member of World History Association
1991–93   served on Executive Council, World History Association
1993   Founder and first president, New England Regional of World History Association

Mein lieber Sohn! Die Briefe von Max von Laue an seinen Sohn Theodor in den Vereinigten Staaten von Amerika. 1937 bis 1946, ed. Jost Lemmerich (2011)

Selected Publications

Leopold Ranke: The Formative Years (1950)
Trans.: Leopold Ranke, *A Dialogue on Politics: Politisches Gespräch* (1950)
Imperial Russia at the Turn of the Century: A Cultural Slope and the Revolution from Without (1961)
Sergei Witte and the Industrialization of Russia (1963)
Why Lenin? Why Stalin? A Reappraisal of the Russian Revolution, 1900–1930 (1964, ²1971, ³1993, rev. ed. 2009)
The Global City: Freedom, Power, and Necessity in the Age of World Revolutions (1969)
with Marvin Perry, *Man's Unfinished Journey: A World History* (1971, ²1974, ³1978)
The World Revolution of Westernization: The Twentieth Century in Global Perspective (1987)
with Marvin Perry, Joseph R. Peden and George W. Bock, *Sources of the Western Tradition*, 2 vols. (1987, ²1989)
with Angela von Laue and Dmitri Baltermants, *Faces of a Nation: The Rise and Fall of the Soviet Union 1917–1991* (1996)
with Marvin Perry, Myrna Chase, James R. Jacob and Margaret C. Jacob, *Western Civilization: Ideas, Politics and Society* (2007, ¹⁰2013)
with Marvin Perry and Joseph R. Peden, *Sources of the Western Tradition*. Vol. 1, *From Ancient Times to the Enlightenment* (2008, ²2013)

George Alexander Lensen

Born 5 November 1923 in Berlin; died 5 January 1979 in Florida
Parents: Alexander and Charlotte Lensen

1939   to the U.S.

1943–46	served in U.S. Army Intelligence
1947	B.A. Columbia University
1948	M.A. Columbia University
1951	Ph.D. Columbia University, "Russia's Japan Expedition of 1852 to 1855"
1949–60	Instructor, assistant to associate professor, Florida State University, Tallahassee
1960–79	Professor of East Asian History, Florida State University, Tallahassee

Ad personam

1947–48	SSRC grant
1948	1961 and 1967: Grant, American Philosophical Society
1953–54	Fulbright scholar, Hokkaido University, Japan
1959	and 1941: SSRC-ACLS grant
1961	Inter-University Committee fellowship at Leningrad State University
1966	established and managed The Diplomatic Press to publish historical documents and monographs
1967–68	NEH senior fellow, Japan
1981	Personal library sold to Slavic Research Center, Hokkaido University, Sapporo, Japan

George Alexander Lensen Manuscripts, 1959–1967, Special Collections Department, Florida State University Libraries, Tallahassee, FL

Selected Publications

Report from Hokkaido: The Remains of Russian Culture in Northern Japan (1954, 1973)
Russia's Japan Expedition of 1852 to 1855 (1955, 1982)
The Russian Push toward Japan: Russo-Japanese Relations, 1697–1875 (1959, 1971)
The World Beyond Europe: An Introduction to the History of Africa, India, Southeast Asia, and the Far East (1960, ²1966)
Russia's Eastward Expansion (1964)
Ed., *Revelations of a Russian Diplomat: The Memoirs of Dmitrii I. Abrikossow* (1964)
Ed., *Korea and Manchuria between Russia and Japan, 1895–1904: The Observations of Sir Ernest Satow, British Minister Plenipotentiary to Japan (1895–1900) and China (1900–1906)* (1966)
The Russo-Chinese War (1967)
Ed., *The d'Anethan Dispatches from Japan, 1894–1910: The Observations of Baron Albert d'Anethan, Belgian Minister Plenipotentiary and Dean of the Diplomatic Corps* (1967)
The Soviet Union: An Introduction (1967)
Ed., *Japanese Diplomatic and Consular Officials in Russia: A Handbook of Japanese Representatives in Russia from 1874 to 1968* (1968)
Ed., *Trading under Sail off Japan, 1860–99: The Recollections of Captain John Baxter Will, Sailing-Master & Pilot* (1968)
Faces of Japan: A Photographic Study (1968)

Japanese Recognition of the U.S.S.R.: Soviet-Japanese Relations, 1921–1930 (1970)
April in Russia: A Photographic Study (1970)
Ed., *War and Revolution: Excerpts from the Letters and Diaries of the Countess Olga Poutiatine* (1971)
The Strange Neutrality: Soviet-Japanese Relations during the Second World War, 1941–1945 (1972)
Ed.: Leonid N. Kutakov, *Japanese Foreign Policy on the Eve of the Pacific War: A Soviet View* (1972)
The Damned Inheritance: The Soviet Union and the Manchurian Crises, 1924–1935 (1974)
Balance of Intrigue: International Rivalry in Korea & Manchuria, 1884–1899, 2 vols. (1982)

Gerda Hedwig Lerner

Born Gerda Kronstein, 30 April 1920 in Vienna; died 2 January 2013 in Madison, WI
Parents: Robert Kronstein and Ilona Neumann
1938 to Liechtenstein, 1939 to the U.S.

1939	trained as x-ray technician, Sydenham Hospital, New York
1939–63	worked in various jobs
1962	provided first course on women's history at New School for Social Research, NY
1963	B.A. New School for Social Research
1963–65	Instructor, New School for Social Research and Long Island University, Brooklyn
1965	M.A. Columbia University
1965–68	Assistant to associate professor, Long Island University
1966	Ph.D. Columbia University, "Abolitionists from South Carolina: A Life of Sarah Angelina Grimke"
1968–	Associate member, faculty Columbia University, seminar on American Civilization
1968–80	Professor, Sarah Lawrence College, Yonkers, NY
1980–90	Robinson-Edwards Professor of History, University of Wisconsin, Madison
1984–90	Wisconsin Alumni Research Foundation Senior Distinguished Research Professor, University of Wisconsin

Ad Personam

1966	Founding member, National Organization for Women
1969–70	Cochair, Coordinating Council for Women in the Historical Profession
1970–71	SSRC fellowship
1972	created first M.A. degree in Women's History at Sarah Lawrence College with a Rockefeller Foundation grant
1974	and 1991: Resident fellow, Rockefeller Foundation, Bellagio, Italy
1977	Resident fellow, Aspen Institute
1978	Member, National Advisory Committee for Women, Education and Culture Task Force

1978–79	Grant, Ford Foundation
1980–81	Guggenheim fellowship
1981–82	President, OAH
1984	created first Ph.D. program in Women's History, University of Wisconsin, Madison
1986	Joan Kelly Prize, AHA, for *The Creation of Patriarchy*
1986	Achievement Award, American Association of University Women
1988	Lucretia Mott Award
1992	Lifetime Achievement Award for Scholarly Distinction, AHA
1994	Member, Wisconsin Academy of Sciences, Arts and Letters
1995	Käthe-Leichter-Preis, Austrian Ministry of Women's Affairs
1995	Austrian Cross of Honor for Science and Art
1998–	Member, AAAS
2002	Roy Rosenzweig Distinguished Service Award, OAH
2002	Bruce Catton Prize for Lifetime Achievement in Historical Writing, The Society of American Historians

Honorary degrees from 17 universities, including Colby-Sawyer College (1981), Reed College (1982), Rutgers University (1988), Brandeis University (1989), Syracuse University (1989), University of Massachusetts-Boston (1992), University of Pennsylvania (1999), Westminster College (1999), Dartmouth College (2002), Hebrew University (2005), Columbia University (2006)
Lerner-Scott Prize for Best Dissertation in U.S. women's history, OAH (since 1992)
Gerda Lerner Scholarship Fund, Sarah Lawrence College
Gerda Lerner Fellowship Fund, University of Wisconsin-Madison
Gerda Lerner Papers, 1924–2006, Radcliffe Institute, Harvard University, Cambridge, MA

Selected Publications

as Margaret Rainer (pseudonym), *Es gibt keinen Abschied. Ein Wiener Roman* (1953, ²1955). English edition: *No Farewell* (1955)
The Grimké Sisters from South Carolina: Rebels against Authority (1967, repr. 1998, ²2004)
Ed., *The Woman in American History* (1971)
Black Women in White America: A Documentary History (1972). French edition 1975
The Lady and the Mill Girl: Changes in the Status of Women in the Age of Jackson (1973)
The Female Experience: An American Documentary (1976)
A Death of One's Own (1978, ²2006). German edition: *Ein eigener Tod. Der Schlüssel zum Leben* (1979, ²2001)
The Majority Finds Its Past: Placing Women in History (1979, repr. 2005). German edition: *Frauen finden ihre Vergangenheit. Grundlagen der Frauengeschichte* (1995)
Teaching Women's History (1981)
Women's Diaries of the Westward Journey (1982)
with Marie Laberge, *Women Are History: A Bibliography in the History of American Women* (1986)
The Creation of Patriarchy (1986). German edition: *Die Entstehung des Patriarchats* (1991, ²1995), Spanish edition 1990
The Creation of Feminist Consciousness: From the Middle Ages to Eighteen-Seventy (1993). German edition: *Die Entstehung des feministischen Bewusstseins. Vom Mittelalter bis zur ersten Frauenbewegung* (1993, ²1995)

Scholarship in Women's History Rediscovered & New (1994)
Ed., with Hilda Smith, Nupur Chaudhuri, and Berenice A. Carroll, *A History of the Coordinating Committee on Women in the Historical Profession: Conference Group on Women's History* (1994)
Why History Matters: Life and Thought (1997). German edition: *Zukunft braucht Vergangenheit. Warum Geschichte uns angeht* (2002)
The Feminist Thought of Sarah Grimké (1998)
Fireweed: A Political Autobiography (2002). German edition: *Feuerkraut. Eine politische Autobiographie* (2009)
Living With History / Making Social Change (2009)

Guenter Lewy

Born 22 August 1923 in Wrocław (Breslau)
Parents: Henry Lewy and Rosel Leipziger
1939 to Palestine, 1947 to the U.S.

1942–46	served in the British Army
1951	B.S.S. City College of New York
1952	M.A. Columbia University
1953–56	Instructor, Department of Government, Columbia University
1957	Ph.D. Columbia University, "Constitutionalism and Statecraft during the Golden Age of Spain: A Study of the Political Philosophy of Juan de Mariana, D.J."
1957–63	Assistant professor of government, Smith College
1964–66	Associate professor of political science, University of Massachusetts, Amherst
1966–85	Professor of political science, University of Massachusetts, Amherst

Ad Personam

1956–57	SSRC fellowship in political theory
1961–62	SSRC faculty research fellowship
1963–64	and 1976–77: Rockefeller Foundation fellowship
1996–97	ACLS fellowship
2001	Sybil Halpern Milton Memorial Prize, German Studies Association, for *The Nazi Persecution of the Gypsies*
2012	Fulbright Senior Scholar, Berlin

Guenter Lewy Collection, 1933–1995, Hoover Institution Library and Archives, Stanford University

Selected Publications

Constitutionalism and Statecraft during the Golden Age of Spain: A Study of the Political Philosophy of Juan de Mariana (1960)

The Catholic Church and Nazi Germany (1964, new ed. 2000). German edition: *Die Katholische Kirche und das Dritte Reich* (1965). Translations into French, Italian, Dutch and Spanish
Religion and Revolution (1974)
America in Vietnam (1978)
False Consciousness: An Essay on Mystification (1982)
The Federal Loyalty-Security Program: The Need for Reform (1983)
Peace and Revolution: The Moral Crisis of American Pacifism (1988)
The Cause That Failed: Communism in American Political Life (1990)
Why America Needs Religion: Secular Modernity and Its Discontents (1996)
The Nazi Persecution of the Gypsies (2000). German edition: *"Rückkehr nicht erwünscht." Die Verfolgung der Zigeuner im Dritten Reich* (2001). Translations into French and Italian
The Armenian Massacres in Ottoman Turkey: A Disputed Genocide (2005). German edition: *Der Armenische Fall. Die Politisierung von Geschichte. Was geschah, wie es geschah und warum es geschah* (2009). Translations into Italian, Spanish, and Turkish
If God is Dead, Everything is Permitted? (2008)
Assisted Death in Europe and America: Four Regimes and Their Lessons (2011)
Essays on Genocide and Humanitarian Intervention (2012)

Peter Jacob Loewenberg

Born 14 August 1933 in Hamburg
Parents: Richard Detlev Lorenz Loewenberg and Sophie Frederike Elisabeth Borowicz
1933 to Shanghai; 1937 to the U.S.

1951–53	A.A. Bakersfield College, CA
1955	B.A. University of California, Santa Barbara
1957	M.A. University of California, Berkeley
1966	Ph.D. University of California, Berkeley, "Walter Rathenau and German Society"
1965	Instructor, San Jose College, CA
1965–77	Assistant to associate professor, University of California, Los Angeles
1966–74	Research clinical associate; since 1971: member, Southern California Psychoanalytic Institute
1974	Certified Psychoanalyst
1977	Ph.D. (Psychoanalysis), Southern California Psychoanalytical Institute
1977–2004	Professor of History, University of California, Los Angeles
2001–06	Dean and Chairman, Education Committee, and Director, Training School of the Southern California Psychoanalytic Institute and the New Center for Psychoanalysis, Los Angeles

Ad Personam

1961–62	Fulbright fellowship, Free University Berlin
1965–66	Leader of the UCLA Grenada Project preparing African-American high school students for school integration in Grenada, Mississippi

1967–68	Ford Foundation fellowship
1968–69	SSRC fellowship
1968–69	University of California Humanities Foundation grant
1967–71	Research Clinical Associate, Southern California Psychoanalytic Institute
1970	Franz Alexander Essay Prize, Southern California Psychoanalytic Institute
1970–71	ACLS fellowship
1971	Fellow, Leo Baeck Institute
1973–75	and 1992–95: Member, editorial board, *Journal of the American Psychoanalytical Association*
1975–77	Chair, Licensure Committee for California Research Psychoanalyst Law
1977–85	Fellow, Center for Advanced Psychoanalytic Studies, Princeton
1979	NEH fellowship
1979	Austrian Ministry of Education grant
1979	Fellow, Rockefeller Foundation, Bellagio
1981	Guggenheim fellowship
1982–91	Pro Helvetia Foundation, Zurich
1989	Austrian Cross of Honor for Science and Art
1993	Cofounder of University of California Interdisciplinary Psychoanalytic Consortium
1994–	Member, editorial board, *Clio's Psyche*
1995	Fellow, Max Planck Institute for History, Göttingen
1995	Training and supervising analyst, American Psychoanalytic Association
1998–2001	Chair, Committee on Research and Special Training, American Psychoanalytic Association
1999	Edith Sabshin Award "for excellence in teaching psychoanalytic concepts"
2001–14	Fellow, Board of Professional Standards of the American Psychoanalytic Association
2006	Sir Peter Ustinov Visiting Professor, University of Vienna
2006–13	Chair, International Psychoanalytic Association (IPA), China Committee
2010	Nevitt Sanford Award, International Society for Political Psychology
2008–11	Editor of the IPA Centenary History Committee (1910–2010)
2013	Honorary member, Deutschen Psychoanalytische Vereinigung (DPV)

"Peter Loewenberg Festschrift," *Clio's Psyche* 19, no. 1 (June 2012)

"A Life Between Homelands," in *The Second Generation: Émigrés from Nazi Germany as Historians*, ed. Andreas W. Daum, Hartmut Lehmann, and James J. Sheehan (2016), 114–129.

Selected Publications

Walther Rathenau and German Society (1966)

Walther Rathenau and Henry Kissinger: The Jew as a Modern Statesman in Two Political Cultures (1980)

Decoding the Past: The Psychohistorical Approach (1983, ²1985, ³1996)

Fantasy and Reality in History (1995)

Ed., with Nellie L. Thompson, *100 Years of the IPA: The Centenary History of the International Psychoanalytical Association 1910–2010. Evolution and Change* (2011)

Otto Max Marx

Born 14 July 1929 in Heidelberg; died 30 August 2012 Townshend, VT
Parents: Richard Marx and Gertrud Fisch
1936 to Holland, 1938 to Palestine, 1950 to the U.S.

1936–38	attended boarding school in Bilthoven, Holland
1938–50	High school in Nahariya, Palestine, and military service
1947	University of London: Matriculation examination with honors
1953	B.A. University of California, Berkeley
1957	M.D. University of California, San Francisco
1957–	Postgraduate training at Washington University Barnes Hospital; residency at Langley Porter Neuropsychiatric Institute and Herrick Memorial Hospital; training in psychiatric administration in Berkeley and in psychotherapy at the University of Zürich
1964–66	Research fellow in the History of Psychiatry, Institute of Medical History at the University of Zürich
1966–67	Research fellow, Johns Hopkins Institute of the History of Medicine
1967–77	Associate to professor of psychiatry, School of Medicine, Boston University
1972–73	Associate professor of psychology, University of Massachusetts, Boston
1972–77	Lecturer in psychiatry, School of Medicine, Harvard University
1977–85	in California and
1985–	in Massachusetts and Vermont: various clinical and academic appointments, also private practice as a psychiatrist
1989–92	Research associate, Boston University, Center for the Philosophy and History of Science

Ad Personam

1969	Visiting professor of medical history, Harvard University
1971	Visiting associate professor of psychology, University of New Hampshire
1990–92	(visiting) professor, Institut für Geschichte der Medizin, University of Heidelberg

Selected Publications

Ed., with Annett Moses, *Emeriti erinnern sich. Rückblicke auf die Lehre und Forschung in Heidelberg*, 2 vols. (1993–94)

Michael Albert Meyer

Born 15 November 1937 in Berlin
Parents: Charles (Karl) Meyer and Susanne Paula Frey
1941 via Spain to the U.S

1959	B.A. University of California, Los Angeles
1960	B.H.L. Hebrew Union College-Jewish Institute of Religion (HUC-JIR), Los Angeles
1964	Ph.D. HUC-JIR, Cincinnati, "From Mendelssohn to Zunz: The Expression of Jewish Self-Consciousness in Germany, 1749–1824"
1964–67	Assistant professor of Jewish history, HUC-JIR, Los Angeles
1967–72	Assistant to associate professor, HUC-JIR, Cincinnati
1972–95	Professor, HUC-JIR, Cincinnati
1995–2009	Adolph S. Ochs Professor of Jewish History, HUC-JIR, Cincinnati
2009–	Adolph S. Ochs Professor of Jewish History Emeritus, HUC-JIR, Cincinnati

Ad Personam

1956–57	President, National Federation of Temple Youth
	Visiting professor at UCLA (1965–67), Antioch College (1968), University of Haifa (1970–71), Ben Gurion University, Beersheba (1971–72), Hebrew University, Jerusalem (1977–78), Hebrew Union College, Jerusalem, and Hebrew University (2000, 2002, 2004, 2006, 2008)
1968	Hilberry Prize and Cohen Award, Jewish Book Council, for *Origins of the Modern Jew*
1969–	Fellow, Leo Baeck Institute, New York
1978–80	President, Association for Jewish Studies
1982	ACLS fellow
1989	Berman Award, Jewish Book Council, for *Response to Modernity*
1991–2013	International president, Leo Baeck Institute
1996	Zeltzer Jewish Cultural Achievement Award, National Foundation for Jewish Culture
1997	Berman Award, Jewish Book Council, for *German-Jewish History in Modern Times*, vol. 2
1997	Fellow, Institute for Advanced Studies at Hebrew University, Jerusalem
2000	Guest professor, Aby Warburg House, Hamburg
2001	Honorary Doctor of Hebrew Letters, Jewish Theological Seminary of America
2003–06	Chair, Academic Advisory Council of the Center for Jewish History, New York
2013–	Chair, Advisory Committee, Zentrum für Jüdische Studien, Berlin
2014	Fellow, Katz Institute for Advanced Judaic Studies, University of Pennsylvania

Mediating Modernity: Challenges and Trends in the Jewish Encounter with the Modern World. Essays in Honor of Michael A. Meyer, ed. Lauren B. Strauss and Michael Brenner (2008)

Selected Publications

The Origins of the Modern Jew: Jewish Identity and European Culture in Germany, 1749–1824 (1967, ⁵1988). German edition: *Von Moses Mendelssohn zu Leopold Zunz. Jüdische Identität in Deutschland. 1749–1824* (1994). New edition: *Die Anfänge des modernen Judentums. Jüdische Identität in Deutschland 1749–1824* (2011). Hebrew edition 1990

Ideas of Jewish History (1974, repr. 1987)
Response to Modernity: A History of the Reform Movement in Judaism (1988, repr. 1995).
  German edition: *Antwort auf die Moderne. Geschichte der Reformbewegung im Judentum* (2000). Hebrew edition 1989
Jewish Identity in the Modern World (1990). German edition: *Jüdische Identität in der Moderne* (1992)
Hebrew Union College—Jewish Institute of Religion: A Centennial History, 1875–1975 (1992)
Ed., with Michael Brenner, *German-Jewish History in Modern Times*, 4 vols. (1996–98).
  German edition: *Deutsch-jüdische Geschichte in der Neuzeit* (1996–98). Hebrew edition 2000–2005
—Vol. 1, *Tradition and Enlightenment: 1600–1780* (1996). German edition: *Tradition und Aufklärung: 1600–1780* (1996)
—Vol. 2, *Emancipation and Acculturation: 1780–1871* (1997). German edition: *Emanzipation und Akkulturation 1780–1871* (1996)
—Vol. 3, *Integration in Dispute: 1871–1918* (1997). German edition: *Umstrittene Integration 1871–1918* (1997)
—Vol. 4, *Renewal and Destruction: 1918–1945* (1998). German edition: *Aufbruch und Zerstörung 1918–1945* (1997)
Ed., with W. Gunther Plaut, *The Reform Judaism Reader: North American Documents* (2001)
Judaism Within Modernity: Essays on Jewish History and Religion (2001). Hebrew edition 2006
Ed., *Leo Baeck Werke*. Vol. 6, *Briefe, Reden, Aufsätze* (2003)
Ed.: Joachim Prinz, *Rebellious Rabbi: An Autobiography: The German and Early American Years* (2007)
Ed., with David N. Myers, *Between Jewish Tradition and Modernity: Rethinking and Old Opposition* (2014)

Alma Maria (Luckau) Molin

Born Alma Maria Luckau, 30 April 1908 in Lamme (Braunschweig); died 2 November 2000 in Poughkeepsie, NY
Parents: Herman Luckau and Ida Heineke
Circa 1930 to the U.S.
Assumed last name Molin after her marriage to Richard Werner Molin in 1955

1932	B.A. Connecticut College
1933	M.A. Connecticut College
1934–40	Research assistant, Carnegie Endowment for International Peace
1940–73	Instructor to full professor (since 1959), Vassar College
1941	Ph.D. Columbia University, "The German Delegation at the Paris Peace Conference: A Documentary Study of Germany's Acceptance of the Treaty of Versailles"
1951	and 1953: With U.S. High Commissioner in Germany Director, International Citizen Education Department, U.S. Department of State

Ad Personam

1936	Research stay in Germany
1949–53	provided summer courses for German students in Germany and Austria
1950–60	Lectures at Free University, Berlin

Selected Publication

(under last name Luckau) *The German Delegation at the Paris Peace Conference* (1941)

Herbert Moller

Born Herbert Möller, 11 April 1909 in Hannover; died 6 February 2001 in Sarasota, FL
Parents: Karl Möller and Frieda Thiemann
1939 to the U.S.

1929–30	attended Heidelberg University
1930–33	attended University of Frankfurt
1936–37	imprisoned in Hannover for assisting illegal emigrants to the Netherlands
1942	Ph.D. in history, Boston University, "Effects of Population Changes on Society"
1943–44	with U.S. Army Special Training Program
1944–45	Instructor, Northeastern University
1945–46	Teacher, George School, Bucks County, PA
1946–50	Instructor, Boston University
1950–61	Assistant to associate professor, Boston University
1961–74	Professor, Boston University

Selected Publication

Ed., *Population Movements in Modern European History* (1964)

George Lachmann Mosse

Born Gerhard Lachmann-Mosse, 20 September 1918 in Berlin; died 22 January 1999 in Madison, WI
Parents: Hans Lachmann and Felicitas Mosse
1933 to the U.K., 1939 to the U.S.

1928–33	attended Schule Schloss Salem
1934	Quaker Bootham School, York, UK
1937–39	attended Cambridge University, UK
1941	B.S. Haverford College
1944	Lecturer, Army Specialized Training Program, State University of Iowa, and University of Michigan, Ann Arbor

1945–55	Assistant to associate professor, State University of Iowa
1947	Ph.D. Harvard University, "The Idea of Sovereignty in England, From Sir Thomas Smith to Sir Edward Coke"
1955–57	Associate professor of European history, University of Wisconsin, Madison
1957–65	Professor, University of Wisconsin, Madison
1965–82	John C. Bascom Professor of European History, University of Wisconsin, Madison
1982–89	Weinstein-Bascom Professor of History and Jewish Studies, University of Wisconsin-Madison
1979–85	Koebner Chair, Hebrew University of Jerusalem
1993–98	A. D. White Professor-at-Large, Cornell University

Ad Personam

1949	Huntington Library grant
1955	Consultant, U.S. High Commissioner, Germany
1961	SSRC grant
1962	and 1969–70, 1972, 1974, 1976, 1978: Visiting professor, Hebrew University
1963–64	Visiting professor, Stanford University
1966–	Coeditor, with Walter Laqueur, *Journal of Contemporary History*
1970	E. Harris Harbison Prize, Danforth Foundation, for gifted teaching
1972	and 1979: Senior fellow, Australian National University
1973–	Member, board, Wiener Library, London
1975	Premio Aqui Storia
1977	Visiting professor, Jewish Theological Seminary of America
1978	Member, board, Leo Baeck Institute, New York
1980	Visiting professor, Kaplan Center for Jewish Research, Capetown University, and University of Amsterdam
1982–83	Visiting professor, University of Munich
1986	Visiting professor, Ecole des Hautes Études, Paris
1988	Goethe Medal, Goethe Institute
1988–92	Visiting professor, University of Amsterdam, Cornell University, Tel Aviv University
1989	Premio Prezzolini
1990–94	Visiting professor, Cambridge University, UK
1994	First Shapiro Senior Scholar in Residence, U.S. Holocaust Memorial Museum, Washington, DC
1996	Award for Scholarly Distinction, AHA
1998	Leo Baeck Medal, Leo Baeck Institute
2000–	George L. Mosse Prize, AHA

Honorary doctorates from: Carthage College (1973), Hebrew Union College Jewish Institute of Religion (1987), Università degli Studi di Camerino (1995), Universität-Gesamthochschule-Siegen (1998), Hebrew University of Jerusalem (1999)

George L. Mosse Collection 1878–2001, Leo Baeck Institute Archives, NY

Selected Publications (for additional, coedited volumes, see the entry on Walter Laqueur)

The Struggle for Sovereignty in England from the Reign of Queen Elizabeth to the Petition of Right (1950)
The Reformation (1953)
The Holy Pretence: A Study in Christianity and Reason of State from William Perkins to John Winthrop (1957)
The Culture of Western Europe: The Nineteenth and Twentieth Centuries. An Introduction (1961, ²1974, ³1988). Italian edition 1986. Spanish edition 1997
The Crisis of German Ideology: Intellectual Origins of the Third Reich (1964; with a new preface 1981; 1997). German edition: *Ein Volk, ein Reich, ein Führer. Die völkischen Ursprünge des Nationalsozialismus* (1979). Italian edition 1984. French edition 2006
Nazi Culture: Intellectual, Cultural and Social Life in the Third Reich (1966, 2003). German edition: *Der nationalsozialistische Alltag* (1978). Spanish edition 1993
Literature and Politics in the Twentieth Century (1967)
Germans and Jews: The Right, the Left, and the Search for a "Third Force" in Pre-Nazi Germany (1970)
The Nationalization of the Masses: Political Symbolism and Mass Movements in Germany from the Napoleonic Wars through the Third Reich (1975, ²1991). German edition: *Die Nationalisierung der Massen. Politische Symbolik und Massenbewegungen von den Befreiungskriegen bis zum Dritten Reich* (1976, 1993). Italian editions 1975–2009. Spanish edition 2005
Nazism: A Historical and Comparative Analysis of National Socialism (1978)
Toward the Final Solution: A History of European Racism (1978). German edition: *Die Geschichte des Rassismus in Europa* (1990). Italian edition 1992. Spanish edition 2005
Masses and Man: Nationalist and Fascist Perceptions of Reality (1980). Italian edition 1988
German Jews beyond Judaism (1985). German edition: *Jüdische Intellektuelle in Deutschland. Zwischen Religion und Nationalismus* (1992)
Nationalism and Sexuality: Respectability and Abnormal Sexuality in Modern Europe (1985). German edition: *Nationalismus und Sexualität. Bürgerliche Moral und sexuelle Normen* (1985)
Fallen Soldiers: Reshaping the Memory of the World Wars (1990). German edition: *Gefallen für das Vaterland. Nationales Heldentum und namenloses Sterben* (1993). Italian edition 1990. French edition 1999
Confronting the Nation: Jewish and Western Nationalism (1993)
The Image of Man: The Creation of Modern Masculinity (1996). German edition: *Das Bild des Mannes. Zur Konstruktion der modernen Männlichkeit* (1997). Italian and French edition 1997. Spanish edition 2001
The Fascist Revolution: Toward a General Theory of Fascism (1999). French edition 2003
Confronting History (2000). German edition: *Aus großem Hause. Erinnerungen eines deutsch-jüdischen Historikers* (2003). Spanish edition 2008

George Hans Nadel

Born Hans Georg Nadel, 26 June 1923 in Vienna; died 19 October 1990 in Sussex
Parents: Alfred Nadel and Alice Pollack Nadel

1939 with a *Kindertransport* to England, 1940 to Australia, 1954 to the US, 1963 to England

1942–45	served in Australian army
1948	B.A. University of Melbourne, Australia
1950	M.A. University of Melbourne, Australia
1955	Ph.D. Harvard University, "Adaptation and Social Culture in Early Colonial Australia"
1955–63	Instructor to assistant professor, Harvard University

Ad Personam

1953–54	Fellowship, Institute of Advanced Studies, National University of Australia, Canberra
1960–65	Editor, *History and Theory*
1961–62	Fellow, Institute for Advanced Studies, Princeton, NJ
1963–66	Honorary Nuffield Commonwealth fellowship, Warburg Institute, London

Selected Publications

Australia's Colonial Culture: Ideas, Men, and Institutions in Mid-Nineteenth Century Eastern Australia (1957)
with Perry Curtis, *Imperialism and Colonialism* (1964)
Ed., *Studies in the Philosophy of History: Selected Essays from History and Theory* (1965)

Gerald David Nash

Born Gerhard Nachschön, 16 July 1928 in Berlin; died 11 November 2000 in Albuquerque, NM
Parents: Alfred Nachschön and Alice Kantorowicz
1937 to Palestine, 1938 to the U.S.
Changed last name to Nash in 1938

1950	B.A. New York University
1952	M.A. Columbia University
1957	Ph.D. University of California, Berkeley, "State Government and Economic Development in California, 1849–1911"
1957–58	Instructor, Stanford University
1958–59	Assistant professor, Northern Illinois University
1959–60	Visiting assistant professor, Stanford University
1960–61	Postdoctoral fellow, Harvard University
1961–68	Assistant to associate professor, University of New Mexico, Albuquerque
1968–94	Professor and since 1985 Distinguished Professor, University of New Mexico, Albuquerque

Ad Personam

1959	Fellow, Newberry Library
1960–61	Resident fellow, Center for the Study of Liberty, Harvard University
1974–	Editor, *The Historian*
1990–91	George Bancroft Professor, University of Göttingen
1994–	Gerald D. Nash Student History Journal Prize Award

Visiting professorships at Summers University (1959, 1961), University of California, Davis (1961), the University of Maryland (1962), the University of California, Berkeley (1965), and New York University (1965–66)

Member, board of editors: *Business Historical Review; New Mexico Historical Review; Agricultural History; Journal of American History*
The American West in 2000: Essays in Honor of Gerald D. Nash, ed. Richard W. Etulain and Ferenc Morton Szasz (2003)

Selected Publications

State Government and Economic Development: A History of Administrative Policies in California, 1849–1933 (1964)
Ed., *Issues in American Economic History: Selected Readings* (1964, ²1972, ³1980)
Ed., *Franklin Delano Roosevelt* (1967)
United States Oil Policy, 1890–1964: Business and Government in Twentieth-Century America (1968)
Perspectives on Administration: The Vistas of History (1969)
The Great Transition: A Short History of Twentieth-Century America (1971)
The American West in the Twentieth Century: A Short History of an Urban Oasis (1973)
The Great Depression and World War II (1979). 2nd edition: *The Crucial Era: The Great Depression and World War II, 1929–1945* (1998)
The American West Transformed: The Impact of the Second World War (1985)
Ed., *Social Security: The First Half-Century* (1988)
The Twentieth Century West: Historical Interpretations (1989)
World War II and the West: Reshaping the Economy (1990)
Creating the West: Historical Interpretations, 1890–1990 (1991, 1993)
A. P. Giannini and the Bank of America (1992)
Ed., with Richard W. Etulain, *Researching Western History: Topics in the Twentieth Century* (1997)
The Federal Landscape: An Economic History of the Twentieth-Century West (1999)
A Brief History of the American West since 1945 (2001)

Toni Fanny Oelsner

Born 5 May 1907 in Frankfurt/M.; died August 1981 in New York, NY
Parents: Salo Oelsner and Betty Oppenheimer
1939 via the U.K. to the U.S.

1931–34	studied at University of Frankfurt
1936–37	Lecturer in modern history, Council of Jewish Women, Frankfurt/M.
1940–42	studied at New School of Social Research, New York
1941–42	Research assistant, Universal Jewish Encyclopedia
1942	M.A. New School of Social Research, "Three Jewish Families in Modern Germany: A Study of the Process of Emancipation"
1944–46	Research fellow, Yidisher Visenshaftlikher Institut, New York

Ad Personam

1943–44	Fellowship, Emergency Committee in Aid of Displaced Foreign Scholars
1959–61	Grant, Conference on Jewish Material Claims against Germany
1960–62	and 1965: Littauer Foundation fellowship
1962	Grant, American Philosophical Society
1963	Grant, Wurzweiler Foundation
1966–67	Grant, Memorial Foundation for Jewish Culture

"Dreams of a Better Life: Interview with Toni Oelsner," *New German Critique* 20, Special Issue 2: *Germans and Jews* (Spring–Summer 1980), 31–56.

Alexander Meier Ospovat

Born 13 March 1923 in Königsberg; died 21 December 2010 in Stillwater, OK
Parents: Samuel Ospovat and Anna Gutmann
1940 to the U.S., then Mexico; 1943 again to the U.S.

1945	B.S. in civil engineering, University of Oklahoma
	worked as an engineer
1958	M.A. University of Oklahoma
1960	Ph.D. in history of science, University of Oklahoma, "The 'Kurze Klassifikation und Beschreibung der verschiedenen Gebirgsarten' of Abraham Gottlob Werner"
1960–62	Assistant professor of history, University of North Dakota
1962–73	Assistant to associate professor, Oklahoma State University
1973–88	Professor, Oklahoma State University

Ad Personam

	Fulbright scholarship
1962–63	ACLS grant
1965–66	National Science Foundation fellowship
1965–66	President, Midwest History of Science Society
1970	Member, International Commission on the History of Geological Sciences
1971–72	Fulbright scholar, University of Nottingham
1987	Abraham Gottlob Werner Silver Pin, Gesellschaft für geologische Wissenschaften der DDR

1990   Honorary doctorate, Bergakademie Freiberg

Selected Publications

Abraham Gottlob Werner, *Short Classification and Description of the Various Rocks*. Trans. with an introduction and notes by Alexander M. Ospovat (1971)

Four Hitherto Unpublished Geological Lectures Given by Sir Humphrey Davy in 1805. From Manuscripts Belonging to the Royal Geological Society of Cornwall. With an introduction and notes by Alexander M. Ospovat (1978)

Peter Paret

Born 13 April 1924 in Berlin
Parents: Hans Paret and Suzanne Aimée Cassirer
1933 to Austria, 1935 to France, 1937 to England and to the U.S.

1943–46	served in the U.S. Army in New Guinea, Luzon (Philippines), Korea
1949	B.A. University of California
1959–60	Resident tutor, Oxford University
1960	Ph.D. University of London, UK, "Hans David Ludwig von York and the Development of Prussian Light Infantry, 1786 to 1812"
1960–62	Research Associate, Center of International Studies, Princeton University
1962–63	Visiting assistant professor, University of California, Davis
1963–66	Associate professor, University of California, Davis
1966–69	Professor, University of California, Davis
1969–77	Professor, Stanford University
1977–86	Raymond A. Spruance Professor of International History, Stanford University
1986–97	Andrew W. Mellon Professor in the Humanities, Institute for Advanced Study, Princeton

Ad Personam

1963	Research associate, Center for International Studies, Princeton University
1966–67	Member, School of Historical Studies, Institute for Advanced Study, Princeton
1968–69	Fellow, Center for Advanced Study in the Behavioral Sciences, Stanford
1970	Moncado Prize, Society for Military History
1971–72	Visiting research fellow, London School of Economics and Political Science
1975	Honorary fellow, London School of Economics
1977–78	Research fellow, Historische Kommission zu Berlin
1980–81	Senior fellow, NEH
1984	Fellow, Leo Baeck Institute
1986–	Fellow, AAAS
1988–	Member, American Philosophical Society (1991–97 member, Council)
1988–93	Senior fellow by courtesy, Hoover Institution on War, Revolution and Peace

1990	Honorary Fellow, the London School of Economics
1993	Thomas Jefferson Medal, American Philosophical Society
1993	Samuel Eliot Morison and Moncado Prizes, Society for Military History
1993–95	Senior fellow, Center for Historical Analysis, Rutgers University
1999	Honorary member, Clausewitz Gesellschaft
2000	Officer's Cross, Order of Merit, Federal Republic of Germany
2008	Lees Knowles Lecturer, Trinity College Cambridge
2009	Guest curator, Princeton University Art Museum
2010	Jack Miller Center Prize, The Historical Society
2013	Great Cross of the Order of Merit, Federal Republic of Germany

Honorary doctorates from University of London (1992), University of South Carolina (1995), The College of Wooster (1996), Humboldt University, Berlin (2007)

"Crossing Borders," *Historically Speaking* 4, no. 2 (November 2002): 8–10.
"External Events, Inner Drives," in *The Second Generation: Émigrés from Nazi Germany as Historians*, ed. Andreas W. Daum, Hartmut Lehmann, and James J. Sheehan (2016), 72–78.

Selected Publications

Internal War and Pacification: The Vendée 1789–1796 (1961)
with John W. Shy, *Guerrillas in the 1960s* (1961, rev. ed. 1962)
French Revolutionary Warfare from Indochina to Algeria: The Analysis of a Political and Military Doctrine (1964)
Yorck and the Era of the Prussian Reform: 1807–1815 (1966)
Ed. and trans. of third edition: Gerhard Ritter, *Frederick the Great: A Historical Profile* (1968, revised ed. 1974)
Ed., *Frederick the Great: A Profile* (1972)
Ed.: Siegfried Bernfeld, *Sisyphus, or: The Limits of Education* (1973)
with Donald Reay, *John Hans Ostwald, Architect* (1975)
Clausewitz and the State: The Man, His Theories, and His Times (1976; rev. ed.1985; reissued, with a new preface by the author 2007). German edition: *Clausewitz und der Staat. Der Mensch, seine Theorien und seine Zeit* (1993). Spanish edition 1979. Japanese edition 1991 (pbk. 2006)
Ed. and trans., with Michael Howard: Carl von Clausewitz, *On War* (1976, rev. ed.1984, 1993, 2011, condensed ed. 2007); abbreviated Spanish edition 1999
Ed. and trans., with Helmuth Fischer: Friedrich Meinecke, *The Age of German Liberation, 1795–1815* (1977)
The Berlin Secession: Modernism and Its Enemies in Imperial Germany (1980). German edition: *Die Berliner Secession. Moderne Kunst und ihre Feinde im kaiserlichen Deutschland* (1981, rev. ed. 1982)
Ed., *Berliner Secession*. Katalog der Ausstellung, Neuer Berliner Kunstverein, West Berlin (1981)
Ed. and trans., with Daniel Moran: Carl von Clausewitz, *Two Letters on Strategy* (1984, 1994)
Ed., *Makers of Modern Strategy: From Machiavelli to the Nuclear Age* (1986). Japanese edition 1990. Italian and Spanish editions 1992. Greek edition 2001 (^{2}2006). Brazilian edition 2002

Art as History: Episodes in the Culture and Politics of Nineteenth-Century Germany (1988, rev. ed. 1989). German edition: *Kunst als Geschichte. Kultur und Politik von Menzel bis Fontane* (1990)
Understanding War: Essays on Clausewitz and the History of Military Power (1992)
Ed., with Daniel Moran: Carl von Clausewitz, *Historical and Political Writings* (1992)
with Beth Irwin Lewis and Paul Paret, *Persuasive Images: Posters of War and Revolution from the Hoover Institution Archives* (1992)
Ed., with Ekkehard Mai, *Sammler, Stifter und Museen. Kunstförderung in Deutschland im 19. und 20. Jahrhundert* (1993)
Imagined Battles: Reflections of War in European Art (1997)
German Encounters with Modernism, 1840–1945 (2001, reprint 2010)
An Artist against the Third Reich: Ernst Barlach, 1933–1938 (2003). German edition: *Ein Künstler im Dritten Reich. Ernst Barlach 1933–1945* (2006)
The Cognitive Challenge of War (2009)
with Helga Thieme, *Myth and Modernity: Barlach's Drawings on the Nibelungen* (2012)
Clausewitz in His Time: Studies in the Cultural History of Thinking about War (2015)

Agnes Gertrude Fischer Peterson

Born 8 March 1923 in Berlin; died 1 September 2008 in Los Altos, CA
Parents: Hermann Otto Laurenz Fischer and Ruth Seckels
1932 to Switzerland, 1937 to Canada, 1948 to the U.S.

1945	B.A., University of Toronto
1949	M.A., Radcliffe College
	Research assistant with the documentary film program, National Film Board of Canada, and the California Historical Society, San Francisco
1952–58	Associate, Hoover Institution Library, Stanford
1958–93	Curator of the Central and Western European Collections, Hoover Institution Library

Ad personam

1980	Order of Leopold II (Belgium)
1986	Hoover Institution research fellow
1990	Distinguished Service Award, Stanford University Library Council

Agnes F. Peterson Papers. Schlesinger Library, Radcliffe Institute, Harvard University

Selected Publications

with Grete Heinz, *NSDAP Hauptarchiv: Guide to the Hoover Institution, Microfilm Collection* (1964)

with Gábor Erdélyi, *German Periodical Publications: A Checklist of German Language Series and Series Currently Received in the Stanford University Libraries* (1967)
with Grete Heinz, *The French Fifth Republic: An Annotated Bibliography of the Holdings at the Hoover Institution.* Vol. 1, *Establishment and Consolidation: 1958–1965* (1970); vol. 2, *Continuity and Change, 1966–1970* (1974)
Western Europe: A Survey of Holdings at the Hoover Institution on War, Revolution and Peace (1970)
with Bradley F. Smith, *Heinrich Himmler. Geheimreden 1933 bis 1945 und andere Ansprachen.* French edition 1978

Theodore K. Rabb

Born Theodor Kwasnik Rabinowicz, 5 March 1937 in Teplice-Šanov (Teplitz-Schönau)
Parents: Oskar Rabinowicz and Rosa Oliner
1939 to the U.K., 1959 to the U.S.

1951–55	attended Clifton College, Bristol
1958	B.A. The Queen's College, Oxford
1960	M.A. Princeton University
1961	Ph.D. Princeton University, "The Early Life of Sir Edwin Sandys and Jacobean London"
1961	Instructor, Princeton University
1961–62	Instructor, Stanford University
1962	M.A. Oxford University
1962–63	Instructor, Northwestern University
1963–67	Assistant professor, Harvard University
1967–76	Associate professor, Princeton University
1976–2006	Professor, Princeton University
1974–2001	Director, Princeton University Community College Internship Program
1977–2006	Director, Mid-Career Fellowship Program, Princeton University

Ad Personam

1960	Fellowship, Folger Shakespeare Library, Washington, DC
1965	Fellowship, American Philosophical Society
1965–66	SSRC fellowship
1967–77	Member, AHA Committee on Quantitative Research in History from 1967 to 1977 (chair, 1975–77)
1969	and 1976: ACLS fellowship
1970	Guggenheim fellowship
1969	Visiting associate professor, Johns Hopkins University
1970–	Founder and coeditor, *Journal of Interdisciplinary History*
1972–73	Visiting associate professor, SUNY Binghamton
1972–76	Member, Behavioral Science Assembly, National Research Council

1976–   Member, board of consultants, NEH
1989–96   Member, New Jersey Council for the Humanities (chair: 1994–96)
1992–2000   and 2008–09: Chair, board of trustees, National Council for History Education
1993   Historical advisor and writer, PBS television series *Renaissance*
2008   Board of Governors, Hebrew University of Jerusalem
            Fellow, Royal Historical Society

Theodore K. Rabb Papers on the National Council for History Education, Princeton University Archive

Selected Publications

Ed., *The Thirty Years' War: Problems of Motive, Extent, and Effect* (1964, ²1972, 1981)
Enterprise & Empire: Merchant and Gentry Investment in the Expansion of England, 1575–1630 (1967)
Ed., with Jerrold E. Seigel, *Action and Conviction in Early Modern Europe: Essays in Memory of E. H. Harbison* (1969)
Ed., with Robert I. Rotberg, *The Family in History: Interdisciplinary Essays* (1971, 1976)
with Mortimer Chambers, Barbara Hanawalt, David Herlihy, Isser Woloch, Raymond Grew, and Lisa Tiersten, *The Western Experience* (1974, ¹⁰2010)
The Struggle for Stability in Early Modern Europe (1975)
Ed., with Robert I. Rotberg, *Marriage and Fertility: Studies in Interdisciplinary History* (1980)
Ed., with Robert I. Rotberg, *Industrialization and Urbanization: Studies in Interdisciplinary History* (1981)
with Nancy W. Bauer, *The Origins of Modern Nations* (1981, 1993)
Ed., with Robert I. Rotberg, *Climate and History: Studies in Interdisciplinary History* (1981)
Ed., with Robert I. Rotberg, *The New History, the 1980s and Beyond: Studies in Interdisciplinary History* (1982)
Ed., with Robert I. Rotberg, *Hunger and History: The Impact of Changing Food Production and Consumption Patterns on Society* (1983)
with Anatole Gregory Mazour and John M. Peoples, *People and Nations: A World History* (1983, rev. ed. 1987)
Ed., with Robert I. Rotberg, *Population and Economy: Population and History from the Traditional to the Modern World* (1986)
Ed., with Robert I. Rotberg, *Art and History: Images and their Meaning* (1986)
Ed., with Robert I. Rotberg, *The Origin and Prevention of Major Wars* (1988)
Origins of the Modern West: Essays and Sources in Renaissance & Early Modern European History (1993)
Renaissance Lives: Portraits of an Age (1993)
Jacobean Gentleman: Sir Edwin Sandys, 1561–1629 (1998)
Ed., with Ezra N. Suleiman, *The Making and Unmaking of Democracy: Lessons from History and World Politics* (2003). French edition 2005
The Last Days of the Renaissance and the March to Modernity (2006)
Ed., with Byron Hollinshead, *I Wish I'd Been There: Twenty Historians Revisit Key Moments in History* (2008)

Trans., with an introduction: Hans Sachs, *A Sixteenth-Century Book of Trades: Das Ständebuch* (2009)
The Artist and the Warrior: Military History through the Eyes of the Masters (2011)

Valentin Hanno Rabe

Born 30 January 1930 in Hanover; died 29 November 2008 in Geneseo, NY
Parents: Michael Rabe and Margarete Beer
1940 to the U.S.

1953–55	served in U.S. Army
1953	A.B. Tufts University
1957	M.A. Harvard University
1965	Ph.D. Harvard University, "The American Protestant Foreign Mission Movement, 1880–1920"
1961–67	Instructor to assistant professor, Drexel Institute of Technology, Philadelphia
1967–91	Professor, SUNY Geneseo

Ad Personam

1967	Grant-in-aid, ACLS
1968	and 1972: SUNY Research Foundation, summer faculty fellow
–1991	Academic Delegate, United University Professions
1991–2008	Executive board, Livingston County Historical Society
	Valentin Rabe Undergraduate Paper Award

Selected Publications

American-Chinese Relations, 1784–1941: Books and Pamphlets Extracted from the Shelf Lists of Widener Library (1960)
The Home Base of American China Missions, 1880–1920 (1978)

Harald Anton Thrap Reiche

Born 14 February 1922 in Germany; died 25 July 1994 in Massachusetts
Parents: Johannes Reiche and Olga Maria Thrap Olsen
1938 via Switzerland and France to the U.S.

	studied in Switzerland prior to emigration
1943	A.B. in classics, Harvard University
1944	A.M. Harvard University
1946–47	served in U.S. Army
1949–51	Teaching fellow, Harvard

1955	Ph.D. Harvard University, "A History of the Concepts 'Theoprepes' and 'Hieroprepes'"
1955–66	Assistant to associate professor of classics and philosophy, MIT
1966–91	Professor of classics and philosophy, MIT
1980–90	Faculty resident, Baker House, MIT

Ad Personam

1953–55	Carnegie fellowship in the humanities
1958–61	Visiting lecturer of history, Brandeis University
1961–63	and 1970: Visiting lecturer of humanities, Suffolk University, Boston
1963–64	Guggenheim fellowship, Athens
1967–68	Ford Foundation visiting professor, Institute of Archaeology, Technical University of Berlin

Selected Publications

Trans., with Harry T. Moore and Karl W. Deutsch (bibliography, notes, and index prepared by Harald A. T. Reiche): Karl Jaspers, *Tragedy Is Not Enough* (1953)

with Giorgio de Santillana, *Aristotle and Science: A Critical Controversy* (1959)

Empedocles' Mixture, Eudoxan Astronomy and Aristotle's Connate Pneuma: With an Appendix "General Because First." A Presocratic Motif in Aristotle's Theology (1960)

Joachim Remak

Born Heinrich Joachim Remak, 4 December 1920 in Berlin; died 16 June 2001 in Santa Barbara, CA
Parents: Heinrich Remak and Gertrud Kronthal
1939 to England and the U.S.

1942	B.A. University of California, Berkeley
1944-46	served in U.S. Navy
1946	M.A. University of California, Berkeley
1947-51	Historian, U.S. Department of State
1954-58	Instructor, Stanford University
1955	Ph.D. Stanford University, "Germany and the United States, 1933–1939"
1958–65	Assistant to associate professor, Lewis and Clark College, Portland
1965–67	Associate professor, University of California, Santa Barbara
1967–84	Professor, University of California, Santa Barbara

Ad Personam

1960	Borden Award, Hoover Institution, and Danforth Faculty Grant

1963–64	Visiting associate professor, Indiana University, Bloomington
1966–67	Guggenheim fellowship
1970	Higby Prize, AHA, for best article

Selected Publications

Sarajevo: The Story of a Political Murder (1959)
The Gentle Critic: Theodor Fontane and German Politics, 1848–1898 (1964)
The Origins of World War I, 1871–1914 (1967)
The First World War: Causes, Conduct, Consequences (1971)
The Origins of the Second World War (1976)
The Nazi Years: A Documentary History (1986)
Ed., *War, Revolution and Peace: Essays in Honor of Charles B. Burdick* (1987)
A Very Civil War (1992). German edition: *Bruderzwist nicht Brudermord. Der Schweizer Sonderbundskrieg von 1847* (1997)

Wilhelm Reuning

Born 26 August 1924 in Mainz; died 3 March 2013 in Selinsgrove, PA
Parents: Wilhelm Reuning and Sophia May
1937 to the U.S.

1942–43	attended University of Pennsylvania
1943–45	served in U.S. Army
1948	B.S. and M.S. University of Pennsylvania
1948–51	Assistant professor, University of Pennsylvania
1951–59	Assistant to associate professor of history and political science, Elizabethtown College, PA
1956	Ph.D. University of Pennsylvania, "The History of Article VII of the Triple Alliance, 1875–1915"
1959–89	Professor of history and (1959–71) dean of faculty, Susquehanna University
1971–78	Vice president for academic affairs, Susquehanna University

Ad Personam

1967	Honorary doctorate, Susquehanna University
1971	John E. Wilkinson Award for Administrative Excellence
1984	Susquehanna's Silver Quarter Century Cup
2009	Establishment of the Wilhelm and Ruth S. Reuning Library Endowment

John Edward Rodes

Born 3 May 1923 in Frankfurt/M.; died 26 December 2000 in Pasadena, CA

Parents: Charles Anthony Rosenthal and Olivia Veit
1938 to Switzerland, 1940 to Colombia, 1941 to the U.S.

1937–38	attended American School in Berlin
1938–40	attended schools in Switzerland
1940–41	attended school in Bogotá, Colombia
1943	B.A. University of Southern California
1943–46	served in U.S. Army as translator
1947	Certificat d'études supéerieures, Sorbonne, Paris
1948	M.A. University of Southern California
1948–50	Instructor in German, Simmons College, Boston
1949	M.A. Harvard University
1950–51	Instructor, Occidental College, Los Angeles, CA
1951–61	Assistant to associate professor, Occidental College
1953–64	Head, History of Civilization program, Occidental College
1954	Ph.D. Harvard University, "Stanislas Leszczynski: An Evaluation"
1961–93	Professor, Occidental College

Ad Personam

1974–75	Fulbright visiting professor, University of Saarbrücken
1977–78	Visiting professor, University of Puget Sound
1994	Annual Alumni Seal for Faculty Emeritii, Occidental College

Selected Publications

Germany: A History (1964)
A Short History of the Western World (1970)
The Quest for Unity: Modern Germany 1848–1970 (1971)

Hans (Jack) Rogger

Born Hans Rosenbaum, 9 September 1923 in Herford; died 11 January 2002 in Los Angeles, CA
Parents: Max Rosenbaum and Berni Heilbronn
1939 to the U.S.

1943–46	served in U.S. Navy
1948	B.A. Sarah Lawrence College
1950	M.A. Soviet Area Studies, Harvard University
1953–61	Faculty, Sarah Lawrence College, New York; also teaching fellow Harvard University
1956	Ph.D. Harvard University, "National Consciousness in 18th Century Russia"
1957–60	Lecturer, School of General Studies, Columbia University
1961	Associate professor, Department of History, University of California, Los Angeles

| 1962–66 | Director, Center for Russian and East European Studies, UCLA |
| 1965–83 | Professor, UCLA |

Ad Personam

1964–65	Guggenheim fellowship
1975–76	NEH fellowship
1982–85	Director-at-large, American Association for Slavic Studies
1984–88	Member, academic council, Kennan Institute for Advanced Russian Studies
	Member, editorial boards, *Slavic Review* and *American Historical Review*

Jewish Social Studies 11, no. 1 (Fall 2004) contains several articles in honor of Hans Rogger

Selected Publications

National Consciousness in Eighteenth-Century Russia (1960, repr. 1969)
Ed., with Eugene Weber, *The European Right: A Historical Profile* (1965)
Russia in the Age of Modernisation and Revolution, 1881–1917 (1983, repr.1997)
Jewish Policies and Right-Wing Politics in Imperial Russia (1986)

Gunther Erich Rothenberg

Born 11 July 1923 in Berlin; died 26 April 2004 in Canberra, Australia
Parents: Erich Abraham Rothenberg and Lotte Cohn
1937 to the Netherlands, 1939 to Palestine, 1949 via Canada to the U.S.

1941–46	served in British Army in North Africa, Italy, and Yugoslavia
1946–48	Civilian employee, U.S. intelligence, Austria
1948–49	Captain in the Haganah
1949–55	served in U.S. Air Force intelligence
1954	B.A. University of Illinois
1956	M.A. University of Chicago
1959	Ph.D. University of Illinois Champaign-Urbana, "Antechristianitatis: The Austrian Military Border in Croatia, 1522–1749"
1958	Instructor, Illinois State University
1958–62	Assistant professor, Southern Illinois University, Carbondale
1963–73	Associate to full professor, University of New Mexico, Albuquerque
1973–98	Professor, Purdue University

Ad Personam

1961	and 1965, 1967, 1970 and 1975: Grants, American Philosophical Society
1962	and 1968, 1973 and 1977: ACLS-SSRC grants
1962–63	Guggenheim fellowship

1985	Visiting Fulbright fellow, Australian Royal Military College, Duntroon, Australia
1995–2001	Visiting fellow, School of Historical Studies, Monash University, Australia
2001–03	Visiting professor, School of History, University of New South Wales Canberra, Australia
2003–04	Visiting professor, School of Humanities and Social Sciences, University of New South Wales, Canberra, Australia
2003–04	Member, editorial advisory board, *Australian Army Journal*

Selected Publications

The Austrian Military Border in Croatia, 1522–1747 (1960). German edition: *Die österreichische Militärgrenze in Kroatien 1522 bis 1881* (1970)
The Military Border in Croatia, 1740–1881: A Study of an Imperial Institution (1966). German edition: *Die österreichische Militärgrenze in Kroatien. 1522–1881* (1970)
Congregation Albert, 1897–1972, Albuquerque, New Mexico (1972)
The Army of Francis Joseph (1976)
The Art of Warfare in the Age of Napoleon (1977)
The Anatomy of the Israeli Army: The Israel Defence Force, 1948–78 (1979)
Ed., with Béla K. Király, *Special Topics and Generalizations on the 18th and 19th Centuries* (1979)
Ed., with Béla K. Király and Peter F. Sugar, *East Central European Society and War in the Prerevolutionary Eighteenth Century* (1982)
Napoleon's Great Adversary: Archduke Charles and the Austrian Army, 1792–1814 (1982, pbk. 2007)
The Napoleonic Wars (2000). French edition 2000
The Emperor's Last Victory: Napoleon and the Battle of Wagram (2004)

Beate Ruhm von Oppen

Born 2 July 1918 in Zurich, Switzerland; died 10 August 2004 in Annapolis, MD
Parents: Dietrich von Oppen and Hilda Lilly Isaac
1934 to the Netherlands, 1936 to the U.K., 1959 to the U.S.

	raised in Germany
1934–37	attended Quaker School, Eerde, Netherlands
1939	B.A. Birmingham University, UK
1939–43	Assistant, Barber Institute of Fine Arts, Birmingham University
1943–	worked on German documents for the British Foreign Office
1959	worked on German documents for the War Documentation Project, Alexandria, VA
1959	affiliated with the Centre for International Affairs, Harvard University
1960–	taught at St. John's College, Annapolis
1968–69	Fellow, Institute for Advanced Study, Princeton

Ad Personam

1978   NEH grant

"Memorial for Beate Ruhm von Oppen," *The St. John's Review* 48, no. 2 (2005): 5–25.

Selected Publications

Ed., *Documents on Germany under Occupation 1945–1954* (1955)
Trans.: L. F. Rushbrook Williams, *Der Staat Israel* (1959)
Trans.: Konrad Adenauer, *Memoirs: 1945–53* (1964)
Religion and Resistance to Nazism (1971)
Ed. and trans.: Helmuth James von Moltke, *Briefe an Freya. 1939–1945* (1988; exp. ed. 1991; ³2005; repr. 2007). English edition: *Letters to Freya* (1990)
Ed. and trans.: Dorothy von Moltke, *Ein Leben in Deutschland. Briefe aus Kreisau und Berlin. 1907–1934* (1999, ²2011)

Conrad Schirokauer

Born Max Conrad Schirokauer, 29 April 1929 in Leipzig
Parents: Arnold Schirokauer and Erna Selo-Moser
1935 to Italy, 1939 to the U.S.

1950	B.A. Yale University
1952	M.A. Stanford University
1955–57	served in U.S. Army
1960	Ph. D. Stanford University, "The Political Thought and Behaviour of Chu Shi"
1960–62	Instructor, Swarthmore College
1962–77	Assistant to associate professor, CUNY
1977–91	Professor, CUNY
1993–	Senior Scholar and adjunct professor, Columbia University

Ad Personam

1952–54	Ford Foundation overseas research fellow
1957–58	Fulbright grant
1967–68	ACLS-SSRC fellowship
1971–72	CUNY grant
1991	Visiting professor, Kansai University of Foreign Studies, Kyoto and Hirakata

Selected Publications

A Brief History of Chinese and Japanese Civilizations (1978, ²1989; ³2006, ⁴2013 with Miranda Brown, David Lurie, and Suzanne Gay)

Modern China and Japan (1981)
with Stanley Chodorow and Hans W. Gatzke, *A History of the World* (1986)
A Brief History of Chinese Civilization (1991, ²2006, ³2013). Chinese edition 2008
A Brief History of Japanese Civilization (1993, ⁴2011 with David Lurie and Suzanne Gay)
with Robert P. Hymes, *Ordering the World: Approaches to State and Society in Sung Dynasty China* (1993)
with Donald N. Clark, *Modern East Asia: A Brief History* (2004, ²2008)
Trans.: Miyazaki Ichisada, *China's Examination Hell* (1976, pbk. 1981)

Bruno Paul Schlesinger

Born 15 April 1911 in Neunkirchen, Austria; died 2 September 2010 in Santa Barbara, CA
Parents: Max Schlesinger and Della Wolf
Left Austria 1938; via Yugoslavia, Switzerland, and France to the U.S. in 1939

1931–33	attended German School of Drama, Munich
1933–38	studied law and political science at University of Vienna
1942–45	studied at Notre Dame University, IN
1945–2005	from part-time faculty to full professor, St. Mary's College, IN
1949	Ph.D. in political science, Notre Dame University, "Christopher Dawson and the Modern Political Crisis"
1985–2005	Bruno P. Schlesinger Chair in Humanistic Studies, St. Mary's College, IN

Ad Personam

1956	founded Christian Culture Program (since 1968: Humanistic Studies) at St. Mary's College
1958	Spes Unica Excellence in Teaching Award, St. Mary's College

Schlesinger Papers, Archives. St. Mary's College
Bruno Schlesinger: A Life in Learning & Letters at Saint Mary's College, South Bend, Indiana, ed. Rick Regan (2013)

Hans Adolf Schmitt

Born 6 June 1921 in Frankfurt/M.; died 15 February 2006 in Charlottesville, VA
Parents: Julius Schmitt and Elisabeth Dorothea Hamburger
1934 to the Netherlands, 1937 to the U.K., 1938 to the U.S.

1934–37	attended Quaker School, Eerde, Netherlands
1940	A.B. Washington and Lee University, Lexington, VA
1943	M.A. University of Chicago
1943–46	served in U.S. Army
1948–50	Assistant professor, Alabama State Teachers College

1953	Ph.D. Chicago, "Charles Peguy: The History of a Reputation, 1900–1930"
1953–59	Assistant to associate professor, University of Oklahoma
1959–67	Associate to full professor, Tulane University
1967–71	Professor, New York University
1971–91	Professor, University of Virginia

Ad Personam

1951	Louis E. Asher fellowship
1952	Carnegie fellow in teaching
1956	Outstanding Teaching Award, University of Oklahoma
1956–57	Fulbright scholar, Belgium and Luxembourg
1963	George Louis Beer Prize, AHA, for *The Path to European Union*
1971	Member, editorial board, *Societas*
1980–81	Chairman, European Section, Southern Historical Association

Additional Papers of Hans Schmitt 1943–2004, Special Collections, University of Virginia Library

Selected Publications

The Path to European Union: From the Marshall Plan to the Common Market (1962)
Charles Peguy: The Decline of an Idealist (1967)
European Union: From Hitler to De Gaulle (1969)
Ed., *Historians of Modern Europe* (1971)
with John L. Snell, *The Democratic Movement in Germany, 1789–1914* (1976)
U.S. Occupation in Europe after World War II (1978)
The First Year of the Nazi Era: A Schoolboy's Perspective (1985)
Ed., *Neutral Europe between War and Revolution, 1917–23* (1988)
Lucky Victim: An Ordinary Life in Extraordinary Times, 1933–1946 (1989)
Quakers and Nazis: Inner Light in Outer Darkness (1997)

Ismar Schorsch

Born 3 November 1935 in Hannover
Parents: Emil Schorsch and Fanny Rothschild
1938 to the U.K., 1940 to the U.S.

1957	B.A. Ursinus College, Collegeville, PA
1961	M.A. Columbia University
1962	ordained as rabbi by Jewish Theological Seminary (JTS), New York
1962–64	served as chaplain in U.S. Army
1967–68	Instructor of Jewish history, JTS
1968–70	Assistant professor, Columbia University

1969	Ph.D. Columbia University, "Organized Jewish Reactions to German Anti-Semitism, 1870–1914"
1970–76	Associate professor, JTS
1975–	Dean of graduate school, JTS
1976–80	Professor, JTS
1980–	Rabbi Herman Abramovitz Chair in Jewish History, JTS
1986–2006	Sixth chancellor, JTS

Ad Personam

1969	Ansley Award, Columbia University, for dissertation
1973–76	Grant, Memorial Foundation for Jewish Culture
1976	Leo Baeck Memorial Lecture
1989	Honorary doctorate, University of Wittenberg
1990	Honorary doctorate, Ursinua College
1992	Cofounder of Solomon Schechter High School (now Bergen County, NJ)
1994	served in the official U.S. presidential delegation to witness the peace treaty signing between Jordan and Israel
1995	Honorary doctorate, Graetz College
1996	Cofounder, William Davidson Graduate School of Jewish Education
1998	Honorary degree, Russian State University
2000	Honorary degree, Tufts University
2003	Jewish Cultural Achievement Award, National Foundation for Jewish Culture
2008	President, Memorial Foundation for Jewish Culture
	Member, board of directors and executive committee, Leo Baeck Institute

Text and Context: Essays in Modern Jewish History and Historiography in Honor of Ismar Schorsch, ed. Eli Lederhendler and Jack Wertheimer (2005)

Selected Publications

Jewish Reactions to German Anti-Semitism: 1870–1914 (1972)
Ed., *Heinrich Graetz: The Structure of Jewish History and Other Essays* (1975)
On the History of the Political Judgment of the Jew (1976, ²1977)
Thoughts from 3080: Selected Addresses and Writings (1987)
In the Defense of the Common Good: A Philosophy of Conservative Judaism on the Eve of a New Century (1992)
Form Text to Context: The Turn to History on Modern Judaism (1994)
The Sacred Cluster: The Core Values of Conservative Judaism (1995)
Polarities in Balance (2004)
Canon Without Closure: Torah Commentaries (2007)

Reinhold Siegmund Adolf Schumann

Born 24 May 1919, in Düsseldorf; died 13 April 2010 in Concord, MA

Parents: Robert Schumann and Anne Marks
1938 to the U.S., c. 1950–63 in Germany, returned to the U.S. in 1963

1937	attended University of Rome, Italy
1938	attended Harvard University with scholarship
1941	B.A. Harvard University
1942	M.A. Harvard University
1943–45	served in U.S. Army
1949–50	Teaching fellow, Brandeis University
1951	Ph.D. Harvard University, "A Critical History of the Government of Parma and Its Territory in the Early Middle Ages, About 850–1133"
	taught briefly at Brandeis University
c. 1950–63	Businessman at A. Schumann Co. in in Düsseldorf
1963	President, Schumann Co. in Concord, MA
1967–80	Adjunct to assistant and associate professor, Boston University
1980–90	Professor and (1982–89) director of Italian Studies program, Boston University

Ad Personam

1987	Knight of the Republic of Italy

Selected Publications

Authority and the Commune, Parma, 833–1133 (*Impero e comune, Parma 833–1133*) (1973)
Geschichte Italiens (1983)
Italy in the Last Fifteen Hundred Years: A Concise History (1986, ²1992)

Robert Schwarz

Born 6 May 1921 in Vienna
Parents: Samuel and Dora Schwarz
1939 with a *Kindertransport* to England, 1940 to the U.S.

1939	attended high school in Vienna
1939–40	worked in England
1944	A.B. Emory University
1946	M.A. Syracuse University
1948–51	Instructor, Carnegie Institute of Technology
1951–57	Assistant professor, Carnegie Institute of Technology
1951	Ph.D. University of Wisconsin, Madison, "The Rabbinical Responsa as Sources of Medieval Business History"
1964–89	Professor, Florida Atlantic University
1965–76	Chairman, Philosophy Department, Florida Atlantic University
1972–76	Director, General College Majors in the Humanities, Florida Atlantic University

Ad Personam

1954	Distinguished Teacher Award, Carnegie Institute of Technology
1961	Grant, Jewish Claims Commission, for research in Austria
1967	Grant, Memorial Foundation for Jewish Culture, for research in England
1970	Grant, Ludwig Boltzmann Institut für Geschichte der Arbeiterbewegung
1977–93	Guest lectures in Italy, Austria, Australia, Kenya, England, and Mexico
1977	and 1979: Guest professor, Florida State University Study Center in Florence, Italy
1989	Award for Excellence in Undergraduate Teaching, Florida Atlantic University
1990	Guest professor, Moi University, Kenya

Robert Schwarz Collection, 1934–1995, Leo Baeck Institute Archives, New York
AHC interview with Robert Schwarz, Oral History, Leo Baeck Institute Archives, New York

Book Publication

"Sozialismus" der Propaganda: Das Werben des "Völkischen Beobachters" um die österreichische Arbeiterschaft 1938/1939 (1975)

Walter Michael Simon

Born 29 May 1922 in Berlin; died 4 June 1971 in Ashley Heath, U.K.
Parents: Ernst S. Simon and Elisabeth Bauer
1933 to the U.K., 1940 to the U.S., 1965 to the U.K.

1943	B.A. Wesleyan University
1943–46	served in U.S. Army
1948	M.A. Yale University
1949	Ph.D. Yale University, "The Survival of Authoritarian Prussia in the Age of Reform, 1807–1819"
1949–53	Assistant to associate professor, Stanford University
1953–62	Assistant to associate professor, Cornell University
1962–65	Professor, Cornell University
1965–71	Professor, Keele University, Staffordshire, U.K.

Ad Personam

1957	Guggenheim fellowship
1960–61	Fellow, Institute for Advanced Study, Princeton University
1970	Fellow, Royal Historical Society

Selected Publications

The Failure of the Prussian Reform Movement 1807–1819 (1955)

Germany: A Brief History (1966)
Germany in the Age of Bismarck (1968, ²1970)
Ed., *French Liberalism 1789–1848* (1972)

George Henry Stein

Born 18 May 1934 in Vienna; died 13 July 2007 in Ithaca, NY
Parents: Otto and Sloma (Ellen) Stein
1938 to Palestine, 1940 to the U.S.

1953–57	served in U.S. Air Force
1959	B.A. Brooklyn College
1960	M.A. Columbia University
1962–63	Lecturer, CUNY
1963–66	Instructor to assistant professor, Columbia University
1964	Ph.D. Columbia University, "The Waffen SS: A Political Army at War, 1939–1945"
1966–74	Associate professor to professor, SUNY Binghamton
1973–98	Distinguished teaching professor, SUNY Binghamton
1976–87	Vice president for academic affairs, SUNY Binghamton

Ad Personam

1970–71	NEH fellowship
1971	SUNY Research Council Faculty Fellowship
1987	Alumni Association's Distinguished Service Award, SUNY Binghamton

Selected Publications

The Waffen SS: Hitler's Elite Guard at War, 1939–1945 (1966, 1984). German edition: *Geschichte der Waffen-SS* (1967, 1999). French editions 1967 and 1977. Spanish edition 1973. Dutch edition 2010
Ed., *Hitler* (1968)

Fritz Richard Stern

Born 2 February 1926 in Wrocław (Breslau); died 18 May 2016 in New York City
Parents: Rudolf Stern and Kaethe Brieger
1938 to the U.S.

1946	B.A. Columbia College
1948	M.A. Columbia University
1949–51	Instructor, Columbia University

1951–53	Acting assistant professor, Cornell University
1953	Ph.D. Columbia University, "Cultural Despair and the Politics of Discontent: A Study of the Rise of the 'Germanic' Ideology"
1953–63	Assistant to associate professor, Columbia University
1963	Professor, Columbia University
1967–97	Seth Low Professor, Columbia University
1980–83	Provost, Columbia University
1987–88	Acting provost, Columbia University

Ad Personam

1954	Visiting professor, Free University Berlin
1957–58	Fellow, Center for Advanced Study in the Behavioral Sciences, Stanford University
1960–61	SSRC grant
1962–95	Book review editor for Western Europe, *Foreign Affairs*
1963	Visiting professor, Yale University
1966–67	ACLS grant
1966–67	Member, Nuffield and St. Antony's College, Oxford
1966–67	Consultant, U.S. Department of State
1967–	Permanent visiting professor, University of Konstanz
1969–	Member, AAAS
1969–70	and 1983–83, 1985–86, 1988, 1990–91, 1996–97: Member, Institute for Advanced Study, Princeton
1969–70	Guggenheim fellowship
1972–73	Fellow, Netherlands Institute for Advanced Study
1972–75	Member, International Affairs Committee, AHA
1974–77	Member, editorial board, *American Historical Review*
1976–77	Ford Foundation fellowship
1976	Officer's Cross of the Order of Merit, Federal Republic of Germany
1977	Lionel Trilling Book Award for *Gold and Iron*
1978	Great Teacher Award, Columbia University
1978–92	Member, editorial board, *Foreign Affairs*
1979	Élie Halévy Visiting Professor, Fondation Nationale des Sciences Politiques, Paris
1981–90	and 1991–99: Member, board of trustees, German Marshall Fund
1982–	Fellow, Leo Baeck Institute
1983–90	Member, Trilateral Commission
1983–2000	Member, board of trustees, Aspen Institute Berlin
1983–2007	Member, Visiting Committee, Graduate Faculties, The New School for Social Research, New York
1984	Dr. Leopold Lucas Prize, together with Hans Jonas
1984–	Member, editorial board, *The Collected Papers of Albert Einstein*
1985	D.L.H. (Honorary Degree), Oxford University
1985	and 1988: Grant, Alfred P. Sloan Foundation
1985–86	Chairman, Evaluation Committee of Institute for Advanced Study, Hebrew University, Jerusalem

1987–93	Member, Academic Council, Institute for Advanced Study, Berlin
1987–	Academic Advisory Board, Institute for Human Sciences, Vienna (vice chairman since 1994)
1988–	Member, American Philosophical Society
1988–	Corresponding member, Deutsche Akademie für Sprache und Dichtung
1989	and 1993: Visiting scholar, Russell Sage Foundation, New York
1992–2000	Member, Advisory Board, Einstein Forum, Potsdam
1993–2007	Member of the Senate, German National Foundation
1993–94	Senior advisor to the U.S. Embassy, Federal Republic of Germany
1994–96	Consultant, U.S. Embassy, Federal Republic of Germany
1994–	Member, Order Pour le mérite für Wissenschaften und Künste, Federal Republic of Germany
1994–	Corresponding member, Berlin Brandenburg Academy of Sciences and Humanities
1995	Guest professor, University of Munich
1996	Mark van Doren Award, Columbia College
1996	Kulturpreis Schlesien des Landes Niedersachsen
1997–	Member, board of trustees, American Academy, Berlin
1997	Doctor of Letters (honorary degree), New School for Social Research, New York
1997	Bancroft Award for Retiring Professor
1998	Doctor of Letters (honorary degree), Columbia University
1999	Peace Prize of the German Book Trade
1999	Alexander von Humboldt Research Prize
2000–	Member, International Advisory Board, Jena Center on 20th Century History
2000–	Member, Academic Advisory Committee, Jewish Museum, Berlin
2000–	Fellow, New York Institute of the Humanities at New York University
2000–	Fritz Stern Dissertation Prize, German Historical Institute, Washington, DC
2002	Honorary Doctorate, University of Wrocław
2002	Bruno Snell Medal for Exemplary Dedication in Science and Society, Hamburg University
2002–05	Member, Committee on Membership (Social Sciences), American Philosophical Society
2004	Leo Baeck Medal, Leo Baeck Institute, New York
2004	Knight Commander's Cross of the Order of Merit, Federal Republic of Germany
2005	Nationalpreis of the German National Foundation
2005–	Fritz Stern Fellowships, German National Foundation
2006–	Member, Program Board, Center for International Relations, Warsaw
2006	Honorary Degree, Viadrina University, Frankfurt/Oder
2006	Grand Cross of the Order of Merit with Star and Sash, Federal Republic of Germany
2007	Doctor of Humane Letters, Princeton University
2007	Prize for Tolerance and Reconciliation, Jewish Museum, Berlin
2007	Honorary Senator, German National Foundation
2007	Lifetime Achievement Award, AHA
2007	Jacques Barzun Prize for Cultural History, American Philosophical Society

2008   International Brücke Prize
2008   Prize of the "Europastadt" Goerlitz-Subice
2008–   Honorary chairman, American Friends of Marbach
2009   Marion Dönhoff Prize
2013–   Member, Academic Advisory Board, Institute for Human Sciences, Vienna,
2013   Honorary doctorate, Carl von Ossietzky Universität, Oldenburg
2013   Volkmar and Margret Sander Prize

Visiting professor at Free University of Berlin, Yale University, University of Konstanz, Fondation Nationale des Sciences Politiques in Paris, Ludwig-Maximilians-University/ Munich, University of Mainz, University of Jena

Fritz Stern at 70, ed. Marion F. Deshmukh and Jerry Z. Muller (1997)
"A Conversation with Fritz Stern," *Bulletin of the German Historical Institute* 28 (Spring 2001): 37–54.
"Not Exile, But a New Life," in *The Second Generation: Émigrés from Nazi Germany as Historians*, ed. Andreas W. Daum, Hartmut Lehmann, and James J. Sheehan (2016), 79–81.

Selected Publications

The Varieties of History: From Voltaire to the Present (1956, new and enlarged ed. 1973 and 1986). German edition: *Geschichte und Geschichtsschreibung. Möglichkeiten, Aufgaben, Methoden. Texte von Voltaire bis zur Gegenwart* (1966). New German edition with Jürgen Osterhammel, *Moderne Historiker. Ausgewählte Texte von Voltaire bis zur Gegenwart* (2011)
The Politics of Cultural Despair: A Study in the Rise of the Germanic Ideology (1961, ²1974).
    German edition: *Kulturpessimismus als politische Gefahr. Eine Analyse nationaler Ideologie in Deutschland* (1963, 2005). Japanese edition 1988. French edition 1990
Ed., with Leonard Krieger, *The Responsibility of Power: Historical Essays In Honor of Hajo Holborn* (1967, 1970)
The Failure of Illiberalism: Essays on the Political Culture of Modern Germany (1972, ²1992).
    German edition: *Das Scheitern illiberaler Politik. Studien zur politischen Kultur Deutschlands im 19. und 20. Jahrhundert* (1974)
Gold and Iron: Bismarck, Bleichröder, and the Building of the German Empire (1977). German edition: *Gold und Eisen. Bismarck und sein Bankier Bleichröder* (1978, various new editions since then). Italian edition 1989. French edition 1990. Dutch edition 1992
Dreams and Delusions: The Drama of German History (1987). German edition: *Der Traum vom Frieden und die Versuchung der Macht. Deutsche Geschichte im 20. Jahrhundert* (1988, 2006). French edition 1989. Dutch edition 1994
Verspielte Größe. Essays zur deutschen Geschichte (1996, ³2005)
Einstein's German World (1999, pbk. 2001). French and Polish edition 2001. Catalan edition 2003. Brazilian edition and Chinese edition 2004. Spanish edition 2005
Das feine Schweigen. Historische Essays (1999)
Five Germanys I Have Known (2006, pbk. 2007). German edition: *Fünf Deutschland und ein Leben. Erinnerungen* (2007, ⁹2008). Polish edition 2008. Hungarian edition 2009. Czech edition in preparation. Audiobook edition 2008
Der Westen im 20. Jahrhundert. Selbstzerstörung, Wiederaufbau, Gefährdungen der Gegenwart (2008). Catalan edition 2009

with Helmut Schmidt, *Unser Jahrhundert. Ein Gespräch* (2010, ⁶2011)
with Joschka Fischer, *Gegen den Strom. Ein Gespräch über Geschichte und Politik* (2013)
with Elisabeth Sifton, *No Ordinary Men: Dietrich Bonhoeffer and Hans von Dohnanyi, Resisters Against Hitler in Church and State* (2013). German edition: *Keine gewöhnlichen Männer. Dietrich Bonhoeffer und Hans von Dohnanyi im Widerstand gegen Hitler* (2013)
Zu Hause in der Ferne. Historische Essays (2015)

Felix Friedrich Strauss

Born 22 April 1918 in Innsbruck; died 31 December 1990 in New York, NY
1939 to the U.S.

1936	graduated from high school in Austria
1936–37	volunteered in Austrian Army
	studied at the Vienna Hochschule für Welthandel
1942–45	served in U.S. Army
1947	B.A. Hofstra College, Hempstead, NY
1948	M.A. Columbia University
1948–55	Lecturer and instructor, Hofstra College, Hempstead, NY
1955–57	Instructor, Polytechnic Institute of Brooklyn
1957	Ph.D. Columbia University, "Duke Ernst of Bavaria and the Territory of Salzburg, 1540–1554"
1957–67	Assistant to associate professor, Polytechnic Institute of Brooklyn
1967–90	Professor, Polytechnic Institute of Brooklyn (since 1973: Polytechnic Institute of New York; since 1985: Polytechnic University, New York)

Ad Personam

1962	AAAS research grant
1964–65	Research grant, American Philosophical Society

Universität Innsbruck. Forschungsinstitut Brenner-Archiv. Bundeserziehungsanstalten – Sammlung Felix F. Strauss

Selected Publications

Bilder von der Wiener Neustädter Burg zwischen zwei Weltkriegen (1985)
Herzog Ernst von Bayern und der Gasteiner Bergbau um die Mitte des 16. Jahrhunderts (1991)

Gerald Strauss

Born 3 May 1922 in Frankfurt/M.; died 7 March 2006 in Amherst, MA
1939 to the U.S.

	served in U.S. Army
1949	A.B. Boston University
1950	A.M. Columbia University
1951–57	Instructor, Phillips Exeter Academy, NH
1957	Ph.D. Columbia University, "Germania Illustrada: Topographical-Historical Descriptions of Germany in the Sixteenth Century"
1957–59	Assistant professor, University of Alabama
1959–64	Assistant to associate professor, Indiana University, Bloomington
1964–89	Professor and, since 1983, Distinguished Professor, Indiana University, Bloomington

Ad Personam

1960	and 1962: ACLS grant
1961–62	Fulbright exchange professor, Trinity College, University of Dublin
1964–65	Visiting professor, Cornell University
1965–66	and 1972–73: Guggenheim fellowship
1975–76	and 1983–84: Member, Institute for Advanced Study, Princeton
1979	NEH fellowship
1979	1981 and 1986: Director, NEH Summer Seminar for College Teachers
2007	Gerald Strauss Book Prize, Sixteenth Century Society and Conference

Germania Illustrata: Essays on Early Modern Germany Presented to Gerald Strauss, ed. Andrew C. Fix and Susan C. Karant-Nunn (1992)

Selected Publications

Sixteenth-Century Germany: Its Topography and Topographers (1959)
Historian in an Age of Crisis: The Life and Work of Johannes Aventinus, 1477–1534 (1963)
Nuremberg in the Sixteenth Century (1966). Rev. ed.: *Nuremberg in the Sixteenth Century: City Politics and Life between Middle Ages and Modern Times* (1976)
Manifestations of Discontent in Germany on the Eve of the Reformation: A Collection of Documents (1971)
Pre-Reformation Germany (1972)
Luther's House of Learning: Indoctrination of the Young in the German Reformation (1978)
Law, Resistance, and the State: The Opposition to Roman Law in Reformation Germany (1986)
Enacting the Reformation in Germany: Essays on Institution and Reception (1993)

Herbert Arthur Strauss

Born 1 June 1918 in Würzburg; died 11 March 2005 in New York, NY
Parents: Benno Strauss and Magdalena Hinterneder
1943 to Switzerland, 1946 to the U.S.

1936–42	studied at Hochschule für die Wissenschaft des Judentums, Berlin (concluded with examination as rabbi and religious teacher)
1940–42	Auxiliary rabbi, Jüdische Gemeinde Berlin
1942–43	hiding in Berlin
1943	Flight to Bern, Switzerland
1946	Dr. phil. University of Bern, "Staat, Bürger, Mensch. Die Grundrechtsdebatte der Deutschen Nationalversammlung zu Frankfurt 1848/49"
1946–48	Resident fellow, Commission on European Jewish Cultural Reconstruction
1948–51	Fellow, project on Concentration Camps for United States Public Health Service Postgraduate studies at Columbia University New School of Social Research, New York
1948–54	Lecturer to instructor, City College of New York
1954–60	Assistant to associate professor, Juilliard School of Music, New York
1960–71	Assistant to associate professor, City College, CUNY
1971–	Professor, CUNY
1982–90	Founding director, Center for Research on Antisemitism (Zentrum für Antisemitismusforschung), Technical University Berlin
1990	returned to the U.S.

Ad Personam

1944–46	Representative of Jewish refugees, Bern
1946	Member, Swiss delegation to the conference of World Union for Progressive Judaism, London
1956	1960 and 1963: Grants, Memorial Foundation for Jewish Culture
1961	Teaching and Leadership Award, CUNY
1963	Fellowships from ACLS, SSRC, and the Leo Baeck Institute
1964–	Executive director, then vice president, American Federation of Jews from Central Europe
1972	founded Research Foundation for Jewish Immigration, collaborated with Institute for Contemporary History, Munich
1977	NEH grant
1981–	Corresponding member, Historische Kommission zu Berlin
1986	Walter-Meckauer-Plakette

Antisemitismus und jüdische Geschichte. Studien zu Ehren von Herbert A. Strauss, ed. Rainer Erb and Michael Schmidt (1987)

The Herbert A. Strauss Memorial Seminar at the Leo Baeck Institute, New York, March 29, 2006, ed. Werner Bergmann, Christhard Hoffmann, and Dennis E. Rohrbaugh (2006)

See also the autobiography by Herbert Strauss's wife, Lotte Schloss, *Over the Green Hill* (1999). German edition: *Über den grünen Hügel. Erinnerungen an Deutschland* (1997)

Selected Publications

Staat, Bürger, Mensch. Die Debatten der deutschen Nationalversammlung 1848/1849 über Grundrechte (1947)

Trans.: Hannah Vogt, *The Burden of Guilt: A Short History of Germany, 1914–1945* (1964)
Ed., with Hanns G. Reissner, *Jubilee Volume Dedicated to Curt C. Silberman* (1969)
Ed., with Kurt R. Grossmann, *Gegenwart im Rückblick. Festgabe für die jüdische Gemeinde zu Berlin 25 Jahre nach dem Neubeginn* (1970)
Ed., *Conference on American-Jewish Dilemmas: Papers Delivered at the Fifth Lerntag of the American Federation of Jews from Central Europe* (1971)
Ed., *Conference on Intellectual Policies in American Jewry* (1972)
Ed., *Leo Baeck Memorial Conference on Jewish Social Thought: Papers Delivered at the Seventh Lerntag and the Annual Meeting of the American Federation of Jews from Central Europe, inc., 1973–1974* (1974)
Ed., *Jewish Immigrants of the Nazi Period in the U.S.A*, 6 vols. (1978–92)
Ed., *Biographisches Handbuch der deutschsprachigen Emigration nach 1933 = International Biographical Dictionary of Central European Émigrés 1933–1945*, 3 vols. (1980–83)
Ed., *Antisemitismus. Von der Judenfeindschaft zum Holocaust* (1984)
Ed., with Christhard Hoffmann, *Juden und Judentum in der Literatur* (1985)
Ed., with Norbert Kampe, *Lerntag über den Holocaust in der politischen Kultur seit 1945* (1985)
Ed., *Current Research on Antisemitism*, 3 vols. (1987–93)
Ed., with Tilmann Buddensieg and Kurt Düwell, *Emigration. Deutsche Wissenschaftler nach 1993: Entlassung und Vertreibung* (1987)
Ed., *Bibliographie zum Antisemitismus. Die Bestände der Bibliothek des Zentrums für Antisemitismusforschung der Technischen Universität Berlin*, 4 vols. (1989–93)
Ed., with Werner Bergmann and Christhard Hoffmann, *Lerntag über Gewalt gegen Juden. Die Novemberpogrome von 1938 in historischer Perspektive* (1989)
Ed., with Werner Bergmann and Christhard Hoffmann, *Lerntag über Ausländerpolitik 1989. Das Ende der Integration?* (1990)
Ed., *Der Antisemitismus der Gegenwart* (1990)
Ed., *Die Emigration der Wissenschaften nach 1933. Disziplingeschichtliche Studien* (1991)
with Jacob Goldstein and Irving F. Lukoff, *Individuelles und kollektives Verhalten in Nazi-Konzentrationslagern. Soziologische und psychologische Studien zu Berichten ungarisch-jüdischer Überlebender* (1991)
Ed., *Hostages of Modernization: Studies on Modern Antisemitism, 1870–1933/39* (1993)
In the Eye of the Storm: Growing Up Jewish in Germany, 1918–43. A Memoir (1999). German edition: *Über dem Abgrund. Eine jüdische Jugend in Deutschland 1918–1943* (1997)
Die Juden und die jüdischen Gemeinden Preußens in amtlichen Enquêten des Vormärz, 4 vols. (1998)

Gerard Charles Thormann

Born Gerhard Thormann, 30 September 1922 in Frankfurt/M.; died 11 January 2011 in Nyack, NY
Parents: Werner Ernst Thormann and Charlotte Forschner
1933 to France, 1941 to the U.S.

1940	served in French Army
1941	Studies at University of Aix-Marsailles

1942–46	served in U.S. Army, in unit of the "Ritchie Boys"
1946	B.A. Columbia University
1947	M.A. Columbia University
1948–59	Lecturer and assistant to associate professor, Notre Dame College, Staten Island
1958–59	Assistant professor, School of Education, Fordham University
1951	Ph.D. Columbia University, "Christian Trade Unionism in France: A History of the French Confederation of Christian Workers"
1959–68	Associate professor, Manhattanville College
1968–90	Professor, Manhattanville College

Ad Personam

c. 1952–62	United Nations Representative of the International Federation of Christian Trade Unions
	Honorary doctorate, Manhattan College
1990–	Gerard Thormann Award for Achievement in European History, Manhattanville

Gerard Thormann Collection, Manhattanville College
Nachlass Werner E. Thormann, Deutsches Exilarchiv, Frankfurt/M.

Hans Louis Trefousse

Born 18 December 1921 in Frankfurt/M.; died 8 January 2010 in Staten Island, NY
Parents: George L. Trefousse and Elizabeth Albersheim
1936 to the U.S.

1942	B.A. City College of New York
1942–45	served in U.S. Army
1946	Instructor, Brooklyn College
1947	M.A. Columbia University, "Survey of German-American Relations, 1933–1939"
1947–48	Instructor, Hunter College
1949–50	Instructor, Adelphi College
1950	Ph.D. Columbia University, "Germany and American Neutrality, 1939–1941"
1950–58	Instructor, Brooklyn College
1958–66	Assistant to associate professor, Brooklyn College
1966	Professor, Brooklyn College

Ad Personam

| | Red Bronze Star and Purple Heart for service in U.S. Army |
| 1959 | and 1968: Visiting professor, University of Wisconsin, Milwaukee |

1960   Distinguished Teaching Award, Brooklyn College
1963   Visiting professor, University of Minnesota, Minneapolis
1964   Visiting professor, Johns Hopkins University
1975   ACLS grant
1977–78   Guggenheim fellowship

Selected Publications

Germany and American Neutrality: 1939–1941 (1951, ²1969)
Ben Butler: The South Called Him Beast (1957, ²1974)
What Happened at Pearl Harbour? Documents Pertaining to the Japanese Attack of December 7, 1941, and Its Background (1958)
Ben Wade and the Failure of the Impeachment of Johnson (1960)
Benjamin Franklin Wade: Radical Republican from Ohio (1963)
The Cold War: A Book of Documents (1963)
The Radical Republicans: Lincoln's Vanguard for Racial Justice (1969)
Reconstruction: America's First Effort at Racial Democracy (1971, ²1999)
Background for Radical Reconstruction: Testimony Taken from the Hearings of the Joint Committee on Reconstruction, The Select Committee on the Memphis Riots and Massacres, and the Select Committee on the New Orleans Riots, 1866 and 1867 (1970)
The Causes of the Civil War (1971)
Ed., with Edward McPherson and Harold M. Hyman, *The Political History of the United States of America during the Period of Reconstruction: April 18, 1865–July 15, 1870* (1972)
Impeachment of a President: Andrew Johnson, the Blacks and Reconstruction (1975)
Lincoln's Decision for Emancipation (1975)
with Béla Király, *Ferenc Deák* (1975)
Toward a New View of America: Essays in Honour of Arthur C. Cole (1977)
Ed., with Abraham Seldin Eisenstad, and Ari Arthuer Hoogenboom, *Before Watergate: Problems of Corruption in American Society* (1978)
Germany and America: Essays on Problems of International Relations and Immigration (1980, ²1981)
Pearl Harbour: The Continuing Controversy (1982)
Carl Schurz: A Biography (1982, 1998)
The Great Emancipator (1988)
Andrew Johnson: A Biography (1989)
Historical Dictionary of Reconstruction (1991)
Thaddeus Stevens: Nineteenth Century Egalitarian (1997)
Rutherford B. Hayes (2002)
"First Among Equals": Abraham Lincoln's Reputation during His Administration (2005)

Ilza Fanny Veith

Born 13 May 1912 in Ludwigshafen; died 8 June 2013 in Tiburon, CA
1937 to the U.S.

1934–36	studied medicine in Geneva and Vienna
1944	M.A. Johns Hopkins University
1947	first Ph.D. in history of medicine in the U.S., Johns Hopkins University, "Huang Ti nei ching su wên. The Yellow Emperor's Classic of Internal Medicine. Chapters 1–34 Translated from the Chinese with an Introductory Study"
1949–51	Lecturer, history of medicine, University of Chicago
1951–64	Assistant to associate professor, University of Chicago
1964–79	Professor of history of health science, University of California, San Francisco
1967–79	concurrent professor of psychiatry, University of California, San Francisco

Ad Personam

1951–53	Editor for biology and medicine, University of Chicago Press
1954	President, Society of the History of Medicine of Chicago
1958	Visiting professor, Los Angeles Medical Center, University of California
1958–62	Member, council, American Association for the History of Medicine
1968	Visiting professor, Chicago Medical School
1971	Officer's Cross, Order of Merit, Federal Republic of Germany
1975	Igaku hakase (honorary M.D., D.M.S.), Juntendo University, Tokyo

Ilza Veith Papers, 1965–81, Archives and Special Collections. Library, University of California, San Francisco

Selected Publications

Huang Ti nei ching su wên. The Yellow Emperor's Classic of Internal Medicine. Chapters 1–34 Translated from the Chinese with an Introductory Study (1949, new ed. 1966)

The University of Chicago Clinics and Clinical Departments, 1927–1952: A Brief Outline of the Origins, the Formative Years, and the Present State of Medicine at the University of Chicago (1952)

Ed., *Perspectives in Physiology: An International Symposium, 1953* (1954)

with Leo M. Zimmermann, *Great Ideas in the History of Surgery* (1961, 2nd ed. 1967, rev. ed. 1983)

Hysteria: The History of a Disease (1965, paperback 1983)

with Leo M. Zimmermann, *American Medicine*. 2 vols. (1967)

with Leong T. Tan and Margaret Y.-C. Tan, *Acupuncture Therapy: Current Chinese Practice* (1973, 2nd revized and enlarged ed. 1976))

Can You Hear the Clapping of One Hand? Learning to Live with a Stroke (1988, pbk. 1997)

Robert Vogel

Born 4 November 1929 in Vienna; died 3 April 1994 in Montréal, Quebec
Parents: Frederick and Helen Vogel
1939 to the U.K., 1949 to Canada

1941–49	attended grammar school in Abergavenny and Cardiff
1949	declined scholarship from Oxford University, joined family in Canada
1952	B.A. Sir George Williams University, Montréal, Quebec
1954	M.A. McGill University, "The Diplomatic Career of Sir Fairfax Cartwright from 1906 to 1913"
1955–58	Lecturer, Sir George Williams University
1958–69	Lecturer and assistant to associate professor, McGill University
1959	Ph.D. McGill University, "British Diplomatic Blue Books, 1919–1939"
1969–94	Professor, McGill University
1971–81	Dean, Faculty of Arts and Sciences, McGill University

Ad Personam

1952	Governor-General's Silver Medal for History
	Distinguished Teaching Award, McGill University
1990	with J. Terry Copp, C. P. Stacey Award for excellence in the study of Canadian military history

McGill University Archives Private Fonds, 1960–94
Leadership and Responsibility in the Second World War: Essays in Honour of Robert Vogel, ed. Brian P. Farrell (2004)

Selected Publications

A Breviate of British Diplomatic Blue Books, 1919–1939 (1963)
with J. T. Copp, *Maple Leaf Route: Caen* (1983); *Maple Leaf Route: Falaise* (1983); *Maple Leaf Route: Antwerp* (1984); *Maple Leaf Route: Scheldt* (1985); *Maple Leaf Route: Victory* (1988)

Werner Ernst Warmbrunn

Born 3 July 1920 in Frankfurt/M.; died 19 July 2009 in Claremont, CA
Parents: David Warmbrunn and Lilly Guckenheimer
1936 to the Netherlands, 1941 to the U.S.

1939	graduated from Hervormd Lyceum, Amsterdam, Netherlands
1942	B.A. Cornell University
1944–47	taught history in Putney School, Vermont
1948	M.A. Stanford University
1949–52	Principal, Peninsula School Menlo Park, CA
1952–54	Foreign student advisor, Stanford University
1955	Ph.D. Stanford University, "The Netherlands under German Occupation, 1940–1945"
1957–64	Director, Bechtel International Student Center, Stanford University
1964–66	Associate professor, Pitzer College, Claremont, CA

1966–   Professor of history, Pitzer College, Claremont, CA

Ad Personam

1948–49   Abraham Rosenberg fellowship
1960   Asia Foundation Travel Grant
1963–64   President, National Association for Foreign Student Affairs
1970–71   Senior Fulbright fellow, Federal Republic of Germany
1985   Pitzer College Alumni Association's Academic Excellence Award
           Fulbright Senior Research fellowship (research on Belgium under German Occupation)

Werner Warmbrunn Collection 1885–2006, Leo Baeck Institute, New York

Selected Publications

The Dutch under German Occupation, 1940–1945 (1963). Dutch edition 1964
The German Occupation of Belgium 1940–1945 (1993)

Renée Neu Watkins

Born Eva Renate Nelly Neu, 7 February 1932 in Berlin
Parents: Kurt Max Neu and Ruth Anna Warburg
1936 to the Netherlands, 1940 to Portugal, 1941 to the U.S.

1953   B.A. Radcliffe College
1954   M.A. Harvard University
1959   Ph.D. Radcliffe College, "Leon Battista Alberti, Social Class and Self-Image"
1961–63   Substitute assistant professor, Ithaca College
1963–67   Assistant professor, Smith College
1967–71   Assistant professor, University of Massachusetts, Boston
1971–91   Associate professor, University of Massachusetts, Boston

Ad Personam

1959–60   Fulbright scholarship, Florence

Selected Publications

Trans.: Leon Battista Albert, *The Family in Renaissance Florence* (1969, 1994)
Trans., with Catherine Lord: *Storefront Day Care Centers: The Radical Berlin Experiment* (1973)
Ed. and trans., *Humanism & Liberty: Writings on Freedom from Fifteenth-Century Florence* (1978)

Trans.: Leon Battista Alberti, *The Use and Abuse of Books* (1999)
Trans.: Bartolomeo Scala, *Essays and Dialogues* (2008)

Gerhard Ludwig Weinberg

Born 1 January 1928 in Hannover
Parents: Max B. Weinberg and Kaethe S. Came
1938 to the U.K., 1940 to the U.S.

1946–47	served in U.S. Army in Japan
1948	B.A. New York State College for Teachers, Albany
1949	M.A. University of Chicago
1951	Ph.D. University of Chicago, "German Relations with Russia, 1939–1941"
1951–54	Columbia University research analyst, War Documentation Project, Alexandria, VA
1954–55	Visiting lecturer, University of Chicago
1955–56	Visiting lecturer, University of Kentucky
1956–57	Director, Project for Microfilming Captured German Documents, AHA
1957–59	Assistant professor, University of Kentucky
1959–74	Associate to full professor, University of Michigan
1974–99	William Rand Kenan Jr. Professor of History, University of North Carolina at Chapel Hill

Ad Personam

1962–63	Rockefeller Foundation and SSRC fellowships
1965–66	ACLS fellowship
1971	ACLS grant
1971	George Louis Beer Prize, AHA, for *The Foreign Policy of Hitler's Germany, 1933–1936*
1971–72	Guggenheim fellowship
1978–79	NEH fellowship
1981	Halverson Prize, German Studies Association, for *The Foreign Policy of Hitler's Germany, 1937–1939*
1982–83	Chairman, Conference Group for Central European History of the AHA
1982–84	Vice president for research, AHA
1983	Fulbright professor, University of Bonn
1989	Honorary Doctor of Humane Letters, University at Albany
1989	Order of Merit First Class of the Federal Republic of Germany
1990–91	Visiting professor, U.S. Air Force Academy
1994	George Louis Beer Prize, AHA, for *A World at Arms: A Global History of World War II*
1995	Distinguished Book Award, Society for Military History; and the 1994 Herbert Hoover Book Award for *A World at Arms: A Global History of World War II*
1996–	Member, AAAS

1996–98	President, German Studies Association
2001	Honorary Doctor of Philosophy, University of Hanover
2001–02	Shapiro Senior Scholar in Residence, U.S. Holocaust Memorial Museum
2009	Pritzker Military Library Literature Award for lifetime excellence in military writing, Tawani Foundation Chicago
2011	Samuel Eliot Morison Award for Lifetime Achievement of the Society for Military History, 2011
2012	Spencer-Tucker Award of ABC-Clio for publications in military history

Served as a member of the editorial boards of *Journal of Modern History, Central European History, International History Review, Journal of Intelligence History*

The Impact of Nazism: New Perspectives on the Third Reich and Its Legacy, ed. Alan E. Steinweis and Daniel E. Rogers (2003)

"Some Issues and Experiences in German-American Scholarly Relations," in *The Second Generation: Émigrés from Nazi Germany*, ed. Andreas W. Daum, Hartmut Lehmann, and James J. Sheehan (2016), 97–101.

Selected Publications

Guide to Captured German Documents (1952, 2010)

Germany and the Soviet Union (1954, ²1972)

Hitlers zweites Buch. Ein Dokument aus dem Jahr 1928 (1961). New edition: *Hitler. Reden, Schriften Anordnungen, Februar 1925 bis Januar 1933*, Vol. II.A (1995). English edition: *Hitler's Second Book: The Unpublished Sequel to Mein Kampf* (2003, ²2010)

The Foreign Policy of Hitler's Germany: Diplomatic Revolution in Europe, 1933–36 (1970; with a new preface 1993, combined volume 2010)

Ed., *Transformation of a Continent: Europe in the Twentieth Century* (1975)

The Foreign Policy of Hitler's Germany: Starting World War II 1937–1939 (1980; with a new preface 1993; combined volume 2010)

World in the Balance: Behind the Scenes of World War II (1981)

A World at Arms: A Global History of World War II (1994, ²2005). German edition: *Eine Welt in Waffen. Die globale Geschichte des Zweiten Weltkrieges* (1995, rev. ed. 2002). Spanish, Polish, and Italian editions. Swedish and Korean editions forthcoming

Germany, Hitler, and World War II: Essays in Modern German and World History (1995)

Visions of Victory: The Hopes of Eight World War II Leaders (2005). Polish, Greek, and Turkish editions

Hitler's Foreign Policy 1933–1939: The Road to World War II (2005, 2010)

Dora Bierer Weiner

Born 16 May 1924 in Fürth; died 7 January 2018 in Santa Monica, CA
Parents: Ernst and Emma Bierer
1938 to France, 1942 to the U.S.

1945	B.A. Smith College

1946	M.A. Columbia University, "Intellectual Cooperation under the League of Nations"
1949–51	Lecturer and instructor, Columbia University
1951	Ph.D. Columbia University, "Ernest Renan: His Role in the Culture of Modern France"
1951–56	Lecturer and instructor, Barnard College
1957–62	Instructor, Sarah Lawrence College
1962–63	Visiting lecturer, Teacher's College, Columbia University
1962–65	Research associate, Einstein College of Medicine
1965–78	Associate professor, Manhattanville College
1978–82	Professor of history, Manhattanville College
1982–	Professor of the medical humanities, Department of Psychiatry and Biobehavioral Sciences, UCLA
1996–	Joint appointment in History Department, UCLA

Ad Personam

1956–57	Fellow, American Association of University Women, Johns Hopkins University
1962	SSRC grant-in-aid
1962–64	and 1966–69: U.S. Public Health Service research grant
1972	NEH Senior humanist fellow
1972–74	Consultant, National Institute of Health
1973–76	Distinguished Scholar Award for the History of Medicine, National Library of Medicine
1973	Consulting editor, *Clio Medica*

Selected Publications

Raspail: Scientist and Reformer (1968)
Ed., with William R. Keylor, *From Parnassus: Essays in Honor of Jacques Barzun* (1976)
Ed., with Philippe Pinel, *The Clinical Training of Doctors: An Essay of 1793* (1980)
The Citizen-Patient in Revolutionary and Imperial Paris (1993)
Ed.: Jacques Tenon, *Memoirs on Paris Hospitals* (1996)
Comprendre et soigner: Philippe Pinel, 1745–1826. La médecine de l'esprit (1999)
Ed., with Simon Varey and Rafael Chabrán, *Searching for the Secrets of Nature: The Life and Works of Dr. Francisco Hernández* (2000)

Karl Joachim Weintraub

Born 31 December 1924 in Darmstadt; died 25 March 2004 in Chicago
Parents: Mischa Weintraub and Elisabeth Anders-Hammel
1935 to the Netherlands, 1948 to the U.S.

	attended Quaker School, Eerde, Netherlands
1949	B.A. University of Chicago

1952	M.A. University of Chicago
1954	Teaching intern, University of Chicago, Western Civilization Program
1957	Ph.D. University of Chicago, "The Thought of Johan Huizinga on the Nature of History"
1963–2001	Professor; later: Thomas E. Donnelley Distinguished Service Professor, University of Chicago
1973–84	Dean, Division of Humanities, University of Chicago

Ad Personam

1960	and 1986: Quantrell Awards for Excellence in Undergraduate Teaching, University of Chicago
1967	E. Harris Harbison Award for Distinguished Teaching, Danforth Foundation
1978–2002	Trustee, Art Institute of Chicago
1995	Award for Distinguished Contributions to Undergraduate Teaching, Amoco Foundation
2001	Norman Maclean Alumni Award, University of Chicago

Festschrift: *Cultural Visions: Essays in the History of Culture*, ed. Penny Schine Gold and Benjamin C. Sax. (2000)

Selected Publications

Visions of Culture: Voltaire, Guizot, Burckhardt, Lamprecht, Huizinga, Ortega y Gasset (1966)
The Value of the Individual: Self and Circumstance in Autobiography (1978)

Chapter 24

Selected Bibliography

Reference Works

Biographisches Handbuch der deutschsprachigen wirtschaftswissenschaftlichen Emigration nach 1933, ed. Harald Hagemann and Claus-Dieter Krohn with the assistance of Hans Ulrich Esslinger. 2 vols., Munich, 1999.

Directory of American Scholars. 4th edition (1963); 5th edition (1969); 6th edition (1974); 7th edition (1978); 8th edition (1982); 9th edition (1999); 10th edition (2002).

Epstein, Catherine. *A Past Renewed: A Catalogue of German-Speaking Refugee Historians in the United States after 1933*. New York, 1993.

Fischer, Ernst. *Verleger, Buchhändler & Antiquare aus Deutschland und Österreich in der Emigration nach 1933. Ein biographisches Handbuch*. Elbingen, 2011.

International Biographical Dictionary of Central European Émigrés 1933–1945 = Biographisches Handbuch der deutschsprachigen Emigration nach 1933, ed. Werner Röder and Herbert A. Strauss. 3 vols. in 4. Munich, New York, 1980–83.

Wendland, Ulrike. *Biographisches Handbuch deutschsprachiger Kunsthistoriker im Exil. Leben und Werk der unter dem Nationalsozialismus verfolgten und vertriebenen Wissenschaftler*. 2 vols., Munich, 1999.

Who's Who in American Education: various editions since 1962.

Electronically Accessible Databases (Selection)

Ancestry.com
Biography Reference Bank
JSTOR
LexisNexis
Munzinger Archiv. Internationales Biographisches Archiv
Neue Deutsche Biographie
Obituaries.com
ProQuest Dissertations & Theses
20th Century German History Online: National Socialism, Holocaust, Resistance and Exile 1933–1945
World Biographical Information System
WorldCat

Published Sources and Autobiographical Texts

Adelson, Roger, ed. *Speaking of History: Conversations with Historians*. East Lansing, 1997.

Angress, Werner T. *Generation zwischen Furcht und Hoffnung. Jüdische Jugend im Dritten Reich.* Hamburg, 1985. English edition: *Between Fear and Hope: Jewish Youth in the Third Reich.* New York, 1988.

———. *. . . . immer etwas abseits. Jugenderinnerungen eines jüdischen Berliners 1920–1945.* Berlin, 2005. English edition: *Witness to the Storm: A Jewish Journey from Nazi Berlin to the 82nd Airborne, 1920–1945*; trans. Werner T. Angress with Christine Granger. Durham, NC, 2012.

Ascher, Abraham. *A Community under Siege: The Jews of Breslau under Nazism.* Stanford, 2007.

Bell, Susan Groag. *Between Worlds: In Czechoslovakia, England, and America.* New York, 1991.

———. "Visiting the Place that was Home." In *Gender, Exil, Schreiben*, ed. Julia Schöll. Würzburg, 2002, 21–36.

Bendix, Reinhard. *From Berlin to Berkeley: German-Jewish Identities.* New Brunswick, NJ, 1986. German edition: *Von Berlin nach Berkeley. Deutsch-jüdische Identitäten.* Frankfurt/M., 1985.

Blumenthal, Henry. *Challenges along My Twentieth Century Odyssey.* New York, 1981.

Boris, Eileen, and Nupur Chaudhuri, eds. *Voices of Women Historians: The Personal, the Political, the Professional.* Bloomington, 1999.

Clive, John Leonard. *Not by Fact Alone: Essays on the Writing and Reading of History.* Boston, 1991.

Eyck, Frank. *A Historian's Pilgrimage: Memoirs and Reflections*, ed. Rosemarie Eyck. Calgary, 2009.

Eyck, F. Gunther. *Pantha Rei: A Century's Memoir.* Baltimore, 2010.

Friedländer, Saul. *When Memory Comes*; trans. Helen R. Lane. New York, 1979. German edition: *Wenn die Erinnerung kommt.* Munich, 1998, ^{5}2007.

Gay, Peter. "At Home in America." *The American Scholar* 46, no. 1 (Winter 1977): 31–42.

———. *My German Question: Growing Up in Nazi Berlin.* New Haven, 1998. German edition: *Meine deutsche Frage. Jugend in Berlin 1933–1939.* Munich, 1999.

Gilbert, Felix. *A European Past: Memoirs 1905–1945.* New York, 1988. German edition: *Lehrjahre im alten Europa. Erinnerungen 1905–1945.* Berlin, 1989.

Grab, Walter. *Meine vier Leben. Gedächtniskünstler, Emigrant, Jakobinerforscher, Demokrat.* Cologne, 1999.

Grossmann, Walter. *Abschied von Österreich. Ein Bericht.* Wien, 1975.

———. "Farewell to Austria: A Memoir." *Journal of Refugee Studies* 1 (1988): 308–16.

Hamerow, Theodore S. *Remembering a Vanished World: A Jewish Childhood in Interwar Poland.* New York, 2001.

Hilberg, Raul. *The Politics of Memory: Journey of a Holocaust Historian.* Chicago, 1996. German edition: *Unerbetene Erinnerung. Der Weg eines Holocaust-Forschers.* Frankfurt/M., 1994.

Hirsch, Helmut. *Onkel Sams Hütte. Autobiographisches Garn eines Asylanten in den U.S.A.* Mit einem Geleitwort von Lew Kopelew. Leipzig, 1994.

Hobsbawm, Eric J. *Interesting Times: A Twentieth-Century Life.* London, 2002. German edition: *Gefährliche Zeiten. Ein Leben im 20. Jahrhundert.* Munich, 2003.

Iggers, Georg G., and Wilma A. Iggers. *Zwei Seiten der Geschichte. Lebensbericht aus unruhigen Zeiten.* Göttingen, 2002. English edition: *Two Lives in Uncertain Times: Facing the Challenges of the 20th Century as Scholars and Citizens.* New York, 2006.

Iggers, Wilma A. "Refugee Women from Czechoslovakia in Canada: An Eyewitness Report." In *Between Sorrow and Strength: Women Refugees of the Nazi Period*, ed. Sibylle Quack. New York, 1995, 121–28.
Huttenbach, Henry R. "Vita Felix, Via Dolorosa: An Academic Journey Towards Genocide." In *Pioneers of Genocide Studies*, ed. Samuel Totten and Steven Leonard Jacobs. New Brunswick, 2002, 47–58.
Klemperer, Klemens von. *Voyage Through the Twentieth Century: A Historian's Recollections and Reflections*. New York, 2009.
Kormann, Gerd. *Nightmare's Fairy Tale: A Young Refugee's Home Fronts, 1938–1948*. Madison, WI, 2005.
Kraut, Alan M., and David A. Gerber, eds. *Ethnic Historians and the Mainstream: Shaping the Nation's Immigration Story*. New Brunswick, 2013.
Laqueur, Walter. *Thursday's Child Has Far to Go: A Memoir of the Journeying Years*. New York, 1992. German edition: *Wanderer wider Willen. Erinnerungen 1921–1951*. Berlin, 1995.
———. *Best of Times, Worst of Times: Memoirs of a Political Education*. Waltham, MA, 2009. German edition: *Mein 20. Jahrhundert. Stationen eines politischen Lebens*. Berlin, 2009.
Lerner, Gerda. *A Death of One's Own*. New York, 1978. German edition: *Ein eigener Tod. Der Schlüssel zum Leben*. Düsseldorf, 1979. New ed. Königstein/Ts., 2001.
———. *Why History Matters: Life and Thought*. New York, 1997.
———. "Gespräch mit Gerda Lerner." *Emma* (May/June 2000), http://www.emma.de/artikel/gespraech-mit-gerda-lerner-ich-bin-ein-alien-266112 (8 September June 15, 2014).
———. *Fireweed: A Political Autobiography*. Philadelphia, 2002.
———. *Living With History / Making Social Change*. Chapel Hill, 2009.
Loewenberg, Peter. "Selbstreflexionen zur Identitaet eines amerikanisch-deutsch-jüdischen Psychoanalytikers und Historikers." In *"Denk ich an Deutschland . . .": Sozialpsychologische Reflexionen*, ed. Ulrich Bahrke. Frankfurt/M., 2010, 78–86.
Meyer, Michael A. "Four Decades at HUC-JIR." *The Chronicle* 62 (2003): 22, 24.
Mosse, George L. *"Ich bleibe Emigrant": Gespräche mit George L. Mosse*, ed. Irene Runge and Uwe Stelbrink. Berlin, 1991.
———. *Confronting History: A Memoir*. Madison, WI, 2000. German edition: *Aus großem Hause. Erinnerungen eines deutsch-jüdischen Historikers*. Munich, 2003.
Nash, Gerald D. "Autobiography: Roads to the West." In *The American West in 2000: Essays in Honor of Gerald D. Nash*, ed. Richard W. Etulain and Ferenc Morton Szasz. Albuquerque, 2003, 6–16.
[Oelsner, Toni]. "Dreams of a Better Life: Interview with Toni Oelsner." *New German Critique* 20, Special Issue 2: *Germans and Jews* (Spring–Summer 1980): 31–56.
Paret, Peter. "Crossing Borders." *Historically Speaking* 4, no. 2 (November 2002): 8–10.
Peck, Abraham J., ed. *The German-Jewish Legacy in America, 1938–1988: From Bildung to the Bill of Rights*. Detroit, 1989. [includes essays, among others, by Peter Gay, Georg G. Iggers, Manfred Jonas, Henry L. Feingold, Herbert A. Strauss, Michael A. Meyer, Henry R. Huttenbach, and Renate Bridenthal]
Ruhm von Oppen, Beate. "The Tuning Fork." *The St. John's Review* 48, no. 2 (2005): 27–41.
Schmitt, Hans A. *Lucky Victim: An Ordinary Life in Extraordinary Times, 1933–1946*. Baton Rouge, 1989.
Schwarz, Egon. *Refuge: Chronicle of a Flight from Hitler*; trans. Philip Boehm. Riverside, CA, 2002. German edition: *Keine Zeit für Eichendorff. Chronik unfreiwilliger Wanderjahre*. Frankfurt/M., 1992.

[Stern, Fritz]. "A Conversation with Fritz Stern." *Bulletin of the German Historical Institute* 28 (Spring 2001): 37–54.
Stern, Fritz. *Five Germanys I Have Known*. New York, 2006. German edition: *Fünf Deutschland und ein Leben. Erinnerungen*. Munich, 2007, ⁹2008.
Stolper, Toni. *Ein Leben in Brennpunkten unserer Zeit. Wien, Berlin, New York, Gustav Stolper, 1888–1947*. 2nd ed., Tübingen, 1960.
Strauss, Herbert A. *In the Eye of the Storm: Growing Up Jewish in Germany, 1918–43. A Memoir*. New York, 1999. German edition: *Über dem Abgrund. Eine jüdische Jugend in Deutschland 1918–1943*. Rev. ed. Berlin, 1999.
Suedfeld, Peter, ed. *Light from the Ashes: Social Science Careers of Young Holocaust Refugees and Survivors*. Ann Arbor, 2001.

Secondary Literature

Alter, Peter, ed. *Out of the Third Reich: Refugee Historians in Post-War Britain*. London, New York, 1998.
Aschheim, Steven E. "George Mosse at 80: A Critical Laudatio." *Journal of Contemporary History* 34 (1999): 295–312.
———. *Beyond the Border: The German-Jewish Legacy Abroad*. Princeton, NJ, 2007.
Ash, Mitchell G., and Alfons Söllner. *Forced Migration and Scientific Change: Émigré German-Speaking Scientists and Scholars after 1933*. New York, 1996.
Baets, Antoon de. *Censorship of Historical Thought: A World Guide, 1945–2000*. Westport, CT, 2002.
Barkow, Ben. *Alfred Wiener and the Making of the Holocaust Library*. London, 1997.
Bauerkämper, Arnd. "Americanisation as Globalisation? Remigrés to West Germany after 1945 and Conceptions of Democracy: The Cases of Hans Rothfels, Ernst Fraenkel and Hans Rosenberg." *Leo Baeck Institute Yearbook* 49 (2004): 153–70.
Bauerkämper, Arnd, Konrad H. Jarausch, and Marcus M. Payk, eds. *Demokratiewunder. Transatlantische Mittler und die kulturelle Öffnung Westdeutschlands 1945–1970*. Göttingen, 2005.
Benz, Wolfgang, ed. *Das Exil der kleinen Leute. Alltagserfahrungen deutscher Juden in der Emigration*. Frankfurt/M., 1994.
———, ed. *Flucht aus Deutschland. Zum Exil im 20. Jahrhundert*. Munich, 2001.
———, ed. *Die Kindertransporte 1938/39. Rettung und Integration*. Frankfurt/M., 2003.
Berghahn, Volker R. "Deutschlandbilder 1945–1965. Angloamerikanische Historiker und moderne deutsche Geschichte." In *Deutsche Geschichtswissenschaft nach dem Zweiten Weltkrieg (1945–1965)*, ed. Ernst Schulin. Munich, 1989, 239–72.
Berghahn, Volker R., and Charles S. Maier. "Modern Europe in American Historical Writing." In *Imagined Histories: American Historians Interpret the Past*, ed. Anthony Molho and Gordon Wood. Princeton, NJ, 1998, 393–414.
Bergmann, Werner, and Christhard Hoffmann."Herbert A. Strauss—eine wissenschaftliche Biographie." *Jahrbuch für Antisemitismusforschung* 14 (2005): 17–38.
Bleek, Wilhelm. *Geschichte der Politikwissenschaft in Deutschland*. Munich, 2001.
Christmann, Hans Helmut, and Frank-Rutger Hausmann. *Deutsche und österreichische Romanisten als Verfolgte des Nationalsozialismus*. Tübingen, 1989.

Cornelißen, Christoph. *Geschichtswissenschaft im Geist der Demokratie. Wolfgang J. Mommsen und seine Generation*. Berlin, 2010.

Coser, Lewis A. *Refugee Scholars in America: Their Impact and Their Experiences*. New Haven, 1984.

Daum, Andreas W. "German Historiography in Transatlantic Perspective: Interview with Hans-Ulrich Wehler." *Bulletin of the German Historical Institute* 26 (Spring 2001): 117–25.

———. "The Second Generation: German Émigré Historians in the Transatlantic World, 1945 to the Present." *Bulletin of the German Historical Institute* 51 (Fall 2012): 116–21.

———. "Was Clausewitz mit Kleist und Schiller verbindet: Unmodisch und frei. Der Historiker Peter Paret feiert seinen neunzigsten Geburtstag." *Frankfurter Allgemeine Zeitung*, no. 84 (9 April 2014): N 3 [English translation in *Michigan War Studies Review*, 7 May 2014, at http://www.miwsr.com/2014-041.aspx].

Daum, Andreas W., Sabine Hacke, and Bradley Prager, eds., *The GSA at Forty*. Special Issue of *German Studies Review* 39, no. 3 (2016).

Deshmukh, Marion F., and Jerry Z. Muller, eds. *Fritz Stern at 70*. Washington, DC, 1997.

Eakin-Thimme, Gabriela Ann. *Geschichte im Exil. Deutschsprachige Historiker nach 1933*. Munich, 2005.

Eckel, Jan. *Hans Rothfels. Eine intellektuelle Biographie im 20. Jahrhundert*. Göttingen, 2005.

Edgcomb, Gabrielle Simon. *From Swastika to Jim Crow: Refugee Scholars at Black Colleges*. Malabar, FL, 1993.

Epstein, Catherine. "Introduction." In *A Past Renewed: A Catalogue of German-Speaking Refugee Historians in the United States after 1933*. New York, 1993, 1–20.

———. "*Schicksalsgeschichte*: Refugee Historians in the United States." In *An Interrupted Past: German Speaking Refugee Historians in the United States after 1933*, ed. Hartmut Lehmann and James J. Sheehan. New York, 1991, 116–35.

———. "Fashioning Fortuna's Whim: German-Speaking Women Emigrant Historians in the United States." In *Between Sorrow and Strength: Women Refugees of the Nazi Period*, ed. Sibylle Quack. Cambridge, 1995, 301–23.

———. "German Historians at the Back of the Pack: Hiring Patterns in Modern European History, 1945–2010." *Central European History* 46, no. 3 (2013): 599–639.

Etzemüller, Thomas. "How to Make a Historian: Problems in Writing Biographies of Historians." *Storia della Storiografia* 27, no. 53 (2008): 47–58.

Evans, Richard J. *Cosmopolitan Islanders: British Historians and the European Continent*. Cambridge, 2009.

Fair-Schulz, Axel, and Mario Kessler, eds. *German Scholars in Exile*. Lanham, MA, 2011.

Feichtinger, Johannes. *Wissenschaft zwischen den Kulturen. Österreichische Hochschullehrer in der Emigration 1933–1945*. Frankfurt/M., 2001.

Fermi, Laura. *Illustrious Immigrants: The Intellectual Migration from Europe, 1930–1941*. 2nd ed., Chicago, 1971.

Friedländer, Saul. "Mosse's Influence on the Historiography of the Holocaust." In *What History Tells: George L. Mosse and the Culture of Modern Europe*, ed. Stanley Payne, David J. Sorkin, and John S. Tortorice. Madison, WI, 2004, 134–47.

Gay, Peter. *Moritz Fröhlich—Morris Gay: A German Refugee in the United States*. Washington, DC, 1999.

———. "Reflections on Hitler's Refugees in the United States: Keynote Speech." *Leo Baeck Institute Yearbook* 53 (2008): 117–26.

Gerber, David A. "Introduction." In *Ethnic Historians and the Mainstream: Shaping the Nation's Immigration Story*, ed. Alan M. Kraut and David A. Gerber. New Brunswick, 2013, 1–16.

The Herbert A. Strauss Memorial Seminar at the Leo Baeck Institute, New York, March 29, 2006, ed. Werner Bergmann, Christhard Hoffmann, and Dennis E. Rohrbaugh. Berlin, 2006.

Hoffmann, Christhard. "The Contribution of German-Speaking Jewish Immigrants to British Historiography." In *Second Chance: Two Centuries of German-Speaking Jews in the United Kingdom*, ed. Werner Mosse. Tübingen, 1991, 153–75.

———, ed. *Preserving the Legacy of German Jewry: A History of the Leo Baeck Institute, 1955–2005*. Tübingen, 2005.

Hübinger, Gangolf. "Fritz Stern zwischen Europa und Amerika. Eine Fallstudie zum Geschichts-Intellektuellen." In *Intellektuelle im Exil*, ed. Peter Burschel. Göttingen, 2011, 219–40.

Iggers, Georg G. "Die deutschen Historiker in der Emigration." In *Geschichtswissenschaft in Deutschland. Traditionelle Positionen und gegenwärtige Aufgaben*, ed. Bernd Faulenbach. Munich, 1974, 97–111.

———. *Geschichtswissenschaft im 20. Jahrhundert. Ein kritischer Überblick im internationalen Zusammenhang*. New ed., Göttingen, 2007.

———. *Refugee Historians from Nazi Germany: Political Attitudes towards Democracy*. Washington, DC, 2006.

Ingles, Ken. "From Berlin to the Bush." *The Monthly: Australian Politics, Society & Culture* 59, at http://www.themonthly.com.au/monthly-essays-ken-inglis-berlin-bush--2638 (8 September 2015).

Ingrisch, Doris. *Der dis/kontinuierliche Status des Seins. Über vom Nationalsozialismus aus Österreich vertriebene (und verbliebene) intellektuelle Kulturen in lebensgeschichtlichen Kontexten*. Frankfurt/M., 2004.

Jarausch, Konrad H. "German Social History—American Style." *Journal of Social History* 19 (1985): 349–59.

———. "Die Provokation des 'Anderen.' Amerikanische Perspektiven auf die deutsche Vergangenheitsbewältigung." In *Doppelte Zeitgeschichte. Deutsch-deutsche Beziehungen 1945–1990*, ed. Arnd Bauerkämper, Martin Sabrow, and Bernd Stöver. Bonn, 1998, 432–47.

Jarausch, Konrad H., and Rüdiger Hohls, eds. *Versäumte Fragen. Deutsche Historiker im Schatten des Nationalsozialismus*. Stuttgart, 2000.

Jarausch, Konrad H., and Martin Sabrow, eds., *Die historische Meistererzählung. Deutungslinien der deutschen Nationalgeschichte nach 1945*. Göttingen, 2002.

Jütte, Robert. *Die Emigration der deutschsprachigen "Wissenschaft vom Judentum". Die Auswanderung jüdischer Historiker nach Palästina 1933–1945*. Stuttgart, 1991.

Jay, Martin. *Permanent Exiles: Essays on the Intellectual Migration from Germany to America*. New York, 1986.

Kaplan, Marion A. *Between Dignity and Despair: Jewish Life in Nazi Germany*. New York, 1998.

———. "Revealing and Concealing: Using Memoirs to Write German-Jewish History." In *Text and Context: Essays in Modern Jewish History and Historiography in Honor of Ismar Schorsch*, ed. Eli Lederhendler and Jack Wertheimer. New York, 2005, 383–410.

Katz, Ethan. "Displaced Historians, Dialectical Histories: George L. Mosse, Peter Gay, and Germany's Multiple Paths in the Twentieth Century." *Journal of Modern Jewish Studies* 7, no. 2 (July 2008): 135–55.

Keßler, Mario. *Exilerfahrung in Wissenschaft und Politik. Remigrierte Historiker in der frühen DDR.* Cologne, 2001.

———, ed. *Deutsche Historiker im Exil (1933–1945). Ausgewählte Studien.* Berlin, 2005.

Kielmansegg, Peter Graf, Horst Mewes, and Elisabeth Glaser Schmidt, eds. *Hannah Arendt and Leo Strauss: German Émigrés and American Political Thought after World War II.* New York, 1995.

Kraus, Elisabeth. *Die Familie Mosse. Deutsch-jüdisches Bürgertum im 19. und 20. Jahrhundert.* Munich, 1999.

Krieger, Leonard. "European History in America." In *History: Professional Scholarship in America*, ed. John Higham. Baltimore, 1989, 233–313.

Krohn, Claus-Dieter, ed. *Handbuch der deutschsprachigen Emigration 1933–1945.* Darmstadt, 1998.

———. "Geschichtswissenschaften." In *Handbuch der deutschsprachigen Emigration 1933–1945.* Darmstadt, 1998, 747–61.

———. *Intellectuals in Exile: Refugee Scholars and the New School for Social Research*; trans. Rita Kimber and Robert Kimber. Amherst, 1993.

Lahme, Tilmann, *Golo Mann. Biographie.* 3rd ed., Frankfurt/M., 2009.

Lamberti, Marjorie E. "German Antifascist Refugees in America and the Public Debate on 'What Should be Done with Germany after Hitler,' 1941–1945." *Central European History* 40 (2007): 279–305.

———. "The Search for the 'Other Germany': Refugee Historians from Nazi Germany and the Contested Historical Legacy of the Resistance to Hitler." *Central European History* 47 (2014): 402–29.

Laqueur, Walter. *Generation Exodus: The Fate of Young Jewish Refugees from Nazi Germany.* Hanover, NH, 2001.

Lederhendler, Eli, and Jack Wertheimer, eds. *Text and Context: Essays in Modern Jewish History and Historiography in Honor of Ismar Schorsch.* New York, 2005.

Leeman, Merel. "The Transatlantic Reconstruction of 'Western' Culture: George Mosse, Peter Gay, and Development of the German Tradition of *Geistesgeschichte*." In *Bulletin of the German Historical Institute* 54, Supplement 10 (2014), 139–59.

Lehmann, Hartmut, ed. *Felix Gilbert as Scholar and Teacher.* Washington, DC, 1992.

Lehmann, Hartmut, and James Van Horn Melton, eds. *Paths of Continuity: Central European Historiography from the 1930s to the 1950s.* New York, 1994.

Lehmann, Hartmut, and James J. Sheehan, eds. *An Interrupted Past: German Speaking Refugee Historians in the United States after 1933.* New York, 1991.

Melhuish, Kathleen Joy. "The German-Jewish Emigrant and the Historian's Craft." In *From the Emancipation to the Holocaust: Essays on Jewish Literature and History in Central Europe,* ed. Konrad Kwiet. Kensington, 1987, 155–65.

Meyer, Michael A., with Michael Brenner, eds., *German-Jewish History in Modern Times,* 4 vols. New York, 1996–98. German edition 1996–98.

Meyer, Michael A. "Ismar Schorsch, the Historian: A Critical Appreciation." In *Text and Context: Essays in Modern Jewish History and Historiography in Honor of Ismar Schorsch,* ed. Eli Lederhendler and Jack Wertheimer. New York, 2005, 3–23.

Micale, Mark S., and Robert L. Dietle, eds. *Enlightenment, Passion, Modernity: Historical Essays in European Thought and Culture.* Stanford, CA, 2000.

Michels, Karen. *Transplantierte Kunstwissenschaft. Deutschsprachige Kunstgeschichte im amerikanischen Exil.* Berlin, 1999.

Mitchell, Allan. *Fleeing Nazi Germany: Five Historians Migrate to America.* Trafford, 2011.

Mommsen, Wolfgang J. *The Return to the Western Tradition: German Historiography since 1945*. Washington, DC, 1991.
Mosse, Werner E., ed. *Second Chance: Two Centuries of German-Speaking Jews in the United Kingdom*. Tübingen, 1991.
Muller, Jerry Z. "American Views of German History Since 1945." In *Whose Brain Drain? Immigrant Scholars and American Views on Germany*, ed. Frank Trommler and Peter Hohendahl. Washington, DC, 2001, 14–27.
Müller-Kampel, Beatrix, ed. *Lebenswege und Lektüren. Österreichische NS-Vertriebene in den USA und Kanada*. Tübingen, 2000. [includes interviews with Walter Sokel, Peter Heller, Herbert Lederer, Hans Eichner, Egon Schwarz, Harry Zohn, Dorrit Claire Cohn, Ruth Klüger, and Evelyn Toron Beck]
Nattermann, Ruth. *Deutsch-jüdische Geschichtsschreibung nach der Shoah. Die Gründungs- und Frühgeschichte des Leo Baeck Institute*. Essen, 2004.
Payne, Stanley G., David J. Sorkin, and John S. Tortorice, eds. *What History Tells: George L. Mosse and the Culture of Modern Europe*. Madison, WI, 2004.
Peck, Abraham J., ed. *The German-Jewish Legacy in America, 1938–1988: From Bildung to the Bill of Rights*. Detroit, 1989.
Popkin, Jeremy D. *History, Historians, & Autobiography*. Chicago, 2005.
Quack, Sibylle, ed. *Between Sorrow and Strength: Women Refugees of the Nazi Period*. New York, 1995.
Raphael, Lutz. *Geschichtswissenschaft im Zeitalter der Extreme. Theorien, Methoden, Tendenzen von 1900 bis zur Gegenwart*. Munich, 2003.
Regan, Rick, ed. *Bruno Schlesinger: A Life in Learning & Letters at Saint Mary's College, South Bend, Indiana*. Raleigh, NC, 2013.
Ritter, Gerhard A. "Hans Rosenberg, 1904–1988." *Geschichte und Gesellschaft* 15 (1989): 282–302.
———. "Die emigrierten Meinecke-Schüler in den Vereinigten Staaten. Leben und Geschichtsschreibung im Spannungsfeld zwischen Deutschland und der neuen Heimat: Hajo Holborn, Felix Gilbert, Dietrich Gerhard, Hans Rosenberg." *Historische Zeitschrift* 284 (2007): 59–102.
———, ed. *Friedrich Meinecke. Akademischer Lehrer und emigrierte Schüler. Briefe und Aufzeichnungen, 1910–1977*. Munich, 2006. English edition: *German Refugee Historians and Friedrich Meinecke: Letters and Documents, 1910–1977*, ed. Gerhard A. Ritter; trans. Alex Skinner. Leiden, 2010.
Schulin, Ernst. ed. *Deutsche Geschichtswissenschaft nach dem Zweiten Weltkrieg. 1945–1965*. Munich, 1989.
Schulze, Winfried. *Deutsche Geschichtswissenschaft nach 1945*. Munich, 1989.
Srubar, Ilja, ed. *Exil, Wissenschaft, Identität. Die Emigration deutscher Sozialwissenschaftler 1933–1945*. Frankfurt/M., 1988.
Söllner, Alfons. *Deutsche Politikwissenschaftler in der Emigration. Studien zu ihrer Akkulturation und Wirkungsgeschichte*. Opladen, 1996.
Sonnert, Gerhard, and Gerald Holton. *What Happened to the Children Who Fled Nazi Persecution*. New York, 2006.
———. "The Grand Wake for Harvard Indifference: How Harvard and Radcliffe Students Aided Young Refugees from the Nazis." *Harvard Magazine* (September–October 2006): 50–55.
Sorkin, David. "The Émigré Synthesis: German-Jewish History in Modern Times." *Central European History* 34 (2001): 531–59.

Stelzel, Philipp. "Working Toward a Common Goal? American Views on German Historiography and German-American Scholarly Relations during the 1960s." *Central European History* 41 (2008): 639–71.

———. "Rethinking Modern German History: Critical Social History as a Transatlantic Enterprise, 1945–1989." Ph.D. diss., University of North Carolina at Chapel Hill, 2010.

Stern, Fritz. "German History in America, 1884–1984." *Central European History* 19 (1986): 131–63.

———. "Lessons from German History." *Foreign Affairs* 84 (May/June 2005): 14–18.

Strauss, Herbert A. *Essays on the History, Persecution and Emigration of German Jews*. New York, Munich, 1987.

Trommler, Frank, and Peter Hohendahl, eds. *Whose Brain Drain? Immigrant Scholars and American Views on Germany*. Washington, DC, 2001.

Volkov, Shulamit. "How German and How Jewish Were the German Jews? Reflections on the Problem of Identity." In *Text and Context: Essays in Modern Jewish History and Historiography in Honor of Ismar Schorsch*, ed. Eli Lederhendler and Jack Wertheimer. New York, 2005, 411–31.

———. *Die Juden in Deutschland 1780–1918*. Munich, 2010.

Walther, Peter Th. "Von Meinecke zu Beard? Die nach 1933 in die U.S.A emigrierten deutschen Neuhistoriker." Ph.D. diss., State University of New York at Buffalo, 1989.

———. "Die deutschen Historiker in der Emigration und ihr Einfluss in der Nachkriegszeit." In *Geschichtswissenschaft um 1950*, ed. Heinz Duchhardt and Gerhard May. Mainz, 2002, 37–47.

Wehler, Hans-Ulrich, ed., *Deutsche Historiker*. Vol. 1–9, Göttingen, 1973–82.

Wolf, Heinz. *Deutsch-jüdische Emigrationshistoriker in den U.S.A und der Nationalsozialismus*. Bern, 1988.

INDEX

Abraham, Claude K., 332
Abraham, David, 238
Abraham, Karl, 126
Ackerknecht, Erwin H., 37
Adenauer, Konrad, 14
Adorno, Theodor, 218, 331
Alexander, Paul J., 37
Allen, Willie, 123
Altmann, Alexander, 37
Altmann, Berthold, 37
Amann, Peter H., 13, 24, 33, 36, 339–40
American Historical Association (AHA), 28, 98, 134–35, 137, 247, 287
American Jewish Committee, 198
Anderson, Bonnie, 131
Anderson, Margaret Lavinia, 309
Angress, Werner (Tom), 10–11, 19, 28, 33, 36, 40n. 3, 120, 144, 148, 167, 340–41
Anschluss, 5, 245, 264
Antisemitism in Germany, 11, 15–6, 24, 26, 82, 131, 149, 160–61, 163, 180, 186, 188–89, 198–206, 245, 250, 252, 254, 268, 329
Antisemitism in the United States, 20–21, 57, 84, 104, 112, 116, 163
Appel, John J., 33, 36, 341–42
Appleby, Joyce, 137
Apsler, Alfred, 37
Arendt, Hannah, 65, 105, 177, 197, 236, 331
Arnade, Charles W., 15–16, 33, 36, 342–43
Arnstein, Walter L., 16, 21, 24, 33, 36, 343–44
Arieli, Joshua, 263, 268
Aron, Raymond, 69

Ascher, Abraham, 11, 24, 33, 36, 68, 344–45
Aschheim, Steven, 32, 149, 202, 297
Auerbach, Erich, 105, 146, 211, 219–20
Auschwitz-Birkenau, 19, 58, 131, 161–62, 188–89, 229, 238–9, 330
Australia, 6, 156, 276

Bach, Max, 332
Badian, Ernst, 15, 24, 33, 36, 345–47
Bailyn, Bernard, 222
Bankier, David, 232
Bar-Hillel, Yehoshua, 268
Barkin, Kenneth, 4
Barkow, Ben, 65
Baron, Hans, 3, 27, 37, 107, 111, 276
Barlach, Ernst, 76
Bartov, Omer, 203
Barzun, Jacques, 80
Bauer, Otto, 126
Bauman, Zygmunt, 231
Beard, Charles, 107, 161, 215, 217, 249
Beard, Mary, 249
Bebel, August, 314
Beck, Ann Frank, 4, 18, 25, 33, 36, 331, 347
Beck, Curt F., 331
Becker, Carl, 211, 214–17
Beer, Yzchak, 263, 265
Bell, Bishop George, 272
Bell, Susan Groag, 10, 18, 24–25, 30–1, 33, 36, 43n. 20, 159, 337n. 11, 347–48
Benda, Harry, 15, 22, 33, 36, 43n. 20, 348–49
Bendix, Reinhard, 331
Benjamin, Walther, 223

Bentley, Jerry, 137–38
Berge, Nicholas, 198
Berger, Alan, 156–57, 162, 169
Berghahn, Marion, xii, 159
Berghahn, Volker, 4
Bergstraesser, Arnold, 146
Berkner, Lutz, 121
Berlin, 5, 7–13, 15, 18–9, 21, 26, 28–30, 33–5, 37–39, 72, 75, 89, 103–4, 111, 120, 136, 158, 161, 163, 166–67, 187, 211, 218, 222, 229, 239, 262–63, 266, 272, 276, 279–80, 304–10, 312–14, 318–20, 329, 331
Berman, Paul, 205
Bernstein, Eduard, 185, 210–12
Berthold, Werner, 89
Besterman, Theodore, 219
Beveridge, William, 276
Bickerman, Elias J., 37
"The Bielefeld School of Social History," 182, 306, 319
Bieler, Arthur, 332
Binion, Rudolf, 133
Binswanger, Ludwig, 126
Bittner, Egon, 203
Black, Max, 217
Bleuler, Eugen, 126
Bloch, Charles, 261, 266
Blumenthal, Gerda R., 332
Blumenthal, Henry, 15, 33, 36, 349–50
Blumenthal, Michael W., 331
Blumenthal, Uta-Renate, 330
Bodenheimer, Rosy R, 37
Boehm, Eric H., 22–23, 33, 36, 350–51
Böhme, Helmut, 290–91
Bohnstedt, John W., 33, 36, 351
Boia, Lucian, 90
Bolivia, 1, 15–16, 310
Bonhoeffer, Dietrich, 223
Booms, Hans, 99
Borinski, Ernst, 319–20
Bourdieu, Pierre, 30
Bowlby, John, 116
Bracher, Dorothee, 222–23
Bracher, Karl Dietrich, 28, 56, 81, 167–68, 198–200, 222–23, 308
Brandt, Willy, 166, 332
Braudel, Fernand, 88

Braun, Rudolf, 306
Brazil, 15
Breitman, Richard, 57, 201
Brenner, Michael, 24, 310
Breslau, 5, 11, 26, 33–35, 37, 60, 162, 263, 267, 321
Bridenthal, Kenneth, 133
Bridenthal, Renate, 2, 6, 23, 25, 33, 36, 147–48, 158–59, 166, 352–53
Brieger, Gert H., 25, 33, 36, 353
Broch, Hermann, 106
Brodie, Fawn McKay, 122
Brown, Edmund G. (Gerry), 124
Browning, Christopher, 161, 201–2, 237
Broszat, Martin, 177, 290, 297, 332
Bruck, Eberhard F., 37
Bruehl, Henry J., 37
Brunson, Edward, 118
Buber, Martin, 223
Büsch, Otto, 304, 318
Bullock, Alan, 65, 80
Burke, Edmund, 218
Burlingham, James, 116
Butzer, Karl W., 331
Buzanski, Peter, 6, 33, 36, 353–54
Bynum, Caroline Walker 137

Callis, Helmut G., 37
Campbell, Joan (Johanna Stolper), 5, 18, 33, 36, 354
Cammett, John, 134
Canada, 13, 18–19, 29, 84, 86, 111, 229, 236, 276, 328–30, 332
Caplan, Jane, 136
Carbonell, Charles-Olivier, 90
Carlebach, Julius, 283
Carr, E.H., 31, 282
Carroll, Berenice, 134
Carsten, Francis, 166, 169, 279–83, 311
Caspari, Fritz, 37
Caspary, Gerard, 24, 109, 355
Cassirer, Ernst, 32, 105, 211–17
Caughey, John, 123
Center for Advanced Study in the Behavioral Sciences, 27, 222
Chakrabarty, Dipesh, 93
Chatfield, Leroy, 124
Chavez, César, 124

Czechoslovakia, 5, 10–11, 31, 84, 89–90, 93, 130, 159, 203, 268, 272, 330–31
Cherikover, Avigdor, 263, 265
Chickering, Roger, 309
China, 15, 89–90, 93, 114–16, 120, 125–27, 131, 331
Chodorow, Nancy, 125
Chrobog, Jürgen, 100
Civil Rights Movement in the United States, 32, 84–94, 123–34, 148, 164, 247–48, 319–20
Clausewitz, Carl von, 75
Clive, Geoffrey, 10
Clive, John L., 9–10, 24, 33, 36, 109, 355–56
Cohn, Dorrit, 332
Cold War, 132, 167, 211
Communism, 132, 166, 250, 265
Confino, Michael, 268
Congress of American Women, 251–53
Conversion, 9, 11
Conze, Werner, 297
Cooper, Sandi, 134
Coordinating Committee on Women in the Historical Profession, 245
Coser, Lewis A., 331
Craig, Gordon A., 67, 80, 147, 309
Cramer, Frederick H., 37
Cuba, 13, 162, 230
Cuppers, Martin, 204–5
Czerniakow, Adam, 231

Dahrendorf, Ralf, 28, 81, 67, 167, 181
Dallin, Alexander, 7, 24, 33, 36, 356–58
Darnton, Robert, 222
Darwin, Charles, 216
Davis, Natalie, 137
Dawidowicz, Lucy, 197–98, 236–37
Degras, Jane, 66
Demetz, Peter, 332
Deter, Adolf, 121
Deutsch, Karl W., 331
Dilthey, Wilhelm, 212
Dinburg (Dinur), Ben-Zion, 263
Dittmar, Henry G., 37
Documents, Captured German, 23, 97–100, 145, 232
Dorpalen, Andreas, 37

Döscher, Hans-Jürgen, 98–99
Droysen, Johann Gustav, 77
DuBois, W. E. B., 88, 198
Duggan, Stephen, 103

Eckstein, Harry H., 331
Edelstein, Ludwig, 37, 106
Edgcomb, Gabrielle S., xi, 33, 36, 48, 337n. 11, 358
Eerde School, 14–16
Eichner, Hans, 332
Eisenhower, Dwight D., 87
Eisenstein, Samuel, 119, 122–23
Eisler, Colin T., 331
Eitner, Lorenz, 331
Elbogen, Ismar, 37
Eliach, Yaffa, 236
Elias, Norbert, 279
Elkana, Yehuda, 58
Elpeleg, Zvi, 204
Elton, Geoffrey (Gottfried Ehrenberg), 278–79, 282–83, 312
Emergency Committee for the Relief of Displaced Foreign Scholars, 103–4
Engel-Janosi, Friedrich, 37
Epstein, Catherine, xi-xii, 4, 329, 332–3
Epstein, Fritz T., xi, 3, 23, 37, 55–56, 98, 108, 143, 145, 147, 155, 276
Epstein, Klaus, xi, 17, 23, 56, 67, 109, 143–46, 289–96, 309, 358–59
Erdmann, Karl Dietrich, 293–94
Eschwege, Helmut, 198
Ettinger, Shumel, 268
Euthanasia Program, National Socialist, 233, 238
Evans, Richard, 67
Eyck, Erich, 10, 24, 276, 280
Eyck, Frank, 10, 14, 19, 33, 36, 337n. 11, 359–60
Eyck, F. Gunther, 10, 33, 36, 360–61

Faber, Karl-Georg, 289
Fay, Sidney B., 55–56
Federal Bureau of Investigation (FBI), 83, 89, 148
Fehl, Philipp, 332
Feingold, Henry L., 23, 33, 36, 361–62
Feldman, Gerald, 287, 309

Feldman, Leon A., 331
Fengli, Luo, 127
Ferber, Marianne A., 331
Ferguson, Niall, 67
Feuchtwanger, Edgar, 271, 278, 281, 283, 312
Finkelstein, Norman, 237
First generation of refugee historians, 2–3, 26, list, 37–39. *See also* second generation, relations to first
Fischer, Fritz, 12, 56, 89, 147, 179, 266, 288–94, 331
Fischer, Wolfram, 306
Fleming, Donald, 222
Fraenkel, Eduard, 111
Fraenkel, Ernst, 180, 306–8, 321, 331
Franck, Erich, 105, 108
Franklin, John Hope, 198
Franz, Günther, 289
Freddi, Giorgio, 119
Free University of Berlin, 120, 167, 221, 304, 306–8, 318
Frei, Norbert, 205
Freimann, Aron, 37
Freitag, Sandria, 137
Freud, Anna 116, 124
Freud, Sigmund, 26, 31, 126, 201, 210, 213, 221–22
Freudenberger, Herman, 16, 33, 36, 362–63
Freudenheim, Tom L., 332
Freund, Gerald, 22, 33, 36, 363–64
Fried, Paul, 364
Friedländer, Saul, 23, 29, 197, 201, 230, 235, 296, 330
Friedlander, Albert, 157
Friedlander, Henry, 23, 33, 36, 100, 149, 229–43, 329, 365–66
Friedmann, Robert, 37
Friedrich, Carl F., 331

G.I.Bill, 20, 70
Gann, Lewis, 19, 366–67
Gans, Herbert J., 331
Gatzke, Hans, 12, 23, 33, 36, 55, 144, 290–91, 336n. 3, 367–68
Gaupp, Frederick Ernest, 37
Gay, Peter, 11, 13, 22, 24–25, 28–32, 33, 36, 133, 148–49, 158–59, 161–62, 168, 177–206, 210–28, 289, 294, 321, 368–70
Gay, Ruth, 223–24
gender, 2, 7, 10, 16, 18, 20, 23, 25, 31, 246, 252
generation
  concept, 55, 152–55
  definition, 1, 3–4, 181–82, 184, 328–9
Gensicke, Klaus, 204
Gentile,Emilio, 199
George, Stefan, 223
Gerhard, Dietrich, 37, 106, 145, 308
German Democratic Republic, 89–90, 121, 132, 136, 198, 205, 314
German Historical Institute (London), 312
German Historical Institute (Washington, D.C.), xi-xii, 28, 238, 333
German Marshall Fund, 28
German Studies Association (GSA), 28, 90, 99–100
Gerlach, Alf, 127
Gerschenkron, Alexander, 37
Gerth, Hans, 203
Gettleman, Marvin, 134
Geyl, Pieter, 68
Gibbon, Edward, 61, 188, 214, 218
Gilbert, Felix, xi, 3, 27, 37, 55–57, 77, 80 106, 108, 111, 146, 184, 276, 321
Gilmore, Myron, 111
Glanz, Glanz, 37
Glaser, Edward, 332
Glazer, Nathan, 224
Globke, Hans, 222
Goda, Norman, 204
Goebbels, Joseph, 11, 76, 106, 201
Göring, Hermann, 76
Goldhagen, Daniel, 160–61, 204, 235
Goldhagen, Erich, 204
Goldway, David, 134
Gombrich, Ernst, 67, 111
Grab, Walter, 261, 264–66, 268 314
Grab family, 264
Grass, Günther, 181
Graham, Ruth, 135
Gray, Hanna Holborn, 2, 17, 24, 27, 33, 36, 370–72
Grebing, Helga, 304

Grenville, John (Hans Gubrauer), 278–79, 281, 283
Gross, Hanns, 24, 33, 36, 372–73
Grossmann, Atina, 136, 203
Grossmann, Maria, 12, 18, 22, 24, 33, 36, 373
Grossmann, Walther, 12, 34, 36, 373–74
Gruber, Helmut, 34, 36, 374–75
Gruen, Erich S., 24, 34, 36, 375–76
Grün, Karl, 134
Gundersheimer, Hermann, 6
Gundersheimer, Werner, 6, 24, 34, 36, 376–77
Gunther, Gerald, 331
Gurevich, Aaron, 92
Gutman, Joseph, 332 *Gymnasium*, German high school, 8, 10–11, 14, 30, 49, 245, 264

Haas, Arthur, 34, 36, 336n. 3, 377–78
Haber, Fritz, 9
Habermas, Jürgen, 28, 181
Hackett, Amy, 136
Hahn, Fred, 37
Haj Amin El Husseini, 205
Hallgarten, George W., 37, 98
Hamerow, Theodore, 7, 34, 36, 40n. 20, 147, 166, 289–90, 329, 378–79
Harsegor, Michel, 262, 268
Hassell, Ulrich von, 75
Hausen, Karin, 306
Haushofer, Albrecht, 75
Hayes, Peter, 203
Hebrew Immigrant Aid Society, 83
Heichelheim, Fritz M., 37, 276
Heidegger, Martin, 201
Heilbronner, Hans, 34, 36, 379
Helleiner, Karl F., 37
Heller, Emmy, 37
Heller, Erich, 332
Heller, Peter, 332
Hennock, E. P., 278, 281, 283, 313
Herbert, Ulrich, 205
Herbst, Jurgen, 330
Hering, Rainer, 100
Hertz, Deborah, 136
Herzfeld, Hans, 292, 294, 305, 311

Herzl, Theodor, 121
Hess, Moses, 314
Heuss, Elly, 10
Heuss, Theodor, 5, 10
Heymann, Frederick G., 38
Heymann, Michael, 121
Hilberg, Raul, 5, 7, 22–23, 34, 36, 145, 149, 197–206, 229–43, 379–81
Hindemith, Paul, 105
Hintze, Otto, 223, 304
Hirsch, Felix, E., 38
Hirsch, Helmut, 21, 38
Hirschman, Albert O., 27, 321, 331
Hitler, Adolf, 5, 15, 23, 59, 61, 82, 106, 114, 145, 153, 160, 167, 187–90, 200–6, 231, 273
Hobsbawm, Eric, 3, 67, 279
Hochschule für Politik, Berlin, 103, 307
Hoffmann, Christhard, 4, 277, 281–82
Hoffmann, Peter, 330
Hoffmann, Stanley, 330
Hoffs, Joshua, 123
Hofstadter, Richard, 80, 211–12, 219, 222
Hoggan, David, 291
Holborn, Hajo, 3, 27, 38, 55–56, 79–80, 102–12, 144, 146, 164, 184, 219–20, 278, 287, 289
Holdheim, Wolfgang W., 331
Holocaust, 1, 4, 8, 13, 15–6, 23, 26, 28, 57–58, 65, 69, 88, 143, 145, 148–49, 155–57, 160, 163, 179–80, 188, 190, 197–206, 218, 229–43, 282, 318, 320
Holtfrerich, Carl Ludwig, 309
Holton, Gerald, 6, 25, 30, 34, 36, 245–46, 381–83
Horkheimer, Max, 218
Horowitz, David, 119, 121
Hovannisian, Richard, 118
Howard, Michael, 74
Hudson, James, 123
Hughes, H. Stuart, 56–57, 80
Huizinga, Johan, 153
Hume, David, 214
Hungary, 159, 184, 330
Hunt, Lynn, 137
Huttenbach, Henry, 23–24, 34, 36, 149, 383–84

Huttenback, Robert, 13, 34, 36, 384–85

Iggers, Georg, xii, 2, 10, 17, 22, 25, 32, 34, 36, 145, 164, 287, 295, 311, 320–21, 385–87
Iggers, Wilma A., 10, 34, 36, 40n. 20, 84–94, 164, 320, 332, 387–88
Indonesia, 15
Interdisciplinary Psychoanalytic Consortium, 125–25
Institute for Advanced Study (Princeton), xi, 27, 219, 321
Institute for Social Research (Hamburg), 206
International Congress of the Historical Sciences, 90, 137, 305
Israel, 1, 4, 19, 28, 15, 17, 59–61, 121, 162–63, 184, 189–91, 198–204, 230, 261–69, 313–15, 328
Italy, 13, 16, 74, 200, 276, 280, 310, 330

Jacob, Ernest I., 38
Jacobs, Wilbur, 118–19
Jaeckel, Berhard, 198–99
Jaeger, Hans, 155
Jaffe, Else, 111
Jarausch, Konrad, 29, 330
Jaspers, Karl, 65
Jens, Walter, 181
Jessner, Sabine, 24, 34, 36, 388–89
Jockusch, Laura, 199
Joll, James, 80–81
Jolles, Charlotte, 271–72
Jonas, Manfred, 11, 23, 25, 34, 36, 389–90
Jones, Arnita, 137
Jong, Loe de, 62–63
Journal of Contemporary History, 65–67, 182, 199, 201, 310
Jung, Carl Gustav, 126

Kaelble, Hartmut, 306
Kahler, Erich von, 38
Kann, Robert A., 38
Kant, Immanuel, 214, 221
Kantorowicz, Ernst H., 3, 27, 38, 74, 106, 276
Kaplan, Marion, 136, 162, 203
Karajan, Herbert von, 222

Kater, Michael H., 330
Katz, Friedrich, 24, 34, 36, 390–91
Katz, Jacob, 267
Kautsky, Karl, 212
Kehr, Eckart, 38, 56, 223
Kelly, Joan, 134
Kelman, Herbert C., 331
Kelsen, Hans, 27, 74
Kerber, Linda, 137
Kessler, Harry Graf, 223
Kindertransport (children's transport), 1, 6, 8, 16, 278
Kirk, Russell, 218
Kisch, Guido, 38
Kissinger, Henry, 19, 22, 25, 34, 36, 109, 184, 189, 391–94
Klein, Fritz, 287
Kleinmann, Ruth S., 24, 34, 36, 394
Kleist-Schmenzin, Ewald von, 75
Klemperer, Klemens von, 2, 8, 27, 29, 34, 36, 144, 296, 394–96
Kober, Adolf, 38
Kocka, Jürgen, 28, 81, 177, 305–6, 311
Koebner, Richard, 60, 263, 265
Köhler, Horst, 94
Königsberger, Franz, 262
Koenigsberger, Helmut, 278–79, 282–83, 312
Kogan, Arthur, 22, 34, 36, 396
Kohn, Hans, 3, 38, 56, 98, 297
Kohn-Bramstedt, Ernst (Ernest K. Bramstedt), 276
Kojeve, Alexandre, 62
Kollman, Eric C., 38
Kolz, Arno W. F., 330
Koonz, Claudia, 135–36
Korman, Gerd, 7–8, 23, 34, 36, 396–97
Koselleck, Reinhart, 28, 177, 180
Kraushaar, Wolfgang, 205–6
Krautheimer, Richard, 38, 105
Kren, George, 23, 34, 36, 397
Krieger, Leonard, 80, 147, 287, 297
Kristallnacht, 6, 8, 83, 229, 233, 271, 273, 275
Kristeller, Paul O., 3, 27, 38, 105, 111, 276
Kronick, John W., 332
Kronstein, Robert and Ilona, 251
Küntzel, Mathias, 205

Küttler, Wolfgang, 90
Kuttner, Stephan Georg, 38
Kula, Witold, 92

Laan, Leonore, 16, 34, 36, 398
Lachmann Mosse Family, 5
LaCapra, Dominick, 235
Ladner, Gerhart M. A., 38
Laibman, David, 134
Lamb, Ursula, 12, 34, 36, 336n. 3, 398–99
Landauer, Carl, 38
Lane, Nancy, 122
Langer, Lawrence, 235
Langer, William L., 55–57, 144, 147
Lanzmann, Claude, 231–32, 235
Laqueur, Richard, 38, 59, 64
Laqueur, Walter, 2, 8, 15, 23–24, 30–31, 34, 36, 149, 156, 158, 162–63, 177–206, 337n. 11, 399–402
Lassalle, Ferdinand, 264, 314
Latour, Conrad, 22, 402–3
Laue, Max von, 12
Laue, Theodore von, 12, 22, 24, 29, 34, 36, 336n. 3, 403–4
Lazarsfeld, Paul, 80
Lederer, Herbert, 332
Lederer, Ivo John, 330
Lee, David, 125
Lehmann, Hartmut, 28, 182, 333
Leisinger, Albert, 99
Lenel, Edith, 38
Lensen, George A., 7, 34, 36, 404–6
Leo Baeck Institute, 28, 311–12
Lepsius, M. Rainer, 181
Lerner, Carl, 250–51
Lerner, Gerda, 4, 8, 16, 18, 25, 32, 34, 36, 134, 244–58, 406–8
Leschnitzer, Adolf, 38, 308
Lessing, G.E., 105
Levinson, Joseph, 120
Levison, Wilhelm, 278
Levy, Ernst, 38
Lewy, Guenter, 19, 22, 34, 36, 331, 408–9
Leyser, Karl, 278–79, 283
Lichtenberg, Bernhard, 234
Lichtenberg, Georg, 221
Lichtheim, George, 69, 223
Liebknecht, Wilhelm, 314

Littauer-Blaschke, Charlotte, 38
Litvak, Meir, 204
Locke, John, 214
Loewenberg, Anna Sophie, 115
Loewenberg, Josefine, 124–25
Loewenberg, Peter, 2, 25, 28–29, 34, 36, 40n. 3, 147, 409–10
Loewenberg Family, 116
Löwenstein, Karl, 105
Löwenthal, Leo, 331
Löwenthal, Richard, 308
Lovejoy, Arthur, 186
Low, Alfred D., 38
Luckert, Karl Wilhelm, 330
Luxemburg, Rosa, 212

Mackauer, Christian W., 38
McCarthyism, 132–33, 211, 217–18, 253
Maenchen-Helfen, Otto, 38
Maier, Charles S., 26, 67, 287, 297
Mallmann, Klaus, 204
Mankin, Paul A., 332
Mann, Golo, 38
Mann, Thomas, 185
Mannheim, Karl, 153, 222
Marias, Julian 153
Marcuse, Herbert, 105, 108, 112, 331
Markowitz, Gerald, 134
Marschak, Jakob, 105
Marwick, Arthur, 67
Marx, Karl, 26, 84, 134, 216, 245
Marx, Otto M., 25, 34, 36, 411
Marxism, 26, 119–20, 264, 314
Masur, Gerhard, 38
Mayer, Arno J., 29, 144, 287, 330
Mayer, Gustav, 278, 280
Mazower, Mark, 328
Meinecke, Friedrich, xi 26, 55, 57, 80, 91, 106–8, 178, 218–19, 223, 304, 306
Melani, Lilia, 134
Mendels, Franklin, 121–22
Mendl, Wolf, 283
Menze, Ernest A., 330
Meskill, Johanna Menzel, 330
Metcalf, Barbara, 137
Metzger, Michael, 332
Meyer, Michael A., 4, 24, 28, 34, 36, 147, 411–13

Mexico, 1, 156
Michael, Franz H., 38
Michman, Dan, 232
Milgram, Stanley, 235
Milton, Sybil, 233, 238
Mines, Luke, 115
Misch, Carl, 38
Molin, Alma, 22, 34, 36, 329, 413–14
Moller, Herbert, 22, 34, 36, 414
Momigliano, Arnaldo, 111
Mommsen, Hans, 28, 177, 297
Mommsen, Theodor E., 38, 106–8
Mommsen, Wolfgang (archivist), 99
Mommsen, Wolfgang J. (historian), 28, 67, 177, 287, 289
Morgenthau, Hans, 62, 331
Mosse, George L., 4–5, 14, 22–24, 28, 30, 35–6, 63, 66–67, 146, 148–49, 157–58, 166, 169, 177–206, 223, 276, 278, 293–95, 309–10, 321, 414–16
Mosse, Werner, 278–79, 281–83, 312
Muller, Jerry Z., 203
Munich Conference and Agreement 1938, 5–6, 273, 330
Murrow, Edward R., 104

Na'aman, Shlomo, 261, 264–65, 286, 314
Nadel, George, 6, 35–6, 416–17
Nash, Gerald (Gerhard Nachschön), 15, 21, 417–18
National Association for the Advancement of Colored People (NAACP), 32, 84, 86–87
Neilson, Nellie, 137
Nemiroff, Robert, 125
Netherlands, 14, 18–19, 114, 330
Neugebauer, Otto, 38
Neumann, Franz L., 16, 32, 80, 105, 108, 146, 180, 211–13, 221, 230, 236, 331
Neumann, Fritz C., 38
Neumann, Sigmund, 105
Niebuhr, B.G., 134
Nipperdey, Thomas, 28, 81, 91, 180, 202, 310
Nolan, Molly, 136
Nolte, Paul, 182

Nordau, Max, 191
Novick, Peter, 91, 198
Nuremberg Anti-Semitic Laws, 5, 161

O'Donnell, Krista, 138
Oelsner, Toni F., 10, 24, 35–6, 337n. 11, 418–20
Oesterreich, Gerhard, 312
Office of Strategic Services (OSS), 56–57, 80, 107–8, 205
Olden, Peter H., 38
Oncken, Hermann, 15
Organization of American Historians, 245, 247
Orlow, Dietrich, 330
Ortega y Gasset, José, 153
Ospovat, Alexander M., 25, 35–6

Pachter, Henry M., 38
Panofsky, Dora, 105
Panofsky, Erwin, 32, 67, 105, 111, 146, 219, 331
Pappe, Helmut, 281, 283
Paret, Peter, 2, 13, 18, 24, 28, 35–6, 157, 167, 420–22
Pareto, Vilfredo, 165
Parker, Harold, 93
Paucker, Arnold, 281, 312
Payne, Stanley, 67
Peace Movement in the United States, 250
Peterson, Agnes, 22, 35–6, 329, 337n. 11, 422–23
Pevsner, Nikolaus, 67
Pflanze, Otto, 147, 309
Pinson, Koppel, 294
Pius XII, 232, 237
Pipes, Richard, 330
Poland, 5, 7, 92, 163, 232, 268, 291, 330
Political science, 19, 21–22, 62–3, 68, 204, 236, 266, 304, 307, 318, 331
Pollard, Sidney (Siegfried Pollak), 278, 281–83
Portugal, 18
Posner, Ernst, 39
Prawer, Joshua, 263
Psychoanalysis, 25, 29, 73, 120–28, 147, 210, 222, 250–51
Puhle, Hans-Jürgen, 306, 319
Pulzer, Peter, 278, 281–83, 312

Quasten, Johannes, 39
Qi Shirong, 90
Quack, Sybille, xi

Rabb, Theodore K., 10, 24, 35–6, 40n. 20, 423–25
Rabe, Valentin H., 24, 35–6, 425
Rabinbach, Anson, 202
Ranke, Leopold von, 80, 91
Rathenau, Walther, 120
Reagan, Ronald, 32
Reagin, Nancy, 138
Redlich, Fritz, 39, 321
Reiche, Harald, 24, 35–6, 425–26
Reichmann, Eva, 276–78, 311
Reiss, Hans S., 332
Reissner, Hanns Günther, 39
Remak, Henry A. A., 332
Remak, Joachim, 23, 35–6, 426–27
Renner, Karl, 126
Research Psychoanalyst Law, 124–25
Resistance to Nazism, German, 8, 75, 167–68, 223, 234
Reuning, Wilhelm, 22, 35–6, 427
Reutershan, Joan, 136
Riasanovsky, Nicholas, 120
Ricci, Matteo, 127
Richter, Richter, 39
Riesman, David, 217
Rilke, Rainer M., 223
Ringer, Fritz K., 67, 330
"Ritchie Boys," 19, 144
Ritter, Gerhard, 178, 294–96
Ritter, Gerhard A., 28, 318–19
Roberts, Henry, 79–80, 212
Robertson, James, 116
Robertson, Joyce, 116
Rodes, John, 20, 35–6, 427–28
Rogger, Hans, 24, 35–6, 68, 428–29
Romein, Jan, 63
Roosevelt, Franklin D., 106
Roseman, Mark, 153–54
Rosen, Edgar R., 39
Rosenberg, Arthur, 39, 184, 276
Rosenberg, Ethel and Julius, 133
Rosenberg, Hans, 3, 26–27, 39, 106, 120, 144–45, 155, 164, 180, 184, 276, 292–93, 304–6, 315

Rosenmann, Samuel, 57
Rosenstock-Huessy, Eugen, 39
Roth, Guenther, 100
Roth, John, 234
Roth, Joseph, 223
Rothberg, Michael, 235
Rothenberg, Gunther E., 19, 429–30
Rothfels, Hans, 3, 39, 55, 144, 184, 236, 278, 293
Rousseau, Jean-Jacques, 213–14
Rubinstein, Annette, 134
Rubinstein, Nicolai, 111, 278, 280, 283
Rüsen, Jörn, 90
Ruhm von Oppen, Beate, 14, 22, 35–6, 40n. 20, 337n. 11, 430–31
Runciman, Steven, 62–63

Saalmann, Howard, 332
Salm, Peter, 332
Salomon, Albert, 105
Salomon, Richard G., 39
Sauer, Wolfgang, 304
Saxl, Fritz, 67
Schleicher, Rüdiger, 223
Schleier, Hans, 89–90
Schelsky, Helmuth, 153
Schieder, Theodor, 293, 297
Schieder, Wolfgang, 177
Schirokauer, Conrad, 13, 35–6, 431–32
Schissler, Hanna, 100
Schlesinger, Bruno, 11, 20, 22, 35–6, 432
Schmitt, Carl, 201
Schmitt, Hans, 9, 14, 19, 35–6, 157–58, 167, 169, 432–33
Schnabel, Franz, 289
Schoeps, Hans Joachim, 289
Scholem, Gershom, 162, 190
Schorsch, Emil, 11
Schorsch, Ismar, 11, 35–6, 433–34
Schorske, Carl E., 55–56, 80, 119–20, 127, 147, 222, 287
Schulin, Ernst, 287
Schulz, Gerhard, 304, 318
Schumann, Reinhold, 24, 35–6, 336n. 3, 434–35
Schwarz, Dorle, 311
Schwarz, Egon, 310–11, 321, 332
Schwarz, Robert, 6, 35–6, 435–36

Schweitzer, Hans (Mjölnir), 76
Scott, Joan W., 29
Second generation of refugees as historians
  biographies, 33–36, 339–453
  defined, 1–4, 143–44, 328–32
  education in the United States, 21–25, 144–45
  Jewish identity, 5–11, 31–32, 82–83, 93, 158–59, 177–79, 218, 252–53, 278
  language, 8, 17, 79, 104, 109, 131–32, 165, 168–69, 211–12, 233–34, 251, 279
  list of members, 33–36
  relations to "first generation," 26–27, 37–39, 55–56, 77
  military service, 18–19, 73–74, 144, 165–67, 267–68, 279
  names, 82, 184, 211–12, 264, 279, 312
  parents, 1, 4–7, 10, 12, 15–17, 59, 72, 82, 102–12, 114–18, 130–32, 158, 163–64, 251
  return to Germany, 28, 99, 111–12, 120–22, 165–66, 252
  year of emigration, 4–6, 36
Seeley, J.R., 56
Selig, Karl-Ludwig, 332
Sell, Frederick C., 39
Selz, Peter, 332
Sempell, Charlotte, 39
Shamir, Shimon, 262
Sheehan, James J., xi, 4, 81, 287, 309
Siedler, Wolf Jobst, 69
Shils, Edward, 61–62
Shirer, William, 290
Simon, Walter M., 9, 35–6, 144, 436–37
Simonson, Shlomo, 267
Simpson, Esther, 277
Skidmore, Thomas, 147
Slavin, A.J., 121
Smelser, Ronald, 100
Smith, Helmut W., 203
Snell, John, 147
Snowmann, Daniel, 282
Snyder, Timothy, 235
Sokel, Walter, 26, 332
Sonderweg, 32, 146, 148, 179, 199, 288, 295–99, 321

Sonnenfeld, Albert, 332
Sonnert, Gerhard, 245–46
Sontag, Raymond J., 119
Spalding, Hobart Ames, 133
Spender, Stephen, 273
Spiegel, Gabrielle, 137
Spivakovsky, Erika, 39
Stein, George, 23, 35–6, 437
Stern, Fritz, 2, 9, 11, 14, 17, 21, 23, 25, 28–29, 32, 35–6, 56, 144, 146–49, 158, 160–61, 167, 177–206, 289–95, 311, 320–21, 437–41
Stern, Guy, 19, 332
Stern Täuber, Selma, 3, 39
Stiern, Walter, 124
Stolper, Johanna, see Campbell, Joan
Stolper, Gustav, 5
Stolper, Toni, 5
Stourzh, Gerald, 330
Straus, Raphael, 39
Strauss, Bruno, 39
Strauss, Felix, 17, 35–36, 441
Strauss, Gerald, 35–6, 441–42
Strauss, Herbert A., 24, 35–6, 329, 333, 442–44
Strauss, Leo, 62, 331
Strauss, Sylvia, 336n. 4
Switzerland, 5, 13, 15, 43n. 20, 49n. 105, 90, 106–6, 329

Täubler, Eugen, 39
Tal, Uriel, 262, 267
Talmon, Jacob, 218, 263
Tec, Nechama, 230
Thieme, Helga, 76
Thimme, Annelise, 330
Thompson, Mark, 126
Thormann, Gerard, 12, 19, 35–6, 444–45
Thucydides, 233
Tibi, Bassam, 205
Tillich, Paul, 83, 105
Tobias, Sheila, 135
Topolski, Jerzy, 92
Toury, Jacob, 262, 267
Trefousse, Hans, 25, 35–6, 445–46
Trilling, Lionel, 80
Turner, Henry A., 203, 287

Ulich, H. G. Robert, 39
Ulrich, Laurel Thatcher, 137
United States Holocaust Memorial Museum, 205, 238
Urdang, George, 39
Uruguay, 15

Vagts, Alfred, 63, 39, 107
Valentin, Veit, 39, 184, 276–77, 280
Vargas, Getúlio, 15
Veith, Ilza, 25, 35–6, 336n. 3, 446–47
Vienna, 5–8, 11–12, 26, 30, 33–5, 37–38, 49n. 105, 72–3, 120, 126, 159, 229, 245, 249, 251–53, 261–62, 264–65, 267, 310, 314, 330
Viereck, Peter, 56
Vietnam War, 135
Voegelin, Eric, 331
Vogel, Robert, 24, 35–6, 447–48
Volkov, Shulamit, 15, 17, 313–15
Voltaire, 210–18

Wachendorf, Milli, 115
Wachenheim, Hedwig, 39
Wagner, Richard, 30
Wallach, Jehuda, 262, 267–68
Wallach, Luitpold, 39
Wang, Qingjia Edward, 93
Warburg, Aby, 211, 219, 221
Warburg Institute, 111
Warmbrunn, Werner, 10, 20, 35–6, 448–49
Warsaw Ghetto, 231
Watkins, Renée, 18, 24, 35–6, 449–50
Webb, Robert, 122
Weber, Alfred, 111
Weber, Max, 26, 111, 119, 328
Webman, Ester, 204
Webster, Charles, 279
Weckerling, Rudolf, 121
Wehler, Hans-Ulrich, 28, 81, 89, 177, 287, 289, 298, 319
Weidenfeld, George, 66
Weil, Rolf A., 21
Weinbaum, Martin, 39
Weinberg, Gerhard, 2, 17, 23, 28, 35–6, 144–45, 149, 158, 203–4, 229–43, 291, 450–51

Weil, Rolf, 21
Weiner, Dora, 24, 35–6, 451–52
Weinryb, Bernard Dov, 39
Weinstein, Barbara, 137
Weintraub, Karl J., 20, 35–36, 146, 452–535,
Welleck, Rene, 105
White, Hayden, 91–92
Wieckenberg, Ernst Peter, 28
Wiener Library, 28, 64–68 198, 277, 311
Wieruszowski, Helen, 3, 39
Wiesel, Elie, 235
Wildt, Michael, 205
Wilhelm, Hellmut, 39
Winkler, Heinrich August, 177
Winnicott, D.W., 117
Winslade, Bill, 124
Wischnitzer, Mark, 39
Wistrich, Robert, 202, 204
Witt, Peter Christian, 309
Wittfogel, Karl A., 39
Wittkower, Rudolf, 67
Wohl, Robert, 153
Wolfers, Arnold, 105
Wolff, Hans J., 39
Wolff, Kurt, 203
Wolfson, Manfred, 331
Woloch, Isser, 121
Women's history, 8, 18, 25, 134–38, 147, 244–58
Wright, Gordon, 80
Wulf, Joseph, 198
Wyman, David, 57
Wyszanski, Andrzej, 92

Yakobson, Sergius O., 39
Yavetz, Zvi, 263, 313
Yutang, Lin, 126–27

Zhang Zhilian, 90
Ziebura, Gilbert, 304–318
Zimmer, Heinrich, 105
Zionism, 7, 10–11, 19, 63, 82, 121, 159, 164, 190–91, 264–65, 267, 314
Zohn, Harry, 332
Zunkel, Friedrich, 304
Zweig, Arnold, 31

www.ingramcontent.com/pod-product-compliance
Lightning Source LLC
Chambersburg PA
CBHW070041120526
44589CB00035B/2020